IN FOUR BOOKS

LONGMAN ANNOTATED TEXTS

PUBLISHED TITLES

Michael Mason, *Wordsworth and Coleridge: Lyrical Ballads*
Alexandra Barratt, *Women's Writing in Middle English*
Tim Armstrong, *Thomas Hardy: Selected Poems*
René Weis, *King Lear: A Parallel Text Edition*
Randall Martin, *Women Writers in Renaissance England*
Helen Phillips and Nick Havely, *Chaucer's Dream Poetry*
Valerie Rumbold, *Alexander Pope: The Dunciad in Four Books*
Virginia Blair, *Victorian Women Poets*

ALEXANDER POPE

THE DUNCIAD

IN FOUR BOOKS

EDITED BY
VALERIE RUMBOLD

LONDON AND NEW YORK

First published 1999 by Pearson Education Limited
Second edition published 2009

Published 2014 by Routledge
2 Park Square, Milton Park, Abingdon, Oxon OX14 4RN
711 Third Avenue, New York, NY 10017, USA

Routledge is an imprint of the Taylor & Francis Group, an informa business

ISBN 13: 978-1-4082-0416-0 (pbk)

British Library Cataloguing in Publication Data
A CIP catalogue record for this book can be obtained from the British Library

Library of Congress Cataloging-in-Publication Data
Pope, Alexander, 1688–1744.
The Dunciad : in four books / edited by Valerie Rumbold. – 2nd ed.
p. cm. – (Longman annotated texts)
Includes bibliographical references and indexes.
ISBN 978-1-4082-0416-0 (pbk.)
1. Verse satire, English. 2. Literature publishing – Poetry.
3. Authorship – Poetry. I. Rumbold, Valerie. II. Title.
PR3625.A2R86 2008
821′.5–dc22

2008031246

Set by 35 in 9/12pt Stone Serif and 8.75/11pt Amasis

CONTENTS

ACKNOWLEDGEMENTS

This edition would have been impossible to complete without the generous support of friends and colleagues. Howard Erskine-Hill and Roger Lonsdale have been patient in their encouragement of what has seemed at times a very slow project, and I am particularly grateful to them for their time and care in reading the commentary. I am also grateful to J. Paul Hunter, William Kinsley, Sarah Prescott and Bruce Redford for allowing me to see and to quote from their unpublished work. Don Fowler has given invaluable help with classical allusions; and Christine Gerrard, Isobel Grundy, Brean Hammond, Rosamond McGuinness, Isabel Rivers and Ruth Smith have been unstinting in sharing knowledge and ideas.

I have been particularly fortunate in the bibliographical expertise I have been able to draw upon. At the outset of the project James Sutherland responded generously to my enquiries, and David Vander Meulen shared with me some of the detailed results of his work on the bibliography of the *Dunciads*. James McLaverty has been an unfailing source of information and ideas on typography, bookmaking and the book trade; and his indefatigable and judicious reading of text and commentary has saved me from many errors. I am also grateful to David Foxon for arranging for me to examine his fine-paper copy of *The Dunciad in Four Books*, since presented to the Bodleian Library.

Research involving the numbers of eighteenth-century books required for a project of this kind can only be undertaken in a major library, and I am grateful to Bill Tydeman and Tom Corns, my successive heads of department in Bangor, for helping to secure the support of the various bodies whose contributions have made extended library visits possible: the Research Committee of the University of Wales, Bangor, helped with start-up funding; the English Department supplied further financial support and arranged study leave; the British Academy supported the project under its Small Personal Research Grants scheme; and St John's College, Oxford, provided a Summer Visiting Scholarship. Without such practical support this project would not have been feasible.

My bibliography gives some idea of the burdens I have placed on library staff over the years: the staff of the Upper Reserve in the Bodleian Library have been patient and helpful throughout, and Ann Illsley and Marion Poulton in the Main Arts Library in Bangor have contributed invaluable expertise in mobilising resources. In the English Department Office in Bangor I should like to thank Michelle Harrison, Gail Kincaid and Linda Jones, who have helped in all kinds of practical ways.

I would like to thank the Longman editorial team for supporting this project throughout. The enthusiasm of Henry Woudhuysen, academic editor to the series, has been a constant encouragement, and Katy Coutts, my copy-editor, has coped with the complexities of the typescript with remarkable calmness and thoroughness.

No-one is likely to edit *The Dunciad in Four Books* without wondering periodically why they started and how they can ever hope to finish: the line 'Call'd to this work by Dulness, Jove, and Fate' has, in this context, a discomforting ring. I have been fortunate to have had so many tolerant listeners, both in my own department in Bangor and elsewhere. My deepest debt of gratitude, on this score as on so many others, is, as always, to Ian.

The publishers are grateful to the British Library for the illustration on p. viii, the spoof royal arms on pp. 27 and 396, and the monograms on p. 28, all taken from *The Dunciad in Four Books* (Alexander Pope), 1743 edition.

NOTE TO THE SECOND IMPRESSION

For this reimpression, corrections have been made to the following pages: 93, 97, 98, 137, 148, 150, 173, 176, 217, 227, 250, 286, 355, 378, 412, 420, 432. Except for minor changes to the pagination of the bibliography, the original pagination has been preserved throughout.

Book II. The DUNCIAD. 83

With arms expanded Bernard rows his ſtate,
And left-legg'd Jacob ſeems to emulate.
Full in the middle way there ſtood a lake,
Which Curl's Corinna chanc'd that morn to make:
(Such was her wont, at early dawn to drop
Her evening cates before his neighbour's ſhop,)
Here fortun'd Curl to ſlide; loud ſhout the band,
And Bernard! Bernard! rings thro' all the Strand.
Obſcene with filth the miſcreant lies bewray'd,
Fal'n in the plaſh his wickedneſs had laid:

REMARKS.

VER. 70. *Curl's Corinna*] This name, it ſeems, was taken by one Mrs. T——, who procured ſome private letters of Mr. Pope's, while almoſt a boy, to Mr. Cromwell, and ſold them without the conſent of either of thoſe Gentlemen to Curl, who printed them in 12mo, 1727. He diſcovered her to be the publiſher, in his Key, p. 11. We only take this opportunity of mentioning the manner in which thoſe letters got abroad, which the author was aſhamed of as very trivial things, full not only of levities, but of wrong judgments of men and books, and only excuſable from the youth and inexperience of the writer.

VER. 75. *Obſcene with filth, &c.*] Though this incident may ſeem too low and baſe for the dignity of an Epic poem, the learned very well know it to be but a copy of Homer and Virgil; the very words ὄνθος and *fimus* are uſed by them, though our poet (in compliance to modern nicety) has remarkably enriched and coloured his language, as well as raiſed the verſification, in this Epiſode, and in the fol-

IMITATIONS.

VER. 73. *Here fortun'd Curl to ſlide;*]

Labitur infelix, cæſis ut forte juvencis
Fuſus humum viridesque ſuper madefecerat herbas ——
Concidit, immundoque fimo, ſacroque cruore.

Virg. Æn. v. of Niſus.

VER. 70. *And Bernard! Bernard!*]

—*Ut littus, Hyla, Hyla, omne ſonaret.* Virg. Ecl. vi.

L 2

A page from *The Dunciad in Four Books* (1743), showing the complexity of the original layout and typography.

INTRODUCTION

LEVELS OF COMPLEXITY

Reading *The Dunciad in Four Books* can be a marvellously rewarding experience. As the culminating achievement of Pope's career, it engages so memorably with so many aspects of its time that it is regularly cited in discussions of a whole range of aesthetic, ideological, cultural and historical issues. To a novice reader, however, at more than two centuries' distance from the events, assumptions and controversies involved, it can seem bafflingly complex and offputtingly alien. This Introduction aims principally to provide a practical approach to a first reading: once that is achieved, the reader is in a stronger position to explore, evaluate and contest theoretical and critical approaches – including those implicit in this edition and commentary. A few particularly helpful books and articles are marked with asterisks in the Bibliography.

The Dunciad in Four Books is complex both in itself and in its relation to Pope's previous *Dunciads*. The most obvious level of complexity is chronological, since Pope altered and updated the *Dunciads* from one edition to the next over a period of fifteen years. Leaving aside intermediate variants, there were four principal versions:

1. *The Dunciad* of 1728, a poem in three books, with a hero called Tibbald.
2. *The Dunciad Variorum* of 1729, the same poem in a slightly revised version, but with commentary and apparatus (i.e. prefaces, appendices, index, etc.).
3. *The New Dunciad* of 1742, a new book of verse conceived as a sequel to the previous three, with commentary and apparatus. (The first three books were not included in this version.)
4. *The Dunciad in Four Books* of 1743, a revised version of the original three books and a slightly revised version of the fourth book of 1742 with revised commentary and apparatus. A new character, Bays, replaces Tibbald in the role of hero.

We therefore need to be careful how we speak of the *Dunciads*: much that is true of one version will not be true of another, and even the material they have in common takes on altered perspectives as surrounding elements change over time. The present edition gives the text of *The Dunciad in Four Books* of 1743, the fullest and arguably the most interesting of the versions. Other versions are mentioned only as background.[1]

The second major aspect of the texts' complexity is that after 1728 the *Dunciad* ceased to be simply a poem: succeeding versions were composite texts of verse and prose. Lavish care and ingenuity went into the elaboration of annotations, prefaces and appendices, and much of the fun of the *Dunciads* is lost if they are overlooked; moreover, once they began to appear, the reader's experience of the work became vastly more complicated, as eye and judgement were diverted into negotiation between poem and surrounding prose.

A third level of complexity in all *Dunciads* from 1729 onwards relates to authorship; for there are several hints that the commentary, which first appeared in 1729 and developed further in subsequent versions, incorporated contributions from others besides Pope. Although the prefatory *A Letter to the Publisher* suggests that notes were contributed by 'strangers' as well as 'the Author's friends', it seems likely that most of the extra material came from his own circle; but exactly what and how much remains to a large extent unclear (see editor's note on note c) to Appendix I). By the time he was revising for *The Dunciad in Four Books* of 1743, many of his early friends were dead or, in the case of Jonathan Swift (1667–1745), isolated by distance and failing health in the deanery of St Patrick's Cathedral in Dublin. In 1740, however, Pope had met William Warburton (1698–1779), an ambitious clergyman and former attorney whom he rapidly adopted as his authorised editor and commentator. Pope invited Warburton to contribute to the prose of 1743, and after the poet's death Warburton indicated their respective contributions (Warburton 1751: V). These are noted in the present commentary, although it should be borne in mind that they are attributions after the fact, published by someone with a vested interest in emphasising his importance to the project. Any other evidence for the authorship of notes is also recorded: otherwise, although it is overwhelmingly likely that Pope wrote most of the notes himself, I have tried to avoid implying that any particular note is necessarily his.

Readers of Pope have typically found Warburton an unappealing addition to the poet's circle. His characteristic tone is ponderous and over-assertive, and he very obviously used his friendship with Pope to further his career: aided by his status as Pope's authorised editor, he was to marry an heiress to whom Pope had introduced him, rising to become a bishop and a considerable figure in the world of letters. Yet, although his contributions to *The Dunciad in Four Books* often work against the grain, he remains an invited co-author, the last heir of Pope's tradition of collaborative wit.

VALUES AND PERSONALITIES

Origins

Pope was experimenting with motifs which he would later work into the *Dunciads* from his teenage years; but the precise point at which he decided to begin a major satire on the perverse stupidity that he called 'Dulness' remains debatable. He may have been provoked by the promotion of one or other undistinguished poet to a position of distinction, or by what he took to be perverse judgements about contemporary literary history (Vander Meulen 1991: 3–16; McLaverty 1985). In 1726, however, the project took an important turn when the lawyer, translator, playwright and textual scholar Lewis Theobald (1688–1744) offended Pope by finding fault with his edition of Shakespeare in a book provocatively entitled *Shakespeare Restored: or, A Specimen of the Many Errors, as well Committed, as Unamended, by Mr. Pope in his late Edition of this Poet*. This came in the context of Pope's already substantial experience of concerted and bitterly hostile attacks on his character and writing in newspapers and pamphlets (Guerinot 1969: xxi–xxiii). A year later, in 1727, came the coronation of George II, an episode of pomp and pageantry which offered a focus for dissatisfaction with the continuing Hanoverian regime and its effect on the national culture (Rogers 1985: 120–50). In the *Dunciads* Pope is obviously angry about what could be described as personal issues (the success of writers he considers unworthy, and media hostility to his own career); but he is also, from an early stage in the development of the *Dunciads*, angry about wider issues (the state of contemporary literature, culture and politics).

An important pointer to the themes and motivations of the *Dunciads* lies in the dedication to Swift which Pope included from 1729 (I.19–28; and see the anecdote recorded in note a) to Appendix I). Pope and Swift, along with the poet and dramatist John Gay (1685–1732) and John Arbuthnot (1667–1735), satirist and physician to Queen Anne, had been key members of the Scriblerus Club, which had flourished briefly in the second decade of the century (Kerby-Miller 1950: 1–77). It took its name from the fictitious character Martinus Scriblerus, whose mock-biography the club originally intended to compose: he was conceived as 'a man of capacity enough that had dipped in every art and science, but injudiciously in each', a caricature of what the members took to be the ludicrous excesses of modern intellectual life (*OAC*: I, 56). In the event, enthusiasm for this project waned, and Pope was finally left to edit the materials, from which he published *Memoirs of the Extraordinary Life, Works, and Discoveries of Martinus Scriblerus* in 1741. More significant by far had been three parodic satires stimulated by the heady mix of wit, conservative indignation and camaraderie among the collaborators: Swift's *Gulliver's Travels* appeared in 1726, and 1728 saw a double Scriblerian triumph with Gay's *The Beggar's Opera* and Pope's first *Dunciad* (*PW*: II, 174). Pope had earlier that year presented Scriblerus as author of a satirical guide to bad writing, *Peri Bathous: or, Martinus Scriblerus, His Treatise of the Art of Sinking in Poetry*, which Arbuthnot may initially have helped to draft (*PW*: II, 180–81). From 1729 Scriblerus's courteously preposterous interventions also became a key feature in the apparatus of the *Dunciads*.

Ancients and Moderns

There is a strangely belated quality about many of Pope's most heartfelt loyalties: as a young man he tended to adopt as mentors distinguished men whose active careers were largely behind them; and their quarrels often became his quarrels, to be pursued with the intensity that marked his commitment to friendship as an ideal. This is highly relevant to the values espoused with such passion in the *Dunciads*, values which in important ways hark back to issues debated in the late seventeenth century, long before Pope was of an age to be directly involved.

The Quarrel of the Ancients and the Moderns had broken out in the late seventeenth century in France around the question of whether present civilisations could hope to outdo the achievements of the ancient world in the arts and in science and technology. If some contemporaries were excited by the possibility, others realised with horror that aspirations of this kind threatened the educational and cultural structures that Europe's elite had shared ever since the Renaissance rediscovery of the classical past. Such humanistically educated men believed that values derived from Greek and Roman literature provided authoritative standards of virtue, rationality and aesthetic taste, and – quite contrary to our own culture's assumption of the pre-eminent importance of empirical science and the technologies it supports – they assumed that the skills required to read classical texts and interpret their values for the benefit of society must always be superior to the merely mechanical skills of an investigator of the physical world. This faith, so alien to most people today, was the product of an educational system which separated boys of the social elite from girls and from boys of lower rank by immersing them in classical languages and literature almost to the exclusion of other subjects; and once that system and the view of the classics on which it depended was questioned, the way was open (as we might see it now) to new, more democratic forms of literature, notably the novel, and to the triumphs of science and technology; but for those nurtured within the intensely demanding and correspondingly satisfying intellectual world of humanistic classicism, what lay ahead seemed a wilderness without structure or standard, where ignorance would be no bar to literary ambition, and the dissection of a flea could be claimed as a more important endeavour than the understanding of an epic. It is the fear of such a world, and a poignant sense of the beauty and dignity of what is being lost, that fuels the *Dunciads*' onslaught on modernity.

Grub Street

One specifically literary aspect of the modernity attacked in the *Dunciad*s is the milieu metonymically referred to as 'Grub Street', that is, the world of the new breed of writers who – as the stereotype alleged – lived a hand-to-mouth existence by selling the products of their labour in the expanding market for printed books and ephemera. The classic account by Pat Rogers links the actual Grub Street (in an insalubrious area abutting the north-western corner of the City of London) with the careers of actual writers named in the *Dunciads* (Rogers 1972).[2] This remains a suggestive and illuminating treatment of the *Dunciads*' terrain, and of some of their characteristic objects of satire; but it is also important to recognise that – especially in *The Dunciad in Four Books* – Pope's targets extend more widely, indicting, ultimately, the highest in the land as the crucial encouragers of Dulness. At a more mundane level, it should also be noted that some of those named as bad writers in any and all of the *Dunciad*s were too genteel, or too successful, to lodge in anything like the squalor of the actual Grub Street. Grub Street remains, however, a powerful image of shabbiness of way of life, morals and literary standards: it may overlap, in strictly factual terms, with only a small minority of the careers cited as evidence for the triumph of Dulness, but it retains the figurative capacity to smear even the successful with the connotations of their complicity in a new system of literary production which Pope – and others – resented as a betrayal of traditional values.

Literature had formerly been associated with leisure and privilege. It required reserves of learning and an intensity of concentration possible only for those who could combine a gentleman's education with freedom from the need to earn a living. A writer without independent means needed patronage, rendering his work in a sense a vicarious product of the social group conventionally associated with good writing. Literature produced under these conditions assumed an elite readership.

This had never been an unproblematic basis for literary production; and Pope himself – from a middle-class trading background, and excluded by his Roman Catholicism from the conventional schooling of a gentleman – was centrally involved in the changes by which literary works were coming to be seen as a kind of property which a writer could legitimately sell in order to earn a living. As a young man he had shown exceptionally shrewd business sense in organising the sale of his translations of Homer. But the crucial turn in his management of his career was that he used the profit from his Homer not as a basis for proclaiming himself a literary professional in the modern literary marketplace, but as capital on which he could build a self-presentation as independent poet. He fashioned an image of himself as gentleman-poet, a writer as free from pressure from the marketplace as he was of pressure from patrons. In a telling passage in *To Arbuthnot* (1735) he lists the gentlemen and aristocrats who had first encouraged him to publish, contrasting them contemptuously with writers who had attacked him and whom he had attacked in his *Dunciads* (lines 135–46; see Hammond 1986: 70–98). The *Dunciads*, particularly in the games of Book II, construct such writers as commercially driven artisans producing to specification. Their masters are commercial publishers or government propaganda agents; venality in art and venality in politics are typically intertwined.[3]

Yet the *Dunciads* are not simple expressions of contempt. In what is probably the single most stimulating essay ever written on the *Dunciads*, Emrys Jones stresses the seductive relish with which Pope's imagination dwells on what he decries, citing the ostensibly disgusting but in effect 'strangely attractive' sewer-diving competition in Book II (Jones 1968: 641–2). A comparable ambivalence characterises Pope's attitude to the conceptual and technological fecundity of the book trade, with its continual transformation of literary genres, book formats, readerships and marketing structures. Pope's mock-epic *Dunciad in Four Books*, its verse set in classically elegant typography amid the pomp of ample margins, aspires to lofty judgement over the alleged chaos of hack writing; but it is intrinsic to the effect of the work that the verse is surrounded by dense and intricately laid out parody of the supposed excesses of contemporary scholarship, making the whole in effect as hybrid a product and as reliant on sophisticated presentation as any of the mixed genres and theatrical extravaganzas it condemns. Pope clearly wants to diagnose terminal degeneracy, but the work itself suggests a cultural proliferation as exciting as it is threatening.

A plethora of persons

Values and personalities are closely identified in Pope's imaginative construction of his world, whether we look at the positive ideals focused on his early mentors, or the fears of cultural disintegration projected onto a range of modern writers. What strikes readers first about the *Dunciads* is likely to be not so much a structure of values as a plethora of persons: even Swift warned Pope that within a few years or a few miles from London many of the names would be opaque to readers (*Corr.*: II, 504–5). Yet there is also a sense in which a chaos of striving and often unmemorably insignificant individuals is precisely the image of modernity that Pope wants to evoke. Artfully reconstructed in verse and commentary, such persons focus the issues and values which Pope felt to be at stake in current controversies – not least because many of their names become a kind of shorthand allusion to much-resented episodes of personal insult and aggression.[4]

Some of the writers who agitated against Pope had long been his enemies; others rushed into print on seeing themselves and their associates ridiculed in the first *Dunciad*; and Cibber was provoked to sustained attack only when he suspected that he was to be a central target in a new revision. Indeed, Pope deliberately orchestrated the response to his *Dunciads*, as if to obtain indisputable testimony to the antagonism that he wanted to pillory (see editor's note on note a) to Appendix I, and on the preliminary 'Advertisement'). He collected pamphlet attacks and had them bound into volumes, writing at the front of the first the biblical quotation, 'Behold it is my desire, that mine Adversary had written a Book. Surely I would take it on my Shoulder, and bind it as a crown unto me' (Job 31:35–6; Guerinot 1969: li). Pope takes the pamphlets as proof of his case against their authors: in the words of 'A Letter to the Publisher', 'they themselves were at great pains ... to testify under their hands to the truth of it'; or in the phrase that follows the epigraphs to *The Dunciad in Four Books* (all taken from the writings of his attackers), *'Out of thine own Mouth will I judge thee, wicked Scribler!'*

In this connection it is important to realise just how unpleasant some of these writers had been about Pope. What is remarkable about these attacks, as summarised in Guerinot's chronological listing, is not only their unprecedented quantity, but also their routine use of tactics which would today be considered both outrageous and irrelevant. Far from confining themselves to discussion of his writing, his antagonists employed gross vilification of his family (his father was a merchant), his religion (he was a Roman Catholic), and his physical appearance (only four feet six inches tall, he was hunched both forward and to the side). Fictitious allegations about his personal and professional life were made and repeated; and pamphleteers revelled in inventing crude sexual and excremental fantasies. The eagerness to wound and misrepresent was by no means all on Pope's side, although the fame of the *Dunciads* and the relative obscurity of most of his attackers have sometimes made it seem so.

How, though, is the first-time reader of *The Dunciad in Four Books* to cope with this crowd of unknown names? A practicable approach would be to start by getting familiar with a few of the most central figures – those discussed in the paragraphs that follow – and then to read the verse for the first time without pausing over the detail of the original or editorial annotation. In subsequent readings more attention can be paid to the original and editorial commentaries. Thus more detail about issues and individuals can be absorbed into and can adjust the reader's general sense of the shape of the work, until a complex sense emerges of the tensions between the roles that persons and events are made to play and what we might discover about them from other sources and points of view. This can only be done gradually, in repeated readings, for this is not a work that allows even the illusion of a single, unified reading.

Sir William Temple and Jonathan Swift

The Quarrel of the Ancients and the Moderns became personal for Pope through his friendship with men who had supported the ancient side when the quarrel arrived in England. Swift had been secretary to Sir William Temple (1628–99), a retired statesman of traditional humanistic outlook whose confidence in the obvious rightness of the ancient cause had led him to commit himself in print to opinions which were soon to be exposed (not that Swift or Pope would ever have admitted this) as completely erroneous. In *An Essay upon the Ancient and Modern Learning* (1690), Temple had not only demonstrated extremes of scepticism about the recent achievements of empirical science and of credulity about the technology of the ancient world, but had also declared that in the realm of literature 'the oldest books we have are still in their kind the best' (Monk 1963: 56–9, 64). As one of his examples in support of this claim he cited the (to him) evident merits of what he took to be one of the oldest books extant, namely the Epistles of Phalaris.

Richard Bentley

The controversy that followed hinged on whether these Epistles really were the work of Phalaris, a Sicilian of the sixth century BC, or whether they were a later composition falsely attributed to him. The professional classicist Richard Bentley (1662–1742), a pioneering figure in the editing and interpretation of ancient texts, was able to mobilise the kind of evidence that literary scholars now take for granted to show from dialect and internal references that these particular writings could not have been the work of a person living in the time and place of Phalaris.

Such an argument would today be regarded as conclusive, because historicist study is now the accepted foundation for the editing of texts; but at the time Bentley's conclusions outraged those committed to the superiority of the ancients. Opposition centred on Christ Church, an Oxford college at that time headed by Pope's future friend Francis Atterbury (1662–1732). To contemporaries, it was far from obvious that Bentley had won the debate, since his lack of the wit and graceful polish of the gentlemanly advocates of the classics ranged against him was widely mistaken for incompetence: later readers too would hardly judge from Swift's defence of his patron's position in *The Battle of the Books* that Bentley, not Temple, had had the best of the argument. The issues were widely conceived as issues of taste, not fact, since the taste of a classically trained gentleman could, it was assumed, be trusted to discern the essential qualities of the literature in which he had been immersed from boyhood; whereas the taste of a pedant, a person of inferior rank who earned his living by teaching and writing on the classics, could be assumed to have been corrupted by over-emphasis on technicalities which he would lack the instinctive discernment to ignore as irrelevant. Moreover, whereas a gentleman would involve himself in such a controversy only light-heartedly, to display the superiority of his wit and taste, a pedant would exploit the controversy to promote his professional expertise, either by advancing preposterous views or by dredging up unfamiliar works whose novelty depended on their being so tedious or fragmentary that gentlemen had no time for them. Bentley offended on both counts, and his blunt sarcasms, often delivered in language both coarse and archaic, further debarred him from any possibility of promotion to the rank of man of taste. For Swift, Pope and Atterbury, Bentley could no more be considered a gentleman than his techniques of historicist textual analysis and emendation ('verbal criticism') could convince them of unwelcome truths about ancient texts. When, a third of a century later, Bentley published an edition of Milton's *Paradise Lost* which proposed readings apparently in flat contradiction to common sense and probability, he further qualified himself for the direct onslaught that he received in *The Dunciad in Four Books* (Bentley 1732). It remains difficult to be sure exactly what he thought he was doing with Milton's text, which, as a book printed in the author's lifetime, presented radically different editorial problems from the ancient texts whose scattered and fragmentary manuscript traditions he had previously analysed. For sceptical contemporaries, however, this work of his old age confirmed long-held suspicions of his arrogance and perversity.

Lewis Theobald

Lewis Theobald, pilloried in the *Dunciad*s as the hero Tibbald from 1728 until he was replaced in 1743, was closely identified with Bentley's approach to texts at precisely the point that the quarrel impinged on Pope's own career. His *Shakespeare Restored* extended to an English author the principles of historicist analysis established by Bentley in his work on Greek and Latin texts. He showed that reading the books Shakespeare would have known, and comparing his grammar and idioms with those of his contemporaries, produced answers to textual problems very different from those which had resulted from Pope's reliance on taste rooted in assumed universal standards. The quarrel between such taste and the techniques of professional scholarship was thus revived over an English author, and the *Dunciads'* attack on Theobald as a pedantic and self-interested quibbler was one of its results. Again, although the commentary to any modern edition of Shakespeare will confirm that posterity has backed Theobald's belief in the importance of contextual study, if we looked only at the early *Dunciad*s, the most famous contemporary response to his work, we might well be persuaded that his approach was doomed to perish without trace. It is the irony of the *Dunciads*, in common with Scriblerian works more generally, to espouse outmoded positions with such dazzling accomplishment that readers, especially those disposed to cultural nostalgia, have often overlooked their tendentiousness.

Theobald qualified for his role as butt of the early *Dunciad*s by more than his textual scholarship, for though a lawyer by training, he worked as a professional writer; and Pope would repeatedly insist that the mark of a dunce was to neglect some lowlier – and implicitly more appropriate – occupation in the hope of making money by writing. In Vander Meulen's words, 'Theobald was the ideal centerpiece; he perfectly embodied the functions of farce-writing dramatist, occasional poet, periodical journalist, and pedantic editor and critic that Pope in his developing satire was identifying as generators of cultural degradation' (Vander Meulen 1991: 13).

Whigs and Tories

The values and personalities of the *Dunciad*s need also to be understood in relation to contemporary politics, a theme that emerges with particular explicitness in *The Dunciad in Four Books*.

Pope's family background placed him in an ambiguous relation to the political alignments of his time. As a Roman Catholic he was debarred from normal schooling, residence in central London, admission to university, public employment (including the post of Poet Laureate) and the ownership of land. In addition, he was always vulnerable to representation through the stereotypes of anti-Popish propaganda as a traitor to his country. Such a situation alone would have rendered contemporary Whiggism unattractive, since this was a strongly anti-Popish ideology which had at the close of the previous century crystallised around the insistence that no Catholic should be king. The fact that Pope's father was a merchant, belonging to a group seen by Whigs as vital to the expanding economy, might seem a potential counterweight; but Pope's paternal grandfather had been an Anglican royalist clergyman, and although his mother's recently gentrified family had for generations been prominent York tradesmen, Pope, who was only a child when his father retired from business and moved to the country, was to adopt an outlook that had much in common with traditional Toryism. Rather than celebrating business and the values of modernity, this child of a merchant forbidden by law to own land would grow up to celebrate not only a social order of rank and responsibility founded on landownership, but also many other traditional assumptions about literature, art, religion and politics which in retrospect we can recognise as associated with that increasingly obsolescent order. The *Dunciad*s in particular are fundamentally based on such values.

Walpole's regime

When Pope was young the political climate was sufficiently relaxed for him to mix with people of a wide variety of political outlooks. Although the Scriblerians represented a strongly Tory grouping, Pope also counted among his friends committed Whigs like the dramatist and Shakespeare editor Nicholas Rowe (1674–1718), and Joseph Addison (1672–1719), celebrated co-author of *The Spectator* and mentor to a circle of Whig writers. This changed when Queen Anne died in 1714 and was succeeded by the Hanoverian George I, who feared Tories as potential

Jacobites, supporters of the exiled line of Catholic Stuarts. He therefore ensured that they were excluded from power, and placed his government entirely in Whig hands. It was in the context of this hardening of political attitudes that Pope learned that Addison was secretly intriguing against him (*OAC*: I, 60–80). Although he continued for the rest of his life to proclaim his commitment to moderation and his willingness to befriend decent men of both parties, this betrayal marked the end of an era in his personal and political life.

The most powerful politician under George I and his successor George II was Sir Robert Walpole (1676–1745; Earl of Orford from 1742). Walpole, who has often been seen as, in effect, the first Prime Minister – the first to attain a degree of power over sovereign and colleagues which, though now familiar, was then a potentially scandalous usurpation – was a shrewd manager of the individuals and interest groups who sustained his regime, and remained in power until 1742. As a Whig, he was obviously open to conservative accusations of favouring the burgeoning financial and commercial schemes of the period to the detriment of traditional values; but as time went on, the opposition to his policies was swelled also by disaffected Whigs, typically motivated by disgust at his reluctance to use military force to defend British commercial interests (Gerrard 1994). By the time the first *Dunciad* appeared in 1728, opposition to his administration was already endemic among men of letters: what particularly outraged them was his indifference to the long-established expectation that monarchs and ministers should encourage the arts by providing financial support for writers (Goldgar 1976). With Walpole in charge it was clear that the government would do nothing to protect literature from the commercial pressures that were beginning to render obsolete some of the most cherished assumptions of traditional elite culture. From the beginning, Pope's *Dunciad*s implied that Walpole's regime was the necessary condition for the flourishing of Theobald and his like.

Bolingbroke and the Patriot opposition

This is not to assert that Pope was himself a Jacobite, committed to returning the exiled Catholic Stuarts to the throne, although all his *Dunciad*s employ Jacobite allusions as part of their arsenal against the status quo. By the 1730s, indeed, many Whigs as well as Tories, members of a group known as the Patriots, had gathered round the figurehead of Frederick, Prince of Wales, in the hope of establishing a reformed administration when his father should die (Gerrard 1994). Pope never fully committed himself to this opposition group, early suspecting the motives of some of its leaders. In revising the poem for *The New Dunciad* and *The Dunciad in Four Books* he made no attempt to set up the movement as an ideal: it effectively collapsed in the rush for power that greeted Walpole's fall in 1742. On the other hand, the Patriot platform had been to a large extent shaped by Henry St John (1678–1751), first Viscount Bolingbroke, one of Pope's most admired friends and mentors; and much in the politics of the 1742–3 revision rests on Bolingbroke's analysis of Whig corruption. Bolingbroke had served as a Tory minister under Anne and had after her death fled into exile and become for a time a professed Jacobite. More recently he had returned to England and attempted to cast off these associations, arguing that Walpole's regime had made such labels irrelevant. Walpole's Whig government, he claimed, had now assimilated the absolutist faith in its own power and prerogative that had formerly marked the extremes of Tory and royalist ideology, and was attempting to rule without regard for the balance of powers within the constitution (*A Dissertation upon Parties* 1735). The attacks on absolutism in Book IV of *The Dunciad in Four Books* allude to Bolingbroke's analysis; but Pope, apparently thoroughly disillusioned by this stage, does not even hint at a celebration of his positive programme.

Colley Cibber

The greatest surprise to readers in 1743, when Pope finally worked together the text of the earlier three-book *Dunciad* with the *New Dunciad* which had appeared separately in 1742, must have been that there was a new hero: instead of Theobald, the familiar target, the honour passed to Colley Cibber (1671–1757), a figure of undeniable cultural centrality whose ties to Walpole and the King, and to the worlds of playhouse and bookseller, were not only arguably closer than Theobald's had ever been, but were also more topical in the changed circumstances of the 1740s, especially since the publication of his self-satisfied *An Apology for the Life of Mr. Colley Cibber* in 1740. As a lackey of the regime, one who wrote, acted and produced plays, and was besides the King's chosen poet (Pope calls him 'Bays' to emphasise his Laureate status), he presented a potent focus for the alleged vicious circle of Whig corruption, cultural commercialism and the decline of taste.

Warburton and 'Bentley'/Aristarchus

The main problem in substituting Bays for Tibbald was that, unlike Theobald, Cibber was no scholar. The awkwardness shows in the list of medieval and early-modern books carried over from Tibbald's library, books in which Bays would have had little interest (I.135–40). However, Pope now had Warburton working alongside him. Warburton, who had reason to feel uneasy about the markedly friendly discussions he had had with Theobald about literature and editing before he met Pope, had first earned the gratitude of his new mentor by defending him against accusations that the *Essay on Man* was heretical (from 1738: see Warburton 1742). His initial training had been in the law, and his application of close critical reading to the defence of Pope's orthodoxy had about it an aggressive pertinacity not entirely unlike the attitude that Pope deplored in Theobald and Bentley. There is, therefore, a certain irony in Warburton's role in creating the character of 'Bentley'/Aristarchus in *The Dunciad in Four Books*, for which he composed the prefatory essay 'Ricardus Aristarchus of the Hero of the Poem'. He also contributed a distinctive brand of pedantic dogmatism to some of the notes attributed to 'Bentley', and to his predecessor Scriblerus, in the revised commentary.

The development of 'Bentley'/Aristarchus in 1743 was not simply a compensation for the new hero's unsuitability to the scholarly aspect of the satire, for Bentley, as the crucial figure in the English branch of the Quarrel of the Ancients and the Moderns, and also as a staunch supporter of the Whig regime in his later role as head of Trinity College, Cambridge, was far more important to Pope's grievances than the earlier *Dunciads* had revealed: a draft of the verse character of Aristarchus, not printed until 1742 and 1743 (IV.203–74), probably dates from a decade or more earlier.[5] By finally including in *The Dunciad in Four Books* this indictment of Bentley's literary, educational and political record, and by encouraging Warburton to elaborate the caricature of his methods, manner and attitudes, Pope was making explicit the connection between his dislike of modernity and the quarrel over the meaning of the past which had first called into question the gentlemanly taste of his early mentors. Although Bentley was eighty in 1742, and actually died in that year, the ridicule that had greeted his edition of *Paradise Lost* in 1732 had effectively renewed the topicality of what might otherwise have appeared an obsolete antagonism.

EPIC AND MOCK EPIC

The *Dunciads* owe their form to a late seventeenth- and early eighteenth-century hybrid of ancient and modern, the mock-epic or mock-heroic poem. Epic, which reflected on the culture and values of a society by retelling a traditional story of heroes and the gods who protected them, was the earliest narrative verse form known in Europe, the Greek *Iliad* and *Odyssey* attributed to Homer being, along with the Roman *Aeneid* of Virgil, the examples best known in the eighteenth century. Described by John Dryden (1631–1700) as 'the greatest Work which the Soul of Man is capable to perform', the epic or heroic poem (as it was often called) was respected as the highest form of narrative art: both Dryden and Pope translated ancient epic into English heroic couplets (rhyming pairs of lines in iambic pentameter) and aspired to write original epic for their own times ('Dedication of the Aeneis', Hooker 1956–89: V, 267). Neither, however, managed to do so; but both excelled at mock epic (Dryden in *Mac Flecknoe* and Pope in *The Rape of the Lock* and the *Dunciads*), in which a story of modern life was told with all the traditional grandeur of the old heroic poetry. Both indeed executed these poems in what had become the age's favourite metrical form, the heroic couplet, whose very name recalled its use in the translation of the ancient epic: there was no getting away from standards implied by this revered inheritance. The effect of decking out a modern tale in ancient dress has been much debated: does the grandeur shame and belittle modern life, or does it reveal an insufficiently recognised value in modernity? Despite a long tradition of insisting that mock epic (like those transparent but now rather dated frauds, mock cream and mock-turtle soup) never mocks but always pays tribute to the object of its imitation, readers have recently been more willing to concede that it also exposes the inadequacy of ancient models to a full exploration of the modern; and in the light of current interest in the vitality and volatility of eighteenth-century modernity, that inadequacy is no longer seen simply as an implicit condemnation of the modern. With the benefit of hindsight, and from a world in which the classics are even further from being accepted as cultural absolutes, we see that the epic was, by the eighteenth century, effectively finished; that the novel was gaining the ascendancy it still retains among literary forms; and that the combination of ostensibly triumphant wit and elegiac edginess typical of mock epic arises precisely from its precarious straddling of the growing divide.

Pope had already worked with the genre in *The Rape of the Lock*, placing a young society beauty in the structural position occupied in epic by the warrior hero. In the *Dunciads*, which from the beginning featured a kind of progress from the plebeian and mercantile City of London towards the royal and aristocratic Westminster, he signals an overarching allusion to the action of Virgil's *Aeneid*, in which Aeneas leaves the ruins of Troy and sails westward to found the new and greater city of Rome. Pope's perverse hero is still, in 1743, engaged on a version of this project: he is Dulness's 'Son who brings / The Smithfield Muses to the ear of Kings', translating fairground culture to theatres and palaces (I.1–2 and 2n.; and see map). Just as Aeneas has for his mother the powerful goddess Venus, so Pope's hero has Dulness. The classic account of the *Dunciads*' relation to the *Aeneid* is that by Aubrey Williams, who also emphasises Pope's invocation of Milton's *Paradise Lost* as exemplar of the English epic. There is, however, a danger in reading the *Dunciads* primarily as structural allusion to earlier epics, for by overemphasising the elements that correspond, we may pass over too lightly those that do not, making too tidy a set of equivalences. *The Dunciad in Four Books* is not predominantly characterised by sequences of action and speech: much of what passes for action is phantasmagoric; and long stretches of the verse, notably the whole fourth book, contain hardly anything describable as action. Thus we need to be alert to its often disconcerting differences from – even irrelevancies to – the *Aeneid* and the other classical antecedents so lavishly memorialised in its allusions and authorial commentary, as well as noticing its carefully crafted similarities.

This is not in any way to imply that today's reader can afford to ignore the *Dunciads*' classical heritage; and my commentary attempts to give a detailed sense of the beauty and complexity of the allusions with which Pope loads verse and notes alike, as well as of the jokes against ignorance or supposed perversity in classical studies by which he encourages the conventionally educated reader to preen himself on his superiority. After a first reading, it is particularly useful to turn in an accessible modern translation to the Homeric and Virgilian games which underpin much of Book II, and to the Virgilian visit to the underworld which shapes Book III, to get some sense of the structural importance to Pope's work of these poems which every educated male of the upper ranks then knew almost by heart. After examining the way these are refracted through Pope's memory and imagination, a modern reader can begin to see something of the thoroughness with which ancient poetry permeated the creativity of the conventionally educated. From this, even at our historical distance, we may be able to glimpse something of the terrifying prospect that opened up when it became conceivable that these basic building blocks of literate thought might be defaced by crass verbal critics or displaced by ignorant moderns convinced of the sufficiency of their own creations.

THE ACTION OF THE POEM

Although the prose elements of *The Dunciad in Four Books* are integral to its effects, there is at its heart a narrative poem, and new readers in particular may find it helpful to have a summary of its action keyed to line numbers. (Personalities, vocabulary, etc. are not explained here, but should be followed up in the editorial commentary on the relevant passage.)

Book I

The speaker declares Dulness and her son as subject, and invokes the great, her servants, to tell how she brought Britain under her power (1–8). The speaker describes Dulness's origins and ambitions (9–18). The work is dedicated to Jonathan Swift (19–28). In the Cave of Poverty and Poetry, near a lunatic asylum, Dulness reviews a mass of printed matter which testifies to the perversion of morality and literary decorum (29–84). On the evening of a Lord Mayor's Day she reflects how the achievements of the poets formerly employed by the City of London are continued in poets of the present (85–106). Bays, her favourite, is introduced, at a loss how to proceed in his writing and surrounded by worthless books (107–54). He builds an altar of books and places his works on it as a burnt offering, calling on Dulness to remember his lifelong devotion (155–256). Dulness puts out the flames and transports him to her home, where she reveals the processes by which literature degenerates under her care (257–86). She anoints him as her chosen son and prophesies his triumph at court, looking forward to the day when monarch and parliament will also succumb to her power (287–318). The book closes with general acclaim for Bays, prompting a comparison with the fable of the frogs who asked for a king (319–30).

Book II

Bays is enthroned, and Dulness summons Dunces of all ranks and occupations to join in games in his honour (1–30). The booksellers Lintot and Curll chase a phantom poet: Curll falls, sends a petition to Jupiter by way of the divine privy tended by Cloacina, and is inspired to get up and overtake his rival; but as he lays hold on the phantom it vanishes; and Dulness repeats the joke by providing three more phantom writers for a second race (31–130). Dulness advises Curll to learn from her trick how to market his authors under the names of their betters; and she gives him as a consolation prize a tapestry representing the sufferings of her champions, among whom he recognises himself in the act of being tossed in a blanket by the boys of Westminster School (131–56). Eliza is offered as first prize in a urination contest, with a chamber pot as second prize: Osborne's poor performance merits only the latter, while Curll's, impressive enough to be compared to the River Po, secures the first prize (157–90). Authors compete to tickle the patron with their dedications, but he is won over only by the prostitution of the sister of a candidate otherwise without merit (191–220). Dulness proclaims a noise-making contest in two classes: on hearing the equally matched performances in the jabbering class she awards a prize of a catcall to everyone; but in the braying class Blackmore easily outdoes the rest and is awarded the drum (221–68). Dulness then invites journalists to dive into a sewer, offering an ingot of lead as first prize and consolation prizes of coal for everyone else: competitors include Oldmixon,

Smedley, Concanen and Arnall; but Smedley appears to be lost, and emerges only later, relating how the mud-nymphs had revealed to him the underworld where authors from among the clergy spend the afterlife, and how he had been acclaimed there by his predecessor Milbourne (269–364). Dulness finally proposes to see who can stay awake while authors read from their works, offering the winner critical licence to say whatever he likes about literature; but there is no winner, as everyone falls asleep (365–418). Night falls, and the competitors disperse (419–28).

Book III

Meanwhile, Bays lies dreaming in Dulness's lap (1–12). He is led into the underworld by a slovenly sibyl, and is rowed over the Styx, past the souls of dead bad poets, to the place where they wait to be returned to the world in new bodies (13–34). He is greeted by Settle, his poetic father, who explains the metempsychosis of nonsense and promises him visions of the past and future triumphs of Dulness (35–66). Settle begins with a historical survey of the destruction of learning, ranging over China, Alexandria, the Roman Empire and the Islamic world; and he presents religious bigotry as prime cause of the ruin of Roman art and culture both in Rome itself and in medieval Britain (67–122). He prophesies Dulness's coming triumph, localising her in Grub Street among her literary sons; and he goes on to survey individual writers, closing with a warning that though the Dunces should set themselves against everything good, they must still be careful not actually to commit blasphemy (123–224). This advice is ascribed to a transitory flash of reason; and Settle moves on to show Bays apocalyptic scenes of contemporary stage-effects in pantomime, assuring him that all this is destined for him to achieve (225–72). Bays will fulfil what Settle, in a relatively limited career whose high point was the office of poet to the City of London, could only dream of; for Bays will be taken up by the highest in the land; he will be involved with fashionable opera, and will produce theatrical programmes featuring apocalyptic special effects (273–316). Settle closes by acclaiming Bays as agent of the return of Dulness's empire, by identifying the cultural signals of her approach – which include Gay's failure to secure a pension, Swift's exile and Pope's turn from original poetry to translating Homer and editing Shakespeare – and by foreseeing the dissolution of the educational system (317–38). Bays's dream vanishes through the ivory gate (339–40).

Book IV

The speaker implores Chaos and Night to allow him time to conclude (1–9). Amid widespread sickness and infertility Dulness takes her throne, with Bays on her lap and personifed abstractions – the good under restraint and the bad triumphant – grouped around (9–44). Opera warns Dulness to banish Handel (45–70). Dulness summons her supporters (71–100). Seeing editors bringing up the rear, Dulness encourages them to distinguish themselves at their authors' expense (101–34). The schoolmaster emerges from the jostling crowd to celebrate the narrowly verbal learning imposed on schoolboys, prompting Dulness to wish for a return, via verbal quibbling, to arbitrary monarchy (135–88). This rouses the intellectual reactionaries of Oxford and Cambridge, led by Aristarchus, who boasts of his service to Dulness in textual criticism and in educating the young in such a way as to prevent them from understanding anything important; but he falls silent when he sees the young traveller returning from the Grand Tour (189–274). The traveller's tutor presents his pupil and his foreign whore, describing the experiences abroad that have improved the pupil's capacity to serve Dulness (275–336). She notices Paridel among an apathetic group of idlers: her favour only makes him sleepier (336–46). Annius prays to be allowed to cheat by trading in fake antiquities, and when challenged by Mummius to produce medals which he has paid for but which Annius has swallowed, suggests that they dine with Pollio with a view to recovering the treasure (347–97). From a crowd of virtuosi in natural history emerge a horticulturalist and a butterfly collector who argue over a carnation damaged by the collector in his eagerness to capture a butterfly: Dulness commends both and exhorts them to interest others in such hobbies in order to distract them from the worship of the God who creates the objects of their obsessions (397–458). A clergyman of deist leanings with a taste for *a priori* argument promises to take care of the latter project (459–92). Silenus, mentioned at the end of the clergyman's speech, wakes up and explains to Dulness that the returned traveller is the finished product of the education she sponsors: devoid of religious awe and skilled only in empty words, he is ready to submit to arbitrary authority (493–516). The Wizard offers the young a potion which turns them into mere dilettanti, obsessed with distractions from horseracing and hunting, through varieties of self-obsession, to opera and gastronomy (517–64). Dulness confers titles and degrees on her disciples (565–78). She instructs them to cultivate pride, selfishness and dullness, suggests hobbies to distract the ruling class from public responsibilities, and looks forward to the ambition of one of her servants who, by daring to make the monarch his puppet, will bring the whole country under her control (579–604). She is prevented from saying more by a yawn which puts to sleep the church, educational institutions, parliament, government and the armed forces (605–18). The speaker implores the muse to list the victims of the yawn, but his speech lapses into asterisks (619–26). Even the muse succumbs as Dulness arrives in triumph, extinguishing intellectual light and putting to flight the personifications of moral and religious principle: she restores the chaos which existed before the creation, and shuts the curtain on a darkened universe (627–56).

THE DUNCIAD IN FOUR BOOKS AS PHYSICAL OBJECT

Pope was unusually interested in the physical appearance of his works, and controlled the production process carefully. *The Dunciad in Four Books* of 1743 was conceived in the quarto format which he had adopted for his most expensive editions, and many features of its appearance testify to his aspiration to present it as a modern classic, at the same time as parodying what he saw as the excesses of modern editors. The poem itself is printed with a plain dignity which had become established as the appropriate style for prestige editions of Latin poetry, and which

Pope increasingly favoured for his own works: it marks a reaction against the relative fussiness of the conventional format – with routine capitalisation of nouns and extensive italicisation – in which his earliest works had been produced. However, *The Dunciad in Four Books* as a whole is typographically very complex: the verse is elaborately underlaid with double columns of footnotes, with much italic type and substantial quotations in Greek; and even archaic blackletter type is occasionally used. The layout of notes is further complicated by a division between 'Remarks' and 'Imitations'. This somewhat artificial distinction between explanatory notes and citation of passages imitated reflects another aspect of Pope's aspiration to present himself as a classic: it is copied, along with other features of layout and typography, from the 1716 Geneva edition of the much-admired French poet Nicolas Boileau Despréaux (1636–1711: known as Boileau), which had presented, in double columns, a three-decker commentary divided into 'Changemens', 'Remarques' and 'Imitations' (McLaverty 1984: 99–105 and plates on pp. 102–3). (Warburton completed the resemblance after the poet's death by adding a third level of commentary, 'Changes', which recorded the different versions through which particular lines had passed.)

Around the poem and its notes is arranged a complex series of prefaces and appendices. Some parody the methods of scholars in presenting classic Greek and Latin texts. Others parody legal documents. Several reprint documents from previous stages in the text's production and reception history. All in all, the accumulation of supplementary documentation both parodies the modern developments in the volume and the ephemerality of printed matter and implies a claim to be the kind of classic text that generates a documentary and interpretative tradition.

A NOTE ON THE TEXT

Copy text

This edition has been made from British Library 641.l.17 (1.), one of the 100 fine-paper copies of the 1743 *Dunciad in Four Books* (Maslen & Lancaster 1991: Checklist, no. 3138). These were printed on larger, thicker paper than the 1500 ordinary copies, and were presumably intended for presentation. Additional minor corrections were also made between the printing of the ordinary and fine-paper copies. Fine-paper copies are now very rare: apart from the one in the British Library, there is one at Yale, and another was presented to the Bodleian Library by David Foxon in 1997 (Vander Meulen 1989: 309; Bodleian Vet. A4 c. 429(1)).

One particular feature of the fine-paper copies deserves comment: they are not affected as most of the ordinary copies are by the substitution of a cancel which replaced IV.115–18 with four lines of asterisks. The issues surrounding the cancel are complex: allegations about it appeared soon after Pope's death, and have recently been reconsidered by David Vander Meulen (*Gentleman's Magazine* 14 (1745): 611; Vander Meulen 1989: 307–8). However, no cancels were printed for the fine-paper copies, so there is at least a case for believing that Pope wished his most privileged readers not to be deprived of these four lines (Vander Meulen 1989: 309–10).

Copies of 1743 vary in the order in which the titles, preliminaries and introductory essays are bound. It is not easy to see in what order the items were intended to appear, and binders evidently had difficulty in making the two pagination sequences (one roman, one arabic) run properly. The order given here is not that of my copy text: it has been devised to present the items in a plausible sequence compatible with the page-numbering.

General

The aim of this edition is to present *The Dunciad in Four Books* with a full modern commentary set out on the same page, but with a clear visual separation between the modern commentary and the verse and prose of Pope's text.

I present the text largely unmodernised, because there are particularly strong arguments for regarding the accidentals of Pope's *Dunciad*s as part of their meaning: these are texts which discuss the implications of the new market in the printed word, and as they develop they mobilise an increasing range of the resources of early eighteenth-century print technology. I have preserved, with the exceptions listed below, the spelling, capitalisation and italicisation of 1743; and I have made no attempt either to regularise its inconsistencies of referencing or to bring its punctuation into line with modern usage. Two features, however, have been modernised: diphthongs are spelled out as two letters; and contemporary abbreviations for 'et', 'et cetera' and 'verse' which use unfamiliar characters have been modernised. Some additional changes which particularly affect the original footnotes have been dictated by the need to save space: double inverted commas have been changed to single and are not repeated at the beginning of each line of the quotation, and in the light of this omission closing speech marks have been inserted where necessary to prevent confusion; double-column presentation of footnotes has been abandoned; short verse quotations which were originally italicised, indented and spaced off from the prose preceding and following have been set in roman inside inverted commas and set continuously with the prose, with punctuation modified accordingly and slashes inserted to show line divisions; the separate sequences of footnotes originally designated as 'Remarks' and 'Imitations' have been merged, with cues adapted as necessary; the abbreviation 'VER.' before line cues has been omitted and square brackets following cues supplied where absent; and the quotations which follow cues in the original are omitted – with cues adapted accordingly – except in cases where the quotation is necessary to identify the particular word or phrase engaged by the note. Literal errors (mainly miscued notes and incorrect book, page and line references) have been silently corrected.

An annotated edition can assist the reader in many ways, but it can never replace the original book, particularly in the case of so significantly complex a piece of bookmaking as *The Dunciad in Four Books*. Although facsimiles might provide a partial solution, at the time of writing these have been published only for the *Dunciad*s of 1728 and 1729. However, although fine-paper copies of 1743 are rare and access to them is usually restricted, ordinary copies are quite widely distributed among major libraries, and anyone working on *The Dunciad in Four Books* who can arrange to examine one will find that the experience well repays the effort.

NOTES

1. In contrast, James Sutherland's Volume V of *The Twickenham Edition of the Poems of Alexander Pope* collates all four versions, as well as intermediate variants, and produces from them two reading texts. The present text is a variant of Sutherland's B type, but is presented without the need to reconstruct the original and editorial commentaries by cross-referencing to the earlier versions subsumed in his A text.
2. The principal places named in *The Dunciad in Four Books* are marked on the simplified map included in the present edition. A contemporary large-scale map is reproduced and indexed in Hyde 1981.
3. Hammond has recently extended and elaborated his view of Pope's relation to this tension between the ideal of the gentlemanly amateur and the new realities of professional authorship (Hammond 1997).
4. Few readers will be in danger of taking literally a satirical poem which assigns imaginary words and actions to named individuals; but where Pope does assign to a character a name (Tibbald, Bays) which distinguishes him from his historical original (Theobald, Cibber), the distinction is worth preserving. In the case of Richard Bentley (whose role I discuss later in this Introduction), the original commentary assigns to him so many fictitious pronouncements that I have distinguished in my commentary between the real Bentley and the fictionalised 'Bentley'.
5. This formed part of the second of two known manuscripts of *Dunciad* material, which are now extant only in later transcriptions. Dating of the original second manuscript is problematic: Vander Meulen places it in its entirety before the first *Dunciad* of 1728, while McLaverty suggests that some parts, including the Bentley passage, may date from as late as the early 1730s. For discussion see Mack 1982: 339–43; Mack 1984: 98, 127–8; Vander Meulen 1991: 49–59; McLaverty 1993: 9–14.

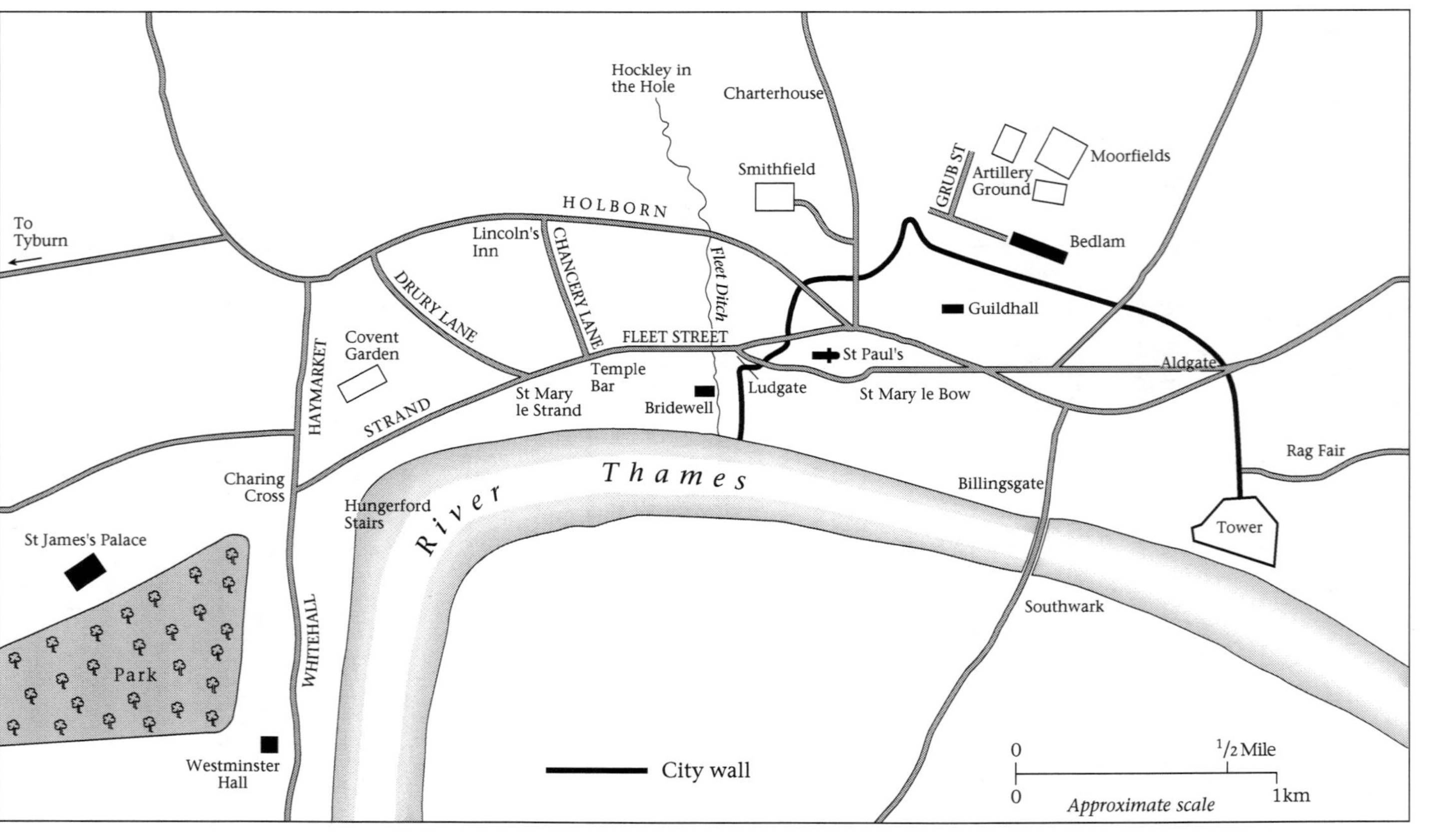

The London area in the 1740s

THE

DUNCIAD,

IN

FOUR BOOKS.

Printed according to the complete Copy found in the Year 1742.

WITH THE

PROLEGOMENA of SCRIBLERUS,

AND

NOTES VARIORUM.

To which are added,

SEVERAL NOTES now first publish'd, the HYPERCRITICS of ARISTARCHUS, and his *Dissertation* on the HERO of the POEM.

Tandem *Phoebus* adest, morsusque inferre parantem
Congelat, et patulos, ut erant, indurat hiatus. OVID.

LONDON,

Printed for M. COOPER at the Globe in Pater-noster-row,

MDCCXLIII.

---

complete Copy found in the Year 1742: *The Dunciad in Four Books* of 1743 first incorporated Book IV (published separately in 1742 as *The New Dunciad*). The claim that the text was 'found' rather than deliberately published by Pope is a transparent pretence.

PROLEGOMENA of SCRIBLERUS: Introductory material provided by the fictitious Martinus Scriblerus.

NOTES VARIORUM: 'Variorum' ('of various people') designates an edition which compiles extracts from the critical tradition, a potentially uncritical procedure from which Bentley, with his emphasis on critical judgement, was moving away (McLaverty 1984: 97). The fiction was that Scriblerus had compiled the 1729 *Dunciad Variorum*: 'Bentley'/Aristarchus is now brought in to challenge and update his work.

HYPERCRITICS of ARISTARCHUS: 'Hypercritics' suggests that the critical input will be excessive and unreasonable. Aristarchus of Samothrace (*c.*215–*c.*143 BC), librarian at Alexandria and reputedly the first professional scholar, produced commentaries on some of the texts later to be edited by Richard Bentley, who had specified the qualities of Aristarchus among the requirements of an editor (Bentley 1711: Praefatio). Pope makes Bentley call himself Aristarchus at IV.210.

Tandem: The Roman poet Ovid (Publius Ovidius Naso: 43 BC–AD 17) describes how Phoebus (Apollo), god of poetry, prevented a serpent from devouring the murdered poet Orpheus: 'At last Phoebus appears, and freezes him as he is about to bite, and turns to stone, just as they were, his gaping jaws' (*Metamorphoses* XI.58, 60). This implies an identification between Orpheus, the Apollonian poet-priest whose song brought order and peace and continued even after his death, and the author of the *Dunciad*, suggesting that Pope's adversaries will find a similarly unwelcome immortality through their representation in the *Dunciad* (Regan 1975; Peterson 1975).

Speedily will be publish'd,

[In the same Paper, and Character, to be bound up with this,]

The ESSAY on MAN,

The ESSAY on CRITICISM,

And the rest of the Author's ORIGINAL POEMS,

With the COMMENTARIES and NOTES of

W. WARBURTON, A. M.

Speedily will be publish'd: When Pope died in 1744 he left his collaborator Warburton 'the property of all such of my Works already printed, as he hath written, or shall write Commentaries or Notes upon' (Nichol 1992: xxxii). For the collaboration and its relation to the publication process of *The Dunciad in Four Books* and to Warburton's subsequent career, see Foxon 1991: 144–52.

Character: type.

ADVERTISEMENT
TO THE
READER.

I *Have long had a design of giving some sort of Notes on the Works of this Poet. Before I had the happiness of his acquaintance, I had written a Commentary on his* Essay on Man, *and have since finished another on the* Essay on Criticism. *There was one already on the* Dunciad, *which had met with general approbation: but I still thought some additions were wanting (of a more serious kind) to the humorous Notes of* Scriblerus, *and even to those written by Mr.* Cleland, *Dr.* Arbuthnot, *and others. I had lately the pleasure to pass some months with the Author in the Country, where I prevailed upon him to do what I had long desired, and favour me with his explanation of several passages in his Works. It happen'd, that just at that juncture was published a ridiculous book against him, full of Personal Reflections which furnished him with a lucky opportunity of improving* This Poem, *by giving it the only thing it wanted, a* more considerable Hero. *He was always sensible of its defect in that particular, and owned he had*

ADVERTISEMENT: This declaration, first used in 1743 and ostensibly by Warburton, was apparently drafted by Pope as part of his 'Project ... to make you in some measure the Editor of this new Edit. of the Dunc. if you have no scruple of owning some of the *Graver Notes* which are now added' (*Corr.*: IV, 427; Leranbaum 1977: 143–4). The 'scruple' might seem to suggest that the notes were actually not by Warburton; but Pope may simply have thought that Warburton might be unwilling to 'own' his participation in a satire potentially embarrassing to a clergyman (compare *Corr.*: IV, 430). By initialling the 'Advertisement' Warburton declared his status as Pope's authorised commentator.

one already: From 1729 the *Dunciad* had a commentary written mostly by Pope, but apparently incorporating contributions from friends and others.

Mr. *Cleland:* Pope's friend Major (called 'Colonel') William Cleland (*c.*1674–1741), who allowed his signature to be put to 'A Letter to the Publisher', and was similarly accommodating in 1731 over a letter defending *To Burlington* (Butt 1954: 32–3; *Corr.*: III, 162, 254–7; Mack 1984: 423). Pope addressed a verse invitation to him (*TE*: VI, 321–2). A Scot, he pursued a military career during the War of the Spanish Succession, and 'after the Peace' concluded at Utrecht in 1713 held civil service posts (Blanchard 1941: 119–20). Pope suggests that he was unjustly dismissed by Walpole (see notes on the conclusion of 'A Letter to the Publisher', and for Pope's response to news of Cleland's death, *Corr.*: IV, 377–8).

a ridiculous book: Cibber's *A Letter from Mr. Cibber, To Mr. Pope* (1742).

a *more considerable hero:* The original hero, Tibbald, caricatured Lewis Theobald, who had given particular offence by his criticism of Pope's Shakespeare in his *Shakespeare Restored* (1726). In 1743 Tibbald was replaced by Bays, caricaturing Colley Cibber, a more compelling focus for increasingly explicit and wide-ranging political and cultural concerns (Rogers 1975: 121). Cibber had been an object of Pope's ridicule from before the publication of the first *Dunciad* in 1728 (see the ironic guide to bad writing *Peri Bathous*: *PW*: II, 197, 230). His

let it pass with the Hero it had, purely for want of a better; not entertaining the least expectation that such an one was reserved for this Post, as has since obtained the Laurel: *But since that had happened, he could no longer deny this justice either to* him *or the* Dunciad.

And yet I will venture to say, there was another motive which had still more weight with our Author: This person was one, who from every Folly (not to say Vice) of which another would be ashamed, has constantly derived a Vanity; *and therefore was the* man in the world who would least be hurt by it.

W. W.

---

appointment as Poet Laureate in 1730 enabled Pope to present him as a buffoon raised from playhouse to court by the corruption of the establishment (for Pope's attitude to the Laureateship, from which he was barred by religion, see Woodman 1990). Once he had decided on the change, Pope had deliberately provoked Cibber into offering apparent justification by attacking him further (*Corr.*: IV, 448–9; *OAC*: I, 111–12, 148–9).

This person was one: Cibber's *Apology*, characterised by frankness about arguably discreditable traits, marked a new departure in the construction of actors as media figures (Straub 1992: 24–46).

W. W.: William Warburton.

By AUTHORITY.

By virtue of the Authority in Us vested by the Act for subjecting Poets to the power of a Licenser, we have revised this Piece; where finding the style and appellation of KING to have been given to a certain Pretender, Pseudo-Poet, or Phantom, of the name of TIBBALD; and apprehending the same may be deemed in some sort a

---

By AUTHORITY. The announcement of the new hero of 1743, a parody of an official proclamation, printed in archaic blackletter type under a spoof royal arms. The royal lion has an exaggerated smirk perhaps indicative of Cibber's self-satisfaction; and, like the unicorn, has suggestively large genitals (Mengel in Mack & Winn 1980: 767–73). The initials on the Garter buckle could be read as 'G' for George II and a reversed 'C' for Colley; while the interlocked 'C's under the text could stand for Colley Cibber (while recalling the 'X' used by the illiterate to sign documents), and a 'Ch.' for Lord Chancellor, anticipating III.324. A monogram of interlocked 'C's was also used by the actual Lord Chamberlain, Charles Fitzroy (1683–1757), second Duke of Grafton, responsible for appointing Cibber as Laureate in 1730, and widely ridiculed for stupidity (Gibbs 1910–40: VI, 45–6).

Act for subjecting Poets: Dramatic verse (only) was subject to licensing, in that by the Act of 1737 plays had to be approved by the Lord Chamberlain before they could be performed. The opposition to Walpole condemned this as oppressive censorship: see IV.35–44 and notes.

KING* to have been given to a certain *Pretender: Since George II had honoured Cibber as Laureate, it would be treasonable to promote any other writer (such as Theobald) ahead of him. 'Pretender' at this time primarily denoted a Jacobite claimant to the throne: in 1745 the 'Young Pretender', Charles Edward Stuart (1720–88), was to lead a rebellion in favour of his father, James Francis Edward Stuart (1688–1766), the 'Old Pretender'.

Phantom: A term used by the literary theorist René Le Bossu (1631–80) to suggest that the importance of the epic hero was representative, not individual. Here it allows Pope to play with the notion that his victim was not even a real person. Scriblerus develops the notion in 'Martinus Scriblerus of the Poem'.

Reflection on Majesty, **or at least an insult on that Legal Authority which has bestowed on another person the** Crown of Poesy: **We have ordered the said** Pretender, Pseudo-Poet, **or** Phantom, **utterly to** vanish **and** evaporate **out of this work: And do declare the said Throne of Poesy from henceforth to be abdicated and vacant, unless duly and lawfully supplied by the** LAUREATE himself. **And it is hereby enacted, that no other person do presume to fill the same.**

ƆC. Ch.

---

abdicated and vacant: A tendentious allusion to the official justification of the accession of William and Mary in 1688 ('The Glorious Revolution'): when James II fled from William's invasion, he was held to have abdicated, and to have left the throne vacant.

DENNIS, Remarks on Pr. ARTHUR.

I Cannot but think it the most *reasonable* thing in the world, to distinguish good writers, by discouraging the bad. Nor is it an *ill-natured* thing, in relation even to the very *persons* upon whom the reflections are made. It is true, it may deprive them, a little the sooner, of a *short profit* and a *transitory reputation*; but then it may have a good effect, and oblige them (before it be too late) to decline that for which they are so very *unfit*, and to have recourse to *something* in which they may be more successful.

CHARACTER of Mr. P. 1716.

THE *Persons* whom Boileau has attacked in his writings, have been for the most part *Authors*, and most of those Authors, *Poets:* And the censures he hath passed upon them have been confirmed by all Europe.

GILDON, Pref. to his NEW REHEARSAL.

IT is the common cry of the *Poetasters* of the town, and their fautors, that it is an *ill-natured thing* to expose the *Pretenders* to wit and poetry. The Judges and Magistrates may with full as good reason be reproached with *Ill-nature* for putting the Laws in execution against a Thief or Impostor. — The same will hold in the republic of Letters, if the Critics and Judges will let every *ignorant pretender* to scribling pass on the world.

DENNIS: John Dennis (1657–1734), literary critic and convinced Whig, was an inveterate and immoderate adversary of Pope who early set the precedent for attacks on his work and character. In *Peri Bathous*, published just before the first *Dunciad* in 1728, Dennis is implied to be among the '*Porpoises*' who cause 'a great turmoil and tempest, but ... are only shapeless and ugly monsters' (*PW*: II, 197). Dennis is ironically made to 'justify' Pope's attack on the victims of the *Dunciad* by a loose quotation from *Remarks on Prince Arthur*, an attack on Sir Richard Blackmore (*d.* 1729), physician, prolific epicist and favourite butt of the wits, responsible for more than twice as many examples of bad writing in *Peri Bathous* as any other writer (Hooker 1939–43: I, 48).

CHARACTER of Mr. P. 1716: *A True Character of Mr. Pope* (1716), an anonymous attack by Dennis, apparently incorporating material by Charles Gildon (1665–1724) (Hooker 1939–43: II, 107; for other grounds of offence see *OAC*: I, 71; II, 625). In *Peri Bathous* Gildon seems to be included both among the '*Porpoises*' alongside Dennis and among the '*Flying Fishes* ... who now and then rise' above their general level of bad writing (*PW*: II, 196–7). ***Boileau:*** Boileau, who had satirised fellow poets, is shown by repeated allusions to be a model for the stance towards contemporary writers adopted in the *Dunciad*.

GILDON: Adapted from the opening of Gildon's anonymously published *A New Rehearsal* (1714). **Poetasters:** worthless poets. ***fautors:*** supporters. ***pass on the world:*** Pass themselves off to the public as what they are not.

THEOBALD, Letter to Mist, June 22, 1728.

ATTACKS may be levelled, either against *Failures* in *Genius*, or against the *Pretensions* of *writing without one*.

CONCANEN, Ded. to the Author of the DUNCIAD.

A *Satyr* upon *Dulness* is a thing that has been *used* and *allowed* in *All Ages*.

Out of thine own Mouth will I judge thee, wicked Scribler!

Mist: *Mist's Weekly Journal*, a paper which specialised in Tory, sometimes Jacobite, political comment (for title changes see *The Weekly Journal: or, Saturday's Post*; Black 1987b).

Concanen: Matthew Concanen (1701–49), writer and Whig propagandist, to whom Pope attributed 'To the Author of the Dunciad', the preface to *A Compleat Collection* (1728).

Out of thine own Mouth: Echoing the words of the master to the servant who buried his one talent rather than investing it ('Out of thine own mouth will I judge thee, thou wicked servant': Luke 19:22). The allusion serves Pope's contention that bad writers refuse to labour at the work nature and education have fitted them for and wrongly aspire instead to an elite activity: cp. his own self-justificatory claim that 'I left no Calling for this idle trade' (*To Arbuthnot*, line 129). By citing his victims' own defences of satire on bad writers, Pope has made them 'justify' the satire he will turn against them.

A

LETTER

TO THE

PUBLISHER,

Occasioned by the first correct

EDITION of the DUNCIAD.

IT is with pleasure I hear, that you have procured a correct copy of the DUNCIAD, which the many surreptitious ones have rendered so necessary; and it is yet with more, that I am informed it will be attended with a COMMENTARY: A Work so requisite, that I cannot think the Author himself would have omitted it, had he approved of the first appearance of this Poem.

Such *Notes* as have occurred to me I herewith send you: You will oblige me by inserting them amongst those which are, or will be, transmitted to you by others; since not only the Author's friends, but even strangers, appear engaged by humanity, to take some care of an Orphan of so much genius and spirit, which its parent seems to have abandoned from the very beginning, and suffered to step into the world naked, unguarded, and unattended.

It was upon reading some of the abusive papers lately published, that my great regard to a Person, whose Friendship I esteem as one of the chief honours of my life, and a much greater respect to Truth, than to him or any man living, engaged me in enquiries, of which the inclosed *Notes* are the fruit.

I perceived, that most of these Authors had been (doubtless very wisely) the first aggressors. They had tried, 'till they were weary, what was to be got by railing at each other: Nobody was either concerned or surprised, if this or that scribler was proved a dunce. But every one was curious to read what could be said to prove

A LETTER TO THE PUBLISHER: Generally supposed to be by Pope, though signed by Cleland. First used in 1729, it was adapted for 1743, after Cleland was dead. Like the 1729 *Dunciad*, it focuses on bad writing and on personal offences against Pope rather than on the larger political concerns stressed in *The Dunciad in Four Books*.

had he approved: In line with the fiction that the *Dunciad* had been published without Pope's consent.

abusive papers: Pope's politics, religion and literary attitudes had long made him a target of printed abuse (listed and described in Guerinot 1969).

***the inclosed* Notes:** Implying that Cleland contributed to the annotation of 1729.

railing at each other: The mutual enmity of bad writers is a key theme of the *Dunciad*.

if this or that scribler was proved a dunce: 'Dunce' derives from the celebrated thirteenth-century scholastic philosopher Duns Scotus. In the Renaissance scholastic thought came to be seen as perverse sophistry, and 'dunce' to imply wrong-headed stupidity.

Mr. Pope one, and was ready to pay something for such a discovery: A stratagem, which would they fairly own, it might not only reconcile them to me, but screen them from the resentment of their lawful Superiors, whom they daily abuse, only (as I charitably hope) to get that *by* them, which they cannot get *from* them.

I found this was not all: Ill success in that had transported them to Personal abuse, either of himself, or (what I think he could less forgive) of his Friends. They had called Men of virtue and honour bad Men, long before he had either leisure or inclination to call them bad Writers: And some had been such old offenders, that he had quite forgotten their persons as well as their slanders, 'till they were pleased to revive them.

Now what had Mr. Pope done before, to incense them? He had published those works which are in the hands of every body, in which not the least mention is made of any of them. And what has he done since? He has laughed, and written the Dunciad. What has that said of them? A very serious truth, which the public had said before, that they were dull: And what it had no sooner said, but they themselves were at great pains to procure or even purchase room in the prints, to testify under their hands to the truth of it.

I should still have been silent, if either I had seen any inclination in my friend to be serious with such accusers, or if they had only meddled with his Writings; since whoever publishes, puts himself on his trial by his Country. But when his Moral character was attacked, and in a manner from which neither truth nor virtue can secure the most innocent, in a manner, which, though it annihilates the credit of the accusation with the just and impartial, yet aggravates very much the guilt of the accusers; I mean by Authors *without names:* then I thought, since the danger was common to all, the concern ought to be so; and that it was an act of justice to detect the Authors, not only on this account, but as many of them are the same who for several years past have made free with the greatest names in Church and State, exposed to the world the private misfortunes of Families, abused all, even to Women, and whose prostituted papers (for one or other Party, in the unhappy divisions of their Country) have insulted the Fallen, the Friendless, the Exil'd, and the Dead.

---

own: admit.

to get that* by *them, which they cannot get* from *them: As these writers cannot gain their patronage, they are reduced to earning money by writing against them.

not the least mention is made of any of them: *Peri Bathous* (1728) had equivocated over the identity of its victims by using initials, allegedly at random. 'Those works which are in the hands of every body' could be read as limiting the field to Pope's most widely read poems and translations.

the prints: the press.

to testify under their hands: By publishing signed proof of their dulness.

only meddled with his Writings: Distinguishing between legitimate criticism of published works, and illegitimate personal attacks.

prostituted papers: Political propaganda written only for money.

unhappy divisions: Pope's society was polarised around oppositions between Whig and Tory, Hanoverian and Jacobite. Though basically Tory in outlook, he prided himself on cultivating friendships across party lines, and even *The Dunciad in Four Books* attempts some semblance of neutrality (e.g. I.207–8).

the Fallen, the Friendless, the Exil'd, and the Dead: Notably three friends highly placed in

Besides this, which I take to be a public concern, I have already confessed I had a private one. I am one of that number who have long loved and esteemed Mr. Pope; and had often declared it was not his capacity or writings (which we ever thought the least valuable part of his character) but the honest, open, and beneficent man, that we most esteemed, and loved in him. Now, if what these people say were believed, I must appear to all my friends either a fool, or a knave; either imposed on myself, or imposing on them; so that I am as much interested in the confutation of these calumnies, as he is himself.

I am no Author, and consequently not to be suspected either of jealousy or resentment against any of the Men, of whom scarce one is known to me by sight; and as for their Writings, I have sought them (on this one occasion) in vain, in the closets and libraries of all my acquaintance. I had still been in the dark, if a Gentleman had not procured me (I suppose from some of themselves, for they are generally much more dangerous friends than enemies) the passages I send you. I solemnly protest I have added nothing to the malice or absurdity of them; which it behoves me to declare, since the vouchers themselves will be so soon and so

---

the Tory regime of Anne's last years, but threatened with prosecution by the Whig administration of George I: Robert Harley (1661–1724), first Earl of Oxford and former Lord Treasurer, was accused of treason (largely because he had ended the War of the Spanish Succession, which the Whigs wished to continue) and sent to the Tower in 1715, but acquitted in 1717; his associate and rival Bolingbroke fled to France and for a time became Foreign Secretary to the Pretender, but was pardoned in 1723; and Francis Atterbury, Bishop of Rochester, was sentenced to exile in 1723 after a Bill of Pains and Penalties was brought against him: this required only a parliamentary vote, rather than a conviction. The government correctly suspected, but could not prove, that he was plotting a Jacobite invasion.

the honest, open, and beneficent man: Pope frequently insisted that friendship and integrity meant more to him than literary fame.

I am as much interested: I have as much at stake.

the confutation of these calumnies: the disproof of these false charges.

in vain: Because no person of taste would buy such works.

closets: Small rooms used for private study and reading.

a Gentleman: Probably Richard Savage (*d.* 1743), a gifted but unstable writer, best known from Samuel Johnson's *Life of Savage* (1744: Tracy 1971). Although Savage claimed his real parents were aristocrats, he lived a hand-to-mouth existence as a writer, and thus knew the less respectable aspects of the literary marketplace in a way that the successful and financially self-sufficient Pope did not. Pope respected Savage's talent and attempted unsuccessfully to help him settle to a more constructive way of life, paying him a regular allowance long after he had exasperated other friends (see Index to Tracy 1971 under 'Pope'). Savage was routinely accused of being Pope's spy on the victims of the *Dunciad* (Guerinot 1969: 93, 162, 233–4, 302, 315).

much more dangerous friends than enemies: The bad writers who provided samples of each other's work (perhaps ultimately bound into Pope's collection of attacks, British Library C.116.b.1–4) were providing evidence against their supposed friends.

I have added nothing: Although the quotations and paraphrases used in the notes are often deftly edited to sharpen the intended application.

the vouchers themselves: The books and pamphlets which vouch for the truth of the quotations are ephemeral rubbish which no-one will think worth preserving.

irrecoverably lost. You may in some measure prevent it, by preserving at least their Titles[a], and discovering (as far as you can depend on the truth of your information) the Names of the concealed authors.

The first objection I have heard made to the Poem is, that the persons are too *obscure* for satyr. The persons themselves, rather than allow the objection, would forgive the satyr; and if one could be tempted to afford it a serious answer, were not all assassinates, popular insurrections, the insolence of the rabble without doors, and of domestics within, most wrongfully chastised, if the Meanness of offenders indemnified them from punishment? On the contrary, Obscurity renders them more dangerous, as less thought of: Law can pronounce judgment only on open facts; Morality alone can pass censure on intentions of mischief; so that for secret calumny, or the arrow flying in the dark, there is no public punishment left, but what a good Writer inflicts.

The next objection is, that these sort of authors are *poor*. That might be pleaded as an excuse at the Old Baily, for lesser crimes than Defamation, (for 'tis the case of almost all who are tried there) but sure it can be none: For who will pretend that the robbing another of his Reputation supplies the want of it in himself? I question not but such authors are poor, and heartily wish the objection were removed by any honest livelihood. But Poverty is here the accident, not the subject: He who describes Malice and Villany to be pale and meagre, expresses not the least anger against Paleness or Leanness, but against Malice and Villany. The Apothecary in Romeo and Juliet is poor; but is he therefore justified in vending poison? Not but Poverty itself becomes a just subject of satyr, when it is the consequence of vice, prodigality, or neglect of one's lawful calling; for then it

[a] Which we have done in a List printed in the Appendix.

at least their Titles: See Appendix II.

assassinates: murderers.

without doors: outside.

domestics: household servants.

Meanness: low social standing.

open facts: Actions to which witnesses can testify.

the arrow flying in the dark: Cp. Psalm 91:5: 'Thou shalt not be afraid for the terror by night; nor for the arrow that flieth by day'.

what a good Writer inflicts: Satire is presented as the only punishment that can be applied to false accusations made anonymously.

the Old Baily: The Old Bailey is the central criminal court in London.

for lesser crimes than Defamation: Poverty is said not to mitigate defamation, since, in contrast with a poor man who by stealing gains what he lacks, a writer who lacks reputation cannot gain one by taking it from someone else.

Poverty is here the accident, not the subject: Poverty is alleged to be an accidental not an essential attribute of the writers accused. For the established poetic tradition of satirising the poverty of writers, see Jones in Mack & Winn 1980: 628–34.

Apothecary in Romeo and Juliet: Shakespeare, *Romeo and Juliet*, Act V.i.

increases the public burden, fills the streets and highways with Robbers, and the garrets with Clippers, Coiners, and Weekly Journalists.

But admitting that two or three of these offend less in their morals, than in their writings; must Poverty make nonsense sacred? If so, the fame of bad authors would be much better consulted than that of all the good ones in the world; and not one of an hundred had ever been called by his right name.

They mistake the whole matter: It is not charity to encourage them in the way they follow, but to get them out of it; for men are not bunglers because they are poor, but they are poor because they are bunglers.

Is it not pleasant enough, to hear our authors crying out on the one hand, as if their persons and characters were too sacred for Satyr; and the public objecting on the other, that they are too mean even for Ridicule? But whether Bread or Fame be their end, it must be allowed, our author, by and in this Poem, has mercifully given them a little of both.

There are two or three, who by their rank and fortune have no benefit from the former objections, supposing them good, and these I was sorry to see in such company. But if, without any provocation, two or three Gentlemen will fall upon one, in an affair wherein his interest and reputation are equally embarked; they cannot certainly, after they have been content to print themselves his enemies, complain of being put into the number of them.

Others, I am told, pretend to have been once his Friends. Surely they are their enemies who say so, since nothing can be more odious than to treat a friend as they have done. But of this I cannot persuade myself, when I consider the constant and eternal aversion of all bad writers to a good one.

Such as claim a merit from being his Admirers I would gladly ask, if it lays him under a personal obligation? At that rate he would be the most obliged humble servant in the world. I dare swear for these in particular, he never desired them to

---

it increases the public burden: Wilful poverty increases the number of paupers who have to be supported by the public.

Clippers, Coiners, and Weekly Journalists: Levelling writers of propaganda with criminals who devalue the currency: clippers (who clipped precious metal from the edges of coins and sold it) and forgers. All three are implied to have forsaken a 'lawful calling'.

consulted: attended to.

not one ... by his right name: The quality of canonical authors would never have been recognised if the poverty of their worthless contemporaries had been held to compensate for their lack of merit.

pleasant: amusing.

two or three: An admission that not *all* the authors ridiculed in the *Dunciad* are poor or of humble birth.

supposing them good: Even if 'the former objections' had been accepted.

pretend to have been once his Friends: Notably the would-be dramatist James Moore Smythe (1702–34), who had initially sought Pope's favour, but is condemned in the *Dunciad* as a plagiarist (see II.35–50). In *Peri Bathous* he is apparently classed with the '*Frogs*', who 'live generally in the bottom of a ditch, and make a great noise whenever they thrust their heads above water' (*PW*: II, 197).

be his admirers, nor promised in return to be theirs: That had truly been a sign he was of their acquaintance; but would not the malicious world have suspected such an approbation of some motive worse than ignorance, in the author of the Essay on Criticism? Be it as it will, the reasons of their Admiration and of his Contempt are equally subsisting, for his works and theirs are the very same that they were.

One, therefore, of their assertions I believe may be true, 'That he has a contempt for their writings.' And there is another, which would probably be sooner allowed by himself than by any good judge beside, 'That his own have found too much success with the public.' But as it cannot consist with his modesty to claim this as a justice, it lies not on him, but entirely on the public, to defend its own judgment.

There remains what in my opinion might seem a better plea for these people, than any they have made use of. If Obscurity or Poverty were to exempt a man from satyr, much more should Folly or Dulness, which are still more involuntary; nay, as much so as personal Deformity. But even this will not help them: Deformity becomes an object of Ridicule when a man sets up for being handsome; and so must Dulness when he sets up for a Wit. They are not ridiculed because Ridicule in itself is, or ought to be, a pleasure; but because it is just to undeceive and vindicate the honest and unpretending part of mankind from imposition, because particular interest ought to yield to general, and a great number who are not naturally Fools, ought never to be made so, in complaisance to a few who are. Accordingly we find that in all ages, all vain pretenders, were they ever so poor or ever so dull, have been constantly the topics of the most candid satyrists, from the Codrus of JUVENAL to the Damon of BOILEAU.

---

some motive worse than ignorance: Observers would have suspected Pope of self-serving flattery if he, the author of a poem demonstrating a refined taste, had pretended to admire such authors' works.

are ... subsisting: still exist.

it cannot consist with his modesty: It would be improper for Pope himself to assert that his poetry deserved its initial success. Only readers can do this by their continued esteem.

as much so as personal Deformity: A pointed comparison, since Pope's physical handicaps *had* been used to ridicule him.

sets up for: claims to be.

it is just to undeceive: Attacks on bad writers are justified as an attempt to protect unsuspecting readers from being imposed upon.

particular interest ought to yield to general: The interest of a few has to give way to the interest of the whole community.

complaisance: politeness, deference.

Codrus of JUVENAL: Juvenal, Roman satirist (flourished early second century AD), attacks in his first satire a tedious poet called Cordus. Pope follows the tradition of assuming Cordus to be the same character as Codrus, an impoverished book-lover in the third satire who lives in the Roman equivalent of a garret. The assimilation of the two suits Pope's insistence that poverty is the dunces' proper punishment for refusing to give up a literary career for which they lack talent (for the use of the name to attack Pope, see *Codrus: or, The Dunciad Dissected* 1728).

Damon of BOILEAU: Although Damon the poor poet, the speaker in Boileau's first satire, is to some extent the author's persona, Pope's desire to present poverty as the ordained punishment of bad poets is best satisfied by treating the account as simple satire.

Having mentioned BOILEAU, the greatest Poet and most judicious Critic of his age and country, admirable for his Talents, and yet perhaps more admirable for his Judgment in the proper application of them; I cannot help remarking the resemblance betwixt him and our author, in Qualities, Fame, and Fortune; in the distinctions shewn them by their Superiors, in the general esteem of their Equals, and in their extended reputation amongst Foreigners; in the latter of which ours has met with the better fate, as he has had for his Translators persons of the most eminent rank and abilities in their respective nations[b]. But the resemblance holds in nothing more, than in their being equally abused by the ignorant pretenders to Poetry of their times; of which not the least memory will remain but in their own Writings, and in the Notes made upon them. What BOILEAU has done in almost all his poems, our author has only in this: I dare answer for him he will do it in no more; and on this principle, of attacking few but who had slandered him, he could not have done it at all, had he been confined from censuring obscure and worthless persons, for scarce any other were his enemies. However, as the parity is so remarkable, I hope it will continue to the last; and if ever he shall give us an edition of this Poem himself, I may see some of them treated as gently, on their repentance or better merit, as Perrault and Quinault were at last by BOILEAU.

In one point I must be allowed to think the character of our English Poet the more amiable. He has not been a follower of Fortune or Success; he has lived with the Great without flattery; been a friend to Men in power, without pensions, from

[b] Essay on Criticism, in French verse, by General Hamilton; the same, in verse also, by Monsieur Roboton, Counsellor and Privy Secretary to king George I. after by the Abbé Reynel, in verse, with notes. Rape of the Lock, in French, by the Princess of Conti, Paris 1728. and in Italian verse, by the Abbé Conti a Noble Venetian; and by the Marquis Rangoni, Envoy Extraordinary from Modena to King George II. Others of his works by Salvini of Florence, *etc.* His Essays and Dissertations on Homer, several times translated in French. Essay on Man, by the Abbé Reynel, in verse, by Monsieur Silhouet, in prose, 1737. and since by others in French, Italian, and Latin.

---

the distinctions shewn them by their Superiors: People of higher rank enhanced the status of both poets by condescending to associate with them.

his Translators: The stress on their status is characteristic of Pope's representation of his admirers. Anthony Hamilton (1645?–1719), Irish Jacobite in exile, sent Pope his translation of the *Essay on Criticism* in manuscript (*Corr.*: I, 192–3). For French translations of the works mentioned, see index to Audra 1931. For Italian translations of *The Rape of the Lock*, see O'Grady 1986: 15–57.

parity: similarity, parallel.

Perrault and Quinault: Charles Perrault (1628–1703) and Philippe Quinault (1635–1688) were writers attacked by Boileau. In the preface to the 1701 edition of his works he attempted to minimise the antagonism. Instances of reconciliation in *The Dunciad in Four Books* are sparse and sometimes equivocal (e.g. editor's note on I.146).

He has not been a follower: Pope prided himself on not seeking patronage for himself, particularly from the Hanoverian establishment (for his refusal of pensions, see *OAC*: I, 99–100). His Catholicism rendered him legally ineligible for many kinds of patronage.

whom, as he asked, so he received no favour, but what was done Him in his Friends. As his Satyrs were the more just for being delayed, so were his Panegyrics; bestowed only on such persons as he had familiarly known, only for such virtues as he had long observed in them, and only at such times as others cease to praise, if not begin to calumniate them, I mean when out of power or out of fashion[c]. A satyr, therefore, on writers so notorious for the contrary practice, became no man so well as

[c] As Mr. Wycherley, at the time the Town declaimed against his book of Poems; Mr. Walsh, after his death; Sir William Trumbull, when he had resigned the Office of Secretary of State; Lord Bolingbroke, at his leaving England after the Queen's death; Lord Oxford in his last decline of life; Mr. Secretary Craggs, at the end of the South Sea year, and after his death: Others only in Epitaphs.

---

what was done Him in his Friends: The favours which the establishment did him by bestowing favours on his friends: he was sometimes prepared to solicit for others as he would not have done for himself (e.g. *OAC*: I, 29–31).

more just for being delayed: Pope's harshest satire comes from relatively late in his career.

so were his Panegyrics ... out of fashion: Asserting that Pope praised his heroes most when they had least power to reward him: it remains true, however, that some of them benefited him substantially by their advice, contacts and influence.

William Wycherley (1640–1716) had been a celebrated dramatist, but his *Miscellany Poems* (1704) were badly received. The young Pope defended the collection in his 'Epigram. Occasion'd by *Ozell's* Translation of *Boileau's Lutrin*', and dedicated the third of his *Pastorals* to Wycherley. Pope also helped to revise his verse; and it was one of Pope's grudges against Theobald, who had attended the dying Wycherley as lawyer and hence came under suspicion of helping to deceive him into a fraudulent and mercenary deathbed marriage, that he had gained possession of the corrected papers, which he had further altered and published in 1728 as Wycherley's *Posthumous Works* (*Corr.*: I, xi–xii; *OAC*: I, 36, 39–40). Pope retaliated in 1729 by publishing what he called *Volume II* (*PW*: II, 305–16).

William Walsh (1663–1708) was a gentleman critic whose guidance Pope acknowledged in the closing lines of the *Essay on Criticism* and in *To Arbuthnot* (lines 135–6) (*OAC*: I, 31–2).

Sir William Trumbull (1639–1716) retired to Windsor Forest after a career in politics and diplomacy. He became a valued friend of Pope, who dedicated the first of his *Pastorals* to him, complimented him in *Windsor Forest* (lines 235–58) and composed an epitaph for him (*OAC*: I, 31).

Pope honoured both Oxford and Bolingbroke after their fall, notably by praising Oxford in his 'Epistle. To Robert Earl of Oxford, and Earl Mortimer' (prefaced to his posthumous edition of the works of their mutual friend Thomas Parnell (1679–1718; works published 1722)), and by dedicating the *Essay on Man* to Bolingbroke.

James Craggs (1686–1721), Secretary of State, was in fact praised by Pope when at the height of his career, notably at the close of *To Mr. Addison, Occasioned by his Dialogues on Medals*, first published in 1720; but the lines were re-used in 1727 in an epitaph for his monument in Westminster Abbey, where, despite the suspicions of dishonest dealing in South Sea stock that had gathered around him at the time of his sudden death, Craggs was proclaimed as 'in Honour clear', an expression of loyalty on Pope's part which drew immediate disapproval (*TE*: VI, 205–6, 282–3).

The exiled Atterbury was honoured in an epitaph (*TE*: VI, 343–5).

the contrary practice: Flattering those in power.

himself; as none, it is plain, was so little in their friendships, or so much in that of those whom they had most abused, namely the Greatest and Best of all Parties. Let me add a further reason, that, though engaged in their Friendships, he never espoused their Animosities; and can almost singly challenge this honour, not to have written a line of any man, which, through Guilt, through Shame, or through Fear, through variety of Fortune, or change of Interests, he was ever unwilling to own.

I shall conclude with remarking what a pleasure it must be to every reader of Humanity, to see all along, that our Author in his very laughter is not indulging his own ill-nature, but only punishing that of others. As to his Poem, those alone are capable of doing it justice, who, to use the words of a great writer, know how hard it is (with regard both to his subject and his manner) VETUSTIS DARE NOVITATEM, OBSOLETIS NITOREM, OBSCURIS LUCEM, FASTIDITIS GRATIAM. I am

Your most humble servant,

St. James's
Dec. 22, 1728.

WILLIAM CLELAND[d].

[d] This Gentleman was of Scotland, and bred at the University of Utrecht, with the Earl of Mar. He served in Spain under Earl Rivers. After the Peace, he was made one of the Commissioners of the Customs in Scotland, and then of Taxes in England, in which having shewn himself for twenty years diligent, punctual, and incorruptible, though without any other assistance of Fortune, he was suddenly displaced by the Minister in the sixty eighth year of his age; and died two months after, in 1741. He was a person of Universal Learning, and an enlarged Conversation; no man had a warmer heart for his Friend, or a sincerer attachment to the Constitution of his Country.

---

he never espoused their Animosities: A strategy vital to his ability to resist being limited to one political or literary clique.

not to have written a line of any man: Although Pope *had* published anonymously, the equivocation turns on the despicable motives for doing so that he attributes to the dunces.

not indulging his own ill-nature: Satire is pointedly presented as the administration of justice rather than the indulgence of malice.

a great writer: The quotation (slightly adapted) from the preface to the *Natural History* of Pliny the Elder (AD 23/4–79) may be translated as 'to give novelty to what is ancient, sparkle to what is commonplace, clarity to what is obscure, charm to what is distasteful'. The manner in which it is introduced is a reminder of the assumption, fundamental to the *Dunciad*, that literature is the preserve of the educated gentleman: those who cannot recognise the author of a Latin quotation without being told are implicitly excluded.

St. James's: The royal associations of Cleland's address (close to St James's Palace in Westminster) lend the authority of social distinction to his defence of Pope (*Corr.*: III, 381).

This Gentleman: The note presents Cleland as a victim of the unjust conduct of 'the Minister', Sir Robert Walpole (cp. *Corr.*: IV, 377–8). Cleland is suggestively associated with two eminent but ultimately disaffected servants of Whig regimes: John Erskine (1675–1732), sixth (or twenty-third) Earl of Mar, who became a Jacobite; and Richard Savage (1660?–1712), fourth Earl Rivers. Pope presents Cleland as well informed, 'enlarged' ('liberal', 'enlightened') in attitude, and devoted to 'the Constitution of his Country' – in implied contrast to the regime that slighted him.

MARTINUS SCRIBLERUS
HIS
Prolegomena and Illustrations
TO THE
DUNCIAD:
WITH THE
Hyper-critics of ARISTARCHUS.

TESTIMONIES
OF
AUTHORS
Concerning our POET and his WORKS.
M. SCRIBLERUS Lectori S.

BEFORE we present thee with our exercitations on this most delectable Poem (drawn from the many volumes of our Adversaria on modern Authors) we shall here, according to the laudable usage of editors, collect the various judgments of the Learned concerning our Poet: Various indeed, not only of different authors, but of the same author at different seasons. Nor shall we gather only the Testimonies of such eminent Wits, as would of course descend to posterity, and consequently be read without our collection; but we shall likewise with incredible labour seek out for divers others, which, but for this our diligence, could never at the distance of a few months appear to the eye of the most curious. Hereby thou may'st not only receive the delectation of Variety, but also arrive at a more certain judgment, by a grave and circumspect comparison of the Witnesses with each other, or of each with himself. Hence also thou wilt be enabled to draw reflections, not only of a critical, but a moral nature, by being let into many particulars of the Person as well as Genius, and of the Fortune as well as Merit, of our Author: In which if I relate some things of little concern peradventure to thee, and some of as little even to him; I entreat thee to consider how minutely all true

TESTIMONIES OF AUTHORS: A parody of the apparatus of a learned edition, first used in 1729 and later revised.

M. Scriblerus Lectori S.: 'Martin Scriblerus greets his reader' ('S.' is short for Latin *salutem* ('greetings'): understand *dicit* ('says')). The formula, supported by Scriblerus's addressing the reader with the intimate but old-fashioned 'thee', recalls the Latin correspondence of Renaissance humanists. Scriblerus bursts on the reader with a preposterous blend of high-spirited hair-splitting, hyperbole and archaism, fatuously complacent about the value of his work and that of his fellow-critics. However, the style becomes more incisive and the character of the writer less clear-cut as the focus shifts to Pope's sense of the true state of his reputation: esteemed by respectable figures, ludicrously abused by the insignificant, and treated by the venal with an inconsistency which only exposes their lack of integrity.

exercitations: academic exercises.

Adversaria: scholarly notes.

could never at the distance of a few months: Another confident gibe at the ephemeral celebrity of the dunces.

particulars of the Person: physical details.

some things of little concern: A joke on Pope's part against the complacent self-absorption of scholars.

critics and commentators are wont to insist upon such, and how material they seem to themselves, if to none other. Forgive me, gentle reader, if (following learned example) I ever and anon become tedious: allow me to take the same pains to find whether my author were good or bad, well or ill-natured, modest or arrogant; as another, whether his author was fair or brown, short or tall, or whether he wore a coat or a cassock.

We purposed to begin with his Life, Parentage, and Education: But as to these, even his cotemporaries do exceedingly differ. One saith[a], he was educated at home; another[b], that he was bred at St. Omer's by Jesuits; a third[c], not at St. Omer's, but at Oxford; a fourth[d], that he had no University education at all. Those who allow him to be bred at home, differ as much concerning his Tutor: One saith[e], he was kept by his father on purpose; a second[f], that he was an itinerant priest; a third[g], that he was a parson; one[h] calleth him a secular clergyman of the Church of Rome; another[i], a monk. As little do they agree about his Father, whom one[k] supposeth, like the Father of Hesiod, a tradesman or merchant; another[l], a husbandman; another[m], a hatter, *etc.* Nor has an author been wanting to give our Poet

[a] Giles Jacob's Lives of Poets, vol. ii. in his Life.
[b] Dennis's Reflect. on the Essay on Crit. [c] Dunciad dissected, p. 4.
[d] Guardian, N° 40. [e] Jacob's Lives etc. vol. ii. [f] Dunciad dissected, p. 4.
[g] Farmer P. and his son. [h] Dunc. dissect. [i] Characters of the times, p. 45.
[k] Female Dunc. p. ult. [l] Dunc. dissect.
[m] Roome, Paraphrase on the 4th of Genesis, printed 1729.

a coat or a cassock: Whether he was a layman or in holy orders.

educated at home: With the exception of some periods at small (and illegal) Catholic schools in England, this was the truth, since Roman Catholics were excluded by law from schools and universities.

at St. Omer's by Jesuits: Dennis argued that as a Catholic Pope was tainted with subversion, associating him with the Jesuits (notorious in Protestant propaganda as plotters and spies) and their school at St Omer in France (Hooker 1939–43: II, 415).

no University education at all: Pope wrote the *Guardian* essay himself, perhaps in association with Gay (Appendix V; see also Stephens 1982: 640–41; Nokes 1995: 123). Since the law excluded Roman Catholics from the universities, Pope could only have gained the education his enemies condemned him for lacking by abandoning his religion.

his Tutor: Pope actually had his first lessons from the family priest (*OAC*: I, 10).

his father: Alexander Pope senior (1646–1717) was the posthumous son of a royalist clergyman of the Church of England. He became a cloth merchant, converted to Catholicism, and retired from his business in the City of London shortly after the poet's birth in 1688, settling at Binfield in Berkshire in about 1700.

a secular clergyman: One who lived in the world, rather than as a monk in a religious house.

Hesiod: One of the earliest Greek poets (lived *c.*700 BC). He states in his *Works and Days* that his father had been an unsuccessful sea-trader.

a tradesman or merchant: The source ('p. ult.' is a Latin abbreviation for 'last page') actually claims that Pope's father had been a bankrupt.

another, a hatter: Pope attributed to Edward Roome (*d.* 1729) the anonymous *Dean Jonathan's Parody on the 4th Chap. of Genesis* 1729.

such a father as Apuleius hath to Plato, Jamblicus to Pythagoras, and divers to Homer, namely a Daemon: For thus Mr. Gildon[n]: 'Certain it is, that his original is not from Adam, but the Devil; and that he wanteth nothing but horns and tail to be the exact resemblance of his infernal Father.' Finding, therefore, such contrariety of opinions, and (whatever be ours of this sort of generation) not being fond to enter into controversy, we shall defer writing the life of our Poet, 'till authors can determine among themselves what Parents or Education he had, or whether he had any Education or Parents at all.

Proceed we to what is more certain, his Works, tho' not less uncertain the judgments concerning them; beginning with his ESSAY on CRITICISM, of which hear first the most ancient of Critics,

Mr. JOHN DENNIS.

'His precepts are false or trivial, or both; his thoughts are crude and abortive, his expressions absurd, his numbers harsh and unmusical, his rhymes trivial and common; — instead of majesty, we have something that is very mean; instead of gravity, something that is very boyish; and instead of perspicuity and lucid order, we have but too often obscurity and confusion.' And in another place: 'What rare *numbers* are here! Would not one swear that this youngster had espoused some antiquated muse, who had sued out a divorce from some superannuated sinner,

[n] Character of Mr. P. and his Writings, in a Letter to a Friend, printed for S. Popping, 1716. p. 10. Curl, in his Key to the Dunciad (first edit. said to be printed for A. Dodd) in the 10th page, declared Gildon to be author of that libel; though in the subsequent editions of his Key he left out this assertion, and affirmed (in the Curliad, p. 4. and 8.) that it was writ by Dennis only.

---

such a father: In saying that Plato (Greek philosopher, 427–347 BC) and Pythagoras (Greek mathematician and mystic, sixth century BC) were sons of daemons (i.e. divine spirits), later writers such as Apuleius (*fl. c.* AD 155) and Iamblichus (*d. c.* AD 330) intended a compliment to their genius. In contrast, Gildon, whom John Dennis seems to quote in his anonymous *A True Character of Mr. Pope*, thinks Pope is 'demonic' in the modern sense, i.e. he is a son of Satan (Hooker 1939–43: II, 105).

thus Mr. Gildon: The reference is to *A True Character* 1716. Sarah Popping, a trade publisher, was associated with Edmund Curll (1675–1747), the entrepreneurial publisher and long-time adversary of Pope to whose explanatory keys the note refers (*A Compleat Key* 1728; Curll 1729; Straus 1927; Sherburn 1934: 149–85; Rogers 1985: 26).

this sort of generation: The begetting of children by demons.

most ancient of Critics: Dennis had led the pamphlet attacks on Pope with his furious response to gibes at himself in the *Essay on Criticism* (lines 584–7; Dennis 1711; Guerinot 1969: xlvi–xlvii, 1–11).

numbers: metre.

mean: low, vulgar.

perspicuity: clarity.

Would not one swear: Dennis's metaphor reeks of sexual innuendo. Pope's muse is said to have been infected with venereal disease by an older poet from whom she has obtained a

upon account of impotence, and who, being poxed by her former spouse, has got the gout in her decrepid age, which makes her *hobble so damnably*[o].' No less peremptory is the censure of our hypercritical Historian

Mr. Oldmixon.

'I dare not say any thing of the Essay on Criticism in verse; but if any more curious reader has discovered in it something *new* which is not in Dryden's prefaces, dedications, and his essay on dramatic poetry, not to mention the French critics, I should be very glad to have the benefit of the discovery[p].'

He is followed (as in fame, so in judgment) by the modest and simple-minded

Mr. Leonard Welsted;

Who, out of great respect to our poet not naming him, doth yet glance at his

[o] Reflections critical and satyrical on a Rhapsody called An Essay on Criticism. Printed for Bernard Lintot, octavo.

[p] Essay on Criticism in prose, octavo, 1728. by the author of the Critical History of England.

---

divorce 'upon account of impotence'. Despite Dennis's immoderate tone, Pope found some of his specific criticisms to be well-founded enough to justify revision (Guerinot 1969: 7–11).

our hypercritical Historian: The Whig John Oldmixon (1673–1742), author of *The Critical History of England* (1724–26), offended Pope by his representation of recent history (see notes on II.283). He responded to Pope's *Essay on Criticism* by making the familiar point that it summarises traditional literary theory rather than revolutionising it, and pointed to the prose of John Dryden (1631–1700) and to French literary criticism as obvious influences (Oldmixon 1728a; Pope's notes often cite the format of an edition, in this case spelled out as 'octavo', though he also uses abbreviations in the forms '8to.' or '8°'). In *Peri Bathous* initials which may refer to Oldmixon appear under the '*Porpoises*' alongside the initials of Dennis and Gildon (*PW*: II, 197); and in the frontispiece to the 1729 *Dunciad Variorum* his name appears on one of the books carried by the ass as 'OLD MIXON' (a 'mixen' is a dungheap), a pun repeated at II.283.

the modest and simple-minded Mr. Leonard Welsted: Leonard Welsted (1688–1747), translator of Longinus (reputed author of the first-century AD Greek literary treatise *On the Sublime*) and an established defender of the regime and antagonist of Pope, had been attacked for writing verse that was 'harmless', 'easy', and tedious in its vacuous praise of women (Mack 1969: 123–6; Morrice 1721). Cowler comments that his preface to Longinus 'epitomized everything that Pope despised in contemporary modernist theory' (*PW*: II, 174). Pope attacks him at III.169–72 and in *Peri Bathous*, where he also seems to figure among the '*Didappers*' who 'come up now and then where you least expected them' and the '*Eels*' who 'wrap themselves up in their own mud, but are mighty nimble and pert' (*PW*: II, 197, 203, 209).

great respect: Professing to take Welsted's contemptuous claim not to know who wrote the *Essay on Criticism* as a mark of respect. He dismisses Pope's views on language change (line 483) with a contemptuous 'whoever this Writer is, he certainly judg'd the Matter wrong' (Welsted 1724: x).

Essay, together with the Duke of Buckingham's, and the Criticisms of Dryden, and of Horace, which he more openly taxeth[q]: 'As to the numerous treatises, essays, arts, *etc.* both in verse and prose, that have been written by the moderns on this ground-work, they do but *hackney the same thoughts over again,* making them still more *trite.* Most of their pieces are nothing but a pert, insipid heap of *common place.* Horace has even in his Art of Poetry thrown out several things which plainly shew, he thought an Art of Poetry was of no use, even while he was writing one.'

To all which great authorities, we can only oppose that of

Mr. Addison.

'[r]The Art of Criticism (saith he) which was published some months since, is a master-piece in its kind. The observations follow one another, like those in Horace's Art of Poetry, without that methodical regularity which would have been requisite in a prose-writer. They are some of them *uncommon,* but such as the reader must assent to, when he sees them explain'd with that ease and perspicuity in which they are delivered. As for those which are the *most known* and the most *receiv'd,* they are placed in so beautiful a light, and illustrated with such apt allusions, that they have in them all the graces of novelty; and make the reader, who was before acquainted with them, still more convinc'd of their truth and solidity. And here give me leave to mention what Monsieur Boileau has so well enlarged upon in the preface to his works: That wit and fine writing doth not consist so much in advancing things that are new, as in giving things that are known an agreeable turn. It is impossible for us who live in the latter ages of the world, to make observations in criticism, morality, or any art or science, which have not been touch'd upon by others; we have little else left us, but to represent the common sense of mankind in more strong, more beautiful, or more uncommon lights. If a reader examines Horace's Art of Poetry, he will find but

[q] Preface to his Poems, p. 18, 53. [r] Spectator, N° 253.

the Duke of Buckingham's: Pope revised the *Essay on Poetry* by John Sheffield (1648–1721), first Duke of Buckingham, for his posthumous edition of the Duke's works (Pope 1723).

Horace: Quintus Horatius Flaccus, Roman poet (65–8 BC), author of the *De arte poetica* ('Art of Poetry').

this ground-work: The established maxims of good writing.

hackney: A hack, or hackney, is a hired horse; hence to hackney is to make stale by repetition.

great authorities: Intended ironically.

Mr. Addison: The approval of Addison counters denigration by lesser writers.

The Art of Criticism: Pope's *Essay on Criticism.*

***the most* receiv'd:** the most generally accepted.

what Monsieur Boileau has so well enlarged upon in the preface to his works: In the edition of 1701.

few precepts in it, which he may not meet with in Aristotle, and which were not commonly known by all the poets of the Augustan age. His way of expressing, and applying them, not his invention of them, is what we are chiefly to admire.

Longinus, in his Reflexions, has given us the same kind of sublime, which he observes in the several passages that occasioned them: I cannot but take notice that our English author has after the same manner exemplify'd several of the precepts in the very precepts themselves.' He then produces some instances of a particular beauty in the numbers, and concludes with saying, that 'there are three poems in our tongue of the same nature, and each a master-piece in its kind; The Essay on Translated Verse; the Essay on the Art of Poetry; and the Essay on Criticism.'

Of WINDSOR FOREST, positive is the judgment of the affirmative

Mr. JOHN DENNIS,

'[s]That it is a wretched rhapsody, impudently writ in emulation of the Cooper's Hill of Sir John Denham: The author of it is obscure, is ambiguous, is affected, is temerarious, is barbarous.'

But the author of the Dispensary

Dr. GARTH,

in the preface to his poem of Claremont, differs from this opinion: 'Those who have seen these two excellent poems of Cooper's Hill, and Windsor Forest, the

[s] Letter to B. B. at the end of the Remarks on Pope's Homer, 1717.

Aristotle: Greek philosopher (384–322 BC). His *Poetics* is a foundation text in literary theory and criticism.

the poets of the Augustan age: Latin poetry was thought to have reached its peak in the works of Virgil, Horace and Ovid, produced under the rule of Gaius Octavius (63 BC–AD 14), the first Emperor of Rome, who took the title of Augustus.

invention: discovery, power of generating something new.

The Essay on Translated Verse: By Wentworth Dillon (1633?–85), fourth Earl of Roscommon.

the Essay on the Art of Poetry: The *Essay on Poetry* by John Sheffield (Pope 1723).

the Essay on Criticism: By Pope.

positive: confident, dictatorial.

affirmative: dogmatic.

the Cooper's Hill of Sir John Denham: A celebrated topographical poem by Denham (1615–69).

temerarious: reckless.

the Dispensary: Mock-epic poem by Sir Samuel Garth (1661–1719), physician and friend of Pope (Lord 1963–75: VI, 58–128; *OAC*: I, 44–5). For its influence on the *Dunciad*, see Brooks-Davies 1985: 84; Colomb 1992.

Claremont: The anonymously issued *Claremont* (1715).

one written by Sir John Denham, the other by Mr. Pope, will shew a great deal of candour if they approve of this.'

Of the Epistle of ELOISA, we are told by the obscure writer of a poem called Sawney, 'That because Prior's Henry and Emma charm'd the finest tastes, our author writ his Eloise, *in opposition to it*; but forgot innocence and virtue: If you take away her tender thoughts, and her fierce desires, all the rest is of no value[t].' In which, methinks, his judgment resembleth that of a French taylor on a Villa and gardens by the Thames: 'All this is very fine, but take away the river, and it is good for nothing.'

But very contrary hereunto was the opinion of

Mr. PRIOR

himself, saying in his *Alma*[v],

O *Abelard!* ill fated youth,
Thy tale will justify this truth.
But well I weet thy cruel wrong
Adorns a nobler Poet's song:
Dan *Pope*, for thy misfortune griev'd,
With kind concern and skill has weav'd
A silken web; and ne'er shall fade
Its colours: gently has he laid
The mantle o'er thy sad distress,
And Venus shall the texture bless, *etc.*

[t] Printed 1728, p. 12. [v] Alma, Cant. 2.

candour: generosity of spirit (Garth implies his poem is inferior to its two models).

this: *Claremont* 1715.

the obscure writer of a poem called Sawney: James Ralph (*d.* 1762), antagonist of Pope, would-be poet and, in later life, a leading opposition journalist, attacked Pope and some of his closest friends in 1728 in the anonymously published *Sawney* (a vulgar diminutive of 'Alexander'; see Guerinot 1969: 124–7; and for a full account of Ralph's career, Shipley 1963).

Prior's Henry and Emma: A narrative of chaste love by Matthew Prior (1664–1721), poet, diplomat and friend of Pope (Wright & Spears 1971: I, 278–300).

If you take away: Paraphrasing Ralph's blank verse satire, which denigrates Pope's *Eloisa to Abelard* as a gratuitously lewd imitation of *Henry and Emma* (*Sawney* 1728: 11–12). The French tailor, a stereotype of superficial judgement, is introduced to enforce the point that the sexual element in the poem is as integral to its artistic effect as the river is to a riverside villa (but for Pope's pruning of a sexually explicit couplet, see *TE*: II, 340).

***in his* Alma:** Ralph's suggestion that *Eloisa* was an implicit insult to Prior is undercut by showing that he admired it. 'Cant.' stands for 'canto', one of the sections into which the poem is divided.

weet: know.

Dan: A mock-medieval title of respect, equivalent to 'Master'.

Come we now to his translation of the ILIAD, celebrated by numerous pens, yet shall it suffice to mention the indefatigable

Sir RICHARD BLACKMORE, Kt.

Who (tho' otherwise a severe censurer of our author) yet styleth this a 'laudable translation[w].' That ready writer

Mr. OLDMIXON,

in his forementioned Essay, frequently commends the same. And the painful

Mr. LEWIS THEOBALD

thus extols it[x], 'The spirit of Homer breathes all through this translation. — I am in doubt, whether I should most admire the justness to the original, or the force and beauty of the language, or the sounding variety of the numbers: But when I find all these meet, it puts me in mind of what the poet says of one of his heroes, That he alone rais'd and flung with ease a weighty stone, that two common men could not lift from the ground; just so, one single person has performed in this translation, what I once despaired to have seen done by the force of several masterly hands.' Indeed the same gentleman appears to have chang'd his sentiment in his Essay on the Art of sinking in reputation, (printed in Mist's Journal, March 30, 1728.) where he says thus: 'In order to sink in reputation, let him take it into his head to descend into Homer (let the world wonder, as it will, how the devil

[w] In his Essays, vol. 1. printed for E. Curl. [x] Censor, vol. ii. n. 33.

ILIAD: Pope's translation (1715–20) of Homer's epic, financed by subscription, was a major element in gaining him public recognition and financial security (Foxon 1991: 51–101; Rogers 1993a: 190–227).

a 'laudable translation': Pope shows that even his enemies admit his worth on occasion (Blackmore 1716–17: I, vi). Pope seems at first to have been on good terms with Blackmore, but the older poet reacted with horror to the publication of Pope's bawdy parody of the first Psalm (*Corr.*: I, 218; see II.268 and notes).

frequently commends: Oldmixon suggests that smoothness of versification is the only merit of his translation, and hints that Pope used other translations to supplement a deficient command of Greek (Oldmixon 1728a).

painful: Taking pains, or giving pain to the reader? For Pope's contempt for Theobald's kind of textual criticism, see *To Arbuthnot*, lines 163–4; for sneers at his original writing, see *Peri Bathous*, where he seems to be classed both as a fly-catching swallow and as a muddy but 'mighty nimble and pert' eel (*PW*: II, 197, 199, 211, 223).

extols it: Theobald is accused of bad faith: though he admires Pope's translation (Theobald 1714: II, no. 33), he attacks it when it suits his purpose (*Mist's Weekly Journal*, 30 March 1728: unsigned, but attributed by Pope to Theobald; reprinted in *A Compleat Collection* 1728).

one of his heroes: Diomedes (*Iliad* V.302–4).

the Art of sinking in reputation: The title of the anonymous article in *Mist's Weekly Journal* of 30 March 1728 alludes to the subtitle of *Peri Bathous* ('*the Art of Sinking in Poetry*').

he got there) and pretend to do him into English, so his version denote his neglect of the manner how.' Strange Variation! We are told in

MIST'S JOURNAL, June 8.

'That this translation of the Iliad was not in all respects conformable to the fine taste of his friend Mr. Addison; insomuch that he employed a *younger muse*, in an undertaking of this kind, which he supervised himself.' Whether Mr. Addison did find it conformable to his taste, or not, best appears from his own testimony the year following its publication, in these words:

Mr. ADDISON, FREEHOLDER, N° 40.

'When I consider myself as a British freeholder, I am in a particular manner pleased with the labours of those who have improved our language with the translations of old Greek and Latin authors. — We have already most of their Historians in our own tongue, and what is more for the honour of our language, it has been taught to express with elegance the greatest of their Poets in each nation. The illiterate among our own countrymen may learn to judge from Dryden's Virgil of the most perfect Epic performance. And those parts of Homer which have been published already by Mr. Pope, give us reason to think that the Iliad will appear in English with as little disadvantage to that immortal poem.'

As to the rest, there is a slight mistake, for this *younger muse* was an *elder:* Nor was the gentleman (who is a friend of our author) employ'd by Mr. Addison to translate it *after him*, since he saith himself that he did it *before*[y]. Contrariwise that

[y] Vid. pref. to Mr. Tickel's translation of the first book of the Iliad, 4to.

MIST'S JOURNAL, June 8: Pope attributed the issue for 8 June 1728, which is signed 'W. A.', to Theobald and his associates (*Mist's Weekly Journal*, 8 June 1728).

***he employed a* younger muse**: The note seeks to play down Addison's attempt to sabotage Pope's Homer translation by privately backing a rival translation by Thomas Tickell (1686–1740), which was rumoured to be in part at least by Addison himself, and is treated by Pope as such when he quotes its infelicities of expression in *Peri Bathous* (Tickell 1715 (the first and only instalment published); *PW*: II, 217; *OAC*: I, 60–72). This intrigue, following closely on the accession of George I and the exclusion of the Tories from government, ended a period in which it had seemed possible for Pope and other Tories to associate on friendly terms with the Whig writers grouped around Addison (Sherburn 1934: 126–33; Mack 1985: 275–6). For Felicity Rosslyn's transcription of Pope's marginalia to Tickell's version, see Mack 1982: 443–56.

FREEHOLDER: A periodical by Addison (Leheny 1979).

illiterate: Those ignorant of Greek and Latin.

Dryden's Virgil: Dryden had translated Virgil's *Aeneid* into heroic couplets (1697).

***this* younger muse *was an* elder**: Tickell was two years older than Pope.

a friend of our author: Pope apparently blamed Addison rather than Tickell (*OAC*: I, 68–71).

***he did it* before**: By accepting this statement, Scriblerus reinforces the erroneous impression that Tickell and his backers respected Pope too much to risk competition.

Contrariwise: Stressing Addison's ostensible support for Pope's Homer, mentioned by Pope in his preface to the *Iliad* (*PW*: I, 253) and attested by letters from Addison himself (although

Mr. Addison engaged our author in this work appeareth by declaration thereof in the preface to the Iliad, printed some time before his death, and by his own letters of October 26, and November 2, 1713. where he declares it is his opinion, that no other person was equal to it.

Next comes his Shakespear on the stage: 'Let him (quoth one whom I take to be

Mr. THEOBALD, Mist's Journal, June 8, 1728.)

publish such an author as he has least studied, and forget to discharge even the dull duty of an editor. In this project let him lend the bookseller his name (for a competent sum of money) to promote the credit of an exorbitant subscription.' Gentle reader, be pleased to cast thine eye on the *Proposal* below quoted, and on what follows (some months after the former assertion) in the same Journalist of June 8. 'The bookseller proposed the book by subscription, and raised some thousands of pounds for the same: I believe the gentleman did *not* share in the profits of this extravagant subscription.'

After the Iliad, he undertook (saith

MIST'S JOURNAL, June 8, 1728.)

the sequel of that work, the Odyssey; and having secured the success by a numerous subscription, he employed some *underlings* to perform what, according to his proposals, should come from his own hands.' To which heavy charge we can in truth oppose nothing but the words of

---

the originals do not survive, internal evidence suggests that they are at least partly authentic: *Corr.*: I, 196).

engaged our author in this work: Encouraged him to undertake it.

Shakespear: Pope's edition of Shakespeare (Pope 1725).

one, whom I take to be Mr. THEOBALD: The date given is incorrect: the reference is to the unsigned 'Arts of a Poet's Sinking in Reputation' in the issue of 30 March 1728 (Guerinot 1969: 116–22). Its offensiveness has been toned down.

the dull duty of an editor: A quotation – understandably offensive to serious textual critics – from Pope's preface to his edition of Shakespeare (*PW*: II, 24).

competent: adequate.

Proposal: The initial advertisement for a subscription project.

the same Journalist: *Mist's Weekly Journal.*

The bookseller: the publisher.

the gentleman did* not *share: Another hostile witness is made to speak in Pope's defence.

Odyssey: Sequel to the *Iliad*. Pope's translation of Homer's epic appeared between 1725 and 1726.

***he employed some* underlings:** Pope translated only half of the *Odyssey* himself, the rest being drafted by Elijah Fenton (1683–1730) and William Broome (1689–1745) and revised by Pope. Broome also wrote the commentary. All three at first colluded in the fiction that the work was principally Pope's, but the truth was widely suspected. The charge that Pope profited by passing off inferior poets under his own name is countered by citing his mention of '*two of my friends*' in the Proposal – although this text of the Proposal is known only from this

Mr. POPE'S PROPOSAL for the ODYSSEY, (printed by J. Watts, Jan. 10, 1724.)

'I take this occasion to declare that the subscription for Shakespear belongs wholly to Mr. Tonson: And that the benefit of *this Proposal* is not solely for my own use, but for that of *two of my friends*, who have *assisted me in this work*.' But these very gentlemen are extolled above our poet himself in another of Mist's Journals, March 30, 1728. saying, 'That he would not advise Mr. Pope to try the experiment again of getting a great part of a book done by assistants, lest those extraneous parts should unhappily ascend to the sublime, and retard the declension of the whole.' Behold! these *Underlings* are become good writers!

If any say, that before the said Proposals were printed, the subscription was begun without declaration of such assistance; verily those who set it on foot, or (as their term is) secured it, to wit, the right honourable the Lord Viscount HARCOURT, were he living, would testify, and the right honourable the Lord BATHURST, now living, doth testify the same is a falshood.

Sorry I am, that persons professing to be learned, or of whatever rank of authors, should either falsely tax, or be falsely taxed. Yet let us, who are only reporters, be impartial in our citations, and proceed.

MIST'S JOURNAL, June 8, 1728.

'Mr. Addison raised this author from obscurity, obtained him the acquaintance and friendship of the *whole body of our nobility*, and transferred his powerful interests with those great men to this rising bard, who frequently levied by that means

---

citation, and the word 'assisted' is deliberately vague (Foxon 1991: 93, Fig. 51(b)) – and by showing that hostile commentators professed to believe the assistants better poets than Pope. Mack concludes that 'the deception had cast a shadow on his reputation that was real and had given enemies an opening for attacks that would not readily be closed' (*TE*: VII, xliii–xliv; Mack 1985: 412–17).

Jan. 10, 1724: The archaic dating system used for legal documents began the year on 25 March; in ordinary dating the year would be 1725.

Mr. Tonson: The publishers Jacob Tonson the elder (1656?–1736) and his nephew Jacob Tonson the younger (*d.* 1735) claimed copyright in the edition of Shakespeare by Nicholas Rowe which formed the basis of Pope's edition. After paying Pope and his principal assistants, they kept the balance of the subscription money (Foxon 1991: Figs. 49 and 50).

another of Mist's Journals: The 'Arts of a Poet's Sinking in Reputation' attributed to Theobald (30 March 1728).

declension: decline. It is suggested that Pope's apparent intention of sinking his reputation is in danger of being foiled by unacknowledged collaboration with poets better than himself.

If any say: Pope *did* use influential friends to recruit subscribers for the *Odyssey* before the appearance of published proposals in January 1725: it is not clear at what point these subscribers learned Pope was not doing all the translation himself (Rogers 1993a: 204; Foxon 1991: 99–101). Pope refers – as if to guarantee the respectability of the undertaking – to the part played by his friends Simon Harcourt (1661–1727), first Viscount Harcourt, a former Lord Chancellor; and Allen Bathurst (1684–1775), first Earl Bathurst, dedicatee of Pope's *To Bathurst.*

unusual contributions on the public.' Which surely cannot be, if, as the author of The Dunciad dissected reporteth; 'Mr. Wycherley had before introduced him into a familiar acquaintance with the *greatest Peers* and *brightest Wits* then living.'

'No sooner (saith the same Journalist) was his body lifeless, but this author, reviving his resentment, libelled the memory of his departed friend; and, what was still more heinous, made the scandal public.' Grievous the accusation! unknown the accuser! the person accused no witness in his own cause; the person, in whose regard accused, dead! But if there be living any one nobleman whose friendship, yea any one gentleman whose subscription Mr. Addison procured to our author; let him stand forth, that truth may appear! *Amicus Plato, amicus Socrates, sed magis amica veritas*. In verity, the whole story of the libel is a lye; witness those persons of integrity, who several years before Mr. Addison's decease, did see and approve of the said verses, in no wise a libel, but a friendly rebuke sent privately in our author's own hand to Mr. Addison himself, and never made public, 'till after their own Journals, and Curl had printed the same. One name alone, which I am here authorised to declare, will sufficiently evince this truth, that of the right honourable the Earl of BURLINGTON.

Next is he taxed with a crime (in the opinion of some authors, I doubt, more heinous than any in morality) to wit, Plagiarism, from the inventive and quaint-conceited

JAMES-MOORE SMITH Gent.

'[z]Upon reading the third volume of Pope's Miscellanies, I found five lines which I thought excellent; and happening to praise them, a gentleman produced a

[z] Daily Journal, March 18, 1728.

unusual contributions: Pope's subscription projects.

the author of The Dunciad dissected: Pope believed Edmund Curll and Elizabeth Thomas (1677–1731) to be the authors of *Codrus: or, The Dunciad Dissected* 1728.

the same Journalist: *Mist's Weekly Journal*, 8 June 1728.

his body: Addison's.

this author: Pope.

libelled the memory: Implying that Pope would not have dared to criticise Addison to his face as he did in the 'Atticus' portrait in his *To Arbuthnot* (lines 193–214), published in 1735. However, by that time Addison had been dead for fifteen years; and Pope testified that he *had* confronted Addison with the portrait at the time of their original estrangement (*OAC*: I, 71–3).

the person accused no witness: Pope has not been allowed to state his defence.

Amicus Plato: 'Plato is a friend, Socrates is a friend, but truth is a greater friend', traditional paraphrase from Aristotle, *Nichomachean Ethics* (I.vi.1).

BURLINGTON: Richard Boyle (1694–1753), third Earl of Burlington, a key figure in the promotion of architecture and opera, a close friend of Pope, and addressee of *To Burlington*.

JAMES-MOORE SMITH: Pope quotes a letter signed 'Philo-Mauri' ('one who loves Moore') which accuses Pope of plagiarising from Moore Smythe's *The Rival Modes* (*A Collection of Several Curious Pieces* 1728). Pope accused Moore Smythe of having written the letter himself (Guerinot 1969: 105–6). Pope had at Moore Smythe's request first given but later withdrawn

modern comedy (the Rival Modes) published last year, where were the same verses to a tittle.

These gentlemen are undoubtedly the first plagiaries, that pretend to make a reputation by stealing from a man's works in his own life-time, and out of a Public print.' Let us join to this what is written by the author of the Rival Modes, the said Mr. James-Moore Smith, in a letter to our author himself, who had informed him, a month before that play was acted, Jan. 27, 1726/7, that 'These verses, which he had before given him leave to insert in it, would be known for his, some copies being got abroad. He desires, nevertheless, that, since the lines had been read in his comedy to several, Mr. P. would not deprive it of them,' *etc.* Surely if we add the testimonies of the Lord BOLINGBROKE, of the Lady to whom the said verses were originally addressed, of Hugh Bethel Esq. and others, who knew them as our author's, long before the said gentleman composed his play; it is hoped, the ingenuous that affect not error, will rectify their opinion by the suffrage of so honourable personages.

And yet followeth another charge, insinuating no less than his enmity both to Church and State, which could come from no other informer than the said

Mr. JAMES-MOORE SMITH.

'[a]The Memoirs of a Parish clerk was a very dull and unjust abuse of a person who wrote in defence of our Religion and Constitution, and who has been dead many years.' This seemeth also most untrue; it being known to divers that these

[a] Daily Journal, April 3, 1728.

---

permission for the disputed lines to be used in the play before he had published them himself. They were first published in a revision of his verses on Martha Blount's birthday, but later became part of *Characters of Women* (lines 243–8; see *TE*: VI, 244–7).

first plagiaries: greatest plagiarists.

in a letter: Not extant (*Corr.*: III, 10).

the Lady: Pope's close friend Martha ('Patty') Blount (1690–1763).

Hugh Bethel: (*d.* 1748), a close friend of Pope and Martha Blount, assigned a speaking role in *Imitations of Horace*: *Satires* II.ii.

the ingenuous that affect not error: fair-minded people with no taste for being in the wrong.

suffrage: opinion.

enmity both to Church and State: Roman Catholics were widely assumed to desire the overthrow of the Protestant Church of England and the constitution of which it formed a major element.

which could come from no other informer: Pope attributes another hostile letter to Moore Smythe, this one signed 'Philo-Ditto' in allusion to the previous 'Philo-Mauri' (*A Collection of Several Curious Pieces* 1728; Guerinot 1969: 105–6).

The Memoirs of a Parish clerk: A Scriblerian parody of the Whig propagandist Gilbert Burnet (1643–1715), Bishop of Salisbury, whose *History of his Own Times* was published posthumously in 1724. The attempt to deny the allusion is unconvincing (*PW*: II, 99–128, particularly pp. 104, 107).

divers: various people.

memoirs were written at the seat of the Lord Harcourt in Oxfordshire, before that excellent person (bishop Burnet's) death, and many years before the appearance of that history, of which they are pretended to be an abuse. Most true it is, that Mr. Moore had such a design, and was himself the man who prest Dr. Arbuthnot and Mr. Pope to assist him therein; and that he borrowed those Memoirs of our author, when that History came forth, with intent to turn them to such abuse. But being able to obtain from our author but one single hint, and either changing his mind, or having more mind than ability, he contented himself to keep the said Memoirs, and read them as his own to all his acquaintance. A noble person there is, into whose company Mr. Pope once chanced to introduce him, who well remembereth the conversation of Mr. Moore to have turned upon the 'Contempt he had for the work of that reverend prelate, and how full he was of a design he declared himself to have of exposing it.' This noble person is the Earl of PETERBOROUGH.

Here in truth should we crave pardon of all the foresaid right honourable and worthy personages, for having mentioned them in the same page with such weekly riff-raff railers and rhymers; but that we had their ever-honoured commands for the same; and that they are introduced not as witnesses in the controversy, but as witnesses that cannot be controverted; not to dispute, but to decide.

Certain it is, that dividing our writers into two classes, of such who were acquaintance, and of such who were strangers, to our author; the former are those who speak well, and the other those who speak evil of him. Of the first class, the most noble

JOHN Duke of BUCKINGHAM

sums up his character in these lines:

'[b]And yet so wond'rous, so sublime a thing,
As the great Iliad, scarce could make me sing,
Unless I justly could at once commend
A *good companion*, and as *firm a friend*;
One *moral*, or a mere *well-natur'd deed*,
Can all desert in sciences exceed.'

[b] Verses to Mr. P. on his translation of Homer.

the seat of the Lord Harcourt: At Stanton Harcourt, where Pope had worked on the Homer translation.

either changing his mind, or having more mind than ability: Playing on different senses of 'mind' in the expressions 'change one's mind' and 'have a mind to do something'.

the Earl of PETERBOROUGH: Charles Mordaunt (1658–1735), third Earl of Peterborow (his preferred spelling), soldier, diplomat and friend of Pope.

not to dispute, but to decide: Invoking the social standing of his supporters as a touchstone of moral authority.

JOHN Duke of BUCKINGHAM: For full text, see Pope 1723.

desert in sciences: merit in learning.

So also is he decyphered by the honourable

SIMON HARCOURT.

'[c]Say, wond'rous youth, what column wilt thou chuse,
What laurel'd arch, for thy triumphant Muse?
Tho' each great ancient court thee to his shrine,
Tho' ev'ry laurel thro' the dome be thine,
Go to the *good* and *just*, an awful train!
Thy soul's delight. ——

Recorded in like manner for his virtuous disposition, and gentle bearing, by the ingenious

Mr. WALTER HART,

in this apostrophe:

'[d]O! ever worthy, ever crown'd with praise!
Blest in thy *life* and blest in all thy *lays*.
Add, that the Sisters ev'ry thought refine,
And ev'n thy *life*, be *faultless* as thy line.
Yet envy still with fiercer rage pursues,
Obscures the *virtue*, and defames the Muse.
A soul like thine, in pain, in grief, resign'd,
Views with just scorn the malice of mankind.'

The witty and moral satyrist

Dr. EDWARD YOUNG,

wishing some check to the corruption and evil manners of the times, calleth out upon our poet to undertake a task so worthy of his virtue:

[c] Poem prefix'd to his works. [d] In his Poems, printed for B. Lintot.

---

decyphered: interpreted.

SIMON HARCOURT: (1683–1720), second son of the first Viscount Harcourt. This was one of the complimentary poems prefaced to Pope's 1717 edition of his *Works*.

Mr. WALTER HART: Harte (1709–74) was a writer, clergyman and admirer of Pope (Harte 1727).

apostrophe: address.

lays: songs, i.e. poems.

Sisters: the nine Muses.

just scorn: The text in Harte's *Poems on Several Occasions* reads 'vain scorn', which somewhat undermines the eulogy (Harte 1727).

Dr. EDWARD YOUNG: (1683–1765), clergyman and poet, now best known for his *Night Thoughts* (1742–5). The quotation is from his satirical sequence *The Love of Fame, the Universal Passion* (Young 1728).

'[e]Why slumbers Pope, who leads the Muse's train,
Nor hears that *Virtue*, which he *loves*, complain?'

Mr. MALLET,

In his epistle on Verbal Criticism:

'Whose life, severely scan'd, transcends his lays;
For wit supreme is but his second praise.'

Mr. HAMMOND,

That delicate and correct imitator of Tibullus, in his Love Elegies, Elegy xiv.

'Now, fir'd by Pope and *Virtue*, leave the age,
  In low pursuit of self-undoing wrong,
And trace the author thro' his moral page,
  Whose blameless life still answers to his song.'

Mr. THOMSON,

In his elegant and philosophical poem of the Seasons:

'Altho' not sweeter his own Homer sings,
Yet is his *life* the more endearing song.'

To the same tune also singeth that learned clerk of Suffolk

Mr. WILLIAM BROOME.

'[f]Thus, nobly rising in fair *Virtue*'s cause,
From thy own *life* transcribe th' *unerring laws*.'

And, to close all, hear the reverend Dean of St. Patrick's:

[e] Universal Passion, Satyr i. [f] In his Poems, and at the end of the Odyssey.

Mr. Mallet: David Mallet (1705?–1765), a writer helped by Pope. His anonymously issued *Of Verbal Criticism* (1733) supports Pope against Theobald and Bentley.

Mr. Hammond: James Hammond (1710–42), poet.

Tibullus: Roman love poet (*c*.55–19 BC).

Mr. Thomson: James Thomson (1700–48), Scottish poet, a disaffected Whig opposed to Walpole, now best known as the author of 'Rule Britannia' and of *The Seasons*, from which the quotation is taken ('Winter', as expanded in 1730, lines 553–4; Sambrook 1986: 143, 273).

Mr. William Broome: Broome, a clergyman and collaborator on Pope's Homer, published his verse compliment in his *Poems on Several Occasions* (1727) and at the end of his notes to the *Odyssey* translation.

Dean of St. Patrick's: From Swift's 'A Libel on Dr. Delany and a Certain Great Lord': Pope omits the parts of the compliment that stressed his disdain for the Hanoverian establishment more openly than seemed prudent.

'A Soul with ev'ry virtue fraught,
By Patriots, Priests, and Poets taught.
Whose filial Piety excells
Whatever Grecian story tells.
A genius for each bus'ness fit,
Whose meanest talent is his Wit,' *etc.*

Let us now recreate thee by turning to the other side, and shewing his Character drawn by those with whom he never conversed, and whose countenances he could not know, though turned against him: First again commencing with the high voiced and never enough quoted

Mr. John Dennis;

Who, in his Reflections on the Essay on Criticism, thus describeth him: 'A little affected hypocrite, who has nothing in his mouth but candour, truth, friendship, good-nature, humanity, and magnanimity. He is so great a lover of falshood, that, whenever he has a mind to calumniate his cotemporaries, he brands them with some defect which is just *contrary to some good quality*, for which all their *friends and their acquaintance* commend them. He seems to have a particular pique to *People of Quality*, and authors of that rank. — He must derive his religion from St. Omer's.' — But in the Character of Mr. P. and his writings (printed by S. Popping, 1716.) he saith, 'Though he is a professor of the worst religion, yet he *laughs at it*;' but that 'nevertheless, he is a *virulent Papist*; and yet a *Pillar* for the *Church of England*.'

Of both which opinions

Mr. Lewis Theobald

seems also to be; declaring, in Mist's Journal of June 22, 1728. 'That, if he is not shrewdly abused, he made it his practice to cackle to both *parties* in their own sentiments.' But, as to his *pique* against *People of quality*, the same Journalist doth not

---

Whose filial Piety excells: Pope's care for his aged mother was much admired. Mack cites Homer as influencing his conception of the filial role (Mack 1969: 29).

recreate: refresh (by a change of subject).

with whom he never conversed: This is not literally true of all (e.g. Dennis and Cibber); but the addition of 'whose countenances he could not know' effectively stresses the anonymous publication of many of their attacks.

high voiced: loud.

Quality: rank.

Character of Mr. P.: i.e. Dennis's anonymous *A True Character of Mr. Pope* (1716).

the worst religion: In Dennis's bigoted view, Roman Catholicism (Hooker 1939–43: II, 103). Although Dennis means to imply cynical and opportunistic hypocrisy on Pope's part, his listing of contradictory positions touches interestingly on Pope's frequently declared strategy of flexible moderation (see especially *Imitations of Horace*: *Satires* II.i.63–8).

***cackle to both* parties:** Pope's insistence that people of goodwill could maintain friendships across party lines looked to some like unprincipled hypocrisy.

agree, but saith (June 8, 1728.) 'He had, by some means or other, the *acquaintance* and *friendship* of the *whole body of our nobility*.'

However contradictory this may appear, Mr. Dennis and Gildon, in the character last cited, make it all plain, by assuring us, 'That he is a creature that reconciles all contradictions; he is a beast, and a man; a Whig, and a Tory; a writer (at one and the same time) of [g]Guardians and Examiners; an Assertor of liberty, and of the dispensing power of kings; a Jesuitical professor of truth; a base and a foul pretender to candour.' So that, upon the whole account, we must conclude him either to have been a great hypocrite, or a very honest man; a terrible imposer upon both parties, or very moderate to either.

Be it as to the judicious reader shall seem good. Sure it is, he is little favoured of certain authors, whose wrath is perilous: For one declares he ought to have a *price set on his head*, and to be hunted down as a *wild beast*[h]. Another protests that he does not know *what may happen*; advises him to *insure his person*; says he has *bitter enemies*, and expressly declares it will be well if he *escapes with his life*[i]. One desires he would *cut his own throat, or hang himself*[k]. But Pasquin seemed rather inclined it should be done by the Government, representing him engaged in grievous designs with a Lord of Parliament, then under prosecution[l]. Mr. Dennis

[g] The Names of two weekly Papers. [h] Theobald, Letter in Mist's Journal, June 22, 1728.
[i] Smedley, Pref. to Gulliveriana, p. 14, 16. [k] Gulliveriana, p. 332. [l] Anno 1723.

---

the character last cited: *A True Character of Mr. Pope* 1716 (Hooker 1939–43: II, 103).

Guardians and Examiners: There is no evidence that Pope wrote for the Tory *Examiner*, but he did contribute to the *Guardian*, run by the Whig Richard Steele (1672–1729). Pope recognised that this 'rendered me a suspected Whig' in the eyes of some Tories (*Corr.*: I, 194). *Guardian* 40 (Appendix V of the *Dunciad in Four Books*) is Pope's ironic comparison of his own pastorals with those of the Whig favourite Ambrose Philips (1674–1749), praised in the *Guardian* in essays which Pope may have attributed to Steele, but were probably by Tickell (Sherburn 1934: 117–21; Mack 1985: 214–18). Editors vary in their attribution to Pope of specific *Guardian* essays (*PW*: I, lvi–lxxii, 75–151; Stephens 1982: 25–6).

an Assertor of liberty: The liberty of the subject was a central tenet of Whig ideology.

the dispensing power of kings: A doctrine associated with Stuart absolutism, and hence with high Tory doctrine, which asserted that the monarch might suspend the law at pleasure. Pope is accused of paying hypocritical lip-service to incompatible political positions.

a Jesuitical professor of truth: In Protestant polemic, Jesuits were proverbially guileful.

candour: generosity of spirit.

Another protests: Pope attributed the anonymous *Gulliveriana* to Jonathan Smedley (1671–1729), Irish Whig clergyman, writer and antagonist of Swift.

Pasquin: 20 February 1723, sometimes attributed to Edward Roome. (The title alludes to a traditional character under whose name satires could be circulated.)

a Lord of Parliament: Atterbury, who as a bishop sat in the House of Lords, was exiled by a Bill of Pains and Penalties in 1723 (Bennett 1975). Pope, who seems to have known that he was involved in Jacobite intrigue, gave evidence on his behalf, thus putting a further weapon into the hands of enemies who already associated him, as a Catholic, with subversion of the state (*OAC*: I, 102–3; Erskine-Hill 1988: 204–9). 'Anno' in the note is Latin for 'in the year', used in citing dates.

himself hath written to a *Minister*, that he is one of the most *dangerous persons in this kingdom*[m]; and assureth the public, that he is an *open* and *mortal enemy* to his *country*; a monster, that *will*, one day, shew as *daring a soul* as a *mad Indian*, who runs a *muck* to kill the first Christian he meets[n]. Another gives information of *Treason* discovered in his poem[o]. Mr. Curl boldly supplies an imperfect verse with *Kings* and *Princesses*[p]. And one Matthew Concanen, yet more impudent, publishes at length the Two most SACRED NAMES in this Nation, as members of the Dunciad[q]!

This is prodigious! yet it is almost as strange, that in the midst of these invectives his greatest Enemies have (I know not how) born testimony to some merit in him.

Mr. THEOBALD,

in censuring his Shakespear, declares, 'He has so great an *esteem* for Mr. Pope, and so high an *opinion* of his *genius* and *excellencies*; that, notwithstanding he professes a *veneration almost rising to Idolatry* for the writings of this inimitable poet,

[m] Anno 1729.

[n] Preface to Rem. on the Rape of the Lock, p. 12. and in the last page of that treatise.

[o] Page 6, 7. of the Preface, by Concanen, to a book intitled A Collection of all the Letters, Essays, Verses, and Advertisements, occasioned by Pope and Swift's Miscellanies. Printed for A. Moore, octavo, 1712.

[p] Key to the Dunciad, 3d edit. p. 18.

[q] A List of Persons, *etc.* at the end of the forementioned Collection of all the Letters, Essays, *etc.*

***hath written to a* Minister:** Reference unidentified, but presumably the attack mentioned in the Dedication, signed by Savage but probably by Pope, to *A Collection of Pieces* ('one wrote a Letter to a great Minister, assuring him Mr. *Pope* was the greatest Enemy the Government had': Savage 1732: vi; Tracy 1971: 46–8).

assureth the public: See Hooker 1939–43: II, 322, 325, 351.

Another gives information: Pope attributed the Preface to *A Compleat Collection* 1728 to Concanen.

Mr. Curl boldly supplies: Curll's anonymously published *A Compleat Key* (three editions in 1728) supplied names for the asterisks and initials under which Pope had originally veiled his targets. In the second and third editions Curll suggested 'Kings and Princesses' for the asterisks in III.299, a satire on the vulgar taste of the ruling elite. This was embarrassingly near the mark, for as a Catholic and Tory Pope had to equivocate carefully when attacking the establishment (Guerinot 1969: 110–14; see note on the 1728 III.299 in *TE*: V, 184; the corresponding line in 1743 is III.297).

the Two most SACRED NAMES: The line could even more compromisingly be filled by the royal names 'George' and 'Caroline', described in the Preface to *A Compleat Collection* (1728: Preface attributed by Pope to Concanen) as 'Names, which of all mortal Names ought to be the most Sacred, and the most exempt from any Ridicule in *English* Poetry' (*TE*: V, 184). Curll extended the charge from treason to blasphemy by including the royal pair in a list of Pope's victims which began with 'ALMIGHTY GOD' (Guerinot 1969: 122).

he would be very loth even to do *him* justice, at the expense of that *other gentleman*'s character[r].'

Mr. Charles Gildon,

after having violently attacked him in many pieces, at last came to wish from his heart, 'That Mr. Pope would be prevailed upon to give us Ovid's Epistles by his hand, for it is certain we see the original of Sappho to Phaon with much more life and likeness in his version, than in that of Sir Car. Scrope. And this (he adds) is the more to be wished, because in the English tongue we have scarce any thing truly and naturally written upon Love[s].' He also, in taxing Sir Richard Blackmore for his heterodox opinions of Homer, challengeth him to answer what Mr. Pope hath said in his preface to that poet.

Mr. Oldmixon

calls him a great master of our tongue; declares 'the purity and perfection of the English language to be found in his Homer; and, saying there are more good verses in Dryden's Virgil than in any other work, excepts this of our author only[t].'

The Author of a Letter to Mr. Cibber

says, '[v]Pope *was* so good a versifier [*once*] that his predecessor Mr. Dryden, and his cotemporary Mr. Prior excepted, the harmony of his numbers *is* equal to any body's. And, that he *had* all the merit that a man can have that way.' And

[r] Introduction to his Shakespear restored, in quarto, p. 3.
[s] Commentary on the Duke of Buckingham's Essay, octavo, 1721, p. 97, 98.
[t] In his prose Essay on Criticism. [v] Printed by J. Roberts, 1742. p. 11.

***that* other gentleman's:** Pope's.

at last: In *The Laws of Poetry* (Gildon 1721).

Ovid's Epistles: Ovid's *Heroides*, one of which was translated by Pope as 'Sapho to Phaon', take the form of letters, mostly from famous heroines to the lovers who have deserted them, and provide a model for Pope's *Eloisa to Abelard.*

Sir Car. Scrope: Sir Carr Scrope (1649–80), author of the best-known verse translation of 'Sappho to Phaon' before Pope.

heterodox opinions of Homer: Gildon thought Blackmore too severe in his criticisms of Homer, and challenged him to refute the orthodoxy represented by Pope and other more approving critics (Gildon 1721: 257–71).

Mr. Oldmixon: Selective paraphrase conceals Oldmixon's slighting suggestion that Pope's Homer has only superficial elegance to compensate for its lack of spirit and substance (Oldmixon 1728a).

The Author of a Letter to Mr. Cibber: John Hervey (1696–1743), Baron Hervey of Ickworth, confidant of Queen Caroline and antagonist of Pope from the early 1730s, was the target of Pope's 'A Letter to a Noble Lord' and 'A Most Proper Reply', and was satirised as 'Sporus' in *Epistle to Dr. Arbuthnot* (*PW*: II, 431–98; *To Arbuthnot*, lines 305–33). Pope here omits the

Mr. THOMAS COOKE,

after much blemishing our author's Homer, crieth out,

'But in his other works what beauties shine!
While sweetest Music dwells in ev'ry line.
These he admir'd, on these he stamp'd his praise,
And bade them live to brighten future days[w].'

So also one who takes the name of

H. STANHOPE,

the maker of certain verses to Duncan Campbell[x], in that poem, which is wholly a satyr on Mr. Pope, confesseth,

''Tis true, if finest notes alone could show
(Tun'd justly high, or regularly low)
That we should fame to these mere vocals give;
Pope more than we can offer should receive:
For when some gliding river is his theme,
His lines run smoother than the smoothest stream,' *etc.*

MIST'S JOURNAL, June 8, 1728.

Although he says, 'The smooth numbers of the Dunciad are all that recommend it, nor has it any other merit;' yet that same paper hath these words: 'The author is allowed to be a perfect master of an easy and elegant versification. *In all his works* we find the most *happy turns*, and *natural similes*, wonderfully short and thick sown.'

The Essay on the Dunciad also owns, p. 25. it is very full of *beautiful images*. But

[w] Battle of Poets, folio, p. 15.
[x] Printed under the title of the Progress of Dulness, duodecimo, 1728.

---

insulting twist of the original: 'when other People thought for him (that is, when he was a Translator) he had all the Merit that a Man can have in the Execution of a Task where Genius is not necessary, and to which no Man of true Genius can, or will submit' (*A Letter to Mr. C–b–r* 1742: 11–12; Guerinot 1969: 297).

Mr. Thomas Cooke: (1703–56), author of the anonymous *The Battle of the Poets. An Heroick Poem* (1725, revised, even more offensively, 1729: Guerinot 1969: 91–3, 160–64). His verse is quoted for its inanity in *Peri Bathous* (*PW*: II, 209, 215–16). He worked for Curll.

one who takes the name of H. Stanhope: Pseudonym of the author of the first item in the anonymous *The Progress of Dulness* (1728), identified by Curll as William Bond (*d.* 1735), dramatist, journalist and poet (Guerinot 1969: 123). The poem makes an unfavourable contrast between Pope (writer of 'Sound without Sense, and Body without Soul') and Duncan Campbell (1680?–1730), a deaf and dumb fortune-teller.

The Essay on the Dunciad: Anonymous pamphlet (1728).

the panegyric, which crowns all that can be said on this Poem, is bestowed by our Laureate,

Mr. COLLEY CIBBER,

who 'grants it to be a better Poem of its kind than ever was writ;' but adds, 'it was a victory over a parcel of poor wretches, whom it was almost cowardice to conquer. — A man might as well triumph for having killed so many silly flies that offended him. Could he have let them alone, by this time, poor souls! they had all been buried in oblivion[y].' Here we see our excellent Laureate allows the justice of the satyr on every man in it, but *himself*; as the great Mr. Dennis did before him.

The said

Mr. DENNIS and Mr. GILDON,

in the most furious of all their works (the forecited Character, p. 5.) do in concert[z] confess, 'That some men of *good understanding* value him for his rhymes.' And (p. 17.) 'That he has got, like Mr. Bays in the Rehearsal, (that is, like Mr. Dryden) a notable knack at rhyming, and writing smooth verse.'

[y] Cibber's Letter to Mr. Pope, p. 9, 12.

[z] *In concert*] Hear how Mr. Dennis hath proved our mistake in this place; 'As to my writing in *concert* with Mr. Gildon, I declare upon the honour and word of a gentleman, that I never wrote so much as one line in *concert* with any one man whatsoever. And these two Letters from Mr. Gildon will plainly shew that we are not writers in *concert* with each other.

Sir,

— The height of my Ambition is to please Men of the best Judgment; and finding that I have entertained my Master agreeably, I have the extent of the Reward of my Labour.

Sir,

I had not the opportunity of hearing of your excellent Pamphlet 'till this day. I am infinitely satisfied and pleased with it, and hope you will meet with that encouragement your admirable performance deserves, etc.

CH. GILDON.

Now is it not plain, that any one who sends such compliments to another, has not been used to write in partnership with him to whom he sends them?' Dennis, Rem. on the Dunc. p. 50. Mr. Dennis is therefore welcome to take this piece to himself.

---

the forecited Character: *A True Character of Mr. Pope* 1716. Selective quotation masks the insulting context of these remarks (Hooker 1939–43: II, 103, 108).

in concert: Although Dennis probably did not work alongside Charles Gildon on *A True Character* – as he insists in the passage from his *Remarks upon ... the Dunciad* (1729) quoted in the original note – he does seem to have incorporated material by Gildon (Hooker 1939–43: II, 374; Guerinot 1969: 42). For Pope's satire on a pamphlet, not extant, purporting to be jointly by Dennis and Gildon, see *PW*: II, 231, 274.

Mr. Bays in the Rehearsal: *The Rehearsal* by George Villiers (1628–87), second Duke of Buckingham, and others, parodies heroic drama: the character of Mr. Bayes (i.e. the Laureate,

Of his Essay on Man, numerous were the praises bestowed by his avowed enemies, in the imagination that the same was not written by him, as it was printed anonymously.

Thus sang of it even

BEZALEEL MORRIS.

'Auspicious bard! while all admire thy strain,
All but the selfish, ignorant, and vain;
I, whom no bribe to servile flatt'ry drew,
Must pay the tribute to thy merit due:
Thy Muse, sublime, significant, and clear,
Alike informs the Soul, and charms the Ear,' *etc.*

And

MR. LEONARD WELSTED

thus wrote [a] to the unknown author, on the first publication of the said Essay: 'I must own, after the reception which the vilest and most immoral ribaldry hath lately met with, I was surprised to see what I had long despaired, a performance deserving the name of a poet. Such, Sir, is your work. It is, indeed, above all commendation, and ought to have been published in an age and country more worthy of it. If my testimony be of weight any where, you are sure to have it in the amplest manner,' *etc. etc. etc.*

Thus we see every one of his works hath been extolled by one or other of his most inveterate Enemies; and to the success of them all they do unanimously give testimony. But it is sufficient, *instar omnium*, to behold the great critic, Mr. Dennis, sorely lamenting it, even from the Essay on Criticism to this day of the Dunciad! 'A most notorious instance (quoth he) of the depravity of genius and taste, the

[a] In a Letter under his hand, dated March 12, 1733.

---

a hint Pope takes up in casting Cibber as 'Bays') has been taken as a caricature of Dryden (Stone 1969). Cibber distinguished himself in the role in 1717 (before he became real-life Laureate), and claimed that an ad lib he inserted was the origin of his quarrel with Pope (see notes on the Argument to Book I).

BEZALEEL MORRIS: Morrice (*d.* 1749), an adversary of Pope, was tricked into praising his *Essay on Man* by its anonymous publication. See 'To the Author of the *Essay on Man*', prefaced to the anonymously issued *An Essay on the Universe: A Poem* (1733).

thus wrote to the unknown author: The letter, apparently written in ignorance of Pope's authorship of the *Essay on Man*, is not extant (*Corr.*: III, 355). 'Under his hand' implies that the genuineness of the letter can be proved by the handwriting.

instar omnium: 'the image of them all'. Dennis had set the pattern for attacks on Pope with his *Reflections ... upon ... An Essay upon Criticism* (1711).

sorely lamenting it: i.e. Pope's success. The quotations from Dennis are freely adapted (Hooker 1939–43: I, 396; II, 115, 119–22).

approbation this Essay meets with[b] — I can safely affirm, that I never attacked any of these writings, unless they had *success* infinitely beyond their merit. — This, though an empty, has been a *popular* scribler. The epidemic madness of the times has given him *reputation*[c]. — If, after the cruel treatment so many extraordinary men (Spencer, Lord Bacon, Ben. Johnson, Milton, Butler, Otway, and others) have received from this country, for these last hundred years, I should shift the scene, and shew all that penury changed at once to riot and profuseness; and more squandered away upon *one object*, than would have satisfied the greater part of those extraordinary men; the reader to whom this one creature should be unknown, would fancy him a prodigy of art and nature, would believe that all the great qualities of these persons were centered in him alone. — But if I should venture to assure him, that the PEOPLE of ENGLAND had made such a choice — the reader would either believe me a *malicious enemy*, and *slanderer*; or that the reign of the last (Queen Anne's) *Ministry* was designed by fate to encourage *Fools*[d].'

But it happens, that this our Poet never had any Place, Pension, or Gratuity, in any shape, from the said glorious Queen, or any of her Ministers. All he owed, in the whole course of his life, to any court, was a subscription, for his Homer, of 200 *l.* from King George I, and 100 *l.* from the prince and princess.

However, lest we imagine our Author's Success was constant and universal, they acquaint us of certain works in a less degree of repute, whereof, although owned by others, yet do they assure us he is the writer. Of this sort Mr. DENNIS[e] ascribes to him *two Farces*, whose names he does not tell, but assures us that *there is not*

[b] Dennis, Pref. to his Reflect. on the Essay on Criticism. [c] Pref. to his Rem. on Homer.
[d] Rem. on Homer, p. 8, 9. [e] Ibid. p. 8.

so many extraordinary men: Dennis compared Pope's success, which he considered undeserved, with the neglect or disgrace suffered by those he considered greater writers, e.g. Edmund Spenser (1552?–99); Francis Bacon (1561–1626), first Baron Verulam and Viscount St Albans; Ben Jonson (1572–1637); John Milton (1608–74); Samuel Butler (1612–80), author of *Hudibras*; and the dramatist Thomas Otway (1652–85).

***the last (Queen Anne's)* Ministry:** Dennis, writing in 1717, had no need to name the late Queen (*d.* 1714), but Pope has added the parenthesis so that Dennis's sneer at an administration led by Pope's Tory friends Oxford and Bolingbroke should not be lost. Pope is, however, justified in stating that he never received *official* – as opposed to private – support from them.

l.: Abbreviation for pound(s) sterling.

although owned by others: Although other people claim to have written them.

two Farces: Pope's enemies insisted on attributing *The What D'ye Call It* and *Three Hours after Marriage* to him, whereas both were principally the work of Gay, though the former may have incorporated some of Pope's suggestions, and the latter seems to have been written in collaboration with Pope and Arbuthnot (*OAC*: I, 103; Fuller 1983: I, 14–17, 22–4; Winton 1993: 42–56; Nokes 1995: 181–2, 233–6). *The What D'ye Call It* had been a marked success, but *Three Hours*, produced in 1717, fell foul of an orchestrated press campaign, and the part allocated to Cibber contained satire against his own activities as actor-manager which may have contributed to his quarrel with Pope (Cibber 1742: 17–19; Winton 1993: 54; Nokes 1995: 240–43).

one jest in them: And an imitation of Horace, whose title he does not mention, but assures us *it is much more execrable than all his works*[f]. The DAILY JOURNAL, May 11, 1728. assures us, 'He is below Tom. Durfey in the Drama, because (as that writer thinks) the Marriage Hater matched, and the Boarding School are better than the What-d'-ye-call-it;' which is not Mr. P.'s, but Mr. Gay's. Mr. GILDON assures us, in his New Rehearsal, p. 48. 'That he was writing a *play* of the Lady Jane Grey;' but it afterwards proved to be Mr. Row's. We are assured by another, 'He wrote a pamphlet called Dr. Andrew Tripe[g];' which proved to be one Dr. Wagstaff's. Mr. THEOBALD assures us, in Mist of the 27th of April, 'That the treatise of the *Profound* is very dull, and that Mr. Pope is the author of it.' The writer of Gulliveriana is of another opinion; and says, 'the whole, or greatest part, of the merit of this treatise must and can only be ascribed to Gulliver[h].' [Here, gentle reader! cannot I but smile at the strange blindness and positiveness of men; knowing the said treatise to appertain to none other but to me, Martinus Scriblerus.]

We are assured, in Mist of June 8, 'That his own *Plays* and *Farces* would better have adorned the Dunciad, than those of Mr. Theobald; for he had neither genius for Tragedy nor Comedy.' Which whether true or not, is not easy to judge; in as much as he hath attempted neither. Unless we will take it for granted, with Mr. Cibber, that his being once very angry at hearing a friend's Play abused, was

[f] Character of Mr. Pope, p. 7. [g] Character of Mr. Pope, p. 6. [h] Gulliv. p. 336.

an imitation of Horace: For an early imitation of Horace, now lost, see *OAC*: I, 144.

the DAILY JOURNAL: The letter is probably by Dennis (Hooker 1939–43: II, 416–17, 526; Guerinot 1969: 118).

Tom. Durfey: Since the popular ballad-writer and dramatist Thomas D'Urfey (1653–1723) is for Dennis a stock example of a bad writer, his favourable comparison of his work with Gay's *The What D'ye Call It* is particularly insulting (D'Urfey 1691, 1692). According to Nokes, however, 'No other writer had so great an influence on Gay as Durfey' (Nokes 1995: 149). Pope would hardly have held such a staple of popular culture in high esteem, and in *Peri Bathous* D'Urfey is apparently classed with the '*Frogs*' (*PW*: II, 197).

Mr. Row: Nicholas Rowe, playwright, editor of Shakespeare and early friend of Pope.

Dr. Andrew Tripe: Pope attributes *A Letter from the Facetious Doctor Andrew Tripe* (1714) to William Wagstaffe (1685–1725), physician and writer.

Mist of the 27th of April: It does not contain the particular statement quoted.

***the treatise of the* Profound:** Pope's *Peri Bathous: or, ... the Art of Sinking in Poetry.*

Gulliver: The anonymous author of *Gulliveriana* (1728) calls Swift 'Captain Gulliver'. Although Swift is singled out for sustained attack, *Peri Bathous* is also decried.

to none other but to me: The full title of *Peri Bathous* assigns it to the fictitious Martinus Scriblerus, author of 'Testimonies of Authors'.

Mist of June 8: Signed 'W. A.', but attributed by Pope to a group headed by Theobald.

he hath attempted neither: Pope prefers to overlook whatever contribution he may have made, along with Arbuthnot, to Gay's much reviled farce *Three Hours after Marriage*. Characteristically, he decided against further dramatic composition 'from seeing how much everybody that did write for the stage was obliged to subject themselves to the players and the town' (*OAC*: I, 15–16; II, 690–91).

a friend's Play: Cibber was alluding to the judgment of Solomon as to which of two women

an infallible proof the Play was his own; the said Mr. Cibber thinking it impossible for a man to be much concerned for any but himself: 'Now let any man judge (saith he) by this concern, who was the true mother of the child[i]?'

But from all that hath been said, the discerning reader will collect, that it little availed our author to have any Candour, since when he declared he did not write for others, it was not credited; as little to have any Modesty, since, when he declined writing in any way himself, the presumption of others was imputed to him. If he singly enterprised one great work, he was taxed of Boldness and Madness to a prodigy[k]: If he took assistants in another, it was complained of, and represented as a great injury to the public[l]. The loftiest heroics, the lowest ballads, treatises against the state or church, satyrs on lords and ladies, raillery on wits and authors, squabbles with booksellers, or even full and true accounts of monsters, poisons, and murders; of any hereof was there nothing so good, nothing so bad, which hath not at one or other season been to him ascribed. If it bore no author's name, then lay he concealed; if it did, he fathered it upon that author to be yet better concealed: If it resembled any of his styles, then was it evident; if it did not, then disguised he it on set purpose. Yea, even direct oppositions in religion, principles, and politics, have equally been supposed in him inherent. Surely a most rare and singular character! Of which let the reader make what he can.

Doubtless most Commentators would hence take occasion to turn all to their Author's advantage, and from the testimony of his very Enemies would affirm, That his Capacity was boundless, as well as his Imagination; that he was a perfect

[i] Cibber's Letter to Mr. P. p. 19.

[k] Burnet's Homerides, p. 1. of his translation of the Iliad.

[l] The London and Mist's Journals, on his undertaking of the Odyssey.

was the true mother of a disputed child (1 Kings 3.16–28; Cibber 1742: 19). Cibber interprets Pope's anger – which he describes in belittling terms – as proof that he was personally insulted by ridicule of *Three Hours after Marriage* (Fuller 1983: I, 22–4; Ault 1949: 298–301).

the presumption of others: Publications wrongly attributed to him.

If he singly enterprised: The anonymous *Homerides: or, A Letter to Mr. Pope* (1715) was by Thomas Burnet (1694–1753), a Whig diplomat later to become a judge and to be knighted in 1745, and the author and journalist George Duckett (1684–1732), apparently attacked in *Peri Bathous* as one of the '*Didappers*' who 'come up now and then where you least expected them' (*PW*: II, 197). *Homerides* said of Pope's *Iliad* that it was 'somewhat bold, and almost prodigious, for a single Man to undertake a Work, which not all the Poets of our Island durst jointly attempt' (p. 5; Guerinot 1969: 22).

took assistants: The objection was to Pope's failure to acknowledge his collaborators' contributions to the *Odyssey* from the outset (Mack 1985: 412–17, citing the *London Journal*; *Mist's Weekly Journal* repeatedly mentions the affair in 1728).

The loftiest heroics: Despite the disdainful rhetoric, Pope *did* publish ballads, political spoofs, lampoons, epigrams against authors, intrigues against publishers, and even *A Full and True Account of a Horrid and Barbarous Revenge by Poison* (by himself on Edmund Curll) – though often anonymously (*PW*: I, 257–66).

his Capacity was boundless: The reader is teased with a crescendo of astounding claims: Scriblerus ostensibly dissents, while actually highlighting them.

master of all Styles, and all Arguments; and that there was in those times no other Writer, in any kind, of any degree of excellence, save he himself. But as this is not our own sentiment, we shall determine on nothing; but leave thee, gentle reader, to steer thy judgment equally between various opinions, and to chuse whether thou wilt incline to the Testimonies of Authors avowed, or of Authors concealed; of those who knew him, or of those who knew him not.

MARTINUS SCRIBLERUS of the POEM.

THIS poem, as it celebrateth the most grave and ancient of things, Chaos, Night, and Dulness; so is it of the most grave and ancient kind. Homer (saith Aristotle) was the first who gave the *Form*, and (saith Horace) who adapted the *Measure*, to heroic poesy. But even before this, may be rationally presumed from what the Ancients have left written, was a piece by Homer composed, of like nature and matter with this of our poet. For of Epic sort it appeareth to have been, yet of matter surely not unpleasant, witness what is reported of it by the learned archbishop Eustathius, in Odyss. x. And accordingly Aristotle, in his Poetic, chap. iv. doth further set forth, that as the Iliad and the Odyssey gave example to Tragedy, so did this poem to Comedy its first idea.

---

kind: genre.

MARTINUS SCRIBLERUS of the POEM. First used in 1729, this essay was slightly altered for 1743.

Chaos, Night, and Dulness: Dulness, the personification on which the divine machinery of Pope's *Dunciad* is based, is 'Daughter of Chaos and eternal Night' (I.12), echoing Milton's *Paradise Lost*, which states that between hell and earth 'eldest Night / And Chaos, ancestors of Nature, hold / Eternal anarchy' (Fowler 1998: II.894–6). 'Night' in this sense is an aspect of Chaos ('sable-vested Night, eldest of things, / The consort of his reign': II.962–3), not the night which God later creates as opposite of day ('light the day, and darkness night / He named': VII.251–2).

Homer (saith Aristotle): Aristotle cites Homer as the pioneer of epic form (Fyfe & Roberts 1932: *Poetics*, xxiv).

(saith Horace): In the *Art of Poetry* Homer is said to have demonstrated the metre ('*Measure*') suited to epic subjects (lines 73–4).

a piece by Homer composed, of like nature: Scriblerus, following Aristotle (*Poetics*, iv), claims that before composing his epics Homer had written *Margites*, a lost comic epic on the actions of a fool – a compelling precedent for the *Dunciad*. (The attribution is no longer accepted.)

not unpleasant: not unamusing.

witness what is reported of it by the learned archbishop Eustathius: Eustathius (late twelfth century), Byzantine bishop and commentator on Homer, reports that Margites, though sexually well endowed, showed no understanding of what his genitals were for. Finally his mother-in-law suggested to his wife that she describe sexual intercourse to him as a way of repairing the wound she pretended to have suffered to her own genitals (Allen 1946: V, 158–9).

idea: In the sense of 'archetype' or 'pattern'.

From these authors also it should seem, that the Hero, or chief personage of it was no less *obscure*, and his understanding and sentiments no less quaint and strange (if indeed not more so) than any of the actors of our poem. MARGITES was the name of this personage, whom Antiquity recordeth to have been *Dunce the first*; and surely from what we hear of him, not unworthy to be the root of so spreading a tree, and so numerous a posterity. The poem therefore celebrating him was properly and absolutely a *Dunciad*; which though now unhappily lost, yet is its nature sufficiently known by the infallible tokens aforesaid. And thus it doth appear, that the first Dunciad was the first Epic poem, written by Homer himself, and anterior even to the Iliad or Odyssey.

Now, forasmuch as our poet had translated those two famous works of Homer which are yet left, he did conceive it in some sort his duty to imitate that also which was lost: And was therefore induced to bestow on it the same form which Homer's is reported to have had, namely that of Epic poem; with a title also framed after the ancient Greek manner, to wit, that of *Dunciad*.

Wonderful it is, that so few of the moderns have been stimulated to attempt some Dunciad! since, in the opinion of the multitude, it might cost less pain and oil than an imitation of the greater Epic. But possible it is also, that, on due reflection, the maker might find it easier to paint a Charlemagne, a Brute, or a Godfrey, with just pomp and dignity heroic, than a Margites, a Codrus, or a Fleckno.

We shall next declare the occasion and the cause which moved our poet to this particular work. He lived in those days, when (after Providence had permitted the invention of Printing as a scourge for the sins of the learned) Paper also became so cheap, and Printers so numerous, that a deluge of Authors covered the land:

---

the first Dunciad was the first Epic poem: Scriblerus solemnly promotes a genre which gibes at idiots ahead of the martial, celebratory epic traditionally regarded as the highest literary kind, and reverses the common-sense assumption that epic is logically prior to mock epic (see Bogel 1982: 852).

those two famous works of Homer: Pope had translated both the *Iliad* and (with Broome and Fenton) the *Odyssey*.

he did conceive it in some sort his duty: A questionable account of Pope's motivation.

a title also framed after the ancient Greek manner: As the *Iliad* tells of Ilium ('Troy'), so the *Dunciad* tells of dunces.

less pain and oil: The writer is imagined working late by an oil lamp.

a Charlemagne, a Brute, or a Godfrey: Charlemagne, eighth-century King of France, is a presiding figure in the eleventh-century *Chanson de Roland*, the *Orlando Innamorato* by Matteo Maria Boiardo (1441–94) and the *Orlando Furioso* by Ludovico Ariosto (1474–1533). Brutus, mythical Trojan founder of Britain, appears in the twelfth-century *Historia Regum Britanniae* of Geoffrey of Monmouth, and was to have been the hero of an epic planned but never completed by Pope, who knew the work in translation (Thompson 1718; Leranbaum 1977: 155–74; Mack 1985: 771–4). Godfrey of Bouillon is the twelfth-century crusader hero of the *Gerusalemme Liberata* by Torquato Tasso (1544–95).

a Codrus, or a Fleckno: Familiar examples of untalented versifiers. For Codrus/Cordus, see Juvenal's first satire. Richard Flecknoe (*d.* 1678?) was ridiculed by Marvell and Dryden: in the mock-epic *Mac Flecknoe*, an important model for the *Dunciad*, Dryden makes him the poetic father of Thomas Shadwell (1642?–1692).

Whereby not only the peace of the honest unwriting subject was daily molested, but unmerciful demands were made of his applause, yea of his money, by such as would neither earn the one, nor deserve the other. At the same time, the licence of the Press was such, that it grew dangerous to refuse them either; for they would forthwith publish slanders unpunished, the authors being anonymous, and skulking under the wings of Publishers, a set of men who never scrupled to vend either Calumny or Blasphemy, as long as the Town would call for it.

[a]Now our author, living in those times, did conceive it an endeavour well worthy an honest Satyrist, to dissuade the dull, and punish the wicked, *the only way that was left*. In that public-spirited view he laid the plan of this Poem, as the greatest service he was capable (without much hurt, or being slain) to render his dear country. First, taking things from their original, he considereth the Causes creative of such Authors, namely *Dulness* and *Poverty*; the one born with them, the other contracted by neglect of their proper talents, through self-conceit of greater abilities. This truth he wrappeth in an *Allegory*[b] (as the construction of Epic poesy requireth) and feigns that one of these Goddesses had taken up her abode with the other, and that they jointly inspired all such writers and such works. [c]He proceedeth to shew the *qualities* they bestow on these authors, and the *effects* they produce[d]: then the *materials*, or *stock*, with which they furnish them[e]; and (above all) that *self-opinion*[f] which causeth it to seem to themselves vastly greater than it is, and is the prime motive of their setting up in this sad and sorry merchandice.

[a] Vide Bossu, Du Poeme Epique, ch. viii. [b] Bossu, chap. vii. [c] Book I. v. 32, *etc.*
[d] Ver. 45 to 54. [e] Ver. 57 to 77. [f] Ver. 80

Now our author: Scriblerus cites Le Bossu's *Traité du poème épique*, which claims that Homer's *Iliad*, like all epics, presents moral instruction precisely calculated for the needs of the poet's time and place, a point taken up by Thomas Parnell in his prefatory Essay to Pope's *Iliad* (Le Bossu 1695: Bk I, Ch. 8; *TE*: VII, 70–72). Pope, who read Le Bossu in his late teens and also knew him in translation (J. 1695), made his theories the basis for his parodic 'A Receipt to make an *Epic Poem*', and cited them in his prefaces to the *Iliad* and *Odyssey* (*PW*: II, 228–30; *OAC*: I, 20). For the structural and thematic relevance of Le Bossu to *The Dunciad*, see Keener 1991. 'Vide' in the note is Latin for 'see!'

without much hurt: The parenthesis goes some way to undercut claims for Pope's heroism so inflated as to risk derision. Yet there is something uneasy in its humorous ruling out of military heroism, since readers well knew that Pope's physical disabilities made military service unthinkable.

First, taking things from their original: For an analysis of Scriblerus's account of the genesis of the *Dunciad* in terms of Le Bossu's theory, see Keener 1991: 44–9.

an* Allegory *(as the construction of Epic poesy requireth): Although Scriblerus's discussion of the goddesses Dulness and Poverty is compatible with modern definitions of allegory, according to Le Bossu *all* epic characters, even if they have the names of historical persons, function allegorically. Keener argues that this account of the basic plot idea (what Le Bossu calls the 'fable') shows that Dulness, rather than either Theobald or Cibber, was always at the centre of Pope's concern (Keener 1991: 45; and see I.1 and notes).

feigns: imagines.

self-opinion: vanity.

The great power of these Goddesses acting in alliance (whereof as the one is the mother of Industry, so is the other of Plodding) was to be exemplified in some *one, great* and *remarkable Action*[g]*:* And none could be more so than that which our poet hath chosen, *viz.* the restoration of the reign of Chaos and Night, by the ministry of Dulness their daughter, in the removal of her imperial seat from the City to the polite World; as the Action of the Aeneid is the restoration of the empire of Troy, by the removal of the race from thence to Latium. But as Homer singing only the *Wrath* of Achilles, yet includes in his poem the whole history of the Trojan war; in like manner our author hath drawn into this *single Action* the whole history of Dulness and her children.

A *Person* must next be fixed upon to support this Action. This *Phantom* in the poet's mind must have a *Name*[h]: He finds it to be ——; and he becomes of course the Hero of the poem.

The *Fable* being thus, according to the best example, one and entire, as contained in the Proposition; the *Machinery* is a continued chain of Allegories, setting

[g] Ibid. chap. vii, viii. [h] Ibid. chap. viii. Vide Aristot. Poetic. cap. ix.

---

as the one is the mother of Industry, so is the other of Plodding: Dulness's enterprising stupidity, which is 'born with' her dunces, makes them want to be writers, but the poverty consequent on their 'neglect of their proper talents' means that once they begin they cannot afford to stop.

one, great *and* remarkable Action: Le Bossu follows Aristotle in holding that the epic fable should focus on a single action complete in itself (*Poetics*, xxiii).

the restoration of the reign of Chaos and Night: Implying the reversal of Milton's account of creation (cp. Genesis 1:1–5; John 1:1–5; Fowler 1998: *Paradise Lost*, II.890–97; Keener 1991: 46, 54–5).

the removal of her imperial seat: Introducing the transfer of empire from east to west which underlies the *Dunciad*'s allusion to Virgil's *Aeneid*. Aeneas is a prince of Troy (in Asia Minor), but flees westward to Latium (the district of Italy inhabited by the Latins), where his descendants are to found the greater empire of Rome. In line with the traditional contempt of the wits for the mercantile culture and values of the City of London, this is where Dulness's progress begins (although many of her writers and other supporters actually have little or no connection with it): after the City festival of a Lord Mayor's installation she moves towards 'the polite World' of the West End, which includes, crucially, the court at St James's Palace. Pope fears the swamping of elite culture by trends which he associates with a market unconcerned with traditional notions of cultural value.

only the* Wrath *of Achilles: Aristotle had praised Homer because instead of detailing the whole story of Troy in his *Iliad*, he had focused on the anger of Achilles over a slight from his commander (*Poetics*, xxiii). It was traditionally agreed that Homer had successfully integrated the major elements of the Troy story around this focus.

A* Person *must next be fixed upon: Scriblerus draws on a hint from Aristotle as elaborated by Le Bossu, who refers to the hero of the *Iliad* as an abstraction, a 'phantom' for which the poet chooses the name 'Achilles' (Bk I, Ch. 8). Similarly, Cibber is to become, in the hero Bays, a puppet of the poet's predetermined moral and fable – a pointed snub for one for whom the flaunting of personality was his stock in trade.

the Proposition: The statement of the subject at the beginning of an epic.

the* Machinery *is a continued chain of Allegories: Epic machinery is constituted by the

forth the whole Power, Ministry, and Empire of Dulness, extended through her subordinate instruments, in all her various operations.

This is branched into *Episodes*, each of which hath its Moral apart, though all conducive to the main end. The Crowd assembled in the second book, demonstrates the design to be more extensive than to bad poets only, and that we may expect other Episodes of the Patrons, Encouragers, or Paymasters of such authors, as occasion shall bring them forth. And the third book, if well considered, seemeth to embrace the whole World. Each of the Games relateth to some or other vile class of writers: The first concerneth the Plagiary, to whom he giveth the name of More; the second the libellous Novellist, whom he styleth Eliza; the third, the flattering Dedicator; the fourth, the bawling Critic, or noisy Poet; the fifth, the dark and dirty Party-writer; and so of the rest; assigning to each some *proper name* or other, such as he could find.

As for the Characters, the public hath already acknowledged how justly they are drawn: The manners are so depicted, and the sentiments so peculiar to those to whom applied, that surely to transfer them to any other or wiser personages, would be exceeding difficult: And certain it is that every person concerned, being

---

supernatural characters whose actions frame the human action, in this case Dulness, the personification of an abstract quality, whose actions are here presented as primarily allegorical. (Although Pope, like Boileau in *Le Lutrin* and Garth in *The Dispensary*, uses overt personification, it should be remembered that *all* epic characters are, by Le Bossu's theory, capable of allegorical interpretation.) Spenser had described *The Faerie Queene* as 'a continued Allegory, or darke conceit' (Smith & De Selincourt 1912: 'A Letter of the Authors expounding his *whole intention*').

Ministry: Evoking the much-satirised administration of 'the Minister', Sir Robert Walpole.

Episodes: The individual incidents in an epic.

The Crowd assembled in the second book: The 'endless band' comprises not only 'true Dunces' but also 'all who knew those Dunces to reward' (II.21–6).

seemeth to embrace the whole World: Book III foresees Dulness's 'boundless empire' spreading over 'all the nations' (III.67–72).

Each of the Games: In Book II the dunces celebrate Cibber's elevation with mock-heroic games, an allusion to the athletic contests that mark great events in classical epic. Scriblerus insists that the individuals named are of no importance in themselves: the poet has simply assigned to each 'vile class of writers ... some *proper name* or other, such as he could find', i.e. names of real people. James Moore Smythe and Eliza Haywood are presented as two such (see II.50 and II.157). For Pope's use of proper names, see Rogers 1993a: 98–128.

the public hath already acknowledged how justly they are drawn: 1728 designated victims by initials: the fact that many were soon recognised seems to be taken by Scriblerus as proof of the accuracy of the descriptions. Readers were quickly aided by commentaries, notably *A Compleat Key* (1728) by Edmund Curll, who drew on his inside knowledge of the publishing world. From 1729 Pope gave most names in full.

the sentiments so peculiar: 'Peculiar' primarily in the sense of 'specific to an individual', but also implying that only the victims of the *Dunciad* could harbour sentiments so preposterous. The discrimination of characters by their speech is a conventional topic of literary praise: Pope had used it in his Prefaces to the *Iliad* and to Shakespeare (*PW*: I, 229–31; II, 13–14).

consulted apart, hath readily owned the resemblance of every portrait, his own excepted. So Mr. Cibber calls them, 'a parcel of *poor wretches*, so many *silly flies*[i]: but adds, our Author's Wit is remarkably more bare and barren, whenever it would fall foul on *Cibber*, than upon any other Person whatever.'

The *Descriptions* are singular, the *Comparisons* very quaint, the *Narration* various, yet of one colour: The purity and chastity of *Diction* is so preserved, that in the places most suspicious, not the *words* but only the *images* have been censured, and yet are those images no other than have been sanctified by ancient and classical Authority, (though, as was the manner of those good times, not so curiously wrapped up) yea, and commented upon by most grave Doctors, and approved Critics.

As it beareth the name of *Epic*, it is thereby subjected to such severe indispensable rules as are laid on all Neoterics, a strict imitation of the Ancients; insomuch that any deviation, accompanied with whatever poetic beauties, hath always been censured by the sound Critic. How exact that Imitation hath been in this piece, appeareth not only by its general structure, but by particular allusions infinite, many whereof have escaped both the commentator and poet himself; yea divers by his exceeding diligence are so altered and interwoven with the rest, that several have already been, and more will be, by the ignorant abused, as altogether and originally his own.

In a word, the whole poem proveth itself to be the work of our Author, when his faculties were in full vigour and perfection; at that exact time when years have ripened the Judgment, without diminishing the Imagination: which, by good Critics, is held to be punctually at *forty*. For, at that season it was that Virgil finished his Georgics; and Sir Richard Blackmore at the like age composing his Arthurs,

[i] Cibber's Letter to Mr. P. pag. 9, 12, 41.

various, yet of one colour: Despite its variety, the different elements of the narration are all in keeping with each other.

***The purity and chastity of* Diction:** Scriblerus boasts that Pope has avoided offensive language, even on 'suspicious' subjects (e.g. the urination contest in II.161–84), claiming that far more explicit references are accepted in classical literature – but sidestepping the issue of Pope's deliberate emphasis on the scatalogical.

Doctors: learned men.

Neoterics: moderns (a pedantic term).

accompanied with whatever poetic beauties: Scriblerus, the pedantic devotee of 'severe indispensable rules', characteristically sets exact imitation of the classics above the creation of 'poetic beauties' (contrast *Essay on Criticism*, lines 141–80).

particular allusions infinite: An invitation to competent readers to enjoy identifying classical allusions. Incompetent readers will show their ignorance and bad taste by condemning classical imitations under the illusion that they are simply his own invention. Scriblerus boasts of having identified allusions which even the poet and the original commentator are not aware of.

***punctually at* forty:** Pope was forty just after the publication of the first version of the *Dunciad* in 1728.

Virgil finished his Georgics: Virgil was entering his 40s when he published his didactic poem on farming and devoted himself to the *Aeneid*. Brooks-Davies argues that this reference introduces a major pattern of allusion to the *Georgics* (Brooks-Davies 1985: 6, 12–45).

Sir Richard Blackmore: Blackmore, whose year of birth is uncertain, published his epic *Prince*

declared the same to be the very *Acme* and pitch of life for Epic poesy: Though since he hath altered it to *sixty*, the year in which he published his Alfred[k]. True it is, that the talents for *Criticism*, namely smartness, quick censure, vivacity of remark, certainty of asseveration, indeed all but acerbity, seem rather the gifts of Youth than of riper Age: But it is far otherwise in *Poetry*; witness the works of Mr. Rymer and Mr. Dennis, who beginning with Criticism, became afterwards such Poets as no age hath paralleled. With good reason therefore did our author chuse to write his Essay on that subject at twenty, and reserve for his maturer years this great and wonderful work of the Dunciad.

RICARDUS ARISTARCHUS
OF THE
HERO of the POEM.

OF the Nature of *Dunciad* in general, whence derived, and on what authority founded, as well as of the art and conduct of this our poem in particular, the learned and laborious Scriblerus hath, according to his manner, and with tolerable share of judgment, dissertated. But when he cometh to speak of the *Person* of the *Hero* fitted for such poem, in truth he miserably halts and

[k] See his Essays.

Arthur in 1695 and *King Alfred* in 1723, six years before his death. His published views on the ideal age for writing are misrepresented: he had suggested that major works were unlikely to be produced before thirty, but that anyone who was writing well by forty could, so long as he retained his faculties, continue to do so into old age (Blackmore 1716–17: II, 280, 283).

***the talents for* Criticism:** Scriblerus, who equates criticism with savage fault-finding, associates it with an impudent, rash and over-confident approach. This fits his view of the young – except that he concedes the critic also requires a degree of bitterness usually found only in older people.

certainty of asseveration: confidence in making his declarations.

witness the works of Mr. Rymer and Mr. Dennis: Unlike Pope, who dedicated himself to poetry from youth, Thomas Rymer (1641–1713) and John Dennis were essentially critics (and doctrinaire and aggressive ones) who occasionally composed verse: 'such Poets as no age hath paralleled' can be read ironically. Pope was exceptionally precocious both as poet and, in the *Essay on Criticism*, as commentator on critical practice.

RICARDUS ARISTARCHUS: The caricature of Richard Bentley whose 'Hypercritics' and '*Dissertation* on the Hero' were promised on the title page. The essay, new in 1743, was contributed by Warburton.

tolerable share of judgment: Aristarchus's references to fellow scholars range from the patronising to the gratuitously offensive.

dissertated: A pedantic neologism, underlining the pompous awkwardness of the opening sentence.

halts: limps.

hallucinates. For, misled by one Monsieur Bossu, a Gallic critic, he prateth of I cannot tell what *Phantom of a Hero*, only raised up to support the Fable. A putid conceit! As if Homer and Virgil, like modern Undertakers, who first build their house and then seek out for a tenant, had contrived the story of a War and a Wandering, before they once thought either of Achilles or Aeneas. We shall therefore set our good brother and the world also right in this particular, by giving our word, that in the *greater Epic*, the prime intention of the Muse is to exalt Heroic Virtue, in order to propagate the love of it among the children of men; and consequently that the Poet's first thought must needs be turned upon a real subject meet for laud and celebration; not one whom he is to make, but one whom he may find, truly illustrious. This is the *primum mobile* of his poetic world, whence every thing is to receive life and motion. For this subject being found, he is immediately ordained, or rather acknowledged, an *Hero*, and put upon such action as befitteth the dignity of his character.

But the Muse ceases not here her Eagle-flight. Sometimes, satiated with the contemplation of these *Suns* of glory, she turneth downward on her wing, and darts like lightning on the *Goose* and *Serpent* kind. For we may apply to the Muse in her various moods, what an ancient master of Wisdom affirmeth of the Gods in general: *Si Dii non irascuntur impiis et injustis, nec pios utique justosque diligunt. In rebus enim diversis, aut in utramque partem moveri necesse est, aut in neutram. Itaque qui bonos diligit, et malos odit; et qui malos non odit, nec bonos diligit. Quia et diligere*

---

a Gallic critic: Aristarchus betrays his disdain for polite taste by a xenophobic distrust of the French critical tradition represented by Le Bossu, particularly his notion of the epic hero as a 'phantom' whose name and identity are contingent on the poet's predetermined moral and fable.

putid conceit: rotten idea. 'Putid' is an obsolete variant of 'putrid' favoured by Bentley, an instance of vocabulary that struck polite readers as both immoderate and inelegant (Jarvis 1995: 22–3). Although 1743 actually gives the more usual 'putrid', 'putid', which Warburton restored in 1751, was probably the intended reading. Pope had also used it in a manuscript draft of the portrait of Aristarchus in Book IV (Mack 1982: 340–41; Mack 1984: 128).

Undertakers: speculative builders, developers.

Achilles or Aeneas: Heroes respectively of the *Iliad* and the *Aeneid*.

***the* greater Epic:** That is, epic as usually understood (as distinct from 'the little epic' discussed at the beginning of 'Martinus Scriblerus of the Poem').

meet for laud: deserving of praise.

primum mobile: Figuratively, the prime source of action. (In pre-Copernican cosmology, the outermost sphere around the earth, which receives the divine energy and transmits it to the inner parts of the creation.)

her Eagle-flight: Eagles were supposed to be able to look directly at the sun without being blinded.

these* Suns *of glory: epic heroes.

the* Goose *and* Serpent *kind: Figuratively, the stupid and the devious.

an ancient master of Wisdom: Lactantius (*c.* AD 245–*c.*325), Christian apologist, defender of the notion that anger (*ira*) is a necessary attribute of divine justice (Migne 1844: *De Ira Dei*, V). Lactantius refers to the one God of Christianity: the change to 'Gods' may be intended to avoid the imputation of mocking Christian theology.

bonos ex odio malorum venit; et malos odisse ex bonorum caritate descendit. Which in the vernacular idiom may be thus interpreted: 'If the Gods be not provoked at evil men, neither are they delighted with the good and just. For contrary objects must either excite contrary affections, or no affections at all. So that he who loveth good men, must at the same time hate the bad; and he who hateth not bad men, cannot love the good; because to love good men proceedeth from an aversion to evil, and to hate evil men from a tenderness to the good.' From this delicacy of the Muse arose the *little Epic,* (more lively and choleric than her elder sister, whose bulk and complexion incline her to the flegmatic) and for this some notorious Vehicle of vice and folly was sought out, to make thereof an example. An early instance of which (nor could it escape the accurate Scriblerus) the Father of Epic poem himself affordeth us. From him the practice descended to the Greek Dramatic poets, his offspring; who in the composition of their *Tetralogy,* or set of four pieces, were wont to make the last a *Satyric Tragedy.* Happily one of these ancient *Dunciads* (as we may well term it) is come down to us amongst the Tragedies of Euripides. And what doth the reader think may be the subject? Why truly, and it is worth his observation, the unequal Contention of an *old, dull, debauched, buffoon Cyclops,* with the heaven-directed *Favourite of* Minerva; who after having quietly born all the monster's obscene and impious ribaldry, endeth the farce in punishing him with the mark of an indelible brand in his *forehead.* May we not then be excused, if for the future we consider the Epics of Homer, Virgil, and Milton, together with

---

delicacy: refinement or intensity of feeling: the Muse so loves good, that she is compelled to attack evil.

***the* little Epic:** The comic epic described at the beginning of 'Martinus Scriblerus of the Poem', exemplified by the pseudo-Homeric *Margites.*

choleric: easily angered.

complexion: nature, constitution.

flegmatic: phlegmatic, i.e. calm, unemotional.

some notorious Vehicle of vice and folly was sought out: Aristarchus prepares for the introduction of Cibber as hero.

An early instance: The lost poem *Margites,* traditionally attributed to Homer, discussed in 'Martinus Scriblerus of the Poem'.

the Greek Dramatic poets: In competitive festivals of tragedy in Athens each playwright staged three tragedies followed by a semi-comic play featuring a chorus of satyrs. The *Cyclops* of Euripides (*c.*485–406 BC) is the only complete example of a satyr play extant.

***an* old, dull, debauched, buffoon Cyclops:** One-eyed monster of Greek myth, outwitted by Odysseus in Homer's *Odyssey.* Readers are invited to parallel him with Cibber, and Pope with Odysseus, 'the heaven-directed *Favourite of* Minerva' (goddess of wisdom, called Athene by the Greeks). Pope notes in his commentary on the *Odyssey* that Euripides had repeated from Homer a pun which Pope will later accuse Cibber of mistranslating in an opera libretto, further elaborating the association between Cibber and the one-eyed monster (Pope's *Odyssey* IX.432; and see III.305).

May we not then be excused: Introducing the bold claim that the *Dunciad* completes a tetralogy comprising Homer's *Iliad* and *Odyssey,* Virgil's *Aeneid* and Milton's *Paradise Lost*: the *Dunciad* will transpose into a satiric form the values of the three epics commonly seen as underlying humane culture.

this our poem, as a complete *Tetralogy*, in which the last worthily holdeth the place or station of the *satyric* piece?

Proceed we therefore in our subject. It hath been long, and alas for pity! still remaineth a question, whether the Hero of the *greater Epic* should be an *honest man?* or, as the French critics express it, *un honnête homme*[a]; but it never admitted of any doubt but that the Hero of the *little Epic* should *not* be so. Hence, to the advantage of our Dunciad, we may observe how much juster the *Moral* of that Poem must needs be, where so important a question is previously decided.

But then it is not every Knave, nor (let me add) Fool, that is a fit subject for a Dunciad. There must still exist some Analogy, if not Resemblance of Qualities, between the Heroes of the two Poems; and this in order to admit what Neoteric critics call the *Parody*, one of the liveliest graces of the little Epic. Thus it being agreed that the constituent qualities of the greater Epic Hero, are *Wisdom*, *Bravery*, and *Love*, from whence springeth *heroic Virtue*; it followeth that those of the lesser Epic Hero, should be *Vanity*, *Impudence*, and *Debauchery*, from which happy assemblage resulteth *heroic Dulness*, the never-dying subject of this our Poem.

This being confessed, come we now to particulars. It is the character of true *Wisdom*, to seek its chief support and confidence within itself; and to place that support in the resources which proceed from a conscious rectitude of Will. — And are the advantages of *Vanity*, when arising to the heroic standard, at all short of this self-complacence? Nay, are they not, in the opinion of the enamoured owner, far beyond it? 'Let the world (will such an one say) impute to me what Folly or weakness they please; but till *Wisdom* can give me something that will make me more heartily happy, I am content to be GAZED AT[b].' This we see is *Vanity* according to the *heroic* gage or measure; not that low and ignoble species which pretendeth to *Virtues* we *have not*, but the laudable ambition of being *gazed at* for glorifying in those *Vices* which all the world know *we have*. 'The world may ask (says he) why I make my follies publick? Why not? I have passed my time very pleasantly with them[c].' In short, there is no sort of Vanity such a Hero would

[a] Si un Heros Poëtique doit être un honnête homme. Bossu, du Poême Epique, lib. iv. ch. 5.
[b] Dedication to the Life of C. C. [c] Life, p. 2. octavo Ed.

***an* honest man:** 'Honest' in the wider sense of 'honourable'. Le Bossu had argued that the principal character in an epic need not be a pattern of virtue, and cited Homer's practice in making Achilles reprehensibly brutal. Aristarchus despises such Frenchified immorality.

***how much juster the* Moral:** According to Aristarchus, our knowledge that the hero of the 'little epic' *must* be discreditable means that we benefit from unambiguous moral teaching – in comparison with the 'greater epic', where the reader may supposedly be led astray by reasoning like that of Le Bossu. The perversity of this view may be judged by applying it to Pope's previous 'little epic', *The Rape of the Lock*. It was in any case accepted as axiomatic that the major epics were unrivalled for moral teaching.

self-complacence: self-satisfaction.

such an one: Cibber.

gage: gauge.

scruple, but that which might go near to degrade him from his high station in this our Dunciad; namely, 'Whether it would not be *Vanity* in him, to take shame to himself for *not being* a *wise man*[d]?'

Bravery, the second attribute of the true Hero, is Courage manifesting itself in every limb; while, in its correspondent virtue in the mock Hero, that Courage is all collected into the *Face*. And as Power when drawn together, must needs be more strong than when dispersed, we generally find this kind of courage in so high and heroic a degree, that it insults not only Men, but Gods. Mezentius is without doubt the bravest character in all the Aeneis; but how? His bravery, we know, was an high courage of blasphemy. And can we say less of this brave man's, who having told us that he placed 'his *Summum bonum* in those follies, which he was not content barely to possess but would likewise glory in,' adds, '*If I am misguided,* 'TIS NATURE'S FAULT, *and I follow* HER[e].' Nor can we be mistaken in making this happy quality a species of *Courage*, when we consider those illustrious marks of it, which made his *Face* 'more known (as he justly boasteth) than most in the kingdom,' and his *Language* to consist of what we must allow to be the most *daring* Figure of Speech, that which is taken from the *Name of God*.

Gentle Love, the next ingredient in the true Hero's composition, is a mere bird of passage, or (as Shakespear calls it) *summer-teeming Lust*, and evaporates in the heat of *Youth*; doubtless by that refinement it suffers in passing through those *certain strainers* which our Poet somewhere speaketh of. But when it is let alone to work upon the *Lees*, it acquireth strength by *Old age*; and becometh a standing ornament to the little Epic. It is true indeed, there is one objection to its fitness

[d] Life, ibid. [e] Life, p. 23. octavo.

but that which might go near to degrade him: Cibber would be 'degraded' from his eminence as hero if he were vain enough to wish to be wise, which would show a glimmer of sense and thus lose him his role as Dulness's favourite.

***collected into the* Face:** Such a hero's courage consists not in action but in impudence.

Mezentius: Described by Virgil as a cruel atheist (*Aeneid* VII.648).

Summum bonum: highest good. Aristarchus sanctimoniously implies that Cibber's revelling in his natural folly amounts to blasphemy: the implied contrast is with the wise man who seeks grace for the amendment of his fallen nature. Cibber had defended the hilarity that he took to be his natural talent as a relaxation necessary to human happiness.

illustrious marks of it: Implying that it is the folly fearlessly displayed in Cibber's face that has made it famous. Cibber, implying that Pope had difficulty marketing his work, claimed that he deliberately capitalised on Cibber's fame: 'a Lick at the *Laureat* will always be a sure bait ... to catch him little Readers' (Cibber 1740: 31–2).

the most* daring *Figure of Speech: Cibber was noted for casual blasphemy.

as Shakespear calls it: Warburton's emendation of the usual 'summer-seeming' (Alexander 1951: *Macbeth*, IV.iii.86).

***those* certain strainers:** 'Lust, thro' some certain strainers well refin'd, / Is gentle love, and charms all womankind' (*Essay on Man*, II.189–90).

Lees: residue in a bottle of wine.

Old age: Cibber was in his early seventies in 1743.

for such an use: For not only the Ignorant may think it *common*, but it is admitted to be so, even by Him who best knoweth its nature. 'Don't you think (saith he) to say only *a man has his Whore*, ought to go for little or nothing? Because *defendit numerus*, take the first ten thousand men you meet, and I believe you would be no loser if you betted ten to one, that every single sinner of them, one with another, had been guilty of the same frailty[f].' But here he seemeth not to have done himself justice: The man is sure enough a Hero, who has his Lady at fourscore. How doth his Modesty herein lessen the merit of a *whole well-spent* Life: not taking to himself the commendation (which *Horace* accounted the greatest in a theatrical character) of continuing to the very *dregs*, the same he was from the beginning: 'Servetur ad *IMUM* / Qualis ab incepto processerat'.

But let us farther remark, that the calling her *his* whore, implieth she was *his own*, and not his *neighbour's*. Truly a commendable Continence! and such as Scipio himself must have applauded. For how much Self-denial was necessary not to covet

[f] Letter to Mr. P. p. 46.

---

common: Playing on the two senses of 'prevalent' and 'vulgar'. Either might sit uneasily with the distinction (for good or ill) required of a hero.

a man has his Whore: To illustrate his claim that his satire never inhibited its victims from further offending, Pope had written 'And has not *Colly* still his Lord, and Whore?' (*To Arbuthnot*, line 97).

defendit numerus: there is strength in numbers (i.e. everybody does it). Cibber's *Letter* in effect accuses Pope of hypocrisy, claiming that the young Pope had allowed himself to be taken to a brothel by Cibber and the eighteen-year-old Edward Rich (1698–1721), twenty-eighth Earl of Warwick, who wanted to 'see what sort of Figure a Man of his Size, Sobriety, and Vigour (in Verse) would make' (Cibber 1742: 46–9; for the sexual politics of Cibber's attack, see Straub 1992: 44). Cibber claims to have decided that the joke had gone far enough when he reflected that venereal disease would be more than Pope's constitution could survive: in response to Cibber's mocking account of how he intervened to save the English Homer, engravings were published showing him dragging Pope from the arms of a whore, while behind the door Warwick is seen 'tittering without, in hopes the sweet Mischief he came for would have been compleated'. One version has the caption '*And has not* Sawney *too his* Lord *and* Whore?', alluding to the 'Lord, and Whore' attributed to Cibber in *To Arbuthnot* (*OAC*: I, 110–12; Ault 1949: 298–307).

fourscore: Cibber was a decade younger than this when his *Apology* came out in 1740.

his Modesty: In claiming *not* to be the sexual prodigy Aristarchus would make him out to be.

which* Horace *accounted the greatest: Horace declared it a merit in a playwright to 'keep the character right to the end just the same as it was at the beginning' (*De arte poetica*, line 126). Cibber *had* in fact used this quotation, but of his folly, not lechery (Cibber 1740: 17).

Continence: sexual restraint (in the limited sense of his keeping his hands off other men's mistresses).

Scipio: Scipio Africanus, Roman general (236–183 BC), earned his reputation for sexual restraint by freeing a captive princess instead of making her his concubine.

his Neighbour's whore? and what disorders must the coveting her have occasioned, in that Society, where (according to this Political Calculator) *nine* in *ten* of all ages have their *concubines?*

We have now, as briefly as we could devise, gone through the three constituent Qualities of either Hero. But it is not in any, or all of these, that Heroism properly or essentially resideth. It is a lucky result rather from the collision of these lively Qualities against one another. Thus, as from Wisdom, Bravery, and Love, ariseth *Magnanimity*, the object of *Admiration*, which is the aim of the greater Epic; so from Vanity, Impudence, and Debauchery, springeth *Buffoonry*, the source of *Ridicule*, that 'laughing ornament,' as he well termeth it[g], of the little Epic.

He is not ashamed (God forbid he ever should be ashamed!) of this Character; who deemeth, that not *Reason* but *Risibility* distinguisheth the human species from the brutal. 'As Nature (saith this profound Philosopher) distinguished our species from the mute creation by our Risibility, her design MUST have been by *that faculty* as evidently to raise our HAPPINESS, as by OUR *os sublime* (OUR ERECTED FACES) to lift the dignity of our FORM above them[h].' All this considered, how complete a Hero must he be, as well as how *happy* a Man, whose Risibility lieth not barely in his *muscles* as in the common sort, but (as himself informeth us) in his very *spirits?* And whose *Os sublime* is not simply an *erect face*, but a Brazen head, as should seem by his comparing it with one of Iron, said to belong to the late king of Sweden[i]!

But whatever personal qualities a Hero may have, the examples of Achilles and Aeneas shew us, that all those are of small avail, without the constant *assistance of the* GODS: for the subversion and erection of Empires have never been judged the work of Man. How greatly soever then we may esteem of his high talents, we

[g] Letter to Mr. P. p. 31. [h] Life, p. 23, 24. [i] Letter, p. 8.

what disorders: Aristarchus stresses both Cibber's slapdash sociology and his easy acceptance of sexual misconduct. If nine out of ten men maintained whores on an individual basis, this would imply a similar proportion of the female population engaged in prostitution, and a demand so closely matched to supply that any poaching would lead to violence. Cibber is therefore to be congratulated on preferring self-denial to public strife.

Political Calculator: Mocking Cibber's attempt at sociological statistics.

Magnanimity: greatness of soul, celebrated in Aristotle's *Nicomachean Ethics* as including all the other virtues (IV.iii).

***not* Reason *but* Risibility**: Whereas reason was traditionally held to set man above the animals, Cibber defines man by the faculty of laughter.

os sublime: Human beings were traditionally distinguished from animals by the upright carriage of the head.

a Brazen head: Cibber, like the opposition representation of his patron Sir Robert Walpole, is characterised by 'brazen' effrontery.

the late king of Sweden: Charles XII of Sweden (1682–1718) was famous for fighting on against impossible odds, prompting curses against his stubborn 'Head of Iron' (Voltaire 1732: IV, 86).

can hardly conceive his personal prowess alone sufficient to restore the decayed empire of Dulness. So weighty an atchievement must require the particular favour and protection of the GREAT: who being the natural patrons and supporters of *Letters*, as the ancient Gods were of *Troy*, must first be drawn off and engaged in another Interest, before the total subversion of them can be accomplished. To surmount, therefore, this last and greatest difficulty, we have in this excellent man a professed Favourite and Intimado of the Great. And look of what force ancient Piety was to draw the Gods into the party of Aeneas, that, and much stronger is modern Incense, to engage the Great in the party of Dulness.

Thus have we essayed to pourtray or shadow out this noble Imp of Fame. But now the impatient reader will be apt to say, if so many and various graces go to the making up a Hero, what mortal shall suffice to bear this character? Ill hath he read, who sees not in every trace of this picture, that *individual*, ALL-ACCOMPLISHED PERSON, in whom these rare virtues and lucky circumstances have agreed to meet and concentre with the strongest lustre and fullest harmony.

The good Scriblerus indeed, nay the World itself might be imposed on in the late spurious editions, by I can't tell what *Sham-hero*, or *Phantom:* But it was not so easy to impose on HIM whom this egregious error most of all concerned. For no sooner had the fourth book laid open the high and swelling scene, but he recognized his own heroic Acts: And when he came to the words, 'Soft on her lap

---

the GREAT: Stressing the cultural responsibility of the aristocrats and other leading figures who flourished under Walpole. Their decadent taste is exemplified in their patronage of Cibber.

***the natural patrons and supporters of* Letters:** Taking as 'natural' the older assumption that literature ('*Letters*') should be financed by patrons of high rank.

***as the ancient Gods were of* Troy:** For Troy to fall it was necessary for some gods to take the Greek side against it: they are paralleled with the patrons who support Cibber to the detriment of literature.

a professed Favourite and Intimado of the Great: Cibber, son of a craftsman of foreign extraction, revelled in his intimacy with the highest in the land.

look of what force ancient Piety was: The obsolete idiom 'look ... what' ('whatever') insinuates Bentley's taste for obsolete vocabulary (Maxwell 1962). It was the proverbial piety of Aeneas that endeared him to the gods, but the much stronger power of flattery ('modern Incense') that endears Cibber to his patrons and thus recruits them for Dulness.

shadow out: give an outline of.

Imp of Fame: Shakespeare twice applies the phrase to Henry V (Alexander 1951: *Henry IV 2* V.v.42; *Henry V* IV.i.45). 'Imp' means 'offspring'.

Ill hath he read, who sees not: Only an incompetent reader can fail to have recognised Cibber as the possessor of the qualities specified.

concentre: come to a common centre.

late spurious editions: Most previous editions were not spurious, only shorter *Dunciads* with a different hero; but Aristarchus's professional pride demands that only the text he has selected be taken seriously.

Sham-hero, *or* Phantom: Tibbald.

no sooner had the fourth book: Book IV was first published, separately, in 1742 as *The New Dunciad.* The line quoted (IV.20) clearly referred to Cibber as Poet Laureate, even before he had been identified as hero of the first three books.

her Laureat son reclines', (though *Laureat* imply no more than *one crowned with laurel*, as befitteth any Associate or Consort in Empire) he ROAR'D (like a Lion) and VINDICATED HIS RIGHT OF FAME: Indeed not without cause, he being there represented as *fast asleep*; so unbeseeming the eye of Empire, which, like that of Providence, should never slumber. 'Hah! (saith he) fast asleep it seems! that's a little too strong. Pert and dull at least you might have allowed me, but as seldom asleep as any fool[k].' However, the injured Hero may comfort himself with this reflexion, that tho' it be *sleep*, yet it is not the *sleep of death*, but of *immortality*. Here he will[l] *live* at least, tho' not *awake*; and in no worse condition than many an enchanted Warrior before him. The famous *Durandarte*, for instance, was, like him, cast into a long slumber by *Merlin* the *British Bard* and Necromancer: and his example, for submitting to it with so good a grace, might be of use to our Hero. For this disastrous knight being sorely pressed or driven to make his answer by several *persons of quality*, only replied with a sigh, *Patience, and shuffle the cards*[m].

But now, as nothing in this world, no not the most sacred or perfect things either of Religion or Government, can escape the teeth or tongue of Envy, methinks I already hear these carpers objecting to the clear title of our Hero.

'It would never (say they) have been esteemed sufficient to make an Hero for the Iliad or Aeneis, that Achilles was brave enough to overturn one Empire, or Aeneas pious enough to raise another, had they not been Goddess-born, and Princes bred. What then did this Author mean, by erecting a Player instead of one of his Patrons, (a person 'never a hero even on the stage[n],') to this dignity of Collegue

[k] Letter, p. 53. [l] Letter, p. 1. [m] Don Quixote, Part ii. Book ii. ch. 22.
[n] See Life, p. 148.

---

he* ROAR'D *(like a Lion): Like the king of beasts in Spenser's 'Prosopopoia: Or Mother Hubberds Tale', whose roar vindicates his status after his skin has been stolen by usurpers, Cibber's bare assertion establishes beyond all doubt that he is the hero of the *Dunciad* (Oram 1989: 327–79).

unbeseeming the eye of Empire: unbecoming in one who has an empire to oversee.

Durandarte: In Cervantes' *Don Quixote*, the Don reports how he found the hero Durandarte in an enchanted sleep into which he had been cast by Merlin (Riley 1992: Pt II, Ch. 23; for Merlin as figure for Walpole, see editor's note on IV.517). Instead of wanting to be released, Durandarte expressed his resignation in the words quoted – which could also be taken to glance at Cibber's gambling. Aristarchus considers Durandarte's detachment 'of use to our Hero' as an example of how to resist the rash suggestions of one's patrons, for Cibber had stated at the beginning of his *Letter* that he would not have attacked Pope, 'but that I am really driven to it (as the Puff in the Playbills says) *At the Desire of several Persons of Quality*'. However, Cibber's parenthesis recognises that this is simply a stock phrase.

title: right of possession.

to overturn one Empire: Troy.

to raise another: Rome.

Goddess-born: The divine mothers of Achilles and Aeneas were respectively Thetis and Venus.

never a hero even on the stage: Cibber specialised in comic parts, notably fops. For the sexual and cultural politics of his playing the fop on and off the stage, see Straub 1992: 47–68.

in the empire of Dulness, and Atchiever of a work that neither old Omar, Attila, nor John of Leiden could entirely compass.'

To all this we have, as we conceive, a sufficient answer from the Roman historian, *Fabrum esse suae quemque fortunae: Every man is the* Smith *of his own fortune.* The politic Florentine Nicholas Machiavel goeth still farther, and affirms that a man needs but to *believe himself a Hero* to be one of the best. 'Let him (saith he) but fancy himself capable of the highest things, and he will of course be able to atchieve them.' Laying this down as a principle, it will certainly and incontestably follow, that, if ever Hero *was* such a character, OURS *is:* For if ever man *thought* himself such, OURS *doth.* Hear how he constantly paragons himself, at one time to ALEXANDER the Great and CHARLES the XII. of SWEDEN, for the excess and delicacy of his Ambition[o]; to HENRY the IV. of FRANCE, for honest Policy[p]; to the first BRUTUS, for love of Liberty[q]; and to Sir ROBERT WALPOLE, for good Government while in power[r]: At another time, to the godlike SOCRATES, for his diversions and

[o] Life, p. 149. [p] P. 424. [q] P. 366. [r] P. 457.

neither old Omar, Attila, nor John of Leiden: Three examples of threats to established order. Omar b. al-Khattab (sixth–seventh century), second Caliph of Sunnite orthodox Islam, attacked the Persian and Byzantine Empires. Attila (fifth century), king of the Huns, invaded Italy but stopped short of capturing Rome. John of Leiden (*d.* 1536) was declared king of the rebel Anabaptist city of Munster before the regime was crushed by force. Unlike these, Cibber is to succeed 'entirely' in wiping out civilisation.

the Roman historian: The quotation is from the early Roman poet Appius, quoted in *Ad Caesarem Senem De Re Publica Oratio*, which is written as if by the historian Sallust (Gaius Sallustius Crispus, 86–35 BC). The attribution was generally accepted in the eighteenth century, but the work is now thought to be a rhetorical exercise of later date (Rolfe 1920: *Ad Caesarem ... Oratio*, I).

Nicholas Machiavel: Niccolò Machiavelli (1469–1527), Italian political writer, often seen in England as an unprincipled advocate of cruelty and duplicity. The quotation seems to be a loose paraphrase from the closing exhortation of *Il Principe* ('The Prince', Ch. 26).

paragons: parallels, compares.

ALEXANDER the Great and CHARLES the XII. of SWEDEN: Cibber compared his joy on hearing the first prediction of his success as an actor with the feelings of Alexander (fourth century BC) and Charles XII on first commanding their armies.

HENRY the IV. of FRANCE: Cibber admits supporting entertainments of which he did not approve artistically as necessary crowd-pullers, and compares this denial of conscience to the pragmatism of Henry IV (1553–1610), who, though brought up a Protestant, abjured his faith in order to gain the throne. 'Honest Policy' therefore has the ironic sense of 'honourable deceit'.

the first BRUTUS: Lucius Junius Brutus, credited with the expulsion of the corrupt King Tarquin from Rome in 509 BC.

Sir ROBERT WALPOLE: Cibber consoled himself when factions formed against his theatrical management by reasoning that even good Ministers have to cope with opposition. The reader is reminded that Cibber regards Walpole as an example of 'Good Government'.

SOCRATES: Cibber, noting that even the philosopher Socrates (469–399 BC) enjoyed playing with his children, had asked, 'am I oblig'd to be as eminent ... before I am as frolicksome?'

amusements[s]; to HORACE, MONTAIGNE, and Sir WILLIAM TEMPLE, for an elegant Vanity that makes them for ever read and admired[t]; to TWO Lord CHANCELLORS, for Law, from whom, when confederate against him at the bar, he carried away the prize of Eloquence[v]; and, to say all in a word, to the right reverend the Lord BISHOP of LONDON himself, in the art of writing *pastoral letters*[w].

Nor did his *Actions* fall short of the sublimity of his Conceptions. In his early youth he *met the Revolution* at Nottingham[x] face to face, at a time when his betters contented themselves with *following* her. But he shone in Courts as well as Camps: He was *called up* when *the nation fell in labour* of this *Revolution*[y]*:* and was a gossip at her christening, with the Bishop and the ladies[z].

As to his *Birth*, it is true he pretendeth no relation either to Heathen God or Goddess; but, what is as good, he was descended from a *Maker* of both[a]. And that he did not pass himself on the world for a Hero, as well by birth as education, was his own fault: For, his lineage he bringeth into his life as an Anecdote, and is sensible he had it in his power *to be thought no body's son at all*[b]*:* And what is that but coming into the world a Hero.

There is in truth another objection of greater weight, namely, 'That this Hero still existeth, and hath not yet finished his earthly course. For if Solon said well,

[s] P. 18. [t] P. 425. [v] P. 436, 437. [w] P. 52. [x] P. 47. [y] P. 57. [z] P. 58, 59.
[a] A Statuary. [b] Life, p. 6.

HORACE, MONTAIGNE, and Sir WILLIAM TEMPLE: Cibber defends his vanity by pointing to the pleasure readers take in the urbane discussions of self provided by the Roman poet Horace and the essayists Michel Eyquem de Montaigne (1533–92) and Sir William Temple.

TWO Lord CHANCELLORS: Cibber recounts a Chancery suit in which he spoke successfully against Steele, who had two future Lord Chancellors on his side.

the Lord BISHOP of LONDON: Cibber reflected that if he had gone to university as his father had planned, he might have written 'Sermons, and Pastoral Letters' (the latter implying that he would have become a bishop) instead of poems and plays.

met the Revolution *at Nottingham:* A sneer at a turn of phrase taken to imply a more direct involvement in the Glorious Revolution of 1688 than that of more eminent supporters who were content to speak of 'following' the cause.

***when* the nation fell in labour:** Aristarchus insinuates that Cibber combines high pretension with vulgar expression by following through his obstetric metaphor (which actually appears on p. 51): he is made a godparent ('gossip') at the 'christening' of the infant Revolution, as if on a level with the distinguished persons at the centre of events ('the Bishop' was William III's chaplain Gilbert Burnet, later Bishop of Salisbury; 'the ladies' were the future Queen Anne and her attendant Lady Sarah Churchill, later Duchess of Marlborough).

a* Maker *of both: Cibber's father Caius Gabriel Cibber (1630–1700) was a sculptor whose commissions included mythological figures.

no body's son at all: Aristarchus twists Cibber's words to suggest that he may have been illegitimate – like so many of the mythical heroes fathered on mortals by gods. Cibber jested that he named his parents merely 'for fear I should be thought to be no body's Son at all'.

Solon: Sentiment attributed to Solon, Greek poet and statesman (*c.*640–after 561 BC), in the *Histories* of Herodotus (*c.*490–*c.*425 BC) (I.i.32).

that no man could be called happy till his death, surely much less can any one, till then, be pronounced a Hero: this species of men being far more subject than others to the caprices of Fortune and Humour.' But to this also we have an answer, that will be deemed (we hope) decisive. It cometh from *himself*, who, to cut this dispute short, hath solemnly protested that *he will never change or amend*.

With regard to his *Vanity*, he declareth that nothing shall ever part them. 'Nature (saith he) hath amply supplied me in Vanity; a pleasure which neither the pertness of Wit, nor the gravity of Wisdom, will ever persuade me to part with[c].' Our poet had charitably endeavoured to administer a cure to it: But he telleth us plainly, 'My superiors perhaps may be mended by him; but for my part I own myself incorrigible. I look upon my Follies as the best part of my Fortune[d].' And with good reason: We see to what they have brought him!

Secondly, as to *Buffoonry*, 'Is it (saith he) a time of day for me to leave off these fooleries, and set up a new character? I can no more put off my Follies than my Skin; I have often tried, but they stick too close to me; nor am I sure my friends are displeased with them, for in this light I afford them frequent matter of mirth, *etc. etc.*[e].' Having then so publickly declared himself *incorrigible*, he is become *dead in law*, (I mean the *law Epopoeian*) and descendeth to the Poet as his property: who may take him, and deal with him, as if he had been dead as long as an old Egyptian hero; that is to say, *embowel* and *embalm him for posterity*.

Nothing therefore (we conceive) remains to hinder his own Prophecy of himself from taking immediate effect. A rare felicity! and what few prophets have had the satisfaction to see, alive! Nor can we conclude better than with that extraordinary one of his, which is conceived in these Oraculous words, MY DULNESS WILL FIND SOMEBODY TO DO IT RIGHT[f].

[c] P. 424. [d] P. 19. [e] P. 17. [f] Ibid. p. 243. octavo edit.

---

dead in law: Aristarchus argues that unlike the dead, the living can change, so that a portrait made during the subject's lifetime may, with hindsight, be unfair. In Cibber's case, however, he might as well be dead, since he declares that he will never reform.

Epopoeian: epic.

an old Egyptian hero: Egyptian mummies were much sought-after curiosities (see also IV.371–2).

his own Prophecy of himself: Cibber's prophecy, quoted at the end of the paragraph, that he would find a commentator to do justice to his career, is taken to be fulfilled by *The Dunciad*.

Oraculous: prophetic.

BOOK ONE

HEADNOTE. Book I sets the pattern of a prefatory 'Argument' to each book of verse, reminiscent of those provided by Milton for *Paradise Lost*, while Scriblerus and the parodic 'Bentley' are given a weighty presence in the commentary, encumbering with their pedantry the already long-deferred beginning of the poem proper.

Book I is set on a Lord Mayor's Day, when the new mayor processes through the City of London amid festivities which epitomise its mercantile culture (as opposed, implicitly, to that of polite society). For the modelling of earlier versions of the dunces' progress on the mayoral route, see Williams 1955: 29–41; for the suggestion that the traditional route and ceremonies of a coronation were also parodied, see Rogers 1985: 120–50; Brooks-Davies 1985: 108–11; for views of London in Pope's work, see Byrd 1978: 44–79. *The Dunciad in Four Books* was published on 29 October 1743, which was both Lord Mayor's Day and the eve of George II's sixtieth birthday, a juxtaposition arguably contrived to stress the connection (Vander Meulen 1989: 300, 304). Rogers points out that the coronation of George II in 1727 had been celebrated by 'a Lord Mayor's show of unparalleled splendour', at which the royal family was entertained to a dinner at the Guildhall costing £5000, a demonstration that 'the loyal and trusty Hanoverian corporation would ensure that the City of London allied itself in the most open way with the new regime' (Rogers 1985: 131–3, 143).

The principal action of Book I is the adoption by Dulness of her son Bays, the caricature of Cibber who becomes the new hero in 1743. Dulness is called 'Mighty Mother', translating the Latin 'magna mater', and alerting readers to a sinister parody of goddesses associated with (in various combinations) fertility, mysterious rites, night and the moon or stars. These include Aeneas's mother Venus; the Great Mother Cybele; the Egyptian Isis; Ceres/Demeter, patroness of corn and mother of Persephone/Proserpina, abducted from her to become queen of the underworld; Hecate, associated with night, the underworld and the howling of dogs; and Astraea, the constellation Virgo and personification of justice, whose return to earth was to herald the return of the Golden Age (Williams 1955: 26–9; and for detailed claims of mythological influence, see Faulkner & Blair 1980; Brooks-Davies 1985). Allegorised perversities imaged as divinities surrounded by human devotees were an established satirical convention: Dulness figures briefly in Swift's *Battle of the Books* (1704), and as a god of blockheads associated with the owl and the ass in Blackmore's *The Kit-Cats* (1708; see Hodges 1936); and a goddess Oblivion who loves bad books and induces sleep had visited a modern library in the anonymously published *Bibliotheca* (1712) by the Whig poet and denigrator of Pope Thomas Newcomb (Lund 1991: 173–81; for other examples, see e.g. Garth 1699; *Faction Display'd* and *Moderation Displayed* 1704; *The Battle of the Poets* 1725). For the relation between the tableaux in which Pope depicts Dulness and her disciples and Renaissance painting, see Gneiting 1975. Aspects of Dulness are reminiscent of Caroline, George II's queen, notably her tendency to appear more dynamic than her male associate (see Mack 1969: 129; Rogers 1985: 120–50).

Bays's role as child of a divine parent recalls Virgil's Aeneas, son of Venus, and the Christian doctrine of Jesus Christ as Son and creative Word of God, especially as presented in Milton's *Paradise Lost* (for theological implications, see Williams 1955: 144–5; Battestin 1974: 102–18;

for the ominous lack of differentiation between parent and child, see Bogel 1982: 850; for the *Dunciads*' increasing emphasis over time on the dangers posed by apparently weak and muddled entities, see Todd 1982). Constant allusion to the epic myths of Virgil and Milton both adds to the surreal imaginative pleasure of the representation and emphasises Pope's allegations of cultural and spiritual decline.

ARGUMENT
TO
BOOK the FIRST.

THE Proposition, the Invocation, and the Inscription. Then the Original of the great Empire of Dulness, *and cause of the continuance thereof. The College of the* Goddess *in the City, with her private Academy for Poets in particular; the Governors of it, and the four Cardinal Virtues. Then the Poem* hastes into the midst of things, *presenting her, on the evening of a Lord Mayor's day, revolving the long succession of her Sons, and the glories past and to come. She fixes her eye on* Bays *to be the Instrument of that great Event which is the Subject of the Poem. He is described pensive among his Books, giving up the Cause, and apprehending the Period of her Empire: After debating whether to betake himself to the Church, or to Gaming, or to Party-writing, he raises an Altar of proper books, and (making first his solemn prayer and declaration) purposes thereon to sacrifice all his unsuccessful writings. As the pile is kindled, the Goddess beholding the flame from her seat, flies and puts it out by casting upon it the poem of* Thulé. *She forthwith reveals herself to him, transports him to her Temple, unfolds her Arts, and initiates*

THE Proposition, the Invocation, and the Inscription: The declaration of the subject, invocation of presiding powers (usually the muse, but here 'the Great': see I.3), and dedication.

the Poem *hastes into the midst of things:* Echoing Milton's Argument to the first book of *Paradise Lost,* which in turn echoes Horace's perception that Homer 'always goes straight to the action, and hurries the hearer into the middle of things' (Fowler 1998; *De arte poetica,* lines 148–9).

revolving: meditating on.

Bays: Cibber is doubly entitled to the name: before he became Poet Laureate he was already noted for his role as Bays (the Laureate) in a revival in 1717 of the satirical *The Rehearsal,* by George Villiers (1628–87), second Duke of Buckingham, and others (Stone 1969: 39–67; Koon 1986: 85–6). Cibber claimed that an ad lib which he made in this role, alluding to the failure of *Three Hours after Marriage,* was the origin of Pope's quarrel with him (Cibber 1742: 18–19; Ault 1949: 298–301).

Period: end.

Party-writing: writing political propaganda.

proper: suitable.

Thulé: See note on I.258.

him into her Mysteries; then announcing the death of Eusden *the Poet Laureate, anoints him, carries him to Court, and proclaims him Successor.*

---

her Mysteries: In the sense of religious truths beyond the reach of human reason. In the ancient world, initiation into the mysteries of Eleusis, associated with the myth of the abduction of Persephone to the underworld and her return to her mother, the fertility goddess Ceres (to whom Dulness can be read as alluding), was routinely sought by holders of high office (Brooks-Davies 1985: 122–7; and see headnote).

Eusden: Laurence Eusden (1688–1730), the Laureate preceding Cibber. In *Peri Bathous* he seems to be characterised both as one of the '*Ostridges*' (too heavy to fly properly but a fast runner) and as one of the 'slow and chill' tortoises; and he is proposed as 'poetical son' of Blackmore (*PW*: II, 197, 203, 219).

THE

DUNCIAD:

TO

Dr. JONATHAN SWIFT.

Book the First.

The Dunciad, *sic MS.* It may well be disputed whether this be a right reading: Ought it not rather to be spelled *Dunceiad*, as the Etymology evidently demands? *Dunce* with an *e*, therefore *Dunceiad* with an *e*. That accurate and punctual Man of Letters, the Restorer of *Shakespeare*, constantly observes the preservation of this very Letter *e*, in spelling the Name of his beloved Author, and not like his common careless Editors, with the omission of one, nay sometimes of two *ee's*, [as *Shakspear*] which is utterly unpardonable. 'Nor is the neglect of a *Single Letter* so trivial as to some it may appear; the alteration whereof in a learned language is an Atchievement that brings honour to the Critic who advances it; and Dr. Bentley will be remembered to posterity for his performances of this sort, as long as the world shall have any esteem for the remains of Menander and Philemon.' Theobald.

This is surely a slip in the learned author of the foregoing note; there having been since produced by an accurate Antiquary, an *Autograph* of *Shakspeare* himself, whereby it appears

---

THE DUNCIAD: TO Dr. JONATHAN SWIFT.: The dedication is taken up at lines 19–28.

NOTE ON TITLE. ***The Dunciad, sic MS.:*** 'Thus reads the manuscript' (Latin), used to mark scribal errors when transcribing manuscripts. Scriblerus, like the antiquarian Thomas Hearne (1678–1735) whose use of this convention is satirised later in the note, prefers to draw attention to apparent errors in the texts he edits rather than silently correcting them. While this is mere pedantry to Pope, the practice is invaluable to textual scholars.

accurate and punctual: Lewis Theobald (slighted by Pope as 'Tibbald', under which name he had been the 'hero' of previous versions of the *Dunciad*), author of *Shakespeare Restored*, is presented as a pedantic quibbler: 'punctual' belittles his interest in punctuation. His spelling of 'Shakespeare', now standard, seemed to Pope a pedantic deviation from the usual contemporary spelling, 'Shakespear'.

***a* Single Letter:** Theobald cites Bentley's discovery that in reading Greek verse allowance should sometimes be made for a letter (the digamma or vau) which had vanished by the time manuscripts were written, but which would make metrical sense of many lines previously thought defective (Brink 1986: 76).

Menander and Philemon: Greek comic poets (respectively 342–*c*.292 BC and *c*.361–263 BC) whose fragmentary texts were emended by Bentley (*Emendationes in Menandri et Philemonis reliquias . . . auctore Phileleuthero Lipsiensi* 1710).

an accurate Antiquary: It is not clear to whom Pope could be referring as early as 1743 (for dating of the rediscovery of the original and a copy of Shakespeare's will, which is presumably the document in question, see Schoenbaum 1975: 242–5).

that he spelled his own name without the first *e*. And upon this authority it was, that those most Critical Curators of his Monument in Westminster Abby erased the former wrong reading, and restored the true spelling on a new piece of old Aegyptian Granite. Nor for this only do they deserve our thanks, but for exhibiting on the same Monument the first Specimen of an *Edition* of an author in *Marble*; where (as may be seen on comparing the Tomb with the Book) in the space of five lines, two Words and a whole Verse are changed, and it is to be hoped will there stand, and outlast whatever hath been hitherto done in Paper; as for the future, our Learned Sister University (the other Eye of England) is taking care to perpetuate a *Total new Shakespear*, at the Clarendon press. BENTL.

It is to be noted, that this great Critic also has omitted one circumstance; which is, that the Inscription with the Name of Shakspeare was intended to be placed on the Marble Scroll to which he points with his hand; instead of which it is now placed behind his back, and that Specimen of an Edition is put on the Scroll, which indeed Shakspeare hath great reason to point at. ANON.

And upon this authority: The monument to Shakespeare in Westminster Abbey, erected in 1741, was financed by a subscription organised by Pope and other friends committed to the view that the regime of George II and Sir Robert Walpole shamed the nation by failing to honour and reward writers; and the note records how its execution fell short of Pope's intentions (Dobson 1992: 135–9). The Latin inscription, attributed to Pope, incorporates the spelling 'Shakspeare', whereas the then usual spelling, favoured by Pope, was 'Shakespear' (Mack 1985: Plate 86; for the political implications of the inscription, see editor's note on IV.131–2). Theobald insisted on both of the disputed 'e's ('Shakespeare').

***an* Edition *of an author in* Marble:** The next paragraph of the note claims that the Latin inscription placed behind the statue was supposed to have been inscribed on the marble scroll to which Shakespeare points: the scroll was in fact left blank when the monument was first unveiled, which gave anti-Walpole commentators further material for satire (Dobson 1992: 143–6). Within a few months the Dean of Westminster had the blank filled with lines from *The Tempest*: 'Bentley', caricatured as a lover of textual innovation for its own sake, is made to enthuse over its variations from the accepted text (*TE*: VI, 396; Brownell 1978: 354–6, Plate 86).

our Learned Sister University: Oxford ('Bentley' is a Cambridge man). He conceives the two universities as the eyes of England.

***a* Total new Shakespear:** Sir Thomas Hanmer (1677–1746), a Tory supporter of the Hanoverian succession and formerly Speaker of the House of Commons, had apparently been on good terms with Pope when Gay (to whom he was distantly related) listed him as among those congratulating Pope on the completion of his *Iliad* translation (Dearing 1974: 'Mr Pope's Welcome', line 14). Since the disappointment of Tory hopes for a return to royal favour on the accession of George II in 1727, he had devoted himself to literary retirement; and his interest in Shakespeare, originally a topic of friendly discussion with Warburton, had led to a quarrel when it emerged that Hanmer was planning to publish an edition, which Warburton, also planning an edition, feared would make unacknowledged use of his own emendations (Evans 1932: 147–55; *Corr.*: IV, 438–9, 475; Nichol 1992: 140–45; and see Book IV.105–8 and 113–18 and editor's notes). For the deployment of Hanmer in *The Dunciad in Four Books*, see Jarvis 1995: 83–7, 107–28. By calling Hanmer's edition, which was to appear anonymously in 1743 and 1744, 'a *Total new Shakespear*', the note insinuates that contrary to the established expectation that each edition should vary as little as possible from the previous text, Hanmer would indulge in wholesale emendation.

indeed Shakspeare hath great reason: Suggesting that Shakespeare is pointing in indignation at the garbled quotation.

Though I have as just a value for the letter *E*, as any Grammarian living, and the same affection for the Name of this Poem as any Critic for that of his Author; yet cannot it induce me to agree with those who would add yet another *e* to it, and call it the *Dunceiade*; which being a French and foreign termination, is no way proper to a word entirely English, and vernacular. One *e* therefore in this case is right, and two *e's* wrong. Yet upon the whole I shall follow the Manuscript, and print it without any *e* at all; moved thereto by Authority (at all times, with Critics, equal, if not superior to Reason.) In which method of proceeding, I can never enough praise my good friend, the exact Mr. Tho. Hearne; who if any word occur, which to him and all mankind is evidently wrong, yet keeps he it in the Text with due reverence, and only remarks in the Margin *sic MS*. In like manner we shall not amend this error in the Title itself, but only note it *obiter*, to evince to the learned that it was not our fault, nor any effect of our ignorance or inattention. SCRIBLERUS.

This Poem was written in the year 1726. In the next year an imperfect Edition was published at Dublin, and reprinted at London in twelves; another at Dublin, and another at London in octavo; and three others in twelves the same year. But there was no perfect Edition before that of London in quarto; which was attended with Notes. SCHOL. VET.

It was expressly confessed in the Preface to the first edition, that this Poem was not published by the Author himself. It was printed originally in a foreign Country. And what foreign Country? Why, one notorious for blunders; where finding blanks only instead of proper names, these blunderers filled them up at their pleasure.

The very *Hero* of the Poem hath been mistaken to this hour; so that we are obliged to open our Notes with a discovery who he really was. We learn from the former Editor, that this

---

moved thereto by Authority: Scriblerus is represented as too slavishly devoted to 'Authority' to *correct* textual errors – but so anxious that 'the learned' should not blame his 'ignorance or inattention' for the mistakes that he has to mark every one '*obiter*' (Latin, 'in passing').

In the next year: First publication was actually in 1728, not 1727 (compare heading to Appendix I).

in twelves: in duodecimo format.

SCHOL. VET.: 'Scholia vetera' (Latin, 'old marginalia'). A version of this publishing history, probably drafted by Pope's friend Jonathan Richardson the younger (1694–1771), was first included in 1735 (Griffith 1922–7: II, 283).

not published by the Author: Just as the real Bentley had in his edition of Milton blamed the blind poet's assistants for the alleged corruption of *Paradise Lost* (Bentley 1732), his fictitious double claims that Theobald never *was* the hero of the poem: this was only a blunder by the Irish printers of the Dublin edition of 1728.

***The very* Hero:** See the reference to *Sawney* in the note on line 1.

discovery: revelation.

We learn from the former Editor: George II had apparently expressed interest in the *Dunciad* when it first appeared in 1728 (*Corr.*: II, 502). On 12 March 1729 he received from Pope via Walpole a copy of the new *Dunciad Variorum* (*TE*: V, 60). Arbuthnot told Swift, in a jocular account of recent Scriblerian triumphs, that the King had declared the author 'a very honest man'; in 1732 Savage mentioned the presentation in *A Collection of Pieces*; and in 1735 it was incorporated in a note on line 1 below, here attributed to 'the former editor' (Williams 1965: III, 236; Savage 1732: vi). Keener argues from the epic theory of Le Bossu, as embraced by Pope, that the current ruler must inevitably be the addressee of any epic conceived according to his rules: if this were applied also to mock-epic, the hero, whether Tibbald or Bays, would necessarily represent that ruler (Keener 1991: 52–5).

Piece was presented by the Hands of Sir Robert Walpole to King George II. Now the author directly tells us, his Hero is the Man 'who brings / The Smithfield Muses to the ear of Kings.' And it is notorious who was the person on whom this Prince conferred the honour of the *Laurel*.

It appears as plainly from the *Apostrophe* to the *Great* in the third verse, that Tibbald could not be the person, who was never an Author in fashion, or caressed by the Great; whereas this single characteristic is sufficient to point out the true Hero; who, above all other Poets of his time, was the *Peculiar Delight* and *Chosen Companion* of the Nobility of England; and wrote, as he himself tells us, certain of his Works at the *earnest Desire* of *Persons of Quality*.

Lastly, The sixth verse affords full proof; this Poet being the only one who was universally known to have had a *Son* so exactly like him, in his poetical, theatrical, political, and moral Capacities, that it could justly be said of him 'Still Dunce the second reign'd like Dunce the first.' BENTL.

Sir Robert Walpole: Chief Minister of George I and George II and key figure in opposition claims of government corruption, Walpole had resigned in 1742 but remains both metonymically and metaphorically associated with Cibber in *The Dunciad in Four Books*, and is inseparable from Pope's vision of what the nation has become under his government (for satirical parallels between the two men's talents as actor/gambler/stage-manager, see Mack 1969: 158–62). Mack relates the 'unparalleled specificity and boldness' of the political satire of *The New Dunciad* (published 1742, shortly after Walpole's resignation) and of *The Dunciad in Four Books* (published 1743, adapting *The New Dunciad* as Book IV) to the fact that Walpole was no longer a power to be feared (Mack 1969: 150–62).

it is notorious who: Cibber received the Laureateship ('the honour of the *Laurel*') from George II in 1730. Rogers argues that Cibber's prime qualification to replace Theobald as butt of the *Dunciad* lies in his commissioning by the current monarch (Rogers 1985: 125).

***the* Apostrophe *to the* Great:** The address to the nobility in line 3. Cibber had boasted of his titled friends in his *Apology*, and had alluded playfully to the language of theatrical advertising in describing himself as 'driven' to write his *Letter to Mr. Pope* '(as the Puff in the Play-Bills says) *At the Desire of several Persons of Quality*' (Cibber 1742: 5).

a* Son *so exactly like him: A transparent misreading of line 6 (see note below) which evades its subversive force by applying it to Cibber's disreputable son, the actor and writer Theophilus Cibber (1703–58) (see editor's note on III.139).

THE Mighty Mother, and her Son who brings
The Smithfield Muses to the ear of Kings,

1.] The Reader ought here to be cautioned, that the *Mother*, and not the *Son*, is the principal Agent of this Poem: The latter of them is only chosen as her Collegue (as was anciently the custom in Rome before some great Expedition) the main action of the Poem being by no means the Coronation of the Laureate, which is performed in the very first book, but the Restoration of the Empire of Dulness in Britain, which is not accomplished 'till the last.

Ibid.] Wonderful is the stupidity of all the former Critics and Commentators on this work! It breaks forth at the very first line. The author of the Critique prefixed to *Sawney*, a Poem, p. 5. hath been so dull as to explain *the Man who brings, etc.* not of the Hero of the piece, but of our Poet himself, as if he vaunted that *Kings* were to be his readers; an honour which though this Poem hath had, yet knoweth he how to receive it with more modesty.

We remit this Ignorant to the first lines of the *Aeneid*, assuring him that *Virgil* there speaketh not of himself, but of *Aeneas:* 'Arma virumque cano, Trojae qui primus ab oris / Italiam, fato profugus, Lavinaque venit / Littora: multum ille et terris jactatus et alto', *etc.* I cite the whole three verses, that I may by the way offer a *Conjectural Emendation*, purely my own, upon each: First, *oris* should be read *aris*, it being, as we see *Aen.* ii. 513. from the *altar* of *Jupiter Hercaeus* that *Aeneas* fled as soon as he saw *Priam* slain. In the second line I would read *flatu* for *fato*, since it is most clear it was by *Winds* that he arrived at the *shore* of Italy. *Jactatus*, in the third, is surely as improperly applied to *terris*, as proper to *alto*; to say a man *is tost on land*, is much at one with saying *he walks at sea: Risum teneatis, amici?* Correct it, as I doubt not it ought to be, *vexatus*. SCRIBLERUS.

2.] *Smithfield* is the place where Bartholomew Fair was kept, whose shews, machines, and dramatical entertainments, formerly agreeable only to the taste of the Rabble, were, by the

---

1 and n. The Mighty Mother, and her Son: See headnote, and for contextualisation in terms of female fertility/monstrosity, animus against women writers and fear of the feminisation of culture, see Gubar 1977; Ingrassia 1991; Francus 1994. The note, the first paragraph of which was initialled in 1751 as by Warburton, deflects possible objections to the inactivity of the hero and at the same time argues for the formal necessity of the newly added Book IV (see also Keener 1991: 45). **Sawney:** *Sawney: An Heroic Poem* (1728), by James Ralph. Scriblerus's 'corrections', which had also appeared at this point in 1729, derive from 'Virgilius Restauratus', a parody of Bentley's methods of textual emendation, probably by Arbuthnot (Kerby-Miller 1950: 55). Instead of printing it as a separate appendix, as in 1729, *The Dunciad in Four Books* works further elements into the commentary. To correct any suspicion that Pope himself is the hero res-ponsible for bringing vulgarity to court, Scriblerus cites his source, the opening of Virgil's *Aeneid*: everyone knows that 'virum' ('the man'/'hero') is Aeneas, not Virgil (*Aeneid* I). Having quoted the lines ('Arms and the man I sing, who, driven by *fate*, first from the *shore* of Troy reached Italy and the Lavinian strand: he was much *tossed about* by land and by sea'), Scriblerus makes the ingenious but prosaic suggestion that the italicised words should read instead 'wind', 'altar' and 'annoyed'. So sure is he that the accepted version is nonsense that he smugly quotes Horace's enquiry as to how his friend would react to a picture of a monster whose parts were all taken from different animals (*Risum teneatis, amici?*: 'Could you contain your laughter, my friend?' (*De arte poetica*, line 5)). ***an honour which though this Poem hath had:*** For the presentation to George II, see notes on the title.

2. Implying that the 'low' amusements of Smithfield (site of Bartholomew Fair and centre of the London meat trade) have been transplanted to the court and polite society (see

I sing. Say you, her instruments the Great!
Call'd to this work by Dulness, Jove, and Fate;
You by whose care, in vain decry'd and curst,
Still Dunce the second reigns like Dunce the first;
Say how the Goddess bade Britannia sleep,
And pour'd her Spirit o'er the land and deep.
  In eldest time, e'er mortals writ or read,
E'er Pallas issu'd from the Thund'rer's head,

Hero of this poem and others of equal genius, brought to the Theatres of Covent-garden, Lincolns-inn-fields, and the Hay-market, to be the reigning pleasures of the Court and Town. This happened in the Reigns of King George I, and II. See Book 3.

4.] i.e. By their *Judgments*, their *Interests*, and their *Inclinations*.

---

particularly III.231–316.) Elkanah Settle (1648–1724), whose 1702 poem welcoming the Hanoverian succession had prompted Pope's youthful satire 'To the Author of a Poem call'd *Successio*', and who functions in the *Dunciads* as Bays's poetic 'father', was the last of the official City Poets whose task was to provide and commemorate pageants for City occasions: he devised some of the most popular fairground shows, especially one on the fall of Troy (Rogers 1985: 30, 88–91). His election as City Poet in 1691 has been suggested as possible origin of the satiric project which later became the *Dunciad* (*TE*: V, xiv; Mack 1984: 98). Although Cibber himself operated only in leading theatres, his work was performed at Bartholomew Fair, and two of his children acted there.

3. Say you: Calling upon the aristocracy, whom Pope implicitly blames for conniving at corruption under Walpole and the Hanoverians, to fulfil the role usually taken by the muse in recalling the story of the epic poem (compare IV.619–20). A note to an early manuscript draft cites Virgil's address to the muse at the beginning of the *Aeneid* (Mack 1984: 129). Since 'the Great' are responsible for Dulness's advance, they can best tell how it came about. For the refocusing of satire away from authors and onto the aristocracy in 1743, see Keener 1991: 51–2.

4n. Initialled in 1751 as by Warburton.

6. Dunce the second: Alluding to Dryden, 'For *Tom* the Second reigns like *Tom* the first', a reference to the succession of one undistinguished Poet Laureate to another (Kinsley 1958: 'To My Dear Friend Mr Congreve', line 48; Erskine-Hill 1983: 243; Erskine-Hill 1996: 101; Bogel 1982: 850; and for succession as satirical motif, see Seidel 1979: 232–49). Dryden was replaced as Laureate at the Revolution of 1688 on account of his Catholicism, putting him into a situation analogous to Pope's own. Thus Pope's allusion mocks Cibber as no better than his predecessor Eusden, but also suggests the injustice of the religious test by which Pope is excluded from the office of Laureate. The word 'reigns', taken in conjunction with the ordinal numbers, also constitutes an obvious reference to George II, who had succeeded George I in 1727, and had disappointed opposition hopes that he would displace Walpole and set up a less exclusively Whig administration (Rogers 1985: 126).

7–8. For biblical references to the pouring out of God's spirit see Sherbo 1970: 504. A version of lines 7–8 had in 1742 concluded the *New Dunciad*.

9–10. Compare the opening of Dryden's *Absolom and Achitophel*: 'In pious times, e'r Priest-craft did begin / Before *Polygamy* was made a sin' (Sherbo 1988: 223).

10. Pallas Athene (identified by the Romans with Minerva), Greek goddess of arts, crafts and wisdom, sprang full-grown from the head of the thunder-god Zeus (Jupiter/Jove to the Romans).

Dulness o'er all possess'd her ancient right,
Daughter of Chaos and eternal Night:
Fate in their dotage this fair Ideot gave,
Gross as her sire, and as her mother grave,
Laborious, heavy, busy, bold, and blind,
She rul'd, in native Anarchy, the mind.

12.] The beauty of this whole Allegory being purely of the poetical kind, we think it not our proper business, as a Scholiast, to meddle with it: But leave it (as we shall in general all such) to the reader; remarking only, that *Chaos* (according to *Hesiod's* Θεογονία) was the Progenitor of all the Gods. SCRIBLERUS.

15.] I wonder the learned Scriblerus has omitted to advertise the Reader, at the opening of this Poem, that Dulness here is not to be taken contractedly for mere Stupidity, but in the enlarged sense of the word, for all Slowness of Apprehension, Shortness of Sight, or imperfect Sense of things. It includes (as we see by the Poet's own words) Labour, Industry, and some degree of Activity and Boldness: a ruling principle not inert, but turning topsy-turvy the Understanding, and inducing an Anarchy or confused State of Mind. This remark ought to be carried along with the reader throughout the work; and without this caution he will be apt to mistake the Importance of many of the Characters, as well as of the Design of the Poet. Hence it is that some have complained he chuses too mean a subject, and imagined he employs himself, like Domitian, in killing flies; whereas those who have the true key will find he sports with nobler quarry, and embraces a larger compass; or (as one saith, on a like occasion) 'Will see his Work, like Jacob's ladder, rise, / Its foot in dirt, its head amid the skies.' BENTL.

16.] *The native Anarchy of the mind* is that state which precedes the time of Reason's assuming the rule of the Passions. But in that state, the uncontrolled violence of the Passions would

---

12 and n. Dulness has Chaos for father and Night for mother (see line 14), a Miltonic genealogy already suggested at the opening of 'Martinus Scriblerus of the Poem'. As an annotator ('Scholiast') Scriblerus is complacently indifferent to literary qualities, but quick to note an allusion to the *Theogony* of Hesiod.

13–14. Brower compares the mentally retarded protagonist of Dryden's *Cymon and Iphigenia*: 'Fair, Tall, his Limbs with due Proportion join'd, / But of a heavy, dull, degenerate Mind' (lines 52–3; Brower 1959: 327). ***in their dotage:*** Perhaps hinting that feeblemindedness might be expected of the child of such elderly parents. ***fair ... / Gross:*** Queen Caroline was also blonde and ample of figure (Rogers 1985: 133). For line 14 compare Dryden's *Aeneid*: 'Fam'd as his Sire, and as his Mother fair' (Kinsley 1958: III, *Aeneid* VII.1044).

15 and n. Key statements of the case against Dulness as a principle of *active* wrongheadedness. Rogers discusses the imaginative flexibility of Dulness's movement between abstraction and personification, and shows that contemporary usage of 'dull' and 'dulness' stressed slowness of understanding, concluding that 'Pope's conscious departure from this set of associations, whereby the term retains its sense of languor, yet loses that of inactivity, is easily apparent' (Rogers 1993a: 120–28). ***contractedly:*** in a narrow sense. ***Domitian:*** Roman emperor (AD 51–96), whose rule degenerated into a reign of terror: he was reputed to have enjoyed killing flies with a needle. ***Will see his Work:*** An approximate quotation from Dryden (Kinsley 1958: *The Hind and the Panther*, I.220–21).

16 and n. The note, initialled in 1751 as by Warburton, reflects his tendency to paradox and systematisation. It was axiomatic both in art and in psychology that dynamic elements

Still her old Empire to restore she tries,
For, born a Goddess, Dulness never dies.
O Thou! whatever title please thine ear,
Dean, Drapier, Bickerstaff, or Gulliver!
Whether thou chuse Cervantes' serious air,
Or laugh and shake in Rab'lais' easy chair,
Or praise the Court, or magnify Mankind,
Or thy griev'd Country's copper chains unbind;

soon bring things to confusion, were it not for the intervention of Dulness in this absence of Reason; who, though she cannot regulate them like Reason, yet blunts and deadens their Vigour, and, indeed, produces some of the good effects of it: Hence it is that Dulness has often the appearance of Reason. This is the only good she ever did; and the Poet takes particular care to tell it in the very introduction of his Poem. It is to be observed indeed, that this is spoken of the universal rule of Dulness in ancient days, but we may form an idea of it from her partial Government in later times.

17.] This Restoration makes the Completion of the Poem. *Vide* Book 4.

23.] *Ironicè*, alluding to *Gulliver*'s representations of both. — The next line relates to the papers of the *Drapier* against the currency of *Wood*'s Copper coin in *Ireland*, which, upon the great discontent of the people, his Majesty was graciously pleased to recal.

(passion, wit, invention) must be balanced by restraining factors (reason, judgement, design). 'Partial' may be read as a pun, not simply 'incomplete', but also 'biased', implying a sneer at Walpole's government.

18. Garth makes his Sloth exclaim, 'How impotent a Deity am I! / With Godhead born, but curs'd, that cannot die!' (*The Dispensary* 1699: I.105–6).

19–20. Alluding to Swift's position as Dean of St Patrick's Cathedral, Dublin, and to his various literary masks: he wrote as a draper in *The Drapier's Letters* (1724), opposing the imposition on Ireland of a suspect copper coinage (see the 'copper chains' of line 24); he wrote essays under the name of Isaac Bickerstaff; and he wrote *Gulliver's Travels* (1726) as the memoirs of Lemuel Gulliver (Davis 1939–68: X, II, XI).

21–22. Swift is complimented for combining the abilities of two contrasted masters of comic satire: Cervantes, whose *Don Quixote* (1605–15) parodies the solemnities of chivalric romance and was read by Pope as a political satire (Mack 1982: 400–01; Riley 1992), and Rabelais, a favourite author of Swift's though less appreciated by Pope, whose *Gargantua and Pantagruel* (1532–52) is a robustly uninhibited satiric fantasy (*OAC*: I, 55, 217–18). By addressing Swift in these terms, Pope links his friend with the critical comic spirit of Renaissance humanism: a parallel may be discerned between the shared Scriblerian values underlying the *Dunciad* and the humanist friendship which led Desiderius Erasmus (*c.*1467–1536) to dedicate to Sir Thomas More (*c.*1477–1535) his satire *Encomium Moriae* ('*The Praise of Folly*' (1511)), a work in which the characterisation of Folly may be seen as in some ways anticipating Pope's treatment of Dulness (Erskine-Hill 1962: 753–7; Jones in Mack & Winn 1980: 616–21; Levi 1971: 55–61). Pope's early revisions to a poem by Wycherley on the advantages of Dulness provide a suggestive link (Jack 1942: 125; *Corr.*: I, 31–2).

23–4 and n. Ironicè: ironically. **Gulliver's *representations of both:*** Notably in Book II, Chapter VI of *Gulliver's Travels*, when the King of Brobdingnag responds to Gulliver's attempts to 'praise the Court' and 'magnify Mankind' by concluding that Englishmen must be 'the most

From thy Boeotia tho' her Pow'r retires,
Mourn not, my SWIFT, at ought our Realm acquires,
Here pleas'd behold her mighty wings out-spread
To hatch a new Saturnian age of Lead.
  Close to those walls where Folly holds her throne,
And laughs to think Monroe would take her down,

28.] The ancient Golden Age is by Poets styled *Saturnian*; but in the Chemical language *Saturn* is Lead. She is said here only to be spreading her wings to hatch this age; which is not produced completely till the fourth book.

---

pernicious race of little odious vermin that nature ever suffered to crawl upon the surface of the earth'. Sherbo points out that 'magnify' also has a literal sense here, alluding to Swift's creation of the giant Brobdingnagians (Sherbo 1970: 504). ***the papers of the* Drapier:** Swift's pamphlets, written in the person of a draper, against the project promoted by William Wood (1671–1730), with royal backing, for an Irish coinage widely suspected as substandard: the routinely deferential expression 'his Majesty was graciously pleased' is markedly ironic.

25–6. Pope sees Dulness so powerfully at work in England ('our Realm') that he assumes she must have left her proverbial haunts in Ireland ('Boeotia' was originally a part of Greece proverbial for stupidity). Jokes against alleged Irish idiocy ('Irish bulls') were well established in eighteenth-century England. Swift would usually be indignant at English exploitation of Ireland: this time he is not to 'mourn' at England's appropriation of what the Irish will be better off without.

27–8 and n. Alluding to the Holy Spirit who in *Paradise Lost* 'with mighty wings outspread / Dove-like sat'st brooding on the vast abyss / And mad'st it pregnant' (Fowler 1998: I.20–22). Faulkner and Blair argue also for an allusion to the myth of the cosmic egg as the origin of the universe (Faulkner & Blair 1980: 230). Line 28 alludes to the notion of the return of the idyllic golden age, an aspiration characteristic of Virgil's hopes under Augustus, which Dryden in his translation had gone so far as to add even to the more tentative ending of the *Georgics*, a work which stresses the interdependence of political power and artistic patronage in the well-run state, a major theme of ironic comment in the *Dunciad* (*Eclogues* IV.4–7; *Aeneid* VI.791–4; Brooks-Davies 1985: 17–19). Since *Eclogue* IV identifies the return of Astraea, or justice, as the first sign of the return of the golden age, Pope's allusion suggests that Astraea is among the mythical models to which Dulness is an allusion (for a wider view of *Eclogue* IV and the *Dunciad*, see Lawler in Mack & Winn 1980: 732–40). The note points out the ironies of the Saturnian age hatched by Dulness: originally a Roman agricultural deity, Saturn was said to have reigned in the golden age; but he was later identified with the Greek Chronos, who devoured his own children (the gods of Olympus), and was credited in planetary lore with a gloomy, sinister influence (Chaucer, in Benson 1987: *Knight's Tale*, lines 2443–69), and in 'the Chemical language' (i.e. the language of alchemy) with fostering the formation of lead.

29. Cp. Dryden's *Mac Flecknoe*: 'Close to the Walls which fair *Augusta* bind' (line 64; Sherbo 1988: 223).

29–30. The walls of Bethlehem ('Bedlam') lunatic asylum, where the physician James Monro (1680–1752) attempts to dethrone Folly from her usurped dominion in the minds of his patients. For the magnificent asylum building, in Moorfields, just north-west of the City, see Morris 1984: Plate 8, and for notions of madness in the period in relation to the *Dunciad*, see his pp. 270–95. Visiting Bedlam to view the inmates was a popular amusement.

Where o'er the gates, by his fam'd father's hand
Great Cibber's brazen, brainless brothers stand;
One Cell there is, conceal'd from vulgar eye,
The Cave of Poverty and Poetry.

31.] Mr. Caius-Gabriel Cibber, father of the Poet Laureate. The two Statues of the Lunatics over the gates of Bedlam-hospital were done by him, and (as the son justly says of them) are no ill monuments of his fame as an Artist.

33.] The cell of poor Poetry is here very properly represented as a little *unendowed Hall* in the neighbourhood of the Magnific *College* of Bedlam; and as the surest Seminary to supply those learned walls with Professors. For there cannot be a plainer indication of madness than in mens persisting to starve themselves and offend the public by scribling ('Escape in Monsters, and amaze the town') when they might have benefited themselves and others in profitable and honest employments. The *Qualities* and *Productions* of the students of this private Academy are afterwards described in this first book; as are also their *Actions* throughout the second; by which it appears, how near allied Dulness is to Madness. This naturally prepares us for the subject of the third book, where we find them in union, and acting in conjunction to produce the Catastrophe of the fourth; a mad poetical Sibyl leading our Hero through the Regions of Vision, to animate him in the present undertaking, by a view of the past triumphs of Barbarism over Science.

34.] I cannot here omit a remark that will greatly endear our Author to every one, who shall attentively observe that Humanity and Candor, which every where appears in him towards those unhappy objects of the ridicule of all mankind, the bad Poets. He here imputes all scandalous rhymes, scurrilous weekly papers, base flatteries, wretched elegies, songs, and verses (even from those sung at Court to ballads in the streets) not so much to malice or

---

31–2 and n. Pope cites Cibber's pride in his sculptor father's statues of Melancholy and Raving Madness, which flanked the entrance of Bedlam (Morris 1984: Plate 7). Although Cibber objected that the statues were not 'brazen' but stone (Cibber 1743 and see note on II.3), 'brazen' (as in 'brazen impudence') provided an irresistible link with the opposition characterisation of Walpole and hence with the thematic representation of Cibber (Mack 1969: 156–8). In 1742 Pope's printer had suggested changing the word, but Pope insisted on retaining it (*Corr.*: IV, 426).

33 and n. In earlier versions the 'Cell' had been in Rag Fair, near the Tower of London: the change brings it into the neighbourhood of Grub Street, proverbial haunt of hack writers (Rogers 1972: 18–93). The goddess Oblivion in Thomas Newcomb's anonymously published *Bibliotheca* (1712) had also inhabited a 'Cell' in some ways comparable (Lund 1991: 175). Pope's 'Cell' is characterised in the note, which was initialled in 1751 as by Warburton, as a 'little *unendowed Hall*' which supplies 'the Magnific ("magnificent") *College* of Bedlam': in view of Warburton's antagonism to Methodism, he may want to associate the relocated 'Cell' with the disused foundry in what is now Tabernacle Street, used for Methodist worship from 1739. Sutherland speculates that the note may refer to Sion College (*TE*: V, 272). It seems unlikely that Pope intends his richly phantasmagoric 'Cell' as a simple alias for a single, literally existing institution.

34 and n. Pope glances at Theobald's *The Cave of Poverty* (1714), which includes an appeal to poverty as a stimulus to poetic endeavour. The note characteristically insists on taking Pope's persistent association between bad writing and poverty as an expression of 'Humanity

Keen, hollow winds howl thro' the bleak recess,
Emblem of Music caus'd by Emptiness.
Hence Bards, like Proteus long in vain ty'd down,

servility as to Dulness; and not so much to Dulness as to Necessity. And thus, at the very commencement of his Satyr, makes an apology for all that are to be satyrized.

37.] 'Sunt quibus in plures jus est transire figuras: / Ut tibi, complexi terram maris incola, Proteu; / Nunc *violentus aper*, nunc quem tetigisse timerent, / *Anguis* eras, modo te faciebant *cornua Taurum*, / Saepe *Lapis* poteras.' Ovid. Met. viii. Neither Palaephatus, Phurnutus, nor Heraclides give us any steddy light into the mythology of this mysterious fable. If I be not deceived in a part of learning which has so long exercised my pen, by *Proteus* must certainly be meant a hacknied Town scribler; and by his Transformations, the various disguises such a one assumes, to elude the pursuit of his irreconcilable enemy, the Bailiff. Proteus is represented as one bred of the mud and slime of Aegypt, the original soil of Arts and Letters: And what is a Town-scribler, but a creature made up of the excrements of luxurious Science? By the change then into a *Boar* is meant his character of a *furious and dirty Party-writer*; the *Snake* signifies a *Libeller*; and the *Horns of the Bull*, the *Dilemmas* of a *Polemical Answerer*. These are the three great parts he acts under; and when he has completed his circle, he sinks back again, as the last change into a *Stone* denotes, into his natural state of immoveable Stupidity. If I may expect thanks of the learned world for this discovery, I would by no means deprive that excellent Critic of his share, who discovered before me, that in the character of Proteus was designed *Sophistam, Magum, Politicum, praesertim rebus omnibus sese accommodantem*. Which in English is, *A Political writer, a Libeller, and a Disputer, writing indifferently for or against every party in the State, every sect in Religion, and every character in private life*. See my *Fables of Ovid explained*. Abbe Banier.

---

and Candor'. For the role of caves in Pope's creativity, and links with the grotto in his garden, see Mack 1969: 46–7, 60–61.

35–6. Evoking both the worthless poetry written only to pay for the next meal, and the rumblings of an empty stomach. Virgil's Aeolus kept the winds in a cave which may be recalled here: Juno (Hera), mother of the gods, defied her husband Jupiter (Zeus) by opposing Aeneas's mission of founding Rome, and asked Aeolus for a storm to wreck his fleet (*Aeneid* I.52–80; for an explicit parallel between Dulness and Juno, see line 269 below and notes).

37 and n. Like a hack who conceals his identity from creditors by anonymity and pseudonyms, Proteus, unless physically restrained, foiled pursuers by shape-shifting, as described in the quotation from Ovid, which cites his appearance as a boar, a snake, a horned bull and a stone (*Metamorphoses* VIII.732–5). Pope wrote to Warburton, who initialled the note in 1751, 'I like the Note on Proteus much' (*Corr.*: IV, 426). ***Palaephatus, Phurnutus ... Heraclides:*** Palaephatus and Heraclides Ponticus (both fourth century BC) and Phurnutus (alias 'Cornutus', first century AD) wrote on the interpretation of myth. ***mud and slime of Aegypt:*** Animals were popularly believed to be spontaneously generated in the mud left by the Nile floods which guaranteed the fertility of the soil; Egypt was also identified as cradle of ancient civilisation. A parallel is suggested between this source of fertility and 'the excrements of luxurious Science', an image of the rubbishy left-overs of knowledge and speculation rehashed by popular writers which points forward to the excremental themes of Book II. ***that excellent Critic:*** Antoine Banier (1673–1741), over whose name this spoof note appears, had treated Proteus as a figurative depiction of a wily king, speculating that the shape-shifting might refer to his eloquence, to royal insignia derived from animals, or to contemporary magical beliefs

Escape in Monsters, and amaze the town.
Hence Miscellanies spring, the weekly boast
Of Curl's chaste press, and Lintot's rubric post:
Hence hymning Tyburn's elegiac lines,
Hence Journals, Medleys, Merc'ries, Magazines:
Sepulchral Lyes, our holy walls to grace,
And New-year Odes, and all the Grub-street race.

40.] Two Booksellers, of whom see Book 2. The former was fined by the Court of King's Bench for publishing obscene books; the latter usually adorned his shop with titles in red letters.

41, 42.] 'Genus unde Latinum, / Albanique patres, atque altae moenia Romae.' Virg. Aen. i.

41.] It is an ancient English custom for the Malefactors to sing a Psalm at their execution at Tyburn; and no less customary to print Elegies on their deaths, at the same time, or before.

42. Magazines,] Miscellanies in prose and verse, in which at some times 'new-born nonsense first is taught to cry'; at others, dead-born Dulness appears in a thousand shapes. These were thrown out weekly and monthly by every miserable scribler; or picked up piece-meal and stolen from any body, under the title of Papers, Essays, Queries, Verses, Epigrams, Riddles, *etc.* equally the disgrace of human Wit, Morality, and Decency.

43.] Is a just satyr on the Flatteries and Falshoods admitted to be inscribed on the walls of Churches, in Epitaphs.

44. New-year Odes,] Made by the Poet Laureate for the time being, to be sung at Court on every New-year's day, the words of which are happily drowned in the voices and instruments. The *New-year Odes* of the Hero of this work were of a cast distinguished from all that preceded him, and made a conspicuous part of his character as a writer, which doubtless induced our Author to mention them here so particularly.

(Banier 1739–40: II, ch. 6, 516–22). The note concludes with a Latin summary of his views on the Proteus myth, expanded in translation to suit the present application.

39. Miscellanies: See original note on line 42. The stress is on the first syllable.

40 and n. Curll capitalised on scandal and obscenity in his publications and smeared Pope's sexual and political character, provoking persistent and ingenious revenge; but Bernard Lintot (1675–1736) had published extensively for Pope – although long after settling his role in the *Dunciad* (which dates back to 1728), Pope had difficulties with his son Henry over financial arrangements for the Homer translation and over copyright clearance for *The Dunciad in Four Books* (Foxon 1991: 146, 248–50). 'Rubric' denotes red-printed title-pages, posted up to advertise new books.

41–2n.: Genus unde Latinum: The quotation suggests an ironic parallel between the 'Cell' as breeding ground of Dulness and Virgil's identification of Troy as source of Roman destiny ('whence the Latin race, the Alban fathers, and the high ramparts of Rome': *Aeneid* I.6–7).

41 and n. Tyburn: Site of hangings, now occupied by Marble Arch.

42 and n. Kinds of ephemeral journalism. 'Mercury', alluding to the messenger of the Olympian gods, was much used in newspaper titles. An adapted version of the note was initialled in 1751 as jointly by Pope and Warburton. ***new-born nonsense:*** Quoting I.60.

44. Grub-street race: For the real Grub Street and its associations with hack writers, see Rogers 1972.

In clouded Majesty here Dulness shone;
Four guardian Virtues, round, support her throne:
Fierce champion Fortitude, that knows no fears
Of hisses, blows, or want, or loss of ears:
Calm Temperance, whose blessings those partake
Who hunger, and who thirst for scribling sake:
Prudence, whose glass presents th' approaching jayl:
Poetic Justice, with her lifted scale,
Where, in nice balance, truth with gold she weighs,
And solid pudding against empty praise.

45.] 'the Moon / Rising in clouded Majesty'. Milton, Book iv. See this Cloud removed, or rolled back, or gathered up to her head, book iv. ver. 17, 18. It is worth while to compare this description of the Majesty of Dulness in a state of peace and tranquillity, with that more busy scene where she mounts the throne in triumph, and is not so much supported by her own Virtues, as by the princely consciousness of having destroyed all other. SCRIBL.

47–8.] 'Quem neque pauperies, neque mors, neque vincula terrent.' Horat.

50.] 'This is an allusion to a text in Scripture, which shews, in Mr. *Pope,* a delight in prophaneness,' said Curl upon this place. But it is very familiar with Shakespear to allude to passages of Scripture: Out of a great number I will select a few, in which he not only alludes to, but quotes the very Texts from holy Writ. In All's well that ends well, *I am no great Nebuchadnezzar, I have not much skill in grass.* Ibid. *They are for the flowery way that leads to the broad gate and the great fire.* Mat. vii. 13. In Much ado about nothing. *All, all, and moreover God saw him when he was hid in the garden.* Gen. iii. 8. (in a very jocose scene.) In Love's labour lost, he talks of Sampson's carrying the gates on his back; in the Merry wives of Windsor, of Goliah and the weaver's beam; and in Henry IV, Falstaff's soldiers are compared to Lazarus and the prodigal son.

The first part of this note is Mr. CURL's, the rest is Mr. THEOBALD's, Appendix to Shakespeare Restored, p. 144.

---

45 and n. Parodying Milton's description of 'the moon / Rising in clouded majesty', but also drawing on classical imagery of cloud-veiled deities, and perhaps also on Lovelace's compliment to the 'clouded Majesty' of a portrait of Charles I in adversity (Fowler 1998: *Paradise Lost* IV.606–7; Wilkinson 1930: 57). The note was initialled in 1751 as by Warburton.

46. Four guardian Virtues: the four cardinal virtues in debased form. Lord Mayors' shows routinely featured such allegorical tableaux. Rogers suggests an allusion to Queen Caroline at her coronation, supported by bishops and ladies of the court (Rogers 1985: 130, 133–4).

47–8 and n. For 'want ... of ears' see note on I.103. The quotation from Horace refers to the man 'whom neither poverty nor death nor chains frighten', one who has achieved freedom by controlling his passions (*Satires* I.vii.84).

50 and n. Alluding to Matthew 5:6. The note plays off two antagonists against each other (loosely quoting Curll's anonymous *A Compleat Key* (1728) and Theobald's *Shakespeare Restored*).

51. Hack writers need to have an eye to the possibility of being imprisoned – possibly for libel or sedition, but more probably for debt.

52–4. By 'Poetic Justice' is usually meant the punishing of vice and rewarding of virtue. However, the kind of justice conceived by a hack poet is presented as a meticulous ('nice')

Here she beholds the Chaos dark and deep,
Where nameless Somethings in their causes sleep,
'Till genial Jacob, or a warm Third day,
Call forth each mass, a Poem, or a Play:
How hints, like spawn, scarce quick in embryo lie,
How new-born nonsense first is taught to cry,
Maggots half-form'd in rhyme exactly meet,

55–6.] That is to say, unformed things, which are either made into Poems or Plays, as the Booksellers or the Players bid most. These lines allude to the following in Garth's Dispensary, Cant. vi: 'Within the chambers of the globe they spy / The beds where sleeping vegetables lie, / 'Till the glad summons of a genial ray / Unbinds the glebe, and calls them out to day.'

---

weighing not of right and wrong, but of useful profit (which might be compassed by such vices as libel or flattery) against the useless esteem which only integrity could earn.

55–78. Dulness, a parody of a fertility goddess, rejoices in a scene of perverse potential reminiscent of Milton's Satan's looking into chaos, 'The womb of nature and perhaps her grave', thus initiating a parody of the biblical and Miltonic creation stories (Fowler 1998: *Paradise Lost*, II.890–920, 911; Battestin 1974: 105–7). The opening section is also reminiscent of the ritual believed to generate bees (one of the concerns of the goddess Ceres) from the carcass of a ritually slaughtered calf, which Virgil makes the climax of his *Georgics* (*Georgics* IV.281–314, 548–58; Brooks-Davies 1985: 28–9; and see editor's notes on 73n. and III.29–34 below).

55–8 and n. dark and deep: Compare Milton on the role of Light in creation: 'thou ... / ... as with a mantle didst invest / The rising world of waters dark and deep' (Fowler 1998: *Paradise Lost* III.9–11). ***in their causes sleep:*** Cp. Garth's 'Here his forsaken Seat old *Chaos* keeps; / And undisturb'd by Form, in Silence sleeps', which in turn draws on a couplet from Cowley's *Davideis* ('Where their vast *Court* the *Mother-waters* keep, / And undisturbed by *Moons* in silence sleep') already parodied by Dryden in a context of cultural decline (*The Dispensary* 1699: VI.96–7; Waller 1905: 244; *Mac Flecknoe*, lines 72–3). The second line also parodies a celebrated conceit by Thomas Carew (1594/5–1640), in which the beloved is seen as containing the ultimate essence of beauty ('Aske me no more where *Iove* bestowes, / When *Iune* is past, the fading rose: / For in your beauties orient deepe, / These flowers as in their causes, sleepe') (Dunlap 1949: 102, 265). ***Garth's Dispensary:*** *The Dispensary* 1699: VI.40–43. ***glebe:*** 'earth', 'land'.

57–8. Compare Milton's account of how on the third day of creation 'over all the face of earth / Main ocean flowed, not idle, but with warm / Prolific humour softening all her globe, / Fermented the great mother to conceive, / Satiate with genial moisture' (Fowler 1998: *Paradise Lost* VII.278–82; Brockbank 1979: 193). Pope repeats the key terms 'warm' and 'genial', punningly attaching them to a theatrical 'third day' (when the playwright received the takings); and recollection of the passage also suggests a further resonance to the term 'great mother', already applied to Dulness (see line 1 and editor's note). ***'Till genial Jacob:*** The 'Somethings' emerge as poems if Jacob Tonson the publisher proves friendly to them ('genial' retains its root sense of 'generative'), or as plays if audience taste allows them to run for the three nights that ensured a profit for the author ('warm' was also a colloquialism for 'wealthy').

59. quick: alive; used specifically of a foetus that has begun to move in the womb.

61. Maggots: Combining the literal sense with the contemporary sense of 'whim' or 'idea'.

And learn to crawl upon poetic feet.
Here one poor word an hundred clenches makes,
And ductile dulness new meanders takes;
There motley Images her fancy strike,
Figures ill pair'd, and Similies unlike.
She sees a Mob of Metaphors advance,
Pleas'd with the madness of the mazy dance:
How Tragedy and Comedy embrace;
How Farce and Epic get a jumbled race;
How Time himself stands still at her command,
Realms shift their place, and Ocean turns to land.
Here gay Description Aegypt glads with show'rs,

63.] It may not be amiss to give an instance or two of these operations of *Dulness* out of the Works of her Sons, celebrated in the Poem. A great Critic formerly held these clenches in such abhorrence, that he declared 'he that would pun would pick a pocket.' Yet Mr. Dennis's works afford us notable examples in this kind: '*Alexander Pope* hath sent abroad into the world as many *Bulls* as his namesake Pope *Alexander*. — Let us take the initial and final letters of his Name, *viz. A. P—E*, and they give you the idea of an *Ape*. — *Pope* comes from the Latin word *Popa*, which signifies a little Wart; or from *poppysma*, because he was continually *popping* out squibs of wit, or rather *Popysmata*, or *Popisms*.' DENNIS on *Hom.* and Daily Journal, *June* 11, 1728.

64.] A parody on a verse in Garth, Cant. I: 'How ductile matter new meanders takes.'

70–72.] Allude to the transgressions of the *Unities* in the Plays of such poets. For the miracles wrought upon *Time* and *Place*, and the mixture of Tragedy and Comedy, Farce and Epic, see Pluto and Proserpine, Penelope, *etc.* if yet extant.

73.] In the lower Aegypt Rain is of no use, the overflowing of the Nile being sufficient to impregnate the soil. — These six verses represent the Inconsistencies in the descriptions of

---

62. poetic feet: Punning on literal and metrical feet. The image is complicated by the fact that maggots are entirely limbless.

63 and n. 'Clenches' are plays on words: the 'great Critic' Dennis is accused of professing to despise them (Victor 1722) but indulging in them in attacking Pope (though of the texts cited, only the *Remarks on Homer* were acknowledged by Dennis: Hooker 1939–43: II, 157, 416; *Daily Journal*, 11 June 1728). '*Bulls*' puns on the senses 'papal edicts' and 'ludicrous errors'.

64 and n. ductile: malleable, flexible. ***Garth, Cant. I:*** *The Dispensary* 1699: I.25.

67–8. The common application of 'mazy' (i.e. 'like a maze') to a dance was not necessarily pejorative (Sherbo 1970: 505). For 'dance'/'advance' rhymes evoking harmonies in ironic contrast with the present couplet, see Bawcutt 1958: 221.

69–70 and 70–72n. Neo-classical theory condemned hybrid genres such as tragi-comedy. The three '*Unities*', a neo-classical elaboration of Aristotelian dramatic theory, stipulated that plays should present only one principal action, and should contain it within only one location and only one day. Examples of the hybrid popular entertainments Pope denounces are *A Dramatic Entertainment, Call'd Harlequin a Sorcerer: With the Loves of Pluto and Proserpine* (1725), by Theobald (see Brooks-Davies 1985: 22), and *Penelope, a Dramatic Opera* (1728), by John Mottley and Thomas Cooke: 'if yet extant' dismisses them as ephemera unlikely to be preserved.

73n. the Guardian, No. 40: Pope's attack on Ambrose Philips's pastorals (Appendix V). The paragraph cited satirises the mixing of flora and fauna of different seasons and countries. Cibber

Or gives to Zembla fruits, to Barca flow'rs;
Glitt'ring with ice here hoary hills are seen,
There painted vallies of eternal green,
In cold December fragrant chaplets blow,
And heavy harvests nod beneath the snow.
  All these, and more, the cloud-compelling Queen
Beholds thro' fogs, that magnify the scene.
She, tinsel'd o'er in robes of varying hues,
With self-applause her wild creation views;
Sees momentary monsters rise and fall,
And with her own fools-colours gilds them all.
  'Twas on the day, when ** rich and grave,
Like Cimon, triumph'd both on land and wave:

poets, who heap together all glittering and gawdy images, though incompatible in one season, or in one scene.

See the Guardian, No. 40. parag. 6. See also *Eusden*'s whole works, if to be found. It would not have been unpleasant to have given Examples of all these species of bad writing from these Authors, but that it is already done in our Treatise of the *Bathos*. SCRIBL.

79.] From Homer's Epithet of Jupiter, νεφεληγερέτα Ζεύς.

85, 86.] Viz. a Lord Mayor's Day; his name the author had left in blanks, but most certainly could never be that which the Editor foisted in formerly, and which no way agrees with the chronology of the poem. BENTL.

The Procession of a Lord Mayor is made partly by land, and partly by water. — Cimon, the famous Athenian General, obtained a victory by sea, and another by land, on the same day, over the Persians and Barbarians.

---

alleged that Philips had publicly threatened to beat Pope in revenge (Cibber 1742: 65; and for part of a relevant note lost during printing, see editor's note on line 324 and *Corr.*: IV, 425; and cp. *OAC*: I, 71). ***if to be found:*** Insinuating that the works of the previous Poet Laureate may already have vanished without trace. ***our Treatise of the* Bathos:** See *PW*: II, 171–276.

74. Zembla (in the Arctic) typifies a frozen waste, Barca (in Libya) an arid one.

77. chaplets: wreaths of flowers. Compare the disruption of the seasons in Shakespeare's *A Midsummer Night's Dream*: 'hoary-headed frosts / Fall in the fresh lap of the crimson rose; / And on old Hiems' thin and icy crown / An odorous chaplet of sweet summer buds / Is, as in mockery, set' (Alexander 1951: II.i.107–11).

79n: The epithet describes the sky- and thunder-god Zeus as 'cloud-gatherer'.

84. fools-colours: Evoking the parti-coloured costume of a professional fool; but see also editor's note on IV.538.

85–6 and n. **: Replacing the earlier reading 'Thorold' (Sir George Thorold, Lord Mayor of London in 1719), a relative anachronism in the new context of Cibber's election to the role of hero. Brooks-Davies suggests links between Thorold and the political themes of the *Dunciad*; Rogers argues that Thorold/** constituted from the beginning a coded reference to George II and the ceremonial of his coronation in 1727 (Brooks-Davies 1985: 106–8; Rogers 1985: 120–50). Pope seems to have deliberately stayed away from the coronation, and regarded popular interest in its ceremonial with distaste (Williams 1965: III, 243–4; *Corr.*: II, 462). ***most certainly could never be:*** 'Bentley' echoes his real-life original, who used chronology as a test of authenticity (notably in exposing the so-called Epistles of Phalaris). He condemns

(Pomps without guilt, of bloodless swords and maces,
Glad chains, warm furs, broad banners, and broad faces)
Now Night descending, the proud scene was o'er,
But liv'd, in Settle's numbers, one day more.
Now May'rs and Shrieves all hush'd and satiate lay,
Yet eat, in dreams, the custard of the day;
While pensive Poets painful vigils keep,
Sleepless themselves, to give their readers sleep.
Much to the mindful Queen the feast recalls

88. Glad chains,] The Ignorance of these Moderns! This was altered in one edition to *Gold chains*, shewing more regard to the metal of which the chains of Aldermen are made, than to the beauty of the Latinism and Graecism, nay of figurative speech itself: *Laetas segetes*, glad, for making glad, *etc.* SCRIBL.

90.] A beautiful manner of speaking, usual with poets in praise of poetry, in which kind nothing is finer than those lines of Mr. Addison: 'Sometimes, misguided by the tuneful throng, / I look for streams immortaliz'd in song, / That lost in silence and oblivion lie, / Dumb are their fountains, and their channels dry; / Yet run for ever by the Muses skill, / And in the smooth description murmur still.'

Ibid.] Settle was poet to the City of London. His office was to compose yearly panegyrics upon the Lord Mayors, and verses to be spoken in the Pageants: But that part of the shows being at length frugally abolished, the employment of City-poet ceased; so that upon Settle's demise there was no successor to that place.

'Thorold' as a false reading 'foisted in' by an editor, recalling Bentley's edition of Milton, in which expressions he disapproved of were dismissed as error or interpolation (Levine 1991: 245–63). ***Cimon:*** Athenian soldier and statesman (*c.*510–*c.*450 BC).

87. Contrasting the harmless self-glorification of a Lord Mayor's procession with the military triumphs celebrated by victors like Cimon.

88 and n. 'Warm' refers objectively to the furred civic robes, but also, colloquially, to the wealth of their wearers; 'broad faces' alludes to the aldermen's reputation for overeating. ***This was altered:*** Scriblerus refers to an edition of 1728 (Griffith 1922–7: no. 220; Foxon 1975: no. P769). '*Laetas segetes*' ('glad harvests') is quoted from the opening of Virgil's *Georgics* as a stock example of such transference of epithets.

90 and n. Pope would have been familiar with traditional scepticism about the longevity of mayoral verse: see John Oldham (1653–83) in Brooks & Selden 1987 ('A Satyr .... Dissuading the Author from the Study of Poetry', lines 63–6; for Pope and Oldham, see *OAC*: I, 202; Selden 1984). A key figure in the *Dunciad*s (see Book III), Settle is introduced with a bathetic downgrading of poets' traditional claims to immortalise their subjects, as typified in Addison's *A Letter from Italy* (Guthkelch 1914: I, lines 47–52; *OAC*: I, 76). In addition to his 'office' ('duty') of writing for civic occasions as City Poet, Settle composed occasional verse in praise of patrons (Brown 1910: 22–3, 42–3). He had died as a pensioner in the Charterhouse in 1724 (Rogers 1985: 87–101).

91. Shrieves: sheriffs.

92. custard: A traditional delicacy at City feasts.

93–4. Anticipated in a letter Pope wrote to Caryll in 1718 ('I charitably take pains for others' ease, and wake to make you sleep!'), and later echoed in a comment to Warburton on his work on the *Dunciad* itself (*Corr.*: I, 462).

What City Swans once sung within the walls;
Much she revolves their arts, their ancient praise,
And sure succession down from Heywood's days.
She saw, with joy, the line immortal run,
Each sire imprest and glaring in his son:
So watchful Bruin forms, with plastic care,
Each growing lump, and brings it to a Bear.
She saw old Pryn in restless Daniel shine,
And Eusden eke out Blackmore's endless line;

98.] *John Heywood,* whose Interludes were printed in the time of Henry VIII.

103.] The first edition had it, 'She saw in Norton all his father shine': a great Mistake! for Daniel De Foe had parts, but Norton De Foe was a wretched writer, and never attempted Poetry. Much more justly is Daniel himself made successor to W. Pryn, both of whom wrote Verses as well as Politics; as appears by the Poem *De jure divino, etc.* of De Foe, and by these lines in Cowley's Miscellanies, on the other: 'One lately did not fear / (Without the Muses leave) to plant Verse here. / But it produced such base, rough, crabbed, hedge- / Rhymes, as e'en set the hearers ears on edge: / Written by *William Prynn Esqui-re, the / Year of our Lord, six hundred thirty three.* / Brave Jersey Muse! and he's for his high style / Call'd to this day the Homer of the Isle.' And both these authors had a resemblance in their fates as well as writings, having been alike sentenced to the Pillory.

104.] Laurence Eusden Poet laureate. Mr. Jacob gives a catalogue of some few only of his

---

96. City Swans: the City Poets, whose office fell into disuse after Settle's death.

97. revolves: meditates on.

98 and n. Cp. Dryden's reflection that although bees have only a short life, 'Th'immortal Line in sure Succession reigns' (Kinsley 1958: *Georgics* IV.303). Thomas Heywood (*d.* 1641), best known for the tragedy *A Woman Killed with Kindness,* also wrote pageants for the City. The note confuses him with John Heywood (*c.*1497–*c.*1580).

99. For a genealogy of bad writing, see *Peri Bathous* (*PW*: II, 203).

100. imprest: imprinted. There may also be an allusion to the image of George II on his coinage (Nicholson 1994: 193; Rogers 1985: 134).

101–2. Bears (traditionally called 'Bruin') were supposed to be born shapeless and to be licked into shape by the 'plastic' ('shaping') tongues of their mothers.

103 and n. Cp. Milton: 'the Son of God was seen / Most glorious, in him all his Father shone / Substantially expressed' (Fowler 1998: *Paradise Lost* III.138–40). ***old Pryn:*** William Prynne (1600–69) had his ears cut off in the pillory for reflecting on the King and Queen in his *Histrio-Mastix* (1632). ***restless Daniel:*** Pope finds Prynne's heir in Daniel Defoe (1661?–1731), 'restless' in political controversy: he was pilloried for his anonymous *The Shortest Way with the Dissenters: or, Proposals for the Establishment of the Church* (Backsheider 1989: 94–119). He seems to be included alongside Eusden as one of the '*Ostridges*' in Pope's *Peri Bathous* (*PW*: II, 197). For a more positive evaluation, especially of *Robinson Crusoe,* see *OAC*: I, 213. ***The first edition:*** In 1728 Defoe's troublesome and undistinguished son Benjamin Norton Defoe (*fl.* 1720) had been identified as his literary heir; but this is now retracted as unfair (*TE*: V, 71). ***both of whom wrote Verses:*** Defoe published political verse, e.g. *Jure Divino* (1706); Prynne composed devotional verse in his imprisonment (Prynne 1641). ***Cowley's Miscellanies:*** The works of the poet Abraham Cowley (1618–67), frequently reprinted.

104 and n. endless line: Punning on the sense of 'lineage'. Discerning lines of poetic

works, which were very numerous. Mr. Cook, in his Battle of Poets, saith of him, 'Eusden, a laurel'd Bard, by fortune rais'd, / By very few was read, by fewer prais'd.' Mr. Oldmixon, in his Arts of Logic and Rhetoric, p. 413, 414. affirms, 'That of all the Galimatia's he ever met with, none comes up to some verses of this poet, which have as much of the Ridiculum and the Fustian in them as can well be jumbled together, and are of that sort of nonsense, which so perfectly confounds all ideas, that there is no distinct one left in the mind.' Farther he says of him, 'That he hath prophecied his own poetry shall be sweeter than Catullus, Ovid, and Tibullus; but we have little hope of the accomplishment of it, from what he hath lately published.' Upon which Mr. Oldmixon has not spared a reflection, 'That the putting the Laurel on the head of one who writ such verses, will give futurity a very lively idea of the judgment and justice of those who bestowed it.' Ibid. p. 417. But the well-known learning of that Noble Person, who was then Lord Chamberlain, might have screened him from this unmannerly reflection. Nor ought Mr. Oldmixon to complain, so long after, that the Laurel would have better become his own brows, or any others: It were more decent to acquiesce in the opinion of the Duke of *Buckingham* upon this matter: 'In rush'd Eusden, and cry'd, Who shall have it, / But I, the true Laureate, to whom the King gave it? / Apollo beg'd pardon, and granted his claim, / But vow'd that 'till then he ne'er heard of his name.' Session of Poets. The same plea might also serve for his successor, Mr. Cibber; and is further strengthened in the following Epigram, made on that occasion: 'In merry old England it once was a rule, / The King had his Poet, and also his Fool: / But now we're so frugal, I'd have you to know it, / That Cibber can serve both for Fool and for Poet.' Of Blackmore, see Book 2. Of Philips, Book I. ver. 258. and Book 3. *prope fin.*

Nahum Tate was Poet Laureate, a cold writer, of no invention; but sometimes translated tolerably when befriended by Mr. Dryden. In his second part of Absalom and Achitophel are above two hundred admirable lines together of that great hand, which strongly shine through the insipidity of the rest. Something parallel may be observed of another author here mentioned.

---

tradition was an interest of the period: in *Peri Bathous* Eusden is proposed as 'poetical son' of Blackmore (*PW*: II, 203). ***Mr. Jacob:*** Eusden is represented as so uncritically prolific that Jacob had room to mention 'some few only' of his works (Jacob 1719–20: I). ***Mr. Cook:*** In the anonymous *The Battle of the Poets* 1725. ***Mr. Oldmixon:*** Oldmixon was condemning Eusden specifically for prophesying the coming of a new golden age, and focused on Pope and Swift as prime evidence that the contrary was the case. ***Galimatia's:*** confused rigmaroles. ***the Ridiculum:*** what deserves to be laughed at. ***Fustian:*** literally, a cheap, napped fabric; metaphorically, pretentious bombast. ***Catullus, Ovid, and Tibullus:*** Roman love poets (respectively *c.*84–*c.*54 BC; 43 BC–AD 17; *c.*55–19 BC). ***that Noble Person:*** While ostensibly defending the Lord Chamberlain who appointed Eusden, the note pillories him as a sponsor of degraded art. He was Thomas Pelham-Holles (1693–1768), first Duke of Newcastle and key dispenser of government patronage, assumed to have appointed Eusden in return for a flattering poem on his marriage. ***the opinion of the Duke of* Buckingham:** By 'the same plea' (the assertion that the choice of Laureate is – nominally at least – the king's, and thus above criticism) Cibber's appointment too would be unassailable (Pope had edited the duke's works: see Pope 1723). ***the following Epigram:*** Cibber accused Pope of writing it himself (Cibber 1742: 39). ***Of Blackmore, see Book 2:*** Where he wins the noise-making competition (II.259–68). ***Of Philips, Book I:*** The original commentary here runs ahead to line 105. Philips, whose initials appear in *Peri Bathous* in the class of 'slow and chill' tortoises who 'like pastoral writers, delight much in gardens', and whose writings (notably the notoriously 'INFANTINE' style in which he addressed the children of his patrons)

She saw slow Philips creep like Tate's poor page,
And all the mighty Mad in Dennis rage.

106.] This is by no means to be understood literally, as if Mr. Dennis were really mad, according to the Narrative of Dr. Norris in Swift and Pope's Miscellanies, vol. 3. No — it is spoken of that *Excellent* and *Divine Madness*, so often mentioned by Plato; that poetical rage and enthusiasm, with which Mr. D. hath, in his time, been highly possessed; and of those *extraordinary hints and motions* whereof he himself so feelingly treats in his preface to the Rem. on Pr. Arth. [See notes on Book 2. ver. 268.]

Mr. Theobald, in the Censor, vol. ii. N. 33. calls Mr. Dennis by the name of Furius. 'The modern Furius is to be looked upon as more an object of pity, than of that which he daily provokes, laughter and contempt. Did we really know how much this *poor* man *(I wish that reflection on* poverty *had been spared)* suffers by being contradicted, or, which is the same thing in effect, by hearing another praised; we should, in compassion, sometimes attend to him with a silent nod, and let him go away with the triumphs of his ill nature. — *Poor* Furius *(again)* when any of his cotemporaries are spoken well of, quitting the ground of the present dispute, steps back a thousand years to call in the succour of the Ancients. His very panegyric is spiteful, and he uses it for the same reason as some Ladies do their commendations of a dead beauty, who would never have had their good word, but that a living one happened to be mentioned in their company. His applause is not the tribute of his *Heart*, but the sacrifice of his *Revenge*,' *etc.* Indeed his pieces against our poet are somewhat of an angry

---

are cited among the treatise's examples of bad verse more frequently than those of any writer except Blackmore, wrote the fragmentary *Thulè*, which has an appropriately cold theme for extinguishing fire: its eponymous heroine is a daughter of Venus and Adonis who was apparently to be banished to the frozen north in order to give the island its name (Philips 1748: 112–16; III.326 ('prope fin.' means 'near the end'); *PW*: II, 197, 202–3, 214–15, 220). ***Nahum Tate:*** The relationship between Dryden and the dramatist, translator of the Psalms and former Poet Laureate Nahum Tate (1652–1715), whose *The Second Part of Absolom and Achitophel* contains material contributed by Dryden, is likened to that between Addison and Philips, whose translations from Greek were suspected to have been made by Addison (Elwin & Courthope 1871–86: IV, 316; Bond 1965: II, 367). Tate had been further satirised in *Peri Bathous*, and in early manuscript drafts of the *Dunciad* (*PW*: II, 203; Mack 1984: 116, 131, 146).

105. Philips's laboriousness is contrasted with Eusden's facility (cp. *To Arbuthnot*, line 182). See also note on previous line.

106n. as if Mr. Dennis were really mad: Pope's anonymous *Narrative of Dr. Robert Norris* (1713) professes to be an account of Dennis's literal madness written by an asylum keeper (*PW*: I, 153–68). ***that* Excellent *and* Divine Madness:** Plato taught that the soul was in exile in the material world and aspired to return to the eternal world of Ideas: from a neoclassical outlook this kind of other-worldly mysticism seemed a recipe for insanity. ***poetical rage and enthusiasm:*** Dennis's account of creativity (quoted in note to II.268) comes dangerously close to the disapproved mysticism associated with Plato. 'Rage' also suggests the intemperate tone of Dennis's attacks; 'enthusiasm' still carried the negative sense of religious or political extremism. ***Mr. Theobald, in the Censor:*** Published anonymously. Theobald's criticisms of Dennis support the incidental point that Pope's enemies are at odds even with each other; the parentheses are introduced to insinuate that Theobald makes just the kind of cheap jokes against poverty that Pope is accused of making. ***somewhat of an angry character:*** A notable understatement. Under the pretence that such ephemera are 'now

character, and as they are now scarce extant, a taste of his style may be satisfactory to the curious. 'A young, squab, short gentleman, whose outward form, though it should be that of downright monkey, would not differ so much from human shape as his unthinking immaterial part does from human understanding. — He is as stupid and as venomous as a hunchback'd toad. — A book through which folly and ignorance, those brethren so lame and impotent, do ridiculously look very big and very dull, and strut and hobble, cheek by jowl, with their arms on kimbo, being led and supported, and bully-back'd by that blind Hector, Impudence.' Reflect. on the Essay on Criticism, p. 26. 29, 30.

It would be unjust not to add his reasons for this Fury, they are so strong and so coercive: 'I regard him (saith he) as an *Enemy*, not so much to me, as to my King, to my Country, to my Religion, and to that Liberty which has been the sole felicity of my life. A vagary of Fortune, who is sometimes pleased to be frolicksome, and the epidemic *Madness of the times* have given him *Reputation*, and Reputation (as Hobbes says) is *Power*, and *that has made him dangerous*. Therefore I look on it as my duty to *King George*, whose faithful subject I am; to my *Country*, of which I have appeared a constant lover; to the *Laws*, under whose protection I have so long lived; and to the *Liberty* of my *Country*, more dear to me than life, of which I have now for forty years been a constant assertor, *etc.* I look upon it as my duty, I say, to do — *you shall see what* — to pull the lion's skin from this little Ass, which popular error has thrown round him; and to shew that this Author, who has been lately so much in vogue, has neither sense in his thoughts, nor English in his expressions.' DENNIS Rem. on Hom. Pref. p. 2. 91, *etc.*

Besides these public-spirited reasons, Mr. D. had a private one; which, by his manner of expressing it in p. 92. appears to have been equally strong. He was even in bodily fear of his life from the machinations of the said Mr. P. 'The story (says he) is too long to be told, but who would be acquainted with it, may hear it from Mr. Curl, my bookseller. — However, what my reason has suggested to me, that I have with a just confidence said, in defiance of his two clandestine weapons, his *Slander* and his *Poison*.' Which last words of his book plainly discover Mr. D.'s suspicion was that of being *poisoned*, in like manner as Mr. Curl had been before him; of which fact see *A full and true account of a horrid and barbarous revenge, by poison, on the body of Edmund Curl*, printed in 1716, the year antecedent to that wherein these Remarks of Mr. Dennis were published. But what puts it beyond all question, is a passage in a very warm treatise, in which Mr. D. was also concerned, price two pence, called *A true character of Mr. Pope and his writings*, printed for S. Popping, 1716; in the tenth page whereof he is said 'to have insulted people on those calamities and diseases which he himself gave them, by administring *Poison* to them;' and is called (p. 4.) 'a lurking way-laying coward,

---

scarce extant', approximate quotations from some of Dennis's most outrageous abuse are given. ***folly and ignorance:*** Personified by Dennis as brothers protected by the 'blind Hector' ('bully') of 'Impudence'. ***so strong and so coercive:*** Dennis's political hysteria against Pope is ironically presented as persuasive ('coercive'): he cites the perception of the philosopher Thomas Hobbes (1588–1679) that reputation is a kind of power to argue that the vogue for a Catholic poet threatens the very existence of the Protestant state (Oakeshott 1946: *Leviathan*, Ch. X). ***in bodily fear of his life:*** Dennis refers to Pope's revenge on Curll for embarrassing him and his associates by unauthorised publications: Pope slipped an emetic into his drink (written up in *A Full and True Account*; see *PW*: I, 257–66). ***a lurking way-laying coward:*** The note insists on taking Dennis's extreme metaphors literally: the ludicrous notion of the frail and diminutive Pope lurking knife in hand in dark alleys enhances the impression of Dennis's hysteria. The tongue-in-cheek conclusion is that if *that* is the way Mr Pope behaves, he certainly is 'a terror, not to Mr. Dennis only, but to all christian people'.

In each she marks her Image full exprest,
But chief in BAYS's monster-breeding breast;
Bays, form'd by nature Stage and Town to bless,
And act, and be, a Coxcomb with success.

and a stabber in the dark.' Which (with many other things most lively set forth in that piece) must have rendered him a terror, not to Mr. Dennis only, but to all christian people.

For the rest; Mr. John Dennis was the son of a Sadler in London, born in 1657. He paid court to Mr. Dryden: and having obtained some correspondence with Mr. Wycherly and Mr. Congreve, he immediately obliged the public with their Letters. He made himself known to the Government by many admirable schemes and projects; which the Ministry, for reasons best known to themselves, constantly kept private. For his character, as a writer, it is given us as follows: 'Mr. Dennis is *excellent* at Pindaric writings, *perfectly regular* in all his performances, and a person of *sound Learning*. That he is master of a great deal of *Penetration* and *Judgment*, his criticisms, (particularly on *Prince Arthur*) do sufficiently demonstrate.' From the same account it also appears that he writ Plays 'more to get *Reputation* than *Money*.' DENNIS of himself. See Giles Jacob's Lives of Dram. Poets, p. 68, 69. compared with p. 286.

109.] It is hoped the poet here hath done full justice to his Hero's Character, which it were a great mistake to imagine was wholly sunk in stupidity; he is allowed to have supported it with a wonderful mixture of Vivacity. This character is heightened according to his own

---

he immediately obliged the public: 'Obliged' is ironic: Dennis's publication of his correspondence with leading wits could be seen more as a deft piece of self-advertisement than as the expression of a selfless desire to give pleasure to the public (Dennis 1696a). ***many admirable schemes:*** Dennis suggested various policies to government which were not taken up (Hooker 1939–43: I, 506). 'Admirable' (literally 'giving rise to wonder') could in this context be read as 'preposterous'. ***Pindaric writings:*** Imitating the proverbially rapturous and loosely connected odes of the Greek poet Pindar (518–after 446 BC). **perfectly regular:** In the sense 'obedient to the rules', which could suggest a repressed and tedious style, contrasting with Pope's defence of the '*Grace* beyond the Reach of Art' (*Essay on Criticism*, line 155). ***See Giles Jacob's Lives:*** The final reference mentions Dennis as having contributed material about himself: the note invites the reader to conclude that Dennis had himself written the panegyric just quoted. Jacob, who routinely solicited information from his subjects and sent them (Pope included) proofs of their entries, accused Pope of misrepresentation in a letter included in Dennis's *Remarks upon ... the Dunciad*, and retaliated by accusing Pope of approving and enhancing his own entry in proof (Hooker 1939–43: II, 372–3; McLaverty 1985: 26, 29).

107–8. Recalling God the Father in *Paradise Lost*, with Christ as 'the radiant image of his glory' (Fowler 1998: III.63). The 'monsters' bred by Bays are his literary works.

109–10 and n. Stage and Town: Pope points the irony of what he sees as an inappropriate double success: no-one denied that Cibber was a successful comic actor, but did that really qualify him to mix in the best society and be received at court? ('Town' designates fashionable London society, as distinct from the mercantile 'City'.) ***act, and be, a Coxcomb:*** 'Coxcomb' alludes to the flamboyant headdress of a fool or jester. Cibber's public image was strongly coloured by his celebrated role of Sir Novelty Fashion, the fop in his comedy *Love's Last Shift*: in *The Relapse*, a sequel by John Vanbrugh, the character was ennobled as Lord Foppington (Koon 1986: 26–32). ***full justice to his Hero's Character:*** Cibber's defence against the charge of dullness was that he was at least *lively*. In the note his words are

Dulness with transport eyes the lively Dunce,
Remembring she herself was Pertness once.
Now (shame to Fortune!) an ill Run at Play
Blank'd his bold visage, and a thin Third day:
Swearing and supperless the Hero sate,

desire, in a Letter he wrote to our author. 'Pert and dull at least you might have allowed me. What! am I only to be dull, and dull still, and again, and for ever?' He then solemnly appealed to his own conscience, that 'he could not think himself so, nor believe that our poet did; but that he spoke worse of him than he could possibly think; and concluded it must be merely to shew his *Wit*, or for some *Profit* or *Lucre* to himself.' Life of C.C. chap. ii. and Letter to Mr. P. pag. 15. 40. 53.

113. shame to Fortune!] Because she usually shews favour to persons of this Character, who have a three-fold pretence to it.

115. supperless the Hero sate,] It is amazing how the sense of this hath been mistaken by all the former commentators, who most idly suppose it to imply that the Hero of the poem wanted a supper. In truth a great absurdity! Not that we are ignorant that the Hero of Homer's Odyssey is frequently in that circumstance, and therefore it can no way derogate from the grandeur of Epic Poem to represent such Hero under a calamity, to which the greatest, not only of Critics and Poets, but of Kings and Warriors, have been subject. But much more refined, I will venture to say, is the meaning of our author: It was to give us, obliquely, a curious precept, or, what Bossu calls, a *disguised sentence*, that 'Temperance is the life of Study.' The language of poesy brings all into action; and to represent a Critic encompassed with books, but without a supper, is a picture which lively expresseth how much the true Critic prefers the diet of the mind to that of the body, one of which he always castigates, and often totally neglects for the greater improvement of the other. SCRIBL.

But since the discovery of the true Hero of the poem, may we not add that nothing was

---

selected, altered and recombined with characteristic freedom, and the defence is accepted ironically, since it underlines the desired identification of the real Cibber with the fops he plays on stage, and assimilates him to the notion of Dulness as *active* stupidity, 'busy' and 'bold' as well as 'laborious', 'heavy' and 'blind' (I.15).

111. transport: delight, ecstacy.

112. Dulness's youthful impudence marks her distance from the modest reserve expected of young women.

113 and n. ill Run at Play: a run of bad luck at gambling. ***she usually shews favour:*** Bringing to mind the proverbs 'Fortune favours the bold' and 'Fortune favours fools'. A third entitlement to her favour could be Bays's devotion to her as gambler (and as actor?).

114. Blank'd his bold visage: wiped the characteristic smile off his face. ***a thin Third day:*** The playwright received the third night's takings.

115 and n. Swearing: Samuel Johnson claimed that swearing made up half of Cibber's conversation (Hill 1934–5: II, 340). ***supperless:*** Continuing the theme of the deserved poverty of bad writers, although Cibber was far too successful to starve, and had taunted Pope that 'I wrote more to be Fed, than be Famous, and since my Writings still give me a Dinner, do you rhyme me out of my Stomach [appetite] if you can' (Cibber 1742: 9). The epithet had previously been applied to Tibbald (*TE*: V, 76). ***the sense of this hath been mistaken:*** Scriblerus adduces the honourable destitution of the shipwrecked Odysseus, turning to Le Bossu for the notion of the 'disguised sentence' (i.e. an aphorism concealed in narrative:

Blasphem'd his Gods, the Dice, and damn'd his Fate.
Then gnaw'd his pen, then dash'd it on the ground,
Sinking from thought to thought, a vast profound!
Plung'd for his sense, but found no bottom there,
Yet wrote and flounder'd on, in mere despair.
Round him much Embryo, much Abortion lay,
Much future Ode, and abdicated Play;
Nonsense precipitate, like running Lead,
That slip'd thro' Cracks and Zig-zags of the Head;
All that on Folly Frenzy could beget,
Fruits of dull Heat, and Sooterkins of Wit.

so natural, after so great a loss of Money at Dice, or of Reputation by his Play, as that the Poet should have no great stomach to eat a supper? Besides, how well has the Poet consulted his Heroic Character, in adding that he *swore* all the time? BENTL.

---

see Le Bossu 1695: Book VI, Ch. 5), here asserting indifference to food as an emblem of the intellectual life. ***nothing was so natural:*** 'Bentley' interprets 'supperless' as referring to loss of appetite owing to loss of money and reputation (implying cheating) at cards. He takes the swearing in a sense that evokes damaging comparisons: whereas an epic hero swears solemnly to *do* something, Bays just swears.

116. his Gods, the Dice: By taking dice for gods, Bays implicitly adopts a view of life and the universe as random, banishing divine providence and purpose. He has thus made a vacuum which Dulness, the undoer of divine order, is waiting to fill.

118. Sinking from thought to thought: Rochester had described the human mind as misled by aspirations to reason, 'Stumbling from thought to thought' until it 'falls headlong down / Into doubt's boundless sea' (Vieth 1968: 'A Satyr against Reason and Mankind', lines 18–19). ***a vast profound:*** Milton makes Raphael refer to the chaos preceding creation as 'the vast profundity', and Pope several times uses 'vast profound' as periphrasis for 'sea' in the Homer translations (Fowler 1998: *Paradise Lost* VII.229; Sherbo 1970: 505). Pope's *Peri Bathous* (alluding to Longinus's treatise *On the Sublime*) anticipates this punning play with ambiguous qualities such as weightiness (heaviness?) and profundity (bathos?).

119–20. Bays's metaphorical lurching through the chaos of his thoughts recalls Satan's wallowing and plunging through the chaos between Hell and Earth in *Paradise Lost* (Fowler 1998: II.927–42). Compare also Dryden's assessment of the idiot Cymon: 'The more inform'd the less he understood, / And deeper sunk by flound'ring in the Mud' (Kinsley 1958: *Cymon and Iphigenia*, lines 63–4; Brower 1959: 327).

121. The literary productions fostered by Dulness are typically associated with untimely and deformed births (compare I.55–62).

122. The odes required of Bays as Laureate, and the plays which were the foundation of his career. 'Abdicated' suggests plays given up as unfinishable, with perhaps a hint at the failure of the monarchy with which he is associated.

123. Dulness is, paradoxically, both inert and volatile: lead is heavy and dull and difficult to associate with any kind of creativity, but when heated it has the paradoxical quality of fluidity, so that Bays's productions – heavy and dull once they fall to the floor – can be seen as the seepage from the leaky tank of his brain.

126. Following Aristotle, medical theory assumed that bodily heat, associated particularly with the male, was the key factor in procreation (*Generation of Animals*, I.IV.vi). Because Bays's

Next, o'er his Books his eyes began to roll,
In pleasing memory of all he stole,
How here he sipp'd, how there he plunder'd snug
And suck'd all o'er, like an industrious Bug.
Here lay poor Fletcher's half-eat scenes, and here
The Frippery of crucify'd Moliere;
There hapless Shakespear, yet of Tibbald sore,

131. poor Fletcher's half-eat scenes,] A great number of them taken out to patch up his Plays.

132. The Frippery] 'When I fitted up an old play, it was as a good housewife will mend old linnen, when she has not better employment.' Life, p. 217. octavo.

133.] It is not to be doubted but Bays was a subscriber to Tibbald's Shakespear. He was frequently liberal this way; and, as he tells us, 'subscribed to Mr. Pope's Homer, out of pure Generosity and Civility; but when Mr. Pope did so to his Nonjuror, he concluded it could be nothing but a joke.' Letter to Mr. P. p. 24.

This Tibbald, or Theobald, published an edition of Shakespear, of which he was so proud himself as to say, in one of Mist's Journals, June 8, 'That to expose any Errors in it was

---

brain produces only 'dull Heat', the offspring of his fancy are abortive. 'Sooterkins' were supposed to be mouse-sized monsters conceived by Dutch women as a consequence of warming themselves over small stoves placed beneath their skirts: 'Cibber is, in other words, laboring over a misconception' (Sitter 1971: 16).

127–54. The description of Bays's library is reworked from Tibbald's library in earlier versions. For similarities to Thomas Newcomb's anonymously published *Bibliotheca* (1712), see Lund 1991: 174. For the late-Renaissance 'nightmare of dead knowledge', see Jones in Mack & Winn 1980: 635–6.

128. Cibber's staple as a dramatist was the then standard procedure of reworking old or foreign plays.

129–30. snug: Evoking the intimate comfort of his parasitism (compare the proverbial 'snug as a bug in a rug', where the bug is presumably the destructive grub of a clothes-moth).

131. Perhaps insinuating that by using the relatively little-known work of John Fletcher (1579–1625) Cibber hoped to avoid detection.

132 and n. Frippery: rags, tawdry finery. ***crucify'd Moliere:*** Cibber's *The Non-Juror* (1718) was a politically opportunistic reworking of *Tartuffe* by Jean-Baptiste Poquelin, known as Molière (1622–73). Non-jurors were Anglican clergy debarred by conscience from taking the oaths of loyalty to William and Mary after the flight of James II in 1688; but the professed non-juror in the play turns out to be a Roman Catholic priest intent on undermining the family which harbours him by embezzlement and seduction. Cibber also smears Pope by association: the villain refers to the sufferings of Pope's Eloisa in his attempt to seduce the virtuous wife, and the daughter of the endangered house reads aloud from *The Rape of the Lock* and mentions Homer in English, which would imply Pope's translation (Cibber 1718: 7–8, 29, 67; Ault 1949: 309–11). Cibber maliciously highlighted Pope's adverse reaction in his *Letter* (Cibber 1742: 23; see original commentary on I.253). ***When I fitted up an old play:*** Mocking Cibber's 'low' commercial and domestic imagery.

133 and n. of Tibbald sore: Theobald saw his emendations of Shakespeare as restoration ('*Shakespeare Restored*'), not injuries. ***Bays was a subscriber:*** True, though hardly discreditable. ***as he tells us:*** A summary, far from impartial, of Cibber's account. ***This***

Wish'd he had blotted for himself before.
The rest on Out-side merit but presume,
Or serve (like other Fools) to fill a room;
Such with their shelves as due proportion hold,
Or their fond Parents drest in red and gold;
Or where the pictures for the page attone,
And Quarles is sav'd by Beauties not his own.

impracticable.' And in another, April 27, 'That whatever care might for the future be taken by any other Editor, he would still give above five hundred Emendations, that *shall* escape them all.'

134. Wish'd he had blotted] It was a ridiculous praise which the Players gave to Shakespear, 'that he never blotted a line.' Ben Johnson honestly wished he had blotted a thousand; and Shakespear would certainly have wished the same, if he had lived to see those alterations in his works, which, not the Actors only (and especially the daring Hero of this poem) have made on the *Stage*, but the presumptuous Critics of our days in their *Editions*.

135.] This Library is divided into three parts; the first consists of those authors from whom he stole, and whose works he mangled; the second, of such as fitted the shelves, or were gilded for shew, or adorned with pictures; the third class our author calls solid learning, old bodies of Divinity, old Commentaries, old English Printers, or old English Translations; all very voluminous, and fit to erect altars to Dulness.

Tibbald: Theobald is misrepresented in order to make him appear an arrogant fool. The first article cited, signed 'W.A.' but attributed to him by Pope, actually says only that it was 'impracticable' *for Pope* (who is assumed to lack the necessary training in the technicalities of Shakespearean scholarship) to decide whether or not Theobald's textual emendations were correct: it does not claim that Theobald's work was intrinsically above criticism. Similarly, the second article, which *was* signed by Theobald, mentioned not 'any other Editor' but Pope specifically. This was realistic, though hardly tactful.

134 and n. The editors of the First Folio of Shakespeare declared that 'His mind and hand went together: And what he thought, he uttered with that easinesse, that wee have scarse received from him a blot in his papers' (Alexander 1951: xxvii). Compare Pope's attitude in *Imitations of Horace, Epistles* II.i.279–81, where the comment that 'fluent Shakespear scarce effac'd a line' is followed by a reference to 'The last and greatest Art, the Art to blot' (i.e. cross out and correct). ***Ben Johnson:*** Jonson (1573?–1637) makes this retort in his *Timber: or, Discoveries* (Herford & Simpson 1925–52: VIII, 583–4). ***especially the daring Hero:*** Shakespeare was routinely acted in the eighteenth century in texts adapted to contemporary taste: Cibber was responsible for versions of *Richard III* and *King John* (Koon 1986: 37, 105, 166–7; Dobson 1992: see index, 'Cibber, Colley').

135–40 and n. In earlier editions, the library belonged to Tibbald: its medieval and early-modern stock is hardly relevant to Cibber. For the range of Pope's own library, see Mack 1982: 307–21 and Appendix A.

136. like other Fools: Who might be invited to a party just to make up the numbers.

138. red and gold: Luxurious red leather and gilt bindings (typical of presentation copies) which authors lavish on their works, just as doting parents might dress their children in unsuitable finery.

140. Francis Quarles (1592–1644), religious poet, best known for his *Emblems*, mutually dependent visual and verse allegories (a Renaissance mode despised by neo-classical taste).

Here swells the shelf with Ogilby the great;
There, stamp'd with arms, Newcastle shines complete:
Here all his suff'ring brotherhood retire,
And 'scape the martyrdom of jakes and fire:
A Gothic Library! of Greece and Rome
Well purg'd, and worthy Settle, Banks, and Broome.

141.] 'John Ogilby was one, who, from a late initiation into literature, made such a progress as might well style him the prodigy of his time! sending into the world so many *large Volumes!* His translations of Homer and Virgil *done to the life*, and *with such excellent sculptures!* And (what added great grace to his works) he printed them all on *special good paper*, and in a *very good letter.*' WINSTANLY, Lives of Poets.

142.] 'The *Duchess of Newcastle* was one who busied herself in the ravishing delights of Poetry; leaving to posterity in print three *ample Volumes* of her studious endeavours.' WINSTANLY, ibid. Langbaine reckons up *eight* Folios of her Grace's; which were usually adorned with gilded covers, and had her coat of arms upon them.

146.] The Poet has mentioned these three authors in particular, as they are parallel to our Hero in his three capacities: 1. Settle was his Brother Laureate; only indeed upon half-pay,

---

His verse is quoted for its inanity in *Peri Bathous* (*PW*: II, 210; and see *Imitations of Horace*: *Epistles* II.i.386–7). For the incidence of 'not ... own' as a line-ending, see Sherbo 1970: 505.

141 and n. John Ogilby (1600–76), originally a dancing master and theatrical entrepreneur, learned the classical languages and published translations only after losing his livelihood in the Civil War. Although his verse had been a target in *Peri Bathous* (*PW*: II, 203), and although the note ridicules the impact made by his characteristic sumptuousness of presentation, Pope recollected 'with a sort of rapture' that it was reading Ogilby's 'great edition with pictures' ('*such excellent sculptures!*') when he was eight or nine that had first awakened his passion for Homer; and he began his own translation of the *Iliad* with a capital adorned with a miniature copy of the plate that had opened Ogilby's version (*OAC*: I, 13–14; Foxon 1991: 76–80 and Fig. 40). ***Winstanly:*** William Winstanley (1628?–98), compiler of *Lives of the Most Famous English Poets* (1687).

142 and n. Margaret Cavendish (1623–73), Duchess of Newcastle, published poetry, plays, scientific speculation and arguments for the intellectual potential of women, posing a challenge to conventions of rank and gender which contributed to her reputation for ludicrous eccentricity (Blain, Clements & Grundy 1990: 790). 'Newcastle' is accented on the second syllable. ***Langbaine:*** Gerard Langbaine (1609–58), author of *An Account of the English Dramatic Poets* (1691). ***Folios:*** Large-format volumes, formerly used for prestige editions. Pope helped to establish the smaller quarto in this role (Foxon 1991: 63).

143–4. The implicitly worthless works of Bays's brother writers find a safe haven in his library: otherwise they would be torn up for use in privies or as firelighters. The 'martyrdom' metaphor continues the theme that the sufferings of bad writers are brought on by their voluntary persistence in work for which they are unqualified.

145. 'Gothic' (from the Gothic invaders of the Roman Empire) is used as broadly equivalent to 'medieval'; but it also carries the pejorative sense of anything seen as degenerating from the classic authority of 'Greece and Rome'.

146 and n. Cibber is likened to Settle as Laureate (insinuating the parallel between court and city culture); to John Banks (*fl.* 1696) as tragic playwright; and to Richard Brome

But, high above, more solid Learning shone,
The Classics of an Age that heard of none;
There Caxton slept, with Wynkyn at his side,
One clasp'd in wood, and one in strong cow-hide;

for the City instead of the Court; but equally famous for unintelligible flights in his poems on public occasions, such as Shows, Birth-days, *etc.* 2. Banks was his Rival in *Tragedy* (tho' more successful in one of his Tragedies, the *Earl of Essex*, which is yet alive: *Anna Boleyn*, the *Queen of Scots*, and *Cyrus the Great*, are dead and gone. These he drest in a sort of *Beggars Velvet*, or a happy mixture of the *thick Fustian* and *thin Prosaic*; exactly imitated in *Perolla and Isidora*, *Caesar in Aegypt*, and the *Heroic Daughter*. 3. Broome was a serving-man of Ben. Johnson, who once picked up a *Comedy* from his Betters, or from some cast scenes of his Master, not entirely contemptible.

147.] Some have objected, that books of this sort suit not so well the library of our Bays, which they imagine consisted of Novels, Plays, and obscene books; but they are to consider, that he furnished his shelves only for ornament, and read these books no more than the *Dry bodies of Divinity*, which, no doubt, were purchased by his Father when he designed him for the Gown. See the note on v. 200.

149. Caxton] A Printer in the time of Ed. IV, Rich. III, and Hen. VII; Wynkyn de Word, his successor, in that of Hen. VII and VIII. The former translated into prose Virgil's Aeneis, as a history; of which he speaks, in his Proeme, in a very singular manner, as of a book hardly known. 'Happened that to my hande cam a lytyl book in frenche, whiche late was translated out of latyn by some noble clerke of fraunce, whiche booke is named *Eneydos* (made in latyn by that noble poete & grete clerk Vyrgyle) whiche booke I sawe over and redde therein, How after the general destruccyon of the grete Troy, Eneas departed berynge his olde fader anchises upon his sholdres, his lytyl son yolas on his hande, his wyfe with moche other people followynge, and how he shipped and departed; wyth alle thystorye of his adventures that he had er he came to the atchievement of his conquest of ytalye, as all

---

(*c.*1590–1652/3: contemporary accusations of his plagiarising from Jonson seem to be malicious) as comic playwright. Banks's *The Unhappy Favourite: or, The Earl of Essex* was the most frequently performed of his plays in the first half of the eighteenth century (see indexes to Avery 1960, Scouten 1961). By choosing Brome to replace Richard Blome (*d.* 1705), the publisher of large-format illustrated compilations on heraldry and topography who had figured in previous versions, and by using the unusual spelling 'Broome', Pope seems to glance surreptitiously at William Broome, his collaborator on Homer, with whom his relations were strained at best. He seems to have intended Broome as both a parrot and a tortoise in *Peri Bathous*, and included some of his verse (without naming him) among his examples of bathetic writing (*PW*: II, 197, 199). At Broome's request, Pope had previously removed from the *Dunciad* an allusion to him which was capable of an adverse interpretation: this may be a way of getting his own back (see *TE*: V, 78–9, 191, 280–81; *Corr.*: III, 105–6, 510; IV, 2–3). **Perolla and Isidora:** The three plays cited are by Cibber.

147 and n. more solid Learning: As the note partly concedes, the 'Gothick Library' does not fit the new hero. ***designed him for the Gown:*** Cibber relates that his father had hoped he would become a clergyman.

149–50 and n. William Caxton (1422?–91), the first English printer, did in fact know Latin; but as a late-medieval entrepreneur his concern was not with the classics as such but with

There, sav'd by spice, like Mummies, many a year,
Dry Bodies of Divinity appear:
De Lyra there a dreadful front extends,
And here the groaning shelves Philemon bends.
Of these twelve volumes, twelve of amplest size,
Redeem'd from tapers and defrauded pies,
Inspir'd he seizes: These an altar raise:
An hecatomb of pure, unsully'd lays

alonge shall be shewed in this present booke. In whiche booke I had grete playsyr, by cause of the fayr and honest termes & wordes in frenche, whiche I never sawe to fore lyke, ne none so playsaunt ne so well ordred; whiche booke as me semed sholde be moche requysite to noble men to see, as wel for the eloquence as the hystoryes. How wel that many hondred yerys passed was the sayd booke of Eneydos wyth other workes made and lerned dayly in scolis, especyally in ytayle in other places, which historye the sayd Vyrgyle made in metre.'

153.] Nich. de Lyra, or Harpsfield, a very voluminous commentator, whose works, in five vast folios, were printed in 1472.

154.] Philemon Holland Doctor in Physic. He translated *so many books,* that a man would think he had done *nothing else*; insomuch that he might be called *Translator general of his age.* The books alone of his turning into English are sufficient to make a *Country Gentleman* a *complete Library.* WINSTANL.

---

providing English versions of the Burgundian bestsellers of the time, which elaborated classical tales in contemporary terms (Painter 1976: 40–41). Pope regards such texts as worthless corruptions of Virgil; and, imposing his concern to distinguish history from fiction onto the medieval context, he implies that Caxton was simple-minded to present *Eneydos* 'as a history'. His eagerness to discredit Caxton is prompted by Theobald's embarrassing use of Caxton's *Recuyell of the Historyes of Troye* to interpret an allusion in Shakespeare which Pope had misunderstood by attempting to refer it to Homer (Caxton 1473–4; *TE*: V, 213; *Mist's Journal*, 16 March 1728). In 1729 he had printed Caxton's Preface as Appendix III. ***Wynkyn:*** Wynkyn de Worde (*d.* 1535), Caxton's assistant and successor to his printing business. ***wood:*** Used in medieval bookbindings. ***cow-hide:*** A favourite binding material.

151. The books, protected from bookworms by aromatic spices, are compared to embalmed Egyptian mummies.

152. Dry Bodies of Divinity: As well as a general attack on tedious theological works, there is a pointed allusion to the *Complete Body of Divinity* by Thomas Stackhouse (1677–1752), who had offended Pope by writing against Atterbury.

153 and n. The note confuses Nicholas de Lyra (*d.* 1340) with Nicholas Harpsfield (1519?–75), an extreme example of Pope's tendency to collapse the Middle Ages into one undistinguished mass. 'Front' usually denotes 'face' or 'forehead': Pope compares the spine of the book to a face.

154 and n. Philemon Holland (1552–1637).

155. For biblical precedent for an altar of twelve components, see Sherbo 1988: 223.

156. The books might otherwise have been torn up to light candles or line baking tins.

158. hecatomb: major sacrifice, originally of 100 oxen. ***pure, unsully'd lays:*** Just as animals for sacrifice had to be physically unblemished, so are these unsold, unread copies of Bays's poems.

That altar crowns: A folio Common-place
Founds the whole pile, of all his works the base:
Quartos, octavos, shape the less'ning pyre;
A twisted Birth-day Ode completes the spire.
  Then he: Great Tamer of all human art!
First in my care, and ever at my heart;
Dulness! whose good old cause I yet defend,
With whom my Muse began, with whom shall end;
E'er since Sir Fopling's Periwig was Praise,

166.] 'A te principium, tibi desinet.' Virg. Ecl. viii. *Ἐκ Διὸς ἀρχώμεσθα, καὶ εἰς Δία λήγετε, Μοῦσαι.* Theoc. 'Prima dicte mihi, summa dicende Camoena.' Horat.

167.] The first visible cause of the passion of the Town for our Hero, was a fair flaxen full-bottom'd Periwig, which, he tells us, he wore in his first play of the *Fool in fashion.* It attracted, in a particular manner, the Friendship of Col. Brett, who wanted to purchase it. 'Whatever contempt (says he) Philosophers may have for a fine Periwig, my friend, who was not to despise the world but to live in it, knew very well that so material an article of dress upon the head of a man of sense, if it became him, could never fail of drawing to him a more partial Regard and Benevolence, than could possibly be hoped for in an ill-made one. This perhaps, may soften the grave censure which so youthful a purchase might otherwise have laid upon him. In a word, he made his attack upon this Periwig, as your young fellows generally do upon a lady of pleasure, first by a few familiar praises of her person, and then a civil enquiry into the price of it; and we finished our bargain that night over a bottle.' See Life, octavo p. 303. This remarkable Periwig usually made its entrance upon the stage in a sedan, brought in by two chairmen, with infinite approbation of the audience.

---

159. Common-place: Commonplace books were originally personal collections of quotations, but printed ones were also available. Bays relies on one because he has no original ideas.

162. The Laureate was expected to write poems for royal birthdays: Cibber's show him at his weakest. Sutherland suggests that the ode is 'twisted' into 'a fools-cap for George II' (*TE*: V, 282).

163. Bays thinks of 'art' not positively but negatively, as a wild impulse needing to be suppressed by Dulness.

165. good old cause: Literally 'old' because Dulness ruled in prehistoric times, but the phrase was also used to refer pejoratively to the parliamentary cause in the Civil War, since Tories routinely claimed that the Whigs were the heirs of the roundheads and thus a danger to society. (For an otherwise useful discussion, misleading insofar as it rules out Whig ideology as a theme in *The Dunciad*, see Hopkins 1966.)

166n. Three examples of the classical topos parodied by Bays's address to Dulness. Virgil and Horace say that their poetry begins and ends with their respective patrons; the Greek pastoral poet Theocritus (third century BC) sets above even his patron the father of the gods, Zeus (Virgil, *Eclogues* VIII.11; Horace, *Epistles* I.i.1; Theocritus, *Idylls* XVII.1).

167 and n. Pope despised contemporary audiences' delight in lavish costumes (*Imitations of Horace, Epistles* II.i.314–37). Cibber's success in his comedy *Love's Last Shift: or, The Fool in Fashion* is implicitly put down to his wig. Cibber's facetious account of the wig's role in cementing his friendship with Henry Brett (*d.* 1724, member of the Addison circle)

To the last honours of the Butt and Bays:
O thou! of Bus'ness the directing soul!
To this our head like byass to the bowl,
Which, as more pond'rous, made its aim more true,
Obliquely wadling to the mark in view:
O! ever gracious to perplex'd mankind,
Still spread a healing mist before the mind;
And lest we err by Wit's wild dancing light,
Secure us kindly in our native night.
Or, if to Wit a coxcomb make pretence,
Guard the sure barrier between that and Sense;
Or quite unravel all the reas'ning thread,
And hang some curious cobweb in its stead!
As, forc'd from wind-guns, lead itself can fly,
And pond'rous slugs cut swiftly thro the sky;
As clocks to weight their nimble motion owe,
The wheels above urg'd by the load below:
Me Emptiness, and Dulness could inspire,
And were my Elasticity, and Fire.

178, 179.] For *Wit* or *Reasoning* are never greatly hurtful to Dulness, but when the first is founded in *Truth*, and the other in *Usefulness*.

---

works to support Pope's attack on his moral character by its casual references to drinking and whoring.

168. Butt: The allowance of wine received by the Poet Laureate.

170–72. A simile from the game of bowls, in which the skill lies in making allowance for asymmetrical weighting. Pope had inserted a version of these lines into his revision of Wycherley's 'A Panegyrick on Dulness', and the laborious art of a dull writer is said to 'hang on lead, to facilitate and enforce our descent' in *Peri Bathous* (*PW*: II, 190–91; Vander Meulen 1991: 5). Compare the account of Shadwell's genius in Dryden's *Mac Flecknoe*: 'This is that boasted Byas of thy mind, / By which one way, to dullness, 'tis inclin'd' (Kinsley 1958: lines 189–90).

178–9 and n. Insisting on the ingenious pointlessness of activities sponsored by Dulness: however *like* wit or reason they may seem, they are only cobwebs ungrounded in truth or utility. The note was initialled in 1751 as by Warburton.

181–2. A version of this couplet was used in Pope's youthful satire on Settle, 'To the Author of a Poem, intitled, Successio' (lines 17–18), which anticipates several of the themes and persons later brought together in the *Dunciad*. ***slugs:*** bullets. ***cut:*** 'Cut' in this sense is an epic word used of divinities or noble birds (Sherbo 1970: 505). In the satire on Settle Pope had simply used 'move'.

183–4. Spence records that this couplet originated in the epic which Pope had written in his teens but later destroyed (*OAC*: I, 16–19). A version occurs in 'To the Author of a Poem, intitled, Successio' (line 4), and another was introduced into his revision of Wycherley's 'A Panegyrick on Dulness' (Vander Meulen 1991: 5).

186. Elasticity: At this time used primarily of the capacity of gases to expand, the word makes an ironic pairing with 'Emptiness' in the previous line.

Some Daemon stole my pen (forgive th' offence)
And once betray'd me into common sense:
Else all my Prose and Verse were much the same;
This, prose on stilts; that, poetry fall'n lame.
Did on the stage my Fops appear confin'd?
My Life gave ampler lessons to mankind.
Did the dead Letter unsuccessful prove?
The brisk Example never fail'd to move.
Yet sure had Heav'n decreed to save the State,
Heav'n had decreed these works a longer date.
Could Troy be sav'd by any single hand,
This grey-goose weapon must have made her stand.
What can I now? my Fletcher cast aside,
Take up the Bible, once my better guide?

195–7.] 'Me si coelicolae voluissent ducere vitam, / Has mihi servassent sedes.' Virg. Aen. ii. 'Si Pergama dextra / Defendi possent, etiam hac defensa fuissent.' Virg. ibid.

199. My Fletcher] A familiar manner of speaking, used by modern Critics, of a favourite author. Bays might as justly speak thus of Fletcher, as a French Wit did of Tully, seeing his works in a library, 'Ah! mon cher Ciceron! je le connois bien; c'est le même que Marc Tulle.' But he had a better title to call Fletcher *his own*, having made so free with him.

200.] When, according to his Father's intention, he had been a *Clergyman*, or (as he thinks himself) a *Bishop* of the Church of England. Hear his own words: 'At the time that the fate

---

187–8. Presumably in *The Careless Husband*, commended in *Imitations of Horace, Epistles* II.i.91–2. Sherbo compares Dryden's ironic commendation of Shadwell: 'But *Sh*— never deviates into sense' (Kinsley 1958: *Mac Flecknoe*, line 20; Sherbo 1970: 506).

191–4. Bays seeks to justify himself: although his art may sometimes have deviated into 'sense', his life has been a 'brisk Example' of dulness which has inspired others.

195–8 and n. The quotations cited underline the parallel between the empires of Troy and of Dulness. In lines 195–6 Bays echoes the despair of Aeneas's father Anchises at the fall of Troy: 'If the gods had wanted to extend my life, they would have preserved this town' (*Aeneid* II.641–2). He was proved wrong, since he survived his escape from Troy and his son set up a renewed Trojan culture in Italy. Bays will similarly be proved wrong in that the failure of his writings to attain lasting popularity will not mean the end of Dulness's empire. In lines 197–8 Bays's words allude to Aeneas's dream in which the dead Hector warns him that further effort is useless: 'If Troy could have been saved by any hand, it would have been saved by this one' (*Aeneid* II.291–2). Aeneas, however, protected by his goddess mother, *can* in a sense 'save' Troy by escaping to found Rome, and Bays's despair is shown to be unfounded when Dulness appears in person to establish her empire (line 257). Originally Pope had made the 'grey-goose weapon' (quill) Settle's: Settle was notorious for his spectacular version of the Troy story, often staged at Bartholomew Fair (Rogers 1985: 87–101).

199n. a French Wit: a stock figure for arrogant shallowness. ***Tully:*** The traditional name by which the Latin author Marcus Tullius Cicero (106–43 BC) was familiarly known. ***'Ah! mon cher Ciceron! ...':*** 'Oh! my dear Cicero! I know him well: he is the same person as Mark Tully.'

200n. The quotation strategically omits Cibber's admission of his insignificance relative to the great events around him.

Or tread the path by vent'rous Heroes trod,
This Box my Thunder, this right hand my God?
Or chair'd at White's amidst the Doctors sit,
Teach Oaths to Gamesters, and to Nobles Wit?
Or bidst thou rather Party to embrace?
(A friend to Party thou, and all her race;
'Tis the same rope at different ends they twist;
To Dulness Ridpath is as dear as Mist.)
Shall I, like Curtius, desp'rate in my zeal,

of King James, the Prince of Orange and Myself, were on the anvil, Providence thought fit to postpone mine, 'till theirs were determined: But had my father carried me a month sooner to the University, who knows but that purer fountain might have washed my Imperfections into a capacity of writing, instead of Plays and annual *Odes*, Sermons and *Pastoral Letters?*' Apology for his Life, chap. iii.

202.] 'Dextra mihi *Deus*, et telum *quod missile libro*.' Virgil of the Gods of Mezentius.

203.] 'These Doctors had a modest and fair Appearance, and, like true Masters of Arts, were habited in *black* and *white*; they were justly styled *subtiles* and *graves*, but not always *irrefragabiles*, being sometimes examined, laid open, and split.' SCRIBL.

This learned Critic is to be understood allegorically: The *Doctors* in this place mean no more than *false Dice*, a Cant phrase used amongst Gamesters. So the meaning of these four sonorous Lines is only this, 'Shall I play fair, or foul?'

208.] George Ridpath, author of a Whig paper, called the Flying post; Nathanael Mist, of a famous Tory Journal.

---

202 and n. Bays considers turning to gambling: the dice are shaken in the 'Box', producing an ironic echo of Jupiter's thunder. Bays is also likened to Virgil's Mezentius, who put his trust not in the gods but in his right hand and spear (*Aeneid* X.773). For an intermediate source in George Granville's anonymously published *The British Enchanters* (1706), see Todd 1986.

203 and n. The note, initialled in 1751 as by Warburton, is silent about the most obvious allusion, Bays's blasphemous likening of himself to the child Jesus: 'they found him in the temple, sitting in the midst of the doctors, both hearing them, and asking them questions' (Luke 2:46). ***White's:*** A gambling club, of which Cibber was a member. ***Doctors:*** academics, or, more specifically, theological authorities; but also, colloquially, loaded dice. The epithets '*subtiles*', '*graves*' and '*irrefragabiles*' could be applied in different senses to either: academics could be praised as subtle, weighty and impossible to fault; whereas the dice could be condemned as devious, loaded and *not* unbreakable (since they would be split to expose the fraud).

205. Party: factional politics.

208 and n. The declaration that the Whig George Ridpath (*d.* 1726) and the Tory Nathaniel Mist (*d.* 1737) are equally pleasing to Dulness seeks to imply a lofty disdain for *all* party writing (for Ridpath, see *The Flying Post from Paris and Amsterdam*; for Mist, *The Weekly Journal: or, Saturday's Post*; Black 1987b). The *Dunciad*s present their satire not as factional agitation but as part of a universal appeal to traditional pieties.

209–12 and 211n. In his despair over the limited success of his writings, Bays wonders whether to stay loyal to the Whigs (thus sacrificing himself like Marcus Curtius, the legendary

O'er head and ears plunge for the Commonweal?
Or rob Rome's ancient geese of all their glories,
And cackling save the Monarchy of Tories?
Hold — to the Minister I more incline;
To serve his cause, O Queen! is serving thine.

211.] Relates to the well-known story of the geese that saved the Capitol; of which Virgil, Aen. viii: 'Atque hic auratis volitans argenteus anser / Porticibus, Gallos in limine adesse canebat.' A passage I have always suspected. Who sees not the antithesis of *auratis* and *argenteus* to be unworthy the Virgilian majesty? And what absurdity to say a goose *sings? canebat.* Virgil gives a contrary character of the voice of this silly bird, in Ecl. ix: 'argutos *interstrepere* anser olores.' Read it, therefore, *adesse strepebat.* And why *auratis porticibus*? does not the very verse preceding this inform us, 'Romuleoque recens horrebat regia culmo.' Is this *thatch* in one line, and *gold* in another, consistent? I scruple not (*repugnantibus omnibus manuscriptis*) to correct it *auritis*. Horace uses the same epithet in the same sense: '*Auritas* fidibus canoris / Ducere quercus.' And to say that *walls have ears* is common even to a proverb. SCRIBL.

212.] Not out of any preference or affection to the Tories. For what Hobbes so ingenuously confesses of himself, is true of all Party-writers whatsoever: 'That he defends the supreme powers, as the *Geese* by their *cackling* defended the Romans, who held the Capitol; for they favoured them no more than the Gauls their Enemies, but were as ready to have defended the Gauls if they had been *possessed of the Capitol*.' Epist. Dedic. to the Leviathan.

Roman soldier who threw himself into a hole in the Forum when an oracle said that it would close only if Rome's greatest strength was thrown into it), or to capitalise on his inside knowledge of the Whig establishment by selling himself to the Tories. 'Commonweal' in line 210 is contrasted with 'Monarchy' in 212, invoking the divisions of the Civil War as underlying contemporary party politics. ***the well-known story of the geese:*** Their cackling was supposed to have wakened the Romans and thus foiled a night-time attack by the Gauls. ***Atque hic auratis:*** Scriblerus emends Virgil's account of the story, as prophetically represented on the shield of Aeneas (*Aeneid* VIII.655–6). The lines could be literally translated 'And here in a golden portico a silver goose fluttering sang that the Gauls were on the threshold'. Scriblerus seems to find the contrast of gold and silver too gaudy, and cites *Eclogues* IX.36 ('to cackle, a goose among tuneful swans') to show that Virgil did not think geese could sing. He therefore alters 'sang' to 'cackled'. Forgetting that this is a description of a representation in precious metal, and apparently ignorant that Romulus's thatched house was kept up as a monument in later times, he also objects to the supposed contradiction between 'golden portico' and the rough thatch of the previous line ('and the palace of Romulus bristled, newly thatched'): he therefore, against all the manuscript evidence ('*repugnantibus omnibus manuscriptis*'), alters 'a golden portico' to 'a portico with keen hearing'. He supports the attribution of hearing to inanimate objects from Horace (who ascribed to Orpheus, the musician proverbial for bringing inanimate things to life, the power 'to lead the listening oaks with the lyre of his melody': *Odes* I.xii.11–12) and from the English proverb that walls have ears.

212n. The note, initialled in 1751 as by Warburton, uses an extremely free paraphrase from Hobbes's dedication to *Leviathan* to imply that party-writers would write for whichever party was in power (Oakeshott 1946).

213–14. The 'Minister' is Walpole, and 'Queen' in this connection would tend to suggest Queen Caroline (for their working relationship, see Sedgwick 1931: I, 39, 68–9, 151–3, 253–5).

And see! thy very Gazetteers give o'er,
Ev'n Ralph repents, and Henly writes no more.
What then remains? Ourself. Still, still remain
Cibberian forehead, and Cibberian brain.
This brazen Brightness, to the 'Squire so dear;
This polish'd Hardness, that reflects the Peer;
This arch Absurd, that wit and fool delights;

215.] A band of ministerial writers, hired at the price mentioned in the note on book ii. ver. 314. who on the very day their Patron quitted his post, laid down their paper, and declared they would never more meddle in Politics.

218. Cibberian forehead] So indeed all the MSS. read; but I make no scruple to pronounce them all wrong, the Laureate being elsewhere celebrated by our Poet for his great *Modesty* — *modest Cibber* — Read, therefore, at my peril, *Cerberian forehead*. This is perfectly classical, and, what is more, *Homerical*; the *Dog* was the ancient, as the *Bitch* is the modern, symbol of Impudence: (*Κυνὸς ὄμματ' ἔχων*, says Achilles to Agamemnon) which, when in a superlative degree, may well be denominated from *Cerberus*, the *Dog with three heads*. — But as to the latter part of this verse, *Cibberian brain*, that is certainly the genuine reading. BENTL.

215–16 and n. These lines, new in 1743, refer to recent shifts in political journalism. *The Daily Gazetteer* had been from 1735 Walpole's principal organ of propaganda: on his resignation in 1742 it had adopted a less partisan approach (Harris 1987: 124–9). Ralph, who denied that he had ever written for the *Gazetteer* as such (although he had written for its predecessor, the *Daily Courant*) had by 1739 committed himself to anti-ministerial journalism: he took on the previously politically muted *Universal Spectator* and increased its anti-ministerial commitment; he contributed to the opposition *Craftsman*; and he worked with the dramatist and future novelist Henry Fielding (1707–54) on the anti-ministerial *Champion*, of which he took over the direction in 1741 (Shipley 1963: 306–41; Harris 1987: 100). Pope professed to believe that Ralph had been writing for both sides at once (*Corr.*: IV, 255). John Henley (1692–1756), called 'Orator Henley', was a celebrated preacher, eccentric, and attacker of Pope in the government interest, who had ceased publication of the pro-ministerial *Hyp Doctor* in 1741 (Mack 1969: 123–4; Midgley 1973: 217).

217. Echoing Seneca's *Medea* and the play on the same theme by Pierre Corneille (1606–84): although the nurse warns Medea that her allies, her husband and her wealth are all gone, she replies, 'Medea superest' ('There is still Medea') (*Medea* V.166; Warton 1797: V, 110).

218n. Initialled in 1751 as by Warburton. **modest Cibber:** In *Imitations of Horace, Epistles* I.i.6. **Cerberian:** Alluding to Cerberus, the three-headed dog who guarded the Underworld in classical mythology. 'Bentley' insists that the Laureate is too modest to use his own name to characterise his phenomenal impudence ('forehead'), but that he could do it justice by ascribing to himself 'the impudent stare of a dog' (as Achilles insults Agamemnon in the *Iliad*) three times over (I.225). But while his impudence is vast, his brain is not; so it cannot be immodest in him to characterise *that* as 'Cibberian'.

219–24. All levels of society find something to admire in Bays: unsophisticated country gentlemen like his impudent liveliness; aristocrats find in him a reflection of their own sophisticated pragmatism; wits and fools enjoy his supreme absurdity. His character is thus a 'Mess' (stew) combining the debauchery of the lowest (Hockley-in-the-Hole, north of the City, site for such spectacles as bear-baiting) and the highest (White's, an exclusive club). This promiscuous

This Mess, toss'd up of Hockley-hole and White's;
Where Dukes and Butchers join to wreathe my crown,
At once the Bear and Fiddle of the town.
  O born in sin, and forth in folly brought!
Works damn'd, or to be damn'd! (your father's fault)
Go, purify'd by flames ascend the sky,
My better and more christian progeny!
Unstain'd, untouch'd, and yet in maiden sheets;
While all your smutty sisters walk the streets.
Ye shall not beg, like gratis-given Bland,
Sent with a Pass, and vagrant thro' the land;

225.] This is a tender and passionate Apostrophe to his own works, which he is going to sacrifice, agreeable to the nature of man in great affliction; and reflecting like a parent on the many miserable fates to which they would otherwise be subject.

228.] 'It may be observable, that my muse and my spouse were equally prolific; that the one was seldom the mother of a Child, but in the same year the other made me the father of a Play. I think we had a dozen of each sort between us; of both which kinds some *died* in their *Infancy*,' *etc.* Life of C.C. p. 217. 8vo edit.

229.] 'Felix Priamëia virgo! / Jussa mori: quae sortitus non pertulit ullos, / Nec victoris heri tetigit captiva cubile! / Nos, patria incensa, diversa per aequora vectae', *etc.* Virg. Aen. iii.

231–2.] It was a practice so to give the Daily Gazetteer and ministerial pamphlets (in which this B. was a writer) and to send them *Post-free* to all the Towns in the kingdom.

---

mingling of 'Dukes and Butchers' (line 223) is presented as a breach of social order. ***the Bear and Fiddle:*** Bear-baiting was customarily preceded by music on the fiddle; but 'fiddle' could also denote the butt of a joke (see Cibber 1740: 15).

225–7. Playing on original sin, inherited from Adam as father of mankind, and the 'damning' of a play by a hostile audience. The fire in which he proposes to burn his literary offspring evokes the fires of Purgatory, enabling them to 'ascend the sky' despite their sins (Sherbo 1970: 506).

228–30 and 228, 229nn.: Bays contrasts his unsold works, still in unbound sheets as they came from the press, with copies which have been exposed for sale; but 'more christian' also suggests a contrast between the children of his brain and his actual children. Theophilus Cibber had made himself notorious in 1738 for bullying his wife into adultery, living at her lover's expense, and subsequently suing him for adultery (Nash 1977: 108–49; Koon 1986: 145–6). The 'smutty sisters' who 'walk the street' further evoke the unconventional behaviour of his daughter, the cross-dressing actress Charlotte Charke (Charke 1755). In the lines from the *Aeneid* (III.321, 323–5; see 229*n.*), Andromache, widow of Hector, compares her fate as exile and slave to that of her virgin sister-in-law Polyxena, who was killed before leaving Troy ('Happy virgin daughter of Priam! She was sentenced to death: she did not suffer any drawing of lots, nor did she endure as a captive the bed of her victorious master. But as for me, after my home was burnt, I was carried over many seas'). Andromache is paralleled with the shop-soiled copies, Polyxena with the unsold sheets which Bays intends to sacrifice.

231–2 and n. Bays disdains to have his works circulated free of charge like such government newssheets as *The Daily Courant*, to which Henry Bland (*d.* 1746), schoolfriend of Walpole, headmaster of Eton, churchman and propagandist, was a contributor. He is imaged

Not sail, with Ward, to Ape-and-monkey climes,
Where vile Mundungus trucks for viler rhymes;
Not sulphur-tipt, emblaze an Ale-house fire;
Not wrap up Oranges, to pelt your sire!
O! pass more innocent, in infant state,
To the mild Limbo of our Father Tate:
Or peaceably forgot, at once be blest
In Shadwell's bosom with eternal Rest!

233.] 'Edward Ward, a very voluminous Poet in Hudibrastic verse, but best known by the London Spy, in prose. He has of late years kept a public house in the City, (but in a genteel way) and with his wit, humour, and good liquor (ale) afforded his guests a pleasurable entertainment, especially those of the high-church party.' JACOB, Lives of Poets, vol. ii. p. 225. Great numbers of his works were yearly sold into the Plantations. — Ward, in a book called Apollo's Maggot, declared this account to be a great falsity, protesting that his public house was not in the *City*, but in *Moorfields*.

238 & 240. Tate — Shadwell] Two of his predecessors in the Laurel.

---

as a beggar licensed to leave his parish to solicit alms. Pope satirises his style in *Epilogue to the Satires* (I.73–6).

233–4 and n. Edward Ward (1667–1731), high-church Tory tavern-keeper, antagonist of the Whigs, versifier, and writer of *The London Spy* (a periodical as bizarre in the scatological extremism of its partisan, xenophobic, elitist and misogynistic nightmare vision of London life as in its deliberate revelling in 'low' colloquialisms and preposterously accumulated similes), is characterised as a writer appealing to the uncultured taste of the 'Plantations' ('colonies': Ward had also published travel writing featuring a trip to Jamaica), where his works might be traded for 'Mundungus' (low-quality tobacco). For Ward's career, see Hyland 1993: xi–xxvii; for the New England theologian Cotton Mather's denunciation of Ward's works, see Mather 1726: 43. In *Peri Bathous* Ward is apparently classed with the '*Frogs*' who 'live generally in the bottom of a ditch, and make a great noise whenever they thrust their heads above water', and is associated with a tradition of verse by men in low occupations, while *The London Spy* is taken as example of 'the PERT Style' of 'the low in wit' (*PW*: II, 197, 203, 220). The present lines recall Oldham's warning that even poetry which enjoys a brief vogue may soon 'truck for pots of Ale next *Stourbridg*-Fair', and his query 'Then who'l not laugh to see th'immortal Name / To vile *Mundungus* made a Martyr Flame?' (Brooks & Selden 1987: 'A Satyr ... Dissuading the Author from the Study of Poetry', lines 107–9). When a version of this note first appeared in 1729 (I.200), Ward was outraged (Pope had added the parenthetic 'ale' to Jacob's account, implying a low-class establishment) (Ward 1729: 30–31; Guerinot 1969: 179; McLaverty 1985: 30; Colomb 1992: 167–73). Ward is also presented as keen to dissociate himself from the City: Moorfields was in fact just outside, but was, socially, nothing to boast about.

235–6. Bays wants to prevent the unsold sheets from being used as firelighters, or as wrapping for oranges which theatre-goers could buy to pelt him ('your sire').

237–40 and 238–40n. Bays will instead burn the sheets in their purity ('infant state', alluding to the belief that infants who died in innocence went to a Limbo between Heaven and Hell). The good men of pre-Christian Israel were imaged as resting in the bosom of Abraham (Luke 16:22; Sherbo 1970: 506). Both states fall short of the fullness of salvation.

Soon to that mass of Nonsense to return,
Where things destroy'd are swept to things unborn.
  With that, a Tear (portentous sign of Grace!)
Stole from the Master of the sev'nfold Face:
And thrice he lifted high the Birth-day brand,
And thrice he dropt it from his quiv'ring hand;
Then lights the structure, with averted eyes:
The rowling smokes involve the sacrifice.
The op'ning clouds disclose each work by turns,
Now flames the Cid, and now Perolla burns;
Great Caesar roars, and hisses in the fires;
King John in silence modestly expires:

243.] It is to be observed that our Poet hath made his Hero, in imitation of Virgil's, obnoxious to the tender Passions. He was indeed so given to weeping, that he tells us, when Goodman the player swore, if he did not *make a good actor, he'd be damn'd*; 'the surprise of being commended by one who had been himself so eminent on the stage, and in so *positive a manner*, was more than he could support. In a word (says he) it almost took away my breath and (laugh if you please) fairly drew tears from my eyes.' P. 149. of his Life, octavo.

245.] Ovid of Althaea on a like occasion, burning her offspring: 'Tum conata quater flammis imponere torrem, / Coepta quater tenuit.'

250.] 'Jam Deïphobi dedit ampla ruinam / Vulcano superante domus; jam proximus ardet / Ucalegon.'

In the first notes on the Dunciad it was said, that this Author was particularly excellent at Tragedy. 'This (says he) is as unjust as to say I could not dance on a Rope.' But certain it is that he had attempted to dance on this Rope, and fell most shamefully, having produced no less than four Tragedies (the names of which the Poet preserves in these few lines) the three first of them were fairly printed, acted, and damned; the fourth suppressed, in fear of the like treatment.

241–2. Compare Rochester's 'And to that mass of matter shall be swept / Where things destroy'd with things unborn are kept' (Vieth 1968: 'A Translation from Seneca's *Troades*', lines 9–10; Sitter 1971: 20).

243n. Initialled in 1751 as by Warburton. ***obnoxious:*** liable. ***Goodman:*** Cardell Goodman (1649?–99), distinguished actor.

244. sev'nfold Face: Parodying Ovid's allusion to the owner of a sevenfold shield (*Metamorphoses* XIII.1–2 (as alluded to at II.384); for available translations and parodies, see Sambrook 1967). The reminder of the artificiality of an actor's expressions undercuts the solemn emotion.

245. Ovid tells how Althaea was warned that her son Meleager would die when a particular log of wood was burnt. Having saved it carefully to protect him, she finally brought herself to burn it after he had killed her brothers ('then she tried four times to throw the log into the fire, and four times she stopped short': *Metamorphoses* VIII.462–3).

248. involve: roll around, engulf.

250 and n. The quotation from Virgil (*Aeneid* II.310–12) describes palaces burning during the sack of Troy ('now, in the rising flames, the vast home of Deiphobus collapses; now Ucalegon's house next door is on fire'). The note refers to the apparatus of 1729 (I.240), which

No merit now the dear Nonjuror claims,
Moliere's old stubble in a moment flames.
Tears gush'd again, as from pale Priam's eyes
When the last blaze sent Ilion to the skies.

253–4.] A Comedy threshed out of Moliere's Tartuffe, and so much the Translator's favourite, that he assures us all our author's dislike to it could only arise from *disaffection to the Government*: 'Qui meprise Cotin, n'estime point son Roi, / Et n'a, selon Cotin, ni Dieu, ni foi, ni loi.' Boil. He assures us, that 'when he had the honour to kiss his Majesty's hand upon presenting his dedication of it, he was graciously pleased, out of his Royal bounty, to order him two hundred pounds for it. And this he doubts not *grieved* Mr. P.'

256.] See Virgil, Aen. ii. where I would advise the reader to peruse the story of Troy's destruction, rather than in Wynkyn. But I caution him alike in both to beware of a most grievous error, that of thinking it was brought about by I know not what *Trojan Horse*; there never having been any such thing. For, first, it was not *Trojan*, being made by the *Greeks*; and, secondly, it was not a *horse*, but a *mare*. This is clear from many verses in Virgil:

---

had described Cibber as 'particularly admirable in Tragedy', where 'admirable' (etymologically, 'giving cause for wonder') can only be taken ironically, since Cibber was successful neither in the acting nor in the writing of tragedy. The tragedies burned by Bays are *Ximena: or, The Heroick Daughter* (1719: from *Le Cid* by Pierre Corneille (1616–84)), *Perolla and Izadora* (1706), *Caesar in Egypt* (1725) and *Papal Tyranny in the Reign of King John* (an adaptation of Shakespeare's *King John*, finally produced only in 1745 because of its relevance as propaganda in the face of Jacobite invasion, having been cancelled (hence its 'silence') before it could reach the stage in 1722 (Koon 1986: 105, 166–7)).

253–4 and n. Brooks-Davies suggests an allusion to Virgil's recommendation of stubble-burning, suggesting an ironic parallel between the *Georgics*' theme of rebirth and Cibber's revamping of classic plays (*Georgics* I.84–93; Brooks-Davies 1985: 21). The note quotes Boileau: 'Anyone who despises Cotin doesn't respect his King, and, if Cotin is to be believed, is godless, faithless and lawless' (Vercruysse 1969: *Satires* IX.304–6). Cibber had insinuated in his *Letter* that Pope's anger at the anti-Catholic satire in his *The Nonjuror* was evidence of his disloyalty (Cibber 1742: 24).

255. Priam: Last king of Troy.

256n. See Virgil: Implying that it would be in poor taste to prefer a medieval version. The remark is prompted by Pope's discomfiture at Theobald's elucidation of an expression in Shakespeare (Alexander 1951: *Troilus and Cressida*, V.v.14). In a note in 1729 Pope protested, '*Tibbald* quotes a rare passage from him in *Mist's Journal* of *March* 16, 1728, concerning a *straunge and mervayllouse beaste called Sagittarye*, which he would have *Shakespear* to mean rather than *Teucer*, the Archer celebrated by *Homer*' (I.129). Theobald, whose interpretation is followed by modern editors, set Shakespeare in the context of a culture in which medieval romance was still a presence. ***not* Trojan:** The horse was built by the Greeks, who hid inside it and deceived the Trojans into taking it into the city. During the night they sacked the city. ***a* mare:** Scriblerus takes Virgil's metaphors of pregnancy so literally that he feels it necessary to attribute a sex to a piece of woodwork. First he quotes 'and they fill its *womb* with armed men' (*Aeneid* II.20) and 'the Greeks shut in its *womb*' (II.258), asking rhetorically whether the male can be said 'Utero gerere' ('to bear in its womb'). He then quotes 'when its *womb* was struck, the cavity resounded' (II.52–3), and 'and four times weapons clanged in its

Rowz'd by the light, old Dulness heav'd the head;
Then snatch'd a sheet of Thulè from her bed,
Sudden she flies, and whelms it o'er the pyre;
Down sink the flames, and with a hiss expire.
Her ample presence fills up all the place;
A veil of fogs dilates her awful face:
Great in her charms! as when on Shrieves and May'rs
She looks, and breathes herself into their airs.
She bids him wait her to her sacred Dome:
Well pleas'd he enter'd, and confess'd his home.

'*Uterum*que armato milite complent'; 'Inclusos *utero* Danaos'. Can a horse be said *Utero gerere?* Again, '*Utero*que recusso, / Insonuere cavae'; 'Atque *utero* sonitum quater arma dedere.' Nay, is it not expressly said, 'Scandit fatalis machina muros / *Foeta* armis'. How is it possible the word *foeta* can agree with a *horse?* And indeed can it be conceived that the chaste and virgin Goddess *Pallas* would employ herself in forming and fashioning the Male of that species? But this shall be proved to a demonstration in our Virgil restored. SCRIBL.

258. Thulè] An unfinished poem of that name, of which one sheet was printed many years ago, by Amb. Philips, a northern author. It is an usual method of putting out a fire, to cast wet sheets upon it. Some critics have been of opinion that this sheet was of the nature of the Asbestos, which cannot be consumed by fire: But I rather think it an allegorical allusion to the coldness and heaviness of the writing.

263–4.] 'Alma parens confessa Deam; qualisque videri / Coelicolis, et quanta solet'. Virg. Aen. ii. 'Et laetos oculis afflavit honores.' Id. Aen. i.

265.] Where he no sooner enters, but he reconnoitres the place of his original; as Plato says the spirits shall, at their entrance into the celestial regions.

---

womb' (II.243). He also cites 'the fatal contrivance, pregnant with weapons, mounted the walls' (II.237–8), insisting that 'foeta' ('pregnant') can only be used of a mare. Finally, assuming that the gods of Olympus share his prim notions of femininity, he notes that the horse was built 'by the divine art of Pallas' (II.15), and that it would have been unthinkable for the virgin goddess to have designed a male figure. ***our Virgil restored:*** Cp. Theobald's *Shakespeare Restored.*

258n. a northern author: Philips came from Shropshire, but the main point is to insinuate his imaginative frigidity, aptly associated with *Thulè*, whose heroine is banished to Iceland. He had published the fragment in his periodical *The Free-thinker*, describing it as 'not Half finished' (*The Free-thinker* 1722–3: I, 58–64).

262. dilates: magnifies (cp. line 80).

263–4 and n. Reasserting the link between City culture and Dulness, just at the point where she is about to 'adopt' Cibber. 'Airs' may suggest 'give oneself airs'. The quotations from Virgil underline the allusion of the Cibber–Dulness pair to Aeneas and his divine mother: 'my kind parent, revealing her divinity, in form and stature just as she appears to the gods' (*Aeneid* II.591–2); 'and she breathed a joyful dignity into his eyes' (I.591). Pope imitates Dryden's rendering of the former passage: 'Great in her Charms, as when on Gods above / She looks, and breaths her self into their Love' (Kinsley 1958: *Aeneid* II.804–5).

265 and n. sacred Dome: The 'Cell' described at I.29–84. 'Reconnoitre' is used as in French, i.e. 'to recognise' rather than 'to explore'.

So Spirits ending their terrestrial race,
Ascend, and recognize their Native Place.
This the Great Mother dearer held than all
The clubs of Quidnuncs, or her own Guild-hall:
Here stood her Opium, here she nurs'd her Owls,
And here she plann'd th' Imperial seat of Fools.
  Here to her Chosen all her works she shews;
Prose swell'd to verse, verse loit'ring into prose:
How random thoughts now meaning chance to find,

269.] 'Urbs antiqua fuit ... / Quam Juno fertur terris magis omnibus unam / Posthabita coluisse Samo: hic illius arma, / Hic currus fuit: hic regnum Dea gentibus esse / (Si qua fata sinant) jam tum tenditque fovetque.' Virg. Aen. i.

Great Mother] *Magna mater*, here applied to *Dulness*. The *Quidnuncs*, a name given to the ancient members of certain political clubs, who were constantly enquiring *quid nunc?* what news?

267–8. Alluding to the Neoplatonic doctrine that the soul has its origin in heaven and lives in temporary exile in the world, a particularly apt reference in earlier versions when Theobald had been the hero, since he had published a translation from Plato (*TE*: V, 89–90; Kropf 1973: 600). For Miltonic echoes, see Sherbo 1970: 507.

269 and n. Great Mother: 'Magna mater' was the name given to the Asian mother-goddess Cybele on the introduction of her cult to Rome. For detailed arguments for her relation to Dulness's other models among female divinities, see Faulkner & Blair 1980; Brooks-Davies 1985: 15–16. The allusion is specifically to a passage in Virgil's *Aeneid* where Rome is compared to the *magna mater* (*Aeneid* VI.784–7; and see below, III.131). ***Urbs antiqua:*** Virgil describes how Juno (Hera), mother of the gods, cherished ambitions for Carthage, the great adversary of Rome, in opposition to the will of her husband Jupiter (Zeus): 'There was an ancient city ... which it is said Juno loved uniquely, more than all lands, so that even Samos took the second place: here were her weapons, here her chariot: here the Goddess now already tended and nurtured it (if any fate would allow) to be an empire over the peoples' (*Aeneid* I.12–18). Dulness is thus likened to Juno in her opposition to the divine will.

270 and 269n. Quidnuncs: 'Quid nunc?' means 'what now?', applied to those obsessed with the trivia of current affairs (see *Spectator* 625: Bond 1965: V, 136–7; *TE*: VI, 438–9). ***Guild-hall:*** Ceremonial and administrative centre of the City of London.

271. Opium: Used as a painkiller, or to allay the symptoms of hunger, opium is often associated with needy and dissolute writers. ***Owls:*** Ironically, the owl was the emblem of Athena (Minerva), goddess of wisdom, and hence of the city of Athens, but it is also associated with night and its goddesses; and in the *Dunciad*, owls are appropriated to Dulness as emblems of pompous and boring stupidity (Peterson 1975: 443). In 1728 an owl had appeared as frontispiece (reproduced in Vander Meulen 1991, and see pp. 36–7 for a possible allusion to a work on owls published by Curll; see also Mengel in Mack & Winn 1980: 751–3 and Mackenzie 1976). In Boileau's *Le lutrin*, the personification of Night is attended by an owl, characterised as a bird of ill omen, who aids in the prosecution of her schemes (Vercruysse 1969: *Le lutrin*, III.11–84). Brooks-Davies points out that the owl figures in the myth of the fertility goddess Ceres, of whom Dulness is in some respects a parody (Brooks-Davies 1985: 12–13).

Now leave all memory of sense behind:
How Prologues into Prefaces decay,
And these to Notes are fritter'd quite away:
How Index-learning turns no student pale,
Yet holds the eel of science by the tail:
How, with less reading than makes felons scape,
Less human genius than God gives an ape,
Small thanks to France, and none to Rome or Greece,
A past, vamp'd, future, old, reviv'd, new piece,
'Twixt Plautus, Fletcher, Shakespear, and Corneille,
Can make a Cibber, Tibbald, or Ozell.

286. Tibbald,] Lewis Tibbald (as pronounced) or Theobald (as written) was bred an Attorney, and son to an Attorney (says Mr. Jacob) of Sittenburn in Kent. He was Author of some forgotten Plays, Translations, and other pieces. He was concerned in a paper called the Censor, and a Translation of Ovid. 'There is a notorious Idiot, one hight Whachum, who, from an under-spur-leather to the Law, is become an under-strapper to the Play-house, who hath lately burlesqued the Metamorphoses of Ovid by a vile Translation, *etc.* This fellow is concerned in an impertinent paper called the Censor.' DENNIS Rem. on Pope's Hom. p. 9, 10.

Ibid. Ozell.] 'Mr. John Ozell (if we credit Mr. Jacob) did go to school in Leicestershire, where *somebody* left him *something* to live on, when he shall retire from business. He was designed to be sent to Cambridge, in order for priesthood; but he chose rather to be placed

---

279–80. Implying that indexes (much used by scholars like Bentley to facilitate the collation of scattered references, and a fashionable novelty in the book trade at this time) are a substitute for thorough reading. Learning is imaged for students who rely on such aids as slippery; that they can only grasp it by the tail (the index appears at the end) suggests a back-to-front approach, in marked contrast with traditionalists' solid if complacent command of the classical canon.

281. A criminal could attempt to evade sentence by demonstrating that he could read: usually the test passage was the first verse of Psalm 51 in Latin. The practice originated in the fact that medieval clergy were outside the jurisdiction of the secular courts.

283. Condemning writing which fails to imitate the classics of Greece and Rome, and which is only superficially conversant with the French critical tradition so important in English neoclassicism.

284. vamp'd: patched to look new, like a shoe with a new vamp (front panel) fitted.

285. Four dramatists reworked for the eighteenth-century stage. Titus Maccius Plautus (*c.*250–184 BC) was a Roman writer of comedy.

286 and n. Ozell: John Ozell (*d.* 1743), translator from French, Spanish and Italian. Pope had written an early epigram against him, and in *Peri Bathous* placed initials which could be his under the '*Porpoises*' (*TE*: VI, 37–8; *PW*: II, 197). ***Lewis Tibbald (as pronounced):*** This seems to have been a deliberately insulting mispronunciation, which Pope applied to his travesty of Theobald throughout the earlier *Dunciads* (*TE*: V, 75; Seary 1990: 87). ***Sittenburn:*** Sittingbourne. ***a Translation of Ovid:*** Theobald contributed, along with Pope, to a version 'By Several Hands' (Sewell 1717). ***a notorious Idiot:*** Dennis was angry because Theobald had praised Pope's *Iliad* (Theobald 1714: II, no. 33). ***hight:*** called. ***under-spur-leather:*** underling. ***under-strapper:*** underling. ***He was designed to be sent to Cambridge:*** Jacobs's account (which Pope slightly alters) might suggest to one of Pope's

The Goddess then, o'er his anointed head,
With mystic words, the sacred Opium shed.
And lo! her bird, (a monster of a fowl,

in an *office* of *accounts*, in the City, being qualified for the same by his skill in *arithmetic*, and writing the necessary *hands*. He has obliged the world with many translations of French Plays.' JACOB, Lives of *Dram. Poets*, p. 198.

Mr. Jacob's character of Mr. Ozell seems vastly short of his merits, and he ought to have further justice done him, having since fully confuted all Sarcasms on his learning and genius, by an advertisement of Sept. 20, 1729. in a paper called the Weekly Medley, *etc.* 'As to my *learning*, every body knows that the *whole bench of Bishops*, not long ago, were pleased to give me a *purse of guineas*, for discovering the erroneous translations of the Common-prayer in Portuguese, Spanish, French, Italian, *etc.* As for my *genius*, let Mr. Cleland shew better verses in all Pope's works, than Ozell's version of Boileau's Lutrin, which the late Lord Halifax was so pleased with, that he complimented him with leave to dedicate it to him, *etc. etc.* Let him shew better and truer Poetry in the Rape of the Lock, than in Ozell's Rape of the Bucket (*la Secchia rapita.*) And Mr. Toland and Mr. Gildon publicly declared Ozell's translation of Homer *to be*, as it was *prior*, so likewise *superior* to Pope's. — Surely, surely, every man is free to deserve well of his country! JOHN OZELL.

We cannot but subscribe to such reverend testimonies, as those of the *Bench of Bishops*, Mr. *Toland*, and Mr. *Gildon*.

---

outlook both the perversity of preferring bookkeeping to university and the impropriety of a clerk's indulging in literature (though Ozell thus avoided what Pope repeatedly identifies as the prime error of his victims, namely making themselves financially dependent on writing to order). ***discovering the erroneous translations of the Common-prayer:*** In *Common-Prayer not Common Sense* (Ozell 1722). ***Mr. Cleland:*** Ostensible author of 'A Letter to the Publisher'. ***Ozell's version of Boileau's Lutrin:*** *Le Lutrin* ('The Lectern') is a mock-epic poem about a trivial ecclesiastical disagreement (Ozell 1708). Pope composed an 'Epigram' against the translation. ***the late Lord Halifax:*** Charles Montagu (1661–1715), Earl of Halifax, financier, statesman, poet and would-be literary patron (for Pope's scepticism about his literary judgement, see *OAC*: I, 87–8). ***Ozell's Rape of the Bucket:*** A translation of *La secchia rapita* by Alessandro Tassoni (1565–1635) (Ozell 1710). ***Mr. Toland:*** John Toland (1670–1722), a Whig of republican sympathies and an influential editor of classic texts of Whig thought, was regarded by the orthodox as a scandalous freethinker on account of his deist views (Pocock 1985: 232–40). ***such reverend testimonies:*** Insinuating the incongruity of setting Toland's authority on a par with that of the bishops.

287–8. Echoing the anointings of David and of Saul in Cowley's *Davideis*: both passages use the rhyme 'shed/head' (Waller 1905: 245, 375).

287–91 and 290n. Focusing on Dulness's role in a blasphemous parody of the Christian Trinity (Williams 1955: 141–56). Pope's unholy trinity comprises Dulness (Father), Cibber (Son) and a bird with a face like Heidegger (Holy Spirit), whose visible presence alludes both to the baptism of Jesus and to the anointing of a king, the sacrament of his reception of the gifts of the Holy Spirit (Mark 1:10–11; Brooks-Davies 1985: 99; Rogers 1985: 135). John James Heidegger (1659?–1748), a Swiss immigrant and leading theatrical entrepreneur of notorious ugliness, promoted opera and masquerade, focusing unease about such mixed-genre and implicitly un-British manifestations of commercialised leisure (Rogers 1985: 54–66, 105–9). He had also assisted behind the scenes with George II's coronation celebrations; in a British

Something betwixt a Heideggre and owl,)
Perch'd on his crown. 'All hail! and hail again,
My son! the promis'd land expects thy reign.
Know, Eusden thirsts no more for sack or praise;
He sleeps among the dull of ancient days;
Safe, where no Critics damn, no duns molest,
Where wretched Withers, Ward, and Gildon rest,
And high-born Howard, more majestic sire,

290. A Heideggre] A strange bird from Switzerland, and not (as some have supposed) the name of an eminent person who was a man of parts, and, as was said of Petronius, *Arbiter Elegantiarum.*

296. Withers,] 'George Withers was a great Pretender to Poetical Zeal, and abused the greatest Personages in power, which brought upon him frequent correction. The *Marshalsea* and *Newgate* were no strangers to him.' WINSTANLY, Lives of Poets.

Ibid. Gildon] Charles Gildon, a writer of criticisms and libels of the last age, bred at St. Omer's with the Jesuits; but renouncing popery, he published Blount's books against the divinity of Christ, the Oracles of Reason, *etc.* He signalized himself as a critic, having written some very bad plays; abused Mr. P. very scandalously in an anonymous pamphlet of the Life of Mr. Wycherley, printed by Curl; in another, called the New Rehearsal, printed in 1714; in a third, entituled the Complete Art of English Poetry, in two volumes; and others.

297. Howard,] Hon. Edward Howard, author of the British Princes, and a great number of wonderful pieces, celebrated by the late Earls of Dorset and Rochester, Duke of Buckingham, Mr. Waller, *etc.*

Library copy of an earlier version where his name had been given as 'H—' a contemporary reader has suggested 'Hanover' (p. 135; Vander Meulen 1991: 22). ***as some have supposed:*** In 1728 most names were indicated only by initials, and a Dublin edition had wrongly supplied the name of John Hungerford (*d.* 1729), lawyer and MP. The note makes a compliment to compensate for his accidental involvement in the *Dunciad.* ***Petronius:*** Petronius Arbiter (*d.* AD 65), satirist, author of the *Satyricon* and courtier to the Emperor Nero. In a pun on his name, he was called Nero's 'arbiter of taste'.

292. the promis'd land: Alluding to Moses' mission to lead the Israelites out of bondage, through forty years in the wilderness, into the land promised them by God (Exodus 3:7–8). For a possible Jacobite reading, see Brooks-Davies 1985: 6.

293. sack: White wine, allocated to the Laureate as part of his stipend. Eusden was notorious for hard drinking.

295. duns: debt-collectors. Boileau had made his deserving but unrewarded poet leave the city for a country life 'D'où jamais ni l'huissier ni le sergent n'approche' ('where neither the bailiff nor the constable ever comes') (Sherbo 1951; Vercruysse 1969: *Satire* I.26).

296 and n. wretched Withers: George Withers or Wither (1588–1667), a prolific satirical poet widely regarded as feeble and incompetent. In *Peri Bathous* Defoe is proposed as his 'poetical son' (*PW*: II, 203). ***The* Marshalsea *and* Newgate:** Prisons. ***bred:*** educated. ***Blount's books against the divinity of Christ:*** Charles Blount (1654–93) was notorious for his deist views (Blount & Gildon 1693; 'Lindamour' 1695). ***abused Mr. P.:*** In *A New Rehearsal* 1714; *Memoirs of the Life of William Wycherley* 1718; Gildon 1718.

297. high-born Howard: The Honourable Edward Howard (1624–*c.*1700), whose works,

With Fool of Quality compleats the quire.
Thou Cibber! thou, his Laurel shalt support,
Folly, my son, has still a Friend at Court.
Lift up your Gates, ye Princes, see him come!
Sound, sound ye Viols, be the Cat-call dumb!
Bring, bring the madding Bay, the drunken Vine;
The creeping, dirty, courtly Ivy join.
And thou! his Aid de camp, lead on my sons,
Light-arm'd with Points, Antitheses, and Puns.
Let Bawdry, Bilingsgate, my daughters dear,
Support his front, and Oaths bring up the rear:

'wonderful' for their ineptitude, were widely ridiculed (by, for example, Charles Sackville (1638?–1706), sixth Earl of Dorset; John Wilmot (1647–80), second Earl of Rochester; and John Sheffield, Duke of Buckingham; but the satire on Howard previously attributed to Edmund Waller (1606–87) is more probably by Samuel Butler (Drury 1893)). *Spectator* 43 cites Howard as evidence that 'when Dulness is lodged in a Person of a quick Animal Life, it generally exerts itself in Poetry' (Bond 1965: I, 184–5). He seems to be included alongside Eusden as one of the '*Ostridges*' in Pope's *Peri Bathous* (*PW*: II, 197).

298. Fool of Quality: Lord Hervey, formerly vice-chamberlain to the king's household, confidant of the queen and antagonist of Pope, had died on 5 August 1743. Previous versions had looked forward to this as a future event ("till ** grace the quire'; or, in the octavo edition of the four-book *Dunciad* published in two parts dated 1743 and 1742 respectively, "till H—y grace the quire' (Maslen & Lancaster 1991: Checklist, nos. 3080–81; *TE*: V, 291; Halsband 1973: 304–5)). Pope had also in 1741 introduced 'Lord. H.' into a revised text of *Peri Bathous*, making him one of the '*Swallows*' who are 'eternally skimming and fluttering up and down ... to *catch flies*' (*PW*: II, 197, 250). (Although Sherburn connects Pope's letter to Warburton about revisions in November 1742 with Hervey's death, the date is too early (*Corr.*: IV, 425, n.1)).

299. his Laurel: Eusden's.

301. Parodying Psalm 24:7 ('Lift up your heads, O ye gates ... and the King of glory shall come in') in allusion to Bays's role of mock-Messiah.

302. Violins figured in theatre orchestras, and hostile audiences resorted to blowing squeaky whistles called cat-calls: see *Spectator* 361 (Bond 1965: III, 349–53).

303–4. The bay, vine and ivy are degraded by the epithets 'madding' (suggesting a poetic madness more lunacy than inspiration), 'drunken' (tipping gaiety over into excess: Sherbo cites the pagan bacchanalia (Sherbo 1970: 512)), and, most explicitly, 'creeping, dirty, courtly'. The physical habit of ivy becomes a metaphor for the moral degradation needed to succeed at court.

305. his Aid de camp: Presumably Lord Hervey.

306. Cowler cites evidence that Hervey's verse had a reputation for specious rhetorical tricks (*PW*: II, 476). ***Points:*** Ingenious turns of thought (such as those found in seventeenth-century 'metaphysical' verse), which seemed laboured and inelegant to neoclassical taste. ***Antitheses:*** Cp. Pope's attack on Hervey in *To Arbuthnot*: 'His Wit all see-saw between *that* and *this*, / Now high, now low, now Master up, now Miss, / And he himself one vile Antithesis' (lines 323–5).

307. Bilingsgate: Foul language associated with the fishwives at Billingsgate fish market.

And under his, and under Archer's wing,
Gaming and Grub-street skulk behind the King.
  O! when shall rise a Monarch all our own,
And I, a Nursing-mother, rock the throne,
'Twixt Prince and People close the Curtain draw,
Shade him from Light, and cover him from Law;
Fatten the Courtier, starve the learned band,
And suckle Armies, and dry-nurse the land:
'Till Senates nod to Lullabies divine,

309, 310.] When the Statute against Gaming was drawn up, it was represented, that the King, by ancient custom, plays at Hazard one night in the year; and therefore a clause was inserted, with an exception as to that particular. Under this pretence, the Groom-porter had a Room appropriated to Gaming all the summer the Court was at Kensington, which his Majesty accidentally being acquainted of, with a just indignation prohibited. It is reported, the same practice is yet continued wherever the Court resides, and the Hazard Table there open to all the professed Gamesters in town. '*Greatest* and *justest* SOV'REIGN! know you this? / Alas! no more, than *Thames'* calm *head* can know / Whose meads his *arms* drown, or whose corn o'erflow.' Donne to Queen Eliz.

311.] Boileau, Lutrin, Chant. 2: 'Helas! qu'est devenu cet tems, cet heureux tems, / Où les Rois s'honoroient du nom de Faineans: / S'endormoient sur le trone, et me servant sans honte, / Laissoient leur sceptre au mains ou d'un mair, ou d'un comte: / Aucun soin n'approchoit de leur paisible cour, / On reposoit la nuit, on dormoit tout le jour', *etc.*

309–10 and n. Grub Street is brought to court in the person of Cibber, and gaming in the person of Thomas Archer (*d.* 1743), an architect who also held the office of groom-porter to the king, which entailed furnishing royal apartments. The quotation is altered from the fifth satire of John Donne (1572–1631), originally addressed to Elizabeth I (Brooks-Davies 1985: 100–101). Pope had published modernisations of the second and fourth satires in the early 1730s (*TE*: IV, 23–49, 129–45; Milgate 1967: *Satires* V.28–30).

311–12 and 311n. An ironic allusion to a text from the coronation liturgy: 'Kings shall be thy nursing fathers, and queens shall be thy nursing mothers' (Isaiah 43:23). The speech from *Le lutrin* cited in the note is made by La Mollesse ('Indolence'), who laments that the reforming energy of Louis XIV has put an end to her dominion: 'Alas! what has become of that time, that happy time, when kings were honoured with the name of Do-nothings: They slept on the throne, and, serving me without shame, they left the sceptre in the hands of a majordomo or a count: No care came near their peaceful court, where there was rest by night and sleep all day' (Vercruysse 1969: *Le lutrin*, II.123–8). ('Les rois fainéants' is the name given to a decadent line of French medieval kings.) British antipathy to French absolutism gives added impact to the ironic suggestion that even Louis XIV is preferable to what Dulness envisages.

313–18. Dulness favours an absolutist regime where the king is kept in ignorance of the country's needs and is set above the law (the 'curtain' echoes the 'screen' metaphor applied to Walpole in anti-government polemic): only courtiers and soldiers (including the foreign troops maintained on British pay) profit, while scholars (a threat to ignorance) and the country in general are deprived of necessary resources. ('Suckle' and 'dry-nurse' emphasise how Dulness lulls the powerful into a return to infancy, as she sings even Parliament to sleep.) 'Lullabies divine' insinuates that the higher clergy appointed to preach at court and to Parliament are perverting religion to quiet potential opposition. Line 318 gibes at the tedium of Cibber's official odes.

And all be sleep, as at an Ode of thine.

She ceas'd. Then swells the Chapel-royal throat:
God save king Cibber! mounts in ev'ry note.
Familiar White's, God save king Colley! cries;
God save king Colley! Drury-lane replies:
To Needham's quick the voice triumphal rode,
But pious Needham dropt the name of God;
Back to the Devil the last echoes roll,
And Coll! each Butcher roars at Hockley-hole.
So when Jove's block descended from on high

319.] The Voices and Instruments used in the service of the Chapel-royal being also employed in the performance of the Birth-day and New-year Odes.

324.] A Matron of great fame, and very religious in her way; whose constant prayer it was, that she might 'get enough by her profession to leave it off in time, and make her peace with God.' But her fate was not so happy; for being convicted, and set in the pillory, she was (to the lasting shame of all her great Friends and Votaries) so ill used by the populace, that it put an end to her days.

325.] The Devil Tavern in Fleet-street, where these Odes are usually rehearsed before they are performed at Court.

---

319. the Chapel-royal throat: The singers of the Chapel Royal in St James's Palace. The acclamation may recall their participation in the coronation (Rogers 1985: 142).

321. White's addresses Bays in 'familiar' style because Cibber was a member: it is reported that his arrival would be 'saluted with the loud and joyous acclamation of "O king Coll! Come in, king Coll! Welcome, welcome, king Colley!"' (Davies 1780: II, 353). Whether this was an allusion to the present line, or its inspiration, is unclear; but the cry presumably also punned on the proverbially fun-loving Old King Cole.

322. Drury Lane was noted for theatres and brothels.

323–4 and 324n. Needham's: The brothel run by the notorious Elizabeth Needham (*d.* 1731), depicted in the first plate of Hogarth's *The Harlot's Progress.* 'Pious' is ironic, an irony repeated in the note's 'very religious in her way'. This may have been the note referred to in a letter to Warburton of November 1742, in which Pope complains that the printer has omitted the end of a 'Note at the End of Book I' which was to have recounted a slander about Boileau cited as parallel to Cibber's allegations about Pope: part of the intended anecdote seems to have involved a brothel, and could conceivably have been made to relate to Cibber's story about accompanying Pope to one, via a reference to Needham (*Corr.*: IV, 426–7). ***quick:*** quickly. ***to the lasting shame of all her great Friends:*** Suggesting the hypocrisy of clients who would not risk being identified as such by trying to defend her.

325–6 and n. Compare the expression 'go to the devil'. The couplet recalls Dryden's mock-heroic evocation in *Mac Flecknoe* of the enthusiasm with which Shadwell is acclaimed: 'Echoes from *Pissing-Ally, Sh*— call, / And *Sh*— they resound from *A— Hall*' (Kinsley 1958: lines 47–8).

327. Phaedrus (*c.*15 BC–*c.*AD 50) tells how Aesop responded to the grumbling of the Athenians against their ruler by telling the story of how the frogs asked Jupiter for a king

(As sings thy great forefather Ogilby)
Loud thunder to its bottom shook the bog,
And the hoarse nation croak'd, God save King Log!

328–30.] See Ogilby's Aesop's Fables, where, in the story of the Frogs and their King, this excellent hemistic is to be found.

Our Author manifests here, and elsewhere, a prodigious tenderness for the *bad writers*. We see he selects the only good passage, perhaps, in all that ever Ogilby writ; which shews how candid and patient a reader he must have been. What can be more kind and affectionate than these words in the preface to his Poems, where he labours to call up all our humanity and forgiveness toward these unlucky men, by the most moderate representation of their case that has ever been given by any author? 'Much may be said to extenuate the fault of bad poets: What we call a *genius* is hard to be distinguished, by a man himself, from a prevalent inclination: And if it be never so great, he can at first discover it no other way than by that strong propensity which renders him the more liable to be mistaken. He has no other method but to make the experiment, by writing, and so appealing to the judgment of others: And if he happens to write ill (which is certainly no sin in itself) he is immediately made the object of ridicule! I wish we had the humanity to reflect, that even the worst authors might endeavour to please us, and, in that endeavour, deserve something at our hands. We have no cause to quarrel with them, but for their obstinacy in persisting, and even that may admit of alleviating circumstances: For their particular friends may be either ignorant, or unsincere; and the rest of the world too well bred to shock them with a truth which generally their booksellers are the first that inform them of.'

But how much all indulgence is lost upon these people may appear from the just reflection made on their constant conduct, and constant fate, in the following Epigram:

(Fable II). When he gave them a log, they were at first jubilant; but when they became disillusioned with his inactivity and asked for a different king, Jupiter gave them a water-snake, which ate them up. Ogilby's version stresses the dangerous fickleness of 'th'unsetled vulgar', and can be read as implying that they should have known better than to change Charles I for Cromwell; but more important than any allusion to individuals is Ogilby's underlying respect for kingship as divinely ordained ('Men, beasts, and birds; nay Bees their King obey'), an institution that is altered only at the risk of social disintegration ('Small hope is left well grounded peace t'obtain, / Unless again / Thou hear our prayer / Great King of Kings, and we for Kings declare') (Ogilby 1651: 35–6; see also Brooks-Davies 1985: 97–8). By paralleling Cibber, creature of a regime established by the diversion of the hereditary line, with the log acclaimed by the frogs in Ogilby's version, Pope again makes a gesture subversive of the Hanoverian establishment: Rogers compares the acclamations at the coronation of George II in 1727 (Rogers 1985: 136). Cibber had himself made a political application of the fable in his *Apology*, playing into Pope's hands with the conclusion that 'King *Log* himself must have made but a very simple Figure in History' (Cibber 1740: 20).

328 and 328–30n. thy: Cibber's. ***hemistic:*** half-line. Ogilby had written, 'Then all the bog / Proclame their King, and cry *Jove* save King Log' (Ogilby 1651: 35). The same rhyme and allusion had been used in the anonymous Jacobite satire *The Duumvirate* (*c.*1704), by the Jacobite secretary of state in exile, John Caryll, uncle of Pope's friend of the same name (Erskine-Hill 1996: 102). There it refers to the diversion of the throne from the direct line in the cases of William III and the projected Hanoverian succession: 'They hunt and fish for Kings, like Aesops Logs, / In German Forests, and in Holland Bogs'. ***preface to his Poems:***

Ye little Wits, that gleam'd a while,
When Pope vouchsaf'd a ray,
Alas! depriv'd of his kind smile,
How soon ye fade away!

To compass Phoebus' car about,
Thus empty vapours rise;
Each lends his cloud, to put Him out,
That rear'd him to the skies.

Alas! those skies are not your sphere;
There He shall ever burn:
Weep, weep, and fall! for Earth ye were,
And must to Earth return.

The End of the FIRST BOOK.

The Preface to the *Works* of 1717 (*PW*: I, 290). The tone is complex and at least partly defensive. **Ye little Wits . . .** : The epigram (authorship unknown) compares Pope to Phoebus Apollo (god of the sun and of poetry), and the 'little wits' to vapours which can only rise by his power: if they attempt to eclipse him they will condense and fall back to earth where they belong.

BOOK TWO

HEADNOTE. The games that celebrate Bays's coronation imitate the games held by Aeneas in memory of his father in *Aeneid* V, which in turn imitate the funeral games in *Iliad* XXIII. For similarities to the route of a Lord Mayor's procession, see Williams 1955: 29–41; for Pope's fantasy of celebrating the Mayoralty of the Tory printer and alderman John Barber (1675–1741) with a book trade pageant, see Rogers 1985: 132. An early draft of Book II had included material later reworked as part of Book IV (see headnote).

THE

DUNCIAD:

BOOK the SECOND.

ARGUMENT.

The King being proclaimed, the solemnity is graced with public Games *and sports of various kinds; not instituted by the Hero, as by Aeneas in Virgil, but for greater honour by the* Goddess *in person (in like manner as the games Pythia, Isthmia, etc. were anciently said to be ordained by the Gods, and as Thetis herself appearing, according to Homer, Odyss. 24. proposed the prizes in honour of her son Achilles.) Hither flock the Poets and Critics, attended, as is but just, with their Patrons and Booksellers. The Goddess is first pleased, for her disport, to propose games to the* Booksellers, *and setteth up the Phantom of a Poet, which they contend to overtake. The Races described, with their divers accidents. Next, the game for a* Poetess. *Then follow the Exercises for the* Poets, *of* tickling, vociferating, diving: *The first holds forth the arts and practices of* Dedicators, *the second of* Disputants *and* fustian Poets, *the third of* profound, dark, *and* dirty Party-writers. *Lastly, for the* Critics, *the Goddess proposes (with great propriety) an Exercise, not of their parts, but their patience, in hearing the works of two voluminous Authors, one in* verse, *and the other in* prose, *deliberately read, without sleeping: The various effects of which, with the several degrees and manners of their operation, are here set forth; 'till the whole number, not of Critics only, but of spectators, actors, and all present, fall fast asleep; which naturally and necessarily ends the games.*

---

as by Aeneas in Virgil: In *Aeneid* V.

Pythia, Isthmia: Sites of ancient Greek games.

Thetis herself: When Achilles was killed at Troy, his divine mother Thetis obtained from the gods the prizes for his funeral games (*Odyssey* XXIV.85–6).

Booksellers: Eighteenth-century booksellers combined the now-distinct roles of publisher and bookseller.

disport: entertainment.

vociferating: shouting.

parts: talents.

HIGH on a gorgeous seat, that far out-shone
Henley's gilt tub, or Fleckno's Irish throne,

Two things there are, upon the supposition of which the very basis of all Verbal criticism is founded and supported: The first, that an Author could never fail to use the *best word* on every occasion; the second, that a Critic cannot chuse but know *which that is*. This being granted, whenever any word doth not fully content us, we take upon us to conclude, first, that the author could *never have used it*; and, secondly, that he must have used *that very one* which we conjecture in its stead.

We cannot, therefore, enough admire the learned Scriblerus for his alteration of the text in the two last verses of the preceding book, which in all the former editions stood thus: 'Hoarse thunder to its bottom shook the bog, / And the loud nation croak'd, God save king Log.' He has, with great judgment, transposed these two epithets; putting *hoarse* to the nation, and *loud* to the thunder: And this being evidently the true reading, he vouchsafed not so much as to mention the former; for which assertion of the just right of a Critic, he merits the acknowledgment of all sound Commentators.

1.] Parody of Milton, book 2. 'High on a throne of royal state, that far / Outshone the wealth of Ormus and of Ind, / Or where the gorgeous East with richest hand / Show'rs on her Kings Barbaric pearl and gold / Satan exalted sate'.

2. Henley's gilt tub,] The pulpit of a Dissenter is usually called a Tub; but that of Mr. Orator Henley was covered with velvet, and adorned with gold. He had also a fair altar, and over it is this extraordinary inscription, *The Primitive Eucharist*. See the history of this person, book 3.

Ibid. or Fleckno's Irish throne,] Richard Fleckno was an Irish priest, but had laid aside (as himself expressed it) the mechanic part of priesthood. He printed some plays, poems, letters, and travels. I doubt not our author took occasion to mention him in respect to the Poem of Mr. Dryden, to which this bears some resemblance, though of a character more

---

INTRODUCTORY NOTE. ***Two things there are:*** The passage satirises Bentley's approach to textual emendation as displayed in his edition of *Paradise Lost* (Bentley 1732; and see Jarvis 1995: 91). ***all the former editions:*** The editions of 1728 (the note first appeared in 1729). Pope's change of mind is presented as unacknowledged tampering by Scriblerus, though it should be remembered that Bentley *did* draw attention to the changes he wanted to make to the text of Milton (which were in any case confined to the footnotes), and that the *Dunciad* elsewhere condemns the pedantry of *not* correcting what seem obvious errors (cp. Scriblerus's remarks on Hearne in the note on the title to Book I).

1 and n. The allusion to the opening of *Paradise Lost* II makes a key identification between Bays and Satan (for the parody of Christian doctrine of which the *Dunciad*'s allusions to Milton form part, see Williams 1955: 131–58). For parallel epic elevations of leaders, see Sherbo 1970: 507. Rogers compares the enthronement of George II in 1727 (Rogers 1985: 136; and see editor's note on lines 5–8). For comparison with the 'Parnassus' painted by Raphael (Raffaello Santi: 1483–1520), see Gneiting 1975: 424–5 and plate 4.

2 and n. Henley's gilt tub: 'Orator' Henley's preaching was notoriously eccentric both in theology and in presentation (Midgley 1973). He figures more prominently at III.195–212. ***Fleckno's Irish throne:*** In Dryden's *Mac Flecknoe* Flecknoe is 'High on a Throne of his own Labours rear'd' (Kinsley 1958: line 107). ***the mechanic part of priesthood:*** Implying contempt for the practical duties of a priest, such as preaching, pastoral care and officiating at the sacraments. ***to which this bears some resemblance:*** Dryden's *Mac Flecknoe* is claimed as a model

Or that where on her Curls the Public pours,
All-bounteous, fragrant Grains and Golden show'rs,
Great Cibber sate: The proud Parnassian sneer,
The conscious simper, and the jealous leer,
Mix on his look: All eyes direct their rays
On him, and crowds turn Coxcombs as they gaze.

different from it than that of the Aeneid from the Iliad, or the Lutrin of Boileau from the Defait de Bouts rimées of Sarazin.

It may be just worth mentioning, that the Eminence from whence the ancient Sophists entertained their auditors, was called by the pompous name of a Throne; — *ἐπὶ Θρόνου τινὸς ὑψηλοῦ μάλα σοφιστικῶς καὶ σοβαρῶς*. Themistius, Orat. i.

3.] Edmund Curl stood in the pillory at Charing-cross, in March 1727–8.

Mr. Curl loudly complained of this note, as an untruth; protesting 'that he stood in the pillory, not in March, but in February.' And of another on ver. 152. saying, 'he was not tossed in a *Blanket*, but a *Rug*.' Curliad, duodecimo, 1729, p. 19, 25. Much in the same manner Mr. Cibber remonstrated that his Brothers at Bedlam, mentioned Book i. were not *Brazen*, but *Blocks*; yet our author let it pass unaltered, as a trifle, that no way lessened the Relationship.

---

for the *Dunciad*, though Pope is said to have refined his model more than Virgil refined that of Homer, or Boileau that of Jean-François Sarasin (1614–54), whose *Dulot vaincu ou la défaite des bouts-rimés* (1649) was a satire on the fashion for bouts-rimés, i.e. the composition of verse to fit a sequence of paired rhymes given to the poet in advance. ***Sophists:*** Greek teachers of rhetoric of the fifth century BC. Teaching the arts of political success, they were often denigrated as manipulative cynics: the allusion implies a similar slur on the enthroned Bays. ***Themistius:*** Greek teacher of philosophy and travelling rhetorician (*c.* AD 317–*c.*388). In Oration 21 he asks his audience (who already know him as a philosopher) whether they are surprised to see him speaking 'on a certain high throne, very sophistically and haughtily', i.e. in the manner of a rhetorician (Schenkl 1965–74: II, 243.B.i).

3 and n. Or that: the pillory. Curll was sentenced to this punishment in 1728 for publishing the politically sensitive memoirs of a retired spy. He claimed that he had a royal warrant for the publication, and seems to have persuaded the crowd not to torment him – which Pope chooses not to mention (Straus 1927: 112–21). ***Mr. Cibber remonstrated:*** See I.31–2 and n.

4. fragrant Grains and Golden show'rs: Wet malted barley discarded after brewing, and eggs (presumably rotten, although it appears that the crowd turned on the only person who threw an egg at Curll).

5–8. An early manuscript draft had clearly identified the king (Tibbald, until the installation of Bays in 1743) with George II: characterised by 'His Strut his Grin, and his dead Stare' and 'his stupid Eye', he was surrounded by the 'Laurelld Train' as 'With Kingly Joy he hears their Loyal Lies'; and his placing not on a throne but on a 'Bed of State' may have suggested not only the ceremony of a royal levee, but also Queen Caroline's notorious personal influence over royal policy (Mack 1982: 342–3). The published *Dunciad*s are relatively restrained.

5–6. Parnassian sneer: Alluding to Parnassus, home of the Muses; cp. *To Arbuthnot*, line 96. ***jealous leer:*** cp. Satan's 'jealous leer malign' (Fowler 1998: *Paradise Lost* IV.503).

8. In 'To Sir Godfrey Kneller, on his Picture of the King', Addison suggested that George I should make a royal progress through Britain, envisaging how the 'crowds' would 'grow

His Peers shine round him with reflected grace,
New edge their dulness, and new bronze their face.
So from the Sun's broad beam, in shallow urns
Heav'ns twinkling Sparks draw light, and point their horns.
  Not with more glee, by hands Pontific crown'd,
With scarlet hats wide-waving circled round,
Rome in her Capitol saw Querno sit,
Thron'd on sev'n hills, the Antichrist of wit.

15.] Camillo Querno was of Apulia, who hearing the great Encouragement which Leo X. gave to poets, travelled to Rome with a harp in his hand, and sung to it twenty thousand verses of a poem called Alexias. He was introduced *as a Buffoon* to Leo, and promoted to the honour of the *Laurel*; a jest which the court of Rome and the Pope himself entered into so far, as to cause him to ride on an elephant to the Capitol, and to hold a solemn festival on his coronation; at which it is recorded the Poet himself was so transported as to *weep for joy**. He was ever after a constant frequenter of the Pope's table, drank abundantly, and poured forth verses without number. PAULUS JOVIUS, Elog. Vir. doct. chap. lxxxii. Some idea of his poetry is given by Fam. Strada, in his Prolusions.

* See Life of C.C. chap. vi. p. 149.

---

loyal as they gaze' (Guthkelch 1914: line 22). Even after Pope's prudent removal of direct allusions to George II, the parody retains the focus on Cibber as agent of Hanoverian corruption.

9. ***His Peers:*** Bays's fellow dunces; but also with a glance at Cibber's much-vaunted supporters among the nobility.

10. 'Edge' highlights the paradoxically active element in Pope's conception of dulness; 'bronze' echoes Cibber's 'brazen' effrontery.

11–12. The other dunces reflect Bays's dulness, just as the 'shallow urns' of the stars reflect 'the Sun's broad beam'. Cp. Milton: 'Hither as to their fountain other stars / Repairing, in their golden urns draw light, / And hence the morning planet gilds his horns', where horns is a specific reference to the horned appearance of the planet Venus (Fowler 1998: *Paradise Lost* VII.364–6). Its application to 'twinkling Sparks' (a belittling periphrasis for stars, recalling the colloquial use of 'spark' to denote a young man with pretensions to style) allows a casual insinuation of cuckoldry.

13–16 and 15n. Comparing Cibber to the buffoon Camillo Querno, acclaimed laureate in jest by the Renaissance Pope Leo X (see Appendix VI, 'Of the Poet Laureate'). ***Pontific:*** Alluding to the Pope as sovereign pontiff. ***scarlet hats:*** Worn by cardinals. ***Capitol:*** One of the hills of Rome. ***Thron'd on sev'n hills:*** In Revelation 17:9 appears a female figure of apocalyptic evil mounted on a beast with seven heads, representing the seven hills of Rome. The buffoon Querno is presented as 'Antichrist of Wit' (Antichrist being the demonic adversary of Christ who heralds the end of the world). ***Camillo Querno:*** The note is a loose selection from the authorities cited (Jovius 1557: 178–81; Strada 1631: 226–7). Well-informed readers might recall, in line with the *Dunciad*'s insistence on poverty as the just reward of writing without genius, that Querno died in poverty after the death of his patron. ***to weep for joy:*** Although these words had been used in 1729, when Tibbald, not Bays, was compared to Querno, they match so well Cibber's account of his tears of joy on first being commended by a respected actor that a reference to his *Apology* has been added to clinch the resemblance.

And now the Queen, to glad her sons, proclaims
By herald Hawkers, high heroic Games.
They summon all her Race: An endless band
Pours forth, and leaves unpeopled half the land.
A motley mixture! in long wigs, in bags,
In silks, in crapes, in Garters, and in rags,
From drawing rooms, from colleges, from garrets,
On horse, on foot, in hacks, and gilded chariots:
All who true Dunces in her cause appear'd,
And all who knew those Dunces to reward.
Amid that area wide they took their stand,
Where the tall may-pole once o'er-look'd the Strand;
But now (so ANNE and Piety ordain)

17–18. Cp. Pope on the funeral games called for Achilles by his divine mother: '*Thetis* herself to all our peers proclaims / Heroic prizes and exequial games' (*Odyssey* XXIV.107–8). For an account of the games sensitive to the warmth and sheer fun of their evocation of noise and filth, see Jones in Mack & Winn 1980: 637–43. ***the Queen:*** Dulness. ***herald Hawkers:*** Presumably crying newspapers and other ephemera in which the games are imagined as announced.

19–20. ***all her Race:*** All those who, like Bays, look to Dulness as mother.

21–2. The social mix is indicated by an assortment of contrasted styles of dress. 'Long wigs' appealed more to the older generation, 'bags' (which confined the back hair in a silk pouch) more to the young and fashionable; 'silks' were worn by the rich (although the sense 'robes of a King's Counsel' would work neatly here, *OED* has no citation before 1812); 'crapes' (a thin woollen fabric) by the less well-off (and specifically by the clergy); and the royally bestowed Order of the Garter distinguished the highest in society as 'rags' did the lowest.

23. Stressing the diverse social origins of the dunces. 'Drawing rooms' suggests the formal receptions attended by the social elite, notably the royal drawing room where the King and Queen received the most favoured and highly placed of their subjects. Other dunces come from an academic background, or from the cheap garret lodgings proverbially inhabited by impoverished writers.

24. Again, the dunces' means of transport show their social range: some hire 'hacks' (hackney carriages), some can afford to maintain their own 'gilded chariots' (a key status symbol). The contemporary pronunciation of 'chariots' seems to have rhymed with 'garrets'.

25–6. Dulness's progress is laid at the door of wealthy patrons. Cp. Dryden: 'Those who, to worth, their Bounty did extend; / And those who knew that Bounty to commend' (Kinsley 1958: *Aeneid* VI.901–2). An early manuscript draft cites the Virgilian original: 'the devoted bards . . . and those who made others remember them for their merits' (Mack 1984: 137; *Aeneid* VI.662, 663).

27. ***that area wide:*** Occupied by the church of St Mary le Strand, one of the new churches erected in the second decade of the century at the express desire of Queen Anne.

29. ***ANNE and Piety:*** Contrasting the drive to make public spaces respectable – typified by Queen Anne's church-building projects – with their former role as sites of communal merrymaking: a particularly large maypole was erected on the site at the Restoration, and a new and more elaborate one replaced it in 1713, only to be removed when the church was built, and given to Sir Isaac Newton, who gave it in turn to the rector of Wanstead to mount the then largest telescope in Europe (Knight 1842: 157; Elwin & Courthope 1871–86: IV, 325;

A Church collects the saints of Drury-lane.
  With Authors, Stationers obey'd the call,
(The field of glory is a field for all.)
Glory, and gain, th' industrious tribe provoke;
And gentle Dulness ever loves a joke.
A Poet's form she plac'd before their eyes,
And bade the nimblest racer seize the prize;
No meagre, muse-rid mope, adust and thin,
In a dun night-gown of his own loose skin;

35.] This is what Juno does to deceive Turnus, Aen. x. 'Tum Dea nube cava, tenuem *sine viribus umbram* / In faciem Aeneae (visu mirabile monstrum!) / Dardaniis ornat telis, clypeumque jubasque / Divini assimilat capitis ... / ... Dat *inania verba*, / Dat *sine mente sonum*'. The reader will observe how exactly some of these verses suit with their allegorical application here to a Plagiary: There seems to me a great propriety in this Episode, where such an one is imaged by a phantom that deludes the grasp of the expecting Bookseller.

Rogers 1972: 70–72; Stallybrass & White 1986: 112). Despite the *Dunciad*'s generally negative view of popular recreations, the new use of the site is treated with some irony, insinuating the naivety and pointlessness of providing so lavishly for the devotional needs of a district noted for theatres, printing houses and – as Pope specifically notes – prostitution ('saints'). The anonymous *Essay on the Dunciad* took offence at the 'Blasphemy and Disloyalty' of what it saw as the suggestion 'that Queen Anne built the New Church in the *Strand* on purpose for the Reception of all the Strumpets of *Drury-Lane*' (*An Essay on the Dunciad* 1728).

31. Stationers: booksellers, i.e. publishers, who are to compete in the first game.

34. a joke: The prize is only an illusion.

35 and n. A Poet's form: The motif of the phantom poet alludes to Juno's creation of Aeneas's phantom double in order to decoy his enemy Turnus away from danger ('Then the goddess, using a hollow cloud, armed with Trojan spears a thin shade that had no strength but looked like Aeneas (an amazing prodigy to see!), imitating the shield carried by the goddess-born hero and the crest of his helmet ... She gave the illusion empty words, she gave it a voice without any intellect behind it': *Aeneid* X.636–40). For a comparable episode in Swift's *Battle of the Books*, see Davis 1939–68: I, 158. By raising the issue of plagiarism, the note anticipates the identification of the phantom as James Moore Smythe at line 50; but it had originally been intended to impersonate John Gay, thus satirising the invented 'Joseph Gay' under whose name *The Confederates* and *A Complete Key to the Non-Juror* had been published (editor's note on III.149–50; *TE*: V, 103; Mack 1984: 104–5, 138, 140). This supposed author, though dismissed as a mere phantom by Concanen, had been praised by Giles Jacob (McLaverty 1985: 27–9). The real author of the pieces was John Durant Breval (1680?–1738), who turned to writing after his dismissal from a fellowship at Trinity College, Cambridge, on a charge of adultery aggravated by assault on his mistress's husband. He also supported himself by serving in the army and acting as tutor to young men undertaking the Grand Tour, in which role he has often been associated with the tutor featured in Book IV (see IV.272 and editor's notes).

37. adust: dessicated, wretched.

38. night-gown: Not a garment for sleeping in, but a loose gown, usually wrapped in front, for informal morning wear; hence the typical attire of the writer at ease in his study. A marginal note to an early manuscript draft seems to suggest an allusion to Shakespeare's Falstaff, who complains that 'my skin hangs about me like an old lady's loose gown' (Mack

But such a bulk as no twelve bards could raise,
Twelve starv'ling bards of these degen'rate days.
All as a partridge plump, full-fed, and fair,
She form'd this image of well-body'd air;
With pert flat eyes she window'd well its head;
A brain of feathers, and a heart of lead;
And empty words she gave, and sounding strain,
But senseless, lifeless! idol void and vain!
Never was dash'd out, at one lucky hit,
A fool, so just a copy of a wit;
So like, that critics said, and courtiers swore,
A Wit it was, and call'd the phantom More.

39.] 'Vix illud lecti bis sex ... / Qualia nunc hominum producit corpora tellus.' Virg. Aen. xii.

44.] i.e. 'A *trifling head*, and a *contracted heart*', as the poet, book 4. describes the *accomplished* Sons of Dulness; of whom this is only an *Image*, or Scarecrow, and so stuffed out with these corresponding materials. SCRIBL.

47.] Our author here seems willing to give some account of the possibility of *Dulness* making a Wit (which could be done no other way than by *chance*.) The fiction is the more reconciled to probability, by the known story of Apelles, who being at a loss to express the foam of Alexander's horse, dashed his pencil in despair at the picture, and happened to do it by that fortunate stroke.

50. and call'd the phantom More.] CURL, in his Key to the Dunciad, affirmed this to be James-More Smith esq. and it is probable (considering what is said of him in the *Testimonies*) that some might fancy our author obliged to represent this gentleman as a plagiary, or to pass for one himself. His case indeed was like that of a man I have heard of, who, as he was sitting in company, perceived his next neighbour had stolen his handkerchief. 'Sir (said the thief, finding himself detected) do not expose me, I did it for mere want; be so good but to take it privately out of my pocket again, and say nothing.' The honest man did so, but the other cry'd out, 'See, gentlemen, what a thief we have among us! look, he is stealing my handkerchief!'

The plagiarisms of this person gave occasion to the following Epigram: 'More always smiles whenever he recites; / He smiles (you think) approving what he writes. / And yet in this no

---

1984: 137; Alexander 1951: *Henry IV 1*, III.iii.3). Compare the apparition of the poet Spenser which warns of the miseries of being a poet in Oldham's 'A Satyr. ... Dissuading the Author from the Study of Poetry': 'Famish'd his Looks appear'd, His Eyes sunk in, / Like Morning-Gown about him hung his Skin' (Brooks & Selden 1987: lines 9–10).

39–40 and n. The quotation describes Turnus's throwing a huge stone at Aeneas ('Scarcely could twelve picked men have lifted that stone, men with the kind of bodies that the earth now produces': *Aeneid* XII.899–900). For parallels from Dryden's and Pope's epic translations which also use the 'raise'/'days' rhyme, see Sherbo 1970: 507.

44n. The note, initialled in 1751 as by Warburton, cites IV.504.

47n. Apelles: Ancient Greek painter (fourth century BC), from whom Alexander the Great commissioned portraits.

50 and n. call'd the phantom More: James Moore Smythe is accused of plagiarism in 'Testimonies of Authors'. As plagiarist, he only *appears* to be an author. ***CURL, in his Key:*** *A Compleat Key* 1728. ***the following Epigram:*** Since this has been altered from its first

All gaze with ardour: Some a poet's name,
Others a sword-knot and lac'd suit inflame.
But lofty Lintot in the circle rose:
'This prize is mine; who tempt it are my foes;
With me began this genius, and shall end.'
He spoke: and who with Lintot shall contend?
Fear held them mute. Alone, untaught to fear,

vanity is shown; / A modest man may like what's not his own.' His only work was a Comedy called the Rival Modes; the town condemned it in the action, but he printed it in 1726–7, with this modest Motto, 'Hic caestus artemque repono.'

It appears from hence, that this is not the name of a real person, but fictitious. *More* from *μῶρος, stultus, μωρία, stultitia,* to represent the folly of a plagiary. Thus Erasmus, *Admonuit me* Mori *cognomen tibi, quod tam ad* Moriae *vocabulum accedit quam es ipse a re alienus.* Dedication of Moriae Encomium to Sir Tho. More; the farewell of which may be our author's to his plagiary, *Vale,* More! *et moriam tuam gnaviter defende.* Adieu, More! and be sure strongly to defend thy own folly. SCRIBL.

53.] We enter here upon the episode of the Booksellers: Persons, whose names being more known and famous in the learned world than those of the Authors in this poem, do therefore need less explanation. The action of Mr. Lintot here imitates that of Dares in Virgil, rising just in this manner to lay hold on a *Bull*. This eminent Bookseller printed the *Rival Modes* before mentioned.

---

appearance (*The Flying Post*, 12 April 1729), Sutherland suspects that it is Pope's own composition (*TE*: V, 102). ***the town condemned it in the action:*** Audiences condemned it to close by showing their disapproval when it was acted. ***1726–7:*** Between 1 January and 24 March 1727 (the last day of 1726 in the archaic legal calendar). ***this modest Motto:*** In fact an extraordinarily arrogant one for a novice author, since these are the parting words of the aged hero Eutellus, who has just given an awe-inspiring demonstration of his skill against a much younger rival: 'here I lay down the boxing glove and my art' (*Aeneid* V.484). ***not the name of a real person:*** Punning on the resemblance between Moore and the Greek words for 'stupid' and 'stupidity' (cp. 'moron'). The Dutch humanist Desiderius Erasmus (*c.*1467–1536) had made the same pun in dedicating his *Encomium Moriae* (*The Praise of Folly* (1511)) to Sir Thomas More (1478–1535) in the words quoted ('Your surname of More gave me the idea, because it comes as close to the word "moria" ("folly") as you are distant from the thing itself').

51–2. When, at the draft stage, the phantom had represented Gay, 'a poet's name' (the phrase 'ye authors fame' was also considered) would clearly have referred to the 'Joseph Gay' deception (Mack 1984: 105, 138). In all the published versions the application is weakened, as 'More' did not bring any famous poet to mind. As it stands, the phrase could perhaps be glossed 'the fact that he calls himself a poet'. If this attracts some publishers, others are attracted by his superior style of dress ('a sword-knot' was a fashionable ornament on the hilt of a dress sword; the lace on a suit could be its most expensive component).

53–4 and 53n. lofty Lintot: Young described Bernard Lintot as 'a great sputtering fellow' (*OAC*: I, 342). Early manuscript drafts show that Jacob Tonson the elder had first been considered for this role (Mack 1984: 105, 138). ***more known and famous:*** Not only a hit at the insignificance of the authors in question, but also a condemnation of the commercialisation of literature which tended to place authors in a subordinate position to entrepreneurial publishers. ***Dares in Virgil:*** The boxer Dares thinks that no-one dare fight him, and thus

Stood dauntless Curl; 'Behold that rival here!

*58. **Stood dauntless Curl;]*** We come now to a character of much respect, that of Mr. Edmund Curl. As a plain repetition of great actions is the best praise of them, we shall only say of this eminent man, that he carried the Trade many lengths beyond what it ever before had arrived at; and that he was the envy and admiration of all his profession. He possessed himself of a command over all authors whatever; he caused them to write what he pleased; they could not call their very *Names* their own. He was not only famous among these; he was taken notice of by the *State*, the *Church*, and the *Law*, and received particular marks of distinction from each.

It will be owned that he is here introduced with all possible dignity: He speaks like the intrepid Diomed; he runs like the swift-footed Achilles; if he falls, 'tis like the beloved Nisus; and (what Homer makes to be the chief of all praises) he is *favoured of the Gods*; he says but three words, and his prayer is heard; a Goddess conveys it to the seat of Jupiter: Though he loses the prize, he gains the victory; the great Mother herself comforts him, she inspires him with expedients, she honours him with an immortal present (such as Achilles receives from Thetis, and Aeneas from Venus) at once instructive and prophetical: After this he is unrivalled and triumphant.

The tribute our author here pays him is a grateful return for several unmerited obligations:

---

claims the prize – a bull – as his own; but when a challenger emerges he is defeated (*Aeneid* V.362–472). 'Bull', however, can also mean 'cheat', or 'mistake', implying that Lintot made a bad bargain over Moore Smythe's *The Rival Modes*: he paid an extraordinary £105, more than twice the price obtained for Gay, Pope and Arbuthnot's *Three Hours after Marriage* (Nichols 1812–15: VIII, 301). The allusion to the games in *Aeneid* V, however, underlines the allusion to that text and its model in *Iliad* XXIII which underlies the ensuing race between the publishers. The point is further made by echoes of Pope's own translation ('But this, my Prize, I never shall forego; / This, who but touches, Warriors! is my Foe' (*TE*: VIII, *Iliad* XXIII.633–4)).

58n. many lengths beyond what it ever before had arrived at: Attacking Curll's defiance of scruple and decency, but also suggesting the genuine – and to Pope offensive – modernity of his ruthlessly commercial exploitation of literature as a commodity. ***He possessed himself of a command over all authors whatever:*** He organised his own authors like factory outworkers, producing to order, and as he had no scruples about misleading purchasers as to the authorship of what they were buying, even authors too distinguished to work for him could find themselves credited with the work of nonentities, or embarrassed by unauthorised publication of privately circulated manuscripts (see original commentary on II.128; *PW*: II, 89–93; Straus 1927: 24–6). ***by the* State, *the* Church, *and the* Law:** The various penalties ('marks of distinction') imposed on Curll characteristically related to obscenity, libel or publishing without the author's permission (*TE*: V, 104; Stephen & Lee 1885–1900; Straus 1927; Foxon 1964: 14–15). ***like the intrepid Diomed:*** Alluding to Homer's regular epithet for Diomede, 'he of the brave war-cry' (*Iliad* X.219). ***like the swift-footed Achilles:*** 'Swift-footed' is Homer's regular epithet for Achilles (*Iliad* I.84). ***like the beloved Nisus:*** Trojan athlete, celebrated for his friendship with Euryalus. Just when he seemed to be winning the race, Nisus slipped on offal from a sacrifice (*Aeneid* V.315–33). ***but three words:*** just a few words (II.79–82). ***an immortal present:*** The 'shaggy Tap'stry' (line 143) is paralleled with the gifts of armour forged by Haephestus/Vulcan and given to Achilles by Thetis and to Aeneas by Venus. Achilles' shield showed scenes of human life in the context of the forces of nature; Aeneas's shield showed scenes prophetic of Roman destiny (*Iliad* XVIII.478–617; *Aeneid* VIII.608–731). ***The tribute our author here pays:*** The note ranges evasively over a long

The race by vigour, not by vaunts is won;
So take the hindmost, Hell.' —— He said, and run.
Swift as a bard the bailiff leaves behind,

Many weighty animadversions on the public affairs, and many excellent and diverting pieces on private persons, has he given to his name. If ever he owed two verses to any other, he owed Mr. Curl some thousands. He was every day extending his fame, and enlarging his Writings: Witness innumerable instances; but it shall suffice only to mention the *Court Poems*, which he meant to publish as the work of the true writer, a Lady of quality; but being first threatned, and afterwards punished for it by Mr. Pope, he generously transferred it from *her* to *him*, and ever since printed it in his name. The single time that ever he spoke to C. was on that affair, and to that happy incident he ow'd all the favours since received from him: So true is the saying of Dr. Sydenham, 'that any one shall be, at some time or other, the better or the worse, for having but *seen* or *spoken* to a good or bad man.'

60.] 'Occupet extremum scabies; mihi turpe relinqui est.' Horat. de Arte.

61, etc.] Something like this is in Homer, Il. x. v. 220. of Diomed. Two different manners of the same author in his similies are also imitated in the two following; the first, of the Bailiff, is short, unadorned, and (as the Critics well know) from *familiar life*; the second, of

---

history of mutual offence, starting in March 1716 with Curll's publication of *Court Poems*, three satirical town eclogues, principally by Lady Mary Wortley Montagu (1689–1762), which he suggested were by Pope, Gay or a lady of quality. (Lady Mary had been close to both at the time, and commentators differ as to the extent of their possible contributions: see for example Nokes 1995: 223–9; but cp. the forthcoming biography of Lady Mary by Isobel Grundy.) The satire, which could be read as reflecting on the royal family and their intimates, was highly embarrassing to all three: although Pope's religion ruled out any substantial appointment, he was not yet as estranged from the court as he was later to become, and both Gay and Lady Mary were actively seeking royal favour. Pope responded by meeting Curll in a tavern ('the single time that ever he spoke to C') and taking the opportunity to slip an emetic into his drink. He then wrote up the consequences in the anonymous *A Full and True Account*. In revenge, Curll published two lighthearted pieces by Pope which he represented as compromising his religious and political principles (hence the 'favours since received from him'; but the note is evasive in suggesting, at the beginning of this paragraph, that Curll had annoyed him by false attributions, rather than by embarrassingly accurate ones). For accounts of the affair of the *Court Poems* and its consequences, see Straus 1927: 49–64; *PW*: I, 257–66; *TE*: VI, 161–6; Halsband & Grundy 1977: 182–200; Mack 1985: 295–301; Rumbold 1989: 133–5. ***Dr. Sydenham:*** Humphrey Sydenham (1591–1650?), royalist clergyman and theologian. The emphasis on 'having but *seen* or *spoken* to' contrasts ironically with the reader's expected recall of what Pope had *actually* done to Curll.

59. Cp. *Iliad* XVI.631.

60n. Horace makes the would-be poet who will not study the craft shout his defiance in the manner of Roman children playing tag: '"May the hindmost get the itch"; I find it embarrassing to be left behind [and confess that I'm utterly ignorant of what I've never bothered to learn]' (*De arte poetica*, line 417). Classically educated traditionalists resented the power exercised by publishers over literature of whose classical basis they were ignorant (see II.151–2 and n. for Curll's punishment by schoolboys for printing Latin with mistakes in it; and *Corr.*: I, 373–4 for Pope's report of Lintot's methods of keeping his translators in what he took to be a due state of dependency).

61n. Something like this: Diomede declares his desire to undertake a daring mission, which relates to Curll's words at lines 58–60. ***as the Critics well know:*** Introducing a pun on

He left huge Lintot, and outstrip'd the wind.
As when a dab-chick waddles thro' the copse
On feet and wings, and flies, and wades, and hops;
So lab'ring on, with shoulders, hands, and head,
Wide as a wind-mill all his figure spread,
With arms expanded Bernard rows his state,
And left-legg'd Jacob seems to emulate.
Full in the middle way there stood a lake,
Which Curl's Corinna chanc'd that morn to make:

the Water-fowl, more extended, picturesque, and from *rural life*. The 59th verse is likewise a literal translation of one in Homer.

64, 65.] 'So eagerly the Fiend / O'er bog, o'er steep, thro' streight, rough, dense, or rare, / With head, hands, wings, or feet pursues his way, / And swims, or sinks, or wades, or creeps, or flies.' Milton, Book 2.

67, 68.] Milton, of the motion of the Swan: 'rows / His state with oary feet.' And Dryden, of another's: 'With two left legs'.

70. Curl's Corinna] This name, it seems, was taken by one Mrs. T—, who procured some private letters of Mr. Pope's, while almost a boy, to Mr. Cromwell, and sold them without the consent of either of those Gentlemen to Curl, who printed them in 12mo, 1727. He discovered her to be the publisher, in his Key, p. 11. We only take this opportunity of men-

---

'familiar': the image of a bailiff is 'familiar' in the sense of being taken from common life (as contrasted with elevated public affairs); but it is also uncomfortably 'familiar' to anyone whose debts have led to a visit from the bailiffs – as hack critics, it is insinuated, will know from experience. ***one in Homer:*** See editor's note on line 59.

63. dab-chick: the little grebe, a water bird awkward on land.

64, 65n. Echoing Satan's struggling through chaos (Fowler 1998: *Paradise Lost* II.947–50).

67–8 and n. rows his state: See Fowler 1998: *Paradise Lost* VII.439–40. ***left-legg'd Jacob:*** Alluding to the clumsy gait of Jacob Tonson the elder (Mack 1985: 121–4). Tonson had been the outstanding poetry publisher of his time, and had helped to launch Pope's career by offering to publish his 'Pastorals' (*Poetical Miscellanies: The Sixth Part* 1709; *Corr.*: I, 17). For the quotation from Dryden, see Kinsley 1958: 'Lines on Tonson'. In notes to early manuscript drafts Pope had cited Virgil's description of Aeneas's young son's efforts at keeping up with his father as they flee from Troy: 'he follows his father but not with equal steps' (Mack 1984: 106, 138; *Aeneid* II.724).

69–70 and 70n. Corinna: The name of a celebrated woman poet of ancient Greece (*c*.220 BC?), bestowed on the miscellaneous writer Elizabeth Thomas by Dryden (Ward 1942: 125–6). By calling her 'Curl's Corinna', however, Pope evokes the better-known Corinna celebrated as the poet's mistress in Ovid's *Amores*, insinuating a sexual slur in line with the traditional imaging of female publication as lack of chastity (Rumbold 1989: 163). Other witnesses assert her high moral character: at least some of the case routinely made against her rests on spurious evidence. ***some private letters:*** Pope's grudge against Thomas arose from her selling to Curll of some early letters from Pope to her friend Henry Cromwell (1628–74), which Cromwell had given to her (*Miscellanea* 1727 (actually 1726); *Corr.*: II, 437–8, 439–41; III, 458–9). Since the letters dated from a time when the young Pope was experimenting with his image as wit and rake, they had since come to embarrass him as both pretentious and indecent, and this unwelcome publication was important in turning his thoughts to methods

(Such was her wont, at early dawn to drop
Her evening cates before his neighbour's shop,)
Here fortun'd Curl to slide; loud shout the band,
And Bernard! Bernard! rings thro' all the Strand.
Obscene with filth the miscreant lies bewray'd,
Fal'n in the plash his wickedness had laid:

tioning the manner in which those letters got abroad, which the author was ashamed of as very trivial things, full not only of levities, but of wrong judgments of men and books, and only excusable from the youth and inexperience of the writer.

73.] 'Labitur infelix, caesis ut forte juvencis / Fusus humum viridesque super madefecerat herbas ... / Concidit, immundoque fimo, sacroque cruore.' Virg. Aen. v. of Nisus.

74.] 'Ut littus, Hyla, Hyla, omne sonaret.' Virg. Ecl. vi.

75.] Though this incident may seem too low and base for the dignity of an Epic poem,

---

of controlling the image presented by his letters, leading ultimately to a publication overseen – although secretly – by himself (*Corr.*: I, xii–xviii). An early manuscript draft seems to cast Thomas as 'Cromwell's Harlot' (Mack 1984: 106). ***in his Key:*** *A Compleat Key* 1728.

71–2. Such was her wont: Overlaying the association between bad writing and excrement with that between women writers, filth and promiscuity. In Thomas's case the allusion may have been the more wounding because of the spectacularly unpleasant digestive problems she suffered from injuries caused by swallowing a chicken bone (Thomas 1731–2: II, 93–6). The emptying of chamber pots into the street would at this time have been common practice. ***cates:*** delicacies. ***his neighbour's shop:*** Corinna shows an ironic delicacy in fouling the neighbour's frontage rather than that of her protector. Since the race takes place in the Strand (II.28), the incident, which had appeared in all editions of the *Dunciad*, may be envisaged as occurring 'over against Catherine Street in the Strand', where Curll had traded from about 1720, although by the time the passage was incorporated into *The Dunciad in Four Books* he had moved again (*TE*: V, 106; Mack 1985: 657).

73–8. For imitation of Spenser, see Sherbo 1970: 507–8.

73 and n. Curll's fall alludes to the misfortunes of the leading runners in the races in the *Iliad* and the *Aeneid*, both of whom slip on blood and entrails left from sacrifices (*Iliad* XXIII.773–7; *Aeneid* V.327–33). The note quotes lines 329–30 and 333 of the latter: 'The unlucky man slipped, as by chance the blood poured out where cattle had been slaughtered had soaked the ground and the green grass — He fell, right in the filthy dung and the blood of sacrifice'.

74 and n. Now that Lintot is alone in the field, the crowd cheers him on. The line imitates Virgil's account of the Argonauts' calling out for Hylas, who had been abducted by nymphs when he went to a spring to fetch water: 'They cried out until the whole shore rang "Hylas! Hylas!"' (*Eclogues* VI.44; for the *Dunciads*' use of the Hylas story, see Lawler in Mack & Winn 1980: 740–48). There is a play on 'strand' ('shore') and the name of the street.

75–6 and 75n. Obscene: Cp. Pope's translation of the fall of Ajax in Homer's footrace: 'Besmear'd with Filth, and blotted o'er with Clay, / Obscene to sight, the ruefull Racer lay' (*Iliad* XXXIII.911–12). ***bewray'd:*** exposed. ***his wickedness:*** Had Curll not spent the night with Corinna, she would not have been there next morning to create the 'plash' (puddle) in which he slipped. The line goes back to 1728 and the affair of the Cromwell letters referred to in the note; but Pope had more recently enjoyed punishing Curll's further surreptitious attempts to print his private correspondence by fraudulently manoeuvring Curll into publishing an edition of Pope's correspondence which Pope had actually prepared himself (Mack 1985: 653–7). In effect, the puddle got deeper as the years passed. ***the very***

Then first (if Poets aught of truth declare)

the learned very well know it to be but a copy of Homer and Virgil; the very words ὄνθος and *fimus* are used by them, though our poet (in compliance to modern nicety) has remarkably enriched and coloured his language, as well as raised the versification, in this Episode, and in the following one of Eliza. Mr. Dryden in *Mack-Fleckno,* has not scrupled to mention the *Morning Toast* at which the fishes bite in the Thames, *Pissing Alley, Reliques of the Bum, etc.* but our author is more grave, and (as a fine writer says of Virgil in his Georgics) *tosses about his* Dung *with an air of Majesty.* If we consider that the exercises of his *Authors* could with justice be no higher than *tickling, chattering, braying,* or *diving,* it was no easy matter to invent such games as were proportioned to the meaner degree of *Booksellers.* In Homer and Virgil, Ajax and Nisus the persons drawn in this plight are *Heroes;* whereas here they are such with whom it had been great impropriety to have joined any but vile ideas; besides the natural connection there is between Libellers and common Nusances. Nevertheless I have heard our author own, that this part of his Poem was (as it frequently happens) what cost him most trouble and pleased him least; but that he hoped it was excusable, since levelled at such as understand no delicate satyr: Thus the politest men are sometimes obliged to *swear,* when they happen to have to do with porters and oyster-wenches.

---

words: The note cites the Greek and Latin words for 'dung', used by Homer and Virgil in their accounts of the falling athlete (see notes on line 73). ***remarkably enriched and coloured his language:*** Implying that elegant periphrasis makes disgusting matter less so. On the other hand, there is a recurrence of human excrement in Book II that cannot be explained by one solitary reference to animal dung in each of Homer and Virgil; and Pope's elaborate verbal play could be objected to precisely because by defamiliarising bodily functions it stimulates the reader to dwell on them with a new vividness. ***raised the versification:*** Drawing attention to the conscious mastery of couplet form that enhances the contrast between matter and manner. ***the following one of Eliza:*** Beginning at line 157. ***Mr. Dryden in* Mack-Fleckno:** A precedent for Pope's association of bad writing with excrement. 'The *Morning Toast*' refers to the contents of chamber pots, emptied in the morning into the river; '*Pissing Alley*' is mentioned in the couplet 'Echoes from *Pissing-Ally Sh*— call, / And *Sh*— they resound from *A— Hall*' (where '*Sh*—' stands ostensibly for 'Shadwell'); '*Reliques of the Bum*' are unwanted books torn up for use in privies (Kinsley 1958: *Mac Fleckno*, lines 47–50, 101). ***a fine writer:*** Addison, in 'An Essay on Virgil's Georgics' (Guthkelch 1914). Despite the ostensible parallel, the allusion accentuates the disparity between a workaday attitude to agricultural muck-spreading and the *Dunciad*'s pretendedly 'grave' but in fact riotously exuberant fantasy of transgressing basic bodily decorums. **tickling, chattering, braying, *or* diving:** Competitions for authors later in Book II. ***the meaner degree of* Booksellers:** Insisting on a superiority of author to publisher which the commercial power of a Lintot or a Curll threatened to subvert. ***common Nusances:*** indecent or unhygienic acts in public places. ***what cost him most trouble and pleased him least:*** An attempt to evade the suspicion that Pope enjoys writing about excrement. Instead it is presented as an unpleasant necessity imposed by the need to speak the only language publishers can understand – an unconvincing use of the satirist's traditional claim to be motivated by the desire to reform his readers. ***porters and oyster-wenches:*** As people who spent their lives in the street (transporting goods or hawking oysters – then a cheap food), both groups were proverbial – among the polite – for coarseness.

77. In a note to an early manuscript draft Pope cites the closing line of Ovid's *Metamorphoses*, part of a claim to poetic immortality of precisely the kind which Pope's text posits as compromised by Dulness: '[I shall be current in the mouths of the people, and

The caitiff Vaticide conceiv'd a pray'r.
  Hear Jove! whose name my bards and I adore,
As much at least as any God's, or more;
And him and his, if more devotion warms,
Down with the Bible, up with the Pope's Arms.
  A place there is, betwixt earth, air, and seas,
Where, from Ambrosia, Jove retires for ease.
There in his seat two spacious vents appear,
On this he sits, to that he leans his ear,
And hears the various vows of fond mankind;

82.] The Bible, Curl's sign; the Cross-keys, Lintot's.

83.] See Lucian's Icaro-Menippus; where this fiction is more extended.

Ibid.] 'Orbe locus medio est, inter terrasque, fretumque, / Coelestesque plagas'. Ovid. Met. xii.

---

through all ages in fame,] if the prophecies of bards have any truth in them[, I shall live]' (Mack 1984: 139; *Metamorphoses* XV.879).

78. The caitiff Vaticide: Curll is denounced as a wretched ('caitiff') murderer of poets (*vates* is Latin for a poet or bard): he murders them either by starving them when they write for him, or – metaphorically – by mangling them in his publications. ***conceiv'd a pray'r:*** A common motif in the games described by Homer and Virgil.

79–80. Insinuating that the hackneyed poetic convention of invoking Jupiter and the classical pantheon is as near as Curll and his writers get to the practice of religion.

81–2 and 82n. Curll is saying that *if* Jupiter finds more devotion in Lintot and his employees, then Lintot deserves to win the prize. Even in 1729 Curll had pointed out that he no longer used the Bible in his sign; and by the time the passage was incorporated in *The Dunciad in Four Books* he had adopted the sign of the Pope's Head, an inflammatory pun which Pope here declines to acknowledge (Curll 1729; Straus 1927: 183). Lintot's sign of the Cross Keys alludes to Christ's commissioning of Peter to hold the keys of the kingdom, hence 'the Pope's Arms' (Matthew 16:19).

83 and n. A place there is: Alluding to Ovid's description of the house of rumour, which receives and disseminates news both true and false: 'There is a place in the centre of the world, between the earth and the sea and the wide spaces of the sky' (*Metamorphoses* XII.39–40). Pope had previously treated the theme, via its transformation in Chaucer's *Hous of Fame*, in his early dream vision, *The Temple of Fame*. ***Lucian's Icaro-Menippus:*** A fantasy by the Greek satirist Lucian (*c.* AD 115–after 180) in which the earlier Greek satirist Menippus (third century BC) is the main character (*Icaromenippus*, paragraphs 25–6). Like Icarus in myth, he puts on artificial wings and flies into the heavens. He finds Zeus sitting on a golden throne listening at a hole in the floor of heaven through which prayers rise from earth. Lucian is not responsible for the fantasy of the divine privy; but human prayers *are* laid out 'On two Close-Stools which *Jove*'s Back-Closet grac'd' in Ozell's *La secchia rapita: The Trophy-bucket, A Mock-Heroic Poem*, translated from the Italian of Alessandro Tassoni (1565–1635) (Ozell 1710: 51). For Lucian and the Scriblerians, see Jones in Mack & Winn 1980: 618–19.

84. Ambrosia: the food of the gods. ***ease:*** 'House of ease' was a contemporary euphemism for privy.

87. vows: Offered in furtherance of prayers. ***fond:*** foolish (as in the line following, where people ask irreconcilable favours).

Some beg an eastern, some a western wind:
All vain petitions, mounting to the sky,
With reams abundant this abode supply;
Amus'd he reads, and then returns the bills
Sign'd with that Ichor which from Gods distils.
  In office here fair Cloacina stands,
And ministers to Jove with purest hands.
Forth from the heap she pick'd her Vot'ry's pray'r,
And plac'd it next him, a distinction rare!
Oft had the Goddess heard her servant's call,
From her black grottos near the Temple-wall,
List'ning delighted to the jest unclean
Of link-boys vile, and watermen obscene;
Where as he fish'd her nether realms for Wit,
She oft had favour'd him, and favours yet.
Renew'd by ordure's sympathetic force,

92.] Alludes to Homer, Iliad v: '*ῥέε δ' ἄμβροτον αἷμα Θέοιο, / Ἰχὼρ, οἷος πέρ τε ῥέει μακάρεσσι Θεοῖσιν.*' 'A stream of nect'rous humour issuing flow'd, / Sanguine, such as celestial sp'rits may bleed.' Milton.

93.] The Roman Goddess of the common-sewers.

101.] See the preface to Swift's and Pope's Miscellanies.

---

91. bills: notes, documents.

92 and n. Homer states that the gods bleed ichor, not mere human blood: 'there flowed the immortal blood of the goddess, ichor such as flows in the blessed gods' (*Iliad* V.339–40). Pope extends the doctrine to the divine excrement. The note also adds an imitation of the Homeric passage from Milton's account of the wounding of Satan (Fowler 1998: *Paradise Lost* VI.332–3).

93 and n. In office: Punning on the senses 'on duty' and 'privy' ('house of office'). ***Cloacina:*** Named from the Latin *cloaca* ('sewer'), and not among the principal classical deities. In Gay's London mock-georgic *Trivia: or, The Art of Walking the Streets of London* (1716), cited in a note to an early manuscript draft of this passage, she is associated with Fleet Ditch (Dearing 1974: *Trivia* II.107–216; Mack 1984: 107; Nokes 1995: 212–17). For Brooks-Davies *Trivia* is a key influence on Pope's evocation of dark goddesses whose more auspicious manifestations, notably absent from the *Dunciad*, recall lost ideals of government (Brooks-Davies 1985: 34–9).

95–100. Cloacina shows special favour to Curll as 'her Vot'ry' or devotee. Although he prayed directly to Jupiter on this occasion, she knows of his habitual devotion at her 'black grottos', Thames coal-wharves south of the Strand, adjacent to the Temple, where he listens for 'the jest unclean' of such denizens of the streets as 'link-boys' (whose job was to carry torches through the unlit streets to light the way for travellers at night) and 'watermen' (who ferried goods and passengers up and down the Thames).

101 and n. Implying that he finds inspiration for his obscene publications in Cloacina's 'nether [i.e. 'lower'] realms', i.e. the sewers. The note recalls Swift's and Pope's allegation that 'It has been humourously said, that some have fished the very Jakes, for Papers left there by Men of Wit' (*PW*: II, 91).

103. sympathetic: Implying Curll's affinity with excrement.

As oil'd with magic juices for the course,
Vig'rous he rises; from th' effluvia strong
Imbibes new life, and scours and stinks along;
Re-passes Lintot, vindicates the race,
Nor heeds the brown dishonours of his face.
  And now the victor stretch'd his eager hand
Where the tall Nothing stood, or seem'd to stand;
A shapeless shade, it melted from his sight,
Like forms in clouds, or visions of the night.
To seize his papers, Curl, was next thy care;
His papers light, fly diverse, tost in air;
Songs, sonnets, epigrams the winds uplift,
And whisk 'em back to Evans, Young, and Swift.
Th' embroider'd suit at least he deem'd his prey;
That suit an unpay'd taylor snatch'd away.

104.] Alluding to the opinion that there are ointments used by witches to enable them to fly in the air, *etc.*

108.] 'faciem ostentabat, et udo / Turpia membra fimo'. Virg. Aen. v.

111.] 'Effugit imago / Par levibus ventis, volucrique simillima somno.' Virg. Aen. vi.

114.] Virgil, Aen. vi. of the Sibyls leaves: 'Carmina ... / Turbata volent rapidis ludibria ventis.'

116.] Some of those persons whose writings, epigrams, or jests he had owned. See Note on ver. 50.

118.] This line has been loudly complained of in Mist, June 8, Dedic. to Sawney, and

---

106. scours: runs quickly.

107. vindicates the race: claims victory in the race.

108 and n. Typical of Pope's euphemistic diction, heightened by comparison with Virgil's franker description of Nisus: 'He displayed his face, and his limbs filthy with wet dung' (*Aeneid* V.337–8). For established connotations of the key terms here, see Tillotson 1950: 154–6. Compare also Parnell's mock-heroic 'Homer's Battle of the Frogs and Mice', in which mud thrown at a combatant 'Dishonours his brown face' (Rawson & Lock 1989: III.86).

110. For parallels to this line-ending in Dryden and Pope, see Sherbo 1970: 508.

111n. Citing Aeneas's attempt to embrace his dead father's shade: 'The image fled like light winds, and very like a winged dream' (*Aeneid* VI.701–2).

114 and n. fly diverse: in different directions. The phrase is used by Milton to describe the flight of Sin and Death through chaos (Fowler 1998: *Paradise Lost* X.284). ***the Sibyls leaves:*** The Sibyl was Apollo's prophetess, consulted by Aeneas, who asked that his answer should not be entrusted to leaves 'lest the verses should fly away in confusion, the playthings of the swift wind' (*Aeneid* VI.74–5).

115. sonnets: Short poems, not necessarily in the fourteen-line form to which the term is now restricted.

116. Abel Evans (1679–1737), clergyman, wit and acquaintance of Pope, is cited with Young and Swift as the kind of writer whose work a plagiarist like Moore Smythe would purloin and a publisher like Curll would pirate.

118 and n. an unpay'd taylor: It was customary for tradesmen to supply goods on credit. The line insinuates that the clothes of a well-dressed hack writer are unlikely to have been paid for. ***loudly complained of:*** Authors less successful than Pope were quick to sense

No rag, no scrap, of all the beau, or wit,
That once so flutter'd, and that once so writ.
  Heav'n rings with laughter: Of the laughter vain,
Dulness, good Queen, repeats the jest again.
Three wicked imps, of her own Grubstreet choir,
She deck'd like Congreve, Addison, and Prior;

others, as a most inhuman satyr on the *poverty* of *Poets:* But it is thought our author would be acquitted by a jury of *Taylors*. To me this instance seems unluckily chosen; if it be a satyr on any body, it must be on a bad *paymaster*, since the person to whom they have here applied it, was a man of fortune. Not but poets may well be jealous of so great a prerogative as *non-payment*; which Mr. Dennis so far asserts, as boldly to pronounce that 'if Homer himself was not in debt, it was because nobody would trust him.' Pref. to Rem. on the Rape of the Lock, p. 15.

124.] These authors being such whose names will reach posterity, we shall not give any account of them, but proceed to those of whom it is necessary. — Besaleel Morris was author of some satyrs on the translators of Homer, with many other things printed in news-papers. — 'Bond writ a satyr against Mr. P—. Capt. Breval was author of The Confederates, an ingenious dramatic performance to expose Mr. P. Mr. Gay, Dr. Arb. and some ladies of quality,' says Curl, Key, p. 11.

---

injustice in his recurrent references to their poverty (*Mist's Weekly Journal*, 8 June 1728; *Sawney* 1728: Dedication; and see the attempted defence mounted in the prefatory 'Letter to the Publisher'). ***would be acquitted by a jury of*** **Taylors:** Tradesmen were easily ruined by customers who had no means or intention of paying. ***this instance seems unluckily chosen:*** This seems at first to imply that the writers' employers (the publishers) are the ones really to blame, since they refuse to pay a living wage; but with the mention of 'a bad paymaster' a specific gibe at Moore Smythe emerges: he had inherited from his grandfather the lucrative post of paymaster of the King's Gentlemen Pensioners (who formed a royal guard on state occasions), which entitled him to invest the funds set aside for payments and keep the interest. Despite being made 'a man of fortune' in this way, he was unable to remain solvent. ***poets may well be jealous:*** Implying that Dennis aims to prove poets above the obligation of paying their debts by the example of Homer. In fact, Dennis had accused Pope of 'the Impudence to infer ... Want of merit from ... Want of Fortune'; and he concluded that Pope 'owes his little Substance to a *vile Translation* of a *poor* but *excellent* Poet, who if he was not *in Debt*, it was because no Body would trust him', accurately identifying the Homer translation as basis of the financial security which in Pope's eyes vindicated his claim to write independently and with integrity (Dennis 1728; Hooker 1939–43: II, 326–7).

121–2. Recalling the laughter of the gods at the clumsiness of the lame god Haephestus in Homer's *Iliad* (I.599–600). Dulness 'proves her title by simply repeating the same joke' (Morris 1984: 276).

123. her own Grubstreet choir: The poets who sing her praises.

124 and n. Congreve, Addison, and Prior: The publisher could market hack work more successfully by attributing it to such illustrious authors as the dramatist William Congreve (1670–1729), Addison and Prior (for Curll's frauds concerning these authors, see Straus 1927: 25–6, 266–7; *Corr.*: II, 434; *PW*: II, 91–2). ***of whom it is necessary:*** A typical assertion of the ephemeral nature of Grubstreet fame. ***some satyrs on the translators of Homer:*** *An Epistle to Mr. Welsted* 1721; *On the English Translators of Homer* 1733. ***Bond writ a satyr:*** *The Progress of Dulness* 1728. ***Capt. Breval:*** *The Confederates*, Breval's satire on the

Mears, Warner, Wilkins run: delusive thought!
Breval, Bond, Besaleel, the varlets caught.
Curl stretches after Gay, but Gay is gone,
He grasps an empty Joseph for a John:
So Proteus, hunted in a nobler shape,
Became, when seiz'd, a puppy, or an ape.
To him the Goddess: Son! thy grief lay down,

*125. **Mears, Warner, Wilkins]*** Booksellers, and Printers of much anonymous stuff.

*126. **Breval, Bond, Besaleel,]*** I foresee it will be objected from this line, that we were in an error in our assertion on ver. 50. of this book, that More was a fictitious name, since these persons are equally represented by the poet as phantoms. So at first sight it may seem; but be not deceived, reader; these also are not real persons. 'Tis true, Curl declares Breval, a captain, author of a piece called The Confederates; but the same Curl first said it was written by Joseph Gay: Is his second assertion to be credited any more than his first? He likewise affirms Bond to be one who writ a satyr on our poet: But where is such a satyr to be found? where was such a writer ever heard of? As for Besaleel, it carries forgery in the very name; nor is it, as the others are, a surname. Thou may'st depend upon it, no such authors ever lived: all phantoms. SCRIBL.

128.] *Joseph Gay*, a fictitious name put by Curl before several pamphlets, which made them pass with many for Mr. Gay's.

---

collaboration of Pope and Arbuthnot with Gay on *Three Hours after Marriage*, contains gross insults to Pope, with a caricature of him, readily identifiable by its small size and deformity, prominent on the title-page (*The Confederates* 1717). In citing Curll's comment, the note suppresses a direct reference to *Three Hours*, an episode of his youth from which Pope was always keen to divert attention (*A Compleat Key* 1728).

125 and n. Mears, Warner, Wilkins: William Mears (*fl.* 1713–29) published poetry by several victims of the *Dunciad*; Thomas Warner (active from 1716) and William Wilkins (*d.* 1756) published pro-government tracts and newspapers (*TE*: V, 447, 457–8, 459).

126 and n. varlets: rogues. ***I foresee it will be objected:*** Scriblerus argues that the three 'imps' who imitate Congreve, Addison and Prior are no more real than Moore Smythe (the phantom prize of the previous race). The title-page of Breval's *The Confederates* attributed it to 'Mr. Gay', and the dedication was signed 'Joseph Gay', a fiction meant to be mistaken for the celebrated John Gay; so why should Curll's later attribution to Breval be any more reliable (*The Confederates* 1717; *A Compleat Key* 1728)? Breval also attributed *A Complete Key to the Non-Juror* (which ironically laid an accusation of plagiarism against Cibber) to 'Joseph Gay' (see IV.355 and notes). Bond's satire appeared without a name on the title, but with the fictitious internal signature 'H. Stanhope', and his authorship thus rested on Curll's bare assertion (*The Progress of Dulness* 1728; *A Compleat Key* 1728; Guerinot 1969: 122–4). Finally, Scriblerus pronounces Morrice's unusual biblical Christian name so preposterous as to cast doubt on his real existence.

128 and n. For details of the deceit, see *TE*: V, 111. Compare Pope's translation of the divine rescue of Paris from his adversary, which 'left an empty Helmet in his hand' (*Iliad* III.462). There is a pun on 'Joseph', a contemporary term for a long cloak.

130. a puppy, or an ape: The former was a contemporary term of abuse for an insolent young person; the latter suggests empty mimicry.

And turn this whole illusion on the town:
As the sage dame, experienc'd in her trade,
By names of Toasts retails each batter'd jade;
(Whence hapless Monsieur much complains at Paris
Of wrongs from Duchesses and Lady Maries;)
Be thine, my stationer! this magic gift;
Cook shall be Prior, and Concanen, Swift:

132.] It was a common practice of this bookseller to publish vile pieces of obscure hands under the names of eminent authors.

138. Cook shall be Prior,] The man here specified writ a thing called The Battle of Poets, in which Philips and Welsted were the Heroes, and Swift and Pope utterly routed. He also published some malevolent things in the British, London, and Daily Journals; and at the same time wrote letters to Mr. Pope, protesting his innocence. His chief work was a translation of Hesiod, to which Theobald writ notes and half-notes, which he carefully owned.

In the first edition of this poem there were only asterisks in this place, but the names were since inserted, merely to fill up the verse, and give ease to the ear of the reader.

---

132 and n. Dulness comforts Curll by suggesting that he should deceive 'the town' (his potential readers) as she has deceived him.

133–4. The brothel-keeper pretends that even the most decrepit whore ('each batter'd jade') is a society beauty toasted by men of fashion. For parallel allegations from other sources, see Williams 1953b and Bawcutt 1961.

135–6. Developing as an imagined example of the practice described in lines 133–4, this is a semi-private and characteristically unfair allegation about the relationship between Pope's former friend Lady Mary Wortley Montagu and a manipulative Frenchman, Toussaint Rémond de Saint-Mard. Rémond, having elicited a friendly response from Lady Mary to a campaign of epistolary gallantry, came to England and pestered her into investing money on his behalf in the South Sea scheme. When the Bubble burst, he accused her of fraud and threatened to publish her letters and denounce her to her husband (Halsband 1960: see index under Rémond). Pope implausibly implies that Rémond had been her lover and had caught venereal disease from her (for the background to the attack, see Rumbold 1989: 131–61).

138 and n. Savage lists as typical of Curll's methods the commissioning of obscenities to be published as by Prior, Swift and other distinguished authors (*An Author to be Lett* 1729: 3). ***a thing called The Battle of Poets:*** *The Battle of the Poets* 1725. ***wrote letters to Mr. Pope:*** Cooke wrote in 1728 that he was not 'the author of some scurrilous Pieces ... in the Daily Papers'; that he was 'sincerely ashamed' of the *Battle*, which he would not publish again; and, least credibly of all, that 'Your moral character I never heard attacked by any with whom I converse' (*Corr.*: II, 509–10, 519–20). Pope made some attempt to resolve the matter through an intermediary, and finally demanded that Cooke sign a recantation of his attacks on Pope's moral character (III, 8; V, 7). Instead, Cooke's 1729 revision of the *Battle* was even more offensive than the original. ***a translation of Hesiod:*** Cooke 1728. ***which he carefully owned:*** Implying that Theobald is over-keen to take credit for even the tiniest contributions. Cooke says he has acknowledged his friends' contributions lest they should be blamed for his own errors (Cooke 1728: II, 196). ***only asterisks:*** In 1728 (II.118), the names of Cooke and Concanen appeared as '*C—*' and '*C—n*'. ***merely to fill up the verse:*** Stressing their insignificance.

So shall each hostile name become our own,
And we too boast our Garth and Addison.

140.] Nothing is more remarkable than our author's love of praising good writers. He has in this very poem celebrated Mr. Locke, Sir Isaac Newton, Dr. Barrow, Dr. Atterbury, Mr. Dryden, Mr. Congreve, Dr. Garth, Mr. Addison; in a word, almost every man of his time that deserved it; even Cibber himself (presuming him to be author of the Careless Husband.) It was very difficult to have that pleasure in a poem on this subject, yet he has found means to insert their panegyric, and has made even Dulness out of her own mouth pronounce it. It must have been particularly agreeable to him to celebrate Dr. Garth; both as his constant friend, and as he was his predecessor in this kind of satyr. The Dispensary attacked the whole body of Apothecaries, a much more useful one undoubtedly than that of the bad Poets; if in truth this can be a body, of which no two members ever agreed. It also did what Mr. Theobald says is unpardonable, drew in *parts* of *private character*, and introduced *persons independent of his subject*. Much more would Boileau have incurred his censure, who left all subjects whatever, on all occasions, to fall upon the bad poets (which, it is to be feared, would have been more immediately his concern.) But certainly next to commending good writers, the greatest service to learning is to expose the bad, who can only that way be made of any use to it. This truth is very well set forth in these lines addressed to our author:

The craven Rook, and pert Jackdaw,
(Tho' neither birds of moral kind)
Yet serve, if hang'd or stuff'd with straw,
To shew us which way blows the wind.

140n. praising good writers: Dulness's desire to invent a 'Garth and Addison' for her own party is presented as oblique recognition of the merit of the real ones. ***Mr. Locke:*** John Locke (1632–1704), philosopher. ***Sir Isaac Newton:*** Scientist and mathematician (1642–1727). ***Dr. Barrow:*** Isaac Barrow (1630–77), Anglican cleric, mathematician and classicist. ***even Cibber himself:*** See I.187–8 and editor's note. Cibber's dedication to *The Careless Husband* turns accusations that the play was 'not my own' into a compliment to his patron, arguing that its 'more easie Turn of Thought and Spirit' was owing to 'the many stolen Observations I have made from your Grace's manner of Conversing' (Cibber 1705). ***his predecessor in this kind of satyr:*** Garth's *Dispensary*, a mock-heroic attack on members of the Royal College of Physicians who sided with the apothecaries (dispensing chemists) in their opposition to the college's project of a non-profit-making dispensary for the poor. This undercut an important part of the apothecaries' livelihood, the treatment of patients too poor to pay a doctor (Lord 1963–75: VI, 58–61; Colomb 1992: 156–7). ***a much more useful one:*** Implying that if it was acceptable for Garth to attack a group as useful as apothecaries, it would be unreasonable to criticise Pope for attacking one as useless as bad poets. ***of which no two members ever agreed:*** The bad poets are presented as demonstrating their ill nature and lack of true purpose by being always in conflict with each other. ***what Mr. Theobald says is unpardonable:*** In *Mist's Weekly Journal*, 22 June 1728, signed 'W.A.' but attributed by Pope to Theobald. ***would have been more immediately his concern:*** Implying that Theobald would have been personally concerned with what Boileau had to say against bad poets, being one himself. ***to expose the bad:*** Drawing on the traditional satirist's defence against the charge of mere malice, that exposing evil helps to reform society. ***these lines addressed to our author:*** They are said to have appeared in *The Evening Post*, 26–8 June 1729

With that she gave him (piteous of his case,
Yet smiling at his rueful length of face)

Thus dirty knaves, or chatt'ring fools,
Strung up by dozens in thy lay,
Teach more by half than Dennis' rules,
And point instruction every way.

With Aegypt's art thy pen may strive,
One potent drop let this but shed,
And ev'ry Rogue that stunk alive,
Becomes a precious Mummy dead.

141, 142.] 'Risit pater optimus illi ... / Me liceat casum miserere insontis amici ... / Sic fatus, tergum Gaetuli immane leonis', *etc.* Virg. Aen. v.

142. rueful length of face)] 'The decrepid person or figure of a man are no reflections upon his *Genius:* An honest mind will love and esteem a *man of worth,* though he be deformed or poor. Yet the author of the Dunciad hath libelled a person for his *rueful length of face!'* Mist's Journal, June 8. This *Genius* and *man of worth,* whom an honest mind should *love,* is Mr. Curl. True it is, he stood in the Pillory, an incident which will lengthen the face of any man tho' it were ever so comely, therefore is no reflection on the natural beauty of Mr. Curl. But as to reflections on any man's face, or figure, Mr. Dennis saith excellently; 'Natural deformity comes not by our fault; 'tis often occasioned by calamities and diseases, which a man can no more help than a monster can his deformity. There is no one misfortune, and no one disease, but what all the rest of mankind are subject to. — But the deformity of this *Author* is visible, present, lasting, unalterable, and peculiar to himself. 'Tis the mark of God and Nature upon him, to give us warning that we should hold no society with him, as a creature not of our original, nor of our species: and they who have refused to take this warning

---

(Griffith 1922–7: I, 205). **to shew us which way blows the wind:** The dead birds can be hung up as weathercocks. **Aegypt's art:** Just as the ancient Egyptians could transform a decaying corpse into 'a precious Mummy' (often taken in powdered form for its supposed curative properties), so Pope is declared to transform the 'Rogue' who is a nuisance alive into a salutary warning when 'strung up' in his satire.

141–2 and n. Risit pater optimus illi: Citing Aeneas's response to Nisus, who had lost the foot race by slipping in a heap of dung and offal: 'Aeneas, best of fathers, smiled at him' (*Aeneid* V.358, 350–51). Aeneas had previously spoken to Salius ('*me liceat*', etc.), whom Nisus had deliberately tripped up: '"I hope it is all right for me to pity my unfortunate friend". Having said that [he gave him] the huge hide of a Gaetulian lion'.

142n: Mist's Journal: *Mist's Weekly Journal,* 8 June 1728, signed 'W.A.', but attributed by Pope to Theobald. ***the natural beauty of Mr. Curl:*** According to the writer and eccentric Thomas Amory (1691?–1788), 'Curl was in person very tall and thin, an ungainly, aukward, white-faced man. His eyes were a light-grey, large, projecting, gogle and pur-blind. He was splay-footed, and baker-kneed' (knock-knees were supposedly an occupational risk of bakers) (Amory 1770: IV, 138). Laetitia Pilkington (*c.*1705–1760), poet and autobiographer, thought him 'an ugly squinting old Fellow' (Pilkington 1748–54: II, 189). ***Mr. Dennis saith excellently:*** Quoting perhaps the most hurtful of all Dennis's attacks on Pope, but omitting Dennis's allegation that Pope has himself 'upbraided People with their Calamities and Diseases ... which are either false or past, or which he himself gave them by administering Poison to them' –

which God and nature have given them, and have in spite of it by a senseless presumption ventured to be familiar with him, have severely suffered, *etc.* 'Tis certain his original is not from Adam, but from the Devil,' *etc.* DENNIS, Charact. of Mr. P. octavo, 1716.

Admirably it is observed by Mr. Dennis against Mr. Law, p. 33. 'That the language of Billingsgate can never be the language of charity, nor consequently of Christianity.' I should else be tempted to use the language of a Critic; for what is more provoking to a commentator, than to behold his author thus portrayed? Yet I consider it really hurts not *him;* whereas to call some others dull, might do them prejudice with a world too apt to believe it: Therefore, though Mr. D. may call another a *little ass* or a *young toad,* far be it from us to call him a *toothless lion* or an *old serpent.* Indeed, had I written these notes (as was once my intent) in the learned language, I might have given him the appellations of *balatro, calceatum caput, scurra in triviis,* being phrases in good esteem and frequent usage among the best learned: But in our mother-tongue, were I to tax any gentleman of the Dunciad, surely it should be in words not to the vulgar intelligible; whereby christian charity, decency, and good accord among authors, might be preserved. SCRIBL.

The good Scriblerus here, as on all occasions, eminently shews his humanity. But it was far otherwise with the gentlemen of the Dunciad, whose scurrilities were always personal, and of that nature which provoked every honest man but Mr. Pope; yet never to be lamented, since they occasioned the following amiable Verses:

---

a reference to Pope's *Full and True Account* of how he had given Curll an emetic (*A True Character* 1716; Hooker 1939–43: II, 105). ***Admirably it is observed:*** Introducing a summary of a passage from Dennis's *The Stage Defended* (1726), an attack on *The Absolute Unlawfulness of the Stage-entertainment Fully Demonstrated* (1726) by the non-juring clergyman William Law (1686–1761), whose high Tory principles were anathema to Dennis (Hooker 1939–43: II, 316). Dennis is thus convicted by his own words of uncharitable and unchristian behaviour to Pope. ***the language of a Critic:*** Which Scriblerus takes to be characteristically abusive. ***his author:*** Scriblerus adopts a protective and proprietary attitude to Pope. ***it hurts not* him:** Because, Scriblerus assumes, Pope's worth is too well known for such calumnies to be believed. ***the learned language:*** Latin. **balatro, calceatum caput, scurra in triviis:** 'A buffoon, the sort of idiot who puts his shoes on his head, someone who has nothing better to do than hang around at street corners'. Bentley was remarkable for the offensiveness of his denunciations, in Latin, of fellow-scholars (see for examples *Philargyrii Cantabrigiensis Emendationes* 1711; Monk 1833: I, 266–76). ***But in our mother-tongue:*** Since Scriblerus is writing in English, he will say only that if he were to 'tax' (criticise) the authors ridiculed in the *Dunciad,* it would have to be 'in words not to the vulgar intelligible' (Latin), which such authors could not be hurt by because they could not, he insinuates, read it. He concludes ironically with a picture of these authors as an ideal community of Christian harmony, unaffected by insults they would not understand. ***eminently shews his humanity:*** The mock-commentator who takes over at this point accepts Scriblerus's barbed comments as 'humanity', reinforcing the notion that critics are by definition uncharitable. There is an allusion to the notorious insult offered to Bentley by the young Charles Boyle (1676–1731), later fourth Earl of Orrery, who had in 1695 produced the controversial Christ Church edition of the so-called letters of Phalaris (Levine 1991: 47–84). Boyle alleged that Bentley had denied him the use of a manuscript of Phalaris 'pro singulari sua humanitate' ('on account of his singular humanity', i.e. through having no humanity at all) (Boyle 1695: Praefatio). ***every honest man but Mr. Pope:*** Pope professed not to be hurt by such attacks (*OAC*: I, 42). In contrast, Johnson reports the testimony of Jonathan Richardson the younger: 'he attended his father the painter on a visit, when one of Cibber's pamphlets came into the hands of Pope, who said, "These things are my diversion." They sat by him while he perused it, and saw his features writhen with anguish' (Hill 1905: III, 188). ***the following amiable verses:*** Attributed

A shaggy Tap'stry, worthy to be spread
On Codrus' old, or Dunton's modern bed;

While Malice, Pope, denies thy page
Its own celestial fire,
While Critics, and while Bards in rage,
Admiring, won't admire:

While wayward pens thy worth assail,
And envious tongues decry;
These times tho' many a Friend bewail,
These times bewail not I.

But when the World's loud praise is thine,
And spleen no more shall blame,
When with thy Homer thou shalt shine
In one establish'd fame:

When none shall rail, and ev'ry lay
Devote a wreathe to thee;
That day (for come it will) that day
Shall I lament to see.

143. A shaggy Tap'stry,] A sorry kind of Tapestry frequent in old Inns, made of worsted or some coarser stuff; like that which is spoken of by Donne — *Faces as frightful as theirs who whip Christ in old hangings*. The imagery woven in it alludes to the mantle of Cloanthus, in Aen. v.

144.] Of Codrus the poet's bed, see Juvenal, describing his *poverty* very copiously, Sat. iii. ver. 203, *etc: Lectus erat Codro, etc.*

Codrus had but one bed, so short to boot,
That his short Wife's short legs hung dangling out.
His cupboard's head six earthen pitchers grac'd,
Beneath them was his trusty tankard plac'd;

---

by Johnson to David Lewis (1683?–1760), minor poet and acquaintance of Pope, who had printed contributions from Pope in his *Miscellaneous Poems* (Lewis 1730; Savage 1732: Epigrams XXVII; Hill 1934–5: IV, 306–7). The argument is that Pope's detractors give him the opportunity to display his courage and integrity by the manner in which he bears their insults. **rail:** complain abusively.

143n. worsted: The most expensive tapestries were made of silk. Wool is graded either as 'worsted', the relatively fine thread spun from the longer fibres of a fleece (now used principally in suiting), or as woollen, spun from the shorter fibres (the 'coarser stuff' used for blankets and cheap yarns). ***spoken of by Donne:*** Misquoted from Satire IV, of which Pope had published an imitation in 1733 (*TE*: IV, 46–7). ***the mantle of Cloanthus:*** Cloanthus won the boat race, and his prize was a cloak woven with the mythical story of Jupiter's abduction of Ganymede (*Aeneid* V.250–57).

144 and n. Codrus the poet: Identifying Juvenal's poor garret-dweller (Satire III.203–11) with the bad poet Cordus in Satire I. **Codrus had but one bed:** Dryden's translation

Instructive work! whose wry-mouth'd portraiture
Display'd the fates her confessors endure.
Earless on high, stood unabash'd De Foe,

And to support this noble plate, there lay
A bending Chiron, cast from honest clay.
His few Greek books a rotten chest contain'd,
Whose covers much of mouldiness complain'd,
Where mice and rats devour'd poetic bread,
And on heroic verse luxuriously were fed.
'Tis true poor Codrus nothing had to boast,
And yet poor Codrus all that nothing lost. Dryden.

But Mr. Concanen, in his dedication of the letters, advertisements, *etc.* to the author of the Dunciad, assures us that 'Juvenal never satyrized the poverty of Codrus.'

John Dunton was a broken bookseller and abusive scribler; he writ Neck or Nothing, a violent satyr on some ministers of state; a libel on the Duke of Devonshire and the Bishop of Peterborough, *etc.*

(Kinsley 1958: Juvenal, Satire III.332–43), cited as a precedent for Pope's satire on the poverty of bad writers – an application pointed by the italicisation of 'poverty' in the introductory note. ***Mr. Concanen:*** The Preface to *A Compleat Collection* 1728, attributed by Pope to Concanen, claims that Juvenal represented the poverty of poets 'not as a Reproach to themselves, but as an indelible Scandal, and eternal Satire, upon their Patrons, the *Noblesse* of that Age, who suffer'd it'. ***John Dunton:*** Whig eccentric, writer and publisher (1659–1733). For a positive account, contrasting his distinctively modern outlook with the classically oriented Scriblerian mentality, see Hunter 1990: 99–106. ***broken:*** bankrupt. ***Neck or Nothing:*** The anonymously published *Neck or Nothing* 1713. ***some ministers of state:*** Pope's friends Oxford and Bolingbroke. ***a libel on the Duke of Devonshire and the Bishop of Peterborough:*** William Cavendish (1640–1707), first Duke of Devonshire, one of the magnates who supported William of Orange in 1688, had several illegitimate children. White Kennett (1660–1728), Whig cleric, obtained the patronage of the Cavendish family (becoming, ultimately, Bishop of Peterborough) by preaching a funeral sermon which passed over his notorious adulteries, suggested that he had repented on his deathbed, and praised his defence of Whig principles: the sermon was attacked by Dunton in his anonymous *The Hazard of a Death-Bed-Repentance* (1708) (Bennett 1957: 98–100; cp. *Imitations of Horace, Epistles* II.ii.220–23).

145. wry-mouth'd: Because the writers and publishers represented are suffering punishments incurred through their literary activities.

146. her confessors: A play on the sense of 'confessor' as one who professes Christianity under persecution (stress on the first syllable). The tapestry may allude to the Renaissance practice of commissioning paintings of the saints, which could serve as patterns for tapestries (Gneiting 1975: 426–7).

147. Earless on high: Although Defoe had stood in the pillory, he had not had his ears cut off (see editor's note on I.103), but Pope persists with 'Earless' because it reinforces the shameful connotations of the pillory (Colomb 1992: 178–9). Witnesses agree that Defoe's 'unabash'd' demeanour of conscious innocence and the acclaim of the crowd turned the intended disgrace into a triumph: as Pope had noted in an early manuscript draft, Defoe had circulated copies of his *A Hymn to the Pillory* among the bystanders (Lord 1963–75: VI, 585–6;

And Tutchin flagrant from the scourge below.
There Ridpath, Roper, cudgell'd might ye view,
The very worsted still look'd black and blue.
Himself among the story'd chiefs he spies,

148.] John Tutchin, author of some vile verses, and of a weekly paper called the Observator: He was sentenced to be whipped through several towns in the west of England, upon which he petitioned King James II. to be hanged. When that prince died in exile, he wrote an invective against his memory, occasioned by some humane elegies on his death. He lived to the time of Queen Anne.

149. There Ridpath, Roper,] Authors of the Flying-post and Post-boy, two scandalous papers on different sides, for which they equally and alternately deserved to be cudgelled, and were so.

151.] 'Se quoque principibus permixtum agnovit Achivis ... / Constitit, et lacrymans: Quis jam locus, inquit, Achate! / Quae regio in terris nostri non plena laboris?' Virg. Aen. i.

The history of Curl's being tossed in a blanket, and whipped by the scholars of Westminster,

---

Mack 1984: 140; Backscheider 1989: 118–19).

148 and n. Tutchin flagrant from the scourge: John Tutchin (1661?–1707), a Whig propagandist who raised troops for Monmouth's rebellion, was sentenced, among other penalties, to be whipped annually through all the market towns in Dorset, but (despite what is here asserted) was able to bribe his way to a pardon. He is 'flagrant', not only in the sense of burning under the pain of the lash, but also in the sense of 'scandalous', 'notorious'. ***an invective against his memory:*** The anonymous *The British Muse: or, Tyranny Expos'd. A Satyr, occasion'd by all the Fulsome and Lying Poems and Elegies, that have been written on the Death of the Late King James* 1701.

149 and n. George Ridpath ran the Whig *Flying Post.* He was prosecuted for libel under Queen Anne but evaded sentence by escaping to Holland. Pope had offered to mount a verbal attack on him in 1712 for printing a slur on his friend John Caryll (*Corr.*: I, 154). Ridpath returned after the Hanoverian succession, but lived under the shadow of suspicions of bigamy, heresy and illicit financial dealings. He is compared with the Tory journalist Abel Roper (1665–1726), who ran *The Post Boy*, and was threatened with prosecution under George I. In 1716 he was 'decently chastized' by the victim of one of his articles (*The Weekly Journal: or, British Gazetteer*, 8 September 1716). The two men started their papers in the same month, and died within a day of each other. Pope's paralleling of such opposed extremists reflects his insistence on his own political moderation.

151 and n. Himself: Curll. ***story'd chiefs:*** Paralleling incidents in the lives of literary entrepreneurs with the noble 'story' ('history', 'myth') of the 'chiefs' who figure in epic. For Aeneas's self-recognition, see the Virgilian quotation. ***Se quoque:*** Aeneas, shipwrecked with his friend Achates near Carthage after his escape from the sack of Troy, saw buildings decorated with scenes from the Trojan war: 'He also recognised himself in the press of battle with the Greek chiefs – he stopped, and said with tears in his eyes, "What place, Achates, what part of the world is not already full of our sufferings?" ' (*Aeneid* I.488, 459–60). ***Curl's being tossed in a blanket:*** The scholars were taking revenge for Curll's unauthorised and garbled printing of a Latin oration made by the Captain of the School at the funeral of Robert South (1634–1716), a high-church divine and celebrated preacher who had been a Westminster pupil (Straus 1927: 69–76). Pope had reported the event and its press coverage in a letter to

As from the blanket high in air he flies,
And oh! (he cry'd) what street, what lane but knows,
Our purgings, pumpings, blankettings, and blows!
In ev'ry loom our labours shall be seen,
And the fresh vomit run for ever green!
  See in the circle next, Eliza plac'd,

is well known. Of his purging and vomiting, see a full and true Account of a horrid Revenge on the body of Edm. Curl, *etc.* in Swift and Pope's Miscell.

156.] A parody on these of a late noble author: 'His bleeding arm had furnish'd all their rooms, / And run for ever purple in the looms.'

157.] In this game is exposed, in the most contemptuous manner, the profligate licentiousness of those shameless scriblers (for the most part of that Sex, which ought least to be capable of such malice or impudence) who in libellous Memoirs and Novels, reveal the faults or misfortunes of both sexes, to the ruin of public fame, or disturbance of private happiness. Our good poet (by the whole cast of his work being obliged not to take off the Irony) where he could not shew his indignation, hath shewn his contempt, as much as possible; having here drawn as vile a picture as could be represented in the colours of Epic poesy.

SCRIBL.

Ibid.] Eliza Haywood; this woman was authoress of those most scandalous books called the

---

Teresa Blount (*Corr.*: I, 350). In a note to an early manuscript draft he claimed that Curll, once released from the blanket, had asked the boys to translate the Latin they had been chanting during the tossing, 'that (says he) I may print / an account of it' (Mack 1984: 128). ***see a full and true Account:*** *PW*: I, 273–85.

154. pumpings: Informal justice meted out by drenching the offender under a street pump.

155–6 and 156n. In ev'ry loom: Because it will become a standard motif for weavers. ***And the fresh vomit:*** For the relation between pleasure and disgust in this line, see Doody 1985: 216–17. ***A parody on:*** An imitation of (without any pejorative implication). ***a late noble author:*** Introducing a loose recollection of the anonymously published *Epistle to the ... Earl of Dorset* by Charles Montagu, Earl of Halifax, which exhorted Dorset to celebrate the military glory of William III by describing the wounds he had received in battle (*An Epistle* 1690).

157–60. Possibly alluding to Renaissance paintings of the Virgin Mary with the infants Christ and St John the Baptist (Gneiting 1975: 427).

157 and n. in the circle: The prizes for the game are displayed while potential contestants gather round. ***Eliza:*** Eliza Haywood (1693?–1756), novelist, dramatist and journalist (for Pope's attitude to her, see Rumbold 1989: 161–3; for her representation in the *Dunciad*, see Ballaster 1992: 160–65; for revisions to her biography, see Blouch 1991; Firmager 1993: 1–6). ***that Sex, which ought least to be capable:*** Asserting that women's adoption of unscrupulous literary practices is especially disgusting on account of the supposedly greater moral purity of their sex. ***reveal the faults or misfortunes of both sexes:*** Referring to the enormously popular scandal novels which purported to reveal the intrigues of high life under fictitious names. Haywood's *Memoirs of a Certain Island adjacent to ... Utopia* (1725) and *The Court of Carimania* (1727) are leading examples. Pope especially resented a libel on his friend Martha Blount in *A Certain Island*, which not only called her 'the most dissolute and shameless of her Sex', but also seemed to insinuate that she was secretly married to him, that she was profiteer-

Two babes of love close clinging to her waist;
Fair as before her works she stands confess'd,
In flow'rs and pearls by bounteous Kirkall dress'd.
The Goddess then: 'Who best can send on high
The salient spout, far-streaming to the sky;

court of Carimania, and the New Utopia. For the *two babes of love*, see CURL, Key, p. 12. But whatever reflection he is pleased to throw upon this Lady, surely it was what from him she little deserved, who had celebrated Curl's undertakings for *Reformation of manners*, and declared herself 'to be so perfectly acquainted with the *sweetness of his disposition*, and that *tenderness with which he considered the errors of his fellow creatures*; that, though she should find the *little inadvertencies* of her *own life* recorded in his papers, she was certain it would be done in such a manner as she could not but approve.' Mrs. HAYWOOD, Hist. of Clar. printed in the Female Dunciad, p. 18.

158.] 'Cressa genus, Pholoë, geminique sub ubere nati.' Virg. Aen. v.

160.] *Kirkall*, the name of an Engraver. Some of this Lady's works were printed in four volumes in 12mo, with her picture thus dressed up before them.

---

ing from the management of his affairs, and that she was riddled with venereal disease (Haywood 1725: 12–13; Guerinot 1969: 90–91; Rumbold 1989: 162). ***For the* two babes of love:** Haywood declared in documents dated to *c.*1730 that she had made 'an unfortunate marriage', that she had two young children, and that her husband was dead (Blouch 1991). Blouch further suggests that these children were probably illegitimate, and that the elder may have been fathered by Richard Savage – one of Pope's prime links with conditions at the lower end of the literary market. Although the children in the present passage have sometimes been seen as a figurative reference to the two works named in the note, Pope had added to an early draft the note that 'She had 2 Bast: / tards, others say / three' (Ballaster 1992: 160–61; Mack 1984: 141). See also notes on line 158. ***who had celebrated Curl's undertakings:*** Haywood praised the projector (not necessarily Curll) of a periodical to be called 'The Rover' for his aim of showing 'the beautiful Images of *Virtue* in all her proper Shapes, and the Deformities of *Vice* in its various Appearances'. It was commonplace to present scandalous material as morally educative, but the phrase '*Reformation of manners*' ludicrously associates Curll and Haywood with the rigorously pious Societies for the Reformation of Manners, which specialised in bringing prosecutions for such offences as swearing and sabbath-breaking. If Curll *was* the addressee, the trust Haywood expresses in his tact and kindness is preposterous. '*Little inadvertencies*' (i.e. careless slips) might seem something of an understatement if the allegations about the two illegitimate children were taken at face value.

158n. The quotation describes a slave given by Aeneas as a consolation prize: 'Pholoe, of Cretan race, with twin boys at the breast' (*Aeneid* V.285). Cretans were from antiquity denigrated as liars and sexual perverts.

159. confess'd: revealed.

160 and n. No image of Haywood by Elisha Kirkall (1682?–1742) has been traced. Pope may have been thinking of the frontispiece by George Vertue (1684–1756) to Haywood's *Secret Histories, Novels and Poems* (1725 and reprints), which has only one small flower in the hair and no pearls. Belief that Pope was accurately describing an actual frontispiece is not encouraged by his specification in 1728 of 'her fore-buttocks to the navel bare' (*TE*: V, 120).

161–2. Dulness proclaims the urination contest. ***salient:*** leaping.

His be yon Juno of majestic size,
With cow-like udders, and with ox-like eyes.
This China Jordan let the chief o'ercome
Replenish, not ingloriously, at home.'
Osborne and Curl accept the glorious strife,

163.] In allusion to Homer's *Βοῶπις πότνια Ἥρη*.

165.] 'Tertius Argolica hac galea contentus abito.' Virg. Aen. v. In the games of Homer, Il. xxiii. there are set together, as prizes, a Lady and a Kettle, as in this place Mrs. Haywood and a Jordan. But there the preference in value is given to the Kettle, at which Mad. Dacier is justly displeased. Mrs. H. is here treated with distinction, and acknowledged to be the more valuable of the two.

167. Osborne] A Bookseller in Grays-Inn, very well qualified by his impudence to act this part; and therefore placed here instead of a less deserving Predecessor. This man published advertisements for a year together, pretending to sell Mr. Pope's Subscription books of Homer's Iliad at half the price: Of which books he had none, but cut to the size of them (which was

---

163–4 and n. yon Juno: Haywood, likened to the matronly and imposing consort of Jupiter. ***cow-like udders:*** Introduced as a degrading parallel to Homer's customary epithet for Juno, 'ox-eyed' (*Iliad* I.551). Brooks-Davies suggests an allusion to Virgil's account of the competition of two bulls over a beautiful heifer (*Georgics* III.219–41; Brooks-Davies 1985: 27).

165 and n. Jordan: chamber pot. ***Tertius Argolica:*** 'Let he who comes third go away content with this Greek helmet' (*Aeneid* V.314). ***In the games of Homer:*** *Iliad* XXIII.262–5. ***Kettle:*** A deliberately belittling word for the Homeric tripod. ***Mad. Dacier:*** Pope's characteristically ungracious attitude to Anne Tanneguy-Le Fèvre Dacier (*d.* 1720), a leading authority on Homer whose work had very much assisted him in his translation, was conditioned by a defensive concern to establish his own authority, and by her provocative status as a female expert on what was traditionally the preserve of men (Williams 1993: 147–53, 70). She had also embarrassed him during the Atterbury crisis by hinting that he favoured political subversion (Guerinot 1969: 88). Without saying anything directly against her, the note on the kettle drags her into the unsavoury context of the urination contest, where Haywood's presence already highlights the assumed impropriety of female writing. The citation of the protests of the would-be female intellectual (Pope thought it 'great complaisance in that polite nation [the French] to allow her to be a Critic of equal rank' with her husband André) highlights a classical context in which women are literally comparable with other objects of male desire (*Corr.*: I, 492; Rumbold 1989: 163). Deferring with ostensible gallantry to the lady's opinion, the note damningly evaluates Haywood as worth more than a chamber pot.

167 and n. Osborne: Thomas Osborne (*d.* 1767), leading publisher. Johnson, who had worked for him, and had, by his own confession, been provoked to physical violence by his impertinence, reported: 'Osborne was a man entirely destitute of shame, without sense of any disgrace but that of poverty. He told me, when he was doing that which raised Pope's resentment, that he should be put into *The Dunciad*' (Hill 1905: III, 187; Hill 1934–5: I, 154). ***a less deserving Predecessor:*** Earlier versions of this episode had named as Curll's adversary, first, William Rufus Chetwood (*d.* 1766), who published works by Haywood, and, according to Curll, 'in a Drunken-Debauch ... was sent Home with a Jordan, *alias*, a P-ss-Pot

(Tho' this his Son dissuades, and that his Wife.)
One on his manly confidence relies,
One on his vigour and superior size.
First Osborne lean'd against his letter'd post;
It rose, and labour'd to a curve at most.

Quarto) the common books in folio, without Copper-plates, on a worse paper, and never above half the value.

Upon this Advertisement the Gazetteer harangued thus, July 6, 1739. 'How melancholy must it be to a Writer to be so unhappy as to see his works hawked for sale in a manner so fatal to his fame! How, with Honour to your self, and Justice to your Subscribers, can this be done? What an Ingratitude to be charged on the *Only honest Poet* that lived in 1738! and than whom *Virtue* has not had a *shriller Trumpeter* for many ages! That you were once *generally admired and esteemed* can be denied by none; but that you and your works are now despised, is verified by *this fact:*' which being utterly false, did not indeed much humble the Author, but drew this just chastisement on the Bookseller.

169, 170.] 'Ille ... melior motu, fretusque juventa; / His membris et mole valens.' Virg. Aen. v.

---

on his Head'; and, second, Samuel Chapman (active from 1718), who had collaborated in publishing Haywood's collected works and Theobald's *Shakespeare Restored* (*A Compleat Key* 1728: 13; Haywood 1724; Theobald 1726; *TE*: V, 121). ***This man published advertisements:*** Osborne's advertising (see *TE*: V, 303) may have given the impression that the Homer subscriptions had gone badly, leaving superior quarto subscription copies as remainders. Lintot told Pope that Osborne was cutting down folios in order to pass them off as quartos; but although Pope may have believed him, the story is inherently improbable: Lintot had in fact sold on some quarto *Iliad* remainders, and they could have come into Osborne's possession by this route (*Corr.*: IV, 222–3; Foxon 1991: 57). ***in a manner so fatal to his fame:*** The government-subsidised *Gazetteer* takes the chance to denigrate Pope as an opponent of Walpole's regime: the reported remaindering of subscription copies is represented as not only a sign of the project's failure, but also a cheat against the subscribers who paid full price. ***the* Only honest Poet *that lived in 1738:*** Ridiculing the moral pretensions of Pope's *Epilogue to the Satires* (which originally bore that date as its title).

168. Since it fell to Curll's son Henry (active from 1726) to look after his father's business when his boldness got him into difficulties with the law, Henry had understandable motives for dissuading him from risky undertakings. The reference to Osborne's 'Wife' would have had more obvious point in the earlier version in which Chetwood was Curll's opponent, since Chetwood was reputed to be very much under his wife's thumb (*TE*: V, 121).

169–70 and n. Line 169 refers to Osborne, line 170 to Curll. ***Ille ... melior motu:*** Translated by Dryden as 'One on his Youth and pliant Limbs relies; / One on his Sinews, and his Gyant size' (*Aeneid* V.430–31; Kinsley 1958: *Aeneid* V.570–71).

171. his letter'd post: Where he posted his advertisements.

172. It rose: As Warton notes, though without comment, the noun to which 'it' refers is not stated (since it cannot be the 'post' of line 171: see Warton 1797: V, 148). The uncharacteristic grammatical awkwardness, like the euphemistic diction, highlights precisely what it ostensibly seeks to avoid. Sitter discerns a suggestion 'of abiding impotence as well as occasional insufficiency' (Sitter 1971: 27).

So Jove's bright bow displays its wat'ry round,
(Sure sign, that no spectator shall be drown'd)
A second effort brought but new disgrace,
The wild Meander wash'd the Artist's face:
Thus the small jett, which hasty hands unlock,
Spirts in the gard'ner's eyes who turns the cock.
Not so from shameless Curl; impetuous spread
The stream, and smoking flourish'd o'er his head.
So (fam'd like thee for turbulence and horns)
Eridanus his humble fountain scorns;

173, 174.] The words of Homer, of the Rain-bow, in Iliad xi: '*ἅς τε Κρονίων / Ἐν νέφεϊ στήριξε, τέρας μερόπων ἀνθρώπων.*' 'Que le fils de Saturn a fondez dans les nües, pour être dans tous les âges une signe à tous les mortels.' Dacier.

181, 182.] Virgil mentions these two qualifications of Eridanus, Georg. iv: 'Et gemina auratus taurino *cornua* vultu, / Eridanus, quo non alius per pinguia culta / In mare purpureum *violentior* effluit amnis.' The Poets fabled of this river Eridanus, that it flowed through the skies. Denham, Cooper's Hill: 'Heav'n her Eridanus no more shall boast, / Whose fame in thine, like lesser currents lost; / Thy nobler stream shall visit Jove's abodes, / To shine among the stars, and bathe the Gods.'

173–4 and n. The words of Homer: 'rainbows which Zeus fixed in the heavens as a portent' (*Iliad* XI.27–8). ***Que le fils de Saturn:*** 'Which the son of Saturn placed among the clouds, to be for all ages a sign to all mortals' (Dacier 1724: *Iliad* XI). In her note Dacier suggests, in a typical attempt to synthesise Homeric and Christian traditions, that 'perhaps these pagans had even heard of what God said to Noah' (i.e. after the flood, when God showed the rainbow to Noah as a sign 'that the waters shall no more become a flood to destroy all flesh': Genesis 9:8–17), a sense taken up in the blasphemous parody of line 174.

176. Meander: A river in Greece noted for its winding course. ***the Artist's face:*** the performer's face (i.e. Osborne's).

177–8. The simile – concluding in an obvious pun – is of a gardener inexpertly operating a fountain.

179. impetuous: with impetus. It was a favourite word of Dryden when describing 'a large, turbulent body of water' (Sherbo 1970: 508).

180. smoking: vaporising from the heat generated by its swift passage through the air (but see also lines 183–4 and note).

181–2 and n. for turbulence and horns: Although Curll's career featured notorious episodes of 'turbulence', which might justify the horns depicted as part of the iconography of river gods, I know of no evidence for any infidelity on his wife's part which would have afflicted him with the horns of a cuckold. ***Eridanus:*** The Latin name for the River Po. ***his humble fountain scorns:*** The river, instead of being happy to linger around its source, cannot get away fast enough. ***Virgil mentions:*** 'The Po, his bull's head crowned with a pair of golden horns, than whom no river flows with more force through the productive fields into the deep blue sea' (*Georgics* IV.371–3). The note picks out typographically the key points of the comparison. ***Denham:*** An approximate quotation from Denham's praise of the Thames (compare Banks 1969: 'Cooper's Hill', lines 193–6), which Pope had imitated in *Windsor Forest*, lines 227–30.

Thro' half the heav'ns he pours th' exalted urn;
His rapid waters in their passage burn.
  Swift as it mounts, all follow with their eyes:
Still happy Impudence obtains the prize.

183.] In a manuscript Dunciad (where are some marginal corrections of some gentlemen some time deceased) I have found another reading of these lines, thus: 'And lifts his urn, thro' half the heav'ns to flow; / His rapid waters in their passage *glow*.' This I cannot but think the right: For first, though the difference between *burn* and *glow* may seem not very material to others, to me I confess the latter has an elegance, a *je ne sçay quoy*, which is much easier to be conceived than explained. Secondly, every reader of our poet must have observed how frequently he uses this word *glow* in other parts of his works: To instance only in his Homer:

(1.) Iliad. ix. v. 726. — *With one resentment glows.*
(2.) Iliad. xi. v. 626. — *There the battle glows.*
(3.) Ibid. v. 985. — *The closing flesh that instant ceas'd to glow.*
(4.) Iliad. xii. v. 45. — *Encompass'd Hector glows.*
(5.) Ibid. v. 475. — *His beating breast with gen'rous ardour glows.*
(6.) Iliad. xviii. v. 591. — *Another part glow'd with refulgent arms.*
(7.) Ibid. v. 654. — *And curl'd on silver props in order glow.*

I am afraid of growing too luxuriant in examples, or I could stretch this catalogue to a great extent, but these are enough to prove his fondness for this *beautiful word*, which, therefore, let *all future editions* replace here.

I am aware, after all, that *burn* is the proper word to convey an idea of what was said to be Mr. Curl's condition at this time: But from that very reason I infer the direct contrary. For surely every *lover of our author* will conclude he had more *humanity* than to insult a man on such a misfortune or calamity, which could never befal him purely by his *own fault*, but from an unhappy communication with another. This Note is half Mr. THEOBALD, half SCRIBL.

183–4 and 183n. burn: Alluding not only to Virgil's archery contest, in which the winner's arrow kindles with the speed of its flight (*Aeneid* V.525–8), but also to the symptoms of venereal disease. ***In a manuscript Dunciad:*** There is no extant evidence for this variant. The note parodies Theobald's methods in its accumulation of parallel passages to establish an author's patterns of usage, and suggests that no amount of such 'proof' can rule out his use of a less characteristic word on a particular occasion. ***a* je ne sçay quoy:** A somewhat affected Gallicism denoting an admired effect that is difficult to analyse precisely. ***I am afraid of growing too luxuriant:*** Quoted from a lengthy citation of parallels in *Shakespeare Restored* (Theobald 1726: 11). ***which, therefore, let* all future editions *replace here:*** An arrogant piece of false logic (Pope is fond of 'glow'; therefore he must always choose it wherever possible; therefore 'burn' must be altered to 'glow'), expressing Pope's belief that conjectural emendation, rather than restoring the author's verbal decisions, sets them aside in favour of the editor's. ***I am aware:*** Although the note pretends to dismiss the possibility of an allusion to venereal disease, the slur is further highlighted by the critic's naive suggestion that such a condition ought not in any case to be criticised as Curll's '*own fault*'.

186. happy Impudence: Curll's hallmark.

Thou triumph'st, Victor of the high-wrought day,
And the pleas'd dame, soft-smiling, lead'st away.
Osborne, thro' perfect modesty o'ercome,
Crown'd with the Jordan, walks contented home.
But now for Authors nobler palms remain;

187. The high-wrought day,] Some affirm, this was originally, *well p—st day*; but the Poet's decency would not suffer it.

Here the learned Scriblerus manifests great anger; he exclaims against all such *Conjectural Emendations* in this manner: 'Let it suffice, O Pallas! that every noble Ancient, *Greek* or *Roman*, hath suffered the impertinent correction of every *Dutch*, *German*, and *Switz* Schoolmaster! Let our English at least escape, whose intrinsic is scarce of marble so solid, as not to be impaired or soiled by such rude and dirty hands. Suffer them to call their works their own, and after death at least to find rest and sanctuary from Critics! When these men have ceased to *rail*, let them not begin to do worse, to *comment!* Let them not conjecture into nonsense, correct out of all correctness, and restore into obscurity and confusion. Miserable fate! which can befal only the sprightliest wits that have written, and will befal them only from such dull ones as could never write!' SCRIBL.

187n. Some affirm: Despite Scriblerus's angry rebuttal, this is a genuine manuscript reading (Mack 1984: 141). ***O Pallas!:*** Appealing to Pallas Athene, Greek goddess of learning. ***Let our English at least escape:*** Theobald pioneered the application to early modern English literature of the methods applied by Bentley and continental scholars to Greek and Latin texts. 'Schoolmaster' derides the professional scholar or 'pedant', as opposed to the gentlemanly amateur. ***whose intrinsic is scarce of marble so solid:*** Whereas the new textual critics saw all languages at all times as meshed into changing patterns of chronological and regional difference, Pope and the Scriblerians inherited the older concern with fixed linguistic standards (language that seemed 'solid', like 'marble'), usually identified with the language of canonical classical authors. In comparison, English, which had changed from the language of Chaucer to that of Shakespeare within only 200 years, seemed frighteningly transient: as Waller had put it, 'Poets that lasting marble seek, / Must carve in Latin or in Greek' (Drury 1893: 'Of English Verse', lines 13–14). Pope seems to have expected his language to become obsolete within a few generations: 'Our Sons their Fathers' *failing Language* see, / And such as *Chaucer* is shall *Dryden* be' (*Essay on Criticism*, lines 482–3). For Scriblerus, the ephemerality of English makes it particularly dangerous for critics to tamper with it. ***Miserable fate!:*** Stressing the supposed contrast between real writers, 'the sprightliest wits', and 'such dull ones as could never write', who compensate themselves by mutilating the works of those who can.

188. the pleas'd dame: The pleasurable anticipation ascribed to Haywood on becoming the victor's prize focuses the contest's implied parallel between excretory and sexual performance, and sets the seal on the presentation of the 'soft-smiling' Haywood as sexually wanton.

189. This line worked better in its first version, where Chetwood was the subject, since his inhibiting 'modesty' could be ascribed to the subjection to his wife's influence which was part of his characterisation: Osborne, in contrast, had the reputation of shamelessness. Moreover, Curll claimed that it was Chetwood who really had gone home 'Crown'd with' a 'Jordan' (see editor's notes on lines 167–8).

191. for Authors: Marking a change of theme from publishers to authors. ***palms:*** prizes.

Room for my Lord! three jockeys in his train;
Six huntsmen with a shout precede his chair:
He grins, and looks broad nonsense with a stare.
His Honour's meaning Dulness thus exprest,
'He wins this Patron, who can tickle best.'
He chinks his purse, and takes his seat of state:
With ready quills the Dedicators wait;
Now at his head the dextrous task commence,
And, instant, fancy feels th' imputed sense;
Now gentle touches wanton o'er his face,
He struts Adonis, and affects grimace:
Rolli the feather to his ear conveys,

203.] Paolo Antonio Rolli, an Italian Poet, and writer of many Operas in that language, which, partly by the help of his genius, prevailed in England near twenty years. He taught Italian to some fine Gentlemen, who affected to direct the Operas.

192–4. Introducing a type figure through which various specific charges are made. The 'jockeys' and 'huntsmen' would seem to indicate that the nobleman is more interested in racing and hunting than in the arts, and his facial expression suggests low intelligence; but for features of his patronage recalling the Duke of Newcastle, see editor's note on line 203.

196. tickle: flatter.

198. quills: Quills were used for writing; but the image of a feather also fits the tickling motif.

200. fancy feels th' imputed sense: He imagines that he has the mental and moral qualities imputed to him by flattering dedications.

202. As the dedicators tell him he is as handsome as Adonis (mythical lover of Venus), he starts to behave as if he believed it, and at the same time he feigns a modest dislike of hearing himself praised. For parallel uses of 'strut', see Sherbo 1970: 508.

203 and n. **Paolo Antonio Rolli:** Italian poet (1687–1765), first secretary and librettist to the Royal Academy of Music, the joint-stock company set up in 1719 under the patronage of George I to produce Italian operas in London (Milhous & Hume 1986; Gibson 1989: 108–13, 117). Rolli taught Italian to the nobility, including the children of the future George II (Dorris 1967: 124–60). He was unimpressed by George Frederick Handel (1685–1759), for whom he composed opera libretti, in marked contrast with Pope, who praises his oratorios in Book IV (see IV.45–70; Deutsch 1955: *passim*; Dorris 1967: 152). The ironic reference to his 'genius' may glance at the poetical ambition evident in his libretti, which some have seen as detracting from effective dramatic development (Dean & Knapp 1987: 17; LaRue 1995: 187–8). Verse and note represent Rolli as flattering 'fine Gentlemen' into becoming directors (i.e. financial sponsors) of opera: Gibson suggests that the rapid turnover of directors was fuelled by pressure from annual cohorts of young aristocrats returning, full of enthusiasm, from the Grand Tour (Gibson 1989: 26–9). The Academy and its 'Directors of Musick with all their Set of fine Gentlemen of Taste' had been included in a list of targets in an early manuscript draft of Book II, but the motif does not emerge explicitly in the verse until 1742 and 1743, when 'singing Peers' escort Opera to Dulness's throne (Mack 1984: 127; IV.49). The

Then his nice taste directs our Operas:
Bentley his mouth with classic flatt'ry opes,
And the puff'd orator bursts out in tropes.

205.] Not spoken of the famous Dr. Richard Bentley, but of one Thom. Bentley, a small critic, who aped his uncle in a *little Horace*. The great one was intended to be dedicated to the Lord Hallifax, but (on a change of the Ministry) was given to the Earl of Oxford; for which reason the little one was dedicated to his son the Lord Harley. A taste of this *Classic Elocution* may be seen in his following Panegyric on the Peace of Utrecht. *Cupimus Patrem tuum, fulgentissimum illud Orbis Anglicani jubar,* adorare. *O ingens* Reipublicae *nostrae columen! O fortunatam tanto* Heroe *Britanniam! Illi tali tantoque viro* DEUM *per* Omnia *adfuisse, manumque ejus et mentem direxisse,* CERTISSIMUM EST. Hujus *enim* Unius *ferme opera,* aequissimis *et* perhonorificis conditionibus, *diuturno, heu nimium! bello, finem impositum videmus. O*

---

present note goes back to the earliest commentary, 1729, but originally read 'near ten years'. The revision later that year to 'near twenty years' may have been a recognition that the taste actually went back beyond the foundation of the Royal Academy, well into the first decade of the century.

The caricatured patron may recall the Duke of Newcastle, who had patronised all the dedicators mentioned in the corresponding passage in 1729, and as Lord Chamberlain served as the first governor of the Royal Academy (Gibson 1989: 23–4).

205–6 and 205n. Bentley: An early manuscript draft shows that Richard Bentley, whose 'classic flatt'ry' is cited in the note (he had lavished fulsome praise on George II in the unlikely role of patron of learning (Bentley 1726: xx–xxv)), had been the original target, although '**' and 'Welsted' had been specified in published versions until 'B—y' appeared early in 1735, followed by 'Bentley', with the note specifying Bentley's nephew Thomas (1692?–1742) later the same year (*TE*: V, 124, 305–6; Mack 1984: 108–9). This final move was prompted by Thomas Bentley's *A Letter to Mr. Pope, Occasioned by Sober Advice from Horace* (1735), in which he attacked Pope for mocking his uncle by attaching his name to bawdy notes accompanying the indecent Horatian imitation *Sober Advice from Horace*. ***puff'd:*** swollen with pride, but also playing on the sense 'extravagantly praised in booksellers' advertisements'. ***tropes:*** Rhetorical figures of speech. Compare Butler's satire of Hudibras: 'For *Rhetorick*, he could not ope / His mouth, but out there flew a Trope' (Wilders 1967: I.i.81–2). ***a small critic, who aped his uncle:*** Thomas Bentley's small-format annotated edition of Horace used the text established by his uncle – from which Pope had himself incorporated new readings in the Latin version printed in parallel with his *Imitations of Horace* (Bentley 1711; Bentley 1713; Bloom 1948). ***The great one:*** Richard Bentley's large and imposing Horace (Bentley 1711). In 1710 Queen Anne had dismissed prominent Whig ministers and brought in Robert Harley, who moved towards the formation of a Tory ministry. In 1711 he was created Earl of Oxford. Since Halifax, though a considerable literary patron, was a committed Whig, Oxford was in 1711 by far the more prudent choice as dedicatee, especially since Bentley, as Master of Trinity College, Cambridge, was looking for powerful friends to aid him in a long-running dispute with the fellows (Monk 1833: I, 281–2, 297–8, 303–9). ***the little one:*** Thomas Bentley's edition (Bentley 1713), dedicated to Edward Harley (1689–1741), called by courtesy Lord Harley during his father's lifetime, and thereafter second Earl of Oxford. ***the Peace of Utrecht:*** The treaty, negotiated under the last ministry of Queen Anne, in which Pope's friends Oxford and Bolingbroke bore

But Welsted most the Poet's healing balm
Strives to extract from his soft, giving palm;
Unlucky Welsted! thy unfeeling master,
The more thou ticklest, gripes his fist the faster.

Diem aeterna memoria dignissimam! qua terrores Patriae omnes excidit, Pacem*que diu exoptatam toti fere Europae restituit, ille Populi Anglicani Amor, Harleius.*

Thus critically (that is verbally) translated: 'Thy Father, that most refulgent star of the Anglican Orb, we much desire to *adore!* Oh mighty Column of our *Republic!* Oh Britain, fortunate in such an *Hero!* That to such and so great a Man God was ever present, in *every thing,* and all along directed both his hand and his heart, is a *Most Absolute Certainty!* For it is in a manner by the operation of this *Man alone,* that we behold a *War* (alas! how much too long an one!) brought at length to an end, *on the most just and most honourable Conditions.* Oh Day eternally to be memorated! wherein All the Terrors of his Country were ended, and a Peace (long wish'd for by *almost all Europe*) was restored by Harley, the Love and Delight of the People of England.'

But that this Gentleman can write in a different style, may be seen in a letter he printed to Mr. Pope, wherein several Noble Lords are treated in a most extraordinary language, particularly the Lord Bolingbroke abused for that very Peace which he here makes the *single work* of the Earl of Oxford, directed by *God Almighty.*

207.] Leonard Welsted, author of The Triumvirate, or a Letter in verse from Palaemon to Celia at Bath, which was meant for a satyr on Mr. P. and some of his friends, about the year 1718. He writ other things which we cannot remember. Smedley in his Metamorphosis of Scriblerus, mentions one, the Hymn of a *Gentleman* to his *Creator:* And there was another in

---

prime responsibility, brought to an end the War of the Spanish Succession. The quotation from Bentley's dedication (slightly abbreviated) is introduced to suggest hypocrisy: Bentley was a Whig, and the Whigs opposed the treaty. He became an active supporter of the Whig regime installed in 1714 by George I, which tried to have Oxford convicted of treason. Although 'critically (that is verbally) translated' is an obvious gibe at the Bentleys' supposed literal-mindedness, the stiff translation also emphasises the extravagance of Bentley's adulation. ***a letter he printed:*** *A Letter to Mr. Pope, Occasioned by Sober Advice from Horace* 1735.

207–10 and 207n. But Welsted most: In 1728–9 these four lines were meant for Oldmixon, and may have related to his fruitless hopes of becoming Laureate through the patronage of Newcastle (British Library Add. MS 28275, f. 46). In a note to an early manuscript draft Pope makes the additional allegation that Oldmixon had been Curll's tool in embarrassing him over the affair of the *Court Poems* (Mack 1984: 142; see editor's note on line 58). The transfer to Welsted does, however, match a perceived tendency to place-seeking on Welsted's part (Welsted 1724 is dedicated to Newcastle; Morrice 1721 criticises his fawning on the great), and with at least one instance of his apparently offending a patron (Bowles 1806: V, 170–72). ***the Poet's healing balm:*** Money, envisaged as curing all a hack writer's problems. ***giving:*** The hand may 'give' to the touch, but any hope of its 'giving' money is doomed to frustration. ***The Triumvirate:*** An attack on Pope, Gay and Arbuthnot (Nichols 1787: 'Palaemon to Caelia'). ***Smedley in his Metamorphosis of Scriblerus:*** The anonymous *The Metamorphosis: A Poem* 1728, attributed by Pope to Smedley, includes a gibe at Welsted's *Hymn.* ***the Hymn of a* Gentleman *to his* Creator:** In fact, the full title of the anonymously issued *A Hymn to the Creator. Written by a Gentleman, on the Occasion of the Death of his Only*

While thus each hand promotes the pleasing pain,
And quick sensations skip from vein to vein;
A youth unknown to Phoebus, in despair,
Puts his last refuge all in heav'n and pray'r.
What force have pious vows! The Queen of Love
His sister sends, her vot'ress, from above.

praise either of a Cellar, or a Garret. L. W. characterized in the treatise *Περὶ Βάθους*, or the Art of Sinking, as a Didapper, and after as an Eel, is said to be this person, by Dennis, Daily Journal of May 11, 1728. He was also characterized under another animal, a Mole, by the author of the ensuing Simile, which was handed about at the same time:

Dear Welsted, mark, in dirty hole,
That painful animal, a Mole:
Above ground never born to grow;
What mighty stir it keeps below?
To make a Mole-hill all this strife!
It digs, pokes, undermines for life.
How proud a little dirt to spread;
Conscious of nothing o'er its head!
'Till, lab'ring on for want of eyes,
It blunders into Light — and dies.

You have him again in book 3. ver. 169.

213.] The satyr of this Episode being levelled at the base flatteries of authors to worthless wealth or greatness, concludes here with an excellent lesson to such men: That altho' their pens and praises were as exquisite as they conceit of themselves, yet (even in their own mercenary views) a creature unlettered, who serveth the passions, or pimpeth to the pleasures, of such vain, braggart, puft Nobility, shall with those patrons be much more inward, and of them much higher rewarded. SCRIBL.

Daughter (1727) simply conforms to a standard publisher's formula. As abbreviated, however, it suggests an undue attachment to rank on the author's part (especially since, in Pope's eyes, Welsted's gentility was questionable). ***another in praise either of a Cellar, or a Garret:*** Though these are the kind of lodgings Pope obviously regards as Welsted's just deserts, his 'Oikographia' actually describes an unostentatiously comfortable house (Nichols 1787). ***in the treatise:*** i.e. *Peri Bathos* (*PW*: II, 171–276). ***Didapper:*** dabchick, little grebe. ***is said to be this person:*** An attempt to displace onto Dennis the responsibility for Pope's calculated insult to Welsted: in fact Dennis simply assumes, rather than asserts, the self-evident identification. ***the author of the ensuing Simile:*** Not identified. The lines are printed as Epigram 28 in Savage 1732.

213–14 and 213n. unknown to Phoebus: The god of poetry has never heard of him. An early manuscript draft identifies him as 'W—r', i.e. Edward Webster, alleged to have gained the place of chief secretary to Charles Paulet (1661–1722), second Duke of Bolton, Lord Lieutenant of Ireland, by prostituting his daughter (Mack 1984: 109; *TE*: V, 458). ***Puts his last refuge:*** Such a prayer for victory often determines the outcome of contests in Homer and Virgil. ***conceit:*** imagine. ***inward:*** intimate.

215. The Queen of Love: Venus.

As taught by Venus, Paris learnt the art
To touch Achilles' only tender part;
Secure, thro' her, the noble prize to carry,
He marches off, his Grace's Secretary.
  Now turn to diff'rent sports (the Goddess cries)
And learn, my sons, the wond'rous pow'r of Noise.
To move, to raise, to ravish ev'ry heart,
With Shakespear's nature, or with Johnson's art,
Let others aim: 'Tis yours to shake the soul
With Thunder rumbling from the mustard bowl,
With horns and trumpets now to madness swell,
Now sink in sorrows with a tolling bell;

223, 225.] 'Excudent alii spirantia mollius aera, / Credo equidem, vivos ducent de marmore vultus', *etc.* 'Tu regere imperio populos, Romane, memento, / Hae tibi erunt artes'.

226.] The old way of making Thunder and Mustard were the same; but since, it is more advantageously performed by troughs of wood with stops in them. Whether Mr. Dennis was the inventor of that improvement, I know not; but it is certain, that being once at a Tragedy of a new author, he fell into a great passion at hearing some, and cried, ''Sdeath! that is *my* Thunder.'

228.] A mechanical help to the Pathetic, not unuseful to the modern writers of Tragedy.

217–18. Paris won the favour of Venus (Aphrodite) by choosing her as the most beautiful of three goddesses (the others were Juno/Hera and Minerva/Athene). He shot Achilles in the heel, where his mother's hand had held him as she dipped him into the Styx to make him immortal, thus leaving his heel the only vulnerable part of his body.

221. the Goddess: Dulness.

222. the wond'rous pow'r of Noise: The worship of the Magna Mater was notoriously noisy (Williams 1955: 27–8).

223–30. Cp. *Spectator* 44 (Bond 1965: I, 185–91).

223–5 and n. Imitating the prophecy given to Aeneas of Rome's distinctive calling: 'Others will work bronze into softer forms so that it seems to breathe, indeed I believe so; others will draw living faces out of marble ... You must concentrate, Roman as you are, on ruling the peoples with your power: these will be your arts' (*Aeneid* VI.847–52). Whereas the Romans are called in this passage to political rather than artistic achievement, the dunces are called to the crude 'pow'r of Noise' rather than the subtler achievement of earlier playwrights (the contrast between Shakespeare's supposedly unlearned reliance on 'nature' and Jonson's sophisticated 'art' was a critical commonplace: see Pope's Preface to his edition of Shakespeare (*PW*: II, 1–40)).

226 and n. The old method of imitating thunder would have used a pestle and mortar. The new method attributed to Dennis was introduced in his tragedy *Appius and Virginia* (1709), which suggested the name under which Pope satirized him in the *Essay on Criticism* (lines 585–7; Paul 1911: 44–5). The expression 'to steal someone's thunder' apparently derives from this anecdote.

227–8 and 228n. Implying that such 'mechanical help' distracts attention from the inadequacy of the playwright's verbal art in moving the passions. Compare Addison in *Spectator* 44 (Bond 1965: I, 186).

Such happy arts attention can command,
When fancy flags, and sense is at a stand.
Improve we these. Three Cat-calls be the bribe
Of him, whose chatt'ring shames the Monkey tribe:
And his this Drum, whose hoarse heroic base
Drowns the loud clarion of the braying Ass.
  Now thousand tongues are heard in one loud din:
The Monkey-mimics rush discordant in;
'Twas chatt'ring, grinning, mouthing, jabb'ring all,
And Noise and Norton, Brangling and Breval,
Dennis and Dissonance, and captious Art,
And Snip-snap short, and Interruption smart,
And Demonstration thin, and Theses thick,
And Major, Minor, and Conclusion quick.

231. Three Cat-calls] Certain musical instruments used by one sort of Critics to confound the Poets of the Theatre.

238. Norton,] See ver. 417. — *J. Durant Breval*, Author of a very extraordinary Book of Travels, and some Poems. See before, Note on ver. 126.

231–4 and 231n. Improve we these: The competitors in the noise-making competition are to outdo the noise made by 'mechanical help' in the playhouse. ***whose chatt'ring shames the Monkey tribe:*** One prize, the cat-calls, is for high-pitched gibbering like the noise of monkeys, animals seen as mimicking without understanding. ***whose hoarse heroic base:*** The other prize, the drum, is for a bass voice capable of out-braying the proverbially stupid and unmelodious ass. An ass had appeared as frontispiece to the 1729 *Dunciad*: see Mengel in Mack & Winn 1980: 754–8; Berry 1988.

237–40 and 238n. Denying the dunces' individual identities, as their names are assimilated by the verse to mere sound-effects (Mack 1982: 42). ***Norton:*** Benjamin Norton Defoe, journalist. ***Brangling:*** squabbling. ***captious:*** eager to find fault. ***a very extraordinary Book of Travels:*** Breval's *Remarks on Several Parts of Europe* (1726) seems commonplace enough; but 'very extraordinary' may be a sneer at its imposing folio format, and the fact that the author of the insulting *The Confederates* featured such pillars of the Whig establishment as Walpole and Hervey among his subscribers. (Warburton too was among them – but this was before he had attached himself to Pope.)

241–2. Drawing on technical terms from the art of formal disputation, still practised in British universities in Pope's time, and much disapproved of by him as tending to produce a hair-splitting, combative attitude. 'Theses' were the propositions given to students to defend: in this hubbub there are plenty of propositions, but not much 'Demonstration' ('proof'). 'Major, Minor, and Conclusion' are the elements in a syllogism, an argument which consists of a major premiss, a minor premiss and a conclusion. The major premiss contains the predicate (what will be said about the subject in the conclusion), while the minor contains that subject. An example would be: 'Texts consist of words' (major premiss), 'The *Dunciads* are texts' (minor premiss), 'The *Dunciads* consist of words' (conclusion). The speed and din with which the dunces form syllogisms suggests Pope's scepticism about such formal exercises as a means of attaining wisdom.

Hold (cry'd the Queen) a Cat-call each shall win;
Equal your merits! equal is your din!
But that this well-disputed game may end,
Sound forth my Brayers, and the welkin rend.
  As when the long-ear'd milky mothers wait
At some sick miser's triple-bolted gate,
For their defrauded, absent foals they make
A moan so loud, that all the guild awake;
Sore sighs Sir Gilbert, starting at the bray,
From dreams of millions, and three groats to pay.
So swells each wind-pipe; Ass intones to Ass,
Harmonic twang! of leather, horn, and brass;

243.] 'Non nostrum inter vos tantas componere lites, / Et vitula tu dignus, et hic'. Virg. Ecl. iii.

247.] A Simile with a long tail, in the manner of Homer.

243–4 and 243n. The prize for high-pitched chatter is divided equally between Norton Defoe, Breval and Dennis, recalling the judge's inability to choose between the two contestants in one of Virgil's pastoral singing contests: 'It's not for me to settle such a contest between you. You deserve the heifer, and so does he' (*Eclogues* III.108–9). Nokes suggests an allusion to the notorious rivalry between the two leading operatic prima donnas which was fomented by press coverage to the point that in 1727 rival factions in the audience disrupted performances, arguably contributing to the collapse of the Royal Academy, whose role was subsequently taken over by a series of aristocratic associations (Deutsch 1955: 194–227; Gibson 1989: 227–62; Nokes 1995: 409–12; LaRue 1995: 144–81).

246. welkin: sky.

247 and n. the long-ear'd milky mothers: Asses whose foals have been taken away so that their milk can be used as invalid food. For Renaissance uses of the phrase, see Sherbo 1988: 223. ***A Simile with a long tail:*** An epic simile, in which the vehicle is developed well beyond the initial point of comparison.

248. triple-bolted: Because, being a miser, the patient is obsessed with preventing theft.

249. defrauded, absent foals: The foals have been 'defrauded' of the milk purchased by the 'sick miser'.

250. all the guild: Associating the 'miser' and his neighbours with the tradesmen's guilds, and hence with the City of London, rather than with the wit and fashion of districts which considered themselves more refined.

251–2. Sir Gilbert Heathcote (1651?–1733), Whig merchant, Lord Mayor of London, Member of Parliament and co-founder of the Bank of England, was reputedly the richest commoner in England, but was supposed to be miserly over small amounts (this may be unjust: see *TE*: IV, 365). His background and politics would have been sufficient to make Pope unsympathetic to him. His imagined nightmare is having to break into his vast fortune to pay a tiny bill (three groats, at fourpence each, come to only a shilling). Pope presents him as coldly self-righteous towards the poor in *To Bathurst*: 'The grave Sir Gilbert holds it for a rule, / That "every man in want is knave or fool"' (lines 103–4).

253. Ass intones to Ass: The dunces chant to each other.

254. leather, horn, and brass: The blaring of bagpipes, horns and brass instruments.

Such as from lab'ring lungs th' Enthusiast blows,
High Sound, attemp'red to the vocal nose;
Or such as bellow from the deep Divine;
There Webster! peal'd thy voice, and Whitfield! thine.

258.] The one the writer of a News-paper called the Weekly Miscellany, the other a Field-preacher. This thought the only means of advancing Christianity was by the New-birth of religious madness; That, by the old death of fire and faggot: And therefore they agreed in this, though in no other earthly thing, to abuse all the sober Clergy. From the small success of these two extraordinary persons, we may learn how little hurtful *Bigotry* and *Enthusiasm* are, while the Civil Magistrate prudently forbears to lend his power to the one, in order to the employing it against the other.

255–6. Parodying Milton's 'rural ditties ... / Tempered to the oaten flute' (Carey 1968: *Lycidas*, lines 32–3). The claim of the 'Enthusiast', or professedly inspired dissenting preacher, to a revelation not mediated through church hierarchy was a constant irritant to the establishment, particularly in view of the attack on church and king underpinned by such views during the Civil War. For a fuller denunciation, accusing sectarian preachers of using all too natural means to counterfeit spiritual inspiration, of making more sound than sense, and specifically of favouring a nasal delivery, see Swift's *The Mechanical Operation of the Spirit* (Davis 1939–68: I, 171–90). Also relevant is the account of the Aeolists in Section VIII of *A Tale of a Tub* (I, 95–101).

257–8 and 258n. Or such as bellow: This is a new couplet in 1743, inserted into a contest which had been substantially unchanged since 1728. Although Sutherland rightly connects it with wider themes by observing that the pairing of the extremists Webster and Whitefield constitutes 'a sort of Roper and Ridpath of the religious world' (alluding to II.149; *TE*: V, 308), its appearance in 1743 seems connected with Warburton's desire to shift the *Dunciad* in the direction of his own specifically ecclesiastical preoccupations. The note was initialled in 1751 as by Warburton. ***the deep Divine:*** 'Deep' plays on the double sense of 'profound' (bathetic?) and 'bass'; a 'Divine' is a term for a theologian, usually assumed to be a clergyman. ***Webster:*** William Webster (1689–1758), high-church clergyman and journalist in the ministerial interest (Gerrard 1994: 30). Warburton's note chooses not to mention the personal animosity caused by Webster's attacks on his *The Divine Legation of Moses* (see *Remarks on the Divine Legation* 1739; Warburton 1738; Warburton 1738–41: preface to Vol. II). ***Whitfield:*** George Whitefield (1714–70), leading preacher of Calvinist Methodism, celebrated for his open-air addresses to large crowds. For Warburton's disapproval, see Nichols 1812–15: V, 578. Theological controversy between Warburton and Whitefield was to break out in 1763 over Warburton's *The Doctrine of Grace ... Vindicated from ... the Abuses of Fanaticism* (Warburton 1763; Whitefield 1763). ***the New-birth of religious madness:*** The Methodist emphasis on being born again through conversion gave offence to 'sober Clergy' not only by its apparent encouragement of irresponsible emotionalism, but also by its implicit denial of the efficacy of the sacrament of baptism as routinely received in infancy by members of the Church of England. Methodist preachers were also resented as interfering with the relationship between the people and the parish clergy charged with their care. (For a satirical account of these and other aspects of early Methodism, see Richard Graves, *The Spiritual Quixote*: Tracy 1967.) ***the old death of fire and faggot:*** Implying that Webster would have liked to return to the times when dissenters from the established church would have been burned at the stake as heretics. ***while the Civil Magistrate prudently***

But far o'er all, sonorous Blackmore's strain;
Walls, steeples, skies, bray back to him again.
In Tot'nam fields, the brethren with amaze
Prick all their ears up, and forget to graze;
Long Chanc'ry-lane retentive rolls the sound,

260. bray back to him again] A figure of speech taken from Virgil: 'Et vox assensu nemorum ingeminata remugit.' Georg. iii. 'He hears his num'rous herds low o'er the plain, / While neighb'ring hills *low* back to them again.' Cowley. The poet here celebrated, Sir R. B. delighted much in the word *bray*, which he endeavoured to ennoble by applying it to the sound of *Armour, War, etc.* In imitation of him, and strengthened by his authority, our author has here admitted it into Heroic poetry.

262.] 'Immemor herbarum quos est mirata juvenca.' Virg. Ecl. viii. The progress of the sound from place to place, and the scenery here of the bordering regions, Tottenham-fields, Chancery-lane, the Thames, Westminster-hall, and Hungerford-stairs, are imitated from Virgil, Aen. vii. on the sounding the horn of Alecto: 'Audiit et Triviae longe lacus, audiit amnis / Sulphurea Nar albus aqua, fontesque Velini', *etc.*

263.] The place where the offices of Chancery are kept. The long detention of Clients in that Court, and the difficulty of getting out, is humourously allegorized in these lines.

---

forbears: Warburton, with self-conscious moderation, explicitly approves of the increasing disinclination of the civil power to inflict legal penalties for spiritual offences, an attitude which deprives Anglican extremists of a weapon against the Methodists that could have threatened persecution, martyrdom and social turmoil.

259–70. For themes and locations, see Colomb 1992: 112–15.

259. sonorous: Accented on the second syllable.

260n. Et vox assensu ...: 'And the cry, redoubled by the approving groves, roars back' (*remugit* is regularly used of the bellowing of animals: *Georgics* III.45). ***He hears his num'rous herds:*** A loose quotation from Cowley's translation of Horace's commendation of a farmer's life (Gough 1915: 158; *Epodes* II.11–12). ***delighted much in the word* bray:** Blackmore may have been inspired by Milton's sole use of 'bray': 'arms on armour clashing brayed / Horrible discord' (Fowler 1998: *Paradise Lost* VI.209–10). Brooks-Davies suggests that Pope may have had in mind Garth's quotation in the *Dispensary* of lines from Blackmore's Arthurian poems which included the word (Brooks-Davies 1985: 86). Cp. also Pope's evocation of Blackmore's aural qualities in *Imitations of Horace*: 'What? like Sir *Richard*, rumbling, rough and fierce, / With ARMS, and GEORGE, and BRUNSWICK crowd the Verse? / Rend with tremendous Sound your ears asunder, / With Gun, Drum, Trumpet, Blunderbuss & Thunder?' (*Satires* II.i.23–6).

261. Tot'nam fields: Open country north of Westminster. ***the brethren:*** Donkeys, characterised as Blackmore's kin by virtue of his braying; but also suggesting the 'brethren' of the dissenting sects, likely in Pope's view to be impressed by resonant nonsense.

262n. Immemor herbarum ...: 'They so amaze the heifer that she forgets all about the grass' (said in praise of two shepherds engaged in a singing contest: *Eclogues* VIII.2). ***the sounding the horn of Alecto:*** The fury Alecto sounds her horn to stir up violence: 'Diana's lake, far away, heard it; the River Nar white with his sulphurous water and the springs of Velinus heard it' (*Aeneid* VII.516–17).

263 and n. The Court of Chancery in Chancery Lane was a court of justice notorious for its slow and expensive procedures. Its 'retentive' power over litigants was proverbial: for a

And courts to courts return it round and round;
Thames wafts it thence to Rufus' roaring hall,
And Hungerford re-echoes bawl for bawl.
All hail him victor in both gifts of song,
Who sings so loudly, and who sings so long.

268.] A just character of Sir Richard Blackmore knight, who (as Mr. Dryden expresseth it) 'Writ to the rumbling of his coach's wheels', and whose indefatigable Muse produced no less than six Epic poems: Prince and King Arthur, twenty books; Eliza, ten; Alfred, twelve; the Redeemer, six; besides Job, in folio; the whole Book of Psalms; the Creation, seven books; Nature of Man, three books; and many more. 'Tis in this sense he is styled afterwards the *everlasting Blackmore*. Notwithstanding all which, Mr. Gildon seems assured, that 'this admirable author did not think himself upon the *same foot* with *Homer*.' Comp. Art of Poetry,

---

late instance, see Charles Dickens's *Bleak House*. There may be a pun on 'Chancery Rolls', the rolled documents which preserved its records.

265. Rufus' roaring hall: Westminster Hall, built by William II, called 'Rufus' (*d.* 1100), and used for coronations, parliaments, trials and lawsuits (Kingsford 1971: I, 113–18). In Pope's time the 'roaring' was done partly by lawyers and partly by stallholders, including booksellers, who operated in the building.

266. Hungerford re-echoes: Most obviously, Hungerford Market (between the Strand and the Thames, on the site now occupied by Charing Cross Station); but since the name was given as '*H—d*' in 1728 (i.e. it was treated as a surname), there was probably an intended allusion to the lawyer John Hungerford (*d.* 1729), echoing the combination of stallholders' and lawyers' noise in the previous line.

268n. A just character: As knight and personal physician to William III, Blackmore could hardly be accused of writing for hire; but he could be ridiculed for trying to write epic as 'my *Recreation*, and the Entertainment of my idle hours' (Blackmore 1695: Preface). Dryden imagines him composing as he travels between patients, tuning his verse to the lumbering rhythm of the coach (Kinsley 1958: 'Prologue to *The Pilgrim*', line 42). ***no less than six Epic poems:*** Virgil, Spenser and Milton had been content with one each, and even Homer (then believed to be a single individual) had produced only two. However, as described by Blackmore in their titles, only *Prince Arthur, King Arthur* (a total of twenty-two books, not twenty: *King Arthur* has twelve), *Eliza* and *Alfred* qualify as epics. The two poems on Arthur celebrate William III; *Eliza* exhorts Queen Anne to emulate Elizabeth I; *Alfred* exhorts the young Prince Frederick to follow in the footsteps of Alfred the Great. *Creation* is often considered his best work. ***the* everlasting Blackmore:** At II.302. ***Mr. Gildon seems assured:*** A subtle piece of misrepresentation. Gildon presents a dialogue between the ludicrously extreme modern Issachar Lamode (stigmatised as a Jew and a fop) and the more moderate Morisina. Lamode declares 'the *Arthur*'s as good as *Homer*'; but Morisina replies, 'I am very confident, that the *admirable* Author of *the Creation*, has too much *Judgment*, and too much *Modesty*, to have any such Thought himself' (Gildon 1718: I, 106, 108). Unfortunately, Gildon immediately puts his heroine completely beyond the Scriblerian pale by having her concede that Blackmore 'has the Glory of excelling *Lucretius*, it is a Palm gain'd only by him'. (The *De Rerum Natura* ('On the Nature of Things') of Titus Lucretius Carus (98–*c.*55 BC) was traditionally revered as a model of the didactic philosophical poem, despite scandalising Christian orthodoxy by advancing a view of the gods as uninterested in human life.) Pope had reversed such positive comparisons

vol. i. p. 108.

But how different is the judgment of the author of Characters of the times? p. 25. who says, 'Sir Richard Blackmore is unfortunate in happening to mistake his proper talents; and that he has not for many years been *so much as named*, or even *thought of* among writers.' Even Mr. Dennis differs greatly from his friend Mr. Gildon: 'Blackmore's *Action* (saith he) has neither unity, nor integrity, nor morality, nor universality; and consequently he can have no *Fable*, and no *Heroic Poem:* His Narration is neither probable, delightful, nor wonderful; his Characters have none of the necessary qualifications; the things contained in his Narration are neither in their own nature delightful, nor numerous enough, nor rightly disposed, nor surprising, nor pathetic.' — Nay he proceeds so far as to say Sir Richard has *no Genius*; first laying down, that 'Genius is caused by a *furious joy* and *pride of soul*, on the conception of an *extraordinary Hint*. Many Men (says he) have their *Hints*, without these motions of *fury* and *pride of soul*, because they want fire enough to agitate their spirits; and these we call cold writers. Others who have a great deal of fire, but have not excellent organs, feel the forementioned *motions*, without the *extraordinary hints*; and these we call fustian writers. But he declares that Sir Richard had neither the *Hints*, nor the *Motions*.' Remarks on Pr. Arth. octavo, 1696. Preface.

This gentleman in his first works abused the character of Mr. Dryden; and in his last, of Mr. Pope, accusing him in very high and sober terms of profaneness and immorality (Essay on Polite Writing, vol. ii. p. 270.) on a mere report from Edm. Curl, that he was author of a Travestie on the first Psalm. Mr. Dennis took up the same report, but with the addition of what Sir Richard had neglected, an *Argument to prove it*; which being very curious, we shall here transcribe. 'It *was* he who burlesqued the Psalm of David. It is *apparent* to me that Psalm was burlesqued by a *Popish rhymester*. Let rhyming persons who have been brought up *Protestants* be otherwise what they will, let them be rakes, let them be scoundrels, let them be *Atheists*, yet education has made an invincible impression on them in behalf of the sacred

---

in *Peri Bathous* by declaring Blackmore 'the Father of the Bathos, and indeed the Homer of it' (*PW*: II, 196). ***the author of Characters of the times:*** After 1735 Pope dropped his attribution of *Characters of the Times* to Curll and Welsted. The note conceals a reflection on Pope by selective quotation, for the passage reads in full: 'Sir *Richard* has not for many years been so much as nam'd, or even thought of among Writers, as such; and whom no one except *P–pe*, would have had ill-nature enough to revive.' ***Even Mr. Dennis differs:*** Introducing a summary of the opening of Dennis's *Remarks on Prince Arthur* (Dennis 1696b; Hooker 1939–43: I, 46–7). ***in his first works abused the character of Mr. Dryden:*** Blackmore's *Prince Arthur* criticises Dryden under the character of Laurus (Blackmore 1695: *Prince Arthur* VI). ***in his last:*** Blackmore lamented in his 'Essay on Writing' that 'the godless Author has burlesq'd the *First Psalm* of *David* in so obscene and profane a manner' (Blackmore 1716–17: II, 270). ***a mere report from Edm. Curl:*** The report was true, though Curll's presentation of the bawdy parody as 'A Roman Catholick Version of the First Psalm' (1716) was a gratuitous addition to Pope's embarrassment. The note is no more frank about his authorship than he was at the time, when, without literally denying it, he 'equivocated pretty genteelly', as he expressed himself to Teresa Blount (*TE*: VI, 164–6; *Corr.*: I, 350). Curll recalled the circumstances and repeated Blackmore's condemnation in *A Compleat Key* 1728. ***which being very curious:*** The note ridicules Dennis's typically bigoted contention that 'a Popish Rhymester has been brought up with a Contempt for those Sacred Writings in the Language which he understands'. However, it is clear that Pope's parody is aimed specifically at the pedestrian metrical translations of the psalms used at that time in Anglican worship: to Dennis, but not

This labour past, by Bridewell all descend,
(As morning pray'r, and flagellation end)
To where Fleet-ditch with disemboguing streams
Rolls the large tribute of dead dogs to Thames,

writings. But a *Popish rhymester* has been brought up with a contempt for those sacred writings; now shew me another *Popish rhymester* but he.' This manner of argumentation is usual with Mr. Dennis; he has employed the same against Sir Richard himself, in a like charge of *Impiety* and *Irreligion*. 'All Mr. Blackmore's celestial Machines, as they cannot be defended so much as by common received opinion, so are they directly contrary to the doctrine of the church of England; for the visible descent of an Angel must be a miracle. Now it is the doctrine of the Church of England that miracles had ceased a long time before Prince Arthur came into the world. Now if the doctrine of the church of England be true, as we are obliged to believe, then are all the celestial machines in Prince Arthur unsufferable, as wanting not only human, but divine probability. But if the machines are sufferable, that is if they have so much as divine probability, then it follows of necessity that the doctrine of the Church is false. So I leave it to every impartial Clergyman to consider,' *etc.* Preface to the Remarks on Prince Arthur.

270.] It is between eleven and twelve in the morning, after church service, that the criminals are whipt in Bridewell. — This is to mark punctually the *time* of the day: Homer does it by the circumstance of the Judges rising from court, or of the Labourer's dinner; our author by one very proper both to the *Persons* and the *Scene* of his poem, which we may remember commenced in the evening of the Lord-mayor's day: The first book passed in that *night*; the next *morning* the games begin in the Strand, thence along Fleet-street (places inhabited by Booksellers) then they proceed by Bridewell toward Fleet-ditch, and lastly thro' Ludgate to the City and the Temple of the Goddess.

---

to Pope, a hallowed expression of piety (Dennis 1717; Hooker 1939–43: II, 130; see also editor's note on III.187). ***a like charge of* Impiety *and* Irreligion:** Quoting loosely from *Remarks on Prince Arthur* (Dennis 1696b; Hooker 1939–43: I, 53).

269–354. The diving competition alludes at several points to the descent of Aristaeus into the waters of his divine mother in search of a remedy for the death of his bees, a myth of rebirth told by Virgil as origin of the ritual by which bees were supposed to be generated from a ritually killed calf, and one which Gay had reworked in the Cloacina episode of *Trivia* (*Georgics* IV.315–547; Brooks-Davies 1985: 31–3, 38–9; editor's notes on I.55–78).

269. Bridewell: A prison near the Thames where prostitutes were punished.

270 and n. Parodying the Homeric convention of denoting time of day by everyday activities associated with it (as Pope had already done in *The Rape of the Lock*, III.21–4). It may be relevant that this seems to synchronise with the time at which the Lord Mayor's procession reached the Thames (Williams 1955: 39).

271. Fleet-ditch: A navigable waterway which served as an open drain and emptied into the Thames near Bridewell, and was the subject of Jonson's scatological mock-heroic 'On the Famous Voyage' (Rogers 1972: 145–66; Herford & Simpson 1925–52: VIII, 84–9). Cp. Garth's 'Nigh where *Fleet-Ditch* descends in sable Streams / To wash his sooty *Naiads* in the *Thames*' (*The Dispensary* 1699: III.111–12). ***disemboguing:*** emptying out. For its use in Dryden's and Pope's epic translations, see Sherbo 1970: 508–9; for an argument regarding possible influences, see Lund 1984: 298–9.

The King of dykes! than whom no sluice of mud
With deeper sable blots the silver flood.
'Here strip, my children! here at once leap in,
Here prove who best can dash thro' thick and thin,
And who the most in love of dirt excel,
Or dark dexterity of groping well.
Who flings most filth, and wide pollutes around
The stream, be his the Weekly Journals bound,

273.] 'Fluviorum rex Eridanus, / ... quo non alius, per pinguia culta, / In mare purpureum violentior influit amnis.' Virg.

276, 277, 278.] The three chief qualifications of Party-writers; to stick at nothing, to delight in flinging dirt, and to slander in the dark by guess.

280. the Weekly Journals] Papers of news and scandal intermixed, on different sides and parties, and frequently shifting from one side to the other, called the London Journal, British Journal, Daily Journal, *etc.* the concealed writers of which for some time were Oldmixon, Roome, Arnall, Concanen, and others; persons never seen by our author.

273n. Fluviorum rex ....: 'Po, the king of rivers ... than whom none flows with more force through the productive fields into the deep blue sea' (*Georgics* IV.372–3; the passage is also cited at II.181–2).

274. sable: black.

275–8. The diving contest, which focuses on government journalists, draws on the associations still current in such expressions as 'muck-raking' and 'gutter press'. For newspapers in the period, see Black 1987a; for political journalism, see Harris 1987, especially chs. 7 and 8; for opposition journalism, see Varey 1982: xiii–xxxiv; Downie & Corns 1993: 58–77.

276. Cp. Dryden's Doeg (a caricature of Settle) in *The Second Part of Absolom and Achitophel*, who 'Spurd boldly on, and Dash'd through Thick and Thin, / Through Sense and Non-sense, never out nor in' (Kinsley 1958: line 414; for Dryden's composition of this portion, see *OAC*: I, 278).

280 and n. Weekly Journals: A note to an early manuscript draft had specified 'the London Journals subscrib'd / Britannicus', and had identified their author as Benjamin Hoadly (1676–1761), clergyman and Whig propagandist, making more explicit than would have been prudent in print Pope's resentment of Hoadly's attacks on Atterbury (Mack 1984: 143, 145). Hoadly's political and religious views had become a focus for controversy in 1717 when, as Bishop of Bangor, he had preached before the King a sermon later published as *The Nature of the Kingdom, or Church, of Christ* (see line 400). Taking as his text 'Jesus answered, My Kingdom is not of this world' (John 18:36), Hoadly made a tactical equation between the kingdom and the church of Christ, using this as a basis for undermining the authority of the church in such matters as teaching, discipline and interpretation of Scripture. The sacraments were effectively marginalised, since Hoadly defined the individual Christian's membership of the kingdom simply as the keeping of laws plainly laid down by Christ in Scripture. Critics fastened on the kinship between this low-church view and the individualist and Bible-centred sects of the Civil War. Hoadly was typical of the bishops appointed by a Whig regime to undermine the high Anglican doctrine which sustained Tory and Jacobite views of the constitution. ***frequently shifting from one side to the other:*** For an example of the government's buying out of a hostile paper, see Harris 1987: 114. ***concealed writers:*** Journalists

A pig of lead to him who dives the best;
A peck of coals a-piece shall glad the rest.'
In naked majesty Oldmixon stands,

282.] Our indulgent Poet, whenever he has spoken of any dirty or low work, constantly puts us in mind of the *Poverty* of the offenders, as the only extenuation of such practices. Let any one but remark, when a Thief, a Pick-pocket, an Highwayman, or a Knight of the post are spoken of, how much our hate to those characters is lessened, if they add a *needy* Thief, a *poor* Pick-pocket, an *hungry* Highwayman, a *starving* Knight of the post, *etc.*

283.] Mr. John Oldmixon, next to Mr. Dennis, the most ancient Critic of our Nation; an unjust censurer of Mr. Addison in his prose Essay on Criticism, whom also in his imitation of Bouhours (called the Arts of Logic and Rhetoric) he misrepresents in plain matter of fact; for in p. 45. he cites the Spectator as abusing Dr. Swift by name, where there is not the least hint of it; and in p. 304. is so injurious as to suggest, that Mr. Addison himself writ that Tatler, N. 43. which says of his own Simile, that ''Tis as great as ever entered into the mind of man.' 'In Poetry he was not so happy as laborious, and therefore characterised by the Tatler, N. 62. by the name of *Omicron* the *Unborn Poet.*' Curl, Key, p. 13. 'He writ Dramatic

---

writing either anonymously or under pseudonyms. ***Arnall:*** William Arnall (1699?–1736), leading political journalist, who worked closely with Walpole (Harris 1987: 102–3, 108–9, 111).

281. a pig of lead: A lead ingot, continuing the theme of Dulness's 'age of Lead' (I.28).

282 and n. A peck of coals: A peck is a dry measure equivalent to two gallons or about eight litres. The journalists are represented as too poor to afford a fire, an insult which the note typically pretends to take as compassionate extenuation of their offences. ***a Knight of the post:*** One who gives false evidence for pay ('post' is here equivalent to 'whipping post' or 'pillory').

283 and n. Echoing Milton's description of Adam and Eve, who 'In naked majesty seemed lords of all' (Fowler 1998: *Paradise Lost* IV.290). This was before their fall, burlesqued in Oldmixon's impending dive (Erskine-Hill 1972b: 60–61). Rogers points out that the metre demands stress on the second syllable of his name, activating the pun on 'mixen' ('dungheap') (Rogers 1975: 129). ***next to Mr. Dennis:*** Dennis had been the original subject of these lines but had died in 1734. Henceforth Oldmixon took his place, though he too died in 1742, shortly before the publication of *The Dunciad in Four Books.* ***an unjust censurer of Mr. Addison:*** Although expressing broad approval of Addison, Oldmixon criticised the way '*Cato* suspends the Action and the Passion of the Scene to teach the Audience, Philosophy and Morality'; he accused Addison of being unable to take criticism; and he suggested that Addison was in general unduly censorious of other critics (Oldmixon 1728a: 5–16). ***he cites the Spectator:*** Oldmixon gratuitously adds the alleged example 'such as S—t' to Addison's remarks on 'the Ill-natured Man' (Oldmixon 1728b: 45; Bond 1965: II, 167, *Spectator* 169). ***is so injurious as to suggest:*** What Oldmixon actually wrote, after quoting another passage from *Tatler* 43, was: 'I can hardly think Mr. *Addison* wrote that *Tatler*, there being in it a just Complement upon himself' (Oldmixon 1728b: 304). The essay in question is attributed to Steele (Bond 1987: I, 310–11, *Tatler* 43). ***In Poetry he was not so happy as laborious:*** Elaborating Curll's identification of Oldmixon with '*Mr.* Omicron, *the Unborn Poet*' in Steele's *Tatler* 62 (*A Compleat Key* 1728; Bond 1987: I, 433). 'Unborn' was an allusion to a medical quack who advertised himself as 'the unborn doctor' (Bond 1987: I, 120, *Tatler* 14). Several details in the account could be applied to Oldmixon, though Bond considers the identification unlikely, since Steele and Oldmixon were both Whigs. ***Dramatic works, and a***

works, and a volume of Poetry, consisting of heroic Epistles, *etc.* some whereof are very well done,' saith that great Judge Mr. Jacob, in his Lives of Poets, vol. ii. p. 303.

In his Essay on Criticism, and the Arts of Logic and Rhetoric, he frequently reflects on our Author. But the top of his character was a Perverter of History, in that scandalous one of the Stuarts, in folio, and his Critical History of England, two volumes, octavo. Being employed by bishop Kennet, in publishing the Historians in his Collection, he falsified Daniel's Chronicle in numberless places. Yet this very man, in the preface to the first of these books, advanced a *particular Fact* to charge three eminent persons of falsifying the lord Clarendon's History; which fact has been disproved by Dr. Atterbury, late bishop of Rochester, then the only survivor of them; and the particular part he pretended to be falsified, produced since,

---

volume of Poetry: Oldmixon 1700; Oldmixon 1703; *Amores Britannici* 1703. ***that great Judge Mr. Jacob:*** A derisive reference to Jacob 1719–20: II. ***the top of his character:*** the most striking aspect of his character. ***a Perverter of History:*** This section of the note is a compressed and partisan review of a series of charges and counter-charges generated by Oldmixon's histories, notably the anonymous *Critical History* (1724–6) and *History ... of the Royal House of Stuart* (1730). These works offended Pope in general by their Whig propaganda, but they also gave specific offence by blackening the characters of Tory friends.

The matters raised in the note are best taken in chronological order. Edward Hyde (1609–74), first Earl of Clarendon, was an adviser of Charles I, and accompanied the future Charles II into exile. After the Restoration, however, he was exiled on a charge of treason, and devoted himself to revising his *History of the Rebellion and Civil Wars in England,* which was published at Oxford after his death from a manuscript provided by his family (Hyde 1702–4). The preface, by his son, makes it clear that the publication was intended as a vindication of high Tory principle applicable to the contemporary situation. Oldmixon's Preface to *The History ... of the Royal House of Stuart* did not attack Clarendon directly, but 'advanced a *particular Fact*' ('made a specific allegation') against 'three eminent persons' concerned in the publication, all high-church clergy and Oxford dons obnoxious to him, but esteemed by Pope, for their Tory principles. All had additionally earned Pope's esteem by their opposition to Bentley in the Phalaris controversy. Oldmixon accused George Smalridge (1663–1719), Henry Aldrich (1647–1710) and Atterbury (then in exile on accurate but unproven suspicion of Jacobite conspiracy) of employing Edmund Smith (1672–1710) to alter Clarendon's text, to make it more favourable to the royal family and less favourable to those on the parliamentary side, notably John Hampden. Despite evident talent, Smith had been so dissolute that he had been expelled from Christ Church by Aldrich (whom Pope praised as a force for university reform: *OAC*: I, 187); Oldmixon's report of his alleged dying confession rested solely on the anonymous testimony of the Whig MP, journalist and antagonist of Pope George Duckett; and the charge has not been upheld by later scholarship (see for example the disputed characterisation of Hampden in Macray 1888: III, 64). As sole survivor of those accused, Atterbury protested, and was answered by Oldmixon (Atterbury 1731; Oldmixon 1732). An anonymous defender of Atterbury and the Oxford edition then testified to having seen the disputed passages in Clarendon's autograph, and lodged a counter-claim, that Oldmixon, as editor of the composite Whig history written and compiled by John Hughes (1677–1720) and White Kennett, had made 'between two and three Thousand' alterations in the *Collection of the History of England* by Samuel Daniel (1562–1619), a charge dismissed by the nineteenth-century editor of the *Collection* (*Mr. Oldmixon's Reply ... Examin'd* 1732; S.D. 1618; *A Complete History of England* 1706; Grosart 1885–96: V, 295; Bennett 1975: 168–73). Pope's marginalia in his own copy of Clarendon's *History* show that he had personally compared the printed text with the manuscript, to which he presumably had access through his friendship with the

And Milo-like surveys his arms and hands;
Then sighing, thus, 'And am I now three-score?
Ah why, ye Gods! should two and two make four?'
He said, and clim'd a stranded lighter's height,
Shot to the black abyss, and plung'd down-right.
The Senior's judgment all the crowd admire,

after almost ninety years, in that noble author's original manuscript. He was all his life a virulent Party-writer for hire, and received his reward in a small place, which he enjoyed to his death.

He is here likened to Milo, in allusion to that verse of Ovid, 'Fletque Milon senior, cum spectat inanes / Herculeis similes, fluidos pendere lacertos'; either with regard to his Age, or because he was undone by trying to pull to pieces an Oak that was too strong for him. 'Remember Milo's end / Wedg'd in that timber which he strove to rend.' Lord Rosc.

286.] Very reasonably doth this ancient Critic complain: Without doubt it was a fault in the Constitution of things. For the *World*, as a great writer saith, *being given to man for a subject of disputation*, he might think himself mock'd with a penurious gift, were any thing made certain. Hence those superior masters of wisdom, the *Sceptics* and *Academics*, reasonably conclude that *two and two do not make four.* SCRIBL.

But we need not go so far, to remark what the Poet principally intended, the absurdity of complaining of *old age*, which must necessarily happen, as long as we are indulged in our desires of adding one year to another.

Hyde family (Mack 1982: 402). ***a small place:*** A small government post (he was made a collector of taxes at Bridgewater). ***Milo:*** Celebrated wrestler (late sixth century BC). ***that verse of Ovid:*** 'And Milo, now grown older, weeps as he looks at his wasted muscles, once like those of Hercules, now hanging slack' (*Metamorphoses* XV.229–30). ***an Oak that was too strong for him:*** As formerly applied to Dennis, the gibe would relate to Dennis's failure either to silence Pope or to destroy his reputation (compare the previous context in *TE*: V, 135). It is less apt for Oldmixon, whose attacks on Pope were fewer and more casual (see Guerinot 1969: Index, 'Oldmixon'). ***Remember Milo's end:*** From 'An Essay on Translated Verse' (Dillon 1749: 21).

284. A note to an early manuscript draft cites Virgil's description of an aged boxer's preparations for a contest in which he will defeat a younger challenger (Mack 1984: 144; *Aeneid* V.422).

285. George II had his sixtieth birthday the day following publication of *The Dunciad in Four Books* (Vander Meulen 1989: 304).

286n. Initialled in 1751 as by Warburton. ***as a great writer saith:*** Not identified. ***penurious:*** beggarly, stingy. ***the* Sceptics *and* Academics:** The Sceptics were ancient Greek philosophers who asserted that nothing could be known with absolute certainty. They were prominent among the Academics, the members of the school originally set up by Plato near Athens and named the Academy.

287. a stranded lighter's height: Fleet Ditch rose and fell with the tide and was navigable for a considerable distance at high tide. Lighters were flat-bottomed boats used for ferrying goods around the Thames wharves and inlets. Since the lighter is 'stranded', it is low tide, providing the divers with the minimum depth of water and the maximum of mud.

288. down-right: straight down.

Who but to sink the deeper, rose the higher.
  Next Smedley div'd; slow circles dimpled o'er
The quaking mud, that clos'd, and op'd no more.
All look, all sigh, and call on Smedley lost;
Smedley in vain resounds thro' all the coast.
  Then * essay'd; scarce vanish'd out of sight,
He buoys up instant, and returns to light:
He bears no token of the sabler streams,
And mounts far off among the Swans of Thames.

291.] The person here mentioned, an Irishman, was author and publisher of many scurrilous pieces, a weekly Whitehall Journal, in the year 1722. in the name of Sir James Baker; and particularly whole volumes of Billingsgate against Dr. Swift and Mr. Pope, called Gulliveriana and Alexandriana, printed in octavo, 1728.

293.] 'Alcides wept in vain for Hylas lost, / Hylas, in vain, resounds thro' all the coast.' Lord Roscom. Translat. of Virgil's 6th Ecl.

295.] A Gentleman of genius and spirit, who was secretly dipt in some papers of this kind, on whom our Poet bestows a panegyric instead of a satyr, as deserving to be better employed than in Party-quarrels and personal invectives.

---

290. The dive alludes to the favourite Scriblerian irony by which attempted sublimity becomes insanity, attempted profundity bathos.

291 and n. Smedley: Smedley had replaced Eusden ('E—') in this passage in 1729. For a reading of his dive as parodic of the drowning of Hylas and the poetic creativity which makes beauty out of the loss in Virgil's *Eclogue* IV, see Lawler in Mack & Winn 1980: 740–48. ***a Weekly Whitehall Journal:*** First published as *Baker's News: or, The Whitehall Journal*, it soon dropped the first part of the title, which may have referred to a real Sir James Baker, 'a person with whose simplicity several of the quality diverted themselves' ('The Life and Adventures of Mrs. Christian Davies', in Defoe 1855: 494–500). ***whole volumes of Billingsgate:*** For these anonymous attacks, see *Gulliveriana* 1728.

293n. 'Alcides' is a title of the mythical hero Hercules (from his grandfather Alcaeus), who took Hylas on the voyage of the Argonauts and stayed behind to look for him when he was abducted by water nymphs (*Eclogues* VI.43–4; Dillon 1749: 83).

295–8. This passage, distinguishing its subject as superior to the duncely activities in which he is briefly involved, was conceived for the poet, dramatist, journalist and projector Aaron Hill (1685–1750): compare his probable appearance as one of the '*Flying Fishes*' in *Peri Bathous* (*PW*: II, 196). He now becomes one of 'the Swans of Thames' (compare 'swan of Avon', applied to Shakespeare). His relations with Pope went through an intricate succession of offences and reconciliations, resulting in various alterations to the passage over time (*TE*: V, 136–7, 444–5; *Corr.*: III, 164, 165, 170, 174, 177). The asterisk and the form of the note used in 1743 represent a partial compliance with Hill's request to be taken out of the *Dunciad* (in 1728 he had been referred to as 'H—'; and in 1729 the note had been more openly critical). Hill's persistent attempts to make Pope accept him at his own valuation combined with Pope's inability ever to be completely frank with him to produce a superficially friendly but tediously edgy correspondence (*Corr.*: V, 35–6). For Hill's role in the cultural programme of the Patriot opposition of the 1730s, see Gerrard 1994: 48–54; and see also the forthcoming biography by the same author.

True to the bottom, see Concanen creep,
A cold, long-winded, native of the deep:

299.] MATTHEW CONCANEN, an Irishman, bred to the law. Smedley (one of his brethren in enmity to Swift) in his Metamorphosis of Scriblerus, p. 7. accuses him of 'having boasted of what he had not written, but others had revised and done for him.' He was author of several dull and dead scurrilities in the British and London Journals, and in a paper called the Speculatist. In a pamphlet, called a Supplement to the Profund, he dealt very unfairly with our Poet, not only frequently imputing to him Mr. Broome's verses (for which he might indeed seem in some degree accountable, having corrected what that gentleman did) but those of the duke of Buckingham, and others: To this rare piece somebody humourously caused him to take for his motto, *De profundis clamavi*. He was since a hired scribler in the Daily Courant, where he poured forth much Billingsgate against the lord Bolingbroke, and others; after which this man was surprisingly promoted to administer Justice and Law in Jamaica.

---

299 and n. Concanen: Concanen's anonymous *Supplement to the Profund* (1728) presumably qualified him as a 'native of the deep'. The passage was first applied to him in 1729, having previously alluded to 'R—' and 'Wh—', i.e. Edward Roome and the journalist Stephen Whatley (*fl.* 1712–41), who succeeded Ridpath on the *Flying Post* and perhaps edited *The Daily Gazetteer* as an organ of government propaganda (Haig 1960: 8). ***Smedley ... accuses him:*** The note summarises from the anonymous poem *The Metamorphosis* (1728), in which Concanen is made to admit to plagiarism. ***several dull and dead scurrilities:*** *The Speculatist* (1730) reprints articles from the *London Journal* and *British Journal*, according to the Advertisement, 'to refute the Calumny of a rancorous and foul-mouth'd Railer who has asserted in print that the Author of them wrote *several Scurrilities* in those Papers' (a reference to the version of the note given in 1729: see Guerinot 1969: 194; *TE*: V, 113). ***In a pamphlet:*** For a near-contemporary suggestion that Warburton – before he became associated with Pope – may have been involved with Concanen in the *Supplement to the Profund*, see Guerinot 1969: 149. ***Mr. Broome's verses:*** Pope suggested revisions to some of Broome's poems before publication (Broome 1727; *Corr.*: II, 182, 422). ***those of the Duke of Buckingham:*** Prepared for posthumous publication by Pope (Pope 1723). ***somebody humourously caused him:*** The note takes the motto ('Out of the deep have I called': the opening of Psalm 130) as an ironic and unwitting proclamation that the author is sunk in bathos. Concanen presumably meant it simply as an allusion to Pope's *Peri Bathous*, and to the alleged dreadfulness of the examples he cited from Pope and his associates. ***the Daily Courant:*** A government-subsidised paper which made a point of attacking *The Craftsman*, the organ of Bolingbroke's campaign in the late 1720s and early 1730s (after his abandonment of the Jacobite cause and return to England) to unite Tories and dissident Whigs into a 'Patriot' opposition capable of driving Walpole from office (*A Critical History of the Administration* 1743; Haig 1960: 4; Varey 1982: xiii–xxxvi; Harris 1987: 102, 114; Downie & Corns 1993: 58–77). ***this man was surprisingly promoted:*** Hardly surprising – though the note suggests it ought to be – since Concanen was trained in the law and had rendered significant services to government propaganda.

300. In marked contrast with '*' (line 295), Concanen *belongs* in 'the deep': he is 'cold' (the word came into the passage only in 1729, when it was remodelled for him: it not only likens him to a cold-blooded fish, but also insinuates his lack of creative fire, and also his ingratitude to Swift, who had allowed him to print some of his verses in his *Miscellaneous Poems* (1724)); and he is 'long-winded' (as necessary, in its literal sense, for a diver).

If perseverance gain the Diver's prize,
Not everlasting Blackmore this denies:
No noise, no stir, no motion can'st thou make,
Th' unconscious stream sleeps o'er thee like a lake.
Next plung'd a feeble, but a desp'rate pack,
With each a sickly brother at his back:
Sons of a Day! just buoyant on the flood,
Then number'd with the puppies in the mud.
Ask ye their names? I could as soon disclose
The names of these blind puppies as of those.
Fast by, like Niobe (her children gone)
Sits Mother Osborne, stupify'd to stone!

302.] 'Nec bonus Eurytion praelato invidit honori', *etc.* Virg. Aen.

306, 307.] These were daily Papers, a number of which, to lessen the expence, were printed one on the back of another.

311.] See the story in Ovid, Met. vi. where the miserable Petrefaction of this old Lady is pathetically described.

312. Osborne] A name assumed by the eldest and gravest of these writers, who at last being ashamed of his Pupils, gave his paper over, and in his age remained silent.

302n. 'And good Eurytion did not grudge that the prize was awarded to someone else' (*Aeneid* V.541).

305–14 and 306–7n. These lines, sent in draft to Swift in 1739, allude to the subsidised *Daily Gazetteer*, set up in 1735 (*Corr.*: IV, 178–9). Its title deliberately insinuated its authority by its similarity to the *London Gazette*, which published official announcements (Haig 1960: 6–7). Special double issues (two days' issues printed back-to-back) were printed for free national distribution (Haig 1960: 4, 9–10; Harris 1987: 124).

308–10. puppies: Unwanted puppies, drowned before they could open their eyes ('puppy' was also a term of abuse for a young upstart). 'Dead dogs' in the Fleet Ditch were also mentioned at II.272: a confirmed dog-lover, Pope saw dogs as very little inferior to human beings, hated their use for vivisection and saw no compelling reason why they might not have immortal souls (*OAC*: I, 118–19). For line 309, cp. Dryden's translation of Juvenal: 'Ask me their Names, I sooner could relate ...' (Kinsley 1958: *Satires* X.348).

311–12; 311n. and 312n. Niobe: Niobe was so proud of her seven sons and seven daughters that she taunted the goddess Leto (Latona) with having only one of each (i.e. Apollo/Phoebus and Artemis/Diana). In revenge, her children were killed and she was turned into a weeping pillar of stone (*Metamorphoses* VI.146–312). ***Mother Osborne:*** 'Francis Osborne' was a pseudonym used by the Whig journalist and former schoolmaster James Pitt (*d.* 1763) in the *London Journal*, one of the papers absorbed into the *Daily Gazetteer* (Haig 1960: 4–5). The abbreviation 'F. Osborne' could be misread as 'Father Osborne', and 'Mother Osborne' was a derisive play on the misreading originated by *The Craftsman* (*A Critical History of the Administration* 1743: 517; *TE*: V, 311). Pitt is ridiculed in the note as 'this old Lady' (whereas Ovid's Niobe, despite her fourteen children, is still a beautiful woman), and the journalists who are said to have learned from his example are his doomed children (doomed in that their journalism is purely ephemeral) and pupils (alluding to his former career as schoolmaster). His retirement is imaged in his being 'stupify'd to stone'.

And Monumental Brass this record bears,
'These are, — ah no! these were, the Gazetteers!'

314. Gazetteers] We ought not to suppress that a modern Critic here taxeth the Poet with an Anachronism, affirming these Gazetteers not to have lived within the time of his poem, and challenging us to produce any such paper of that date. But we may with equal assurance assert, these Gazetteers not to have lived since, and challenge all the learned world to produce one such paper at this day. Surely therefore, where the point is so obscure, our author ought not to be censured too rashly. SCRIBL.

Notwithstanding this affected ignorance of the good Scriblerus, the *Daily Gazetteer* was a title given very properly to certain papers, each of which lasted but a day. Into this, as a common sink, was received all the trash, which had been before dispersed in several Journals, and circulated at the public expence of the nation. The authors were the same obscure men; though sometimes relieved by occasional essays from Statesmen, Courtiers, Bishops, Deans, and Doctors. The meaner sort were rewarded with Money; others with Places or Benefices, from an hundred to a thousand a year. It appears from the *Report* of the *Secret Committee* for

---

313. Monumental Brass: Beyond the surface meaning of a memorial plaque, for which brass was used in the ancient world, lies the routine anti-Walpole imagery of brazen hypocrisy (Mack 1969: 151–2; Sherbo 1970: 509). A draft dating from 1739 confirms the association by naming Nicholas Paxton (*d.* 1744), Solicitor to the Treasury and Walpole's press officer (*Corr.*: IV, 178–9; Harris 1987: 103–4).

314 and n. The passage, satirising government-subsidised news-sheets as mere ephemera, had taken form by 1739, too early to allude to the collapse of ministerial subsidy that changed *The Gazetteer*'s character after Walpole's fall in 1742 (*Corr.*: IV, 178–9; Haig 1960: 15; Harris 1987: 127–9). For a mock-dedication of the Gazette summarising charges similar to those made in the *Dunciad*, and said to be in Pope's hand, see Prior 1860: 366. ***a modern Critic:*** Alluding to Bentley's use of anachronisms to disprove the alleged dates and attributions of texts (e.g. Bentley 1699). ***challenging us to produce any such paper:*** Most newspaper readers threw away old papers, then as now. The surviving runs of eighteenth-century newspapers now used by scholars represent for the most part the collections of a very few individuals, notably Charles Burney the younger (1757–1817), whose collection is now in the British Library. ***each of which lasted but a day:*** By modern standards, an odd complaint to make against a daily paper. The fact that it is made at all underlines the *Dunciad*'s commitment to an older ideal of literature as a permanent embodiment of value. ***sink:*** drain, sewer. ***before dispersed in several Journals:*** Such as *The Daily Courant*, *The London Journal* and *The Free Briton* (Haig 1960: 4–6). ***circulated at the public expence:*** Making the point that the production and free distribution of government propaganda was all paid for out of taxpayers' money. ***Statesmen, Courtiers, Bishops, Deans, and Doctors:*** As contributors to *The Daily Courant*, *The Gazetteer*'s immediate predecessor, James Ralph listed (evasively as far as the correlation between dashes and missing letters is concerned) 'Dr. Bl——d D—n of D—ham' (Henry Bland (*d.* 1746), Dean of Durham), 'Dr. H——re B——p of Ch—ster' (Francis Hare (1671–1740), Bishop of Chichester: see Kerby-Miller 1950: 270–71), and 'H—ce W—le, brother to the M——re [i.e. 'Minister']' (Horace Walpole (1678–1757), diplomat, brother of Sir Robert) (*A Critical History of the Administration* 1743: 517). Bland may have been a target in an early manuscript draft of II.205 (Mack 1984: 109). ***Places or Benefices:*** Paid appointments, respectively in the state and in the church. ***the* Report *of the* Secret Committee:** After the fall of Sir Robert Walpole from power and his elevation to the peerage as Earl of

Not so bold Arnall; with a weight of skull,
Furious he dives, precipitately dull.

enquiring into the Conduct of R. Earl of O. 'That no less than *fifty-thousand, seventy-seven pounds, eighteen shillings,* were paid to Authors and Printers of News-papers, such as Free-Britons, Daily-Courants, Corn-Cutter's Journals, Gazetteers, and other political papers, between Feb. 10, 1731. and Feb. 10. 1741.' Which shews the Benevolence of One Minister to have expended, for the current dulness of ten years in Britain, double the sum which gained Louis XIV. so much honour, in annual Pensions to Learned men all over Europe. In which, and in a much longer time, not a Pension at Court, nor Preferment in the Church or Universities, of any Consideration, was bestowed on any man distinguished for his Learning separately from Party-merit, or Pamphlet-writing.

It is worth a reflection, that of all the Panegyrics bestowed by these writers on this great Minister, not one is at this day extant or remembred; nor even so much credit done to his Personal character by all they have written, as by one short occasional compliment of our Author. 'Seen him I have; but in his *happier hour* / Of *social pleasure,* ill exchang'd for *Pow'r!* / Seen him, uncumber'd by the Venal Tribe, / *Smile* without *Art,* and *win* without a *Bribe.*'

315.] WILLIAM ARNALL, bred an Attorney, was a perfect Genius in this sort of work. He began under twenty with furious Party-papers; then succeeded Concanen in the British Journal. At the first publication of the Dunciad, he prevailed on the Author not to give him

---

Orford, his enemies in parliament pressed for an enquiry into his alleged corruption, from whose findings the report quotes (*A Further Report* 1742: Appendix 13). The prosecution was not carried through, since Orford was no longer enough of a political force to be worth prolonged harassment. ***the sum which gained Louis XIV. so much honour:*** France, the traditional enemy, is cited to shame Walpole by contrast. Louis XIV used international patronage of scholars and writers to promote his image abroad (Burke 1992: 51–3). ***for his Learning separately from Party-merit:*** Walpole's pragmatic, value-for-money attitude to the subsidy of writing (which he viewed as direct payment for propaganda) represented a break with the policy of previous regimes, and was much resented by writers who conceived their social function in more elevated terms (Goldgar 1976: 8–19). The note conveniently overlooks the political pressures previously exerted on writers through court patronage; under Queen Anne Pope had been in sympathy with the regime, and leading ministers had been among his Scriblerian associates. ***one short occasional compliment:*** Quoting the answer given to the 'Friend' who hints in *Epilogue to the Satires* that Pope might stand to gain by abandoning his opposition to Walpole (I.29–32). Thus the note both incorporates the suggestion that Walpole had suppressed his better nature for the sake of power, and at the same time celebrates Pope's independence.

315 and n. Not so: The insertion of the lines on the Gazetteers in 1743 disrupts the previous contrast between Concanen, who disappears without a ripple (lines 303–4), and the turbulent diver of this passage (formerly Welsted, but since 1735 the leading government journalist Arnall). His style of diving is all splash and flurry, entitling him to the *Journals* (lines 279–80); and his thick skull (Arnall had little schooling and was a poor speller) takes him right to the bottom, entitling him also to the lead (line 281; Harris 1987: 111). ***At the first publication of the Dunciad:*** Such a letter could explain why in 1729 Pope altered his attribution to Arnall and others of an offensive letter printed in *Mist's Weekly Journal* for 8 June 1728, with the remark that Arnall had 'justify'd himself from this and all other offence to Mr. *P*' (*TE*: V, 211). In 1735, however, Pope adapted the present passage to attack Arnall.

Whirlpools and storms his circling arm invest,
With all the might of gravitation blest.
No crab more active in the dirty dance,
Downward to climb, and backward to advance.
He brings up half the bottom on his head,
And loudly claims the Journals and the Lead.
  The plunging Prelate, and his pond'rous Grace,
With holy envy gave one Layman place.
When lo! a burst of thunder shook the flood.
Slow rose a form, in majesty of Mud;

his due place in it, by a letter professing his detestation of such practices as his Predecessor's. But since, by the most unexampled insolence, and personal abuse of several great men, the Poet's particular friends, he most amply deserved a niche in the Temple of Infamy: Witness a paper, called the Free Briton, a Dedication intituled To the Genuine Blunderer, 1732, and many others. He writ for hire, and valued himself upon it; not indeed without cause, it appearing by the aforesaid REPORT, that he received 'for Free Britons, and other writings, in the space of *four years*, no less than *ten thousand nine hundred and ninety-seven pounds, six shillings, and eight pence*, out of the Treasury.'

---

a niche in the Temple of Infamy: *The Dunciad* is cast as parodying the notion of a memorial to the great and good such as the allegorical temple which Pope had in youth crafted in his *The Temple of Fame*, based on parts of Chaucer's *Hous of Fame* (Sitter 1971: 66–117). ***To the Genuine Blunderer:*** An article in *The Free Briton*, 20 July 1732, attacking Bolingbroke. It was reprinted in *The Gentleman's Magazine*, which explained that the title was a retort to the dedication to Walpole as 'the *greatest Blunderer in Christendom*' of a collection of articles from the opposition *Fog's Journal* (Vol. II, 1731: 856, 863–4). ***valued himself upon it:*** was proud of it. ***not indeed without cause:*** Arnall was exceptionally highly paid among government journalists, and worked closely with Walpole (Hanson 1936: frontispiece; Harris 1987: 102–3, 108). The sum quoted is given in Appendix 13 of *A Further Report* 1742.

323. The plunging Prelate: Thomas Sherlock (1678–1761), Bishop of London, who according to a story attributed to his schoolfriend Sir Robert Walpole, had as a boy impressed his classmates by diving straight into icy water while they stood shivering on the bank (Warton 1797: V, 167). Sherlock's support for Walpole and attacks on Bolingbroke probably earned Pope's dislike; but Warburton, who was on good terms with Sherlock, later claimed that Pope had denounced the identification as 'vile and malicious', and pointed out his explicit compliment to Sherlock at III.204 (Warburton 1751: V, 164–5). The compliment is, however, capable of an ironic reading: Pope's response to Warburton's challenge seems evasive. ***his pond'rous Grace:*** Sutherland suggests John Potter (1673?–1747), Archbishop of Canterbury, 'pond'rous' both in figure and in his works of controversy, theology and classical scholarship (*TE*: V, 313). Potter would have been offensive to Pope on account of his Whig politics, and also because he disliked Warburton.

324. Implying that the two bishops resent Arnall's success, since they regard political propaganda as the peculiar preserve of the clergy – a theme further developed at 355–8 (especially the long note on 355).

326. Slow rose a form: Smedley, who disappeared at 291–4. He was actually named in the equivalent passage in 1729; the role had been taken by Eusden in 1728; and the use of Dennis's

Shaking the horrors of his sable brows,
And each ferocious feature grim with ooze.
Greater he looks, and more than mortal stares:
Then thus the wonders of the deep declares.
  First he relates, how sinking to the chin,
Smit with his mien, the Mud-nymphs suck'd him in:
How young Lutetia, softer than the down,
Nigrina black, and Merdamante brown,
Vy'd for his love in jetty bow'rs below,
As Hylas fair was ravish'd long ago.
Then sung, how shown him by the Nut-brown maids

329.] Virg. Aen. vi. of the Sibyl: 'majorque videri, / Nec mortale sonans'.

336.] Who was ravished by the water-nymphs and drawn into the river. The story is told at large by Valerius Flaccus, lib. 3. Argon. See Virgil, Ecl. vi.

---

favourite epithet 'tremendous' in that version may suggest that Pope had previously intended it for him (*TE*: V, 139).

327. Cp. Milton: 'this drear wood, / The nodding horror of whose shady brows / Threats the forlorn and wandering passenger' (Carey 1968: *Comus*, lines 37–9).

329n. *Aeneid* VI.49–50. Cp. Dryden's translation of Virgil's description of the inspired Sybil: 'Greater than Human Kind she seem'd to look: / And with an Accent, more than Mortal, spoke' (Kinsley 1958: *Aeneid* VI.76–7).

330. Echoing Psalm 107:24, citing the seafarers' privilege of witnessing 'the works of the Lord, and his wonders in the deep' (Sherbo 1970: 509).

331. Introducing a parody which combines the loss of Hylas, anticipated at 293–4, with the descent of Aristaeus into the river, attended by his mother's water-nymphs (*Georgics* IV.315–547; Brooks-Davies 1985: 31–3).

332. Smit: smitten. ***mien:*** manner, bearing. ***suck'd him in:*** In a characteristic teasing of refined sensibilities, Pope brings together the kisses of the nymphs with the sensation of being sucked into a quagmire.

333. Lutetia: From Latin *luteus*, 'mud'. Lutetia is the Latin name for the city of Paris. ***softer than the down:*** Emphasising the slime's tactile qualities by a stock erotic comparison, e.g. Ben Jonson's 'A Celebration of Charis in ten Lyrick Peeces': 'Have you felt the wooll o' the Bever? / Or Swans Downe ever?' (Herford & Simpson 1925–52: VIII, 135, lines 25–6).

334. Nigrina: From Latin *nigra* ('black'). ***Merdamante:*** From Latin *merda* ('dung') and *amans* ('loving'), a reminder that the Fleet Ditch functioned as a sewer.

335. jetty: black.

336n. at large: in full. ***Valerius Flaccus:*** Latin poet (late first century AD), author of *Argonautica*, an unfinished account of the voyage of the Argonauts in search of the Golden Fleece (*Argonautica* III.521–610). Erskine-Hill points out that the telling of the Hylas story by Theocritus is closer in some details (Theocritus, *Idylls* XIII; Erskine-Hill 1962: 747–8).

337. Nut-brown maids: Although 'Merdamante brown' sufficiently fixes the immediate reference, the name also recalls, in a further juxtaposition of filth and erotic allure, the late-medieval poem upon which Prior had based his 'Henry and Emma', in which the nutbrown maid wins an earl's son by her courage and fidelity (Chambers & Sidgwick 1907: 34–48; Wright & Spears 1971: 909–10).

A branch of Styx here rises from the Shades,
That tinctur'd as it runs with Lethe's streams,
And wafting Vapours from the Land of dreams,
(As under seas Alphaeus' secret sluice
Bears Pisa's off'rings to his Arethuse)

338.] *Οἵ τ' ἀμφ' ἱμερτὸν Τιταρήσιον ἔργ' ἐνέμοντο*
Ὅς ῥ' ἐς Πηνειὸν προΐει καλλίῤῥοον ὕδωρ,
Οὐδ' ὅγε Πηνειῷ συμμίσγεται ἀργυροδίνῃ,
Ἀλλά τέ μιν καθύπερθεν ἐπιῤῥέει ἠΰτ' ἔλαιον·
Ὅρκοῦ γὰρ δεινοῦ Στυγὸς ὕδατός ἐστιν ἀποῤῥώξ. Homer, Il. ii. Catal.

Of the land of Dreams in the same region, he makes mention, Odyss. xxiv. See also Lucian's True History. *Lethe* and the *Land of Dreams* allegorically represent the *Stupefaction* and *visionary Madness* of Poets, equally dull and extravagant. Of Alphaeus's waters gliding secretly under the sea of Pisa, to mix with those of Arethuse in Sicily, see Moschus, Idyll. viii. Virg. Ecl. x:

---

338 and n. Styx: The main river of the classical underworld, crossed by the newly dead on arrival. Aristaeus had learned the subterranean origins of rivers during his descent (*Georgics* IV.363–73). ***here:*** In Fleet Ditch. ***the Shades:*** the underworld. ***Homer:*** From *Iliad* II: 'They lived in the fields by the lovely Titaressus, who sends forth his fine flowing water into Peneius, but he does not mix with silver-eddied Peneius, but flows underneath it like olive oil; he is a branch of the river Styx, by which oaths are made that cannot be broken' (*Iliad* II.751–5). ***the land of Dreams:*** One of the places spirits pass through on the way to their final resting place (*Odyssey* XXIV.12). ***See also Lucian's True History:*** Lucian's fantastic satire includes a visit to the island of dreams ('A True Story' II, paragraphs 35–9). **Lethe:** A river of the underworld whose name means forgetfulness. '*Lethe*' is said to represent '*Stupefaction*', which makes poets 'dull'; 'the *Land of Dreams*' represents '*visionary Madness*', which makes them 'extravagant' ('fanciful', 'over-imaginative'). Either the 'Poets' satirised by the note are endowed with the paradoxical quality of being both things at once ('equally'), like Dulness herself, who is 'Laborious' and 'heavy' as well as 'busy' and 'bold' (I.15); or two groups are contrasted, 'equally' the 'dull' and the 'extravagant'. The latter is more consistent with line 344. ***Of Alphaeus's waters:*** The passing of the fresh 'water that makes the wild olive grow' untainted through sea water is described by the Greek pastoral poet Moschus (*fl. c.*150 BC) as a love-token sent by Alphaeus to the river Arethusa (*Idylls* VI). Virgil addresses Arethusa as muse, asking in return that if she favours him 'So, when you flow beneath the Sicilian sea, may briny Doris not mingle her waves with yours' (*Eclogues* X.4–5; she plays a small part also in the descent of Aristaeus, *Georgics* IV.351–6). He also makes Aeneas refer to the story: 'There is a tradition that to this place Alphaeus, river of Elis, forced hidden ways under the sea. Now he mingles with the Sicilian waves at your mouth, Arethusa' (*Aeneid* III.694–6). In Ovid's version, Arethusa is a nymph pursued by Alphaeus, the river god: she turns into a river and escapes under the sea to Sicily, with Alphaeus still in pursuit (*Metamorphoses* V.572–641). The closest source, not mentioned here, is Milton's 'Divine Alpheus, who by secret sluice, / Stole under seas to meet his Arethuse' (*TE*: V, 140; Carey 1968: *Arcades*, lines 30–31).

342. Pisa's off'rings: Pisa is a town in Greece, near the Alphaeus. Given that the simile applies to Fleet Ditch, evoked as bearer of sewage and dead dogs, 'off'rings', even in the classical context, takes on a euphemistic note.

Pours into Thames: and hence the mingled wave
Intoxicates the pert, and lulls the grave:
Here brisker vapours o'er the Temple creep,
There, all from Paul's to Aldgate drink and sleep.
  Thence to the banks where rev'rend Bards repose,
They led him soft; each rev'rend Bard arose;
And Milbourn chief, deputed by the rest,

'Sic tibi, cum fluctus subter labere Sicanos, / Doris amara suam non intermisceat undam.' And again, Aen. 3: 'Alphaeum, fama est, ut Elidis amnem / Occultas egisse vias, subter mare, qui nunc / Ore, Arethusa, tuo, Siculis confunditur undis.'

347.] 'Tum canit errantem Permessi ad flumina Gallum, / Utque viro Phoebi chorus assurrexerit omnis; / Ut Linus haec illi divino carmine pastor, / Floribus atque apio crines ornatus amaro, / Dixerit, Hos tibi dant calamos, en accipe, Musae, / Ascraeo quos ante seni', *etc.*

349.] Luke Milbourn a Clergyman, the fairest of Critics; who, when he wrote against Mr. Dryden's Virgil, did him justice in printing at the same time his own translations of him, which were intolerable. His manner of writing has a great resemblance with that of the

---

344. 'Pert' dunces are presumably inspired by 'Vapours from the land of dreams', 'grave' ones by the deadly and soporific qualities of the mixed Styx and Lethe.

345. Young lawyers educated in the Temple are characterised as lively dunces: many miscellaneous writers – including some of the authorial personae of newspapers – claimed to be affiliated to legal institutions.

346. Characterising the City (from St Paul's Cathedral to Aldgate) as lazy and gluttonous. The sumptuousness of official City entertainments was a standard topic for criticism (see I.92–3).

347 and n. Thence: By way of the 'branch of Styx' (line 338). ***the banks where rev'rend Bards repose:*** A part of the underworld set aside for versifying clergymen. ***Tum canit ...:*** Virgil makes the satyr Silenus tell how the Muses honoured Virgil's friend, the poet and soldier Gaius Cornelius Gallus (*c.*69–26 BC): 'Then he sang of how Gallus wandered by the streams of Permessus, and how the whole chorus of Phoebus rose up to greet such a distinguished man; and how Linus, the shepherd of the divine song, his hair adorned with flowers and bitter parsley, said these words to him: "The Muses give you these reeds, take them; they are the reeds they gave before to the old man from Ascra"' (*Eclogues* VI.64, 66–70). The reeds make up a shepherd's pipe, and their previous owner, the man from Ascra, was Hesiod. By this motif Virgil testifies to his faith in Gallus's potential: although his career came to a premature end with his political disgrace and suicide, and his work is almost entirely lost, there are grounds for believing that he was indeed a gifted poet. Linus, of whom various accounts were given in antiquity, was a bardic figure apparently invented to explain the refrain of a traditional Greek song which could be taken to mean 'Alas for Linus!'

349 and n. Milbourn: Pope had already attacked Luke Milbourn (1649–1720) as early as *An Essay on Criticism*, where, speaking of Dryden's antagonists, he asserts: 'Might he return, and bless once more our Eyes, / New *Blackmores* and new *Milbourns* must arise' (lines 462–3). Appendix VIII of *The Dunciad in Four Books*, 'A Parallel of the Characters of Mr. Pope and Mr. Dryden', implies that in Pope Dryden *has* returned – and has the enemies to prove it. ***the fairest of Critics:*** Because by including his own translations of disputed

Gave him the cassock, surcingle, and vest.
'Receive (he said) these robes which once were mine,
Dulness is sacred in a sound divine.'
He ceas'd, and spread the robe; the crowd confess
The rev'rend Flamen in his lengthen'd dress.
Around him wide a sable Army stand,
A low-born, cell-bred, selfish, servile band,

Gentlemen of the Dunciad against our author, as will be seen in the Parallel of Mr. Dryden and him. Append.

355.] It is to be hoped that the satyr in these lines will be understood in the confined sense in which the Author meant it, of such only of the Clergy, who, tho' solemnly engaged in the service of Religion, dedicate themselves for venal and corrupt ends to that of Ministers or Factions; and tho' educated under an entire ignorance of the world, aspire to interfere in

---

passages, he allowed readers to judge for themselves between him and Dryden (Milbourn 1698).

350. surcingle, and vest: In ecclesiastical usage 'surcingle' denotes a belt worn with the cassock, and 'vest' is equivalent to 'vestment'.

352. Implying that people hesitate to challenge the clergy for fear of being accused of blasphemy. 'Sound' in this context suggests not intrinsic value but the prudence that sticks to the party line in religion and politics. Cp. Dryden's Prologue to *Troilus and Cressida*, where Shakespeare's ghost is made to comment that, although unwelcome on the stage, 'Dulness is decent in the Church and State' (Kinsley 1958: line 32).

353. the crowd: the throng assembled by Fleet Ditch. ***confess:*** recognise, acclaim.

354. Flamen: A specific category of priest in ancient Rome. In the context of duncery, it is worth noting that they were distinguished by white conical hats. ***his lengthen'd dress:*** Alluding to the ankle-length cassock, and perhaps hinting that public respect for the clergy is more a case of automatic deference to 'the cloth' (to quote a common phrase) than of discernment of real merit.

355–8 and 355n. a sable Army: the assembled clerical dunces. Spence apparently expected the passage to form part of *The New Dunciad*, reused as the present Book IV, and Osborn reasons that Pope instead slipped it into the existing Book II to render it less noticeable and so avert the anger of the clergy (*OAC*: I, 148; II, 635–6). He wrote to Warburton in 1744, 'I am ... concernd to hear, that some of your clergy [i.e. Anglicans] are offended at a Verse or two of mine, because I have a respect for your Clergy (tho the Verses are harder upon ours [i.e. Roman Catholic]). But if they do not blame *You* for defending those verses, I will wrap myself up in the Layman's Cloak, & sleep under Your Shield' (*Corr.*: IV, 492). ***low-born:*** Hinting that clerical controversialists are using the church as a means of social climbing – a charge that could in fact have been plausibly levelled against Warburton. ***cell-bred:*** Evoking the monastic cell and its seclusion from ordinary life. The slur gains its force from English abhorrence of the influence of the church in medieval and contemporary Catholic Europe (a view which Pope shared, despite being himself a Catholic), and suggests the impropriety of any clerical aspiration to political power. ***servile:*** For an Anglican clergyman to obtain a 'living' (a stipendiary post in a parish) he had to recommend himself to the patron who had the right of presentation; to be chosen as a bishop, he had to win the favour of the monarch and his advisers. Most Catholic clergy in England were, if anything,

Prompt or to guard or stab, to saint or damn,
Heav'n's Swiss, who fight for any God, or Man.
Thro' Lud's fam'd gates, along the well-known Fleet
Rolls the black troop, and overshades the street,

the government of it, and, consequently, to disturb and disorder it; in which they fall short only of their Predecessors, when invested with a larger share of power and authority, which they employed indifferently (as is hinted at in the lines above) either in supporting arbitrary power, or in exciting rebellion; in canonizing the vices of Tyrants, or in blackening the virtues of Patriots; in corrupting religion by superstition, or betraying it by libertinism, as either was thought best to serve the ends of Policy, or flatter the follies of the Great.

359. Lud's fam'd gates,] 'King Lud repairing the City, called it, after his own name, Lud's Town; the strong gate which he built in the west part he likewise, for his own honour, named Ludgate. In the year 1260. this gate was beautified with images of Lud and other Kings. Those images in the reign of Edward VI. had their heads smitten off, and were otherwise defaced by unadvised folks. Queen Mary did set new heads upon their old bodies again. The 28th of Queen Elizabeth the same gate was clean taken down, and newly and beautifully builded, with images of Lud and others, as afore.' *Stow*'s Survey of London.

---

even more intimately constrained by dependence on the families that maintained them as chaplains. ***or to guard or stab:*** either to guard or to stab. ***Swiss:*** Notorious for hiring themselves out as mercenaries. Dryden's Hind had complained that French immigrant protestant clergy were attracted to Britain by material considerations: 'Those *Swisses* fight on any side for pay, / And 'tis the living that conforms, not they' (Kinsley 1958: *The Hind and the Panther*, III.177–8). ***It is to be hoped:*** Introducing an anxious note by Warburton in his role as defender of Pope's orthodoxy, a function Pope had come to rely on him to fulfil since the ingenious defence of the *Essay on Man* which had first recommended Warburton to him (*Corr.*: IV, 163–4; Warburton 1742). Pope's frank criticism of priests had first caused him trouble, with members of his own church, in *An Essay on Criticism* (lines 692–5; *Corr.*: I, 118, 126–8). ***their Predecessors:*** Monks and churchmen who wielded secular power before the Reformation. Pope offended some fellow Catholics by sharing the distaste for presumed clerical tyranny and ignorance as hallmarks of medieval society which was an important element in English protestant ideology. ***Tyrants:*** An expression which could be taken as having a particular application to Walpole. ***Patriots:*** Evoking in particular the anti-Walpole group mobilised by Bolingbroke from the late 1720s (Goldgar 1976: 138–9; Gerrard 1994: 19–45).

359 and n. Where Fleet Street passed through the ancient city wall. The note is summarised from Stow (Kingsford 1971: I, 38–9). The mythical King Lud was supposed to have given his name to London. His reign and supposed burial at Ludgate are described in Geoffrey of Monmouth's *Historia Regum Britanniae* (Thompson 1718: 94–5). Pope knew the work through his acquaintance with its translator, Aaron Thompson, and was amused by Thompson's insistence on accepting it as serious history (*Corr.*: I, 425). The citation of Stow as another believer in Lud's actual existence fits the pattern of Pope's wider disdain for Gothic credulity. Allusion to Ludgate reinforces important themes of the *Dunciad*: it was a decayed Gothic monument distasteful to neo-classical architectural taste; it was a debtors' prison; and its prisoners were exclusively freemen of the City (Maitland 1739: 18–21). An early manuscript draft had identified it as the location of Dulness's 'quarters' (Mack 1984: 115).

'Till show'rs of Sermons, Characters, Essays,
In circling fleeces whiten all the ways:
So clouds replenish'd from some bog below,
Mount in dark volumes, and descend in snow.
Here stopt the Goddess; and in pomp proclaims
A gentler exercise to close the games.
'Ye Critics! in whose heads, as equal scales,
I weigh what author's heaviness prevails;
Which most conduce to sooth the soul in slumbers,
My H—ley's periods, or my Blackmore's numbers;
Attend the trial we propose to make:
If there be man, who o'er such works can wake,
Sleep's all-subduing charms who dares defy,
And boasts Ulysses' ear with Argus' eye;
To him we grant our amplest pow'rs to sit
Judge of all present, past, and future wit;
To cavil, censure, dictate, right or wrong,
Full and eternal privilege of tongue.'
Three College Sophs, and three pert Templars came,

374.] See Hom. Odyss. xii. Ovid, Met. i.

---

361. Characters: For examples see the various entries beginning *Character* in the present bibliography.

362. Contrast the use of 'whiten' in pastoral, denoting the effect of sheep on grass (Sherbo 1970: 509).

364. volumes: Punning on the senses 'masses of cloud' and 'books'. Their works are imagined as made up into 'volumes' with 'dark' bindings, which are then broken up for scrap, showing the white surface of the paper.

370. H—ley's periods: An early manuscript draft shows Pope's hesitation between 'Hoadley', i.e. Bishop Hoadly, and 'Henley', i.e. Orator Henley (Mack 1984: 115). In 1728 the name was given as 'H—'; from 1729 to 1735 as 'H*en*ley' (transferring the ridicule to Orator Henley, as was prudent in view of Hoadly's political influence (Wheeler 1983), but perhaps suggesting by the partial italicisation that this was a blind). The present 'H—ley' leaves the interpretation open. Pope had characterised Henley as an interminable talker in *The Fourth Satire of Dr. John Donne* (line 51).

374 and n. Odysseus (Ulysses) had himself tied to the mast and stuffed the ears of his sailors with wax so that neither captain nor crew could be lured to their deaths by the song of the Sirens (XII.153–200). Argus was a monster covered with eyes: the fifty pairs took it in turns to sleep, thus keeping a constant watch (*Metamorphoses* I.625–7).

375–8. Dulness proposes to endow the winner with 'our amplest pow'rs' to act as an arbitrary and prescriptive critic. Since all the competitors fall asleep, it seems that the prize remains unclaimed.

379. Sophs: Short for 'sophisters', undergraduates in their second or third year of study. ***Templars:*** Barristers or law students who used the buildings on the old Temple site.

The same their talents, and their tastes the same;
Each prompt to query, answer, and debate,
And smit with love of Poesy and Prate.
The pond'rous books two gentle readers bring;
The heroes sit, the vulgar form a ring.
The clam'rous crowd is hush'd with mugs of Mum,
'Till all tun'd equal, send a gen'ral hum.
Then mount the Clerks, and in one lazy tone
Thro' the long, heavy, painful page drawl on;
Soft creeping, words on words, the sense compose,
At ev'ry line they stretch, they yawn, they doze.
As to soft gales top-heavy pines bow low
Their heads, and lift them as they cease to blow:
Thus oft they rear, and oft the head decline,
As breathe, or pause, by fits, the airs divine.

380, 381.] 'Ambo florentes aetatibus, Arcades ambo, / Et certare pares, et respondere parati.' Virg. Ecl. vii.

382.] 'Smit with the love of sacred song'. Milton.

384.] 'Consedere duces, et vulgi stante corona.' Ovid. Met. xiii.

388.] 'All these lines very well imitate the slow drowziness with which they proceed. It is impossible to any one, who has a poetical ear, to read them without perceiving the heaviness that lags in the verse, to imitate the action it describes. The simile of the Pines is very just and well adapted to the subject;' says an Enemy, in his Essay on the Dunciad, p. 21.

380–81n. Virgil describes the competitors in a singing competition in which the first singer developed a motif which the next had to cap: 'They were both in the flower of their age, both Arcadians: they were both equal in competition and ready with an answer' (*Eclogues* VII.4–5. The usual reading is *cantare* ('sing'), not *certare* ('compete').)

382 and n. smit: smitten. ***Prate:*** chatter. ***Smit with the love of sacred song:*** From Milton's description of his inspiration (Fowler 1998: *Paradise Lost* III.29).

384 and n. heroes: The authors whose works are to be read aloud. ***Consedere duces ....:*** Ovid describes the quarrel between the heroes over the arms of the dead Achilles: 'The leaders sat down, the common soldiers stood round in a circle' (*Metamorphoses* XIII.1).

385. Mum: A kind of beer: like the Hanoverian line, it came originally from Brunswick. There is a pun on 'keep mum' ('keep quiet').

386. a gen'ral hum: The crowd seems to be snoring gently even before the reading begins.

387. the Clerks: The three undergraduates and three lawyers, an allusion to their status as educated men.

388–94 and 388n. Pope delights in being able to quote an anonymous 'Enemy' in praise of the remarkable mimetic effects of these lines (*An Essay on the Dunciad* 1728). Compare Statius's comparison of a wrestler to a wind-blown cypress, and Lucan's comparison of the roar of a crowd to the noise of pines bending back and forth in a storm (*Thebaid* VI.854–7; Duff 1928: *Civil War* I.388–91).

And now to this side, now to that they nod,
As verse, or prose, infuse the drowzy God.
Thrice Budgel aim'd to speak, but thrice suppress
By potent Arthur, knock'd his chin and breast.

397.] Famous for his speeches on many occasions about the South Sea scheme, *etc.* 'He is a very ingenious gentleman, and hath written some excellent Epilogues to Plays, and *one small* piece on Love, which is very pretty.' Jacob, Lives of Poets, vol. ii. p. 289. But this gentleman since made himself much more eminent, and personally well-known to the greatest Statesmen of all parties, as well as to all the Courts of Law in this nation.

395–6. The listeners apparently nod to one side for verse, to the other for prose. ***infuse the drowzy God:*** Morpheus, god of sleep, stands for sleep itself, infused into the listeners by the texts being read.

397 and n. Budgel: Eustace Budgell (1686–1737), a cousin of Addison, had a promising career as writer, translator, lawyer and administrator (see his translation of Theophrastus and essays contributed to *The Spectator*: Budgell 1714; Bond 1965: I, li–lii), until he became mentally unstable under pressure of conflict with his superior the second Duke of Bolton (caused by Bolton's patronage of Edward Webster: see editor's note on lines 213–14) and losses in South Sea stock. He finally drowned himself (Kippis & Towers 1778–95: II, 'Budgell'). His writing is mocked as ludicrous and indefatigable in *Imitations of Horace* (*Satires* II.i.27–8, 100). 'Thrice Budgel aim'd to speak' may refer to his futile attempts to have himself elected to parliament. ***his speeches ... about the South Sea scheme:*** Indicating his obsession with his losses (Budgell 1720a; 1720b; 1720c; 1721). Pope mentions his tediousness in *The Fourth Satire of Dr. John Donne* (line 51). ***Epilogues to Plays:*** Particularly successful was his epilogue to Ambrose Philips's tragedy *The Distrest Mother* (Philips 1712; for suspicions that Addison had written it for him, see Bond 1965: III, 250; *OAC*: I, 66–7). **one small *piece on Love:*** Not identified. The note alters the italicisation of the quotation from Jacob (originally 'one small piece *on Love*'), perhaps implying surprise that for once in his life Budgell knew when enough was enough. ***personally well-known to the greatest Statesmen of all parties:*** Despite his Whig affiliations, Budgell came to believe that Walpole's regime was corrupt; and he set the seal on his reputation for lunacy by petitioning the King, in person, to dismiss Walpole (Budgell 1730b; 1730c). He also invited the King to join him for a picnic on the roadside during a royal visit to Newmarket, as mentioned in a note to an early manuscript draft of this passage (Mack 1984: 146). He was said to be a contributor to the opposition *Craftsman*: his poem on the King's visit to Cambridge (which Pope mocked in *Imitations of Horace*: *Satires* II.i.27–8) gave the *Craftsman*'s pseudonymous author Caleb D'Anvers an opening for insinuations regarding Walpole's ambition and his access to the King via the Queen (Budgell 1730a; Kippis & Towers 1778–95: II, 'Budgell'; Varey 1982: xvii–xviii). ***all the Courts of Law:*** Litigation became an outlet for Budgell's gathering obsessions (for specific grievances see *An Epistle to Eustace Budgell* 1734; Preface to Budgell 1730a). The note may also allude to the accusation (never actually brought to court) that Budgell had been party to a spurious will in his favour supposedly made by his friend the deist Matthew Tindal (1653?–1733) (*A Copy of the Will of Dr. Matthew Tindal* 1733; *A Vindication of Eustace Budgell* 1733).

398. potent Arthur: Blackmore's two Arthurian epics are 'potent' only in their power of putting readers to sleep (Blackmore 1695; 1697). If the previous line is taken to refer to Budgell's parliamentary ambitions, there could perhaps also be an allusion to Arthur Onslow (1691–1768), Speaker of the House of Commons.

Toland and Tindal, prompt at priests to jeer,
Yet silent bow'd to Christ's No kingdom here.
Who sate the nearest, by the words o'ercome,
Slept first; the distant nodded to the hum.
Then down are roll'd the books; stretch'd o'er 'em lies
Each gentle clerk, and mutt'ring seals his eyes.
As what a Dutchman plumps into the lakes,
One circle first, and then a second makes;
What Dulness dropt among her sons imprest
Like motion from one circle to the rest;

399.] Two persons, not so happy as to be obscure, who writ against the Religion of their Country.

400. Christ's No kingdom, etc.] This is said by Curl, Key to Dunc. to allude to a sermon of a reverend Bishop.

405.] It is a common and foolish mistake, that a ludicrous parody of a grave and celebrated passage is a ridicule of that passage. The reader therefore, if he will, may call this a parody of the author's own Similitude in the Essay on Man, Ep. iv: 'As the small pebble', *etc.*; but will any body therefore suspect the one to be a ridicule of the other? A ridicule indeed there is in every parody; but when the image is transferred from one subject to another, and the subject is not a *poem burlesqued* (which Scriblerus hopes the reader will distinguish from a *burlesque poem*) there the ridicule falls not on the thing *imitated*, but *imitating*. Thus, for instance, when *Old Edward's armour beams on Cibber's breast*, it is, without doubt, an object ridiculous enough. But I think it falls neither on old king Edward, nor his armour, but on his *armour-bearer* only. Let this be said to explain our Author's Parodies (a figure that has always a good effect in a mock epic poem) either from profane or sacred writers.

---

399 and n. Toland: Toland was offensive to Pope for his rationalist and deistic *Christianity not Mysterious* (1702), which set out a vision of Britain as a rationally protestant nation abjuring priestcraft under a Hanoverian king (Toland 1710; 1711). ***Tindal:*** Matthew Tindal came into the line in 1729, replacing the deist Anthony Collins (1676–1729), whom by 1729 the note was prepared to describe as 'tho' no great friend to the Clergy ... a person of Morals and Ingenuity' (*TE*: V, 144). Tindal had attacked high Anglican claims for the power of the church in *The Rights of the Christian Church* (1706), but became notorious for his *Christianity as Old as the Creation* (1730), which presented the deist case against revealed religion. He was also a defender of the Whig establishment (e.g. *A Defence of our Present Happy Establishment* 1722).

400 and n. Pope's mocking paraphrase of Hoadly's text 'My kingdom is not of this world' (see editor's note on line 370) evokes the defiance of a government apologist warning Christ to mind his own business. Hoadly's doctrine silences Toland and Tindal: he avoided their outright deism, but shared with them a Whig antagonism to the political implications of high Anglican doctrine, and sought accordingly to minimise the importance of church and tradition. ***This is said by Curl:*** Correctly so (*A Compleat Key* 1728). In 1729 the note had begun 'This is scandalously said', and went on to claim – implausibly – that the reference was to Orator Henley. In 1735 the note was used to denounce Hoadly's attacks on Atterbury (*TE*: V, 145).

405–8 and n. Pope had first used the simile of ripples spreading from a stone dropped into water in *The Temple of Fame*, where it forms part of the lecture on the physics of sound adapted from Chaucer (*TE*: II, 284). This was subjected to hostile parody in *Aesop at the*

So from the mid-most the nutation spreads
Round and more round, o'er all the sea of heads.
At last Centlivre felt her voice to fail,

410.] 'A waving sea of heads was round me spread, / And still fresh streams the gazing deluge fed.' Blackm. Job.

411.] Mrs. Susanna Centlivre, wife to Mr. Centlivre, Yeoman of the Mouth to his Majesty. She writ many Plays, and a Song (says Mr. Jacob, vol. i. p. 32.) before she was seven years old. She also writ a Ballad against Mr. Pope's Homer, before he begun it.

Bear-Garden: 'So from a House of Office o'er a Lake, / A T—d falls down, and does a Circle make ... / *Wide and more wide the Excrements advance; / Fill all the watry Place, and to the Margin dance*' (Preston 1715; Guerinot 1969: 24–6). Pope was not deterred from using the simile seriously in *An Essay on Man*, where it illustrates the claim that 'Self-love but serves the virtuous mind to wake' to an all-inclusive love of God and of creatures. (For an interpretation of the link between *An Essay on Man* and the *Dunciads*, see Brown 1985: 147–51.) In all versions of the *Dunciad*, however, Pope includes this imitation of the scatalogical parody from *Aesop*, and in 1743 he echoes the motif again at IV.613. (Dutchmen were the proverbial butt of low humour, and such jokes may also have acquired a political edge after the Revolution which installed the Dutch William III.) No note ever drew attention to the borrowing, and Warburton, who initialled the present note in 1751, seems either not to have known of it or – more likely – to have wished to divert attention from it. Expressing concern that Pope might be thought to be mocking one of the most morally celebratory passages in his *Essay on Man* (which actually postdates the first use of these lines in 1728), Warburton sets out the standard account of such parodic genres as mock epic: the parody implies respect for its original and disrespect for what it is reapplied to (thus *The Rape of the Lock* would express respect for ancient epic and disrespect for contemporary polite society, which many readers would feel to be an over-simplification). Warburton further distinguishes between 'a *poem burlesqued*', where the original poem is burlesqued through parody, and 'a *burlesque poem*', where something else is burlesqued by means of a parodic poem. He interprets Pope's ridicule of audiences' delight in fine theatrical costumes as an image analogous to the working of literary parody – which has the incidental advantage of recalling Pope's gibe at Cibber in *Imitations of Horace* (*Epistles* II.i.319; for Cibber's use of armour said to be borrowed from the Tower of London, see Koon 1986: 115). Warburton's compulsion to confine Pope's meaning within his own notions of propriety is particularly clear in the final sentence.

409. nutation: nodding.

410n. In the passage quoted, Job remembers how in the days of his prosperity people flocked to see him walk down the street (Blackmore 1700: 73). The couplet was mocked for its 'diffus'd circumlocutory manner of expressing a known idea' in *Peri Bathous* (*PW*: II, 201).

411 and n. Centlivre: Susanna Centlivre, *née* Freeman (1667?–1723), playwright and staunch Whig. To define her primarily as wife to the royal cook Joseph Centlivre is to slight an impressive theatrical career, already well established when she married in 1717. Her reputation as child prodigy is probably exaggerated. ***She also writ a Ballad:*** *The Catholick Poet* (1716), convincingly attributed by Curll to Oldmixon (Guerinot 1969: 38–40). Pope misdates it 1715 (see Appendix II), the year in which the first volumes of his *Iliad* appeared, a dating which would support his gibe at a critic who would attack what he could not have read; although even if that date were accepted, 'before he begun it' would remain an obvious exaggeration. In Appendix II Pope also attributes the attack simply to 'Mrs Centlivre, and others', although he had in 1729 noted Curll's attribution to Oldmixon (*TE*: V, 125).

Motteux himself unfinish'd left his tale,
Boyer the State, and Law the Stage gave o'er,

413.] A. Boyer, a voluminous compiler of Annals, Political Collections, *etc.* — William Law A. M. wrote with great zeal against the Stage; Mr. Dennis answered with as great: Their books were printed in 1726. Mr. Law affirmed, that 'The Playhouse is the temple of the Devil; the peculiar pleasure of the Devil; where all they who go, yield to the Devil; where all the laughter is a laughter among Devils; and all who are there are hearing Music in the very Porch of Hell.' To which Mr. Dennis replied, that 'There is every jot as much difference between a true Play, and one made by a Poetaster, as between *two religious books*, the *Bible* and the *Alcoran*.' Then he demonstrates, that 'All those who had written against the Stage were *Jacobites* and *Non-jurors*; and did it always at a time when something was to be done for the *Pretender*. Mr. Collier published his Short View when France declared for the Chevalier; and his Dissuasive, just at the *great storm*, when the devastation which that hurricane wrought, had amazed and astonished the minds of men, and made them obnoxious to melancholy and desponding thoughts. Mr. Law took the opportunity to attack the Stage upon the great

412. Motteux: Peter Anthony Motteux (1663–1718), French Huguenot immigrant, produced translations, opera libretti and journalism. In 1712 he described himself as 'an Author turned Dealer': he ran a warehouse specialising in oriental imports (Bond 1965: III, 25–6, *Spectator* no. 288). To judge by Pope's 'Talkers, I've learn'd to bear; *Motteux* I knew', he was an unstoppable conversationalist as well as a prolific writer (*The Fourth Satire of Dr. John Donne*, line 50). He is apparently classed in *Peri Bathous* as one of the '*Eels* ... that wrap themselves up in their own mud, but are mighty nimble and pert' (*PW*: II, 197).

413 and n. For the numerous victims alluded to in previous versions of this and the following line, see *TE*: V, 146–8. ***Boyer:*** Abel Boyer (1667–1729), Huguenot refugee and former tutor to Pope's friend Bathurst, produced the respected *Dictionnaire royal, françois et anglois* (1702). Pope prefers to highlight his vast compilations on recent history and current affairs, typically produced in instalments, such as his anonymous *The History of the Reign of Queen Anne, Digested into Annals* (1703–13), or *The Political State of Great Britain*, which appeared in monthly instalments from 1711 to his death. He qualifies for Pope's satire not only by the bulk of his works, but also by his Whig commitment and antagonism to Swift and Bolingbroke. ***Law:*** Law was author of *The Absolute Unlawfulness of the Stage-entertainment Fully Demonstrated* (1726). ***A. M.:*** Abbreviation of the degree 'artium magister', 'master of arts'. ***Mr. Law affirmed:*** Introducing a summary of the argument of Law's pamphlet, made more emphatic by compression. ***To which Mr. Dennis replied:*** Dennis compares good plays, which he claims teach morality, with the Bible; bad plays are compared in contrast to the Koran, regarded by Dennis as a blasphemous fraud (Hooker 1939–43: II, 308–9). ***Then he demonstrates:*** Although the (selective) quotation is accurate as to the political sympathies of Law and Jeremy Collier (1650–1726), Dennis's diatribe is cited in order to ridicule his unrestrained indulgence in conspiracy theory: he asserts that attacks on the immorality of the stage were precisely timed to coincide with Jacobite attempts at a restoration ('when something was to be done for the *Pretender*') (Hooker 1939–43: II, 320–21). ***Mr. Collier published his Short View:*** The quotation has been shortened: the original reads, 'when *France* declar'd for the *Chevalier*, upon the Death of *James* II'. Collier's *A Short View of the Immorality and Profaneness of the English Stage* came out in 1698, but James II did not die until 1701, when the French gave renewed impetus to the Jacobite cause by recognising his son ('the Chevalier') as 'James III'. ***his Dissuasive:*** Collier's *Dissuasive from the Play-House* (1703) interpreted a terrible storm as divine retribution for the evils of the theatre. ***obnoxious to:*** vulnerable to. ***Mr. Law took the opportunity:***

Morgan and Mandevil could prate no more;
Norton, from Daniel and Ostroea sprung,

preparations he heard were making abroad, and which the *Jacobites* flattered themselves were designed in their favour. And as for Mr. Bedford's Serious remonstrance, though I know nothing of the time of publishing it, yet I dare to lay odds it was either upon the Duke d'Aumont's being at Somerset-house, or upon the *late Rebellion*.' DENNIS, Stage defended against Mr. Law, p. ult.

414. Morgan] A writer against Religion, distinguished no otherwise from the rabble of his tribe than by the pompousness of his Title; for having stolen his Morality from Tindal, and his Philosophy from Spinoza, he calls himself, by the courtesy of England, a *Moral Philosopher*.

Ibid. Mandevil] This writer, who prided himself as much in the reputation of an *Immoral Philosopher*, was author of a famous book called the Fable of the Bees; which may seem written to prove, that Moral Virtue is the invention of knaves, and Christian Virtue the imposition of fools; and that Vice is necessary, and alone sufficient to render Society flourishing and happy.

415.] Norton De Foe, offspring of the famous Daniel. *Fortes creantur fortibus*. One of the

---

Law's attack on the stage was published in 1726. Jacobites hoped that diplomatic moves on the continent in 1725–6 might lead to backing for an invasion (Jones 1954: 157–63). ***And as for Mr. Bedford's Serious remonstrance:*** Dennis confuses the opposition Whig clergyman Arthur Bedford (1668–1745), author of *A Serious Remonstrance in Behalf of the Christian Religion against the Horrid Blasphemies and Impieties which are still Used in the English Playhouse* (1719), with the nonjuring clergyman Hilkiah Bedford (1663–1724), who had been convicted and imprisoned as the suspected author of *The Hereditary Right of the Crown of England Asserted* (1713), a work of which he was more probably the editor (Hooker 1939–43: II, 510–11). Dennis's frank admission of ignorance regarding the date of *A Serious Remonstrance* sufficiently indicates the slapdash reasoning to which political passion made him vulnerable: both of his suggested contexts are ludicrous in the light of the 1719 publication date. ***the Duke d'Aumont's being at Somerset-house:*** Louis, Duc d'Aumont (1667–1723), French ambassador in London during the negotiations for the Peace of Utrecht in 1712–13, used his position to work for a Jacobite restoration (Stephens 1982: 734). ***upon the* late Rebellion:** The Jacobite rising of 1715.

414 and n. Morgan and Mandeville are new targets in 1743; and since the notes condemning them were initialled by Warburton in 1751, it is to be suspected that their appearance reflects the influence of his concern for religious orthodoxy. ***Morgan:*** The deist Thomas Morgan (*d.* 1743) was author of the anonymous *The Moral Philosopher* (1737). He had offended Warburton by his *A Brief Examination of the Rev. Mr. Warburton's Divine Legation of Moses* (1742). ***Spinoza:*** Benedict de Spinoza (1632–77), philosopher and theologian, offended orthodox opinion by teaching determinism, the denial of an afterlife, and an understanding of God's role in creation which could be represented as pantheistic. ***by the courtesy of England:*** Properly referring to a kind of tenure by which a widower enjoys the use of his late wife's property without having any personal right to it. Warburton means that Morgan had no right to the title. ***Mandevil:*** Bernard Mandeville (1670–1733), Dutch immigrant, became notorious for his *The Fable of the Bees: or, Private Vices, Publick Benefits* (1714), a paradoxical exposition of the conflict between the needs of an expanding economy and traditional Christian ideals of self-restraint.

415–16 and 415n. from Daniel and Ostroea sprung: Benjamin Norton Defoe was alleged by Savage to be Daniel Defoe's illegitimate son by an oyster-seller (*An Author to be Lett* 1729:

Bless'd with his father's front, and mother's tongue,
Hung silent down his never-blushing head;
And all was hush'd, as Folly's self lay dead.
  Thus the soft gifts of Sleep conclude the day,
And stretch'd on bulks, as usual, Poets lay.
Why should I sing what bards the nightly Muse
Did slumb'ring visit, and convey to stews;
Who prouder march'd, with magistrates in state,
To some fam'd round-house, ever open gate!
How Henley lay inspir'd beside a sink,

authors of the Flying Post, in which well-bred work Mr. P. had sometime the honour to be abused with his betters; and of many hired scurrilities and daily papers, to which he never set his name.

418.] Alludes to Dryden's verse in the Indian Emperor: 'All things are hush'd, as Nature's self lay dead.'

Preface). (Oysters were then a cheap food, hawked through the streets: 'Ostroea' was Gay's mock-heroic coinage for an oyster-seller, interpreted by Brooks-Davies as an ironic echo of 'Astraea', or justice, an icon of good government particularly associated with Elizabeth I and Anne (Dearing 1974: I, *Trivia* III.185; Brooks-Davies 1985: 33–4).) Savage's allegation that Norton Defoe was a bastard was included in the 1729 commentary but dropped in 1743: he was in fact the legitimate if wayward son of Daniel Defoe and his wife Mary Tuffley, daughter of a prosperous tradesman (Backscheider 1989: 30–31, 33). ***his father's front:*** his father's impudence. Daniel Defoe was in fact angered by his son's unprincipled journalism: having begun by writing against Walpole (and hence against his father), he was easily bought off, and became a dependant of the government (Backscheider 1989: 499–50). ***mother's tongue:*** Oyster-sellers, as a subspecies of fishwife, are proverbially assumed to be loud and coarse. **Fortes creantur fortibus:** Horace declares that 'Strong men are begotten by strong men' (*Odes* IV.iv.29). ***the Flying Post:*** A government paper. 'Well-bred' is ironic. It was supposedly an 'honour' for Pope to share its obloquy with such distinguished persons as the leaders of the opposition.

417. For Pope's applications of 'never-blushing' in the *Dunciad*, see Sherbo 1988: 223.

418 and n. as: as if. ***All things are hush'd:*** Hooker 1956–89: IX, *The Indian Emperour* III.ii.1.

420. bulks: Stalls built out in front of shops, where vagrants might sleep.

421–2. Parodying Milton's address to the muse of divine poetry, 'yet not alone, while thou / Visitst my slumbers nightly' (Fowler 1998: *Paradise Lost* VII.28–9). The only muse likely to visit these poets is a whore, her only inspiration the idea of adjourning to a brothel.

423–4. These writers are, ironically, 'prouder' because they are escorted, not by a whore, but by an official escort, as they go off to the 'round-house' (lock-up), presumably on charges of vagrancy, drunkenness or disorderly behaviour.

425. Henley: Although an early manuscript draft shows Pope wavering between Dennis and Eusden for this role, published versions had alluded to Eusden, who had been Poet Laureate until his death in 1730, and was reputedly a heavy drinker (Mack 1984: 146). Orator Henley was also said to over-indulge in alcohol (Midgley 1973: 259).

And to mere mortals seem'd a Priest in drink:
While others, timely, to the neighb'ring Fleet
(Haunt of the Muses) made their safe retreat.

426.] This line presents us with an excellent moral, that we are never to pass judgment merely by *appearances*; a lesson to all men who may happen to see a reverend Person in the like situation, not to determine too rashly: since not only the Poets frequently describe a Bard inspired in this posture, ('On Cam's fair bank, where Chaucer lay inspir'd', and the like) but an eminent Casuist tells us, that 'if a Priest be seen in any indecent action, we ought to account it a deception of sight, or illusion of the Devil, who sometimes takes upon him the shape of holy men on purpose to cause scandal.' SCRIBL.

427. Fleet] A prison for insolvent Debtors on the bank of the Ditch.

The End of the SECOND BOOK.

426 and n. mere mortals: The signs of divine presence may not be obvious to the uninitiated. ***a lesson to all men who may happen to see:*** Implying that it is commonplace to see clergymen lying drunk in the street. ***On Cam's fair bank:*** I have been unable to identify the quotation. ***an eminent Casuist:*** Casuistry is the application of Christian principle to the detailed contingencies of actual life; but because of its association with the Catholic tradition of confession and spiritual direction the term came to be used pejoratively, implying a perversion of simple morality. I have been unable to identify the casuist.

428 and 427 n. Haunt of the Muses: In the double sense that Fleet Street is associated with publishing and that the Fleet Prison, sited by a sewer and used to confine debtors, is a likely destination for bad writers.

BOOK THREE

HEADNOTE. Book III takes Bays to the underworld to receive a prophecy of Dulness's triumph from his poetic father Settle, in imitation of Aeneas's visit to the underworld to hear prophecies of Rome's future glory from his father Anchises in *Aeneid* VI (Williams 1955: 42–59). (With regard to Warburton's contributions to the commentary, it is salutary to remember that Book III had largely taken its present shape by 1728, a decade before Pope and Warburton met; and it was not until 1738–40 that Warburton published his theory that *Aeneid* VI should be read as an allegory of the initiation of Augustus into a mystery cult: see editor's notes on line 340, IV.4 and IV.517n.) Also relevant are Milton's reworking of the Virgilian episode in the visions granted Adam in *Paradise Lost* Book XI–XII and the Son of God in *Paradise Regained* Book III (both of which draw on Moses's view of the Promised Land from Mt. Nebo (Pisgah) in Deuteronomy 34), and the related traditions of progress and prospect poems.

THE

DUNCIAD:

BOOK the THIRD.

ARGUMENT.

After the other persons are disposed in their proper places of rest, the Goddess transports the King to her Temple, and there lays him to slumber with his head on her lap; a position of marvellous virtue, which causes all the Visions of wild enthusiasts, projectors, politicians, inamoratos, castle-builders, chemists, and poets. He is immediately carried on the wings of Fancy, and led by a mad Poetical Sibyl, to the Elysian shade; *where, on the banks of* Lethe, *the souls of the dull are dipped by* Bavius, *before their entrance into this world. There he is met by the ghost of* Settle, *and by him made acquainted with the wonders of the place, and with those which he himself is destined to perform. He takes him to a* Mount of Vision, *from whence he shews him the past triumphs of the Empire of Dulness, then the present, and lastly the future: how small a part of the world was ever conquered by Science, how soon those conquests were stopped, and those very nations again reduced to her dominion. Then distinguishing the Island of* Great-Britain, *shews by what aids, by what persons, and by what degrees it shall be brought to her Empire.*

---

virtue: efficacy.

projectors: inventors, entrepreneurs.

inamoratos: the lovesick.

castle-builders: Those whose ambitions are mere castles in the air.

chemists: alchemists.

and poets: A calculated shock, levelling poets with other deranged persons.

Sibyl: A priestess of Apollo, who delivered his oracles. In the sixth book of Virgil's *Aeneid*, an important model for *Dunciad* III, she leads the hero into the underworld so that he can meet his dead father and learn the destiny of his people.

the *Elysian shade:* The Elysian fields in Virgil's underworld are set apart for the souls of the good while awaiting rebirth.

dipped by *Bavius:* Virgil tells how souls about to be reborn drink the water of Lethe to make them forget their former lives (*Aeneid* VI.713–15). Bavius is a poet ridiculed by Virgil, hence a proverbial example of the bad writer who carps at the genuinely talented: he is chosen as a fit person to impart dullness to souls about to be born into duncehood (*Eclogues* III.90).

a *Mount of Vision:* Alluding to the hill from which Adam is shown visions of the future of his race at the close of Milton's *Paradise Lost* (Fowler 1998: XI.366–84).

Science: learning, traditionally constituted principally by the humanities.

reduced to her dominion: reconquered by Dulness.

Some of the persons he causes to pass in review before his eyes, describing each by his proper figure, character, and qualifications. On a sudden the Scene shifts, and a vast number of miracles and prodigies appear, utterly surprising and unknown to the King himself, 'till they are explained to be the wonders of his own reign now commencing. On this Subject Settle *breaks into a congratulation, yet not unmixed with concern, that his own times were but the types of these. He prophesies how first the nation shall be over-run with* Farces, Operas, *and* Shows; *how the throne of Dulness shall be advanced over the* Theatres, *and set up even at* Court: *then how her sons shall preside in the seats of* Arts *and* Sciences: *giving a glimpse, or Pisgah-sight of the future Fulness of her Glory, the accomplishment whereof is the subject of the fourth and last book.*

---

his proper figure: his individual appearance.

qualifications: The particular qualities that fit him to serve Dulness.

the King himself: Bays.

but the types of these: Only foreshadowings of the triumph of Dulness which the vision promises for the present age.

Shows: A disparaging term when applied to the theatre proper, since it usually designated popular dramatic spectacles (also called 'drolls') such as Settle had devised for Bartholomew Fair.

Pisgah: The mountain where at the end of his life Moses was granted a sight of the Promised Land (Deuteronomy 34).

BUT in her Temple's last recess inclos'd,
On Dulness' lap th' Anointed head repos'd.
Him close she curtains round with Vapours blue,
And soft besprinkles with Cimmerian dew.
Then raptures high the seat of Sense o'erflow,
Which only heads refin'd from Reason know.
Hence, from the straw where Bedlam's Prophet nods,
He hears loud Oracles, and talks with Gods:

5, 6, etc.] Hereby is intimated that the following Vision is no more than the chimera of the dreamer's brain, and not a real or intended satyr on the present Age, doubtless more learned, more enlightened, and more abounding with great Genius's in Divinity, Politics, and whatever arts and sciences, than all the preceding. For fear of any such mistake of our Poet's honest meaning, he hath again at the end of the Vision repeated this monition, saying that it all past through the *Ivory gate,* which (according to the Ancients) denoteth Falsity. SCRIBL.

How much the good Scriblerus was mistaken, may be seen from the Fourth book, which, it is plain from hence, he had never seen. BENT.

7, 8.] 'Et varias audit voces, fruiturque deorum / Colloquio'. Virg. Aen. viii.

1–4. The tableau may allude parodically to Renaissance paintings of the Virgin Mary with Christ (Gneiting 1975: 427–8). For possible suggestions of an incestuous relationship, see Ingrassia 1991: 50.

*1. **But:*** Contrasting Bays's pampered seclusion with the outcast situation of the other writers at the close of Book II.

2. Rogers discerns here 'an ironic picture of connubial bliss' alluding to the marriage of George II, anointed at his coronation in 1727, and Queen Caroline (Rogers 1985: 137).

3. Echoing the specifications for the tabernacle to be carried by the wandering Israelites in Exodus 20: 'And thou shalt make a vail *of* blue, and purple, and scarlet ... and the vail shall divide unto you between the holy *place* and the most holy', a passage which Brooks-Davies argues gains added resonance from its reworking in Cowley's *Davideis* (Exodus 20:31, 33; Sherbo 1970: 512; Waller 1905: 261, 372; Brooks-Davies 1985: 81). An early manuscript draft had referred explicitly to the holy of holies of the temple (Mack 1984: 118).

4. Cimmerian: Alluding to the mythical Cimmerii, fabled by the ancients to inhabit a land of perpetual darkness.

5–6 and n. Then raptures high: The 'Cimmerian dew' purges Bays's head of all vestiges of 'Reason' so that he can be filled with the 'raptures high' of visionary dullness. ***Hereby is intimated:*** The part of the note signed by Scriblerus is reprinted from 1729, when there was no Book IV to confirm the ultimate triumph of Dulness. ***chimera:*** monstrous fantasy, illusion. ***the* Ivory gate:** According to Homer and Virgil, there are two gates through which dreams pass into the world, one of horn, through which pass true, prophetic dreams, and one ivory, through which pass the dreams that are mere illusions. At the end of Book III, Bays's vision disappears through the latter, just as Tibbald's had done in previous versions (see line 340 and editor's note). ***How much the good Scriblerus was mistaken:*** The Bentleian voice, while making a characteristically dismissive point against his fellow-commentator, draws attention to the darkening of tone consequent on the addition of Book IV, which describes Dulness's ultimate triumph.

7–8 and n. Hence: From Dulness's 'Cimmerian dew'. ***straw:*** Provided as bedding for the insane in Bedlam. ***Bedlam's Prophet:*** A type figure of the madman convinced that he

Hence the Fool's Paradise, the Statesman's Scheme,
The air-built Castle, and the golden Dream,
The Maid's romantic wish, the Chemist's flame,
And Poet's vision of eternal Fame.
  And now, on Fancy's easy wing convey'd,
The King descending, views th' Elysian Shade.
A slip-shod Sibyl led his steps along,
In lofty madness meditating song;
Her tresses staring from Poetic dreams,
And never wash'd, but in Castalia's streams.

15. A slip-shod Sibyl] This allegory is extremely just, no conformation of the mind so much subjecting it to real *Madness*, as that which produces real *Dulness*. Hence we find the religious (as well as the poetical) Enthusiasts of all ages were ever, in their natural state, most heavy and lumpish; but on the least application of *heat*, they run like lead, which of all metals falls quickest into fusion. Whereas *fire* in a Genius is truly Promethean, it hurts not its constituent parts, but only fits it (as it does well-tempered steel) for the necessary impressions of art. But the common people have been taught (I do not know on what foundation) to regard Lunacy as a mark of *Wit*, just as the Turks and our modern Methodists do of *Holiness*. But if the cause of Madness assigned by a great Philosopher be true, it will unavoidably fall upon the dunces. He supposes it to be the *dwelling over long on one object or idea:* Now as this attention is occasioned either by Grief or Study, it will be fixed by Dulness; which hath not quickness enough to comprehend what it seeks, nor force and vigour enough to divert the imagination from the object it laments.

---

has received privileged inspiration. ***Et varias audit voces ....:*** Virgil says of a priestess through whom oracles are conveyed that 'she hears different voices, and enjoys the conversation of the gods' (*Aeneid* VII.90–91). A note to an early manuscript draft had also included the previous line: 'She sees in marvellous ways many fleeting illusions' (Mack 1984: 147).

10–11. 'Chemist's flame', especially in proximity to 'the golden Dream', suggests the alchemists' belief that base metals could be turned into gold.

*15. **slip-shod:*** Wearing slippers, or shoes down at heel or not properly fastened; hence slovenly in dress, or, metaphorically, careless in writing.

15n. Initialled in 1751 as by Warburton. ***they run like lead:*** Recalling the imagery of Bays's creativity at I.123–4. ***Promethean:*** Alluding to Prometheus, the mythical hero who stole the secret of fire from the gods and gave it to mankind. Hence this is fire seen in its constructive, rather than its destructive, aspect, in line with the analogy with the moulding of steel. ***But the common people have been taught:*** Dismissing the older tradition which associated poetic inspiration with divine possession, and hence with madness. ***the Turks and our modern Methodists:*** Expressing characteristic Warburtonian contempt for religious traditions more open to emotion and mysticism than his own. ***a great Philosopher:*** John Locke (1632–1704) stated that 'a Man, who is very sober, and of a right Understanding in all other things, may in one particular be as frantick, as any in *Bedlam*; if either by any sudden very strong impression, or long fixing his Fancy upon one sort of thoughts, incoherent *Ideas* have been cemented together so powerfully as to remain united' (Nidditch 1975: 161).

*17. **staring:*** standing on end.

*18. **Castalia's streams:*** Castalia is a spring on Mount Parnassus, hence an image of poetic inspiration.

Taylor, their better Charon, lends an oar,
(Once swan of Thames, tho' now he sings no more.)
Benlowes, propitious still to blockheads, bows;
And Shadwell nods the Poppy on his brows.

19.] John Taylor the Water-poet, an honest man, who owns he learned not so much as the Accidence: A rare example of modesty in a Poet! 'I must confess I do want eloquence, / And never scarce did learn my Accidence; / For having got from *possum* to *posset*, / I there was gravel'd, could no farther get.' He wrote fourscore books in the reign of James I. and Charles I. and afterwards (like Edward Ward) kept an Alehouse in Long-Acre. He died in 1654.

21.] A country gentleman, famous for his own bad Poetry, and for patronizing bad Poets, as may be seen from many Dedications of Quarles and others to him. Some of these anagram'd his name, *Benlowes* into *Benevolus:* to verify which, he spent his whole estate upon them.

22.] Shadwell took Opium for many years, and died of too large a dose, in the year 1692.

19–20 and 19n. Taylor: John Taylor (1580–1653), who had in earlier versions been briefly mentioned in Book II, was in 1743 given the new role of Charon, the ferryman of the ancient underworld, who takes the newly arrived souls over the Styx (*TE*: V, 141). As a Thames waterman he is aptly cast as the ferryman; as a person of only rudimentary education who composed the Lord Mayor's pageant in 1634, and published his vigorous, amusing but unsophisticated verse in an elaborate folio edition, he prefigured the kind of writing career attributed to the dunces; yet in his self-promotion as 'the water-poet' and in his experimentation with subscription publishing he also pioneered methods of coping with an increasingly market-orientated literary world which were going to be of vital importance in Pope's career (Capp 1994: 33, 55–61, 64–5). In *Peri Bathous* Edward Ward, a more recent poet of the lower orders, is proposed as his 'poetical son' (*PW*: II, 203). The information here given about him, including the very approximate quotation from his 'Motto' (Taylor 1630: 57), is taken from Winstanley 1687: 167–9 (cp. Capp 1994: 7–8). ***the Accidence:*** The part of Latin grammar which comprises the inflections of words. ***from* possum *to* posset:** He got halfway through the present tense of the verb 'to be able' and got stuck ('gravel'd'). ***He died in 1654:*** From Winstanley (the accepted date is 1653).

21 and n. Benlowes: Edward Benlowes (1602–76), poet and patron, protestant convert from a Catholic family intermarried with the Blounts of Mapledurham (Jenkins 1952). He had been mentioned, with a marginal note on his patronage, anagrams and loss of his estate, in an early manuscript draft of Book I, and again, as patron, in a draft of Book II (Mack 1984: 132–3, 137). ***famous for his own bad Poetry:*** *Theophila*, Benlowes's best-known poem, is an elaborate and ecstatic account of the mystical ascent of the soul to God, lavishly adorned with visual allegories and acrostics (E.B. 1652). Whatever its quality, a work of this kind could only have been stylistically and theologically repellent to Pope. For his patronage, see index to Jenkins 1952: 'Benlowes, Edward, patronage'. ***anagram'd his name:*** Anagrams, despised by neo-classical taste, were an accepted part of the mode in which Benlowes worked. For 'Benevolus', see index to Jenkins 1952: 'Benlowes, Edward, spelling of name'. ***he spent his whole estate upon them:*** In fact the causes of his poverty and reclusiveness in later life were more complex, involving a combination of misfortunes and a yearning for solitary study in the Bodleian Library (Jenkins 1952: 254–303).

22 and n. Poppy: A metonymy for opium. Dryden had written of Shadwell's 'coronation' in *Mac Flecknoe*, 'His Temples last with Poppies were o'erspread, / That nodding seem'd to consecrate his head' (Kinsley 1958: *Mac Flecknoe*, lines 126–7). The preacher of his funeral sermon

Here, in a dusky vale where Lethe rolls,
Old Bavius sits, to dip poetic souls,
And blunt the sense, and fit it for a skull
Of solid proof, impenetrably dull:
Instant, when dipt, away they wing their flight,
Where Brown and Mears unbar the gates of Light,

23.] 'Videt Aeneas in valle reducta / Seclusum nemus ... / Lethaeumque domos placidas qui praenatat amnem', *etc.* 'Hunc circum innumerae gentes', *etc.* Virg. Aen. vi.

24.] Alluding to the story of Thetis dipping Achilles to render him impenetrable: 'At pater Anchises penitus convalle virenti / Inclusas animas, superumque ad lumen ituras, / Lustrabat'. Virg. Aen. vi.

Bavius was an ancient Poet, celebrated by Virgil for the like cause as Bays by our author, though not in so christian-like a manner: For heathenishly it is declared by Virgil of Bavius, that he ought to be *hated* and *detested* for his evil works; *Qui Bavium non* odit; whereas we have often had occasion to observe our Poet's great *Good nature* and *Mercifulness* thro' the whole course of this Poem. SCRIBL.

Mr. Dennis warmly contends, that Bavius was no inconsiderable author; nay, that 'He and Maevius had (even in Augustus's days) a very formidable party at Rome, who thought them much superior to Virgil and Horace: For (saith he) I cannot believe they would have fixed that eternal brand upon them, if they had not been coxcombs in more than ordinary credit.' Rem. on Pr. Arthur, part ii. c. 1. An argument which, if this poem should last, will conduce to the honour of the gentlemen of the Dunciad.

28. Brown and Mears] Booksellers, Printers for any body. — The allegory of the souls of the dull coming forth in the form of books, dressed in calf's leather, and being let abroad in vast numbers by Booksellers, is sufficiently intelligible.

Ibid. Unbar the gates of Light,] An Hemistic of Milton.

---

countered accusations about his use of opium by asserting that he took it only to relieve chronic pain, solemnly recommending his soul to God over each dose (Borgman 1928: 88).

23 and n. Videt Aeneas ...: 'Aeneas sees in a retired valley a secluded grove ... and the River Lethe which flows past the quiet dwellings ... Around it were innumerable peoples' (*Aeneid* VI.703–6).

24 and n. Old Bavius: Since at III.317 Bavius is told to 'take the poppy from thy brow', it may be that he is to be identified with Shadwell (*TE*: V, 151). ***Alluding to the story of Thetis:*** But also, as the quotation immediately following shows, to Virgil's account of souls being prepared for reincarnation: 'But Anchises, Aeneas's father, deep in a green valley, was observing the souls who were imprisoned there, waiting to ascend to the light' (*Aeneid* VI.679–81). Just as Aeneas met his dead father Anchises in the underworld, so Bays will meet Settle. **Qui Bavium non *odit:*** Virgil's shepherd says 'Whoever doesn't hate Bavius, may he love your songs, Maevius, and may he try to yoke foxes and milk he-goats' (Maevius is presumably another bad poet: *Eclogues* III.90–91). ***Mr. Dennis warmly contends:*** Loosely quoted from *Remarks on Prince Arthur* (Hooker 1939–43: I, 70).

26. proof: impenetrability.

27–30. For anticipations of the souls' eagerness, see *Messiah* (lines 88–90) and *The Temple of Fame* (lines 479–82) (Brower 1959: 336). Sitter cites the similar rush of souls in Spenser's Garden of Adonis (Smith & De Selincourt 1912: *Faerie Queene* III.vi.32; Sitter 1971: 22).

28 and n. Brown and Mears: Daniel Brown (*fl.* 1672–1729) published works by such

Demand new bodies, and in Calf's array,
Rush to the world, impatient for the day.
Millions and millions on these banks he views,
Thick as the stars of night, or morning dews,
As thick as bees o'er vernal blossoms fly,
As thick as eggs at Ward in Pillory.

31, 32.] 'Quam multa in sylvis autumni frigore primo / Lapsa cadunt folia, aut ad terram gurgite ab alto / Quam multae glomerantur aves', *etc.* Virg. Aen. vi.

34.] John Ward of Hackney Esq. Member of Parliament, being convicted of forgery, was first expelled the House, and then sentenced to the Pillory on the 17th of February 1727. Mr. Curl (having likewise stood there) looks upon the mention of such a Gentleman in a satyr, as a *great act of barbarity*, Key to the Dunc. 3d edit. p. 16. And another author reasons thus upon it. Durgen. 8vo. p. 11, 12. 'How unworthy is it of *Christian Charity* to animate the *rabble* to abuse a *worthy man* in such a situation? what could move the Poet thus to mention a *brave sufferer*, a *gallant prisoner*, exposed to the view of all mankind! It was laying aside his *Senses*, it was committing a *Crime*, for which the *Law is deficient* not to punish him! nay, a Crime which *Man can scarce forgive*, or *Time efface!* Nothing surely could have induced him

---

authors as Eliza Haywood; his associate Jonas Brown's authors included Theobald. Mears collaborated with Brown and published a wide range of authors despised by Pope. ***Printers for any body:*** Implying that publishers ought to be selective about the authors they are prepared to print. ***An Hemistic:*** A half-line (Fowler 1998: *Paradise Lost* VI.4).

29–34. The connection of calves and bees implies an allusion to the ancient ritual believed to generate bees from a ritually killed calf, and hence parodies the key image of spiritual and cultural rebirth in Virgil's *Georgics* (Brooks-Davies 1985: 28–9; and see editor's note on I.55–78).

29. in Calf's array: Calf leather was commonly used for bookbinding. To call someone a 'calf' was also to imply clumsiness and stupidity.

31–3 and n. The citation from Virgil is odd, insofar as its vision of the dead souls waiting to cross *into* (not out of) the underworld does not feature in any of Pope's specific comparisons ('There were as many as the fallen leaves that drift down in the woods at the first frost of autumn, or as many as the birds that flock to land from the heaving sea' (*Aeneid* VI.309–11)). More relevant to Pope's bee simile is a passage not cited, concerning souls about to be reborn: 'Just as when in the meadows the bees in a calm summer alight on the different flowers and stream around the white lilies' (*Aeneid* VI.707–9).

32. Cp. Milton's description of 'Satan with his powers / ... an host / Innumerable as the stars of night, / Or stars of morning, dewdrops, which the sun / Impearls on every leaf and every flower' (Fowler 1998: *Paradise Lost* V.743–7).

34 and n. John Ward of Hackney: Ward (*d.* 1755), MP, businessman and convicted forger, had outraged Pope by a massive fraud against his friend the Duchess of Buckingham and her son, then a minor (Sedgwick 1970: II, 519–20; Rumbold 1989: 174). ***Mr. Curl:*** When Curll published his identification of the victims of the 1728 *Dunciad*, he at first mistook 'W—d in Pillory' for Edward Ward the writer, pilloried for satirising the Whigs in 1705 (*A Compleat Key* 1728; Guerinot 1969: 113–14). In his second edition he altered the note to read as here quoted; and it remained in this form in the third edition cited by Pope. The 'Satyr' referred to is *To Bathurst.* ***another author:*** Paraphrasing the heroic couplets of Edward

Wond'ring he gaz'd: When lo! a Sage appears,
By his broad shoulders known, and length of ears,

to it but being bribed by a great Lady, *etc.*' (to whom this brave, honest, worthy Gentleman was guilty of no offence but Forgery, proved in open Court.) But it is evident this verse could not be meant of him; it being notorious, that no *Eggs* were thrown at that Gentleman. Perhaps therefore it might be intended of Mr. Edward Ward the Poet when he stood there.

36. And length of ears,] This is a *sophisticated* reading. I think I may venture to affirm all the Copyists are mistaken here: I believe I may say the same of the Critics; Dennis, Oldmixon, Welsted have passed it in silence. I have also stumbled at it, and wondered how an error so manifest could escape such accurate persons. I dare assert it proceeded originally from the inadvertency of some Transcriber, whose head run on the *Pillory*, mentioned two lines before; it is therefore amazing that Mr. Curl himself should over-look it! Yet that *Scholiast* takes not the least notice hereof. That the learned Mist also read it thus, is plain from his ranging this passage among those in which our author was blamed for *personal Satyr* on a *Man's face* (whereof doubtless he might take the *ear* to be a part;) so likewise Concanen, Ralph, the Flying Post, and all the herd of Commentators. — *Tota armenta sequuntur.*

A very little sagacity (which all these Gentlemen therefore wanted) will restore us to the true sense of the Poet, thus, 'By his broad shoulders known, and length of *years*.' See how easy a change; of one single letter! That Mr. Settle was old, is most certain; but he was (happily) a stranger to the *Pillory*. This note partly Mr. THEOBALD'S, partly SCRIBL.

Ward himself, in the anonymously published *Durgen* (Guerinot 1969: 158). ***no offence but Forgery:*** John Ward had altered a note written to him by the young Duke of Buckingham so that it appeared to set aside a covenant regulating a business arrangement (Sedgwick 1970: 519). ***no* Eggs *were thrown at that Gentleman:*** According to *Brice's Weekly Journal* (24 February 1727), a large guard of constables prevented the crowd from pelting John Ward, who had attempted to have his sentence lightened by claiming to be ill (and 'when he was taken down he bled much at the Mouth, and was speechless and senseless for some time'). Curll's mistaken assumption that Edward Ward was meant may also be relevant: 'Who had not one [egg] thrown at him, having committed no other Crime than Writing a merry Burlesque Poem' (*A Compleat Key* 1728). For Pope's alteration of facts in order to engage established thematic patterns, see Colomb 1992: 178.

35. a Sage: Identified at line 37 as Settle, an apt figure to deliver the prophecy of Dulness's triumph since his celebrated fairground show *The Siege of Troy* (published anonymously in 1707) was a version of his opera *The Virgin Prophetess* (1701): the title referred to Cassandra, whose prophecies of Troy's conquest by the Greeks were not believed (for Gay's account of a performance of the *Siege* at Bartholomew Fair in 1726, see Burgess 1966: 53).

36 and n. Settle was said to be tall (Brown 1910: 43). ***length of ears:*** As hinted in the original commentary, this could be taken as an allegation that Settle had had his ears cropped in the pillory (which was not the case). It could alternatively suggest that they were of asinine length. **sophisticated:** altered, corrupted. ***inadvertency:*** carelessness. ***whose head run on the*** **Pillory:** Since one of the punishments that could be inflicted in the pillory was the cropping of ears. ***that Mr. Curl himself should over-look it!:*** Sutherland suggests a pun on Curll's personal experience of the overview to be gained from elevation in the pillory (*TE*: V, 153). ***that*** **Scholiast:** Curll, who in *A Compleat Key* 1728 offered explanatory notes on obscure passages. ***the learned Mist:*** In *Mist's Weekly Journal*, 8 June 1728. **Tota armenta sequuntur:** 'The whole herd follows'. ***wanted:*** lacked. ***This note partly***

Known by the band and suit which Settle wore
(His only suit) for twice three years before:

37.] Elkanah Settle was once a Writer in vogue, as well as Cibber, both for Dramatic Poetry and Politics. Mr. Dennis tells us that 'he was a formidable rival to Mr. Dryden, and that in the University of Cambridge there were those who gave him the *preference*.' Mr. Welsted goes yet farther in his behalf: 'Poor Settle was formerly the *Mighty rival* of Dryden; nay, for *many years*, bore his reputation *above* him.' Pref. to his Poems, 8vo. p. 51. And Mr. Milbourn cried out, 'How little was Dryden able, even when his blood run high, to defend himself against Mr. Settle!' Notes on Dryd. Virg. p. 175. These are comfortable opinions! and no wonder some authors indulge them.

He was author or publisher of many noted pamphlets in the time of king Charles II. He answered all Dryden's political poems; and being cried up on *one side*, succeeded not a little in his Tragedy of the Empress of Morocco (the first that was ever printed with Cuts.) 'Upon this he grew insolent, the Wits writ against his Play, he replied, and the Town judged he had the better. In short, Settle was then thought a very formidable rival to Mr. Dryden; and not only the Town but the University of Cambridge was divided which to prefer; and in both places the younger sort inclined to Elkanah.' DENNIS Pref. to Rem. on Hom.

Mr. THEOBALD's: The note parodies the kind of arguments for emendation offered in *Shakespeare Restored* (Theobald 1726: 19, 26–7).

37–8 and 37n. band: Either a ruff, which would have been very old-fashioned by the time of Settle's death in 1724, or the extended ends of the collar band on a collarless shirt, a feature of legal and ecclesiastical dress. As Settle is said to have had only one suit for the last six years of his life, when he was a pensioner in the Charterhouse (a charity foundation on the site of a Carthusian monastery, now a public school), 'band' could denote part of an institutional uniform. ***as well as Cibber:*** By stressing that Settle was once as much 'in vogue' as Cibber, the note both helps to explain why Settle is chosen to act father Anchises to Cibber's Aeneas, and insinuates that Cibber too will suffer a fall from unmerited prosperity. ***for Dramatic Poetry and Politics:*** A controversy over the relative merits of Settle's and Dryden's heroic drama arose from Settle's comments on Dryden in his dedication to *The Empress of Morocco* (1673), a play which earned him the favour of Charles II at Dryden's expense (Brown 1910: 10–15). When in his turn Settle lost Charles's favour, he turned away from his Tory connections and organised ceremonial Pope-burnings on behalf of the Whig, low-church party which wanted to exclude Charles's brother James from the succession on the grounds of his Catholicism (Brown 1910: 21–2). His anonymous *The Character of a Popish Successor* (1681) painted a negative picture of the consequences of James's accession. Later, however, after the failure of the Whig campaign against James, he compromised himself by producing Tory propaganda, notably the laudatory *An Heroick Poem on the Coronation ... of James II* (1685) (Brown 1910: 24–6). ***Mr. Dennis tells us:*** Summarising from *Remarks upon Mr. Pope's Translation of Homer* (Dennis 1717; Hooker 1939–43: II, 118). Dennis recounts Settle's early vogue and later decline as a lesson 'especially to this little Gentleman [i.e. Pope], not to grow insolent upon Success'. ***comfortable:*** encouraging, offering moral support. Bad authors are presented as drawing comfort from believing that a great author like Dryden could have been seriously challenged by someone like Settle. ***many noted pamphlets:*** Such as *The Character of a Popish Successour* (1681). ***He answered all Dryden's political poems:*** Notably Dryden's *Absolom and Achitophel*, which Settle answered in the anonymous *Absolom Senior* (1682). ***Cuts:*** engravings.

All as the vest, appear'd the wearer's frame,
Old in new state, another yet the same.
Bland and familiar as in life, begun
Thus the great Father to the greater Son.
  Oh born to see what none can see awake!
Behold the wonders of th' oblivious Lake.
Thou, yet unborn, hast touch'd this sacred shore;
The hand of Bavius drench'd thee o'er and o'er.
But blind to former as to future fate,
What mortal knows his pre-existent state?
Who knows how long thy transmigrating soul
Might from Boeotian to Boeotian roll?
How many Dutchmen she vouchsaf'd to thrid?
How many stages thro' old Monks she rid?
And all who since, in mild benighted days,
Mix'd the Owl's ivy with the Poet's bays.
As man's Maeanders to the vital spring
Roll all their tides, then back their circles bring;

50.] Boeotia lay under the ridicule of the Wits formerly, as Ireland does now; tho' it produced one of the greatest Poets and one of the greatest Generals of Greece: 'Boeotum crasso jurares aere natum.' Horat.

54.] 'sine tempora circum / Inter victrices hederam tibi serpere lauros.' Virg. Ecl. viii.

---

40. For a possible allusion to Joseph Hall's *Mundus alter et idem* (1605), see Corse 1991.

42. Cp. Dryden: '*Anchises* then, in order, thus begun / To clear those Wonders to his Godlike Son' (*Aeneid* VI.978–9).

43. Bay's mode of perception is not available to those in full possession of their senses.

44. th' oblivious Lake: Formed by Lethe, river of forgetfulness.

47–8. Alluding to the Neoplatonic doctrine of the pre-existence of the soul (Kropf 1973: 600).

49. transmigrating: Living successively in different bodies.

50n. The great poet is Pindar, the general Epaminondas (fourth century BC). ***Boeotum crasso jurares aere natum:*** 'You would swear that he had been born in the dull air of Boeotia', i.e. he looks stupid (*Epistles* II.i.244). The line concerns rulers who lack literary taste to guide their patronage, a theme of obvious relevance to Bays's destiny: Pope had rendered the passage 'The Hero William, and the Martyr Charles, / One knighted Blackmore, and one pension'd Quarles; / Which made old Ben [i.e. Jonson], and surly Dennis swear, / "No Lord's anointed, but a Russian Bear"' (*Imitations of Horace, Epistles* II.i.386–9).

51. thrid: thread, pass through.

52. stages: sections of a journey by stagecoach. ***old Monks:*** Associated by Pope with ignorance and obscurantism. ***rid:*** rode.

54 and n. Pope adapts a self-deprecating compliment by Virgil to his dedicatee, a successful soldier: 'Let this ivy [i.e. Virgil's poem] twine round your brow amongst the laurels of victory' (*Eclogues* VIII.12–13). Pope associates the ivy with the owl – image of dozy tedium – and makes the laurel the poet's laurel, pointing at such laureates as Cibber.

55–6. For the thematic importance of circular motion in depicting the effects of Dulness, see Sitter 1971: 37–9, 46–8. Pope told Spence that this 'couplet on the circulation of the

Or whirligigs, twirl'd round by skilful swain,
Suck the thread in, then yield it out again:
All nonsense thus, of old or modern date,
Shall in thee centre, from thee circulate.
For this our Queen unfolds to vision true
Thy mental eye, for thou hast much to view:
Old scenes of glory, times long cast behind
Shall, first recall'd, rush forward to thy mind:
Then stretch thy sight o'er all her rising reign,
And let the past and future fire thy brain.
  Ascend this hill, whose cloudy point commands

61, 62.] This has a resemblance to that passage in Milton, book xi. where the Angel 'To nobler sights from Adam's eye remov'd / The film; then purg'd with Euphrasie and Rue / The visual nerve — *For he had much to see.*' There is a general allusion in what follows to that whole Episode.

67. Ascend this hill, etc.] The scenes of this vision are remarkable for the order of their appearance. First, from ver. 67 to 73. those places of the globe are shewn where Science *never* rose; then from ver. 73 to 83, those where she was destroyed by *Tyranny*; from ver. 85 to 95, by inundations of *Barbarians*; from ver. 96 to 106, by *Superstition*. Then Rome, the Mistress

---

blood' (reminiscent of Cowley's 'Ode upon Dr. Harvey', which speaks of 'the winding streams of blood' and 'the Purple reaches' of 'mans *Meander*' (Loane 1944: 37), had originally been written 'word for word, as it is now' in an epic he had written in his teens but later destroyed (Waller 1905: 416; *OAC*: I, 16–19).

57. whirligigs: toys spun by a string.

61–2 and n. The note underlines the importance of the imitation of Adam's prevision of salvation history in *Paradise Lost*, which in turn imitates Anchises' prophecy to Aeneas of the destiny of Rome (Fowler 1998: XI.366–XII.605; *Aeneid* VI.756–892).

67–70. This overview, with its contrasts between polar and equatorial extremes, recalls the vision of British merchant ships ranging the world in *Windsor Forest* (lines 389–92), and, more specifically, a similar passage in the Whig Thomas Tickell's *On the Prospect of Peace* which Pope had singled out for admiration (Tickell 1713; *Corr.*: I, 157). The expression 'burning Line' (i.e. the Equator) also suggests the influence of an earlier Whig panegyric which had envisaged British ships trading from icy pole to aromatic tropics, the English version of Addison's Latin poem on the Peace of Ryswick (1679), in which it is William III who is symbolic unifier of contrasted regions: 'By Nature parted, Worlds together join, / Unite the *Frozen Pole*, and burning *Line*' (Addison 1719: 146; for Sutherland's attribution of the translation to Thomas Newcomb, see *TE*: V, 155).

Rogers suggests that the sequence of panoramic apocalypse which follows may allude to the use of 'cosmic tableau' in Settle's shows: he was especially noted for the burning of Troy (Rogers 1985: 95–6). Burnet and Duckett had insulted Pope's translation of the *Iliad* by suggesting it ought to be advertised by the showman after a puppet-show of the Trojan war (*Homerides* 1715; Guerinot 1969: 22).

67n. Initialled in 1751 as by Warburton. Warton remarks that 'It cannot be believed that our author ever dreamt of the order, which the learned Remarker, has supposed to be observed in this vision' (Warton 1797: V, 186).

Her boundless empire over seas and lands.
See, round the Poles where keener spangles shine,
Where spices smoke beneath the burning Line,
(Earth's wide extremes) her sable flag display'd,
And all the nations cover'd in her shade!
  Far eastward cast thine eye, from whence the Sun
And orient Science their bright course begun:
One god-like Monarch all that pride confounds,
He, whose long wall the wand'ring Tartar bounds;
Heav'ns! what a pile! whole ages perish there,
And one bright blaze turns Learning into air.
  Thence to the south extend thy gladden'd eyes;
There rival flames with equal glory rise,
From shelves to shelves see greedy Vulcan roll,
And lick up all their Physic of the Soul.

of Arts, described in her degeneracy; and lastly Britain, the scene of the action of the poem; which furnishes the occasion of drawing out the Progeny of Dulness in review.

69. See round the Poles, etc.] Almost the whole Southern and Northern Continent wrapt in ignorance.

73.] Our author favours the opinion that all Sciences came from the Eastern nations.

75.] Chi Ho-am-ti Emperor of China, the same who built the great wall between China and Tartary, destroyed all the books and learned men of that empire.

81, 82.] The Caliph, Omar I. having conquered Aegypt, caused his General to burn the Ptolemaean library, on the gates of which was this inscription, *ΨΥΧΗΣ ΙΑΤΡΕΙΟΝ*, the Physic of the Soul.

---

74. orient: Playing on the etymological sense, 'rising', originally of the sun rising, here of the origin of civilisation. In 1751 Warburton explained that the former reading of the line had implied that learning was as old as creation, and had therefore been inconsistent with I.9, where learning is a later development. Given his concern to mould the 1743 text into a consistent system, he may have initiated the revision himself.

75 and n. One god-like Monarch: Ch'in Shih Huang Ti (259–210 BC) ordered in 213 BC the burning of all books except those in his own library, in order to destroy records of Confucian tradition and of the feudal system which had preceded his own centralised despotism, both of which he saw as potential focuses of opposition (Fitzgerald 1986: 137–47; O'Neill 1987: 17–18, 49–50).

76. the wand'ring Tartar: Nomadic peoples of central Asia, separated from China by the Great Wall.

79–82 and 81, 82n. to the south: To the ancient library at Alexandria in Egypt, said to have been founded by the Egyptian King Ptolemy III Euergetes (ruled 246–221 BC). The story of its burning by Omar b. al-Khattab is now discredited: he was reputed to have argued that if the books agreed with the Koran they were superfluous, and if they did not, they were pernicious (Saunders 1965). ***greedy Vulcan:*** Roman god of fire. Jonson writes of a library fire that books make 'a meale for *Vulcan* to lick up' (Herford & Simpson 1925–52: VIII, 206, 'An Execration upon *Vulcan*', line 84). ***Physic of the Soul:*** The inscription is recorded by Diodorus Siculus (*History* I.49).

How little, mark! that portion of the ball,
Where, faint at best, the beams of Science fall:
Soon as they dawn, from Hyperborean skies
Embody'd dark, what clouds of Vandals rise!
Lo! where Maeotis sleeps, and hardly flows
The freezing Tanais thro' a waste of snows,
The North by myriads pours her mighty sons,
Great nurse of Goths, of Alans, and of Huns!
See Alaric's stern port! the martial frame
Of Genseric! and Attila's dread name!
See the bold Ostrogoths on Latium fall;
See the fierce Visigoths on Spain and Gaul!
See, where the morning gilds the palmy shore
(The soil that arts and infant letters bore)
His conqu'ring tribes th' Arabian prophet draws,
And saving Ignorance enthrones by Laws.

96.] Phoenicia, Syria, *etc.* where Letters are said to have been invented. In these countries Mahomet began his conquests.

---

85. Hyperborean: The Hyperboreans ('beyond the North wind') were a fabulous northern race of Greek myth. The reference introduces a vision of the various invaders who poured into Europe at the time of the disintegration of the Roman Empire.

86. Vandals: A Germanic tribe which invaded western Europe in the fourth and fifth centuries AD.

87–8. Johnson records: 'I have been told that the couplet by which he declared his own ear to be most gratified was this', adding 'But the reason of this preference I cannot discover' (Hill 1905: III, 250). Pope was fascinated by accounts of frozen regions (*Corr.*: I, 165–8). ***Maeotis:*** the Sea of Azof. ***Tanais:*** the Don, which flows into the Sea of Azof.

89–92. Milton describes the fallen angels as 'A multitude, like which the populous north / Poured never from her frozen loins, to pass / Rhene or the Danaw, when her barbarous sons / Came like a deluge on the south' (Fowler 1998: *Paradise Lost* I.351–4). ***Goths:*** A Germanic tribe which invaded the eastern and western Roman Empire from the third to the fifth centuries AD. ***Alans:*** A Scythian tribe originating from near the Caspian Sea. ***Huns:*** Asiatic nomads, who invaded Europe from the fourth to the fifth centuries AD. ***Alaric:*** King of the Visigoths, under whom they attacked Rome in AD 410 (see line 94). ***Genseric:*** King of the Vandals, under whom they attacked Rome in AD 455. ***Attila's dread name:*** He was called the scourge of God.

93–4. Ostrogoths: The branch of the Goths that settled in Italy from the late fifth century AD. ***Visigoths:*** The branch of the Goths that set up a kingdom in Spain.

97. th' Arabian prophet: Mohammed (570–632), founder of Islam. Pope himself owned a Latin translation of the Koran (Mack 1982: 395).

98. From the thirteenth century the early glories of Arabic civilisation began to fade in the face of growing distrust for any learning not specifically religious (Saunders 1965: 187–98). Western prejudice assumed that Islam was by its very nature anti-intellectual: a similar process of negative generalisation can be observed in Pope's treatment of the Middle Ages in Europe.

See Christians, Jews, one heavy sabbath keep,
And all the western world believe and sleep.
  Lo! Rome herself, proud mistress now no more
Of arts, but thund'ring against heathen lore;
Her grey-hair'd Synods damning books unread,

102. thund'ring against heathen lore;] A strong instance of this pious rage is placed to Pope Gregory's account. John of Salisbury gives a very odd encomium of this Pope, at the same time that he mentions one of the strangest effects of this excess of zeal in him: *Doctor sanctissimus ille Gregorius, qui melleo praedicationis imbre totam rigavit et inebriavit ecclesiam; non modo Mathesin jussit ab aula, sed, ut traditur a majoribus, incendio dedit probatae lectionis scripta, Palatinus quaecunque tenebat Apollo.* And in another place: *Fertur beatus Gregorius bibliothecam combussisse gentilem; quo divinae paginae gratior esset locus, et major authoritas, et diligentia studiosior.* Desiderius Archbishop of Vienna was sharply reproved by him for teaching Grammar and Literature, and explaining the Poets; because (says this Pope) *In uno se ore cum Jovis laudibus Christi laudes non capiunt: Et quam grave nefandumque sit Episcopis canere quod nec Laico religioso conveniat, ipse considera.* He is said, among the rest, to have burned Livy; *Quia in superstitionibus et sacris Romanorum perpetuo versatur.* The same Pope is accused by Vossius, and others, of having caused the noble monuments of the old Roman magnificence to be destroyed, lest those who came to Rome should give more attention to Triumphal Arches, *etc.* than to holy things. Bayle, Dict.

99–100. Cp. Dryden on the fate of poetry and painting during the Middle Ages: 'Long time the Sister Arts, in Iron sleep, / A heavy Sabbath did supinely keep' (Kinsley 1958: 'To Sir Godfrey Kneller', lines 57–8).

101–2 and 102n. Pope Gregory I becomes the focus for a vision in which Christian philistinism engulfs the West (cp. the view of the Roman heritage in Pope's 'To Mr. Addison, Occasioned by his Dialogues on Medals'). Such views involved Pope in controversy with fellow Catholics (see for example *Corr.*: I, 121–3). Although, as the reference states, the material is derived from Bayle's *Dictionary*, Bayle makes it clear that he regards the allegations concerning the destruction of books and monuments as at best unproven (Bayle 1710: 1464–5). ***John of Salisbury:*** Scholar, churchman and statesman (*d.* 1180). ***encomium:*** praise. **Doctor sanctissimus ...**: 'This most holy teacher Gregory, who refreshed and cheered the whole church with the sweetness of his preaching; not only did he order Mathematics out of his court, but, as it is handed down by our ancestors, he commited to the flames all the classic writing preserved by Palatine Apollo.' The reference is to the temple of Apollo on the Palatine Hill in Rome, which contained a library. **Fertur beatus ...**: 'It is said that blessed Gregory burned the gentile library; by which he hoped that holy scripture would receive higher status, greater authority, and more enthusiastic study'. ***Desiderius:*** See Bayle 1710: 1465. **In uno se ore ...**: 'The praise of Christ does not belong in one and the same mouth with the praise of Jupiter: and do yourself consider how serious and abominable it is for a bishop to recite what is not fitting for a devout layman'. ***to have burned Livy:*** Livy (59 BC–AD 17), Roman historian. The allegation is cited by Bayle from Gerhard Johann Voss (1577–1649), Dutch humanist (Bayle 1710: 1465; Voss 1627). **Quia in superstitionibus ...**: 'Because he is constantly concerned with the superstitious and religious rites of the Romans'.

103. Synods: Meetings of bishops and clergy to decide doctrine and policy. From early times the church condemned books held to be harmful to faith: lists of forbidden books continued to be issued into the twentieth century.

And Bacon trembling for his brazen head.
Padua, with sighs, beholds her Livy burn,
And ev'n th' Antipodes Vigilius mourn.
See, the Cirque falls, th' unpillar'd Temple nods,
Streets pav'd with Heroes, Tyber choak'd with Gods:
'Till Peter's keys some christ'ned Jove adorn,
And Pan to Moses lends his pagan horn;
See graceless Venus to a Virgin turn'd,

109.] After the government of Rome devolved to the Popes, their zeal was for some time exerted in demolishing the heathen Temples and Statues, so that the Goths scarce destroyed more monuments of Antiquity out of rage, than these out of devotion. At length they spared some of the Temples, by converting them to Churches; and some of the Statues, by modifying them into images of Saints. In much later times, it was thought necessary to change the statues of Apollo and Pallas, on the tomb of Sannazarius, into David and Judith; the Lyre easily became a Harp, and the Gorgon's head turned to that of Holofernes.

---

104. Bacon: Roger Bacon (1214?–1294), Franciscan monk, scientist, linguist and philosopher, whose unconventionality placed him under suspicion of magic and heresy. Bayle is sceptical about the legend that he made out of brass a head which could answer questions, but Pope represents him as 'trembling' in fear of the reprisals such a feat could be expected to prompt from obscurantist superiors (Bayle 1710: 461–2).

105. Padua: Birthplace of Livy.

106. Vigilius, eighth-century Bishop of Salzburg, is mourned by the Antipodes because only he believed in their existence, for which he was publicly denounced by the church authorities (Bayle 1710: 1981–2).

107–12. Cp. Pope's evocation of the ruins of Rome in 'To Mr. Addison, Occasioned by his Dialogues on Medals', lines 1–18.

107. Cirque: Circus, i.e. the Coliseum.

109 and n. Peter's keys: Alluding iconographically to Peter's role in founding the church ('And I will give unto thee the keys of the kingdom of heaven', Matthew 16:19). ***Sannazarius:*** Jacopo Sannazaro (1458–1530), Italian poet and humanist, whose Latin verse Pope particularly admired (*OAC*: I, 233). ***the Lyre easily became a Harp:*** Apollo's patronage of poetry was represented by a lyre; this was changed into the harp of David. ***the Gorgon's head turned to that of Holofernes:*** Athena was shown holding the head of the Gorgon Medusa, a snake-haired monster who turned to stone anyone who looked at her. Athena had helped Perseus to kill her by advising him to look only at her reflection in his shield. The statue is adapted to represent the Jewish heroine Judith flourishing the head of the Assyrian chief Holophernes, whose death at her hands is described in the Apocrypha (Judith 8–13).

110. The god Pan is represented with a goat's horns. Owing to an ambiguity in the Vulgate Bible, Moses was thought to have had horns (instead of rays of light) on his head when he returned from speaking with God (Exodus 34:29–35). Pope jokes that statues of Pan could therefore have been taken by the pious for Moses: since the horns were by no means Pan's only goatish feature, this would have required a considerable degree of wilful blindness.

111. graceless: Playing on the conflict between the secular and theological senses of 'grace' as applied to women: as goddess of erotic love, Venus possesses grace in the former sense; but it is the chastity of the Virgin that images the latter.

Or Phidias broken, and Apelles burn'd.
  Behold yon' Isle, by Palmers, Pilgrims trod,
Men bearded, bald, cowl'd, uncowl'd, shod, unshod,
Peel'd, patch'd, and pyebald, linsey-wolsey brothers,
Grave Mummers! sleeveless some, and shirtless others.
That once was Britain — Happy! had she seen
No fiercer sons, had Easter never been.
In peace, great Goddess, ever be ador'd;
How keen the war, if Dulness draw the sword!
Thus visit not thy own! on this blest age
Oh spread thy Influence, but restrain thy Rage.
  And see, my son! the hour is on its way,
That lifts our Goddess to imperial sway;
This fav'rite Isle, long sever'd from her reign,

117, 118.] 'Et fortunatam, si nunquam armenta fuissent.' Virg. Ecl. vi.
Ibid.] Wars in England anciently, about the right time of celebrating Easter.

---

112. The works of Pheidias (*c.*490–432 BC), sculptor, architect and painter, are coupled with those of the painter Apelles as victims of Christian philistinism.

113. yon' Isle: Britain in the Middle Ages, envisaged as overrun with endless varieties of perverse religiosity. Mack cites Pope's attention to satire of the religious orders in the Chaucerian version of the *Romaunt of the Rose* (Mack 1979: 112). ***Palmers:*** pilgrims who wore a branch of palm as sign that they had made the pilgrimage to the Holy Land.

114. cowl'd: wearing a hooded monastic habit.

115. Peel'd: destitute, threadbare, possibly alluding to the monastic tonsure. ***pyebald:*** black and white, a term usually applied to animals; here probably alluding to the habit of the Dominicans or Blackfriars, an order of mendicant preachers founded in the thirteenth century to combat heresy. ***linsey-wolsey:*** Literally, a fabric of wool mixed with flax; hence something shoddy or confused.

116. Mummers: Actors in traditional folk plays. The expression in effect associates medieval forms of religious life with popular drama of the kind by this time relegated to such contexts as Bartholomew Fair.

117–18 and n. had Easter never been: The date of Easter caused acrimonious debate (though hardly war) between the old-established Celtic churches of Britain and the Church of Rome, which progressively gained the ascendancy from the late sixth century. Swift had drawn the controversy to Pope's attention in 1725 (Williams 1965: III, 104). ***Et fortunatam ....:*** In Dryden's version: 'Happy for her if Herds had never been' (*Eclogues* VI.45; Kinsley 1958: *Virgil's Pastorals* VI.69). The reference is to Pasiphae, mythical Queen of Crete, who was cursed with desire for a white bull and gave birth to the monstrous Minotaur.

121. visit: afflict.

122. For the astrological contrast between positive 'influence' (the effect of the stars on human beings) and its negative counterpart, 'rage', see Jonson's 'To the memory of ... Shakespeare': 'Shine forth, thou Starre of *Poets*, and with rage, / Or influence, chide, or cheere the drooping Stage' (Herford & Simpson 1925–52: VIII, 392, lines 77–8).

125. Alluding to the tradition derived from Virgil that sees Britain as 'deeply divided from the whole world' (*Eclogues* I.66). For its use in political panegyric and its adoption by George I in allusion to his joining of Britain to Hanover, see Brooks-Davies 1985: 78.

Dove-like, she gathers to her wings again.
Now look thro' Fate! behold the scene she draws!
What aids, what armies to assert her cause!
See all her progeny, illustrious sight!
Behold, and count them, as they rise to light.
As Berecynthia, while her offspring vye
In homage to the Mother of the sky,
Surveys around her, in the blest abode,
An hundred sons, and ev'ry son a God:

126.] This is fulfilled in the fourth book.

127, 129.] 'Nunc age, Dardaniam prolem quae deinde sequatur / Gloria, qui maneant Itala de gente nepotes, / Illustres animas, nostrumque in nomen ituras, / Expediam.' Virg. Aen. vi.

128.] i.e. Of Poets, Antiquaries, Critics, Divines, Free-thinkers. But as this Revolution is only here set on foot by the first of these Classes, the Poets, they only are here particularly celebrated, and they only properly fall under the Care and Review of this Collegue of Dulness, the Laureate. The others, who finish the great work, are reserved for the fourth book, when the Goddess herself appears in full Glory.

131.] 'Felix prole virûm, qualis Berecynthia mater / Invehitur curru Phrygias turrita per urbes, / Laeta deûm partu, centum complexa nepotes, / Omnes coelicolas, omnes supera alta tenentes.' Virg. Aen. vi.

---

126 and n. Alluding to Jesus' lamentation over Jerusalem ('How often would I have gathered thy children together, even as a hen gathereth her chickens under her wings'); and to Milton's account in *Paradise Lost* of how the Holy Spirit 'Dove-like satst brooding on the vast abyss / And mad'st it pregnant' (Matthew 23:37; Fowler 1998: *Paradise Lost*, I.21–2). Although Warburton did not specifically claim the note, it is of a piece with his concern to assert the systematic coherence of the four-book structure.

127 and n. behold the scene she draws: It seems that Dulness is visualised as drawing a stage-screen on which the scene is represented. (Cp. the theatrical imagery associated with her at lines 231–72, and at IV.655.) ***Nunc age ....:*** Anchises prepares to show Aeneas the destiny of his descendants: 'Now press on; I shall hasten to tell you of the glory which in due course will attend the offspring of Troy, of your descendants of the Italian line who remain to be born, souls who will be illustrious, and will bear our name' (*Aeneid* VI.776–9). Pope may be glancing at the use made of the passage in the dedication to Jacob 1719–20: I (McLaverty 1985: 30–31).

128n. Initialled in 1751 as by Warburton, and manifesting his characteristic systematising urge.

131 and n. Berecynthia: A title of the goddess Cybele, derived from a mountain sacred to her (see editor's note on I.269). ***Felix prole ....:*** Anchises compares Rome to the goddess Berecynthia: 'She is blessed in her heroic offspring, just as Mother Berecynthia, with her crown like a city wall, rides in her chariot through the Phrygian cities, joyful in having given birth to gods, with a hundred descendants in her embrace, all dwellers in heaven, all enthroned in the heights' (*Aeneid* VI.784–7). (Berecynthia's wall-like crown alludes to her role of defending her people in war.) Pope would also remember Denham's application of the passage to Windsor as shrine of British heroes in 'Cooper's Hill' (Banks 1969: lines 59–64).

Not with less glory mighty Dulness crown'd,
Shall take thro' Grub-street her triumphant round;
And her Parnassus glancing o'er at once,
Behold an hundred sons, and each a Dunce.
  Mark first that Youth who takes the foremost place,
And thrusts his person full into your face.
With all thy Father's virtues blest, be born!
And a new Cibber shall the stage adorn.
  A second see, by meeker manners known,
And modest as the maid that sips alone;
From the strong fate of drams if thou get free,

139.] 'Ille vides, pura juvenis qui nititur hasta, / Proxima sorte tenet lucis loca'. Virg. Aen. vi.

141.] A manner of expression used by Virgil, Ecl. viii: 'Nascere! praeque diem veniens, age, Lucifer'. As also that of *patriis virtutibus*, Ecl. iv.

It was very natural to shew to the Hero, before all others, his own Son, who had already begun to emulate him in his theatrical, poetical, and even political capacities. By the attitude in which he here presents himself, the reader may be cautioned against ascribing wholly to the Father the merit of the epithet *Cibberian*, which is equally to be understood with an eye to the Son.

145.] 'si qua fata aspera rumpas, / Tu Marcellus eris!' Virg. Aen. vi.

135–8. For comparison with the visual composition of Raphael's 'Parnassus', see Gneiting 1975: 425–6 and plate 4.

139 and n. that Youth: Theophilus Cibber. In 1728 the allusion would have been principally to the crude bombast of his acting style; but he had more recently made himself notorious by prostituting his wife to a man whom he then sued for adultery: the court awarded him a derisory £10 (Nash 1977: 137–49; Koon 1986: 145–6, 149–50). ***Ille vides ...:*** Anchises shows Aeneas his son-to-be: 'You see that youth, who grasps a headless spear; he as the lots are drawn holds a place next to the light' (*Aeneid* VI.760–61). The headless spear was a trophy given to a warrior on his first success in battle; his place next to the light means that he is soon to be born into the upper world.

141n. Nascere! ...: The pastoral singer calls on Lucifer, the morning star, to rise: 'Be born, Lucifer, and herald the day' (*Eclogues* VIII.17). A play on 'Lucifer' as a name for Satan is presumably intended. **patriis virtutibus:** Virgil's fourth *Eclogue* is a compliment to the Roman statesman, writer and literary patron Gaius Asinus Pollio (76 BC–AD 4), founded on a vision of a golden age restored under a child ruler about to be born. There was a longstanding Christian tradition, continued in Pope's *Messiah*, of reading it as a miraculous revelation of the gospel to a pagan; hence the quotation is related to the evolving theme of Bays as Antichrist. The line may be rendered 'And he shall rule the world that his father's strength has set at peace' (*Eclogues* IV.17). ***ascribing wholly to the Father:*** The language of the note alludes to the Christian doctrine of the Trinity, parodied by the relation of Dulness, Bays and Heidigger at I.287–91.

144. modest: Stock epithet for commending women, ironic when applied to the female secret drinker.

145 and n. Ambiguously applicable either to Edward Ward's 'fate' as the keeper of a tavern, or to allegations of alcoholism. The quotation is from Anchises' lamentation over

Another Durfey, Ward! shall sing in thee.
Thee shall each ale-house, thee each gill-house mourn,
And answ'ring gin-shops sowrer sighs return.
  Jacob, the scourge of Grammar, mark with awe,

147.] 'Te nemus Angitiae, vitrea te Fucinus unda, / Te liquidi flevere lacus.' Virg. Aen. vii. Virgil again, Ecl. x: 'Illum etiam lauri, illum flevere myricae', *etc*.

149.] 'This *Gentleman* is son of a *considerable Maltster* of Romsey in Southamptonshire, and bred to the Law under a *very eminent Attorney:* Who, between his *more laborious* studies, has *diverted* himself with Poetry. He is a great admirer of Poets and their works, which has occasion'd him to try his genius that way. — He has writ in prose the *Lives* of the *Poets, Essays,* and a great many Law-Books, *The Accomplish'd Conveyancer, Modern Justice, etc.*' GILES JACOB of himself, *Lives* of *Poets,* vol. 1. He very grossly, and unprovok'd, abused in that book the Author's Friend, Mr. *Gay*.

149, 150.] There may seem some error in these verses, Mr. Jacob having proved our author to have a *Respect* for him, by this undeniable argument. 'He had once a *Regard* for

---

Marcellus, the chosen heir of Augustus, who died young, and the couplet recalls Dryden's translation: 'Ah, cou'dst thou break through Fates severe Decree, / A new *Marcellus* shall arise in thee!' (*Aeneid* VI.882–3; Kinsley 1958: VI.1220–21).

146. Even if Ward could have escaped his fate, his potential is bathetically held down to the level of a D'Urfey.

147 and n. gill-house: Most probably a tavern where alcohol was sold in small quantities, a gill being a quarter-pint, or sometimes a half. 'Gill' could also denote a malted liquor impregnated with ground ivy, but this seems unduly specific for the context. ***Te nemus ...:*** Quoting from the lamentation over one of the dead in the wars between the invading Trojans and the Latins whom they found in possession on their arrival in Italy: 'The grove of Angitia, the glassy wave of Fucinus, the flowing lakes mourned you' (*Aeneid* VII.759–60). ***Illum etiam ...:*** Virgil writes of his friend Gallus's misery in love: 'even the laurels, even the tamarisks wept for him' (*Eclogues* X.13).

149–50; 149n; 149, 150n; 150n. Jacob: Giles Jacob had annoyed Pope not only in the ways referred to in the note (and see McLaverty 1985), but also by a direct attack in the anonymous *The Mirrour* (1733; see Guerinot 1969: 229–33). There is no good reason why he of all the writers Pope despises should be 'the scourge of Grammar': his *A Law Grammar* was not to appear until 1744. In 1728 the equivalent line had attacked Thomas Woolston (1670–1733), advocate of an allegorical rather than a literal interpretation of the Bible, as 'scourge of Scripture': the figure seems to have outlived its application (*TE*: V, 164). ***This* Gentleman:** The note uses Jacob's own account of himself and his writings (Jacob 1719–20: I, 318; II, 299–30). The italics are added to highlight Jacob's offences against Scriblerian norms, namely his notion that connections with trade could confer honour on a writer, or that poetry could properly be considered as light relief from business. ***He very grossly ... abused:*** Jacob's entry on Gay is scarcely enthusiastic ('by the Strength of his own Genius, and the Conversation of Mr. *Pope*, he has made some Progress in Poetical Writings'), primly declares that *Three Hours after Marriage* 'has some extrordinary Scenes in it, which seem'd to trespass on Female Modesty', and draws attention to Gay's background in trade and his employment as a servant by the Duchess of Monmouth, aspects of his early life that Pope preferred to minimise (Jacob 1719–20: I, 114–15; Nokes 1995: 35, 53). In comparison,

Nor less revere him, blunderbuss of Law.
Lo P—p—le's brow, tremendous to the town,
Horneck's fierce eye, and Roome's funereal Frown.

my *Judgment*; otherwise he would never have subscribed *Two Guineas* to me, for one small Book in octavo.' Jacob's Letter to Dennis, printed in Dennis's Remarks on the Dunciad, pag. 49. Therefore I should think the appellation of *Blunderbuss* to Mr. Jacob, like that of *Thunderbolt* to Scipio, was meant in his honour.

Mr Dennis argues the same way. 'My writings having made great impression on the minds of all sensible men, Mr. P. *repented*, and to *give proof of his Repentance*, subscribed to my two volumes of select Works, and afterward to my two Volumes of Letters.' Ibid. pag. 39. We should hence believe, the Name of Mr. Dennis hath also crept into this poem by some mistake. But from hence, gentle reader! thou may'st beware, when thou givest thy money to such Authors, not to flatter thyself that thy motives are Good-nature or Charity.

150.] Virg. Aen. vi: 'duo fulmina belli / Scipiadas, cladem Libyae!'

152.] These two were virulent Party-writers, worthily coupled together, and one would think prophetically, since, after the publishing of this piece, the former dying, the latter succeeded him in *Honour* and *Employment*. The first was Philip Horneck, Author of a Billingsgate paper call'd The High German Doctor. Edward Roome was son of an Undertaker for Funerals in Fleetstreet, and writ some of the papers call'd Pasquin, where by malicious Innuendos he endeavoured to represent our Author guilty of malevolent practices with a great man then under prosecution of Parliament. P—le was the author of some vile Plays and Pamphlets. He published abuses on our author in a Paper called the Prompter.

Jacob's praise for authors of noble rank was extravagant (McLaverty 1985: 25–6, 30–31). Moreover, he described the fictitious Joseph Gay (alias Breval) as 'Author of an excellent Farce, call'd, *The Confederates* ... written to expose the Obscenity and false Pretence to Wit, in a Comedy call'd, *Three Hours after Marriage*' (p. 289; see editor's note on II.35). ***one small Book:*** Jacob 1719–20: II, which included an account of Pope. ***Dennis's Remarks on the Dunciad:*** Dennis 1729; see Hooker 1939–43: II, 372–3, 370. **Thunderbolt:** One of the attributes of Jupiter, honorifically applied to the distinguished Roman general Scipio Africanus. ***duo fulmina ...:*** 'The two Scipios, thunderbolts in war, the destruction of Libya!' (*Aeneid* VI.842–3).

151. Lo P—p—le's brow: William Popple (1701–64), lawyer, civil servant and playwright. His 'tremendous' attitude may be an allusion to the tone of his preface to his comedy *The Lady's Revenge* (1734), in which he blames 'eight or ten young Fellows' motivated by party feeling for damning the play (which was dedicated to the Prince of Wales and, according to the author, was rumoured to be 'supported by the Court, and therefore to be opposed'). The note on Popple in the original commentary is placed out of sequence at the end of the note on line 152: no 'Pamphlets' known to be by him are now extant, but he collaborated with Aaron Hill on the *Prompter*, which published attacks on Pope in 1735 and 1736.

152 and n. Horneck's fierce eye: Philip Horneck (*d.* 1728), Solicitor to the Treasury, had in 1714 and 1715 abused Pope, Oxford, Bolingbroke and Atterbury in *The High-German Doctor*. ***Roome's funereal Frown:*** Roome, who succeeded Horneck on his death, was notoriously ugly (see Savage 1732: Epigram 29). 'Funereal' also allows a gibe at his family's business, implicitly an unsuitable background for a writer. ***papers call'd Pasquin:*** For a previous allegation of Roome's authorship of this attack on Atterbury, see 'Testimonies of Authors'.

Lo sneering Goode, half malice and half whim,
A Fiend in glee, ridiculously grim.
Each Cygnet sweet of Bath and Tunbridge race,
Whose tuneful whistling makes the waters pass:
Each Songster, Riddler, ev'ry nameless name,
All crowd, who foremost shall be damn'd to Fame.
Some strain in rhyme; the Muses, on their racks,
Scream like the winding of ten thousand jacks:
Some free from rhyme or reason, rule or check,
Break Priscian's head, and Pegasus's neck;
Down, down they larum, with impetuous whirl,
The Pindars, and the Miltons of a Curl.
   Silence, ye Wolves! while Ralph to Cynthia howls,

153.] An ill-natur'd Critic, who writ a Satyr on our Author, call'd *The mock Aesop*, and many anonymous Libels in News-papers for hire.

156.] There were several successions of these sort of minor poets, at Tunbridge, Bath, etc. singing the praise of the Annuals flourishing for that season; whose names indeed would be nameless, and therefore the Poet slurs them over with others in general.

165.] James Ralph, a name inserted after the first editions, not known to our author till he writ a swearing-piece called *Sawney*, very abusive of Dr. Swift, Mr. Gay, and himself. These

---

153 and n. Goode: Barnham Goode (1674–1739), schoolmaster and writer for the government *Daily Courant*, was a friend of Walpole, Theobald and Jacob. According to the Errata included in 1729, Goode had solemnly sworn that he had not written *The Mock Aesop*; to which Scriblerus retorts, '*the Satyr he writ, was call'd not Mock Esop, but* Mack Esop', implying that it would have been a fable of literary paternity, analogous to Dryden's *Mac Flecknoe*. No work of either title is extant.

155. Cygnet: Playing on the image of poet as swan – these are not properly grown up. ***Bath and Tunbridge:*** Fashionable watering places; hence the aptness of characterising the poets of the ephemeral verse generated by such centres as cygnets.

156 and n. tuneful whistling: 'Whistling' (as opposed to 'singing') not only denigrates the occasional verse which supposedly distracts visitors to spa towns from the foul taste of the therapeutic waters, but also alludes to the grooms' trick of whistling to horses to induce them to urinate: cp. Young on the spa poet who 'At *Bath* in *summer* chants the reigning Lass, / And sweetly *whistles*, as the *waters* pass?' (Young 1728: I). ***the Annuals:*** the reigning beauties of the season, likened to annual flowers. There may also be a reference to the annual miscellanies of verse produced by spa-town society, some of which were hostile to Pope's circle (*TE*: V, 327). 'Whose names' seems from what follows to refer to the poets rather than to their subjects.

157. Riddler: Composer of riddles in verse.

160. jacks: Mechanisms by which roasting meat was rotated on the spit.

162. Break Priscian's head: Break the rules of grammar (from the Byzantine grammarian Priscian (AD 491–518)). ***Pegasus's neck:*** Pegasus, the winged horse symbolising the power of poetry, is represented as likely to plummet earthwards under such guidance.

163. larum: Literally, a battle-cry; hence to rush down with loud cries.

165–6 and 165n. Ralph: Alluding to his *Night: A Poem* (1728), a haphazard accumulation of blank verse description and meditation on night and death. Ralph's address to Night

And makes Night hideous — Answer him, ye Owls!
Sense, speech, and measure, living tongues and dead,
Let all give way — and Morris may be read.

lines allude to a thing of his, intitled, *Night*, a Poem: 'Visit thus the glimpses of the Moon, / Making Night hideous'. Shakesp. This low writer attended his own works with panegyricks in the Journals, and once in particular praised himself highly above Mr. Addison, in wretched remarks upon that Author's Account of *English* Poets, printed in a London Journal, Sept. 1728. He ended at last in the common Sink of all such writers, a political News-paper, to which he was recommended by his friend Arnall, and received a small pittance for pay.

168. Morris] *Besaleel*, see Book 2.

---

could almost be mistaken for an appeal to Dulness: 'Wrapp'd in thy shades, companion of thy gloom, / O goddess waft me in thy cloudy wain / To all the lonely limits of thy rule' (Ralph 1728: 4). His Preface, which contrasts the 'thousand difficulties' of writing blank verse with the 'enchanting faculty' offered by couplet verse 'of concealing the errors of the poet', would have struck Pope as both foolhardy and offensive. Pope's couplet, which also sounds an ironic echo of Waller's 'Of the Paraphrase on the Lord's Prayer, written by Mrs. Wharton' ('Silence, you winds! listen, etherial lights! / While our Urania sings what Heaven indites': Drury 1893: II, 136), particularly echoes Ralph's abjuration of prosperity, a theme which could seem somewhat overdone in a needy poet ('Far, far away the baneful gift remove', the poet implores). The passage culminates in a vision of the damnation that Ralph professes to apprehend as the likely consequence of worldly success: 'While owls obscene, portentous scream aloud, / And ev'ry gale, and ev'ry midnight sound, / Rings awful as the horrid call of death' (pp. 72–3). Late and dubious testimony suggests that Ralph claimed his chances of literary employment had been ruined by Pope's gibe (Sherburn 1958: 348). ***Cynthia:*** the moon. ***inserted after the first editions:*** Ralph was first included in 1729, having attacked Pope in 1728 in the anonymous *Sawney*; but Pope mistakenly gave his first name in the index as 'John', presumably a sign that Ralph was otherwise unknown to him (*TE*: V, 165; Shipley 1963: 150). ***Visit thus the glimpses of the Moon:*** *Hamlet*, I.iv.53–4 (Alexander 1951). ***attended his own works with panegyricks:*** *The London Journal* of 14 September 1728 praised Ralph to Addison's disadvantage; the issues of 11 May and 1 June had acclaimed *Night*. Though there is no proof that Ralph wrote these papers, their concern with the advantages of blank verse over rhyme is suspiciously close to his preoccupations in the Preface to *Night*. ***He ended at last:*** In 1735, when this allegation first appeared, the *Daily Courant*, for which Ralph had written pro-ministerial material, was merged into the government-subsidised *Daily Gazetteer*. Ralph later declared that from this point on he had never written for the government, and it is possible that he had been dismissed some time earlier (*TE*: V, 165; Shipley 1963: 303–8). By the end of the decade he was writing for the opposition, although Pope remained sceptical, commenting that 'Mr Ralph is detected of having writt at one & the same time for the Ministry ... and against them ... & he has replyd by owning & defending it' (*Corr.*: IV, 255). Pope would not, therefore, have been surprised that in 1753, after a distinguished career in opposition journalism, Ralph finally allowed himself to be bought off by the government for a pension of £300 per annum (see editor's note on I.215–16; Shipley 1963: 523–31). The mention of his 'small pittance in pay' implies a degrading contrast between venality conditioned by the need to earn a living and Pope's ideal of the writer's independent vocation.

168n. Referring to II.26.

Flow Welsted, flow! like thine inspirer, Beer,
Tho' stale, not ripe; tho' thin, yet never clear;
So sweetly mawkish, and so smoothly dull;
Heady, not strong; o'erflowing, tho' not full.

169.] Of this Author see the Remark on Book 2. ver. 209. But (to be impartial) add to it the following different character of him:

Mr. *Welsted* had, in his youth, rais'd so great expectations of his future genius, that there was a *kind of struggle* between the most eminent in the two Universities, which should have the *honour* of his education. To *compound* this, he (*civilly*) became a member of both, and after having pass'd some time at the one, he removed to the other. From thence he return'd to town, where he became the *darling Expectation* of *all* the polite Writers, whose encouragement he acknowledg'd in his occasional poems, in a manner that *will make no small part of the Fame* of his protectors. It also appears from his Works, that he was happy in the patronage of the most illustrious characters of the present age — Encourag'd by such a *Combination* in his favour, he — publish'd a book of poems, some in the *Ovidian*, some in the *Horatian* manner, in both which the most exquisite Judges pronounce he even *rival'd his masters* — His Love verses have rescued that way of writing from contempt — In his Translations, he has given us the very soul and spirit of his author. His Ode — his Epistle — his Verses — his Love tale — all, are the *most perfect things in all poetry*. WELSTED of *Himself, Char. of the Times*, 8vo 1728. *pag*. 23, 24. It should not be forgot to his honour, that he received at one time the sum of 500 pounds for secret service, among the other excellent authors hired to write anonymously for the Ministry. See Report of the Secret Committee, &c. in 1742.

Ibid. Flow Welsted, flow! etc.] Parody on *Denham, Cooper's Hill:* 'O could I flow like thee, and make thy stream / My great example, as it is my theme: / Tho' deep, yet clear; tho' gentle, yet not dull; / Strong without rage; without o'erflowing, full.'

---

169 and n. Introducing a parody of the much-imitated address to the Thames in Denham's 'Cooper's Hill' (Banks 1969: lines 189–92). ***thine inspirer, Beer:*** There is no evidence that Welsted over-indulged in alcohol; but he had alleged the necessity of wine to poetic inspiration in a poem to his patron lamenting the emptiness of his cellar (Nichols 1787: 113–16). Pope suggests that Welsted's poetry arises instead from the cheaper inspiration of beer. Nichols, Welsted's editor and defender, believed that this slur had ruined Welsted's chances of poetic fame, although he implied at the same time that Welsted had been too much a gentleman to care for such things: 'The ridicule attached to his *supposed* "Inspirer" has had the effect of a magic spell, in depressing what to WELSTED himself seems to have been matter of little concern' (Nichols 1787: Advertisement). Compare also the beer analogy developed in *Peri Bathous*: 'It is with the Bathos as with small Beer, which is indeed vapid and insipid, if left at large and let abroad; but being by our Rules confin'd and well stopt, nothing grows so frothy, pert, and bouncing' (*PW*: II, 191). ***Mr.* Welsted:** An edited quotation from *Characters of the Times* (1728), using italics to highlight the claims most offensive to Pope. From 1735 Pope had dropped his previous attribution to Curll and Welsted; but the attribution to Welsted of his own character persists in this note (Guerinot 1969: 151). ***It should not be forgot:*** The receipt, from 1715, is confirmed by Appendix 10 of *A Further Report* (1742); but Welsted was in fact acting as agent for Steele, who was writing anti-Jacobite propaganda for the newly installed Hanoverian regime (Blanchard 1941: 310–11).

Ah Dennis! Gildon ah! what ill-starr'd rage
Divides a friendship long confirm'd by age?
Blockheads with reason wicked wits abhor,
But fool with fool is barb'rous civil war.
Embrace, embrace my sons! be foes no more!
Nor glad vile Poets with true Critics gore.
Behold yon Pair, in strict embraces join'd;

173.] The reader, who has seen thro' the course of these notes, what a constant attendance Mr. Dennis paid to our Author and all his works, may perhaps wonder he should be mention'd but twice, and so slightly touch'd, in this poem. But in truth he look'd upon him with some esteem, for having (more generously than all the rest) *set his Name* to such writings. He was also a very old man at this time. By his own account of himself in Mr. *Jacob's Lives*, he must have been above three-score, and happily lived many years after. So that he was senior to Mr. *Durfey*, who hitherto of all our Poets enjoy'd the longest Bodily life.

177.] Virg. Aen. vi. 'Ne tanta animis assuescite bella, / Neu patriae validas in viscera vertite vires: / Tuque prior, tu parce ... / ... sanguis meus!'

179.] One of these was Author of a weekly paper call'd *The Grumbler*, as the other was concerned in another call'd *Pasquin*, in which Mr. *Pope* was abused with the Duke of *Buckingham* and Bishop of *Rochester*. They also joined in a piece against his first undertaking to translate the *Iliad*, intitled *Homerides*, by Sir *Iliad Doggrel*, printed 1715.

Of the other works of these Gentlemen the world has heard no more, than it would of Mr. *Pope*'s, had their united laudable endeavours discourag'd him from pursuing his studies. How few good works had ever appear'd (since men of true merit are always the least pre-

---

173–4 and 173n. ill-starr'd rage: Presumably an exaggeration of the annoyance Dennis had shown at Pope's claim that he had written *A True Character of Mr. Pope* (1716) 'in concert' with his protégé Gildon, a matter already raised in 'Testimonies of Authors' (Hooker 1939–43: II, lx, 374–5; Guerinot 1969: 42). ***By his own account of himself:*** Accusing Dennis of having written this complimentary account of himself (Jacob 1719–20: I, 67–70; but for Jacob's use of material contributed by his subjects, see editor's note on I.106). ***above three-score:*** Born in 1657, Dennis was already over 70 when a version of this note was first used in 1729 (*TE*: V, 135). He had died in 1734. ***the longest Bodily life:*** Emphasising that this longevity applies only to the body, not to the works.

175–6. Pope had used a version of this couplet in 1717 in his Prologue to *Three Hours after Marriage* (lines 5–6).

177n. Ne tanta animis ...: Anchises warns Aeneas of the Civil War to be fought between Gaius Julius Caesar (100–44 BC) and Gnaeus Pompeius Magnus (106–48 BC), whose souls are, ironically, united in friendship in their pre-natal existence: 'Do not let your minds become hardened to such wars, and do not turn your strength and vigour against the bowels of your country: you most of all, you must avoid it – my child!' (*Aeneid* VI.832–5). The couplet recalls Dryden's translation: 'Embrace again, my Sons, be Foes no more: / Nor stain your Country with her Childrens Gore' (Kinsley 1958: *Aeneid* VI.1143–4). Unusually, the same rhyme has been continued from the previous couplet.

178. Implying Dulness's patronage of critics as natural enemies of creativity.

179 and n. yon Pair: Thomas Burnet and George Duckett. ***strict:*** close, tight. ***Mr.* Pope *was abused:*** *Pasquin*'s insinuations about Pope's friendship with the Jacobite

How like in manners, and how like in mind!
Equal in wit, and equally polite,
Shall this a Pasquin, that a Grumbler write;
Like are their merits, like rewards they share,

suming) had there been always such champions to stifle them in their conception? And were it not better for the publick, that a million of monsters should come into the world, which are sure to die as soon as born, than that the Serpents should strangle one *Hercules* in his Cradle? C.

After many Editions of this poem, the Author thought fit to omit the names of these two persons, whose injury to him was of so old a date. In the verses he omitted, it was said that one of them had a *pious passion* for the other. It was a literal translation of *Virgil, Nisus amore pio pueri* — and there, as in the original, applied to Friendship: That between *Nisus* and *Euryalus* is allowed to make one of the most amiable Episodes in the world, and surely was never interpreted in a perverse sense. But it will astonish the reader to hear, that on no other occasion than this line, a Dedication was written to that Gentleman to induce him to think something further. 'Sir, you are known to have all that affection for the beautiful part of the creation which God and Nature design'd. — Sir, you have a very fine Lady — and, Sir, you have eight very fine Children,' — *etc.* [*Dedic. to* Dennis *Rem. on the Rape of the Lock.*] The truth is, the poor Dedicator's brain was turn'd upon this article: He had taken into his head, that ever since some books were written against the *Stage*, and since the *Italian Opera* had prevail'd, the nation was infected with a vice not fit to be nam'd: He went so far as to print upon the subject, and concludes his argument with this remark, 'That he cannot help thinking the Obscenity of Plays excusable at this juncture; since, when that execrable sin is spread so wide, it may be of use to the reducing mens minds to the natural desire of women.' DENNIS, *Stage defended* against Mr. *Law*, p. 20. Our author solemnly declared, he never heard any creature but the Dedicator mention that Vice and this Gentleman together.

Ibid.] Virg. Aen. vi: 'Illae autem paribus quas fulgere cernis in armis, / Concordes animae'. And in the fifth: 'Euryalus, forma insignis viridique juventa, / Nisus amore pio pueri.'

Atterbury are again highlighted, this time with an associated grudge over the handling in *Pasquin* nos. 12–13 of Pope's editing of the posthumous works of the Duke of Buckingham, which had been suppressed by the government on account of their (very slight) Jacobite tendency (Sherburn 1934: 225–6). ***than that the Serpents should strangle one* Hercules:** The infant Hercules was said to have strangled two snakes which attacked him: the note implies that it would have been a pity had such attackers as Burnet and Duckett been able to smother Pope's creativity at the outset of his career. ***C.:*** Perhaps an attribution to Cleland. ***It was a literal translation of* Virgil:** Virgil describes Nisus as 'known for his devoted love for Euryalus' (*Aeneid* V.296). ***a Dedication was written to that Gentleman:*** Dennis's dedication of *Remarks on Mr. Pope's Rape of the Lock* (1728) is indeed wholly devoted to a vindication of Duckett's heterosexuality. ***a vice not fit to be nam'd:*** Sodomy. ***Our author solemnly declared:*** An attempt to displace onto Dennis the slur implicit in the earlier version of the passage. ***Illae autem ....:*** 'But those whom you see shining in equal arms, they are souls in harmony' (*Aeneid* VI.826–7). Anchises is stressing the pre-natal affinity between the souls destined to be born as Caesar and Pompey (see line 177n). ***Euryalus ....:*** 'Euryalus was known for his beauty and the flower of his youth, Nisus for his devoted love for the boy' (*Aeneid* V.295–6).

That shines a Consul, this Commissioner.
'But who is he, in closet close y-pent,
Of sober face, with learned dust besprent?'
Right well mine eyes arede the myster wight,

184.] Such places were given at this time to such sort of Writers.

185.] Virg. Aen. vi. questions and answers in this manner, of *Numa:* 'Quis procul ille autem ramis insignis olivae, / Sacra ferens? — nosco crines, incanaque menta', *etc.*

187. arede] *Read,* or *peruse*; though sometimes used for *counsel.* 'READE THY READ, *take thy Counsaile.* Thomas Sternhold, in his translation of the first Psalm into English metre, hath *wisely* made use of this word: "The man is blest that hath not bent / To wicked READ his ear." But in the last spurious editions of the singing Psalms the word READ is changed into *men.* I say *spurious* editions, because not only here, but quite throughout the whole book of Psalms,

---

184 and n. Pope had specified these promotions in a note to an early manuscript draft, but the lofty disdain of the present note is arguably more effective (Mack 1984: 151). Burnet was appointed British Consul in Lisbon in 1719. Later he became a judge, and was knighted in 1745. Duckett held the lucrative post of Commissioner of Excise from 1722 until his death in 1732.

185–8. Mocking the study of medieval language and literature which flourished for the first time in England in the late seventeenth and early eighteenth centuries (Douglas 1939: 15–30). The victim is Thomas Hearne, as quotations in the original commentary make clear. Pope offers a would-be humorous (but inauthentic) evocation of archaic English, as he had also done in correspondence with Lord Oxford's librarian, the Anglo-Saxonist Humphrey Wanley (1672–1726), with whom he was, ostensibly at least, on friendly terms (*Corr.*: II, 304, 312). Unusually among Pope's targets, Hearne was a staunch opponent of the Whig establishment, having refused to take the oaths to George I and George II which would have qualified him for desirable posts in the Bodleian Library (for an argument for his significance in terms of Jacobite politics, see Brooks-Davies 1985: 64).

185n. **Numa:** The second king of Rome, mythical founder of its law and religion. ***Quis procul ....:*** 'But who is the man standing apart, distinguished by a crown of olive and bearing a sacrifice? I recognise his hair and grey beard' (*Aeneid* VI.808–9).

186. besprent: sprinkled. Gay had introduced Wanley as 'with dust besprent' in 'Mr Pope's Welcome from Greece' (1720), making him speak in mock medieval style (Dearing 1974: 'Mr Pope's Welcome', lines 137–44).

187 and n. arede: Despite the gloss given in the original commentary, the line requires the sense 'see', 'perceive'. ***myster wight:*** The gloss assigned to this pseudo-archaic expression is given at the end of the original note. ***READE THY READE:*** Introducing an edited quotation from Hearne's edition of *Robert of Gloucester's Chronicle*, described by Douglas as 'the first workmanlike edition of a Middle-English text' (Hearne 1724: II, 698–700; Douglas 1939: 239). Hearne's characteristic tone of hysterical over-insistence did nothing to enhance his credibility with readers ill disposed to the notion of linguistic historicism. ***Thomas Sternhold:*** Sternhold (*d.* 1549), courtier to Henry VIII, composed metrical versions of the Psalms which were supplemented after his death by John Hopkins (*d.* 1570) and others. They continued to be revised and reissued into the nineteenth century, and were in Pope's lifetime regularly sung (in preference to the unmeasured translations in the Book of Common Prayer) in Anglican worship. Pope, who as a Catholic had no reason to confer the dignity of liturgical status on

On parchment scraps y-fed, and Wormius hight.
To future ages may thy dulness last,

are *strange alterations*, all for the worse; and yet the Title-page stands as it used to do! and all (which is *abominable* in any book, much more in a sacred work) is ascribed to Thomas Sternhold, John Hopkins, and others; I am confident, were Sternhold and Hopkins now living they would proceed against the innovators as cheats. — A liberty, which, to say no more of their intolerable alterations, ought by no means to be permitted or approved of by such as are for *Uniformity*, and have any regard for the *old* English Saxon tongue.' HEARNE, Gloss. on Rob. of Gloc. artic. REDE.

I do herein agree with Mr. Hearne: Little is it of avail to object, that such words are become *unintelligible*; since they are *truly English*, men ought to understand them; and such as are for *Uniformity* should think all alterations in a language, *strange, abominable*, and *unwarrantable*. Rightly therefore, I say, again, hath our Poet used ancient words, and poured them forth as a precious ointment upon good old Wormius in this place. SCRIBL.

Ibid. myster wight,] Uncouth mortal.

188.* Wormius *hight.] Let not this name, purely fictitious, be conceited to mean the learned *Olaus Wormius*; much less (as it was unwarrantably foisted into the surreptitious editions) our own Antiquary Mr. *Thomas Hearne*, who had no way aggrieved our Poet, but on the contrary published many curious tracts which he hath to his great contentment perused.

Most rightly are *ancient Words* here employed, in speaking of such who so greatly delight in the same. We may say not only rightly, but *wisely*, yea *excellently*, inasmuch as for the like practice the like praise is given by Mr. Hearne himself. Glossar. to Rob. of Glocester, Artic. BEHETT; 'Others say BEHIGHT, *promised*, and so it is used *excellently well* by Thomas Norton, in his translation into metre of the 116th Psalm, ver. 14: "I to the Lord will pay my vows, / That I to him *BEHIGHT*." Where the modern innovators, not understanding the propriety of the word (which is *truly English*, from the Saxon) have most *unwarrantably* altered it thus: "I to the Lord will pay my vows / With joy and *great delight*."'

Ibid. hight.] 'In Cumberland they say to *hight*, for to *promise*, or *vow*; but HIGHT, usually signifies *was called*; and so it does in the North even to this day, notwithstanding what is done in Cumberland.' Hearne, ibid.

---

metrical versions which he regarded as feeble doggerel, imitated their style in his notorious parody of the first Psalm (see editor's note on II.268). Thus Hearne's care for their textual purity is taken to manifest his lack of literary taste. ***such as are for* Uniformity:** 'Uniformity' is used in the specific sense of conformity to the liturgy of the established church. The Act of Uniformity of 1662 had reimposed the Book of Common Prayer, thus outlawing the sectarian worship allowed under the Commonwealth. Hearne, a high Tory, sees unauthorised alterations even of the metrical psalms (which are *not* part of the Book of Common Prayer, though often printed with it) as a serious threat to church authority. ***I do herein agree:*** Scriblerus, echoing Hearne's archaic style, presents an ironic defence of his preference for historical authenticity to intelligibility. Pope shared the neo-classical view that linguistic archaism was a disfigurement analogous to rust (see *Imitations of Horace*: *Epistles* II.i.35–6).

188n. Let not this name: An unconvincing disclaimer. ***the learned* Olaus Wormius:** Ole Worm (1588–1654), Danish scholar, published examples of Old Icelandic poetry in runic characters. His name made him an irresistible target for satire against antiquarianism. ***who had no way aggrieved our Poet:*** Hearne seems not to have been so much a personal enemy as

As thou preserv'st the dulness of the past!
There, dim in clouds, the poring Scholiasts mark,
Wits, who like owls, see only in the dark,
A Lumberhouse of books in ev'ry head,
For ever reading, never to be read!
But, where each Science lifts its modern type,
Hist'ry her Pot, Divinity his Pipe,
While proud Philosophy repines to show,
Dishonest sight! his breeches rent below;
Imbrown'd with native bronze, lo! Henley stands,

192.] These few lines exactly describe the right verbal critic: The darker his author is, the better he is pleased; like the famous Quack Doctor, who put up in his bills, *he delighted in matters of difficulty*. Some body said well of these men, that their heads were *Libraries out of order*.

199.] J. Henley the Orator; he preached on the Sundays upon Theological matters, and on the Wednesdays upon all other sciences. Each auditor paid one shilling. He declaimed some years against the greatest persons, and occasionally did our Author that honour. WELSTED, in Oratory Transactions, N. I. published by Henley himself, gives the following account of him. 'He was born at Melton-Mowbray in Leicestershire. From his own Parish school he went to St. John's College in Cambridge. He began there to be uneasy; for it *shock'd* him to find he was *commanded to believe* against his own judgment in points of Religion, Philosophy, *etc.*

---

a representative of scholarly tendencies that Pope disliked. Oxford, who shared Hearne's antiquarian interests, admired him greatly: a letter from Pope to Oxford in June 1730 confirms Pope's intention of alluding to Hearne in the *Dunciad* (*Corr.*: III, 111). ***Thomas Norton:*** Lawyer and poet (1532–84), joint author of the tragedy *Gorboduc*. ***unwarrantably:*** Pope's italics suggest that any sensible person, unlike Hearne, can see exactly why the words had to be changed.

192n. In 1711 Pope had applied this quack-doctor's advertisement to his friend Caryll's attempts to praise *his* poetry (*Corr.*: I, 114).

195–8. An allegorical group satirising modern learning, serving as context for the climactic appearance of Orator Henley at line 199.

195. type: representative figure.

196. The 1728 version of the passage gave a more explicit picture of History as a woman gossiping over a pot of ale, and of Divinity as a tavern idler with pipe and dicebox (*TE*: V, 172, 330). (Since Divinity had previously been male, the 1743 reading 'her Pipe' is probably an error, and is here returned to the former reading.) There was a proverbial association between ale and history.

197. repines: is discontented.

198. Dishonest: disgraceful.

199 and n. Imbrown'd with native bronze: The juxtaposition with Philosophy's split breeches aids the focus on the scatological possibilities of this allusion to brazen impudence. ***J. Henley the Orator:*** In 1726 Henley inaugurated Sunday morning services, which were followed by theological lectures in the afternoon; and on Wednesdays he treated such topics as poetry, elocution, history and natural sciences, although as time went on he devoted these sessions increasingly to political commentary, and advertised them under whimsically provocative titles (Midgley 1973: 92–6). ***Each auditor paid one shilling:*** Henley's scheme of

for his genius leading him freely to *dispute all propositions,* and *call all points to account,* he was impatient under those fetters of the free-born mind. — Being admitted to Priest's orders, he found the examination very short and superficial, and that it was not *necessary to conform to the Christian religion,* in order either to *Deaconship,* or *Priesthood.'* He came to town, and after having for some years been a writer for Booksellers, he had an ambition to be so for Ministers of state. The only reason he did not rise in the Church, we are told, 'was the envy of others, and a disrelish entertained of him, because *he was not qualified to be a compleat Spaniel.'* However he offered the service of his pen to two great men, of opinions and interests directly opposite; by both of whom being rejected, he set up a new Project, and styled himself the *Restorer of ancient eloquence.* He thought it 'as lawful to take a licence from the King and Parliament at one place, as another; at Hickes's-hall, as at Doctors-commons; so set up his Oratory in Newport-market, Butcher-row. There (says his friend) he had the *assurance* to form a Plan, which no mortal ever thought of; he had success against all opposition; challenged his adversaries to fair disputations, and *none would dispute* with him; writ, read, and studied twelve hours a day; composed three dissertations a week on all subjects; undertook to teach in *one year* what schools and Universities teach in *five;* was not terrified by menaces, insults, or satyrs, but still proceeded, matured his bold scheme, and put the *Church,* and *all that,* in *danger.'* WELSTED, Narrative in Orat. Transact. N. I.

After having stood some Prosecutions, he turned his rhetoric to buffoonry upon all public and private occurrences. All this passed in the same room; where sometimes he broke

---

direct charging for admission to services was widely criticised, although Henley pointed out that those who attended the established church also paid, in effect, through such customary charges as tithes and pew rents (Midgley 1973: 79–81). ***occasionally did our Author that honour:*** Henley's attacks on Pope, notably *Why How Now, Gossip* POPE*?* (1736; reprinted 1743), and numerous references in the Oratory's published programmes, seem to have been prompted by the attacks on him in the *Dunciad* from 1728 onwards (Midgley 1973: 170–85). ***WELSTED:*** Not in fact Leonard Welsted, but a pseudonym used by Henley in the 'Narrative' included in the *Oratory Transactions N° 1* (1728). The quotations in the original commentary are loosely edited from this 'Narrative', the final sentence quoted being intended by Henley as a derisive summary of the criticisms levelled against him. Nichols, Welsted's editor, cites Pope's ostensible acceptance of the attribution as an example of his distortion of facts, 'even against his own knowledge, for the sake of insulting Welsted', explaining that 'Orator Henley published a piece called "Oratory Transactions", written by Mr. *Welstede* spelt with an *e* at the end, as an evasion, if Mr. Welsted should call upon him for using his name; and that Mr. Pope could not but know' (Nichols 1787: xi). ***He was born:*** For his early life, see Midgley 1973: chs. 1–3. ***two great men:*** Henley took this accusation to refer to Walpole and William Pulteney (1684–1764; created Earl of Bath in 1742). The two men were initially allies, but a quarrel led, in the mid-1720s, to Pulteney's joining Bolingbroke in opposition and writing extensively for *The Craftsman.* Henley's ties with Walpole are well attested, but there is no evidence that he ever approached Pulteney (Midgley 1973: 49–54). Far from being rejected by Walpole, Henley was retained as a long-term government writer and informer. ***the* Restorer of ancient eloquence:** Satirising Henley's style of preaching. Drawing on classical rhetorical theory, he argued for expressive vocal effects reinforced by gesture; but his practice was decried as indecently theatrical (Midgley 1973: 39–40, 97–9). ***He thought it 'as lawful ...':*** Instead of continuing as a licensed preacher in the Church of England, he took advantage of the provision in the Act of Toleration for the licensing of dissenting preachers, whose ministry had previously been illegal (Midgley 1973: 71–3). ***some Prosecutions:*** In 1728 Henley had been accused of seditious libel, and in 1729 of infringing the terms of

Tuning his voice, and balancing his hands.
How fluent nonsense trickles from his tongue!
How sweet the periods, neither said, nor sung!
Still break the benches, Henley! with thy strain,
While Sherlock, Hare, and Gibson preach in vain.
Oh great Restorer of the good old Stage,
Preacher at once, and Zany of thy age!
Oh worthy thou of Aegypt's wise abodes,
A decent priest, where monkeys were the gods!
But fate with butchers plac'd thy priestly stall,
Meek modern faith to murder, hack, and mawl;

jests, and sometimes that bread which he called the *Primitive Eucharist.* — This wonderful person struck Medals, which he dispersed as Tickets to his subscribers: The device, a Star rising to the meridian, with this motto, AD SUMMA; and below, INVENIAM VIAM AUT FACIAM. This man had an hundred pounds a year given him for the secret service of a weekly paper of unintelligible nonsense, called the Hyp-Doctor.

204.] Bishops of Salisbury, Chichester, and London.

---

the Act of Toleration (Midgley 1973: 131–6). ***Medals:*** Medals in various metals were issued as season tickets to the Oratory (Midgley 1973: 81–3). ***AD SUMMA:*** to the highest. ***INVENIAM VIAM AUT FACIAM:*** 'I shall find a way or make one'. Henley's adoption of this motto may have seemed the more ludicrous from its having been the personal motto of Robert Sidney (1563–1626: brother of Sir Philip), Viscount L'Isle and Earl of Leicester. ***the Hyp-Doctor:*** A pro-government paper, issued 1730–41.

200–202. Alluding to Henley's unconventional use of gesture and vocal pitch in preaching, already a topic of comment in *The Craftsman*; and suggesting that, whereas the rubric to Morning and Evening Prayer in the Book of Common Prayer directs the person presiding to 'say or sing', Henley does something that is not quite either (Hammond 1984: 53).

203. Punning on the musical 'strain' of Henley's attempts at expressive declamation and the physical 'strain' on the furniture of accommodating his large audiences. Juvenal speaks of a theatrical success as breaking the benches (*Satires* VII.86).

204 and n. Three bishops who supported Walpole: their inability to draw congregations to match Henley's is ironically lamented, although Warburton attempted in 1751 to cast a more favourable light on the reference. Edmund Gibson (1669–1748) combined high-church theology with Whig politics, distinguishing himself as an opponent of Atterbury's ecclesiastical politics, and, as Bishop of London, as Walpole's adviser on religious policy. Gibson's strictly orthodox theology and commitment to the legal privileges of the Church of England enabled Walpole to defuse a major source of Tory antagonism, but caused friction with Whigs of an anti-clerical or free-thinking tendency. The strains in this alliance led Gibson to resign in 1736.

206. Zany: clown.

207–8. Juvenal mentions 'the monsters that crazy Egypt worships', instancing 'the golden image of a sacred ape' (*Satires* XV.1–4). (On the relevance of the animal-headed gods of ancient Egypt, see Brooks-Davies 1985: 130–31.) Although 'wise' is here used ironically, it also alludes to the conventional belief in Egypt as ultimate source of many religious traditions.

209–10. with butchers: Henley's first oratory was an upstairs room, already established as a dissenting chapel, in Newport Market: critics implied that a meat market was no place for

And bade thee live, to crown Britannia's praise,
In Toland's, Tindal's, and in Woolston's days.
  Yet oh, my sons! a father's words attend:
(So may the fates preserve the ears you lend)
'Tis yours, a Bacon or a Locke to blame,
A Newton's genius, or a Milton's flame:
But oh! with One, immortal one dispense,
The source of Newton's Light, of Bacon's Sense!
Content, each Emanation of his fires
That beams on earth, each Virtue he inspires,
Each Art he prompts, each Charm he can create,
Whate'er he gives, are giv'n for you to hate.
Persist, by all divine in Man unaw'd,

212.] Of *Toland* and *Tindal*, see book 2. *Tho. Woolston* was an impious madman, who wrote in a most insolent style against the Miracles of the Gospel, in the years 1726, *etc.*

213, etc.] The caution against Blasphemy here given by a departed Son of Dulness to his yet existing brethren, is, as the Poet rightly intimates, not out of tenderness to the ears of others, but their own. And so we see that when that danger is removed, on the open establishment of the Goddess in the fourth book, she encourages her sons, and they beg assistance to pollute the Source of Light itself, with the same virulence they had before done the purest emanations from it.

---

divine worship. In 1729 the Oratory moved to Lincoln's Inn Fields (Midgley 1973: 73–4). ***stall:*** This can be read in two senses: 'seat in a cathedral' (evoking the hierarchy that Henley had rejected), and 'market stall' (implying that Henley had reduced religion to a trade). It is also suggested that his Primitive Eucharist was a blasphemous parody, offering communicants not the body and blood of Christ but of 'Meek modern faith' – a phrase in which 'modern' is characteristically disparaging. (For a sympathetic account of Henley's attempt to reform the liturgy by the practice of the early church, see Midgley 1973: 106–13.) As political and other debates engrossed more of Henley's attention, he seems to have ceased conducting regular religious services.

***212n. Of* Toland *and* Tindal:** Mentioned at II.399. **Tho. Woolston:** See editor's note on lines 149–50.

213–14. the ears you lend: Because blasphemy could be punished by the cutting off of the blasphemer's ears.

213n. The note, initialled in 1751 as by Warburton, refers to IV.453–92.

215. Bacon: The grouping with figures from the seventeenth century identifies this as Francis Bacon (not Roger).

216. flame: inspiration.

217. One: God. ***dispense:*** do without (i.e. the dunces should abstain from attacking God directly).

219. Content: The dunces are to be content that they have been given all God's creatures as objects of their malice, and not to grudge being forbidden to attack God himself. Warton thought the passage 'perhaps the most obscure of any in our poet's writings' (Warton 1797: V, 205).

But, 'Learn, ye DUNCES! not to scorn your GOD.'
Thus he, for then a ray of Reason stole
Half thro' the solid darkness of his soul;
But soon the cloud return'd — and thus the Sire:
See now, what Dulness and her sons admire!
See what the charms, that smite the simple heart
Not touch'd by Nature, and not reach'd by Art.
His never-blushing head he turn'd aside,
(Not half so pleas'd when Goodman prophesy'd)
And look'd, and saw a sable Sorc'rer rise,

224.] Virg. Aen. vi. puts this precept into the mouth of a wicked man, as here of a stupid one: 'Discite justitiam moniti, et non temnere divos!'

Ibid.] See this subject pursued in Book 4.

232.] Mr. Cibber tells us, in his Life, p. 149. that Goodman being at the rehearsal of a play, in which he had a part, clapped him on the shoulder, and cried, 'If he does not make a good actor, I'll be d—d— And (says Mr. Cibber) I make it a question, whether Alexander himself, or Charles the twelfth of Sweden, when at the head of their first victorious armies, could feel a greater transport in their bosoms than I did in mine.'

233. a sable Sorc'rer] Dr. Faustus, the subject of a sett of Farces, which lasted in vogue two or three seasons, in which both Playhouses strove to outdo each other for some years. All the extravagancies in the sixteen lines following were introduced on the Stage, and frequented by persons of the first quality in England, to the twentieth and thirtieth time.

224n. Virgil makes Phlegyas repent after death his crime of burning down the temple of Apollo at Delphi: 'You have been warned: learn justice and do not provoke the gods' (*Aeneid* VI.620).

225–6. Cp. Cowley's description of Hell in *Davideis*: 'Here no dear glimpse of the *Suns* lovely face, / Strikes through the *Solid* darkness of the place' (Waller 1905: 244).

231. His never-blushing head: Presumably Cibber's. Warton comments: 'It is a fault in many, even good writers, not to repeat the substantive intended' (Warton 1797: V, 206).

232n. d—d—: Presumably 'double damned'.

233 and n. a sable Sorc'rer: Introducing an attack on the theatrical vogue for pantomimes featuring dance, mime and elaborate stage effects, envisaged by Pope as an invasion of the legitimate theatre by vulgarities previously confined to the fairground booths in which Settle's shows had been presented. Pantomimes were offered as afterpieces to the main play, contributing to the shift in the early eighteenth century towards theatrical programmes combining different kinds of entertainment (Avery 1960: I, cxvi–cxx; and see original note on 308–9). In 1723 Drury Lane had put on John Thurmond's *Harlequin Doctor Faustus* (published 1724), prompting the noted mime and entrepreneur John Rich (*c.*1692–1761), manager of the theatres at Lincoln's Inn Fields and Covent Garden, and dedicatee of Theobald's *Shakespeare Restored*, to respond with Theobald's *A Dramatic Entertainment, Call'd Harlequin a Sorcerer: With the Loves of Pluto and Proserpine* (published anonymously in 1725), in which Rich played the title role (Avery 1960: II, 746, 806; Sawyer 1972: 85–104; Rogers 1985: 16–18; Koon 1986: 105–6). Pope's 'sable Sorc'rer' alludes to the title of this performance, the elaboration of whose stage effects was indicated by the caution that ''Tis desir'd that no Persons will take it ill, that they are refus'd Admittance behind the Scenes, it being impossible to perform the necessary

Swift to whose hand a winged volume flies:
All sudden, Gorgons hiss, and Dragons glare,
And ten-horn'd fiends and Giants rush to war.
Hell rises, Heav'n descends, and dance on Earth:
Gods, imps, and monsters, music, rage, and mirth,
A fire, a jigg, a battle, and a ball,
'Till one wide conflagration swallows all.
  Thence a new world to Nature's laws unknown,
Breaks out refulgent, with a heav'n its own:
Another Cynthia her new journey runs,
And other planets circle other suns.
The forests dance, the rivers upward rise,

237.] This monstrous absurdity was actually represented in Tibbald's Rape of Proserpine.
244.] 'solemque *suum, sua* sidera norunt'. Virg. Aen. vi.

Decorations, unless the Passages are kept entirely clear' (Avery 1960: II, 806). The satire on the piece had had a more pointed application in versions before 1743, when Tibbald had been the hero addressed by Settle; for Theobald had actually been involved in theatrical collaboration with him (Rogers 1985: 90). Moreover, the substitution of Bays is problematic insofar as Cibber, one of the managers at Drury Lane, strongly disapproved of pantomime even though he felt obliged to satisfy audience demand for it (see lines 266–7). The anti-Walpole paper *The Craftsman* had in 1727 attacked the form, implying that Walpole was himself no more than a manipulative illusionist, and inventing the mock-title 'The Mock Minister: or Harlequin a Statesman' (Hammond 1984: 52–3). ***persons of the first quality:*** On 13 December 1723, for example, there was a performance of *Harlequin Doctor Faustus* at the command of the Prince and Princess of Wales, and on 17 December one 'at the particular Desire of several Ladies of Quality' (Avery 1960: II, 750).

234. According to *The British Stage: or, The Exploits of Harlequin: A Farce* (1724), this was an illusion featured in Rich's performance as the sorcerer.

237n. Tibbald's Rape of Proserpine: A revised issue of *Harlequin a Sorcerer* (Theobald 1727). For its stage effects, see Todd 1989: 24. Settle himself had played a pioneering role in staging cosmic transformations: *The Virgin Prophetess* (1701), on which his spectacular *Siege of Troy* was based, had itself featured shifts between earth, heaven and hell, with elaborate dance scenes (Brown 1910: 103–5; Rogers 1985: 96–7). Pope's lines also recall the gratuitous stage eclipse arranged by a self-congratulatory Bays at the opening of Act V of Buckingham's *The Rehearsal*, in which dancers represent the sun, the moon and the earth (Stone 1969: 64–5).

240–42. one wide conflagration: Theobald made Proserpina's mother set fire to a cornfield (Theobald 1727). Settle's celebrated conflagration in his *Siege of Troy* might also come to mind (Rogers 1985: 93–4). The line evokes apocalyptic expectations that the world would end in fire. ***Thence a new world:*** Continuing the characterisation of pantomime as parodic apocalypse: 'And I saw a new heaven and a new earth: for the first heaven and the first earth were passed away' (Revelation 21:1).

243. Another Cynthia: A moon different from the original one.

244n. According to Virgil, the inhabitants of the groves of the blessed in the underworld 'know a sun of their own, and stars of their own' (*Aeneid* VI.641).

Whales sport in woods, and dolphins in the skies;
And last, to give the whole creation grace,
Lo! one vast Egg produces human race.
  Joy fills his soul, joy innocent of thought;
What pow'r, he cries, what pow'r these wonders wrought?
Son; what thou seek'st is in thee! Look, and find
Each Monster meets his likeness in thy mind.
Yet would'st thou more? In yonder cloud behold,
Whose sarsenet skirts are edg'd with flamy gold,
A matchless Youth! his nod these worlds controuls,
Wings the red lightning, and the thunder rolls.

246.] 'Delphinum sylvis appingit, fluctibus aprum.' Hor.

248.] In another of these Farces Harlequin is hatched upon the stage, out of a large Egg.

251.] 'Quod petis in te est ... / ... Ne te quaesiveris extra.' Pers.

256.] Like Salmoneus in Aen. vi: 'Dum flammas Jovis, et sonitus imitatur Olympi. / ... nimbos, et non imitabile fulmen, / Aere et cornipedum cursu simularat equorum.'

246n. Horace satirises the preposterous imagination of the kind of writer who 'paints a dolphin in the woods, a boar in the sea' (*De arte poetica*, line 30).

248 and n. Rich's mime of hatching from an egg was one of his most famous performances. For the theological and embryological background of the notion, see Todd 1989.

249–52. Echoing Milton's scene between Satan and Sin, when Satan sees for the first time the bridge that Sin and Death have been enabled to build to earth as a consequence of Satan's successful enticement of mankind: 'Great joy was at their meeting, and at sight / Of that stupendous bridge his joy increased' (Fowler 1998: *Paradise Lost* X.350–51). Sin tells him, 'O parent, these are thy magnific deeds, / Thy trophies, which thou viewst as not thine own, / Thou art their author and prime architect' (lines 354–6).

251 and n. Son: Settle replies to Bays's question. ***Quod petis ....:*** 'What you seek is in yourself; don't look beyond yourself', an adapted compound of lines from Horace and Persius (*Epistles* I.11.29; Persius, *Satires* I.7). Horace warns that happiness comes not from travel, but from integrity of mind, while Persius criticises his friend's self-absorbed unwillingness to denounce public taste.

253–6. Cp. Milton's 'mists and exhalations ... / ... dusky or grey, / Till the sun paint your fleecy skirts with gold', and Addison's satire of stage clouds, thunder and lightning in *Spectator* 592 (Fowler 1998: *Paradise Lost* V.185–7; Sherbo 1970: 510; Bond 1965: V, 25–6).

254. sarsenet: A fine silk fabric, here used to make a stage cloud.

255. A matchless Youth!: Rich had been in his thirties even when this line had first appeared in 1728, but he had been strikingly young – about twenty-two – when he took charge of Lincoln's Inn Fields in 1714 (*TE*: V, 178, corrected by information from Sawyer 1972: 85). ***his nod these worlds controuls:*** Alluding to the sign by which Jupiter confirmed his will.

256 and n. Cp. the 'thunder, / Winged with red lightning' with which Milton's God pursues the fallen angels (Fowler 1998: *Paradise Lost* I.174–5). Thunder and lightning were the attributes of Jupiter/Zeus, and, according to Virgil, Salmoneus was punished in the underworld for the blasphemy of imitating them: 'While he mimicked Jupiter's fire and the thunder of Olympus ... he tried to imitate the clouds and the inimitable lightning with brass and the

Angel of Dulness, sent to scatter round
Her magic charms o'er all unclassic ground:
Yon stars, yon suns, he rears at pleasure higher,
Illumes their light, and sets their flames on fire.
Immortal Rich! how calm he sits at ease
'Mid snows of paper, and fierce hail of pease;

258.] Alludes to Mr. Addison's verse, in the praises of Italy: 'Poetic fields encompass me around, / And still I seem to tread on classic ground.' As ver. 264 is a parody on a noble one of the same author in The Campaign; and ver. 259, 260. on two sublime verses of Dr. Y.

261.] Mr. John Rich, Master of the Theatre Royal in Covent-garden, was the first that excelled this way.

---

drumming of horses' hooves' (*Aeneid* VI.586, 590–91). Addison applies the name to a stage technician in *Spectator* 592 (Bond 1965: V, 26).

258 and n. all unclassic ground: Parodying the lines from Addison's *A Letter from Italy* quoted in the original note. Addison is seeing for the first time the actual landscapes familiar to him from Roman poetry (Guthkelch 1914: I, lines 11–12). ***a parody on a noble one of the same author:*** Line 264 is from Addison's *The Campaign* (Guthkelch 1914: I, lines 287–92), which in turn draws on Old Testament images of God (e.g. Nahum 1:3, 'the Lord hath his way in the whirlwind and in the storm'). Addison is celebrating the role played by John Churchill (1650–1722), Duke of Marlborough, as commander of British forces in the War of the Spanish Succession: he is like 'an Angel' who, 'pleas'd th' Almighty's orders to perform, / Rides in the whirl-wind, and directs the storm'. The Tories believed that Marlborough and the Whigs had prolonged the war for personal gain; they welcomed its ending with the Peace of Utrecht (1713); and on the death of Queen Anne in 1714 and the installation of a Hanoverian monarch aligned with the Whigs they saw their leaders (notably Pope's friends Oxford and Bolingbroke) accused of treason, and negotiators of the treaty (Pope's friend Prior) under pressure to incriminate them. By likening Rich to Addison's image of Marlborough as God's 'Angel', Pope insists that Whig politics and a debased drama go hand in hand as Dulness's agents in undoing the divine order. ***on two sublime verses:*** Lines 259–60 allude to Young's *Epistle to the Right Hon. George Lord Lansdowne* (1713). George Granville (1666–1735), Tory (and secretly Jacobite) politician and poet, created Lord Lansdowne by Queen Anne in 1711 as part of a plan to ensure a Tory majority in the House of Lords, was dedicatee of Pope's *Windsor Forest*, and is commemorated as '*Granville* the polite' in the list of his early patrons in *An Epistle to Dr. Arbuthnot* (Handasyde 1933: 117–18; *To Arbuthnot*, line 135; *OAC*: I, 32). Young's flattering address makes the hyperbolic claim that although Anne has been able to elevate Granville's temporal standing, no power on earth could conceive of any enhancement of his spiritual distinction: such a sublime conception would be the prerogative of God alone, 'who the sun's height can raise at pleasure higher, / His lamp illumine, set his flames on fire' (Nichols 1854: I, lines 468–9). An early manuscript draft had been even more deflating: 'three Tapers raisd at pleasure higher / Illuminate their Light, & set their Flames on fire' (Mack 1984: 126).

261. Rich is envisaged as the target of waste paper and dried peas shot from peashooters, both customary resources of disgruntled audiences. Pope may have particularly in mind that Rich's burlesque of Cibber's highly successful spectacular in celebration of the coronation of George II in 1727 had been pelted off the stage (English 1979).

And proud his Mistress' orders to perform,
Rides in the whirlwind, and directs the storm.
But lo! to dark encounter in mid air
New wizards rise; I see my Cibber there!
Booth in his cloudy tabernacle shrin'd,
On grinning dragons thou shalt mount the wind.

266. I see my Cibber there!] The history of the foregoing absurdities is verified by himself, in these words (Life, chap. xv.) 'Then sprung forth that succession of monstrous medleys that have so long infested the stage, which arose upon one another alternately at both houses, out-vying each other in expence.' He then proceeds to excuse his own part in them, as follows: 'If I am asked why I assented? I have no better excuse for my error than to confess I did it against my conscience, and had not virtue enough to starve. Had Henry IV. of France a better for changing his Religion? I was still in my heart, as much as he could be, on the side of Truth and Sense; but with this difference, that I had their leave to quit them when they could not support me. — But let the question go which way it will, Harry IVth has *always been allowed a great man.*' This must be confest a full answer, only the question still seems to be, I. How the doing a thing against one's conscience is an excuse for it? and, 2dly, It will be hard to prove how he got the leave of Truth and Sense to quit their service, unless he can produce a Certificate that he ever was in it.

266, 267.] *Booth* and *Cibber* were joint managers of the Theatre in Drury-lane.

268.] In his Letter to Mr. P. Mr. C. solemnly declares this not to be *literally true*. We hope therefore the reader will understand it *allegorically* only.

---

263. his Mistress' orders: Rich is seen as acting on Dulness's instructions.

265–72. Imaging the competition for audiences between the pantomimes at Drury Lane and those at Lincoln's Inn Fields in the 1720s.

265. Milton compares the confrontation between Satan and Death to the 'dark encounter in mid-air' of two thunderclouds (Fowler 1998: *Paradise Lost* II.718).

266 and n. my Cibber: Previous to Bays's elevation to the role of hero, Cibber had already figured in this passage in his capacity as manager at Drury Lane (*TE*: V, 179). A note is now added, selectively quoting his account of his motives for producing pantomimes despite disapproving of them (Cibber 1740: 423–4). The quotation of Cibber's cynical assertion that 'Harry IVth has *always been allowed a great man*' would recall to readers the satirical title 'the Great Man' as applied to Walpole.

267. Booth: Barton Booth (1681–1733), tragic actor celebrated for his role as Cato in Addison's play, chose the stage in preference to a career in the church. In 1713 he had successfully solicited the Lord Chancellor to be made a manager at Drury Lane, against the will of Cibber and the other managers (Koon 1986: 73–4). ***in his cloudy tabernacle:*** When Moses set up the tabernacle in the wilderness 'A cloud covered the tent of the congregation, and the glory of the Lord filled the tabernacle' (Exodus 40:34). Milton reworks this association of cloud and divine glory in describing how, before the creation of the sun, the principle of light 'in a cloudy tabernacle / Sojourned the while' (Fowler 1998: *Paradise Lost* VII.248–9).

268 and n. For similar epic phraseology, see Sherbo 1970: 510. Commenting on this line, Cibber denied that he had been 'an Encourager of those Fooleries', and added, 'If you intend it literally, that I was Dunce enough to mount a Machine, there is as little Truth in that too' (Cibber 1742: 37).

Dire is the conflict, dismal is the din,
Here shouts all Drury, there all Lincoln's-inn;
Contending Theatres our empire raise,
Alike their labours, and alike their praise.
  And are these wonders, Son, to thee unknown?
Unknown to thee? These wonders are thy own.
These Fate reserv'd to grace thy reign divine,
Foreseen by me, but ah! with-held from mine.
In Lud's old walls tho' long I rul'd, renown'd
Far as loud Bow's stupendous bells resound;
Tho' my own Aldermen confer'd the bays,
To me committing their eternal praise,
Their full-fed Heroes, their pacific May'rs,
Their annual trophies, and their monthly wars:
Tho' long my Party built on me their hopes,
For writing Pamphlets, and for roasting Popes;

282.] *Annual trophies*, on the Lord-mayor's day; and *monthly wars* in the Artillery-ground.

283.] Settle, like most Party-writers, was very uncertain in his political principles. He was employed to hold the pen in the *Character* of a *popish successor*, but afterwards printed his *Narrative* on the other side. He had managed the ceremony of a famous Pope-burning on Nov. 17, 1680. then became a trooper in King James's army, at Hounslow-heath. After the Revolution he kept a booth at Bartholomew-fair, where, in the droll called *St. George for England*, he acted in his old age in a Dragon of green leather of his own invention; he was at last taken into the Charter-house, and there died, aged sixty years.

---

269. Alluding to Milton's depiction of the war in heaven between rebel and loyal angels: 'dire was the noise / Of conflict; over head the dismal hiss / Of fiery darts in flaming volleys flew' (Fowler 1998: *Paradise Lost* VI.211–13).

276. Settle's fairground shows, and the pageants he produced as part of his duties as last of the City Poets, are seen as precursors of fashionable pantomime (Rogers 1985: 88).

277. Lud's old walls: The boundaries of the City of London.

278. Bow's stupendous bells: The City of London was traditionally defined as the area in which the bells of St Mary le Bow could be heard.

281–2 and 282n. Recalling the satire of the pompous and gluttonous celebrations on Lord Mayor's Day at I.87–8: there is an implicit contrast with the triumphs accorded military heroes, and hence with the martial prowess of traditional epic warriors. The 'monthly wars' are the exercises of the City militia, an established target for satire, e.g. Steele's essay in *Tatler* 41 (Rogers 1972: 104; Bond 1987: I, 293–6, 294).

283–4 and n. When Settle says 'my Party', he means the Whigs, for whom he had composed the anonymous anti-Catholic *The Character of a Popish Successour* (1681). Pope would have known this pamphlet and its context from a child, since he told Atterbury that when he was fourteen he had read his father's 'collection of all that had been written on both sides in the reign of King James the second' (*Corr.*: I, 453–4). Settle had also been organiser of the ritual burnings of effigies of the pope which were a regular feature of commemorations of the Gunpowder Plot (5 November) and the accession of Elizabeth I (17 November). Mack points out that Pope's parents, who spent their early married life in the City, had seen such

Yet lo! in me what authors have to brag on!
Reduc'd at last to hiss in my own dragon.
Avert it Heav'n! that thou, my Cibber, e'er
Should'st wag a serpent-tail in Smithfield fair!
Like the vile straw that's blown about the streets,
The needy Poet sticks to all he meets,
Coach'd, carted, trod upon, now loose, now fast,
And carry'd off in some Dog's tail at last.
Happier thy fortunes! like a rolling stone,
Thy giddy dulness still shall lumber on,
Safe in its heaviness, shall never stray,
But lick up ev'ry blockhead in the way.
Thee shall the Patriot, thee the Courtier taste,

297.] It stood in the first edition with blanks, ** *and* **. Concanen was sure 'they must needs mean no body but *King G E O R G E* and *Queen C A R O L I N E*; and said he would insist it was so, 'till the poet cleared himself by filling up the blanks otherwise, agreeably to the context, and consistent with his *allegiance*.' Pref. to a Collection of verses, essays, letters, *etc.* against Mr. P. printed for A. Moor, p. 6.

---

intimidating celebrations of hostility to their faith staged almost on their doorstep (Mack 1985: 5–8). Pope, however, delights in depicting Settle as untrue to these principles, as evidenced by his *A Narrative* (1683) and his joining the army of the monarch whose accession he had agitated against in his *Character* (Brown 1910: 24, 61–3; for his earlier attachment to the Tories, see editor's note on lines 37–8). Further instances of his being 'very uncertain in his political principles' were provided by his writing Whig panegyric at the Revolution but turning during Anne's reign to praise of the Peace of Utrecht, a performance which he dedicated to the Jacobite French Ambassador the Duc D'Aumont; and he later returned under George I to Whig views in a denunciation of the Jacobite rising of 1715 (Brown 1910: 38–9). The original note implies that his time-serving was punished by his being reduced to acting in, rather than simply devising, fairground shows (and his transformation to dragon fitly echoes Milton's Satan's transformation into a serpent on his return to Hell) (Fowler 1998: *Paradise Lost* X.504–45). Although distinguished theatrical figures – including Cibber – worked at Bartholomew Fair without loss of reputation, Settle was in a worse position: his plays had become too great a commercial risk to be put on in the legitimate theatre except by subscription (Brown 1910: 36, 40; Morley 1869: 411; Rogers 1985: 97–8).

291–2. The poet falls from the dignity of a coach to the indignity of being 'carted': prostitutes in particular were punished by being paraded in open carts so that passers-by could hurl abuse and refuse; and carts were also used to take criminals to execution. The poet finally seems, from his being picked up in a dog's tail, to be indistinguishable from the dust of the street.

297 and n. Concanen was claimed by Pope to be the author of the Preface to *A Compleat Collection* (1728). The suggestion that the royal pair were intended by the asterisks of 1728 was uncomfortably close to the real but prudently inexplicit anti-Walpole and anti-Hanoverian drift of the *Dunciad*: Pope had experimented in an early manuscript draft with 'U— & L—' (presumably 'Universities and Lords') and 'Peers and Potentates', and in 1729 with 'Magistrates and Peers' (*TE*: V, 184; Guerinot 1969: 116–22; Mack 1984: 155; Erskine-Hill 1996: 100; for

And ev'ry year be duller than the last.
'Till rais'd from booths, to Theatre, to Court,
Her seat imperial Dulness shall transport.
Already Opera prepares the way,
The sure fore-runner of her gentle sway:
Let her thy heart, next Drabs and Dice, engage,
The third mad passion of thy doting age.
Teach thou the warb'ling Polypheme to roar,
And scream thyself as none e'er scream'd before!

305.] He translated the Italian Opera of Polifemo; but unfortunately lost the whole jest of the story. The Cyclops asks Ulysses his *name*, who tells him his name is *Noman:* After his eye is put out, he roars and calls the Brother Cyclops to his aid: They enquire *who has hurt him?* he answers *Noman*; whereupon they all go away again. Our ingenious Translator made Ulysses answer, *I take no name*, whereby all that follow'd became unintelligible. Hence it appears that Mr. Cibber (who values himself on subscribing to the English Translation of Homer's Iliad) had not that merit with respect to the Odyssey, or he might have been better instructed in the Greek *Pun-nology*.

---

royal interest in pantomime, see editor's note on line 233). The present note attempts to displace the scandal onto Concanen. By filling the blanks with 'Patriot' and 'Courtier' Pope adopts a pose of ostensible moderation, perhaps implying disillusion with the Patriot opposition (see *One Thousand Seven Hundred and Forty*, and Gerrard 1994: 91–3).

301–2. Opera had been identified as forerunner of Dulness from 1728 onwards, but in 1743 the theme is also elaborated in Book IV (*TE*: V, 185; see editor's notes on IV.45–70).

303. Drabs: whores.

305–6 and 305n. the warb'ling Polypheme: Alluding to Nicolò Porpora's opera *Polifemo*, to words by Paolo Rolli, produced in 1735 by the Opera of the Nobility, and based on the Homeric tale of how Odysseus/Ulysses outwitted the cannibal giant Polyphemus (Porpora 1735; Rolli 1734). (For Pope's interpretation of the cyclops as a figure of anarchy, see his *Odyssey*, IX.127–8.) Although the Opera of the Nobility was an opposition enterprise, in contrast with the court-sponsored operas provided by Handel at this time, musical partisanship was not absolutely divided along political lines, and Pope evidently felt no obligation either to be polite about *Polifemo* or to refrain from praising the court favourite Handel (Hume 1988: 359; Gerrard 1994: 61; Gibson 1989: 68–9; Mercer 1935: II, 791–2; cp. IV.45n and IV.65–70). Rolli's text also incorporated the love story that Gay and Handel had used in 1718 in *Acis and Galatea*; and behind the present satire is probably the recollection of a collaboration between poet and composer which could be regarded as a touchstone of appropriate English word-setting. Rolli's libretto for *Polifemo* was sold to operagoers with an English translation, here attributed to Cibber, on facing pages.

'Warb'ling' may register either Pope's sense of the inappropriateness of making a huge, brutal monster express himself in the delicately ornamented and articulated vocal lines typical of operatic arias (inappropriateness which Gay and Handel had turned to witty and touching effect in setting the aria 'O ruddier than the cherry' in *Acis and Galatea*), or it may express a wider disapproval of the relatively high-pitched effect of Italian opera, in which heroic male roles were taken by alto and soprano castrati. Although the role of Polifemo was set for a bass, the published *Favourite Songs in the Opera call'd Polypheme* includes only one aria for him,

To aid our cause, if Heav'n thou can'st not bend,
Hell thou shalt move; for Faustus is our friend:
Pluto with Cato thou for this shalt join,
And link the Mourning Bride to Proserpine.
Grubstreet! thy fall should men and Gods conspire,
Thy stage shall stand, ensure it but from Fire.

308, 309. Faustus, Pluto, etc.] Names of miserable Farces which it was the custom to act at the end of the best Tragedies, to spoil the digestion of the audience.

312.] In the farce of Proserpine a corn-field was set on fire: whereupon the other play-house had a barn burnt down for the recreation of the spectators. They also rival'd each other in showing the burnings of hell-fire, in Dr. Faustus.

---

the rest being for the two castrati who played Ulysses and Acis; whereas in *Acis and Galatea* the weighting had been all the other way, with a bass Polyphemus, two tenors, and the soprano heroine as the only high voice (Burrows 1994: 96–7). For possible political resonances in the trend towards silencing the bass, see an essay generally attributed to Bolingbroke though ostensibly by Rolli in *The Craftsman* in 1733, where the bass who was to sing Polifemo is named in an allegory of the King's management by Walpole (Deutsch 1955: 310–13; Smith 1995: 202–5; Varey 1982: 149–52). Bays is exhorted to 'teach' the monster 'to roar' in allusion to the climax of the story, in which Ulysses burns out the giant's one eye with a torch. There is also a gibe at the notorious stridency of Cibber's voice: although its high pitch enabled him to excel in fop roles, what he called 'the Insufficiency of my Voice' thwarted his early ambition to play heroes (Cibber 1740: 148). ***unfortunately lost the whole jest:*** The note accurately explains the translator's surprising failure to grasp a crucial pun in the Greek, despite its being preserved in the Italian libretto. Since Cibber had gone to some lengths to advertise his magnanimity in subscribing for Pope's *Iliad*, the note takes the opportunity to lament his failure to profit by Pope's subsequent translation of the *Odyssey*, implicitly sneering at Cibber's ignorance of the original Greek (Pope's *Odyssey*: IX.431–4, 479–86; Cibber 1742: 24–6).

307–10 and 308–9n. Recalling Virgil's Juno, who stubbornly opposes her husband Jupiter, and declares 'If I cannot bend the gods above, I shall stir up Hell' (*Aeneid* VII.312). Heaven has obviously no interest in supporting Dulness, but, aptly, Hell is a popular subject for the pantomime afterpieces presented as advancing her conquest. For Faustus, see Thurmond 1724; for Pluto and Proserpina, see Theobald 1727. Addison's *Cato* and Congreve's *The Mourning Bride* are cited as examples of 'the best Tragedies': Pope is outraged at the dissipation of their effect by afterpieces of farce and spectacle. Both were coupled with *Harlequin Doctor Faustus* under Cibber's management at Drury Lane (Avery 1960: II, 769, 789).

312 and n. See editor's note on lines 240–42. Brooks-Davies suggests an allusion to the recommendation of stubble-burning in Virgil's *Georgics*, a work which celebrates Proserpina's mother Ceres, one of Dulness's antitypes, as patroness of fertility and rebirth (Brooks-Davies 1985: 21–2; see editor's note on I.69–70). Fire was always a risk in candle-lit eighteenth-century theatres, as shown by the panic at a false alarm which spoiled the opening of Cibber's spectacular production of Shakespeare's *Henry VIII*, put on to celebrate the coronation of George II in 1727, and which Pope may have had in mind when he first used the line in 1728 (*TE*: V, 185; Koon 1986: 115; Rogers 1985: 131). On-stage conflagrations further increased the danger: Rogers draws attention to a fire which killed eighty people during a provincial

Another Aeschylus appears! prepare
For new abortions, all ye pregnant fair!
In flames, like Semele's, be brought to bed,
While op'ning Hell spouts wild-fire at your head.
  Now Bavius take the poppy from thy brow,
And place it here! here all ye Heroes bow!
This, this is he, foretold by ancient rhymes:
Th' Augustus born to bring Saturnian times.
Signs following signs lead on the mighty year!
See! the dull stars roll round and re-appear.

313.] It is reported of Aeschylus, that when his tragedy of the Furies was acted, the audience were so terrified that the children fell into fits, and the big-bellied women miscarried.

315.] See Ovid. Met. iii.

319, 320.] 'Hic vir, hic est! tibi quem promitti saepius audis, / Augustus Caesar, divum genus; aurea condet / Secula qui rursus Latio, regnata per arva / Saturno quondam'. Virg. Aen. vi. *Saturnian* here relates to the age of *Lead*, mentioned book I. ver. 26.

---

puppet-show production of Settle's version of the St George story, which featured a fire-breathing dragon (Rogers 1985: 98; see original note on line 283). Fire insurance, like other distinctively modern forms of financial speculation in the period, was a routine target for satire: it is, for example, the transparently mercenary suitor who in Mary Leapor's 'Strephon to Celia. A Modern Love-Letter' expresses concern for the insurance of his victim's property (Lonsdale 1989: 50). For the responses of Pope and other Scriblerians to the new financial institutions, see Erskine-Hill 1972a and Nicholson 1994.

313–14 and n. Aeschylus (525–456 BC), the earliest Greek tragedian whose works are now extant, is noted for spectacular stage effects; and the allegations of the terror produced in audiences cited in the note are taken from an ancient scholiast. Stress on such stagecraft suggests a parallel between Aeschylus and the pantomimes under discussion, which is ironic in view of his exemplary classic status and Pope's insistence on locating the pantomimes on 'unclassic ground' (line 258). Theobald, pilloried as a writer of pantomime, had once planned a translation of Aeschylus, and Sutherland suggests that these lines, used from 1728, may have originated in a separate epigram on the project (*TE*: V, 185–6).

315–16 and n. Ovid tells how Juno, jealous of Jupiter's love for Semele, persuaded her to find out who her lover really was by making him promise to reveal himself undisguised: Semele was burned to death by the brightness of his divinity, but her unborn child, Dionysius (from whose cult tragedy was to evolve), was saved, and sewn into Jupiter's thigh until ready to be born (*Metamorphoses* III.259–315). It may be relevant that William Congreve's libretto for *Semele* demanded lavish effects, including thunder and lightning for the climactic scene (Summers 1923: *Semele* III.vii).

319–22 and n. Imitating the rapture of Anchises when, during Aeneas's review of the future destiny of Rome, the Emperor Augustus appears: 'This is the man, this is he! You often hear him promised to you: he is Augustus Caesar, son of a god; he will found an age of gold again in Latium, in the fields once ruled by Saturn' (*Aeneid* VI.791–6). Just as Augustus is the climactic figure in Roman history, so Cibber promises the fulfilment of the empire of Dulness; and an allusion may also be suspected to George II, whose second name was Augustus, and who had appointed Cibber (Rogers 1985: 137–8). (For contrasted views on the use of Augustus

See, see, our own true Phoebus wears the bays!
Our Midas sits Lord Chancellor of Plays!
On Poets Tombs see Benson's titles writ!

325.] W——m Benson (Surveyor of the Buildings to his Majesty King George I.) gave in a report to the Lords, that their House and the Painted-chamber adjoining were in immediate danger of falling. Whereupon the Lords met in a committee to appoint some other place to sit in, while the house should be taken down. But it being proposed to cause some other builders first to inspect it, they found it in very good condition. The Lords, upon this, were going upon an address to the King against Benson, for such a misrepresentation; but the Earl of Sunderland, then secretary, gave them an assurance that his Majesty would remove him, which was done accordingly. In favour of this man, the famous Sir Christopher Wren, who had been Architect to the crown for above fifty years, who built most of the Churches in London, laid the first stone of St. Paul's, and lived to finish it, had been displac'd from his employment at the age of near ninety years.

---

in contemporary political debate, see Weinbrot 1978, and Erskine-Hill 1983: chs. 7 and 9.) For 'the age of *Lead*', see I.27–8 and notes. Cp. Dryden's rendition of the hope of a new golden age in Virgil's fourth *Eclogue*, traditionally believed to prophesy the birth of Christ, and imitated in this sense in Pope's *Messiah*: 'The last great Age, foretold by sacred Rhymes, / Renews its finish'd Course, *Saturnian* times / Rowl round again, and mighty years, begun / From their first Orb, in radiant Circles run' (*Eclogues* IV.4–7; Kinsley 1958: *Virgil's Pastorals* IV.5–8).

323. our own true Phoebus: Cibber, ironically conceived as the 'true' deity of learning, light and poetry; but for a more openly derisive usage of the name, see notes on IV.61.

324. Our Midas: In previous versions the previous line had named Eusden as Laureate, the present line Cibber as 'Lord-Chancellor of Plays' (*TE*: V, 187). Cibber is now presented as Midas, the mythical king who turned all he touched to gold (alluding to Cibber's success in the theatre), and who was cursed by Apollo with ass's ears for preferring Pan (or Marsyas) to him in a singing competition (insinuating Cibber's poor taste in selecting plays for Drury Lane: he is said to have been particularly offensive about a play by Pope's collaborator Elijah Fenton which later succeeded at Lincoln's Inn Fields) (Koon 1986: 104). The Lord Chancellor had the power to ban plays: the implication is that as manager at Drury Lane Cibber 'sits' in similarly lordly authority over the manuscripts submitted to him.

325 and n. On Poets Tombs: The original note is confusing in that it does not address the primary point of the line, namely that William Benson (1682–1754) had in 1737 erected a monument to Milton in Westminster Abbey (see also IV.110–12). The display of his 'titles' (i.e. distinctions) on the monument is represented as the attempt of a nonentity to hitch himself to a great poet.

The note makes explicit other grounds for Pope's contempt. A Whig MP, Benson was appointed in 1718 to succeed Sir Christopher Wren (1632–1723) as Surveyor-General of Works (Sedgwick 1970: I, 455). This was a political appointment, reflecting the Hanoverian distaste for Wren's long service to the Stuarts, including his role – referred to at the end of the note – in rebuilding the City of London after the Great Fire as an expression of the glory of the restored monarchy. When Benson wrongly condemned the House of Lords as unsafe he was dismissed and narrowly escaped prosecution, but he nevertheless received other royal favours. In his post as Surveyor, Benson was responsible to Charles Spencer (1674–1722), fourth Earl of Sunderland, then Secretary for the Northern Department.

Lo! Ambrose Philips is prefer'd for Wit!
See under Ripley rise a new White-hall,
While Jones' and Boyle's united labours fall:

326.] He was (saith Mr. Jacob) 'one of the wits at Button's, and a justice of the peace;' But he hath since met with higher preferment in Ireland: and a much greater character we have of him in Mr. Gildon's Complete Art of Poetry, vol. I. p. 157. 'Indeed he confesses, he dares not set him *quite on the same foot with Virgil*, lest it should *seem* flattery; but he is much mistaken if posterity does not afford him a *greater esteem* than he *at present enjoys*.' He endeavour'd to create some misunderstanding between our author and Mr. Addison, whom also soon after he abused as much. His constant cry was, that Mr. P. was an *Enemy to the government*; and in particular he was the avowed author of a report very industriously spread, that he had a hand in a party-paper call'd the *Examiner:* A falshood well known to those yet living, who had the direction and publication of it.

328.] At the time when this poem was written, the banquetting-house of White-hall, the church and piazza of Covent-garden, and the palace and chapel of Somerset-house, the works of the famous Inigo Jones, had been for many years so neglected, as to be in danger of ruin. The portico of Covent-garden church had been just then restor'd and beautified at the expence of the Earl of Burlington; who, at the same time, by his publication of the designs of that great Master and Palladio, as well as by many noble buildings of his own, revived the true taste of Architecture in this Kingdom.

---

326 and n. prefer'd: promoted. As early as 1725 Pope had been writing to Swift about Philips's hopes of promotion, and quoting the present line as 'a very good conclusion of one of my Satyrs' which would be spoiled if Philips were not promoted (*Corr.*: II, 332). A protégé of Addison, Philips had been made a Justice of the Peace when the Whigs came to power on the accession of George I in 1714, and in 1717 he was made Commissioner for the Lottery. In 1724 he had become secretary to the Primate of Ireland and in Ireland received other preferments. It was a standard complaint of the opposition that whereas previous regimes had supposedly provided for men of letters by granting sinecures without regard to politics, under Walpole such favours were granted only in return for political support – such as Philips had displayed by attacking Pope's friend Atterbury (Goldgar 1976: 6–12, 31–3). ***He was (saith Mr. Jacob):*** Combining material from Jacob 1719–20: I, 204 and II, 139. ***Button's:*** A coffee house set up by Addison and frequented by Whig writers (*OAC*: I, 29). ***a much greater character:*** An abbreviated quotation from Gildon 1718: I, 157. ***He endeavour'd to create some misunderstanding:*** Pope apparently holds Philips partly responsible for his estrangement from Addison: for the quarrel, see 'Testimonies of Authors' and editor's notes. In a letter of 1714 Pope reports at second hand Philips's agitation against him at Button's (*Corr.*: I, 229). There are hints that the relationship between Philips and Addison was vitiated by mutual reservations (*OAC*: I, 67–8; Sherburn 1934: 115). ***a party-paper call'd the* Examiner:** A Tory paper to which there is no evidence that Pope contributed, although the claim was published by Dennis in *A True Character of Mr. Pope* 1716 (Hooker 1939–43: II, 103). ***well known to those yet living:*** By the time this material, originally used in 1729, appeared in 1743, Bolingbroke, the founder of *The Examiner*, was still capable of commenting; but Swift, its principal author, had in 1742 been declared incapable of managing his own affairs, and John Barber, its printer, was dead (Ehrenpreis 1960–83: III, 915).

327–8 and 328n. Thomas Ripley (*d.* 1758) was by training a carpenter, promoted by Walpole to work as an architect both on his own estate and on government contracts. From 1724 to

While Wren with sorrow to the grave descends,
Gay dies unpension'd with a hundred friends,

330.] See Mr. Gay's fable of the *Hare and many Friends*. This gentleman was early in the friendship of our author, which continued to his death. He wrote several works of humour with great success, the Shepherd's Week, Trivia, the What-d'ye-call-it, Fables, and lastly, the celebrated Beggars Opera; a piece of satyr which hit all tastes and degrees of men, from those of the highest quality to the very rabble; That verse of Horace, 'Primores populi arripuit,

---

1726 he worked on a new building for the Admiralty: by the expression 'a new White-hall' Pope contrasts the implicitly shoddy work commissioned from a mere carpenter by a Hanoverian government with the Whitehall built for the Stuarts by the celebrated Inigo Jones (1573–1652). Since a fire at the end of the seventeenth century this had been a ruin, and the present reference also contrasts pointedly with Pope's aspiration in 1713 to see 'a new *White-Hall* ascend' under the patronage of Queen Anne (*Windsor Forest*, line 380). Inigo Jones had also designed Covent Garden, part of which Pope's friend Burlington (whose family name was Boyle) had been responsible for restoring. Pope had celebrated Burlington's public service through such undertakings in *To Burlington*, lines 191–204, concluding with implied criticism of Hanoverian indifference: 'These are Imperial Works, and worthy Kings'. Burlington supported the painter, architect and landscape designer William Kent (1684–1748) in his publication of *The Designs of Inigo Jones* (1727), and his admiration for the Italian Renaissance architect Andrea Palladio (1508–80) resulted in his publication of *Fabbriche antiche designate da A. Palladio* (1730).

329. Alluding to Wren's displacement by Benson (see line 325 and notes).

330 and n. The line and its note date (with slight revisions) from 1729, and focus an account of Gay's career through Pope's vision of the poet's vocation of principled opposition. The imagery of the poet attacking the 'idol' originally anticipated by a decade Pope's posture of defiance to the triumph of Walpolean vice at the close of *Epilogue to the Satires* I. ***unpension'd:*** Gay – who was still alive when this line first appeared in 1729 – had hoped for a court sinecure to support his career as writer when George II came to the throne in 1727; but Gay's patroness, Henrietta Howard (1699–1767), Countess of Suffolk and the new king's mistress, had less power than her friends liked to assume; and Gay was offered only the post of Gentleman Usher to a two-year-old princess, which he declined, taking the offer as a slight to his dignity – although it is at least possible that the choice of post was intended as a compliment to his *Fables*, presented in 1727 to another of the royal children (Rumbold 1989: 208–9, 219, 222–3; Nokes 1995: 398–406). Nokes argues that it was at this time that Gay drafted an inscription for his tomb in a letter to Pope (pp. 398–404; but cp. the date of 1729 assigned in *Corr.*: III, 19). If Nokes's date is accepted, the letter could well have prompted Pope to anticipate Gay's death in the present line. Pope, whose attitudes to court favour were far from unambiguous, especially where Gay was concerned, responded to his disappointment by writing to 'congratulate you on this happy dismission from all court-dependence': 'unpension'd' in the present line implies a tribute to Gay's independence as well as a criticism of the regime's failure to recognise his claims (*Corr.*: III, 453; cp. *Imitations of Horace*, *Satires* II.i.116). ***Mr. Gay's fable:*** Gay attacked the hypocrisy of those who claimed to be his supporters at court by casting himself as the hare. She thought she had friends; but when she was in danger from the hounds, none of them did anything to help: each of them said the others would (Dearing 1974: II, 368–70; Nokes 1995: 389–90). ***That verse of Horace:*** 'He brought the leaders of the people to justice, as well as the common people' (*Satires* II.i.68–9). Pope approvingly

populumque tributim', could never be so justly applied as to this. The vast success of it was unprecedented, and almost incredible: What is related of the wonderful effects of the ancient music or tragedy hardly came up to it: Sophocles and Euripides were less follow'd and famous. It was acted in London sixty-three days, uninterrupted; and renew'd the next season with equal applauses. It spread into all the great towns of England, was play'd in many places to the thirtieth and fortieth time, at Bath and Bristol fifty, *etc.* It made its progress into Wales, Scotland, and Ireland, where it was performed twenty four days together: It was lastly acted in Minorca. The fame of it was not confined to the author only; the ladies carried about with them the favourite songs of it in fans; and houses were furnished with it in screens. The person who acted Polly, till then obscure, became all at once the favourite of the town; her pictures were engraved, and sold in great numbers; her life written, books of letters and verses to her, published; and pamphlets made even of her sayings and jests.

Furthermore, it drove out of England, for that season, the Italian Opera, which had carried all before it for ten years. That idol of the Nobility and the people, which the great Critic Mr. Dennis by the labours and outcries of a whole life could not overthrow, was demolished by a single stroke of this gentleman's pen. This happened in the Year 1728. Yet so great was his modesty, that he constantly prefixed to all the editions of it this motto, *Nos haec novimus esse nihil.*

---

elaborated this passage celebrating the satirist's vocation of attacking the vices of the great in *Imitations of Horace* (*Satires* II.i.105–22). *The Beggar's Opera* suggested comparisons between a thieves' kitchen and the highest circles of government, and was perceived by contemporaries – but not so confidently by recent scholarship – as attacking individual ministers (Fuller 1983: I, 47–8; Winton 1993: 92–3, 99, 103–7; Nokes 1995: 433–6). ***Sophocles:*** Paralleled with Euripides as a highly successful Greek tragedian (*c*.496–406/5 BC). The derivation of opera from Greek drama, which had also combined music, poetry and action, was a commonplace of critical discussion. ***It was acted in London:*** Avery records a total of 62 performances during the 1727–8 season at Lincoln's Inn Fields, 32 of them consecutive (Avery 1960: II, 931; see also Burgess 1966: 72–3; Winton 1993: 98–103). Despite Pope's obvious pride in his friend's success, Nokes suggests it caused tension in a relationship posited on Gay's need for support and protection, and that Pope saw the *Opera* as in some sense a competitor with the *Dunciad*, the first version of which also appeared in 1728 (Nokes 1995: 446, 452). ***houses were furnished with it in screens:*** Screens (used to protect the inhabitants from draughts, or from the direct heat of a fire) were decorated with scenes from the play. ***The person who acted Polly:*** Polly, one of the two principal women's roles in *The Beggar's Opera*, was acted by Lavinia Fenton (1708–60), whose instant celebrity led to her becoming mistress of Charles Paulet (1685–1754), third Duke of Bolton, and giving up her stage career (Burgess 1966: 72–3, 76; Nokes 1995: 419–20). In 1751 the death of Bolton's first wife – whom he had apparently married only for her money and immediately deserted – enabled him to make Fenton his Duchess. For published lives see *The Life of Lavinia Beswick, alias Fenton, alias Polly Peachum* (1728) and *The Whole Life of Polly Peachum* (1730?); for letters and verses see *Letters in Prose and Verse, to the Celebrated Polly Peachum* (1728), *A Letter to Polly. To One of her Own Tunes* (1728) and *A New Ballad Inscrib'd to Polly Peachum* (1728); for her jests see *Polly Peachum's Jests* (1728). ***That idol of the Nobility:*** The 1727–8 season of opera financed by aristocratic subscription under the auspices of the Royal Academy of Music (of which Burlington was a director) floundered amidst difficulties of finance and temperament: the note attributes the failure entirely to the vogue for *The Beggar's Opera*, an interpretation now widely contested (*Corr.*: II, 474, 478; Avery 1960: II, 931; Sadie 1980: VIII, 89–92; Burrows 1994: 125–6; Nokes 1995: 423–7). It seems unlikely that Gay intended his ballad opera, written in English, and using many familiar English melodies, simply as hostile

Hibernian Politics, O Swift! thy fate;
And Pope's, ten years to comment and translate.
  Proceed, great days! 'till Learning fly the shore,
'Till Birch shall blush with noble blood no more,

331.] See book I. ver. 26.

332.] The author here plainly laments that he was so long employed in translating and commenting. He began the Iliad in 1713, and finished it in 1719. The Edition of Shakespear (which he undertook merely because no body else would) took up near two years more in the drudgery of comparing impressions, rectifying the Scenary, *etc.* and the Translation of half the Odyssey employed him from that time to 1725.

333.] It may perhaps seem incredible, that so great a Revolution in Learning as is here prophesied, should be brought about by such *weak Instruments* as have been [hitherto] described in our poem: But do not thou, gentle reader, rest too secure in thy contempt of

---

parody of Italian opera; although it may have caused a cooling of his friendship with Burlington (*Corr.*: II, 474, 478; Rogers 1988: 147–62; Winton 1993: 1121–7; Nokes 1995: 316–17, 334, 426–9). Pope, however, remained on good terms with Burlington despite expressing contempt for Italian opera here and at IV.45–70.

The limiting phrase 'for that season' was introduced only in 1735. Though the admission of opera's survival detracts from the vision of Gay's absolute triumph, it also makes plausible the extended critique of opera in *The New Dunciad* of 1742, which became Book IV in 1743. ***the great Critic Mr. Dennis:*** Dennis's antipathy to opera was expressed particularly in his *Essay on the Opera's after the Italian Manner* (1706) (Hooker 1939–43: I, 382–93). **Nos haec novimus esse nihil:** 'I know this is only a trifle'. The choice of motto superficially proclaims what Nokes characterises as Gay's 'occupational tone of inoffensive servility', a self-presentation which was easily assimilable to Pope's tendency to think of him as a relative innocent in need of advice and protection; but if read in context the quotation from the Roman epigrammatist Martial (*c.* AD 40–103/4) emerges as somewhat more assertive: the poet defies criticism, asserting that he is fully aware of the limitations of his work – but he adds that he is also fully aware that it is not altogether without merit to a reader who approaches it in the right spirit (*Epigrams* XIII.ii.8; Nokes 1995: 5–8 and *passim*).

331 and n. Pope implies regret that Swift, whose *Gulliver's Travels* (1726) had begun the triumphant series of Scriblerian productions which concluded in 1728 with Gay's *Beggar's Opera* and the first version of the *Dunciad*, never received the preferment in the Church of England that would have enabled him to return to England. As his hopes of such preferment faded he committed himself increasingly to Ireland, where he had become Dean of St Patrick's Cathedral, Dublin, in 1713; and his last visit to England had been in 1727. Pope's health would not permit a sea crossing, and he felt the separation acutely.

332 and n. Although Pope owed his financial independence to his Homer translations, the experience had been irksome and laborious, as well as inhibiting major original projects over a long period. The reference to the Shakespeare edition, the hostile reception of which had been crucial to the genesis of the *Dunciad*, expresses a typically dismissive attitude to textual scholarship. By 'rectifying the Scenary' he designates the task of sorting out act and scene divisions.

333–4 and 333n. Proceed, great days: Alluding to Virgil's prophecy of the return of the Saturnian (golden) age: 'incipient magni procedere menses' ('the great months shall begin their progress': *Eclogues* IV.12). ***'till Learning fly the shore:*** Settle is made to prophesy the degeneracy of the most distinguished educational institutions as part of Dulness's triumph.

'Till Thames see Eaton's sons for ever play,
'Till Westminster's whole year be holiday,
'Till Isis' Elders reel, their pupils sport,
And Alma mater lie dissolv'd in Port!
  Enough! enough! the raptur'd Monarch cries;
And thro' the Iv'ry Gate the Vision flies.

these Instruments. Remember what the Dutch stories somewhere relate, that a great part of their Provinces was once overflowed, by a small opening made in one of their dykes by a single *Water-Rat.*

However, that such is not seriously the judgment of our Poet, but that he conceiveth better hopes from the Diligence of our Schools, from the Regularity of our Universities, the Discernment of our Great men, the Accomplishments of our Nobility, the Encouragement of our Patrons, and the Genius of our Writers in all kinds (notwithstanding some few exceptions in each) may plainly be seen from his conclusion; where causing all this vision to pass through the Ivory Gate, he expressly, in the language of Poesy, declares all such imaginations to be wild, ungrounded, and fictitious. SCRIBL.

340.] 'Sunt geminae Somni portae; quarum altera fertur / Cornea, qua veris facilis datur exitus umbris; / Altera candenti perfecta nitens elephanto, / Sed falsa ad coelum mittunt insomnia manes.' Virg. Aen. vi.

The End of the THIRD BOOK.

Birch: Used for flogging schoolboys. ***such is not seriously the judgment of our Poet:*** When a version of this note had been used previously, Scriblerus's naivety had been left more open to interpretation, since there had been no Book IV to assert Dulness's final triumph against the implied optimism of letting the vision escape through the ivory gate (the gate of false visions: see notes on line 340).

335. Eaton: Eton College, located on the Thames.

336. Westminster: Westminster School.

337–8. 'Till Isis' Elders reel: The senior members of Oxford University, located on the River Isis, visualised as reeling, presumably under the influence of alcohol, and thus unable to discipline their students. A note to an early manuscript draft may suggest that Swift contributed line 338 (Mack 1984: 155). ***Alma mater:*** 'Kindly mother' was a title of Ceres and Cybele, later used of the Virgin Mary, and applied to universities by their students. Cambridge University – which seems here to be paralleled with Oxford in the previous line – used on the title-page of its publications the motto 'Alma mater Cantabrigia' ('Cambridge is our kind mother'), with the image of a lactating woman holding the sun in one hand and a chalice in the other (McKenzie 1966: I, 360–61). ***lie dissolv'd in Port:*** Punning on a fleet's lying idle in port and the alcoholic dissipation of the personified university.

339. the raptur'd Monarch: Bays, inspired by the vision of Dulness's triumph.

340 and n. 'There are twin gates for dreams; it is said that one of them is made of horn, and through it shadows of truth find easy passage; the other gleams, being fashioned of white elephant tusk, but through it the spirits send false visions to the upper world' (*Aeneid* VI.893–6; cp. *Odyssey* XIX.559–67). Some commentators took Virgil's decision to send Aeneas through the ivory gate as bringing into question the truth of the prophecies granted him (for a survey, see Austin 1977: 274–6; and for Warburton's reading in terms of his theory that *Aeneid* VI was an allegory of initiation into a mystery cult, see Warburton 1738–41: I, 226–9).

BOOK FOUR

HEADNOTE. This book is adapted from *The New Dunciad,* separately published in 1742. Pope declared that he had shifted his focus towards 'the whole polite world' and away from 'the Dunces of a lower Species', attacking 'all Imposition either Literary, Moral, or Political' with 'General, not particular Satire' (*Corr.*: IV, 377, 396). Although *The New Dunciad* and *The Dunciad in Four Books* both appeared after the fall of Walpole in February 1742, there is no explicit allusion to this long-awaited event in 1743, rather a new boldness in attacking the minister and the regime he served (Mack 1969: 152–3; Goldgar 1976: 210–16). Various topics in Book IV had at a much earlier stage been envisaged as part of a procession to the throne of the new king in Book II (Mack 1982: 339–43; Mack 1984: 98, 127–8; and for dating of this section of the draft material, see Vander Meulen 1991: 49–59; McLaverty 1993: 9–14). These topics, including the Grand Tour, aristocratic opera enthusiasts, virtuosi, Bentley, and the universities, typically reflect on the culture of the ruling class; and the draft attacks George II in more offensive and personal terms than anything admitted into any of the published *Dunciads* (Erskine-Hill 1996: 103–4). The existence of this early draft qualifies the claim made by Warburton, who had met Pope only in 1740, that 'it was at my request he laid the plan of a fourth Book', although Pope had written flatteringly to him that 'the Encouragement you gave me to add the fourth book, first determind me to do so: & the Approbation you seemd to give it, was what singly determind me to print it' (Warburton 1751: vii; *Corr.*: IV, 434). In Warburton's view, the principal importance of Book IV is its defence of religious orthodoxy (Warburton 1751: vii). Many readers, perhaps over-influenced by his claims, have regarded the extra book as a damaging addition (e.g. Warton 1797: V, 224–5). The extent of his influence on the verse of Book IV is unclear (see for example *Corr.*: IV, 357), but his contributions to the commentary are marked by pedantic display, allegorising or summarising of extended passages, laborious wit, and insistence on philosophical and theological controversy.

Among the many formal models proposed for aspects of Book IV are the ancient allegory known as the 'Table of Cebes' (Williams 1953a: 807–10; Fitzgerald & White 1983); the temple designed for Augustus at the beginning of Virgil's *Georgics* III (lines 10–39); Chaucer's *Hous of Fame* (as imitated in Pope's *Temple of Fame*: see Sitter 1971: 66–97); sessions poems, such as Rochester's 'Session of the Poets' or the anonymous *The Session of Musicians* (1724), in which aspirants compete for the approval of a presiding deity (Williams 1953a: 810–13); the ambitious goddess Faction and her votaries in Shippen's *Moderation Display'd* and *Faction Display'd* (both 1704: see Lord 1963–75: VI, 651–3, 668–70; VII, 23); the God of Dulness's review of suppliants in Blackmore's *The Kit-Cats* (1708); the goddess Alecto's allegorical supporters in *Rufinus* (1712), attributed to William King (Lund 1984: 296–8); and the assemblies of suitors to the Goddess Nonsense and to Queen Ignorance in Fielding's *The Author's Farce* and *Pasquin* (Fielding 1730, 1736). Visual models may include Renaissance depictions of the Virgin Mary's assumption into heaven (Gneiting 1975: 428–30), or representations of virtues surmounting chained vices (Sitter 1971: 44). There are also echoes of such social events as masquerades, degree givings and the receptions held by the King and Queen on their birthdays (Jack 1942: 119; Williams 1953a; Sherburn in Mack 1964: 670–73; Sitter 1971: ch. 3; Rogers 1985: 103, 115–16).

THE DUNCIAD:

BOOK the FOURTH.

ARGUMENT.

The Poet being, in this Book, to declare the Completion *of the* Prophecies *mention'd at the end of the former, makes a new* Invocation; *as the greater Poets are wont, when some high and worthy matter is to be sung. He shews the Goddess coming in her Majesty, to destroy* Order *and* Science, *and to substitute the* Kingdom of the Dull *upon earth. How she leads captive the* Sciences, *and silenceth the* Muses; *and* what *they be who succeed in their stead. All her Children, by a wonderful attraction, are drawn about her; and bear along with them divers others, who promote her Empire by connivance, weak resistance, or discouragement of Arts; such as Half-wits, tasteless Admirers, vain Pretenders, the Flatterers of Dunces, or the Patrons of them. All these crowd round her; one of them offering to approach her, is driven back by a Rival, but she commends and encourages both. The first who speak in form are the* Genius's *of the* Schools, *who assure her of their care to advance her Cause, by confining Youth to* Words, *and keeping them out of the way of real Knowledge. Their Address, and her gracious Answer; with her Charge to them and the Universities. The* Universities *appear by their proper Deputies, and assure her that the same method is observ'd in the progress of* Education; *The speech of* Aristarchus *on this subject. They are driven off by a band of young Gentlemen return'd from* Travel *with their* Tutors; *one of whom delivers to the Goddess, in a polite oration, an account of the whole Conduct and Fruits of their* Travels: *presenting to her at the same time a young Nobleman perfectly accomplished. She receives him graciously, and indues him with the happy quality of* Want of Shame. *She sees loitering about her a number of* Indolent Persons *abandoning all business and duty, and dying with laziness: To these approaches the Antiquary* Annius, *intreating her to make them* Virtuosos, *and assign them over to him: But* Mummius, *another Antiquary, complaining of his*

Science: learning.

vain Pretenders: Those who aspire beyond the reach of their talents. An allusion to Jacobite attempts to reinstate the Stuarts is also implied. Walpole had exploited such plots to justify the Whigs' monopoly of power.

in form: formally.

Genius's: attendant spirits.

Charge: instructions.

indues him with: gives him.

Virtuosos: connoisseurs of the fine arts.

fraudulent proceeding, she finds a method to reconcile their difference. Then enter a Troop of people fantastically adorn'd, offering her strange and exotic presents: Amongst them, one stands forth and demands justice on another, who had deprived him of one of the greatest Curiosities in nature: but he justifies himself so well, that the Goddess gives them both her approbation. She recommends to them to find proper employment for the Indolents *before-mentioned, in the study of* Butterflies, Shells, Birds-nests, Moss, *etc. but with particular caution, not to proceed beyond* Trifles, *to any useful or extensive views of Nature, or of the Author of Nature. Against the last of these apprehensions, she is secured by a hearty Address from the* Minute Philosophers *and* Freethinkers, *one of whom speaks in the name of the rest. The Youth thus instructed and principled, are delivered to her in a body, by the hands of* Silenus; *and then admitted to taste the Cup of the* Magus *her High Priest, which causes a total oblivion of all Obligations, divine, civil, moral, or rational. To these her Adepts she sends* Priests, Attendants, *and* Comforters, *of various kinds; confers on them* Orders *and* Degrees; *and then dismissing them with a speech, confirming to each his* Privileges *and telling what she expects from each, concludes with a* Yawn *of extraordinary virtue: The Progress and Effects whereof on all Orders of men, and the Consummation of all, in the Restoration of* Night *and* Chaos, *conclude the Poem.*

Minute Philosophers: For the application of this term to those who challenged religious orthodoxy, see editor's note on lines 459–92.

Adepts: initiates.

Comforters: supporters, with a blasphemous glance at Jesus' prophecy of the sending of the Holy Spirit to his disciples: 'And I will pray the Father, and he shall give you another Comforter' (Luke 14:16).

YET, yet a moment, one dim Ray of Light
Indulge, dread Chaos, and eternal Night!

The* Dunciad*, Book IV.] This Book may properly be distinguished from the former, by the Name of the Greater Dunciad, not so indeed in Size, but in Subject; and so far contrary to the distinction anciently made of the *Greater* and *Lesser Iliad*. But much are they mistaken who imagine this Work in any wise inferior to the former, or of any other hand than of our Poet; of which I am much more certain than that the *Iliad* itself was the Work of *Solomon*, or the *Batrachomuomachia* of *Homer*, as *Barnes* hath affirmed. Bent.

1, etc.] This is an Invocation of much Piety. The Poet willing to approve himself a genuine Son, beginneth by shewing (what is ever agreeable to *Dulness*) his high respect for *Antiquity* and a *Great Family*, how dull, or dark soever: Next declareth his love for *Mystery* and *Obscurity*; and lastly his Impatience to be *re-united* to her. Scribl.

---

note on title. Initialled in 1751 as jointly by Pope and Warburton. ***the distinction anciently made:*** A Greek poem, now lost, offered a brief continuation of the story of the *Iliad*, and was distinguished by the title of *The Little Iliad*. This distinction is the reverse of that proposed between *Dunciad* I–III and its continuation in *Dunciad* IV, since in this case the continuation is claimed to be the more important. ***of any other hand:*** Book IV had originally appeared in 1742 as a separate and anonymous pamphlet entitled *The New Dunciad*, which might have suggested that it was another writer's response to earlier versions of the *Dunciad*. ***of which I am much more certain:*** 'Bentley' is represented as so credulous as to accept the biblical King Solomon's authorship of the *Iliad* – an attribution made, presumably in jest, by the classical scholar Joshua Barnes (1654–1712; the tradition that it was part of an attempt to persuade his wife to support his edition of the poem out of her own income would be more persuasive were his argument not presented in nearly 300 parallel Greek and Latin hexameters: see Monk 1833: I, 291; Emmanuel College Cambridge MS 147) – along with the erroneous but in the eighteenth century widely accepted attribution to Homer of the playful imitation of Homeric epic, *Batrachomyomachia* (*The Battle of the Frogs and Mice*). Pope's opinion on the latter point is unclear: his friend Thomas Parnell, who had translated *The Battle* with mock-critical apparatus satirising attacks on Pope's Homer translation, was, to judge by the 'Essay on the Life, Writings and Learning of Homer' which he wrote for Pope, and which Pope himself revised, not entirely convinced (*Homer's Battle of the Frogs and Mice* 1717; *TE*: VII, 47, 52; Rawson & Lock 1989: 64–108, 442–6). Barnes, however, had accepted it in his edition of Homer's works, which Pope owned and used (Barnes 1711: II, 'De Homeri Batrachomyomachia'; *TE*: X, 441 and index to Vol. X, under 'Barnes'; Mack 1982: 418). The note had in 1742 been signed by Scriblerus, a far more fitting author than 'Bentley', since Bentley, far from tending to credulity towards Barnes's views on attribution, had contested his belief in the genuineness of letters attributed to Euripides (Monk 1833: I, 52–4; Levine 1991: 48). Barnes and Bentley had been paired as exemplars of 'the poring race' in an early manuscript draft of III.191–4 (Mack 1984: 125).

1 and n. The note (initialled in 1751 as jointly by Pope and Warburton) deals with lines 1–8. Scriblerus represents the poet as 'a genuine Son' of Dulness: he addresses her respectfully, promises to 'sing' the restoration of her 'Mysteries', and bids her finally 'take at once the Poet and the Song'. (Doody, in contrast, calls the 'Poet' who speaks here 'an ironic dummy who admires what Pope condemns' (Doody 1985: 190).) Dulness is of 'a *Great Family*' in that her parents are the most ancient of things, Chaos and Night: despite Pope's treasured associations with members of great families he was proud of his independence from noble patrons

Of darkness visible so much be lent,
As half to shew, half veil the deep Intent.
Ye Pow'rs! whose Mysteries restor'd I sing,
To whom Time bears me on his rapid wing,

2. dread Chaos, and eternal Night!] Invoked, as the Restoration of their Empire is the Action of the Poem.

4.] This is a great propriety, for a dull Poet can never express himself otherwise than by *halves*, or imperfectly. SCRIBL.

I understand it very differently; the Author in this work had indeed a *deep Intent*; there were in it *Mysteries* or ἀπόῤῥητα which he durst not fully reveal, and doubtless in divers verses (according to *Milton*) 'more is meant than meets the ear.' BENT.

6.] Fair and softly, good Poet! (cries the gentle *Scriblerus* on this place.) For sure in spite of his unusual modesty, he shall not travel so fast toward Oblivion, as divers others of more Confidence have done: For when I revolve in my mind the Catalogue of those who have the most boldly promised to themselves Immortality, *viz. Pindar, Luis Gongora, Ronsard, Oldham,*

---

and expressed scepticism about the principle of hereditary distinction (e.g. *Essay on Man* IV.205–16). Warburton, whose rise from relatively humble origins would not have been possible without powerful friends, prided himself on his frankness to his patrons (*OAC*: I, 216–17; 373).

2n. Initialled in 1751 as jointly by Pope and Warburton.

3. darkness visible: Alluding to Milton's paradoxical evocation of the medium of sight in Hell, 'yet from those flames / No light, but rather darkness visible' (Fowler 1998: *Paradise Lost* I.62–3).

4 and n. The line implies that under Dulness's dominion, it would be possible for the poet to express only part of his (her?) intention, even if she favoured his attempt (for a reading in terms of the underlying theme of 'the undoing of structure by undifferentiation', compare Bogel 1982: 846, 849). This limitation could represent the inadvisability under the Hanoverian regime moulded by Walpole of speaking out plainly against it; but Scriblerus takes it simply as a confession of incompetence on the part of the poet, whom he takes to be a devotee of Dulness. The political implication is, however, hinted at in the note (initialled in 1751 as jointly by Pope and Warburton): 'Bentley' glosses 'Mysteries', i.e. secret rites which assured the participants of life after death, by its Greek equivalent. Warburton, who believed the mysteries were designed by legislators to enforce the doctrine of a future state of rewards and punishments, was involved in controversy regarding possible links between the ancient mysteries and Christianity – which applied the term 'mystery' to doctrines held to be beyond the scope of human reason (Warburton 1738–41: I, 133–58; Howard 1968; and see Warburton's note on line 517). Milton – of whose *Paradise Lost* Bentley had published a notorious edition – had in 'Il Penseroso' referred to chivalric romances in which 'more is meant than meets the ear', presumably having in mind the allegories of Spenser's *The Faerie Queene* and its Italian forebears: the quotation prepares the reader for an allegorical or symbolic reading of the fantasy of *Dunciad* IV, and also for a close scrutiny of 'divers verses' in which a subversive meaning may be discerned (Carey 1968: 'Il Penseroso', line 120).

6 and n. The line alludes to Milton's sonnet beginning 'How soon hath time the subtle thief of youth, / Stol'n on his wing my three and twentieth year!', where he speaks of the 'lot ... / Toward which time leads me' (Carey 1968: Sonnet VII). In the note, initialled in 1751 as

Lyrics; *Lycophron, Statius, Chapman, Blackmore,* Heroics; I find the one half to be already dead, and the other in utter darkness. But it becometh not us, who have taken upon us the office of Commentator, to suffer our Poet thus prodigally to cast away his Life; contrariwise, the more hidden and abstruse is his work, and the more remote its beauties from common Understanding, the more is it our duty to draw forth and exalt the same, in the face of Men and Angels. Herein shall we imitate the laudable Spirit of those, who have (for this very reason) delighted to comment on the Fragments of *dark* and *uncouth* Authors, preferred *Ennius* to *Virgil*, and chosen to turn the dark Lanthorn of *Lycophron*, rather than to trim the everlasting Lamp of *Homer*. SCRIBL.

---

jointly by Pope and Warburton, Scriblerus offers to save the poet from oblivion by elucidating his obscurities. He lists poets whose expectations of being remembered after their deaths have in his view come to nothing, demonstrating his lack of discrimination by coupling, for example, the classic Pindar with Blackmore. It is worth noting, however, that to neo-classical taste, all those listed had significant stylistic flaws: even Pindar could be criticised for neglect of logical connection in his rapturous odes. The Spanish poet Luis de Góngora y Argote (1561–1627), like the French poet Pierre de Ronsard (1524–85), evolved an elaborate Renaissance style of the kind routinely disparaged by neo-classicists. John Oldham (1653–83), noted for his anti-Catholic satires written during the Popish Plot, preceded Pope in satires imitating classical models: Pope, who owned and annotated his works, considered him 'too rough and coarse', 'a very undelicate writer', who had 'strong rage, but 'tis too much like Billingsgate' (Mack 1982: 431–2; *OAC*: I, 202). The Hellenistic Greek poet Lycophron (*b. c.*320 BC), little of whose work survives, was noted for obscurity of style; and the Roman poet Publius Papinius Statius (*c.* AD 45–*c.*96), the first book of whose *Thebaid* Pope had translated in youth, wrote in extravagantly rhetorical terms. George Chapman (1559?–1634), poet and dramatist, whom Pope classed with Shakespeare in his tendency 'to stiffen his style with high words and metaphors for the speeches of his kings and great men' because 'He mistook it for a mark of greatness', made a translation of Homer which Pope owned, used and annotated (Chapman 1611; *TE*: X, 441, 474–91; *OAC*: I, 183; Mack 1982: 415). ***those, who have (for this very reason) delighted:*** Scriblerus's self-congratulatory delight in obscurity constitutes an attack on scholars, most notably Bentley, who studied authors considered peripheral to the canon in order to establish a fuller context for understanding the development of classical languages and culture (see also lines 223–8). The early Roman poet Quintus Ennius (239–169 BC) composed epic, tragedy and comedy: he was noted for a deliberately grand style, and by later standards his verse could be considered metrically clumsy. Lycophron had been edited with extensive commentary in 1697 (reprinted 1702) by Warburton's enemy the classical scholar and Archbishop of Canterbury John Potter (1673?–1747), a pupil, like Bentley, of Wakefield grammar school (Evans 1932: 67, 104). Potter refers in his Dedication to his subject as 'poetam hunc prae caeteris obscurum' ('this poet who is obscure beyond the rest'); and in his 'Lectori S.' ('To the Reader') counters criticism of his choice by listing great scholars who have thought Lycophron worthy of their attention – an argument which would tend to confirm the traditional humanist's suspicion of philology as a self-sustaining conspiracy of futility. Potter's father (like Pope's) was a draper; his background laid him open to sneers at a professional approach to scholarship which could be represented as careerist pedantry (a charge which could also, with some adjustment, be levelled at Warburton). Potter, like Bentley, was a Whig, and preached at the coronation of George II a sermon which effectively fudged the anomalies in the succession by appealing to the implied sanctity of his hereditary right; but in ecclesiastical politics he retained a high sense of church prerogative which set him against Hoadly in the Bangorian controversy (Gerrard 1994: 189; and see editor's note on 175–88).

Suspend a while your Force inertly strong,
Then take at once the Poet and the Song.
Now flam'd the Dog-star's unpropitious ray,
Smote ev'ry Brain, and wither'd ev'ry Bay;
Sick was the Sun, the Owl forsook his bow'r,
The moon-struck Prophet felt the madding hour:
Then rose the Seed of Chaos, and of Night,
To blot out Order, and extinguish Light,
Of dull and venal a new World to mold,

7. Force inertly strong,] Alluding to the *Vis inertiae of Matter*, which, tho' it really be no Power, is yet the Foundation of all the Qualities and Attributes of that sluggish Substance.

11, 12.] The Poet introduceth this, (as all great events are supposed by sage Historians to be preceded) by an *Eclipse of the Sun*; but with a peculiar propriety, as the Sun is the *Emblem* of that intellectual light which dies before the face of Dulness. Very apposite likewise is it to make this *Eclipse*, which is occasioned by the *Moon's predominancy*, the very time when *Dulness* and *Madness* are in *Conjunction*; whose relation and influence on each other the poet hath shewn in many places, Book I. ver. 29. Book 3. ver. 5, *et seq.*

14.] The two great Ends of her Mission; the one in quality of Daughter of *Chaos*, the other as Daughter of *Night*. *Order* here is to be understood extensively, both as Civil and Moral, the distinctions between high and low in Society, and true and false in Individuals: *Light*, as Intellectual only, Wit, Science, Arts.

15. Of dull and venal] The Allegory continued; *dull* referring to the extinction of Light or Science, *venal* to the destruction of Order, or the Truth of Things.

Ibid. a new World] In allusion to the Epicurean opinion, that from the Dissolution of the

---

The final comparison likens Lycophron to a dark lantern (with a slide for concealing the light when desired), and Homer to an ordinary – but everlasting – lamp. Turning the slide of the former reveals the narrow beam previously concealed, while trimming the wick of the latter brightens its existing light and prevents smoke.

7 and n. Note initialled in 1751 as jointly by Pope and Warburton. *Vis inertiae* ('Power of inertia') denotes the tendency of matter to resist being moved when at rest, or to resist being stopped once in motion.

8. Implicitly conceding that in the face of Dulness's triumph there are no longer grounds to believe that poems will outlast their makers. Erskine-Hill suggests that Pope is here 'speaking of his own death, which in 1741–2 cannot have seemed far distant' (Erskine-Hill 1972b: 61).

9. the Dog-star's unpropitious ray: The heat of late summer was thought to give rise to disease and insanity, and to be caused by the influence of Sirius, the dog-star.

10. wither'd ev'ry Bay: put a stop to the writing of poetry.

11–12 and n. The note, initialled by Warburton in 1751, is a typical example of the laboured wit which, under his influence, sets the tone of commentary for Book IV.

13. Seed: offspring, i.e. Dulness.

14n. Initialled in 1751 as jointly by Pope and Warburton.

15. venal: Identifying those prepared to sacrifice principle to personal advantage as key figures in the establishment of Dulness's 'new World'.

15n. Both parts of the note were initialled in 1751 as jointly by Pope and Warburton. ***the Epicurean opinion:*** Epicurus (341–271 BC) advanced a mechanistic conception of the

And bring Saturnian days of Lead and Gold.
  She mounts the Throne: her head a Cloud conceal'd,
In broad Effulgence all below reveal'd,
('Tis thus aspiring Dulness ever shines)
Soft on her lap her Laureat son reclines.

natural World into Night and Chaos, a new one should arise; this the Poet alluding to, in the Production of a new moral World, makes it partake of its original Principles.

16. **Lead** ***and*** **Gold.***]* *i.e.* dull and venal.

18. all below reveal'd,] Vet. Adag. **The higher you climb, the more you shew your A—** Verified in no instance more than in Dulness aspiring. Emblematized also by an Ape climbing and exposing his posteriors. Scribl.

20. her Laureat son reclines.] With great judgment it is imagined by the Poet, that such a Collegue as Dulness had elected, should sleep on the Throne, and have very little share in

---

universe, according to which all phenomena were accounted for by the combinations and recombinations of a fixed number of immutable atoms. His belief that wise living consisted in the rational pursuit of well-being was from ancient times misrepresented as advocating immoral hedonism, since his materialist philosophy and insistence that the gods did not intervene or take an interest in human affairs gave offence to traditional religion and, in due course, to the Christian church. ***its original Principles:*** Night and chaos.

16. See I.28 and notes.

16n. Initialled in 1751 as jointly by Pope and Warburton.

17–18. her head a Cloud conceal'd: Evoking both intellectual fog and the clouds used by Homeric deities to conceal their activities from mortal sight. Sherbo cites the enthronement of Satan, whose disguise gradually disperses, revealing him to the fallen angels who welcome him on his supposedly triumphant return after the fall of man: 'At last as from a cloud his fulgent head / And shape star-bright appeared' (Sherbo 1970: 510; Fowler 1998: *Paradise Lost* X.449–50). Also relevant is the revelation of God to Moses in Exodus 33:9, 'the cloudy pillar descended, and stood at the door of the tabernacle, and the Lord talked with Moses'. Like the allusion to an adjacent biblical passage in the following line (see below), this contributes to the presentation of Dulness as perversion of the Christian God. ***all below reveal'd:*** In 1742 and again in 1751 the note included the claim that 'It was the opinion of the Ancients, that the Divinities manifested themselves to men by their Back-parts', supported by a passage from Virgil which told how Aeneas recognised his mother Venus through her disguise by the gleam of her neck as she turned away from him (*Aeneid* I.402). This may have been intended to avert accusations of blasphemy on account of the more obvious echo of the words of God to Moses in Exodus 34:23: 'thou shalt see my back parts: but my face shall not be seen'.

18n. Initialled in 1751 as jointly by Pope and Warburton. Vet. Adag. stands for the Latin 'vetus adagium' ('old proverb').

20n. In 1751 Scriblerus's paragraph was initialled as jointly by Pope and Warburton; the first paragraph attributed to 'Bentley' as by Pope; the second attributed to 'Bentley' as jointly by Pope and Warburton. ***With great judgment:*** Scriblerus presents Bays's inactivity –

Beneath her foot-stool, *Science* groans in Chains,
And *Wit* dreads Exile, Penalties and Pains.

the Action of the Poem. Accordingly he hath done little or nothing from the day of his Anointing; having past through the second book without taking part in any thing that was transacted about him, and thro' the third in profound Sleep. Nor ought this, well considered, to seem strange in our days, when so many *King-consorts* have done the like. SCRIBL.

This verse our excellent Laureate took so to heart, that he appealed to all mankind, 'if he was not as *seldom asleep as any fool?*' But it is hoped the Poet hath not injured him, but rather verified his Prophecy (p. 243. of his own Life, 8vo. ch. ix.) where he says *'the Reader will be as much pleased to find me a* Dunce *in my* Old age, *as he was to prove me a* brisk blockhead *in my* Youth.' Wherever there was any room for Briskness, or Alacrity of any sort, *even in sinking*, he hath had it allowed him; but here, where there is nothing for him to do but to take his natural rest, he must permit his Historian to be silent. It is from their *actions* only that Princes have their character, and Poets from their *works:* And if in *those* he be *as much asleep as any fool*, the Poet must leave him and them to *sleep to all eternity*. BENT.

***Ibid.* her Laureat]** 'When I find my Name in the satyrical works of this Poet, I never look upon it as any malice meant to me, but PROFIT to himself. For he considers that *my Face* is more *known* than most in the nation; and therefore *a Lick at the Laureate* will be a sure bait *ad captandum vulgus*, to catch little readers.' Life of Colley Cibber, chap. ii.

Now if it be certain, that the works of our Poet have owed their success to this ingenious expedient, we hence derive an unanswerable Argument, that this Fourth DUNCIAD, as well as the former three, hath had the Author's last hand, and was by him intended for the Press: Or else to what purpose hath he crowned it, as we see, by this finishing stroke, the profitable *Lick* at the *Laureate?* BENT.

21, 22.] We are next presented with the pictures of those whom the Goddess leads in

---

problematic for readers intent on evaluating *The Dunciad in Four Books* by epic conventions – not as a defect, but as a mark of verisimilitude. ***so many* King-consorts:** Implying that Bays resembles George II in that both are only nominally important, depending for their initiatives in reality on a dominating female power – Dulness in the case of Bays, Caroline in the case of George II (for her collaboration with Walpole in managing the King, see editor's note on I.213–14). '*King-consorts*' is an insulting parallel to 'Queen Consort', where 'Queen' is merely a courtesy title for the wife of the reigning king: the force of 'King' is never undermined by being used in this way (compare the case of William III, whose use of the title reflected a constitutional accommodation which made him a joint monarch with his wife Mary II). ***This verse our excellent Laureate took so to heart:*** Cibber's appeal, lightly adapted in the direction of gracelessness, is cited as in itself a damaging admission (Cibber 1742: 53). ***Alacrity of any sort:*** Alluding to Falstaff's confession in Shakespeare's *The Merry Wives of Windsor* that 'you may know by my size that I have a kind of alacrity in sinking' (Alexander 1951: *Merry Wives of Windsor* III.v). ***we hence derive an unanswerable Argument:*** Deliberately attributing to 'Bentley' a nonsensical proof. ***last hand:*** final revisions.

21–2 and n. For a possible source in Joseph Beaumont's religious allegory *Psyche: or, Loves Mysterie* (1648: Canto XVI.84), see Notzon 1979. Beaumont shows personifications of human wisdom tied up around the throne in order to represent their limitations in comparison with the doctrine of the church. ***Exile, Penalties and Pains:*** For the dangers of writing against

There foam'd rebellious *Logic*, gagg'd and bound,
There, stript, fair *Rhet'ric* languish'd on the ground;
His blunted Arms by *Sophistry* are born,
And shameless *Billingsgate* her Robes adorn.
Morality, by her false Guardians drawn,
Chicane in Furs, and *Casuistry* in Lawn,
Gasps, as they straiten at each end the cord,

Captivity. *Science* is only depressed and confined so as to be rendered useless; but *Wit* or *Genius*, as a more dangerous and active enemy, punished, or driven away: *Dulness* being often reconciled in some degree with Learning, but never upon any terms with Wit. And accordingly it will be seen that she admits something *like* each Science, as Casuistry, Sophistry, *etc.*

27.] Morality is the Daughter of *Astraea*. This alludes to the Mythology of the ancient Poets; who tell us that in the *Gold* and *Silver* ages, or in the *State of Nature*, the Gods cohabited with Men here on Earth; but when by reason of human degeneracy men were forced to have recourse to a *Magistrate*, and that the Ages of *Brass* and *Iron* came on, (that is, when Laws were wrote on brazen tablets and inforced by the Sword of Justice) the Celestials soon retired from Earth, and Astraea last of all; and then it was she left this her Orphan Daughter in the hands of the *Guardians* aforesaid. SCRIBL.

---

the culture and morality fostered by Walpole's regime, and for strategies of evasion, see *Imitations of Horace*: *Satires* II.i, especially lines 143–56. There is also, however, a specific allusion to the Act of Pains and Penalties by which Atterbury had been exiled in 1723. The regime did not risk an ordinary prosecution for Jacobite plotting because the evidence was insufficient to ensure a conviction, but for such a bill 'all that had to be done was to persuade a majority in each House that it was expedient to pass into law a bill inflicting criminal penalties on an individual' (Bennett 1975: 264). For Pope's knowledge of Atterbury's involvement, see Erskine-Hill 1988: 204–9. The line averts attention from the treason charge, suggesting that it was Atterbury's status as connoisseur of literature ('*Wit*') that was obnoxious to the government: cp. James Miller, who characterises wit as a rebel forced by the regime to submit to pains and penalties (*Are These Things So?* 1740). The note, initialled in 1751 as jointly by Pope and Warburton, glosses over the political point with bland moral allegory.

23–6. Logic and its perversion, Sophistry, are personified as male; while Rhetoric and its perversion, Billingsgate (i.e. foul language), are personified as female. For a possible allusion to the allegory known as 'The Table of Cebes', see Williams 1953a: 809.

27 and n. Rogers suggests an allusion to the representatives of law and religion who processed in front of Queen Caroline at her coronation in 1727 (Rogers 1985: 141). The note, initialled in 1751 as by Warburton, elaborates Pope's allegory by reference to the myth of Astraea (goddess of justice, whose return was to inaugurate the return of the Golden Age).

28. Chicanery (legal trickery) wears the ermine of a judge, Casuistry the fine linen of a bishop.

29. straiten: tighten. Morality is strangled by a cord wrapped around her neck and pulled in opposite directions.

And dies, when Dulness gives her Page the word.
Mad *Mathesis* alone was unconfin'd,
Too mad for mere material chains to bind,
Now to pure Space lifts her extatic stare,
Now running round the Circle, finds it square.
But held in ten-fold bonds the *Muses* lie,

30. gives her* Page *the word.] There was a Judge of this name, always ready to hang any man, of which he was suffered to give a hundred miserable examples during a long life, even to his dotage. — Tho' the candid *Scriblerus* imagined *Page* here to mean no more than a *Page* or *Mute*, and to allude to the custom of strangling State Criminals in *Turkey* by Mutes or Pages. A practice more decent than that of *our Page*, who before he hanged any person, loaded him with reproachful language. SCRIBL.

31. Mad* Mathesis*] Alluding to the strange Conclusions some Mathematicians have deduced from their principles concerning the *real Quantity of Matter*, the *Reality of Space, etc.*

33. pure Space] i.e. pure and defaecated from Matter. — *extatic Stare*, the action of men who look about with full assurance of seeing what does not exist, such as those who expect to find *Space* a real being.

34.] Regards the wild and fruitless attempts of *squaring the Circle.*

---

30 and n. The note was initialled in 1751 as jointly by Pope and Warburton: the attribution of the whole to Scriblerus is awkward, since it explicitly discusses his views, which in 1742 had simply been given over his name at this point. Sir Francis Page (1661?–1741), Whig lawyer, was active as a judge until his death. His name was, perhaps undeservedly, a byword for brutality: Pope, who may have met him socially in 1739, alluded to his supposedly routine infliction of 'Hard Words or Hanging' in *Imitations of Horace* (*Corr.*: IV, 189; *Satires* II.i.82). Scriblerus is 'candid', i.e. reluctant to find fault, in declining to read the line as an attack on an individual. '*Mute*' alludes to the belief that Turkish rulers cut out the tongues of their executioners so that they could not testify against their masters.

31 and n. '*Mathesis*' personifies Mathematics. The note, initialled in 1751 as jointly by Pope and Warburton, recalls the preposterous theorising undertaken by Martinus Scriblerus (Kerby-Miller 1950: 167). Warton questions the propriety of pronouncing the word with a short (i.e. unstressed) 'e' as required by the metre (Warton 1797: V, 233).

33. extatic: frenzied.

33n. Initialled in 1751 as by Warburton, the note follows Pope's friend the anti-materialist philosopher and clergyman George Berkeley (1685–1753), Bishop of Cloyne, in deriding Newton's notion of absolute space, i.e. space conceived without reference to any body against which it could be measured (Schwartz 1979: 259–60). For Berkeley, such space would have qualities (e.g. eternity, infinity) that could properly be attributed only to God (Cajori 1962: II, 668–9). ***defaecated:*** refined.

34 and n. The note was initialled in 1751 as jointly by Pope and Warburton. To demonstrate that a square could exist which would have the same area as a given circle remains a classic eccentric project: Martinus Scriblerus had produced numerous proofs (Kerby-Miller 1950: 166).

35. Sitter suggests a pun on 'lie' (Sitter 1971: 43).

35–8 and 36n. The note, whose comments on stage censorship apply also to lines 37–42, was initialled in 1751 as jointly by Pope and Warburton. The Licensing Act of 1737 ruled that

Watch'd both by Envy's and by Flatt'ry's eye:
There to her heart sad Tragedy addrest
The dagger wont to pierce the Tyrant's breast;
But sober History restrain'd her rage,

36.] One of the misfortunes falling on Authors, from the *Act* for subjecting *Plays* to the power of a *Licenser*, being the false representations to which they were expos'd, from such as either gratify'd their Envy to Merit, or made their Court to Greatness, by perverting general Reflections against Vice into Libels on particular Persons.

39. But sober* History*] History attends on Tragedy, Satyr on Comedy, as their substitutes in the discharge of their distinct functions: the one in high life, recording the crimes and punishments of the great; the other in low, exposing the vices or follies of the common people. But it may be asked, How came *History* and *Satyr* to be admitted with impunity to minister comfort to the Muses, even in the presence of the Goddess, and in the midst of all her triumphs? A question, says *Scriblerus*, which we thus resolve: *History* was brought up in her infancy by Dulness herself; but being afterwards espoused into a noble house, she forgot (as is usual) the humility of her birth, and the cares of her early friends. This occasioned a long estrangement between her and Dulness. At length, in process of time, they met together in a Monk's Cell, were reconciled, and became better friends than ever. After this they had a second quarrel, but it held not long, and are now again on reasonable terms, and so are like to continue. This accounts for the connivance shewn to History on this occasion. But the boldness of *Satyr* springs from a very different cause; for the reader ought to know, that she alone of all the sisters is unconquerable, never to be silenced, when truly inspired and animated (as should seem) from above, for this very purpose, to oppose the kingdom of Dulness to her last breath.

---

plays had to be licensed by the Lord Chancellor. Thus the personification of tragedy, which had routinely implied parallels between historical crises and the present day, contemplates suicide; and Thalia, the Muse of Comedy, collapses as if dead, thus signalling an end to the capacity of comedy to mount any critique of the establishment. The note affects to deny such plays' specific political allusions, an ironic position in the light of Pope's assertion in 1735 in the Advertisement to *To Arbuthnot* that '*a Nameless Character can never be found out, but by its* Truth *and* Likeness'. Pope had countered Arbuthnot's unease at his attacks on individuals with the claim that 'General Satire in times of General Vice has no force, & is no Punishment ... And in my low Station, with no other Power than this, I hope to deter, if not to reform' (*Corr.*: III, 417–23; *To Arbuthnot*, especially lines 69–104).

39n. Warburton, who initialled the note in 1751, elaborates the tableau of the two dramatic genres and their non-dramatic analogues according to the ancient distinction between tragedy's role of exposing the failings of the great and comedy's those of ordinary people. The allegory attributed to Scriblerus is not entirely clear: a possible reading is that Dulness oversaw the beginnings of post-classical history in the monastic chronicles, but lost control when history was taken up by Clarendon ('espoused into a noble house'), only to regain dominion in the histories written by French ecclesiastics (and perhaps in the cleric Burnet's *History of his Own Times*). The 'second quarrel' seems to imply that promising recent efforts to write history have proved abortive. (For further background, see *TE*: V, 344.)

Warburton's eulogy of satire, the only one of 'the sisters' (Muses) who cannot be silenced because her inspiration comes 'from above', has affinities, despite its less political focus, with Pope's defiance of Walpole's regime in the role of satirist, notably at the climax of *Epilogue to the Satires* II.

And promis'd Vengeance on a barb'rous age.
There sunk Thalia, nerveless, cold, and dead,
Had not her Sister Satyr held her head:
Nor cou'd'st thou, CHESTERFIELD! a tear refuse,
Thou wept'st, and with thee wept each gentle Muse.
  When lo! a Harlot form soft sliding by,

43.] This Noble Person in the year 1737, when the Act aforesaid was brought into the House of Lords, opposed it in an excellent speech (says Mr. *Cibber*) 'with a lively spirit, and uncommon eloquence.' This speech had the honour to be answered by the said Mr. *Cibber*, with a lively spirit also, and in a manner very uncommon, in the 8th Chapter of his *Life and Manners*. And here, gentle Reader, would I gladly insert the other speech, whereby thou mightest judge between them: but I must defer it on account of some differences not yet adjusted between the noble Author and myself, concerning the *True Reading* of certain passages.

SCRIBL.

45.] The Attitude given to this Phantom represents the nature and genius of the *Italian* Opera; its affected airs, its effeminate sounds, and the practice of patching up these Operas with favourite Songs, incoherently put together. These things were supported by the sub-

---

43. CHESTERFIELD: Philip Dormer Stanhope (1694–1773), fourth Earl of Chesterfield, wit and politician, was an anti-Walpole Whig dismissed from court in 1733, partly on account of the Queen's dislike of his friendship with the King's mistress Henrietta Howard (1688–1767), who was widely regarded as a patroness of opposition interests. Hervey described his speech against the Licensing Act as 'one of the most lively and ingenious speeches ... I ever heard in Parliament, full of wit, of the genteelest satire, and in the most polished, classical style' (Sedgwick 1931: III, 738–9). Sherbo points out that his 'tear' alludes to the convention in ancient epitaphs of asking the passer-by to weep over the grave (Sherbo 1970: 510).

43n. Initialled in 1751 as jointly by Pope and Warburton. ***in a manner very uncommon:*** Pope would have been outraged by Cibber's comparison between the stabbing of Oxford by a French spy under interrogation in 1711, which left him seriously ill for some weeks, and recent attacks on Walpole's character in stage satire: Cibber argues that since reputation is as dear as life to a minister, offences against it should be treated by the law with equal severity – although never formally prosecuted, Oxford's attacker had died of injuries received during his arrest (Cibber 1740: 233–7). ***some differences:*** Parliamentary privilege forbade the direct transcription of debates, but the writer in the *Gentleman's Magazine* for 1737 claims to give a fuller version of Chesterfield's speech than had previously appeared (*Gentleman's Magazine* VII, 409–11). Scriblerus's arrogance in textual criticism will not allow him to concede that Chesterfield knows best which version is closest to the speech he actually made.

45–50 and 45n. In 1742 a note had suggested that the passage on opera was a 'detach'd piece', possibly inserted out of sequence (*TE*: V, 345). The present note was initialled in 1751 as jointly by Pope and Warburton. Older accounts of Pope's attitude to opera tended to take his views as normative, but since the 1970s a revival of scholarship and performance has given rise to more positive analysis of *opera seria* (Dorris 1967: 36–123; Dean & Knapp 1987; Strohm 1985; LaRue 1995). For Pope's antagonism towards Italian opera, see Rogers 1985: 43–54, 102–19; Ness 1986; and III.301–7; for his attitude to music in general, see Brownell 1976. *The Craftsman* had warned that Italian opera paved the way for (implicitly Hanoverian)

With mincing step, small voice, and languid eye;
Foreign her air, her robe's discordant pride
In patch-work flutt'ring, and her head aside:
By singing Peers up-held on either hand,
She tripp'd and laugh'd, too pretty much to stand;

scriptions of the Nobility. This circumstance that Opera should prepare for the opening of the grand Sessions, was prophesied of in Book 3. ver. 301: 'Already Opera prepares the way, / The sure fore-runner of her gentle sway.'

---

tyranny, and a host of objectors had stigmatised it as effeminate (since it featured highly paid women sopranos and, in male heroic roles, male castrati); un-English (since it was performed in Italian by Italians); and meaningless (since syllables were routinely extended over a long run of notes, and since most London audiences could not understand Italian). Thomas Newcomb, despite his loyalty to the Whig regime, had in his anonymously published *Bibliotheca* (1712) similarly attributed the importation of opera to his goddess Oblivion (Lund 1991: 177). Cp. also the prominent role given to 'Signior Opera' in Fielding's satire of the court of the Goddess of Nonsense in Act III of *The Author's Farce* (Fielding 1730). The connotations of opera were complicated, however, by the fact that the King and courtiers were not its only supporters: enthusiasts also included Pope's friends Burlington and Arbuthnot and the Patriot Pulteney (Carretta 1983: 145; Hammond 1984: 52; Milhous & Hume 1986; Nokes 1995: 408–9). Pope himself had attended an opera at least once (Handel's *Admeto* in 1727), but was ill the next day – whether because of the opera itself or because of the crush and the late hours is not clear (Williams 1965: III, 243–4).   ***a Harlot form:*** Pope personifies Opera at the extreme of conventional femininity, a 'Harlot' whose feebleness is calculated to beguile the 'singing Peers'. Opera could not be produced without the subscriptions of wealthy patrons, and the Royal Academy of Music, founded with royal backing in 1719 to produce opera, was in effect a joint-stock company of a kind routinely denounced by the opposition to Walpole, and one which did not escape comparison with the contemporary South Sea scheme (for the finances and management of the Academy, see Milhous & Hume 1986; Gibson 1989; for its role in Pope's early sketch of the *Dunciad*, see Mack 1984: 97–100). Opera's 'mincing step' and 'small voice', along with the 'effeminate sounds' referred to in the note, focus disapproval of the high-pitched vocal texture obtained by concentrating on soprano heroines and castrato heroes to the detriment of natural male voices (Rosselli 1992: 33–4, 125).   ***patch-work:*** So-called 'pasticcio' operas recombined the most popular arias from previous operas.   ***favourite Songs:*** The standard expression for published collections of operatic arias.   ***subscriptions of the Nobility:*** Conceivably a specific gibe at the opposition-based Opera of the Nobility (Rogers 1985: 110; but cp. the reference to opera as 'idol of the Nobility and the people' in the note to III.330, which predates the Opera of the Nobility; and for the scheme and its connotations, see editor's note on III.305–6).   ***This circumstance:*** Warburton is characteristically anxious to assert the internal coherence of *The Dunciad in Four Books*. One piece of evidence against the suspicion that Book IV is a mere afterthought which he does not use would have been the inclusion of some of its themes, including opera, in Pope's early sketch: Vander Meulen suggests that if Warburton knew about this, he may have kept silent in order to avoid compromising his claim to have been the key collaborator in the genesis of Book IV, since he had met Pope only in 1740 (Vander Meulen 1991: 59).

Cast on the prostrate Nine a scornful look,
Then thus in quaint Recitativo spoke.
  O *Cara! Cara!* silence all that train:
Joy to great Chaos! let Division reign:

54. let Division reign:] Alluding to the false taste of playing tricks in Music with numberless divisions, to the neglect of that harmony which conforms to the Sense, and applies

---

*51. **the prostrate Nine:*** the Muses.

*52. **Recitativo:*** The use of sung instead of spoken dialogue was, to many English critics, a ridiculous affectation, especially since they could not understand the words. For this reason, and because it offered relatively little melodic interest, English opera audiences seem to have been easily bored by recitative, and composers working in London were under pressure to keep it to a minimum (Dorris 1967: 42–3; Burrows 1994: 304).

53. **Cara!**: 'Dear!' Opera takes for granted her intimacy with the Goddess. Her use of Italian implies affectation. ***all that train:*** the Muses and their supporters.

*54. **great Chaos:*** Dulness's father. The address echoes D'Urfey's 1681 song, 'Joy to Great Caesar', which supported the cause of Charles II against the Whigs: see Addison in *Guardian* 67 (Stephens 1982: 254, 663–4). This was one of D'Urfey's many settings of English words to Italian tunes, which prompted Addison to comment that D'Urfey 'turned ... the Pope's Musick against himself'. A possible link between D'Urfey's song and anti-operatic satire may be that the tune of 'Joy to Great Caesar' was known as 'Farinel's ground' after its composer Michel Farinel or Farinelli (1649–after 1696), a name which may have reminded Pope of the celebrated castrato Carlo Broschi, known as Farinelli, a performer with the Opera of the Nobility (Schnapper 1957: 'Farinelli (Michel)'; Sadie 1980: 'Farinel (2)'). ***Division:*** Punning on Opera's preference for incoherence and on quickly executed vocal ornaments, which divide up the melodic line and the individual syllables of the text. Interest focused particularly on the singer's skill in ornamenting the repetition of the opening melody which formed the conclusion of the standard *da capo* aria.

54n. Initialled in 1751 as jointly by Pope and Warburton, the note runs ahead towards line 70 and pronounces on a range of complex issues relating to music, anticipating in particular the later view, now discredited, that Handel found his vocation only when he abandoned Italian opera and turned instead to English oratorio, an unstaged form of music drama usually on a sacred subject. (This seems to have been a shrewd response to market conditions on Handel's part (Deutsch 1955: 602; Taylor in Sadie & Hicks 1987: 165–81; Burrows 1994: 165–214; Smith 1995: 37–8). Pope's respect for his English word settings probably went back to at least 1718, when Gay was collaborating with Handel on *Acis and Galatea*, with Pope probably providing the text for the chamber work later revised as *Esther* (Beeks in Sadie & Hicks 1987: 209–21; Rogers in Lewis & Wood 1989: 153; Smith 1995: 277–81).) The account of Handel in 1743 remains unaltered from 1742: Handel returned from his Dublin triumph with *Messiah* in 1742, but only after the publication of *The New Dunciad*, and after *The Dunciad in Four Books* had begun to go to press. Despite Pope's fears, Handel's decision to base future London seasons on oratorio proved successful over the longer term (Burrows 1994: 280–84, 300–301). ***Alluding to the false taste:*** Asserting a natural standard of musical excellence deriving from the power of harmony over the mind, a view characteristic of early eighteenth-century English literary opinion: according to this increasingly outdated body of theory, the function of music is to imitate extra-musical phenomena and to express the passions according

Chromatic tortures soon shall drive them hence,
Break all their nerves, and fritter all their sense:

to the Passions. Mr. *Handel* had introduced a great number of Hands, and more variety of Instruments into the Orchestra, and employed even Drums and Cannon to make a fuller Chorus; which prov'd so much too manly for the fine Gentlemen of his age, that he was obliged to remove his Music into *Ireland*. After which they were reduced, for want of Composers, to practise the patch-work above mentioned.

55. Chromatic tortures] That species of the ancient music called the *Chromatic* was a variation and embellishment, in odd irregularities, of the *Diatonic* kind. They say it was invented about the time of *Alexander*, and that the *Spartans* forbad the use of it, as languid and effeminate.

---

to an agreed set of quasi-rhetorical conventions (see Bukofzer 1939; Winn 1981: 197–9, 200–201, 232–7, 241–9). In contrast, the actual practice of the century saw composers moving towards relative independence from text and notions of referentiality, unfolding structures of purely musical logic at unprecedented length (e.g. in symphony and sonata). ***Mr.* Handel *had introduced:*** It does not suit the *Dunciad*'s agenda to admit that Handel had been the most important composer of Italian opera for the London stage. Instead he is aligned with a 'manly' taste (i.e. oratorio, with 'a fuller Chorus', massed orchestration with military associations, and appreciated only in a part of the British Isles innocent of false sophistication), which is contrasted with 'false taste' (i.e. opera, with its virtuoso solo singers, effeminacy and foreignness). ***Drums and Cannon:*** The oratorio *Saul*, produced in 1739, used kettledrums (not actual 'Cannon') borrowed from the Tower of London (Sadie 1980: VIII, 95–7; Burrows 1994: 242–6). ***he was obliged:*** Contrary to older biographies, there is no evidence that bankruptcy or threatened bankruptcy impelled Handel to take his new oratorio *Messiah* to Dublin for the 1741–2 season (see index to Deutsch 1955: 'Handel, bankruptcy (alleged)'; Hume 1988; Burrows 1994: 202–14, 259–84). An official invitation from the Lord Lieutenant may have been a factor in his decision, as may the desire to avoid being pressed into unviable operatic schemes by former patrons. Contemporary reports, however, may have given Pope the impression that Handel was being driven out for good by 'fine Gentlemen' whom he had offended – conceivably by refusing to act as composer for their operatic ventures (Deutsch 1955: 515–17; and see Taylor in Sadie & Hicks 1987: 169). ***After which they were reduced:*** The practice of making up pasticcio operas from existing materials was a well-established one in which Handel had himself participated, not simply a desperate response to his absence. This note is the closest that any version of the *Dunciad* comes to acknowledging that Handel had composed operas.

55 and n. The application of 'Chromatic tortures' is problematic, since the verse seems less concerned with the internal pitch relations of the scale than with high-speed division of syllables, a concern highlighted in the 1742 reading 'My Racks and', replaced by 'Chromatic' in 1743. 'Chroma' ('quaver' in Italian) had the contemporary sense 'a graceful way of singing or playing with Quavers and Trilloes', and Pope, characteristically alert to modish foreign borrowings, may have had this sense in mind (Grassineau 1740: 27; for usage suggesting that concepts of quaver and semitone were not always distinct, see Strahle 1995: 'chroma' and 'chromatic'). The note, initialled in 1751 as by Warburton, takes the term in the more familiar sense as referring to pitch relations; but the difference between the chromatic kind of the ancients and the modern chromatic scale was not clearly understood at the time, which renders Warburton's classicising gloss problematic, despite its rhetorical utility in reinforcing the

One Trill shall harmonize joy, grief, and rage,
Wake the dull Church, and lull the ranting Stage;
To the same notes thy sons shall hum, or snore,
And all thy yawning daughters cry, *encore*.
Another Phoebus, thy own Phoebus, reigns,
Joys in my jiggs, and dances in my chains.
But soon, ah soon Rebellion will commence,
If Music meanly borrows aid from Sense:
Strong in new Arms, lo! Giant Handel stands,
Like bold Briareus, with a hundred hands;

61.] 'Tuus jam regnat Apollo.' Virg. Not the ancient *Phoebus*, the God of Harmony, but a modern *Phoebus* of *French* extraction, married to the Princess *Galimathia*, one of the handmaids of Dulness, and an assistant to Opera. Of whom see *Bouhours*, and other Critics of that nation. SCRIBL.

---

theme of effeminacy (for the difficulties experienced by Charles Burney in dealing with the chromatic in his *General History of Music*, see Lonsdale 1965: 144–9; for his uneasy but irresistible urge to assimilate ancient to modern conceptions of scale, see Mercer 1935: I, 40; for the three kinds of scale (i.e. diatonic, chromatic, enharmonic) recognised by the Greeks, see West 1992: 162). The Greeks believed that music formed character, and that the different kinds of scale had different effects: earlier writers tend to contrast the supposedly firm and plain qualities of the enharmonic with the more insinuating chromatic; but as the enharmonic became less current, theorists transferred its attributes to the diatonic, producing a polarity which could be read as a contrast between manliness and effeminacy (Mercer 1935: I, 40–42; West 1992: 246–53). Hence the military-minded Spartans are presented as condemning the chromatic kind.

57–8. Implying that opera fails to match music to mood and subject. The internal rhyme of line 58 underlines the irony of an antithesis that reduces all to a dull mediocrity of feeling; but the line also draws on the conventional assumption that church music required a restrained and reverent idiom distinct from the theatricality of the playhouse.

60. For the new custom of the 'encore' and a humorous plea for the English term 'again' to be used instead, see *Spectator* 314 (Bond 1965: III, 138–9).

61 and n. Echoing Virgil's acclamation of the returning Golden Age, 'Now your own Apollo reigns', and possibly Fielding's use of a 'modern Apollo' to oversee drama and poetry in *The Historical Register* I.i (*Eclogues* IV.10; Fielding 1737). The note, initialled in 1751 as jointly by Pope and Warburton, echoes Oldmixon's elaboration of a passage from Dominique Bouhours (1628–1702), explaining the French idiom which applied the god's name to pretentious and superficially plausible nonsense, a kind of nonsense of which opera is cited as example (Oldmixon 1728b: 365, 372). Such elaborate nonsense is then contrasted with the plain and obvious nonsense denoted by 'galimatia', a word of unknown origin whose apparent connection with things gallic the note proceeds to exploit.

65–70. Handel's status as 'one of the very few recipients of praise in the fourth book of the *Dunciad*' can be related to the range of cultural, artistic and religious concerns, including the specific political agenda of the Patriot opposition, that oratorio was seen as addressing (Smith 1995: 76 and *passim*). ***Briareus:*** In Greek mythology, a giant with 100 arms who

To stir, to rouze, to shake the Soul he comes,
And Jove's own Thunders follow Mars's Drums.
Arrest him, Empress; or you sleep no more —
She heard, and drove him to th' Hibernian shore.

And now had Fame's posterior Trumpet blown,
And all the Nations summon'd to the Throne.
The young, the old, who feel her inward sway,
One instinct seizes, and transports away.
None need a guide, by sure Attraction led,

71.] Posterior, viz. her *second* or *more certain* Report: unless we imagine this word *posterior* to relate to the position of one of her Trumpets, according to *Hudibras:* 'She blows not both with the same Wind, / But one before and one behind; / And therefore modern Authors name / One good, and t'other evil Fame.'

***75. None need a* guide, *— None want a* place,]** The sons of Dulness want no instructors in study, nor guides in life: they are their own masters in all Sciences, and their own Heralds and Introducers into all places.

---

defended Zeus against attack by other gods. ***Jove's own Thunders:*** Thunder is the attribute of the sky-god Zeus/Jupiter, assimilated in Christianising neo-classical tradition to God the Father. Thus the reference goes beyond the literal loudness of Handel's oratorio orchestra to imply, in line with the previous reference to Handel as Zeus's defender Briareus, that he speaks for God: in the 1739 oratorio *Israel in Egypt*, for example (a subject with strong opposition connotations: see Smith 1995: 213–15, 288–92), Handel uses a substantial chorus and an exceptionally large orchestra featuring drums and brass to set biblical texts highlighting the performative language of divine ordinance, thus giving expression to a conception of God's creative word crucial to the cultural values that Dulness aims to undo. The analogy between divine and human creativity is also stressed in the treatment of David's soothing of Saul's madness by his music in *Saul* (also 1739), a work which invokes conservative piety in its treatment of themes of kingship and succession which also underlie *The Dunciad in Four Books* (Smith 1995: 327–33). ***Mars's Drums:*** The kettledrums used in *Saul* could be so called with particular propriety, since they had reputedly been captured by Marlborough at the battle of Malplaquet (Deutsch 1955: 472–3). *Israel in Egypt* depicted God not only as the sky-god of the thunder imitated by drums, but also as the 'man of war' whose acts are celebrated by military brass and trumpets (Exodus 15:3), a theme related to the Patriot pressure for war with Spain to which Walpole, after long resistance, was finally forced to submit. ***Hibernian:*** Irish.

71 and n. The line looks back to the two trumpets of Fame in Chaucer's *House of Fame* (one of brass which proclaims evil reputation, and one of gold which proclaims good reputation), overlaid with the vulgar identification suggested by the approximate quotation from Butler's *Hudibras* cited in the note, initialled in 1751 as jointly by Pope and Warburton (Benson 1987: *House of Fame*, lines 1573–82, 1636–56, 1678–87; see also Pope's reworking in *The Temple of Fame*, lines 306–17, 332–41; Wilders 1967: *Hudibras* II.i.69–76).

75 and n. Dulness enacts a malign parody of the conventional moral and religious connotations of Newtonian theories of 'Attraction' and 'gravity' (Kinsley 1975). The note, initialled in 1751 as jointly by Pope and Warburton, passes over the political sense of 'none want a place' (line 77), with its gibe at the appointment of Dulness's sons to public office.

And strong impulsive gravity of Head:
None want a place, for all their Centre found,
Hung to the Goddess, and coher'd around.
Not closer, orb in orb, conglob'd are seen
The buzzing Bees about their dusky Queen.
  The gath'ring number, as it moves along,
Involves a vast involuntary throng,
Who gently drawn, and struggling less and less,
Roll in her Vortex, and her pow'r confess.

76 to 101.] It ought to be observed that here are three classes in this assembly. The first of men absolutely and avowedly dull, who naturally adhere to the Goddess, and are imaged in the simile of the Bees about their Queen. The second involuntarily drawn to her, tho' not caring to own her influence; from ver. 81 to 90. The third of such, as, tho' not members of her state, yet advance her service by flattering Dulness, cultivating mistaken talents, patronizing vile scriblers, discouraging living merit, or setting up for wits, and Men of taste in arts they understand not; from ver. 91 to 101. In this new world of Dulness each of these three classes hath its appointed station, as best suits its nature, and concurs to the harmony of the System. The *first* drawn only by the strong and simple impulse of Attraction, are represented as falling directly down into her; as conglobed into her substance, and resting in her centre: 'All their centre found, / Hung to the Goddess, and coher'd around.' The *second*, tho' within the sphere of her attraction, yet having at the same time a different motion, they are carried, by the composition of these two, in planetary revolutions round her centre, some nearer to it, some further off: 'Who gently drawn, and struggling less and less, / Roll in her Vortex, and her pow'r confess.' The *third* are properly *excentrical*, and no constant members of her state or system: sometimes at an immense distance from her influence, and sometimes again almost on the surface of her *broad effulgence*. Their use in their Perihelion, or nearest approach to Dulness, is the same in the moral World, as that of *Comets* in the natural, namely to refresh and recreate the Dryness and decays of the system; in the manner marked out from ver. 91 to 98.

76–101n. This note, typically Warburtonian in its schematising and generalising tendency, was in 1751 divided into two: down to 'ver. 91 to 101' it was initialled as jointly by Pope and Warburton; the remainder was claimed by Warburton. ***to own:*** to admit. **excentrical:** moving at an irregular distance from the centre of the system. ***Perihelion:*** the point at which a heavenly body comes closest to the sun. **Comets:** Newton suggested that the tails of comets attracted by planetary gravity might be the source of the atmospheric moisture essential to maintain life (Cajori 1962: II, 529–30, *Principia Mathematica* III, Proposition XLI, Problem XXI).

79–80. Dulness is likened to a queen bee, which both recalls her role as parody of Ceres, patroness of bees, and alludes to her wider political influence through an ironic reference to the commonplace comparison of the hive to a well-ordered state (Brooks-Davies 1985: 16, 28). Aspirants to fame are compared to bees both in Chaucer's *House of Fame* and in Pope's *Temple of Fame* (Benson 1987: *House of Fame*, lines 1520–25; *Temple of Fame*, lines 282–7).

82. Involves: In the literal sense of rolling them in.

84. Vortex: Dulness is imaged as a cosmic whirlpool drawing in victims, implying an allusion to the theory of solar and planetary vortices advanced by the philosopher René Descartes

Not those alone who passive own her laws,
But who, weak rebels, more advance her cause.
Whate'er of dunce in College or in Town
Sneers at another, in toupee or gown;
Whate'er of mungril no one class admits,
A wit with dunces, and a dunce with wits.
  Nor absent they, no members of her state,
Who pay her homage in her sons, the Great;
Who false to Phoebus, bow the knee to Baal;
Or impious, preach his Word without a call.
Patrons, who sneak from living worth to dead,

***93. false to* Phoebus,]** Spoken of the ancient and true *Phoebus*, not the *French Phoebus*, who hath no chosen Priests or Poets, but equally inspires any man that pleaseth to sing or preach. SCRIBL.

(1596–1650) (Nicolson & Rousseau 1968: 199–206; Kinsley 1975: 27; and see editor's note on 475–6).

85–6. There is an underlying political allusion to factors sustaining the Hanoverian status quo. 'Passive obedience' towards the monarch was traditionally impressed on the subject by Church of England teaching (i.e. the subject was bound not to resist, if not actively to cooperate with, acts of the monarch which he could not in conscience approve): regarded as a Tory doctrine (hence a focus of debate in 1688), it here acts ironically as a scruple supportive of the Hanoverian establishment, bringing into awkward focus the conflict between that establishment and such traditional doctrines of royal succession and authority. To insist on that conflict could imply, for committed Whigs, that Tories were potential traitors; or, for Jacobites, that the Stuarts should be restored. Line 86, however, hints at the evident truth that unsuccessful Jacobite plots and risings merely served to entrench the current regime: Walpole was adept at using the Jacobite threat to discredit any kind of opposition (compare Erskine-Hill 1996: 105).

88. Fashionable town dunces wear the 'toupee', an elaborate wig featuring a top-knot; college dunces wear the academic 'gown' (for Pope's decision fifteen years earlier not to use the then-new word 'toupee' in the three-book *Dunciad*, see Mack 1984: 100; for satirical comment in *Peri Bathous*, see *PW*: II, 207).

89. mungril: mongrel.

91–2. The construction is not entirely clear: the Warburtonian note on 99–100 takes 'The idolizers of Dulness in the Great' as subject of the sentence.

93 and n. Baal: A god worshipped by the Canaanite neighbours of the Israelites, who periodically turned to such cults. The couplet suggests that the misapplication of artistic patronage is equivalent to such apostasy. ***the ancient and true* Phoebus:** For the distinction, see original note and editor's note on line 61.

94. Alluding to the blasphemy of preaching not from a genuine vocation but for personal advancement.

95–6. Conventional mockery of patrons who spend on the commemoration of dead writers money with which they could have helped them while alive (cp. *To Arbuthnot*, lines 231–48). Queen Caroline's setting up of five busts in her Grotto at Richmond in 1732 had prompted the comment that 'Our frugal Queen to save her Meat / Exalts the Heads that cannot eat' (Williams 1958: II, 662–3).

With-hold the pension, and set up the head;
Or vest dull Flatt'ry in the sacred Gown;
Or give from fool to fool the Laurel crown.
And (last and worst) with all the cant of wit,
Without the soul, the Muse's Hypocrit.
  There march'd the bard and blockhead, side by side,
Who rhym'd for hire, and patroniz'd for pride.
Narcissus, prais'd with all a Parson's pow'r,
Look'd a white lilly sunk beneath a show'r.

99, 100.] In this division are reckoned up I. The Idolizers of Dulness in the Great — 2. Ill Judges, — 3. Ill Writers, — 4. Ill Patrons. But the *last and worst,* as he justly calls him, is the *Muse's Hypocrite,* who is as it were the Epitome of them all. He who thinks the only end of poetry is to amuse, and the only business of the poet to be witty; and consequently who cultivates only such trifling talents in himself, and encourages only such in others.

---

97. Alluding to ecclesiastical patrons who repay flattery with preferment, as in the promotion of White Kennett (see editor's note on II.144). It may, however, be relevant here that Pope told Spence he had drafted, but decided to omit, a couplet for Book IV which named Alured Clarke (1696–1742), Dean of Exeter: 'Let Clarke make half his life the poor's support; / But let him give the other half to Court' (*OAC*: I, 148). Clarke was a royal chaplain and protégé of Queen Caroline, whose death in 1737 he lamented in a fulsome memoir (the anonymously published *An Essay towards the Character of her Late Majesty Caroline* 1738, alluded to in *Epilogue to the Satires* II.164–5). The remark to Spence suggests that although Pope thought there was more praise than blame in his couplet, he was uneasy that he might be seen as attacking a man as celebrated for his charities as he was notorious for place-seeking.

98. Alluding to the transfer of the laureateship from Eusden, appointed by the first Duke of Newcastle in 1718, to Cibber, appointed by the second Duke of Grafton in 1730. Cp. the final lines of a satirical ballad, thought by Ault to be by Pope, in which Cibber is made to draw an analogy between his own situation and that of the King: 'So shall the *Crown,* and *Laurel* too, / Descend from F—l to F—l' (Ault 1949: 318).

99–100n. Initialled in 1751 as by Warburton. ***this division:*** i.e. from line 91.

103–4. Cp. Dryden's 'Like a white Poppy sinking on the Plain, / Whose heavy Head is overcharg'd with Rain', and Pope's translation of the death of a Homeric warrior: 'As full blown Poppies overcharg'd with Rain / Decline the Head, and drooping kiss the Plain; / So sinks the Youth' (Kinsley 1958: III, *Aeneid* IX.583–4; Pope's *Iliad* VIII.371–3). Lord Hervey had been fulsomely flattered by the 'Parson' Conyers Middleton (1683–1750) in the dedication to his *History of the Life of Marcus Tullius Cicero* (1741), to which Pope and Warburton were subscribers. A long-standing friendship between Middleton and Warburton was coming under increasing strain at this time owing to differences of opinion on the history of religion (Evans 1932: Index, 'Middleton, Conyers'). Pope had satirised Middleton's style in *Epilogue to the Satires* (I.73–6). Like the classical Narcissus, who fell in love with his own reflection in water, Hervey is attracted by the image of himself reflected in Middleton's eulogy. Narcissus was transformed into the white flower that bears his name: Hervey, who never enjoyed robust health, and nursed himself on a diet of milk and vegetables, presented a languid image readily assimilated to satire of his bisexuality (Halsband 1973: 56–7). Compared to Pope's attack on Hervey as Sporus, the present couplet is markedly restrained (*To Arbuthnot,* lines 305–33).

There mov'd Montalto with superior air;
His stretch'd-out arm display'd a Volume fair;
Courtiers and Patriots in two ranks divide,
Thro' both he pass'd, and bow'd from side to side:
But as in graceful act, with awful eye
Compos'd he stood, bold Benson thrust him by:
On two unequal crutches propt he came,
Milton's on this, on that one Johnston's name.
The decent Knight retir'd with sober rage,

***110. bold* Benson]** This man endeavoured to raise himself to Fame by erecting monuments, striking coins, setting up heads, and procuring translations, of *Milton*; and afterwards by a great passion for *Arthur Johnston*, a *Scotch* physician's Version of the Psalms, of which he printed many fine Editions. See more of him, Book 3. ver. 325.

105–8. For Sir Thomas Hanmer, who had quarrelled with Warburton over their respective aspirations as editors of Shakespeare, see editor's note on the original note on the title, which immediately precedes the original commentary on the first line of Book I. By calling him 'Montalto', Pope implies a loftiness of demeanour which Sutherland suggests may allude to Hanmer's habit of processing to church with his household while his tenants stood ranked on either side (*TE*: V, 351). The 'Volume fair' alludes to Hanmer's lavish edition of Shakespeare: he presented his concern with its appearance as what was owed to the author's dignity, but Pope and Warburton suggest that the editor's vanity is really at stake (Evans 1932: 147–55; Hanmer 1743–4; Jarvis 1995: 83). Hanmer's bowing equally to the court party and to the Patriot opposition alludes to his refusal, as a Hanoverian Tory, to commit himself unambiguously to either party.

110–12 and n. The note was initialled in 1751 as jointly by Pope and Warburton. For Benson, see editor's note on III.325. He is 'bold' in that he dedicated his edition of the Latin translation of the Psalms by the physician and protégé of the Stuart court Arthur Johnston (1587–1641) to the future George III (Johnston 1741). Benson testified his admiration for Milton by erecting a monument in Westminster Abbey, by commissioning a commemorative medal, and by paying £1000 for a translation of *Paradise Lost* into Latin. The text of the Milton monument could only have annoyed Pope, since it stressed Benson's personal initiative in commemorating the poet, and his Hanoverian credentials as servant of George I and II (Dobson 1992: 137). His sponsorship of the translation of *Paradise Lost* may also have annoyed Pope, since the translator had previously been engaged to translate the *Essay on Man*; but Pope agreed to let him break off the arrangement so that he could take up Benson's more lucrative offer (*OAC*: I, 137–8). Benson's devotion to Johnston was shown by publishing his Psalms at his own expense, with Benson's own *Prefatory Discourse* to the work, and by commissioning a bust (Johnston 1741; *A Prefatory Discourse to a New Edition of the Psalms* 1741). For evidence of his connoisseurship in Latin prosody, collected, ironically, by Pope's friend Spence, see *OAC*: I, 364–7.

113–14 and 114n. Lines 113–14 may allude to Hanmer's claim to have given up thoughts of financing an edition of Shakespeare – which in an attempt to pacify Warburton, he implied was to have been Warburton's, not his own – when he found out how expensive it would be (Evans 1932: 152–5). Warburton did not believe him, and later echoed the language of the note to line 114 (initialled in 1751 as jointly by Pope and Warburton) when he stated that

'What! no respect, he cry'd, for Shakespear's page?'
But (happy for him as the times went then)
Appear'd Apollo's May'r and Aldermen,
On whom three hundred gold-capt youths await,
To lug the pond'rous volume off in state.
  When Dulness, smiling — 'Thus revive the Wits!
But murder first, and mince them all to bits;
As erst Medea (cruel, so to save!)
A new Edition of old Aeson gave.
Let standard-Authors, thus, like trophies born,

114, etc. Sh —— r's page?] An Edition of that Author, with his Text arbitrarily altered throughout, was at this time printing at the University Press by the encouragement of the Vice-Chancellor, and certain Heads of Houses, who subscribed for three hundred, to be taken off by the Gentlemen Commoners.

119.] The Goddess applauds the practice of tacking the obscure names of Persons not eminent in any branch of learning, to those of the most distinguished Writers; either by printing *Editions* of their works with impertinent alterations of their Text, as in the former instances, or by setting up *Monuments* disgraced with their own vile names and inscriptions as in the latter.

***122. old* Aeson]** Of whom Ovid (very applicably to these restored authors): '*Aeson* miratur, / *Dissimilemque animum* subiit'.

Hanmer 'was at the expence of his purse in procuring cuts [illustrations] for his edition; and at the expence of his reputation in employing a number of my emendations on the text, without my knowledge or consent' (pp. 147–51).

115–18. In some ordinary copies of 1743, but not in the luxury large paper copies, these lines are replaced by asterisks, inserted on a cancel. They refer to the scheme for financing Hanmer's Shakespeare described in 114n. (*Corr.*: IV, 438–9). By referring to the Vice-Chancellor and heads of houses as 'Apollo's May'r and Aldermen' ('one of Dr. Warburton's witticisms', according to contemporary suspicions recorded by Warton (Warton 1797: V, 257)), Pope implies that they have brought themselves down to the level of the City dignitaries ridiculed in previous books of the *Dunciad*. The 'gold-capt youths' are gentlemen commoners, wealthy undergraduates distinguished by gold tassels on their caps. Pope was also angry with the University of Oxford because it had in 1741 offered honorary doctorates to him and to Warburton, but had then reneged on the offer to Warburton because of objections from his enemies in the university (*Corr.*: IV, 357, 436–7). Pope responded by refusing the honour for himself.

119n. Initialled in 1751 as jointly by Pope and Warburton.

121–2 and 122n. The note was initialled in 1751 as jointly by Pope and Warburton. Warton records but does not confirm contemporary suggestions that Warburton composed these lines (Warton 1797: V, 257). The sorceress Medea rejuvenated the aged Aeson by cutting his throat and replacing his blood with a magic potion. The quotation from Ovid awkwardly combines parts of two widely separated lines: the sense is to the effect that 'Aeson was amazed, and remembered how different he used to be' (*Metamorphoses* VII.170, 292).

123–4. Punning on two senses of 'standard', i.e. received texts of canonical authors, and military banners – which would be revered precisely for the damage which testifies to the danger of the battles in which they have been carried.

Appear more glorious as more hack'd and torn,
And you, my Critics! in the checquer'd shade,
Admire new light thro' holes yourselves have made.
  Leave not a foot of verse, a foot of stone,
A Page, a Grave, that they can call their own;
But spread, my sons, your glory thin or thick,
On passive paper, or on solid brick.
So by each Bard an Alderman shall sit,
A heavy Lord shall hang at ev'ry Wit,
And while on Fame's triumphal Car they ride,
Some Slave of mine be pinion'd to their side.
  Now crowds on crowds around the Goddess press,

128.] For what less than a Grave can be granted to a dead author? or what less than a Page can be allow'd a living one?

Ibid. A Page,] *Pagina*, not *Pedissequus*. A Page of a Book, not a Servant, Follower, or Attendant; no Poet having had a *Page* since the death of Mr. Thomas Durfey. SCRIBL.

131.] Vide the *Tombs of the Poets*, Editio Westmonasteriensis.

125–6. Cp. Milton's 'many a youth, and many a maid, / Dancing in the chequered shade' (Carey 1968: 'L'Allegro', lines 95–6), and Waller's reflection on the wisdom of old age: 'The soul's dark cottage, battered and decayed, / Lets in new light through chinks that time has made' (Drury 1893: II, 'Of the Last Verses in the Book', lines 13–14).

128n. The note, initialled in 1751 as jointly by Pope and Warburton, alludes to the aged D'Urfey's habit of going about attended by a servant, to which Steele had drawn teasing attention by implying that a man of his noble lineage (he was descended from French aristocrats) might more properly have been attended by a whole retinue (Blanchard 1959: 142). The note also touches – somewhat ironically in view of D'Urfey's associations with popular rather than high culture – on the theme of the social debasement of a once dignified vocation.

131–2 and n. The note, initialled in 1751 as jointly by Pope and Warburton, directs attention to poets' monuments in Westminster Abbey ('in the Westminster Edition'). For Benson's monument to Milton, see lines 110–12 and editor's note. Barber, a wealthy printer and alderman, had erected a monument to Samuel Butler which recorded that he had been responsible for it (*TE*: VI, 396). Although Barber was ostensibly on good terms with Pope, Warburton testified that he had offended Pope by offering him money to compliment him in verse (*OAC*: I, 161). Of Shakespeare's monument, erected in 1741 with Pope as one of its sponsors, Pope wrote: 'THUS Britain lov'd me; and preserv'd my Fame, / Clear from a *Barber*'s or a *Benson*'s Name' (*TE*: VI, 395–7). Pope is said to have insisted that this monument should be credited simply to 'amor publicus' ('public esteem'): the organisers, intent on implying that the people were more committed to their heritage than the regime that purported to represent them, had raised a public subscription (*Gentleman's Magazine* XI, 105; Dobson 1992: 135–9).

133–4. A Roman triumph included one of the victor's chained captives. Horace Walpole cites Juvenal's satire of the pomp of a consul: 'at, sibi consul / ne placeat, curru servus portatur eodem' ('and, lest the consul should feel too pleased with himself, a slave rides in the same chariot': *Satires* X.41–2; Fraser 1876: 96).

Each eager to present the first Address.
Dunce scorning Dunce beholds the next advance,
But Fop shews Fop superior complaisance.
When lo! a Spectre rose, whose index-hand
Held forth the Virtue of the dreadful wand;

137, 138.] This is not to be ascribed so much to the different manners of a Court and College, as to the different effects which a pretence to Learning, and a pretence to Wit, have on Blockheads. For as Judgment consists in finding out the *differences* in things, and Wit in finding out their *likenesses*, so the Dunce is all discord and dissension, and constantly busied in *reproving, examining, confuting, etc.* while the Fop flourishes in peace, with Songs and Hymns of Praise, *Addresses, Characters, Epithalamiums, etc.*

140. the dreadful wand;] A Cane usually born by Schoolmasters, which drives the poor Souls about like the wand of Mercury. SCRIBL.

---

136. Address: A testimonial of loyalty offered to a ruler.

137–8n. Initialled in 1751 as by Warburton.

138. complaisance: courtesy, deference.

139–74. The first to address Dulness is a schoolmaster, presented as laying the foundations for her reign by confining boys to learning words by rote, and by discouraging the exploration of the realities which it is implied they ought to represent (for the perceived threat of the separation of words from things, see Williams 1955: 111–23). An early manuscript draft of Book II had made educators boast to Dulness of 'what they have done in bringing up ye Youth to such Ends for ye Next Age' (Mack 1984: 127). Pope's schoolmaster alludes to the traditional perception of Richard Busby (1606–95), headmaster of Westminster School almost half a century earlier, whose reliance on the then usual methods of memorisation, verse composition in the classical languages and flogging did not prevent many of his pupils (e.g. Dryden, Atterbury and Locke) from going on to do creative and original work in adult life (for Busby and contemporary education, see Rivers 1979; for his regime and its impact on Dryden, see Winn 1987: 36–47; for the sexual and cultural connotations of schoolboy floggings, see Straub 1992: 69–80). Pope uses Busby to focus a vision of narrowly verbal pedantry which leads easily into the more topical caricature of Bentley from line 203. A satirical analogy between the recitation of lessons by rote at Westminster School and in the nearby House of Commons may also be implied (Carretta 1983: 152).

The satire on schools – first conceived as part of a projected cycle of philosophical poems – needs to be set in the context of Pope's exclusion from the system by his religion: for the most part he had educated himself at home with some early help from a tutor, largely by reading and translating in pursuit of his own enthusiasms, a method which fed directly into his early attempts at composition; and he felt in contrast that he had learned little from his brief spells at illegal Catholic schools – although even there he had found time to develop such creative pursuits as drawing, and writing and producing a play (*OAC*: I, 8–15, 21–2, 151; Leranbaum 1977: 131–50; Mack 1985: 44–52). Yet the benefits of self-education had come at the price of exclusion; and it seems no accident that Busby's brilliant pupils are passed over, while his rote-learning is made to usher in Walpole's world of words emptied of truth. See also Rousseau in Rousseau & Rogers 1988: 199–239 (especially pp. 216–20 on parallels with the educational views of Busby's pupil Locke); and for a political reading, Carretta 1983: 146–61.

139. index-hand: right hand (from its use in pointing).

140 and n. Virtue: power. ***wand of Mercury:*** *Odyssey* XXIV opens with the god Hermes

His beaver'd brow a birchen garland wears,
Dropping with Infant's blood, and Mother's tears.
O'er ev'ry vein a shudd'ring horror runs;
Eton and Winton shake thro' all their Sons.
All Flesh is humbled, Westminster's bold race
Shrink, and confess the Genius of the place:
The pale Boy-Senator yet tingling stands,
And holds his breeches close with both his hands.
  Then thus. Since Man from beast by Words is known,
Words are Man's province, Words we teach alone.
When Reason doubtful, like the Samian letter,

148.] An effect of Fear somewhat like this, is described in the 7th Aeneid: 'Contremuit nemus ... / Et trepidae matres pressere ad pectora natos', nothing being so natural in any apprehension, as to lay close hold on whatever is suppos'd to be most in danger. But let it not be imagined the author would insinuate these youthful Senators (tho' so lately come from school) to be under the undue influence of any *Master*. SCRIBL.

151. like the Samian letter,] The letter *Y*, used by Pythagoras as an emblem of the different roads of Virtue and Vice: 'Et tibi quae Samios diduxit litera ramos.' Persius.

(called Mercury by the Romans) using his golden wand to drive the spirits of the recently dead from the world of the living into the underworld. The note was initialled in 1751 as jointly by Pope and Warburton.

141. beaver'd brow: Felt hats were made of compressed beaver fur: a portrait of Busby shows him wearing one with a very wide brim (reproduced in Winn 1987: 38). Busby, though a zealous royalist, was supposed to have kept his hat on when showing Charles II round the school, so as not to undermine his pupils' belief in his supreme authority. ***birchen:*** Made of birch, used for beating schoolboys.

142. Recalling Milton's image of the god Moloch, 'horrid king besmeared with blood / Of human sacrifice, and parents' tears, / ... / Their children's cries unheard, that passed through fire / To his grim idol' (Fowler 1998: *Paradise Lost* I.392–6).

144. Pupils of Eton and Winchester shudder at remembered floggings, an indication that the satire is intended not simply of Busby's regime at Westminster, but of elite schools in general. For the idiom, compare '*Troy*, at the Loss, thro' all her Legions shook' (Pope's *Iliad* XVI.672).

147–8 and 148n. Boy-Senator: Even after they have entered parliament, ex-pupils instinctively cringe at fear of punishment. The note on 148, initialled in 1751 as jointly by Pope and Warburton, develops the implication that when such young men leave school Walpole takes on the absolute power of a Busby over them, making a nonsense of their supposed role as representatives of a free people. ***Contremuit nemus ....:*** 'The grove shuddered – and trembling mothers hugged their children to their breasts' (*Aeneid* VII.515, 518). ***any* Master:** Alluding to Walpole's management of parliament.

151–2 and n. The note was initialled in 1751 as jointly by Pope and Warburton. Pythagoras was supposedly from Samos: his allegory originally referred to the different angles of ascent of the branches of the character as written in antiquity, the path of virtue being the steeper; but the present allusion is overlaid by an ironic reference to the biblical injunction to 'Enter ye in at the strait gate: for ... narrow is the way, which leadeth into life' (Matthew 7:13–14).

Points him two ways, the narrower is the better.
Plac'd at the door of Learning, youth to guide,
We never suffer it to stand too wide.
To ask, to guess, to know, as they commence,
As Fancy opens the quick springs of Sense,
We ply the Memory, we load the brain,
Bind rebel Wit, and double chain on chain,
Confine the thought, to exercise the breath;
And keep them in the pale of Words till death.
Whate'er the talents, or howe'er design'd,
We hang one jingling padlock on the mind:
A Poet the first day, he dips his quill;

153.] This circumstance of the *Genius Loci* (with that of the Index-hand before) seems to be an allusion to the *Table of Cebes*, where the Genius of human Nature points out the road to be pursued by those entering into life. *Ὁ δὲ γέρων ὁ ἄνω ἑστηκὼς ἔχων χάρτην τινὰ ἐν τῇ χειρὶ, καὶ τῇ ἑτέρᾳ ὥσπερ δεικνύων τί οὗτος Δαίμων καλεῖται, etc.*

159. to exercise the breath;] By obliging them to get the classic poets by heart, which furnishes them with endless matter for Conversation, and Verbal amusement for their whole lives.

162.] For youth being used like Pack-horses and beaten on under a heavy load of Words, lest they should tire, their instructors contrive to make the Words jingle in rhyme or metre.

Ramsay explains the Pythagorean allegory in his note on the passage cited from Persius, 'and to you is known the letter which spreads its branches' (Persius, *Satires* III.56).

153n. The note, initialled in 1751 as jointly by Pope and Warburton, looks back to lines 139 and 146, where 'Genius Loci' is rendered by referring to Busby as 'the Genius of the place'. The 'Table of Cebes' is a Greek allegorical text, an exposition of an imaginary picture, implausibly ascribed to Cebes, an associate of Socrates. The passage cited runs: 'The old man standing up here – who has a scroll in one hand and who appears to be pointing at something with the other – is called Daimon' (for commentary see Fitzgerald & White 1983: IV).

157. ply: use, work vigorously at.

159n. Initialled in 1751 as jointly by Pope and Warburton.

160. pale: enclosure.

161. howe'er design'd: whatever career the pupils are intended to take up. Their education takes no more account of the varying demands life will make of them than it does of their varying talents.

162. Alluding to the conclusion of Prior's 'An English Padlock', which advises a jealous husband to give up the futile attempt to keep his wife in confinement, and instead to leave her free to find out by experience how much her marriage is to be preferred to the shallow promiscuity of the fashionable world: this is recommended as the only way to 'clap your PADLOCK – on her Mind' (Bawcutt 1958: 221; Wright & Spears 1971: I, 229).

162n. The note, initialled in 1751 as by Warburton, likens the versified mnemonics used in rote-learning to the bells put onto draught horses' bridles – a comparison which Pope had applied to his poetry in a letter of 1713 (*Corr.*: I, 191).

163. Alluding to standard exercises in verse composition, whether in the classical languages, or from them into English.

And what the last? a very Poet still.
Pity! the charm works only in our wall,
Lost, lost too soon in yonder House or Hall.
There truant WYNDHAM ev'ry Muse gave o'er,
There TALBOT sunk, and was a Wit no more!
How sweet an Ovid, MURRAY was our boast!
How many Martials were in PULT'NEY lost!
Else sure some Bard, to our eternal praise,
In twice ten thousand rhyming nights and days,
Had reach'd the Work, the All that mortal can;

***166. in yonder* House *or* Hall.*]** Westminster-hall and the House of Commons.

167–70. Implying that all four devoted themselves to something more important than elegant versification: all were associated with political opposition. Sir William Wyndham (1687–1740), a lifelong Tory, educated at Eton, was Chancellor of the Exchequer under Anne, partisan of Bolingbroke and conspirator in the Jacobite rising of 1715, leader of the Tory opposition under George I and George II, and hence a key figure in the Patriot alliance. His death prompted Pope to bitter reflections on how little the so-called Patriots he led seemed to mourn him (Gerrard 1994: 91). Charles Talbot (1685–1737), Baron Talbot, a Whig, also educated at Eton, had been Solicitor-General and was in 1733 appointed Lord Chancellor by Walpole, but became disaffected when his ecclesiastical protégé was refused preferment on account of the theological objections of Walpole's high-church ecclesiastical adviser Edmund Gibson (Gerrard 1994: 27–30). Talbot was Thomson's patron, and his son emerged in 1734 as a member of the Prince of Wales's opposition. His 'Sense' is cited as proverbial in *Imitations of Horace, Epistles* II.ii.134. William Murray (1705–93), later first Earl of Mansfield, a Tory, was educated at Westminster, and despite the Jacobitism of other members of his family, became Solicitor-General in 1742 and later Attorney-General and Lord Chancellor. As an undergraduate he was distinguished for his skill in Latin; and his eloquence as a lawyer was widely praised. A close friend of Pope and his adviser on copyright law, praised in *Imitations of Horace*, he was also Martha Blount's legal adviser (*Imitations of Horace, Odes* IV.i.9–30, *Epistles* II.ii.131–2). Pulteney, a Whig, also educated at Westminster, was an enthusiast for the classics with a lively taste for verbal wit, and had been a friend of Gay (Nokes 1995: 252–3). In 1725 he quarrelled with Walpole, and soon joined Bolingbroke in the Patriot opposition; but widespread suspicions of his sincerity were borne out when in 1742, in the scramble for office that followed Walpole's fall, he was created Earl of Bath and abandoned the Patriot programme (*OAC*: I, 152–3; Gerrard 1994: 12, 19, 44–5). Pope wrote that 'He foams a Patriot to subside a Peer' (*One Thousand Seven Hundred and Forty*, line 10). During his Patriot phase Pulteney was noted for his witty and versatile contributions to *The Craftsman*, including epigrams, which prompts the comparison with Martial.

173–4 and 174n. The note was initialled in 1751 as jointly by Pope and Warburton. Dryden had begun the Dedication of his *Aeneid* translation with a conventional tribute to the supremacy of epic: 'A heroick Poem, truly such, is undoubtedly the greatest Work which the Soul of Man is capable to perform', a sentiment echoed by Pope in *Peri Bathous* (Kinsley 1958: 1003; *PW*: II, 228). South, a celebrated royalist preacher, sought to commend brevity in prayer (in contrast with what he saw as the extempore ramblings of dissenters) by analogy with other disciplines, e.g. 'in matters of wit, and the finenesses of imagination, *epigram*'; and he con-

And South beheld that Master-piece of Man.
Oh (cry'd the Goddess) for some pedant Reign!

174. that Master-piece of Man.] viz. an *Epigram*. The famous Dr. *South* declared a perfect Epigram to be as difficult a performance as an Epic Poem. And the Critics say, 'an Epic Poem is the greatest work human nature is capable of.'

175.] The matter under debate is how to confine men to Words for life. The instructors of youth shew how well they do their parts; but complain that when men come into the world they are apt to forget their Learning, and turn themselves to useful Knowledge. This was an evil that wanted to be redressed. And this the Goddess assures them will need a more extensive Tyranny than that of Grammar schools. She therefore points out to them the remedy, in her wishes for *arbitrary Power*; whose interest it being to keep men from the study of *things*, will encourage the propagation of *words* and *sounds*; and to make all sure, she wishes for another *Pedant Monarch*. The sooner to obtain so great a blessing, she is willing even for once to violate the fundamental principle of her politics, in having her sons taught at least *one thing*; but that sufficient, the *Doctrine of Divine Right*.

Nothing can be juster than the observation here insinuated, that no branch of Learning

---

cluded that in each discipline 'brevity and succinctness of speech' exemplified 'the greatest and the noblest things that the mind of man can show the force and dexterity of its faculties in' (South 1842: I, 338). The note attempts to wrest this into a perverse attack on the hierarchy of genres.

175–88. Dulness evokes the memory of James I, implying a connection between his advocacy of the divine right of kings (the doctrine that kings were chosen by God and answerable only to God) and his alleged pedantry, a connection contextualised by the commentary's polarisation of 'words' against 'things' and 'learning' against 'knowledge'. (For the sexual and cultural politics of Pope's treatment of James, see Straub 1992: 80–82; for a similar account in Thomson's *Liberty*, IV.956–81, see Sambrook 1986: 118–19; Carretta 1983: 149–51.) Pope told Spence that his reign 'was absolutely the worst reign we ever had – except perhaps that of James the Second' (*OAC*: I, 242–3). The condemnation of the political legacy of the founder of the Stuart line helps to counterbalance the equivocating criticism of the Hanoverians and the evasive play with Jacobite allusions that characterise the *Dunciad*. The scorn expressed in this section and its commentary for key principles of traditional Toryism is in line with Bolingbroke's focusing of the Patriot opposition around the claim that the old distinctions between Whig and Tory were no longer meaningful, and that the true division was now between those who accepted the absolutism implicit in Walpole's control of parliament and those prepared to defend parliamentary independence as a necessary part of the balance of the constitution (*A Dissertation upon Parties* 1735: 235–42; Murray 1968; Dickinson 1970: 184–211; Gerrard 1994: 75; and for Walpole as '*Tibbald* of the State', see *The State Dunces* 1733 and Jarvis 1995: 86). The use of the language of divine right in verse panegyrics on George II and Caroline, the reassertion by George II of his hereditary right, and the stress on the subject's obedience in coronation sermons also show that the Hanoverians were ready to appropriate traditional figurations of royal privilege despite the anomaly of their succession (Gerrard 1994: 173, 188–9). ***pedant Reign:*** An ironic juxtaposition of royal status with the lowly profession of schoolmaster. The note on line 176 cites two anecdotes in which James I implicitly demeans himself by taking this role.

175n. Initialled in 1751 as by Warburton. ***amuse:*** divert, distract. ***Cardinal Richelieu:*** Armand-Jean du Plessis (1585–1642), Cardinal Richelieu, chief minister of Louis XIII.

Some gentle JAMES, to bless the land again;

thrives well under Arbitrary government but *Verbal*. The reasons are evident. It is unsafe under such Governments to cultivate the study of things of importance. Besides, when men have lost their public virtue, they naturally delight in trifles, if their private morals secure them from being vicious. Hence so great a Cloud of Scholiasts and Grammarians so soon overspread the Learning of Greece and Rome, when once those famous Communities had lost their Liberties. Another reason is the *encouragement* which arbitrary governments give to the study of *words*, in order to busy and amuse active genius's, who might otherwise prove troublesome and inquisitive. So when Cardinal Richelieu had destroyed the poor remains of his Country's liberties, and made the supreme Court of Parliament merely *ministerial*, he instituted the *French Academy*. What was said upon that occasion, by a brave Magistrate, when the letters-patent of its erection came to be verified in the Parliament of Paris, deserves to be remembered: He told the assembly, that *this adventure put him in mind after what manner an Emperor of Rome once treated his Senate; who when he had deprived them of the cognizance of Public matters, sent a message to them in form for their opinion about the best Sauce for a Turbot.*

176.] Wilson tells us that this King, *James* the first, took upon himself to teach the Latin tongue to Car, Earl of Somerset; and that Gondomar the Spanish Ambassador wou'd speak false Latin to him, on purpose to give him the pleasure of correcting it, whereby he wrought himself into his good graces.

This great Prince was the first who assumed the title of *Sacred Majesty*, which his loyal Clergy transfer'd from *God* to *Him*. 'The principles of Passive Obedience and Non-resistance (says the Author of the Dissertation on Parties, Letter 8.) which before his time had skulk'd perhaps in some old Homily, were talk'd, written, and preach'd into vogue in that inglorious reign.'

---

merely* ministerial:** purely executive (i.e. of the royal will), rather than representative of the people. There is a glance at Walpole, familiarly known as 'the Minister'. For Richelieu's contest with what remained of France's representative institutions, see Knecht 1991: 135–41. ***he instituted the* French Academy:** For this aspect of Richelieu's mobilisation of patronage in the service of royal prestige, see Knecht 1991: 190–93. The Academy's best-known function was to lay down rules for French grammar and spelling. ***the letters-patent of its erection came to be verified: the royal edict ('patent' in being addressed to the public rather than to an individual) declaring the foundation of the Academy came to the parliament to be ratified (i.e. not debated). **an Emperor of Rome:** Juvenal tells how the tyrannical Emperor Domitian received a turbot so large that it would have been deemed treasonable for any mere subject to eat it, and how the senators, with a prudent concern for their personal safety, solemnly deliberated as to the best method of cooking it (Juvenal, *Satires* IV).

176n. The note, initialled in 1751 as jointly by Pope and Warburton, cites anecdotes implying that James I compromised the dignity of a king by behaving like a schoolmaster. He is said to have undertaken to educate the pageboy Robert Carr (*c.*1587–1645), who became his favourite and was created Earl of Somerset in 1613; and he is also said to have laid himself open to an ambiguous compliment from the Spanish ambassador, who used to make mistakes in his Latin deliberately so that he could offer the King the ostensible compliment that he 'spoke Latin like a Pedant, but I speak it like a Gentleman' (Wilson 1653: 54–5, 145). ***The principles of Passive Obedience and Non-resistance:*** The traditional high-Tory political precepts that obliged subjects to renounce active opposition to the royal will. Bolingbroke, author of the *Dissertation*, which had first appeared as letters to *The Craftsman*, was seeking to distance the Patriot opposition from the high-Tory doctrines that would previously have seemed the obvious alternative to Whig ideology (and that were awkwardly associated with the Jacobitism Bolingbroke had previously espoused (Dickinson 1970: 134–53)). He argued

To stick the Doctor's Chair into the Throne,
Give law to Words, or war with Words alone,
Senates and Courts with Greek and Latin rule,
And turn the Council to a Grammar School!
For sure, if Dulness sees a grateful Day,
'Tis in the shade of Arbitrary Sway.

181, 182.] And grateful it is in Dulness to make this confession. I will not say she alludes to that celebrated verse of Claudian, 'nunquam *Libertas* gratior extat / Quam sub *Rege pio*'. But this I will say, that the words *Liberty* and *Monarchy* have been frequently confounded and mistaken one for the other by the gravest authors. I should therefore conjecture, that the genuine reading of the forecited verse was thus, 'nunquam *Libertas* gratior exstat / Quam sub *Lege* pia', and that *Rege* was the reading only of Dulness herself: And therefore she might allude to it. SCRIBL.

I judge quite otherwise of this passage: The genuine reading is *Libertas,* and *Rege:* So Claudian gave it. But the error lies in the first verse: It should be *Exit,* not *Exstat,* and then the meaning will be, that Liberty was never *lost,* or *went away* with so good a grace, as under a good King: it being without doubt a tenfold shame to lose it under a bad one.

This farther leads me to animadvert upon a most grievous piece of nonsense to be found in all the Editions of the Author of the Dunciad himself. A most capital one it is, and owing to the confusion above mentioned by Scriblerus, of the two words *Liberty* and *Monarchy*. Essay

---

instead that the real threat of absolutism now lay in Walpole's corruption of parliament through his control of places and pensions (*A Dissertation upon Parties* 1735: xx–xxiii, 81, 241–2; for the relation of such Patriot polemic to established traditions of Whig and Tory argument, see Pocock 1985: 215–53; Gerrard 1994: 3–45).

177. Doctor: In the etymological sense of 'teacher'.

178. James I had no taste for an aggressive foreign policy, preferring to rest his reputation on maintaining peace.

180. Council: The Privy Council, which advised the monarch on policy.

181–2 and n. The note, initialled in 1751 as jointly by Pope and Warburton, puns on 'grateful', used by Dulness in its etymological sense of 'pleasant' and by the note in its more modern sense of 'expressing thanks'. Scriblerus then picks up the root word *gratis* in a quotation from Claudian traditionally associated with defences of patriarchal authority in the state: 'Liberty never shows itself to better effect than under a good king' ('De Consulatu Stilichonis' III.114–15; Murray 1968). He argues that liberty and monarchy are words easily confused (an indirect attack on flatterers of royal power, 'the gravest authors' who defend authoritarian government), and suggests that Claudian really meant *lex* ('law') rather than *rex* ('king'). 'Bentley' (in real life a Whig) then suggests a rival emendation, which brings his commitment to liberty into doubt insofar as he seems to regard it as acceptable for it to be lost under a good king, thus aligning him with the court Whiggery decried by Bolingbroke. ***This farther leads me:*** Lines 90–91 of *An Essay on Criticism* had up to 1743 read 'Monarchy', reflecting the now distant context of the poem's composition in the reign of Anne; 'Bentley's' 'Liberty', which Pope actually introduced in the edition of 1744 (printed at the same time as *The Dunciad in Four Books* and often bound with it), was more in line with the terms of constitutional debate as redefined by Pope's Patriot friends (*TE*: I, 249). The second line of the couplet is also slightly altered as given in the note; but this is not reflected in editions of the *Essay*. The usual joke against 'Bentley' for forcing in emendations '*repugnantibus omnibus*' ('even

O! if my sons may learn one earthly thing,
Teach but that one, sufficient for a King;
That which my Priests, and mine alone, maintain,
Which as it dies, or lives, we fall, or reign:
May you, may Cam, and Isis preach it long!
'The Right Divine of Kings to govern wrong.'
  Prompt at the call, around the Goddess roll
Broad hats, and hoods, and caps, a sable shoal:
Thick and more thick the black blockade extends,
A hundred head of Aristotle's friends.

on Crit.: 'Nature, like *Monarchy*, is but restrain'd / By the same Laws herself at first ordain'd.' Who sees not, it should be, *Nature like* Liberty? Correct it therefore *repugnantibus omnibus* (even tho' the Author himself should oppugn) in all the impressions which have been, or shall be, made of his works. Bentl.

192.] The Philosophy of *Aristotle* had suffered a long disgrace in this learned University:

---

though all the authorities oppose it') is complicated by the fact that 'Liberty' is, by this date, Pope's own chosen reading. 'Bentley' pointedly defies 'the Author himself', but Pope denies him the pleasure of a contest.

185. mine alone: Identifying clergy who still preach traditional doctrines of submission to the royal will as agents of Dulness – but whereas this might at one time have been understood only of high Tories and Jacobites, it now points primarily, according to Bolingbroke's redefinition of absolutism, at court Whigs among the clergy.

187. The Universities of Cambridge and Oxford, metonymically identified by their rivers. An early manuscript draft of Book II had already specified the universities among its targets, and indicates that Bentley had originally been envisaged as speaking for Cambridge, with a blank left for an equivalent spokesman for Oxford (Mack 1984: 127).

188. The doctrine of divine right did not, technically speaking, give the king the right to do wrong; but it did insist that it was for God alone (not for his subjects) to judge him. The distinction carried little weight with advocates of the rights of representative institutions.

190. Broad hats, and hoods, and caps: As worn by scholars in universities. ***shoal:*** Punning on the connected term 'school'.

192 and n. The note, initialled in 1751 as by Warburton, oversimplifies for polemical ends a complex situation in the teaching of philosophy at Oxford, where controversy focused on the challenge to traditional methods of academic disputation posed by Locke's advocacy of empirically based reasoning (Aston 1984–94: V, Ch. 20; see also line 196). Whereas up to the eighteenth century the typical manuals of logic used in teaching had been 'compendia, essentially of Aristotle's and later scholastic logical principles and rules', from the middle of the eighteenth century there appeared manuals based on Locke, whose works 'were in almost every college' (pp. 575–6, 591). In 1703 Bodley's librarian had asked him in flattering terms to provide copies of his works for the Bodleian Library, and Locke had been glad to oblige: the meeting of heads of houses in that year alluded to in the note on line 196 was merely an unofficial and ineffective rearguard action by traditionalists (De Beer 1976–89: VII, 743–4, 755; VIII, 220–22, 269–70). For Pope's resentment of the University's recent snub to Warburton, see editor's note on lines 115–18. ***this learned University:*** Oxford.

being first expelled by the *Cartesian*, which, in its turn, gave place to the *Newtonian*. But it had all this while some faithful followers in secret, who never bowed the knee to *Baal*, nor acknowledged any strange God in Philosophy. These, on this new appearance of the Goddess, come out like Confessors, and make an open profession of the ancient faith in the *ipse dixit* of their Master. Thus far SCRIBLERUS.

But the learned Mr. *Colley Cibber* takes the matter quite otherwise; and that this *various fortune of Aristotle* relates not to his *natural*, but his *moral* Philosophy. For speaking of that University in his time, he says, *they seemed to have as implicit a Reverence for Shakespear and Johnson, as formerly for the* ETHICS *of Aristotle*. See his Life, p. 385. One would think this learned professor had mistaken *Ethics* for *Physics*; unless he might imagine the Morals too were grown into disuse, from the relaxation they admitted of during the time he mentions, *viz.* while He and the Players were at Oxford.

Ibid. A hundred head, etc.] It appears by this the Goddess has been careful of keeping up a Succession, according to the rule, 'Semper enim refice: ac ne post amissa requiras, / Anteveni; et sobolem *armento* sortire *quotannis*'. It is remarkable with what dignity the Poet here describes the *friends* of this ancient Philosopher. Horace does not observe the same decorum with regard to those of another sect, when he says *Cum ridere voles Epicuri de* grege *Porcum*. But the word *Drove*, *Armentum*, here understood, is a word of honour, as the most noble *Festus* the *Grammarian* assures us, *Armentum id genus pecoris appellatur, quod est idoneum opus* armorum. And alluding to the temper of this *warlike breed*, our poet very appositely calls them *a hundred head*. SCRIBL.

Cartesian: As taught by Descartes. ***who never bowed the knee to* Baal:** Likening these reactionaries to the saving remnant of Israel who refused to worship the foreign god Baal (1 Kings 19:18). ***like Confessors:*** With all the dignity of those who have suffered for their faith. ***the* ipse dixit *of their Master:*** The Aristotelians are dismissed as bigots who have no interest in empirical enquiry: for them it is enough to cite Aristotle's words to prove a proposition ('ipse dixit', 'he himself has said'). ***the learned Mr.* Colley Cibber:** Mocking Cibber for his slip in implying that it was Aristotle's moral rather than philosophical and scientific teaching that was now considered outmoded (Cibber 1740: 385). **Johnson:** Ben Jonson. ***It appears by this:*** Drawing attention to Pope's counting of the academics as if they were cattle by citing Virgil's advice on selective breeding: 'Therefore, always renew your stock: and so that you don't regret afterwards what you've lost, think ahead, and select young stock for the herd every year' (*Georgics* III.70–71). ***Horace does not observe the same decorum:*** Arguing that *grex* is a less dignified word than *armentum* for a herd – though the contempt in Pope's use of 'head', once extracted from the honorific 'head of house', is obvious. Horace was referring playfully to himself, telling a friend 'If you feel like laughing, laugh at me, a pig from Epicurus's herd' (*Epistles* IV.16). ***the most noble* Festus *the* Grammarian:** Sextus Pompeius Festus (second century AD) transcribed part of the otherwise lost *De Significatu Verborum* ('On the Meaning of Words') by Verrius Flaccus (*d.* AD 14), who, as the tutor chosen by Augustus for the imperial household, was respected as an authority on Latin usage of what was considered its best period. He comments that 'That kind of livestock is called a herd [*armentum*, which the note renders as 'drove', and which Festus derives from *arma*, 'weapons'] which is most apt for warfare', the point presumably being that cattle seem better equipped for aggression than sheep (Lindsay 1913: 4). Thus Scriblerus demonstrates that this is the correct term for university Aristotelians.

Nor wert thou, Isis! wanting to the day,
[Tho' Christ-church long kept prudishly away.]
Each staunch Polemic, stubborn as a rock,
Each fierce Logician, still expelling Locke,
Came whip and spur, and dash'd thro' thin and thick
On German Crouzaz, and Dutch Burgersdyck.
As many quit the streams that murm'ring fall

194.] This line is doubtless spurious, and foisted in by the impertinence of the Editor; and accordingly we have put it between Hooks. For I affirm this College came as early as any other, by its *proper Deputies*; nor did any College pay homage to Dulness in its *whole body*.
BENTL.

196.] In the year 1703 there was a meeting of the heads of the University of Oxford to censure Mr. Locke's Essay on Human Understanding, and to forbid the reading it. See his Letters in the last Edit.

198.] There seems to be an improbability that the Doctors and Heads of Houses should ride on horseback, who of late days, being gouty or unweildy, have kept their coaches. But these are horses of great strength, and fit to carry any weight, as their German and Dutch extraction may manifest; and very famous we may conclude, being honour'd with *Names*, as were the horses Pegasus and Bucephalus. SCRIBL.

199. the streams] The River Cam, running by the walls of these Colleges, which are particularly famous for their skill in Disputation.

---

193. Implying that Oxford was well represented.

194 and n. Pope exempts Christ Church from the initial rush towards Dulness in compliment to its attack on Bentley, under Atterbury's direction, in the Phalaris controversy. The note, initialled in 1751 as jointly by Pope and Warburton, is attributed to 'Bentley', who cannot agree, and therefore decides (as in the celebrated case of Milton) that the offending line is an interpolation. His claim that Christ Church entered Dulness's service 'by its *proper Deputies*' alludes to the prominence of its members in ridiculing Bentley's (correct) assertion that the so-called letters of Phalaris could not be genuine (Levine 1991: 47–84). The last part of the note may reflect a desire on Warburton's part to exempt his own friends in Oxford from criticism.

195. Polemic: controversialist.

196 and n. See editor's note on line 192 and n.

198 and n. Crouzaz: Jean Pierre de Crousaz (1663–1750), actually Swiss. A philosopher and mathematician, he attacked Pope's *Essay on Man*, which he knew only in translation, as an example of modern secularising heresy, and thus furnished Warburton with an opportunity to recommend himself to Pope by defending his orthodoxy (Mack 1985: 736–9). ***Burgersdyck:*** Francis Burgersdijk (1590–1635), Dutch professor of philosophy, produced manuals of scholastic philosophy for the use of Protestants which were still in use in Oxford in the mid-eighteenth century (Aston 1984–94: V, 584–5). ***But these are horses of great strength:*** The note, initialled in 1751 as jointly by Pope and Warburton, relies on the traditional caricature of Germanic intellectuals as heavy and tedious. Pegasus was the mythical winged horse representing poetic inspiration; Bucephalas ('ox-head') was the favourite horse of Alexander the Great.

To lull the sons of Marg'ret and Clare-hall,
Where Bentley late tempestuous wont to sport
In troubled waters, but now sleeps in Port.
Before them march'd that awful Aristarch;
Plow'd was his front with many a deep Remark:
His Hat, which never vail'd to human pride,
Walker with rev'rence took, and lay'd aside.

202. sleeps in Port.] viz. 'now retired into harbour, after the tempests that had long agitated his society.' So *Scriblerus*. But the learned *Scipio Maffei* understands it of a certain Wine called *Port*, from *Oporto* a city of Portugal, of which this Professor invited him to drink abundantly. SCIP. MAFF. *de Compotationibus Academicis*.

205–8.] The Hat-worship, as the Quakers call it, is an abomination to that sect: yet, where it is necessary to pay that respect to man (as in the Courts of Justice and Houses of Parliament) they have, to avoid offence, and yet not violate their conscience, permitted other people to uncover them.

---

200. Marg'ret and Clare-hall: St John's College, Cambridge (Bentley's undergraduate college), founded by Lady Margaret Beaufort, and Clare College, Cambridge (not the more recently founded Clare Hall).

201–2 and 202n. It seems that Pope first conceived a speech by Bentley on education as part of Book II: the early manuscript draft is even more explicit in connecting Bentley with political corruption (Mack 1982: 340–41; Mack 1984: 127–8; for the wider context of Pope's antagonism, see Levine 1991: 241–4; for similarities with Thomas Newcomb's anonymously published *Bibliotheca* (1712), see Lund 1991: 174–5). He is introduced with a reminiscence of his controversy as Master of Trinity College, Cambridge, with the Fellows over the extent of their respective privileges (for the litigation, which had ended only in 1738, see Monk 1833: II, Index, 'Trinity College'). The pun on 'Port' (see Tillotson 1950: 153–4) alludes to his particular fondness for it (Monk 1833: II, 401). The note, initialled in 1751 as jointly by Pope and Warburton, refers to a visit made to the aged Bentley in Cambridge in 1736 by the Italian poet and historian Scipio Maffei (1675–1755), Marquis of Verona, an advocate of a nationalist reformation of the Italian theatre of particular interest to the Patriot opposition, who was also warmly received by Prince Frederick and by Pope, who, however, concluded that Maffei did not live up to his reputation (*OAC*: I, 236; Gerrard 1994: 51, 53). Maffei's travelling companion reported that Bentley appeared to be devoting his retirement entirely to alcohol, hence the spoof title *de Compotationibus Academicis* ('On Academic Drinking Parties') (Dorris 1967: 235–6).

204. Recalling Satan's battle-scars ('his face / Deep scars of thunder had intrenched') and the furrowed brow of Beelzebub ('deep on his front engraven / Deliberation sat and public care': Fowler 1998: *Paradise Lost* I.600–601; II.302–3). 'Remark' typically figured in the titles of polemics such as those published by Bentley and his opponents – although it could also denote commentary on a text (as in the original layout of the 1743 commentary, which distinguished 'Remarks' from 'Imitations').

205–6 and 205–8n. Aristarchus would presumably have kept his hat on in Dulness's presence had it not been removed for him (Bentley apparently wore a wide-brimmed hat to shade his eyes, even indoors: see Monk 1833: II, 401). Richard Walker (1679–1764), Vice-Master of Trinity, took his side in the contest with the Fellows (II, Index, 'Walker, Richard'). Monk records

Low bow'd the rest: He, kingly, did but nod;
So upright Quakers please both Man and God.
Mistress! dismiss that rabble from your throne:
Avaunt —— is Aristarchus yet unknown?
Thy mighty Scholiast, whose unweary'd pains
Made Horace dull, and humbled Milton's strains.
Turn what they will to Verse, their toil is vain,
Critics like me shall make it Prose again.
Roman and Greek Grammarians! know your Better:

207. He, kingly, did but nod;] Milton: 'He, kingly, from his State / Declin'd not'.

210. is* Aristarchus *yet unknown?] 'Sic notus *Ulysses?*' Virg. 'Dost thou not feel me, *Rome?*' Ben. Johnson.

Ibid. Aristarchus] A famous Commentator, and Corrector of Homer, whose name has been frequently used to signify a complete Critic. The Compliment paid by our author to this eminent Professor, in applying to him so great a Name, was the reason that he hath omitted to comment on this part which contains his own praises. We shall therefore supply that loss to our best ability. SCRIBL.

215.] Imitated from Propertius speaking of the Aeneid: 'Cedite, *Romani* scriptores, cedite *Graii!* / Nescio quid majus *nascitur Iliade.*'

---

how Bentley, annoyed by a guest at dinner, called Walker to bring his hat and left abruptly (II, 406–7). The note, which looks ahead to lines 207–8 and was initialled in 1751 as jointly by Pope and Warburton, had in 1742 accused Quakers more directly of hypocrisy: such a slur is out of keeping with Pope's usual willingness to recognise virtue among Quakers (cp. *Epilogue to the Satires* I.131–40; II.94–7). Binfield, where Pope spent his adolescence, sheltered Quakers as well as Roman Catholic recusants; and he owned a presentation copy of a defence of Quaker doctrine (Mack 1982: 311).

207 and n. Aristarchus's pride refuses a full obeisance even to the Goddess. The Miltonic allusion is to the archangel Michael, coming to tell Adam of his expulsion from Eden: 'Adam bowed low, he kingly from his state / Inclined not' (Fowler 1998: *Paradise Lost* XI.249–50).

208. upright: Punning on the physical and moral senses.

210 and n. Avaunt: Be off! The expression is both archaic and rude. ***Sic notus* Ulysses:** When the Trojans welcome the wooden horse, only Laocoön realises that their experience of Odysseus's guile suggests that it is a trap, and he asks 'Is this what you know about Odysseus?' (*Aeneid* II.44). The opening line of Jonson's *Catiline* evokes the dead tyrant whose ghost is speaking (Herford & Simpson 1925–52: V, 435). ***A famous Commentator:*** This part of the note was initialled in 1751 as jointly by Pope and Warburton.

212. Alluding to Bentley's edition of Horace (1711), and of Milton's *Paradise Lost* (1732), which 'humbled' many lines of Milton by denouncing them as the work of an interpolator (but for Pope's incorporation of Bentley's readings into the text printed with his *Imitations of Horace*, see Bloom 1948; for the value of Bentley's tough reading to Milton criticism, see Ricks 1963: Index, 'Bentley, R.'; and for a rhetorical reading of the interpolator figure, see Brink 1986: 82).

213–14. Although Bentley's exceptional sensitivity to poetic rhythms underlay some of his most striking emendations (see Brink 1986: 63 and editor's note on lines 217–18).

215n. Propertius pays Virgil's *Aeneid* the compliment 'Make way, Roman writers, make way you Greeks! Something greater than the *Iliad* is coming to birth' (*Elegies* II.xxxiv.65–6). Pope

Author of something yet more great than Letter;
While tow'ring o'er your Alphabet, like Saul,
Stands our Digamma, and o'er-tops them all.
'Tis true, on Words is still our whole debate,
Disputes of *Me* or *Te*, of *aut* or *at*,
To sound or sink in *cano*, O or A,

217, 218.] Alludes to the boasted restoration of the Aeolic Digamma, in his long projected Edition of Homer. He calls it *something more than Letter*, from the enormous figure it would make among the other letters, being one Gamma set upon the shoulders of another.

220. of Me *or* Te,*]* It was a serious dispute, about which the learned were much divided, and some treatises written: Had it been about *Meum* or *Tuum* it could not be more contested, than whether at the end of the first Ode of Horace, to read, Me *doctarum hederae praemia frontium*, or, Te *doctarum hederae* —

---

had applied the lines to the *Dunciad* in a letter to Swift in 1728, commenting, 'I mean than *my Iliad*; and I call it *Nescio quid*, which is a degree of modesty; but however if it silence these fellows, it must be something greater than any Iliad in Christendome' (*Corr.*: II, 481).

216–18 and 217, 218n. Echoing a deflating context for such eminence from the translation of Addison's Latin mock-heroic 'The Battel of the Pygmies and Cranes': 'the MONARCH of the *Pygmy* Throng ... / Tow'rs o'er his Subjects, and o'erlooks 'em all. / A *Giant-Pygmy*, whose high Spirits swell, / Elated with the Size of *half an Ell*' (Addison 1719: 40; for Sutherland's attribution of the translation to Thomas Newcomb, see *TE*: V, 364).

The note was initialled in 1751 as jointly by Pope and Warburton. Bentley realised that some awkward metrical effects in Homeric verse could be accounted for by positing the disappearance from the language, before the text came to be written down, of a consonant essential to the original metrical scheme. This consonant, equivalent to 'w', was called the digamma ('double gamma') from its resemblance to one gamma written above another, and is hence called 'yet more great than Letter' (Monk 1833: II, 360–67; Brink 1986: 76). The printer of Bentley's Milton, having no type for it, used upper-case F to represent it, thus making it out of scale with his other Greek letters (Bentley 1732: Homeric quotation in note on p. 212; see Kinsley in Mack & Winn 1980: 723–4). It may seem surprising that Pope should disparage a discovery that so powerfully enhanced Homer's claim to poetic artistry – although Bentley did carry his theory to excess by proposing to insert the digamma where it was not needed. ***like Saul:*** When the Israelites insisted on having a king, God chose Saul: 'from his shoulders and upward he was higher than any of the people' (1 Samuel 9:2).

220 and n. An expanded version of this note was initialled in 1751 as by Warburton. ***of* Me *or* Te:** whether the object of the verb is 'me' or 'you'. ***of* aut *or* at:** 'either' or 'but'. **Meum *or* Tuum:** 'mine or yours'. ***at the end of the first Ode of Horace:*** Addressed to Horace's patron, the passage may be translated 'As for me, the ivy that is the reward of skilled heads exalts me among the gods above' (*Odes* I.i.29–30). If 'me' were changed to 'te', the ivy wreath would be transferred from poet to patron. For the suggestion that 'Dr. Douglas was preparing a Treatise on this Subject, but was prevented by his Death', see Dyce 7747; see also editor's note on lines 393–4.

221–2 and 222n. According to Warburton, who initialled this note as his in 1751, the satire reflects Pope's annoyance over a tedious evening spent with John Carteret (1690–1763), later first Earl Granville. A Whig, he joined the Patriot opposition but after Walpole's fall success-

Or give up Cicero to C or K.
Let Freind affect to speak as Terence spoke,
And Alsop never but like Horace joke:

222.] Grammatical disputes about the manner of pronouncing Cicero's name in Greek. It is a dispute whether in Latin the name of Hermagoras should end in *as* or *a*. Quintilian quotes Cicero as writing it *Hermagora*, which Bentley rejects, and says Quintilian must be mistaken, Cicero could not write it so, and that in this case he would not believe Cicero himself. These are his very words: *Ego vero Ciceronem ita scripsisse ne Ciceroni quidem affirmanti crediderim. — Epist. ad Mill. in fin. Frag. Menand. et Phil.*

223, 224.] Dr. Robert Freind, master of Westminster-school, and canon of Christ-church — Dr. Anthony Alsop, a happy imitator of the Horatian style.

---

fully regained the favour of George II. Educated at Westminster School and Christ Church, he was an admirer of Bentley and prided himself on his classical expertise. Warburton told Spence that when Carteret met Pope, 'the two hours were wholly taken up by his Lordship in debating and settling how the first verse in the *Aeneid* was to be pronounced (Canò), and whether we should say Cicero or Kikero' (Monk 1833: II, 324, 364; *OAC*: I, 149–50). The point of the first controversy is that Latin metres are organised around quantity, i.e. the classification of syllables as either long or short: although reconstruction of the historical pronunciation of Latin verse is problematic and contemporary distinctions between quantity and stress hard to pin down, it appears that English readers have often assimilated the patterns to native habits of stress and pronunciation (Attridge 1974: 7–40). Spence's grave accent suggests that Carteret made the second syllable long (perhaps stressed) and the first short (perhaps unstressed) – neither of which would have been at all controversial (pp. 13, 21–2). Warburton's claim that the issue about the pronunciation of 'Cicero' related to the pronunciation of the Roman name *in Greek* may reflect a confusion with the point following (the Latin rendition of Greek names), since neither line 222 nor Warburton's testimony to Spence mentions Greek. There has been much controversy as to whether the Romans pronounced 'c' as hard or soft: the current consensus is that it was hard, but in familiar names and phrases the traditional soft pronunciation persists. There may be a reference to the mispronunciation of 'Cibber' as 'Kibber' which Pope seems to have encouraged (Tucker 1959; Rogers 1993b: 704). ***Grammatical:*** 'linguistic', 'philological'. ***Hermagoras:*** 'Hermagoras' has the usual nominative ending for a Greek noun of its class. No class of Latin nouns has 'as' in the nominative, but one class has 'a'. The Roman rhetorician Quintilian (Marcus Fabius Quintilianus, *b. c.* AD 35), states that Latin writers including Cicero took advantage of this to accommodate such Greek names to Latin usage by dropping the 's' (*Institutio Oratoria* I.v.61–2). ***which Bentley rejects:*** Bentley pointed out that Cicero used the 's' in a number of comparable Greek names, suggested that Quintilian had seen a corrupt manuscript, and concluded, in the words loosely quoted in the note, 'But I would not have believed that Cicero wrote it like that even if Cicero had told me so himself' ('Epistola ad Joannem Millium': 70, as printed with Bentley 1713).

223–4 and n. The note was initialled in 1751 as jointly by Pope and Warburton. Although Aristarchus's contempt may seem to imply a compliment to Robert Freind (1667–1751) and Anthony Alsop (1671?–1726), both of whom were educated at Westminster (of which Freind became headmaster) and Christ Church (where they joined the attack on Bentley over

For me, what Virgil, Pliny may deny,
Manilius or Solinus shall supply:
For Attic Phrase in Plato let them seek,
I poach in Suidas for unlicens'd Greek.
In ancient Sense if any needs will deal,
Be sure I give them Fragments, not a Meal;
What Gellius or Stobaeus hash'd before,
Or chew'd by blind old Scholiasts o'er and o'er.

226. Manilius or Solinus] Some Critics having had it in their choice to comment either on Virgil or Manilius, Pliny or Solinus, have chosen the worse author, the more freely to display their critical capacity.

228, etc. Suidas, Gellius, Stobaeus] The first a Dictionary-writer, collector of impertinent facts and barbarous words; the second a minute Critic; the third an author, who gave his Common-place book to the public, where we happen to find much Mince-meat of old books.

232.] These taking the same things eternally from the mouth of one another.

Phalaris), Pope told Spence, 'Those two lines on Alsop and Freind have more of satire than of compliment in them, though I find they are generally mistaken for the latter only' (*OAC*: I, 150). The implication is presumably that their classicism amounts to pedantic excess. An early manuscript draft of III.191–4 seems to class Alsop alongside Bentley (Mack 1984: 125).

225–6 and 226n. The note, initialled in 1751 as jointly by Pope and Warburton, makes explicit the assumption that only authors of the traditional canon are worthy of critical attention. Bentley had published an edition of the poem on astrology by Marcus Manilius (*fl.* early first century AD: Bentley 1739). The note implies that critics choose to work on authors like Manilius or the summariser of works on geography and natural history Julius Solinus (probably writing around AD 200) only because their obscurity allows free play to critical ingenuity.

227–8 and 228n. Attic: The dialect of Attica (around Athens) enjoyed particular prestige and came to form the basis of the language as used throughout the Greek empire. ***poach:*** Cp. Oldham: 'Turn o're dull *Horace*, and the Classick Fools, / To poach for Sense' (Brooks & Selden 1987: 'A Satyr. ... Dissuading the Author from the Study of Poetry', lines 222–3). ***Suidas:*** The name traditionally but mistakenly thought to be that of the author of a Greek literary encyclopaedia (now known as *The Suda*), edited in 1710 by the German scholar Ludolph Küster (1670–1716), assisted by Bentley (Monk 1833: I, 154, 190). It preserved excerpts from a wide range of lost texts. 'Unlicens'd' implies that the usage of periods other than that which sets the approved standard is less than legitimate. ***The first a Dictionary-writer:*** The note, initialled in 1751 as jointly by Pope and Warburton, disparages *The Suda*, along with the compilations made by Aulus Gellius (*c.* AD 130–180?) and Johannes Stobaeus (early fifth century AD), both of which preserve extracts from texts that are otherwise lost. 'Impertinent' ('irrelevant') and 'barbarous' deny value to fragments actually invaluable for reconstructing the history of language.

229. Implying that he is more interested in the forms of words than in the 'sense' they express.

231. See editor's note on lines 227–8.

232n. Initialled in 1751 as jointly by Pope and Warburton.

The critic Eye, that microscope of Wit,
Sees hairs and pores, examines bit by bit:
How parts relate to parts, or they to whole,
The body's harmony, the beaming soul,
Are things which Kuster, Burman, Wasse shall see,
When Man's whole frame is obvious to a *Flea*.
  Ah, think not, Mistress! more true Dulness lies
In Folly's Cap, than Wisdom's grave disguise.
Like buoys, that never sink into the flood,
On Learning's surface we but lie and nod.

239, 240.] By this it would seem the Dunces and Fops mentioned ver. 137, 138. had a contention of rivalship for the Goddess's favour on this great day. Those got the start, but these make it up by their Spokesmen in the next speech. It seems as if Aristarchus here first saw him advancing with his fair Pupil. SCRIBL.

241, 242.] So that the station of a *Professor* is only a kind of legal Noticer to inform us where the *shatter'd hulk* of Learning lies at anchor; which after so long unhappy navigation,

---

233. Cp. Pope's 'Thoughts on Various Subjects': 'The eye of a Critick is often like a Microscope, made so very fine and nice, that it discovers the atoms, grains, and minutest particles, without ever comprehending the whole, comparing the parts, or seeing all at once the harmony' (*PW*: II, 164; and see editor's note on line 238). Microscopes enjoyed a vogue as curiosities among people not otherwise interested in scientific investigation: Pope took his mother to see one as a curiosity, and Martha Blount had one of her own (*Corr.*: I, 465).

237. Kuster: See editor's note on lines 227–8. ***Burman:*** Bentley's friend the Dutch scholar Peter Burman (1668–1741) had arranged for the first publication of his emendations of Menander and Philemon (*Philargyrii Cantabrigiensis emendationes* 1711). ***Wasse:*** The Cambridge scholar Joseph Wasse (1672–1738) had, like Bentley, aided Küster in his work on *The Suda*, and had published editions of Sallust (1710) and the Greek historian Thucydides (*c*.457–*c*.399 BC) (1731). He and Bentley admired each other's learning (Monk 1833: II, 169–70).

238. Cp. *Essay on Man* I.193–6: 'Why has not Man a microscopic eye? / For this plain reason, Man is not a Fly. / Say what the use, were finer optics giv'n, / T' inspect a mite, not comprehend the heav'n?' The image emphasises the connection between the literary insistence on a unified and professedly comprehensive sense of the meaning of ancient literature – a possibility undermined by the historical specificity and interest in non-canonical authors of the new philologists – and the religious and philosophical need to affirm an overarching coherence and purpose in the universe. The ability to perceive such large structures is characterised as distinctively human: philologists are perversely labouring to rejoin the lower animals.

239–40n. Initialled in 1751 as by Warburton.

241–2 and n. The note, initialled in 1751 as by Warburton, attempts awkwardly to tie the allusion specifically to Bentley, ignoring both his death and the prompt appointment of a new Master of Trinity (see *TE*: V, 366–7, 472). Warburton cites Horace's address to the ship of state: 'Don't you see how your sides are stripped of their oars? You have no sails that are still in one piece; you have no gods to call on when you are in trouble again. Though made of Pontic pine, daughter of a noble forest, you boast a descent and a name which can do you no good' (*Odes* XIV.3–4, 9–13). The emphasis given to 'genus' ('descent') and 'nomen inutile' ('useless name') is Warburton's, perhaps suggesting both that Bentley belongs to a useless cat-

Thine is the genuine head of many a house,
And much Divinity without a *Νοῦς*.
Nor could a BARROW work on ev'ry block,
Nor has one ATTERBURY spoil'd the flock.

and now without either Master or Patron, we may wish, with Horace, may *lie there still.*

——— *Nonne vides, ut*
Nudum remigio latus?
—— *non tibi sunt integra lintea;*
Non Dî, *quos iterum pressa voces malo,*
Quamvis pontica pinus,
Sylvae filia nobilis,
Jactes et genus, *et* nomen inutile. Hor. SCRIBL.

244.] A word much affected by the learned Aristarchus in common conversation, to signify *Genius* or natural *acumen*. But this passage has a farther view: *Νοῦς* was the Platonic term for *Mind*, or the *first Cause*, and that system of Divinity is here hinted at which terminates in blind Nature without a *Νοῦς*: such as the Poet afterwards describes (speaking of the dreams of one of these later Platonists): 'Or that *bright Image* to our Fancy draw, / Which *Theocles* in raptur'd Vision saw, / That *Nature* ...' *etc.*

245, 246. Barrow, Atterbury,] Isaac Barrow Master of Trinity, Francis Atterbury Dean of Christ-church, both great Genius's and eloquent Preachers; one more conversant in the sublime Geometry, the other in classical Learning; but who equally made it their care to advance the polite Arts in their several Societies.

---

egory (that of textual critic) and that his academic rank and title had proved useless in his contest for supremacy in Trinity College. Presumably Warburton intends the ship to stand for the College, and the warning buoy for Bentley, who retained a professorship even when the legality of his mastership had been brought into doubt (see editor's note on lines 201–2).

243–4. Warton records but does not confirm contemporary suggestions that Warburton composed these lines, 'as containing some common cant words peculiar to the university' (Warton 1797: V, 257). ***genuine head:*** Probably alluding to Bentley's contested status as head of Trinity, although the line goes on to spread the accusation more widely. *Νοῦς:* Greek for 'mind' (pronounced to rhyme with 'house'), a key term in Neoplatonic doctrine. The line puns on the notion of someone who has studied theology without attaining wisdom, and a theology that does away with the principle of a divine mind underlying existence (Kropf 1973: 593–602).

244n. The note, initialled in 1751 as jointly by Pope and Warburton, begins by accusing Bentley of pedantically using Greek in conversation, but goes on to anticipate the later attack on the deistic conception of a universe from which God, its creator, is entirely separate (lines 459–92), quoting 487–8, 491. Neoplatonism as developed in the Renaissance had proved to a large extent assimilable to Christian philosophy, but 'later Platonists' is a gibe at contemporary deists: cp. *OAC*: I, 135).

245–6 and n. BARROW: Isaac Barrow (1630–77) held professorships of Greek and of mathematics, excelled as a preacher and theologian, and was considered a prodigy both of learning and of piety. He died young, having held the mastership of Trinity College, Cambridge, for only five years. Aristarchus reassures Dulness that educators like Barrow and Atterbury are too rare to represent a substantial threat to her empire. The note was initialled in 1751 as jointly by Pope and Warburton.

See! still thy own, the heavy Canon roll,
And Metaphysic smokes involve the Pole.
For thee we dim the eyes, and stuff the head
With all such reading as was never read:
For thee explain a thing till all men doubt it,
And write about it, Goddess, and about it:
So spins the silk-worm small its slender store,
And labours till it clouds itself all o'er.

247. the heavy Canon] Canon here, if spoken of *Artillery*, is in the plural number; if of the *Canons of the House*, in the singular, and meant only of *one:* in which case I suspect the *Pole* to be a false reading, and that it should be the *Poll*, or *Head* of that Canon. It may be objected, that this is a mere *Paranomasia* or *Pun*. But what of that? Is any figure of Speech more apposite to our gentle Goddess, or more frequently used by her, and her Children, especially of the University? Doubtless it better suits the Character of Dulness, yea of a Doctor, than that of an Angel; yet *Milton* fear'd not to put a considerable quantity into the mouths of his. It hath indeed been observed, that they were the Devil's Angels, as if he did it to suggest the Devil was the Author as well of false Wit, as of false Religion, and that the Father of Lies was also the Father of Puns. But this is idle: It must be own'd a Christian practice, used in the primitive times by some of the Fathers, and in later by most of the Sons of the Church; till the debauch'd reign of Charles the second, when the shameful Passion for *Wit* overthrew every thing: and even then the best Writers admitted it, provided it was obscene, under the name of the *Double entendre*. SCRIBL.

248.] Here the learned Aristarchus ending the first member of his harangue in behalf of *Words*; and entering on the other half, which regards the teaching of *Things*; very artfully connects the two parts in an encomium on METAPHYSICS, a kind of *Middle nature* between words and things: communicating, in its obscurity with *Substance*, and in its emptiness with *Names*. SCRIBL.

---

247 and n. The pun overlays the image of a dull, overfed cathedral canon (Oxford Cathedral is located within Christ Church, known as 'the House') with the image of heavy artillery suggested by 'smokes' ('cannon' could still be spelled 'canon'). For the suggested identification 'Dr. G—g—y of C.C. Ox.', i.e. David Gregory (1696–1767), a canon of Christ Church who wrote in praise of George I and George II and adorned Christ Church with their busts, see Dyce 7747. Further evidence of his Hanoverian and courtly credentials was his marriage to the daughter of the Duke of Kent (see editor's note on lines 511–12). Another canon of Christ Church, John Gilbert, is attacked by name at line 608.

The note, initialled in 1751 as jointly by Pope and Warburton, suggests an additional pun, on 'Pole' referring to the heavens and 'poll' meaning 'head', and closes with a typical expression of distaste for puns as symptomatic of Restoration decadence (cp. *Essay on Criticism*, lines 530–43; *Imitations of Horace, Epistles* II.i.139–54).

248 and n. The line does not seem to require an individual application, although the pun on 'poll' could indicate the dean as head of the cathedral clergy. ***member:*** part. ***encomium:*** speech of praise.

253–4. By the simile of the silkworm Aristarchus expresses not only the energy and ingenuity of scholars in creating obscurity, but also its value in Dulness's eyes (something that the more familiar image of the spider could not evoke: cp. *Essay on Criticism*, lines 440–45). The

What tho' we let some better sort of fool
Thrid ev'ry science, run thro' ev'ry school?
Never by tumbler thro' the hoops was shown
Such skill in passing all, and touching none.
He may indeed (if sober all this time)
Plague with Dispute, or persecute with Rhyme.
We only furnish what he cannot use,

255 to 271.] Hitherto Aristarchus hath displayed the art of teaching his Pupils words, without things. He shews greater skill in what follows, which is to teach things, without profit. For with the *better sort of fool* the first expedient is, ver. 255 to 258, to run him so swiftly through the circle of the Sciences that he shall stick at nothing, nor nothing stick with him; and though some little, both of words and things, should by chance be gathered up in his passage, yet he shews, ver. 255 to 260, that it is never more of the one than just to enable him to *persecute with Rhyme*, or of the other than to *plague with Dispute*. But, if after all, the Pupil will needs *learn* a Science, it is then provided by his careful directors, ver. 261, 262, that it shall either be such as he can never *enjoy* when he comes out into life, or such as he will be obliged to *divorce*. And to make all sure, ver. 263 to 268, the useless or pernicious Sciences, thus taught, are still applied perversely; the man of Wit *petrified* in Euclid, or *trammelled* in Metaphysics; and the man of Judgment *married*, without his parents consent, to a *Muse*. Thus far the particular arts of modern Education, used partially, and diversified according to the Subject and the Occasion: But there is one general Method, with the encomium of which the great Aristarchus ends his speech, ver. 266 to 268, and that is AUTHORITY, the universal *Cement*, which fills all the cracks and chasms of *lifeless* matter, shuts up all the pores of *living* substance, and brings all human minds to *one dead level*. For if Nature should chance to struggle through all the entanglements of the foregoing ingenious expedients to *bind rebel wit*, this claps upon her one sure and entire cover. So that well may Aristarchus defy all human power to *get the Man out* again from under so impenetrable a crust. The Poet alludes to this Master-piece of the Schools in ver. 501, where he speaks of *Vassals to a name.*

---

silkworm is artful in that it is only 'small' and its internal resources are only a 'slender store'; but it can produce from that a vast length of silk – precisely the argument that the 'modern' spider advances for his pretended superiority over the 'ancient' bee in Swift's *Battle of the Books* (Davis 1939–68: I, 147–51). Dryden had applied the image similarly in *The Conquest of Granada* II (Hooker 1956–89: XI, 118; Means 1983).

255–71n. The note, initialled in 1751 as by Warburton, is typically systematising. The verse does not specify that such studies as the geometry of the Greek mathematician Euclid (lived *c.*300 BC), or poetry, or metaphysics are specifically chosen for those whose talents point in other directions (lines 261–6); nor does it unambiguously identify the 'Cement' of line 267 with 'AUTHORITY'.

257–8. According to Warton, 'These two verses are verbatim from an epigram of Dr. Evans, of St. John's College, Oxford; given to my father twenty years before the Dunciad was written' (Warton 1797: V, 259). Evans, mentioned as a wit worth imitating at II.116, had died in 1737. The image is reminiscent of Pope's ironic commendation of modernity, that 'learned Athens to our Art must stoop, / Could she behold us tumbling thro' a hoop' (*Imitations of Horace, Epistles* II.i.47–8).

Or wed to what he must divorce, a Muse:
Full in the midst of Euclid dip at once,
And petrify a Genius to a Dunce:
Or set on Metaphysic ground to prance,
Show all his paces, not a step advance.
With the same Cement, ever sure to bind,
We bring to one dead level ev'ry mind.
Then take him to devellop, if you can,
And hew the Block off, and get out the Man.
But wherefore waste I words? I see advance
Whore, Pupil, and lac'd Governor from France.

264. petrify a Genius] Those who have no Genius, employ'd in works of imagination; those who have, in abstract sciences.

270. And hew the Block off,] A notion of Aristotle, that there was originally in every block of marble, a Statue, which would appear on the removal of the superfluous parts.

272. lac'd Governor] Why *lac'd?* Because Gold and Silver are necessary trimming to denote the dress of a person of rank, and the Governor must be supposed so in foreign countries, to be admitted into Courts and other places of fair reception. But how comes Aristarchus to know by sight that this Governor came from France? Why, by the laced coat. SCRIBL.

Ibid. Whore, Pupil, and lac'd Governor] Some Critics have objected to the order here, being of opinion that the Governor should have the precedence before the Whore, if not before the Pupil. But were he so placed, it might be thought to insinuate that the Governor led the Pupil to the Whore: and were the Pupil placed first, he might be supposed to lead the Governor to her. But our impartial Poet, as he is drawing their Picture, represents them in the order in which they are generally seen; namely, the Pupil between the Whore and the Governor; but placeth the Whore first, as she usually governs both the other.

---

262. Because most students will need to apply their minds to occupations other than poetry when they leave college.

264n. Initialled in 1751 as jointly by Pope and Warburton.

265–6. Like a horse in a riding school going through its paces on the spot, the college metaphysician is only going through the motions. The image had been used by Lord Hervey in *Some Remarks on the Minute Philosopher* 1732: 32–3.

267. Cement: The metre requires the older pronunciation with the stress on the first syllable.

270n. The note, initialled in 1751 as jointly by Pope and Warburton, attributes to Aristotle an aphorism reminiscent of ideas in the sonnets of the artist and sculptor Michelangelo Buonarrotti (1475–1564) (Bull & Porter 1987: 153, 156; *TE*: V, 370).

272 and n. The 'Pupil' is a young gentleman who has just completed the Grand Tour under the supervision of a 'Governor' or tutor. 'Governors to Travelling Noblemen' and 'A French Refugee Governor with his Pupils' had been included in a list of targets in an early manuscript draft of Book II (Mack 1984: 127). The Tour functioned as an exclusive male rite of passage, and its vogue at this time was related to the low esteem in which contemporary university education was held except as a professional training for clergy and academics (Redford 1996: 7–9, 15–16). Dyce 7747 identifies the pupil as 'D—uke of K—ngst—n or Ld M—dd—x', i.e. Evelyn Pierrepont (1711–73), second Duke of Kingston, or Charles Sackville (1711–69),

Walker! our hat — nor more he deign'd to say,
But, stern as Ajax' spectre, strode away.
In flow'd at once a gay embroider'd race,
And titt'ring push'd the Pedants off the place:
Some would have spoken, but the voice was drown'd

274.] See Homer Odyss. xi. where the Ghost of Ajax turns sullenly from Ulysses. A Passage extremely admired by Longinus.

276.] Hor.: 'Rideat et pulset lasciva decentiùs aetas.'

---

later Duke of Dorset, at this time Earl of Middlesex; and he later identifies his mistress as 'Mad. La Touche', who accompanied the Duke of Kingston on his return from the Tour (Lewis 1937–83: VI, 130). As a prominent opera promoter, cricketer and reputed rake, Middlesex might seem to exemplify all that Pope despised in young aristocrats; but in fact he seems to have been personally well disposed towards him, and instrumental in securing for his friend Spence the post of governor for his Grand Tour (*Corr.*: III, 241). Sutherland cites a report of a lost autograph which further complicates any attempt at identification: the pupil evidently reminded contemporary readers of a range of individuals (Elwin & Courthope 1871–86: IV, 360; *TE*: V, 370–71). Several of the topics treated by Pope in relation to the Tour had already been featured in *The Man of Taste. Occasion'd by an Epistle of Mr. Pope's on that Subject* (1733), anonymously published by Pope's own printer and bookseller James Bramston (1694?–1744), an admirer who had on at least one occasion shown him work before publication (*Corr.*: III, 173). ***Why* lac'd?:** The note, initialled in 1751 as jointly by Pope and Warburton, draws attention to the lowly status of such tutors, alleging that since as mere academics they would not normally be received in company as distinguished as that into which they are expected to introduce their charges during the Tour, they travel in clothes trimmed with gold and silver lace that imply a higher status than is really theirs. Hence Aristarchus can tell by the lace that this one has just come from abroad: at home it would be clear from his drab costume that he was not of the same rank as his pupil. (For the suggestion that the Governor may allude to Breval, whom Bentley had dismissed from his Trinity fellowship for misdemeanours arising from his affair with a married woman, see *TE*: V, 372, and editor's notes on lines 281, 327.) The manuscript draft's reference to 'A French Refugee Governor' could also be construed as a sneer at Breval's background (Mack 1984: 127). ***Some Critics have objected:*** The note, initialled in 1751 as jointly by Pope and Warburton, insinuates a range of possible patterns of sexual connivance among the three. Tutors, often clergymen, were supposed to ensure their pupils' good conduct.

273. For the story of the hat, see editor's note on lines 205–6.

274 and n. A longer version of the note was initialled in 1751 as by Warburton. Ajax was supposed to have died of resentment at seeing the armour of the dead Achilles awarded to Odysseus instead of to himself: when in the *Odyssey* Odysseus calls up his spirit, it refuses to speak to him (XI.543–65). Longinus praised the sublimity of the ghost's silence (Murray 1919: *Odyssey* XI.543–65).

275. a gay embroider'd race: Young men just back from the Tour.

276 and n. The note was initialled in 1751 as jointly by Pope and Warburton. Horace praised the wisdom of accepting old age and death gracefully: in Pope's version, 'Walk sober off; before a sprightlier Age / Comes titt'ring on, and shoves you from the stage' (*Epistles* II.ii.216; *Imitations of Horace, Epistles* II.ii.324–5).

By the French horn, or by the op'ning hound.
The first came forwards, with as easy mien,
As if he saw St. James's and the Queen.
When thus th' attendant Orator begun.
Receive, great Empress! thy accomplish'd Son:
Thine from the birth, and sacred from the rod,
A dauntless infant! never scar'd with God.

279.] This Forwardness or Pertness is the certain consequence, when the Children of Dulness are spoiled by too great fondness of their Parent.

280.] Reflecting on the disrespectful and indecent Behaviour of several forward young Persons in the Presence, so offensive to all serious men, and to none more than the good Scriblerus.

281. th' attendant Orator] The Governor abovesaid. The Poet gives him no particular name; being unwilling, I presume, to offend or do injustice to any, by celebrating one only with whom this character agrees, in preference to so many who equally deserve it. SCRIBL.

284.] Hor.: 'sine Dis Animosus Infans.'

---

278. the French horn: In France at this time the French horn was primarily a hunting horn, though sometimes used for orchestral special effects: it had been known in England as a hunting horn since the Restoration, and in an early draft of II.227 Pope had referred to the use of 'French Horns' as a theatrical gimmick (Mack 1984: 112). Its first orchestral use in England seems to have been by Handel in the second decade of the eighteenth century; and in France it became an orchestral instrument only in the late 1740s (Sadie 1980: VIII, 704–6). Hence it seems more likely that the young man has brought one back as part of his hunting equipage, although the possibility that he intends to play it as a musical instrument cannot be ruled out – and with its associations with the kennels it would be a particularly undignified choice for a nobleman. ***the op'ning hound:*** a hound giving tongue.

279n. Initialled in 1751 as by Warburton.

280 and n. As well as expressing general distaste for the precocious assurance of young aristocrats, the note, initialled in 1751 as jointly by Pope and Warburton, may allude to the notoriously bad relations between Frederick, Prince of Wales, and his parents. 'The Presence' denotes the royal presence. It may be that Scriblerus and 'all serious men' are ridiculed for their assumption that George II and Caroline should be approached with reverence: Pope himself was associated, if less than wholeheartedly, with the Prince of Wales's opposition (Gerrard 1994: 68–95).

281–330. For the classical allusions evoked, see Brower 1959: 30–34.

281 and n. Pope thought 'the travelling Governor's speech one of the best things in my new addition to the *Dunciad*' (*OAC*: I, 150). The note, which seems to hint at an individual application, was initialled in 1751 as jointly by Pope and Warburton. For the possibility that Breval is intended, see editor's note on line 272.

283. sacred from the rod: He has never been beaten, implying by early eighteenth-century norms that he is a complete stranger to discipline. There is a play between 'sacred' and 'scarred' (the word we might have expected), extending to 'scared' in the following line.

284 and n. The note ironically drops the negative from Horace's idyllic account of the infant poet's upbringing by the muses: whereas the poet was 'a fearless child, *not* without the gods', this youth owes his fearlessness to his ignorance of any power greater than himself

The Sire saw, one by one, his Virtues wake:
The Mother begg'd the blessing of a Rake.
Thou gav'st that Ripeness, which so soon began,
And ceas'd so soon, he ne'er was Boy, nor Man.
Thro' School and College, thy kind cloud o'ercast,
Safe and unseen the young Aeneas past:
Thence bursting glorious, all at once let down,
Stunn'd with his giddy Larum half the town.
Intrepid then, o'er seas and lands he flew:

288. he ne'er was Boy, nor Man.] Nature hath bestowed on the human species two states or conditions, *Infancy* and *Manhood*. Wit sometimes makes the *first* disappear, and Folly the *latter*; but true Dulness annihilates *both*. For, want of *apprehension* in Boys, not suffering that conscious ignorance and inexperience which produce the awkward bashfulness of youth, makes them *assured*; and want of *imagination* makes them *grave*. But this *gravity* and *assurance*, which is beyond *boyhood*, being neither wisdom nor knowledge, do never reach to *manhood*. SCRIBL.

290–91.] See Virg. Aen. I: 'At Venus obscuro gradientes aëre sepsit, / Et multo nebulae circum Dea fudit amictu, / Cernere ne quis eos; — I. neu quis contingere possit; / 2. Molirive moram; — aut 3. veniendi poscere causas.' Where he enumerates the causes why his mother took this care of him: to wit, I. that no-body might touch or correct him: 2. might stop or detain him: 3. examine him about the progress he had made, or so much as guess why he came there.

(*Odes* III.iv.20). It was generally considered important to teach children about divine judgment: when the adult Samuel Johnson told his mother that he remembered her first teaching him about Heaven and Hell when he was two, she expressed surprise at having left it so late (McAdam 1958: 10).

285–6. With fashionable aristocratic perversity the father hails his son's implicitly undesirable characteristics as 'Virtues', while the mother hopes he will grow up a rake.

288n. Initialled in 1751 as by Warburton.

289–90 and 290–91n. Venus makes her son Aeneas and his companion invisible so that they can enter Carthage unobserved: 'But Venus muffled them as they walked in a dim atmosphere and, goddess that she was, lapped round them a great cloak of cloud, so that no-one could see them, nor could anyone touch them or delay them or ask them why they had come' (*Aeneid* I.411–14). The pupil presumably passed 'safe and unseen' through his education by being utterly undistinguished, but this will not stop him from making an exhibition of himself later.

291. let down: set down by his mother.

293. Introducing a satirical account of the Grand Tour, advocated in the first half of the eighteenth century as completing the education of members of the ruling class, but also routinely attacked for introducing foreign corruptions in politics, religion and culture, as well as allowing poorly supervised young men to indulge in unrestrained debauchery (Black 1992: 287–305). Although some contemporaries complained that the youths were too inexperienced to make the most of the Tour's educational opportunities, it usefully filled the gap between school or university and the age at which full adult responsibilities could be assumed (pp. 208–10). Pope, already debarred by religion from most aspects of an eighteenth-century

Europe he saw, and Europe saw him too.
There all thy gifts and graces we display,
Thou, only thou, directing all our way!
To where the Seine, obsequious as she runs,
Pours at great Bourbon's feet her silken sons;
Or Tyber, now no longer Roman, rolls,
Vain of Italian Arts, Italian Souls:
To happy Convents, bosom'd deep in vines,
Where slumber Abbots, purple as their wines:
To Isles of fragrance, lilly-silver'd vales,

303. lilly-silver'd vales,] Tuberoses.

---

gentleman's education, was also too frail to travel, but would have heard much about the Tour from friends such as Thomson and Spence, who had both acted as governors (*OAC*: I, 12–13, 22–3; Sambrook 1991: 106–18). From Pope's detailed and enthusiastic reading about the classical antiquities to be seen in Italy it is clear that this aspect at least of the Tour would have appealed enormously to him: in contrast he stresses that the 'young Aeneas', far from travelling to reinvigorate his culture, is simply picking up more diversions and vices with which to intensify Dulness's power (Mack 1982: 313–14). For a range of similar concerns, see *Spectator* 364 and James Miller's *Of Politeness* (Bond 1965: III, 366–70; Miller 1738).

294. Virgil had prophesied that the child whose birth is anticipated in his fourth *Eclogue* would (in Dryden's translation) 'lead the life of Gods, and be / By Gods and Heroes seen, and Gods and Heroes see' (*Eclogues* IV.15–16; Kinsley 1958: *Virgil's Pastorals* IV.18–19). Horace Walpole attributed a similar play on words to the Patriot MP Sir John Barnard (1685–1764): 'S[r] John Barnard's Son desiring an Allowance to travel and see the world, he replied, He would give double the Summ to have the world not see him' (Fraser 1876: 100). Sir James Prior records as from a draft of Pope's intended satire on education the couplet 'Desirous to see all the world they seem, / And ne'er consider that the world sees them' (Prior 1860: 367).

297. obsequious: Transferring to the river that flows through Paris the political behaviour deplored by British commentators as the consequence of arbitrary government. It was widely assumed that the young pupil would be stimulated to the defence of British liberty by his disgust at the absolutist regimes he would see on the Continent: in this vein the Patriot Whig Thomson wrote *Liberty* after making the Grand Tour as governor to a son of Charles Talbot (Sambrook 1991: 106–56; for other responses to continental politics, see Black 1992: 213–32). The Patriot sense that tyranny was flourishing in Britain, however, complicates this tradition: the young man destined for service under Walpole takes to continental absolutism like a duck to water. Pope's friend Gilbert West had in his anonymously published satire *A Canto of the Fairy Queen* (1739) told how Redcross Knight crossed the sea only to encounter allegories of corruption reminiscent of England under Walpole (Gerrard 1994: 177–80).

298. Bourbon: The family name of the kings of France.

299–300. Whereas Roman civilisation is an object of reverence to Pope, the Italian culture that now occupies its ancient sites is not (the Tiber, much mentioned in Roman literature, flows through Rome). For modern Italians to be proud of their culture is by implication to have forgotten the true glories of their past.

301. Echoing Milton's 'Towers, and battlements it sees / Bosomed high in tufted trees' (Carey 1968: 'L'Allegro', lines 77–8).

303 and n. The tuberose has a white flower of overwhelming fragrance.

Diffusing languor in the panting gales:
To lands of singing, or of dancing slaves,
Love-whisp'ring woods, and lute-resounding waves.
But chief her shrine where naked Venus keeps,
And Cupids ride the Lyon of the Deeps;
Where, eas'd of Fleets, the Adriatic main
Wafts the smooth Eunuch and enamour'd swain.
Led by my hand, he saunter'd Europe round,
And gather'd ev'ry Vice on Christian ground;
Saw ev'ry Court, hear'd ev'ry King declare
His royal Sense, of Op'ra's or the Fair;
The Stews and Palace equally explor'd,
Intrigu'd with glory, and with spirit whor'd;
Try'd all *hors-d'oeuvres*, all *liqueurs* defin'd,

308.] The winged Lyon, the Arms of Venice. This Republic heretofore the most considerable in Europe, for her Naval Force and the extent of her Commerce; now illustrious for her *Carnivals*.

---

305. Implying that absolute rulers in effect render their subjects slaves, who, far from attempting to gain liberty, are content to waste their lives in dissipation.

307–8 and n. For contextualisation of Pope's references to Venice, see Redford 1996: 5–25. The 'naked Venus' may allude not only to Venice's reputation for offering unrivalled opportunities for sexual indulgence (Black 1992: 196), but also, in a sadly ironic parody, to the cult of the Virgin Mary formerly associated with the maritime prowess of the Venetian Republic. 'Venus' and 'Venice' were pronounced almost indistinguishably (Redford 1996: 6). The note, initialled in 1751 as jointly by Pope and Warburton, emphasises the Republic's decadence: Venetian carnivals involving masking and fancy dress constituted a transgression of social decorums comparable to the popular but much-censured London masquerades (Castle 1986: 1–51). Venice, in decline despite a proud tradition of liberty, could be seen as a specific warning to Britain (Redford 1996: 7, 25, 63–5).

309. eas'd of Fleets: Noting the absence of the Adriatic fleet crucial to Venice's former commercial and military power.

310. The Eunuch's smoothness refers to his lack of beard, but also contributes to the theme of excessive polish. Redford notes the silence as to whom the 'swain' is 'enamour'd' of, which leaves open the possibility of the homosexual effeminacy widely feared as a likely consequence of exposure to Italian culture; but the 'swain' could also allude to the Doge of Venice, 'enamour'd' of the sea, to which he was married in an annual ceremony symbolic of the city's claims to maritime dominion (Redford 1996: 7).

313–14. The opportunity to be received at foreign courts was a key justification of the Grand Tour's claim to further the political and diplomatic skills of young men destined for a role in government (Black 1992: 216–19). Although many young travellers did in fact make a point of attending opera, the suggestion that kings care only to talk of opera and mistresses has an obvious application to George II (pp. 252–7; for Pope's views on opera, see lines 45–70 and notes).

315. Stews: brothels.

317. This line provides the earliest uses of the italicised expressions recorded in *OED*: they evidently represented for Pope the height of Frenchified affectation. 'Define' suggests an affectation of gastronomic expertise.

Judicious drank, and greatly-daring din'd;
Dropt the dull lumber of the Latin store,
Spoil'd his own language, and acquir'd no more;
All Classic learning lost on Classic ground;
And last turn'd *Air*, the Echo of a Sound!
See now, half-cur'd, and perfectly well-bred,

318. greatly-daring din'd;] It being indeed no small risque to eat thro' those extraordinary compositions, whose disguis'd ingredients are generally unknown to the guests, and highly inflammatory and unwholsome.

322.] Yet less a Body than Echo itself; for Echo reflects *Sense* or *Words* at least, this Gentleman only *Airs* and *Tunes: 'Sonus* est, qui vivit in *illo*'. Ovid. Met. So that this was not a Metamorphosis either in one or the other, but only a Resolution of the Soul into its true Principles, its real Essence being Harmony; according to the Doctrine of Orpheus, the Inventor of Opera, who first perform'd to a choice assembly of Beasts. SCRIBL.

---

318 and n. greatly-daring din'd: Alluding to the conclusion of Sheffield's elegy on a man whose aspiration to the hand of the Spanish Infanta cost him his life: 'If from the glorious Height he falls, / He greatly daring dies; / Or mounting where bright Beauty calls, / An Empire is the Prize' (Pope 1723: I, 66). Although French cookery, which offered a variety of ingredients and presentation contrasting sharply with the traditional British preference for large, plainly roasted joints, was becoming fashionable in England, the note, initialled in 1751 as jointly by Pope and Warburton, expresses traditional patriotic contempt for French cookery, characterised as a fraudulent use of sauces to disguise small quantities of poor ingredients (Black 1992: 149–50).

319. Ideally, the pupil would have consolidated his classical training by deciphering ancient inscriptions and relating what he saw to his previous reading. Cp. Addison's enthusiastic response on his first visit to Italy: 'Poetick fields encompass me around, / And still I seem to tread on Classic ground' (Guthkelch 1914, 'A Letter from Italy', lines 11–12).

320. The opportunity to perfect one's knowledge of modern languages was a standard argument in favour of the Grand Tour. Pope suggests, in line with a common fear that modish gallicisms were corrupting the English language, that the pupil is more likely to adopt a few foreign words into his native speech than to learn a foreign language properly.

322 and n. 'Air' (punning also on the young man's role as 'heir') was the usual translation for the Italian *aria*: the youth's humming of tunes from Italian opera is punningly presented as a kind of evaporation into thin air. The note, initialled in 1751 as by Warburton, makes explicit the allusion to Ovid's story of Echo, who, spurned by Narcissus, wasted away until only her voice remained: 'a sound is all that survives of her' (*Metamorphoses* III.401. Warburton has changed the gender.) The note goes on to make an ironic allusion to the idea that harmony is the essence of the soul (for the background in Plato and Aristotle, see West 1992: 248–52), arguing that the changing of Echo and of the young traveller into sound does not amount to real change, but is only a resolution of each person into his or her essence. (A pun on the musical sense of 'resolution', i.e. movement from discord into concord, is also implied.) The heavy-handed joke about Orpheus alludes to his power of charming non-human audiences, and looks forward to the allusion to Circe's transformation of men to beasts at lines 517–78.

323. half-cur'd: half-dehydrated, like food salted for preservation.

With nothing but a Solo in his head;
As much Estate, and Principle, and Wit,
As Jansen, Fleetwood, Cibber shall think fit;
Stol'n from a Duel, follow'd by a Nun,
And, if a Borough chuse him, not undone;
See, to my country happy I restore
This glorious Youth, and add one Venus more.
Her too receive (for her my soul adores)
So may the sons of sons of sons of whores,

324.] With nothing but a *Solo?* Why, if it be a *Solo,* how should there be any thing else? Palpable Tautology! Read boldly an *Opera,* which is enough of conscience for such a head as has lost all its Latin. BENTL.

326.] Three very eminent persons, all Managers of *Plays;* who, tho' not Governors by profession, had, each in his way, concern'd themselves in the Education of Youth; and regulated their Wits, their Morals, or their Finances, at that period of their age which is the most important, their entrance into the polite world. Of the last of these, and his Talents for this end, see Book I. ver. 199, *etc.*

331.] This confirms what the learned Scriblerus advanced in his Note on ver. 272, that the Governor, as well as the Pupil, had a particular interest in this lady.

332.] Virg: 'Et nati natorum, et qui nascentur ab illis.' Aen. iii.

Ibid. sons of whores,] For such have been always esteemed the ablest supports of the

---

324 and n. Though used in English from the beginning of the century, the word 'solo' had not yet lost its air of Italianate affectation. The note was initialled in 1751 as jointly by Pope and Warburton.

326 and n. Jansen: Henry Janssen (*d.* 1766), son of one of the disgraced directors of the South Sea Company, was a notorious gambler suspected of cheating a young duke of a vast sum (*TE*: IV, 141–3, 366; Lewis 1937–83: XVIII, 124). The note, initialled in 1751 as jointly by Pope and Warburton, puns on 'play', signifying in Janssen's case not drama but gambling. For gambling on the Grand Tour, see Black 1992: 204–6. ***Fleetwood:*** Charles Fleetwood (*d.* 1747), unlike Janssen but like Cibber, was a theatrical manager. Pope expressed contempt for his policies at Drury Lane when his correspondent Aaron Hill had a play rejected by him (*Corr.*: IV, 165–6, 167–8). Fleetwood had run through a considerable fortune, and was notorious for sharp practice, even in dealings with his supposed friends.

327. a Duel: Duelling, increasingly disapproved of in Britain, was particularly associated with continental codes of honour. ***follow'd by a Nun:*** The notion that convents were seething with imperfectly repressed sexuality was one on which the patriotic British anti-Catholic imagination loved to dwell. Horace Walpole comments, 'Capt. Breval a travelling Governor had a nun escap'd to him from a Convent at Milan, where she had been plac'd against her will; and afterwards went to Rome and pleaded her cause & was acquitted there and married Breval' (Fraser 1876: 101–2; and see editor's notes on lines 272, 281). For the French mistress brought back by the Duke of Kingston, see editor's note on 272.

328. If he is elected a Member of Parliament (a virtual certainty, provided he has suitable connections) he will be immune from arrest for debt.

331n. Initialled in 1751 as jointly by Pope and Warburton.

332–4 and n. In another allusion to the destiny of Aeneas, the note, initialled in 1751 as

Prop thine, O Empress! like each neighbour Throne,
And make a long Posterity thy own.
  Pleas'd, she accepts the Hero, and the Dame,
Wraps in her Veil, and frees from sense of Shame.
  Then look'd, and saw a lazy, lolling sort,
Unseen at Church, at Senate, or at Court,
Of ever-listless Loit'rers, that attend
No Cause, no Trust, no Duty, and no Friend.
Thee too, my Paridel! she mark'd thee there,

Throne of *Dulness*, even by the confession of those her most *legitimate* Sons, who have unfortunately wanted that advantage. The illustrious *Vanini* in his divine encomium on our Goddess, intitled *De Admirandis Naturae Reginae Deaeque mortalium Arcanis,* laments that he was not born a Bastard: *O utinam extra legitimum ac connubialem thorum essem procreatus! etc.* He expatiates on the prerogatives of a *free birth,* and on what he would have done for the *Great Mother* with those advantages; and then sorrowfully concludes, *At quia Conjugatorum sum soboles his orbatus sum bonis.*

341.] The Poet seems to speak of this young gentleman with great affection. The name is taken from Spenser, who gives it to a *wandering Courtly 'Squire,* that travell'd about for the same reason, for which many young Squires are now fond of travelling, and especially to *Paris.*

---

by Warburton, cites the prophecy that 'your sons' sons, and the children they beget' would rule the world (*Aeneid* III.98). Redford sets contemporary fears about sexual indulgence on the Grand Tour in the context of a demographic crisis in which many distinguished families were failing to reproduce themselves (Redford 1996: 22). The reference to 'each neighbour Throne' seems to point at foreign courts as reliant on noble houses founded by the ennoblement of illegitimate children of royal mistresses, but the accusation was equally relevant to the English court: a case in point was the Duke of Grafton, who had appointed Cibber as laureate and was the grandson of a mistress of Charles II. Warburton introduces in the note an ironic allusion to the ancient question as to whether illegitimate children were stronger and more talented than legitimate, and if so, why: he cites the discussion by Lucilio (called 'Julius Caesar') Vanini (1585–1619), Italian priest and free-thinking philosopher working in France, who was condemned to death on a charge of atheism, astronomy and magical practices. The passages cited constitute a humorous interjection in an otherwise serious dialogue on sexuality and reproduction, as the speaker speculates on what he might have been had he been the child of youthful fornication rather than of late marriage: 'O if only I had been begotten outside the lawful marital bed! But because I am the offspring of a married couple I am bereft of these benefits' (Vanini 1616: 321–2). Despite Warburton's sneer at the book as written in praise of 'our Goddess' (i.e. Dulness), the title describes its subject as 'the admirable secrets of Nature, queen and goddess of mortals'.

341 and n. Spenser's Paridell is a seducer whose name combines the sense of 'Paris' (seducer of Helen, traditionally stigmatised as effete, over-sophisticated and unfit for war) and 'idle' (Smith & De Selincourt 1912, from *Faerie Queene* III.viii.44ff; Fowler 1959: 585; Williams 1993: 96–9). Pope, whose treatment of Paris in the *Iliad* translation is relatively mild, explicitly links him with knight-errantry: 'Upon the whole, this is no worse than the Picture of a *gentle Knight,* and one might fancy the Heroes of the modern Romance were form'd upon the Model of *Paris*' (*Iliad* III.86). Pope would also have been familiar with an erotic ceiling

Stretch'd on the rack of a too easy chair,
And heard thy everlasting yawn confess
The Pains and Penalties of Idleness.
She pity'd! but her Pity only shed
Benigner influence on thy nodding head.
  But Annius, crafty Seer, with ebon wand,

342–3.] Virg. Aen. vi: 'Sedet, *aeternumque sedebit,* / Infelix Theseus, Phlegyasque *miserrimus* omnes / Admonet'.

347. Annius,] The name taken from Annius the Monk of Viterbo, famous for many Impositions and Forgeries of ancient manuscripts and inscriptions, which he was prompted to by mere Vanity, but our Annius had a more substantial motive.

---

painting of Paridell and Hellenore in the Temple of Venus at Stowe, where its homage to love in idleness would have been implicitly qualified by the more robustly moral and political symbolism of other garden features (Gerrard 1994: 178). These associations seem more relevant here than the coldly exploitative seductions of Spenser's Paridell: the allusion of line 341 focuses explicitly on idleness. Erskine-Hill, however, points out that in Spenser's poem Paridell narrates the transfer of empire from Troy to Britain, alluding to a key theme in the *Dunciad*'s imitation of Virgil's *Aeneid* (Hamilton 1990: 555–6). The note, initialled in 1751 as jointly by Pope and Warburton, seems somewhat at variance with the verse: its second sentence, with its pun on *Paris*, highlights the idea of the traveller in search of sex. This seems inappropriate in that the first sentence of the note strongly suggests an individual application; and the most plausible candidate is Henry Hyde (1710–53), Viscount Cornbury, who could reasonably be accused of inaction, but hardly of philandering. Cornbury had in the 1730s been a Jacobite activist, and was a close associate of Bolingbroke admired by Pope for his political incorruptibility; but by 1740 he seems to have been less in favour, probably on account of his refusal to join the campaign against Walpole's Excise Bill: Pope says of Britain, 'That those who bind and rob thee, would not kill, / Good C— hopes, and candidly sits still' (*Imitations of Horace, Epistles* I.v.60–62; *One Thousand Seven Hundred and Forty*, lines 17–18; *Corr.*: IV, 272; *OAC*: I, 145; Cruickshanks 1986). Cornbury's health was poor, and he spent time at foreign spas. (A less convincing identification of Paridel by Horace Walpole is partly dependent on an equally unconvincing identification of Pollio at line 350 (Fraser 1876: 102–3; *TE*: V, 376).)

342 and n. Pope may have had in mind Boileau's reference to 'Le pénible fardeau de n'avoir rien à faire' ('The painful burden of having nothing to do', Vercruysse 1969: *Epistles* XI.86). Theseus had tried to abduct Proserpine, stolen from the upper world to be queen of the underworld, while Phlegyas had burned down Apollo's temple in retribution at the god's rape of his daughter: the Virgilian allusion may be intended to present them not as offenders against piety, but as men unequal to the task of standing up against oppression by the higher powers. The quotation says of them: 'He sits, and for ever he shall sit, unhappy Theseus, and that most wretched man Phlegyas warns everyone' (*Aeneid* VI.617–19). Theseus was sometimes said to have grown into a rock where he sat down to rest, while Phlegyas was supposed to be imprisoned under a rock which seemed always about to fall. Warburton elsewhere reads the passage as a denunciation of sacrilege (Warburton 1738–41: I, 217–19).

345–6. Dulness's pity only made him sleepier.

347 and n. Introducing a satire on virtuosi, i.e. collectors of antiquities, works of art and curiosities of nature (for the rise of the virtuosi from the late sixteenth century and the

And well dissembled em'rald on his hand,
False as his Gems, and canker'd as his Coins,
Came, cramm'd with capon, from where Pollio dines.
Soft, as the wily Fox is seen to creep,
Where bask on sunny banks the simple sheep,
Walk round and round, now prying here, now there;
So he; but pious, whisper'd first his pray'r.
  Grant, gracious Goddess! grant me still to cheat,
O may thy cloud still cover the deceit!

355–6.] Hor.: 'Da, pulchra Laverna, / Da mihi fallere ... / Noctem peccatis et fraudibus objice nubem.'

Ibid.* still *to cheat,] Some read *skill*, but that is frivolous, for Annius hath that skill already; or if he had not, *skill* were not wanting to cheat such persons. BENTL.

---

tradition of satire against them, see Tinniswood 1989: 53–62; for their political treatment in *A Canto of the Fairy Queen* see Gerrard 1994: 178). An early manuscript draft of Book II had included 'useless' virtuosi among its targets (Mack 1984: 127). The note (initialled in 1751 as jointly by Pope and Warburton) refers to Annius of Viterbo (*c.*1432–1502), who attributed texts of his own invention to ancient historians. He gives his name to a character plausibly identified by Horace Walpole as a caricature of Sir Andrew Fountaine (1676–1753), who specialised in the collection of coins and antiquities, spent much time abroad, and acted as agent for English collectors (Fraser 1876: 103). The 'ebon wand' would then allude to the rod of office carried by Fountaine as vice-chamberlain to Queen Caroline. Fountaine was also connected with coins by his wardenship of the Royal Mint. For possibilities of theological parody, see Chambers 1964; for connections with other objects of Pope's cultural disapproval, see Nash 1992.

348. dissembled: simulated.

349. canker'd: corroded.

350. capon: A cockerel castrated in order to fatten it for the table. ***Pollio:*** Gaius Asinius Pollio (76 BC–AD 4), statesman, writer and patron of Virgil, the dedicatee of Virgil's fourth Eclogue, is presented as type of the statesman worthy of commemoration at the close of Pope's 'To Mr. Addison, Occasioned by his Dialogues on Medals' (lines 63–72). In the present context, however, the connection with ancient artefacts is given a satirical turn, since this Pollio is Annius's dupe. Although Horace Walpole suggests a reference to Burlington, it seems unlikely that Pope would thus satirise his friend, especially in the light of his ridicule in *To Burlington* of collectors who rely on the taste of experts because they have none of their own (Fraser 1876: 102–3; *To Burlington*, lines 3–12). More likely is Henry Herbert (1693–1751), ninth Earl of Pembroke, a celebrated collector mentioned in 'To Burlington' who was on good terms with Fountaine.

355–6n. The note, initialled in 1751 as jointly by Pope and Warburton, cites (slightly adapted) Horace's satire of the man who prays secretly to the goddess of theft: 'Grant, fair Laverna, grant that I may cheat ... cast darkness over my sins and cloud over my deceits' (*Epistles* I.xvi.60–62). Breval, in an attack on Cibber for plagiarism fraudulently attributed to 'Joseph Gay' (see II.35 and editor's note), had used the same rhymes as Pope's couplet in applying the passage to Cibber: '*Laverna*, lovely Goddess of *Deceit*, / Grant me the happy Privilege to Cheat' (*A Complete Key to the Non-Juror* 1718: 24). That the lines had been applied to Cibber

Thy choicer mists on this assembly shed,
But pour them thickest on the noble head.
So shall each youth, assisted by our eyes,
See other Caesars, other Homers rise;
Thro' twilight ages hunt th' Athenian fowl,
Which Chalcis Gods, and mortals call an Owl,
Now see an Attys, now a Cecrops clear,
Nay, Mahomet! the Pigeon at thine ear;
Be rich in ancient brass, tho' not in gold,
And keep his Lares, tho' his house be sold;
To headless Phoebe his fair bride postpone,
Honour a Syrian Prince above his own;
Lord of an Otho, if I vouch it true;
Blest in one Niger, till he knows of two.

361. hunt th' Athenian fowl,] The Owl stamp'd on the reverse of the ancient money of Athens. 'Which *Chalcis* Gods, and Mortals call an *Owl*' is the verse by which Hobbes renders that of Homer: '*Χαλκίδα κικλήσκουσι Θεοὶ, ἄνδρες δὲ Κύμινδιν.*'

363. Attys and Cecrops.] The first Kings of Athens, of whom it is hard to suppose any Coins are extant; but not so improbable as what follows, that there should be any of Mahomet, who forbad all Images. Nevertheless one of these Annius's made a counterfeit one, now in the collection of a learned Nobleman.

---

is thematically convenient; that this was done by a writer who had attempted to plagiarise not a single text but the very identity of Pope's friend imparts a particular piquancy.

360. other Caesars, other Homers: Statues or coins fraudulently passed off as images of famous people.

361n. The note, initialled in 1751 as jointly by Pope and Warburton, slightly misquotes the translation of Homer into alternate rhyming quatrains by the philosopher Hobbes, which was generally considered an absurd effort by an old and poetically unqualified person in an unsuitable form (Hobbes 1676: 211; *Iliad* XIV.291; *OAC*: I, 193).

363 and n. Attys was the mythical founder of the royal house of Lydia, Cecrops the mythical first King of Athens. The note, a longer version of which was initialled in 1751 as jointly by Pope and Warburton, emphasises that a collector would have to be exceptionally credulous to accept such claims, and looks ahead to the next line, alluding to the traditional anti-Islamic propaganda that Mohammed had a pigeon trained to pick grain out of his ear, which he passed off as an angel or the Holy Spirit (cp. Sandys 1615: 53; J.B. 1729: 76).

366. Lares: Domestic gods worshipped in ancient Rome as protectors of the home. The implication is that buying such antiquities may ironically leave the purchaser unable to pay for a roof over his head.

367. Although the statue of Phoebe (a title of the goddess Diana) is mutilated, he prefers it to his bride: cp. the collector of coins in 'To Mr. Addison': 'Curio, restless by the Fair-one's side, / Sighs for an Otho, and neglects his bride' (lines 43–4).

369–70. Examples of extremely rare coins (see *TE*: V, 472). Marcus Salvius Otho (AD 32–69), former husband of the wife of the Roman emperor Nero, attempted to succeed him on his death in AD 68, but never gained the acclamation of more than part of the army and committed suicide without realising his ambition. Gaius Pescennius Niger Justus was governor of

Mummius o'erheard him; Mummius, Fool-renown'd,
Who like his Cheops stinks above the ground,
Fierce as a startled Adder, swell'd, and said,

371. Mummius] This name is not merely an allusion to the Mummies he was so fond of, but probably referred to the Roman General of that name, who burn'd Corinth, and committed the curious Statues to the Captain of a Ship, assuring him, 'that if any were lost or broken, he should procure others to be made in their stead:' by which it should seem (whatever may be pretended) that Mummius was no Virtuoso.

372. Cheops] A King of Egypt, whose body was certainly to be known, as being buried alone in his Pyramid, and is therefore more genuine than any of the Cleopatra's. This Royal Mummy, being stolen by a wild Arab, was purchas'd by the Consul of Alexandria, and transmitted to the Museum of Mummius; for proof of which he brings a passage in Sandys's Travels, where that accurate and learned Voyager assures us that he saw the Sepulchre empty, which agrees exactly (saith he) with the time of the theft above mention'd. But he omits to observe that Herodotus tells the same thing of it in his time.

Syria, where in AD 191 his legions declared him emperor; but he proved unable to sustain his claim and was killed in 193 or 194.

371 and n. Mummius: A satire on the long-established vogue for collecting Egyptian mummies: suggested identifications have included the noted physicians and collectors Richard Mead (1673–1754: see Dyce 7747) and Richard Woodward (*c.*1665–1728); but an Egyptian Club, founded in about 1740, testifies that this was far from an individual aberration (*TE*: V, 379, 449–50; for the leading members of the Egyptian Club, see Nichols 1812–15: V, 334; for the suggestion that John Montagu (1718–92), fourth Earl of Sandwich, the founder and president, may be intended, see line 374 and editor's note; for the suggestion that Pope may have known about the Club through Warburton's contacts, see Rogers 1993a: 257). Despite Mead's being both a Whig and one of Bentley's closest friends, Pope respected him both as a friend and as a physician; and Woodward, though long dead, remains the most likely individual target: he had been a key figure in the development of Pope's scepticism towards antiquarianism, and he had been mocked in the figure of Dr. Fossile in *Three Hours after Marriage*, in which Cibber had acted the part of Plotwell, who disguises himself as a mummy in order to woo Fossile's bride (Nicolson & Rousseau 1968: 123–9; Levine 1977: 127, 238–40, 257–8, 344–5).

The note, initialled in 1751 as jointly by Pope and Warburton, gives a version of the story of the Roman Mummius (*fl.* 142–6 BC) similar to that given in a note to John Breval's *Henry and Minerva*, an allegory of Henry VIII's banishing superstition and restoring learning which Pope owned, in which Mummius, who sacked Corinth and took its treasures to Rome, appears among destroyers of antiquities: he is made to warn the sailors not to put him to the expense of getting new statues made (J.B. 1729: 57; there is no mention of Egyptian mummies). The present note uses the story to insinuate fakery, an interpretation supported by a note of 1751, attributed to Pope, which glossed 'Fool-renown'd' as '*renown'd by fools*, or *renown'd for making Fools*'.

372. Cheops: The Egyptian Pharaoh Khufu (reigned 2789–2767 BC), builder of the Great Pyramid at Giza (Lepre 1990: 61–132). His mummy (the fate of which remains unknown) would therefore have been of extraordinary value. ***stinks:*** The mummy is so bad a fake that putrefaction has not been arrested. Its owner 'stinks' in the sense of conniving at the fraud.

372n. Initialled in 1751 as jointly by Pope and Warburton. ***was certainly to be known:*** could be identified with certainty. ***was purchas'd by the Consul:*** See editor's note on line 371. ***Sandys's Travels:*** The early seventeenth-century traveller George Sandys reported

Rattling an ancient Sistrum at his head.
Speak'st thou of Syrian Princes? Traitor base!
Mine, Goddess! mine is all the horned race.
True, he had wit, to make their value rise;
From foolish Greeks to steal them, was as wise;
More glorious yet, from barb'rous hands to keep,
When Sallee Rovers chac'd him on the deep.
Then taught by Hermes, and divinely bold,
Down his own throat he risqu'd the Grecian gold;
Receiv'd each Demi-God, with pious care,
Deep in his Entrails — I rever'd them there,
I bought them, shrouded in that living shrine,
And, at their second birth, they issue mine.

375.] The strange story following which may be taken for a fiction of the Poet, is justified by a true relation in Spon's Voyages. Vaillant (who wrote the History of the Syrian Kings as it is to be found on medals) coming from the Levant, where he had been collecting various Coins, and being pursued by a Corsaire of Sallee, swallowed down twenty gold medals. A sudden Bourasque freed him from the Rover, and he got to land with them in his belly. On his road to Avignon he met two Physicians, of whom he demanded assistance. One advis'd Purgations, the other Vomits. In this uncertainty he took neither, but pursued his way to Lyons, where he found his ancient friend, the famous Physician and Antiquary Dufour, to whom he related his adventure. Dufour first ask'd him *whether the Medals were of the higher Empire?* He assur'd him they were. Dufour was ravish'd with the hope of possessing such a treasure, he bargain'd with him on the spot for the most curious of them, and was to recover them at his own expence.

***383. each* Demi-God,]** They are called *Θεῖοι* on their Coins.

---

seeing an empty tomb in the pyramid in question, and recounts various details taken from Herodotus (Sandys 1615: 130–31). Herodotus did not explicitly state that this tomb was empty, but reported that Cheops's mummy was said to be in the adjacent pyramid built by his brother (II, paragraph 127).

374. Sistrum: An ancient Egyptian percussion instrument used in the worship of Isis. At meetings of the Egyptian Club 'A sistrum was laid before the President as the insigne of office' (Nichols 1812–15: V, 334).

375n. The note, initialled in 1751 as jointly by Pope and Warburton, cites a story in Spon's *Voyage* about Jean-Foi Vaillant (1632–1706), who was sent abroad by the King of France to obtain medals (Spon 1678: 1, 15, 17–22). Vaillant's swallowing of the medals is described, however, as motivated solely by his fear of being sold into slavery when, after leaving 'the Levant' ('the east') his ship was chased by 'a Corsaire of Sallee' ('Moorish pirate'), since he hoped that the medals would enable him to buy himself out of slavery. After the 'sudden Bourasque' ('squall') enabled his ship to escape he recovered the medals by recourse to a diet of spinach. One was an Otho (see lines 369–70 and notes).

376. horned race: See editor's note on line 387.

380. See editor's note on the note attributed to Pope and Warburton on line 375.

381. taught by Hermes: The god Hermes/Mercury was patron of trickery.

383n. The note, initialled in 1751 as jointly by Pope and Warburton, quotes the Greek word for 'gods' as used on the coinage of these kings.

Witness great Ammon! by whose horns I swore,
(Reply'd soft Annius) this our paunch before
Still bears them, faithful; and that thus I eat,
Is to refund the Medals with the meat.
To prove me, Goddess! clear of all design,
Bid me with Pollio sup, as well as dine:
There all the Learn'd shall at the labour stand,
And Douglas lend his soft, obstetric hand.
The Goddess smiling seem'd to give consent;
So back to Pollio, hand in hand, they went.
Then thick as Locusts black'ning all the ground,

387. Witness great* Ammon!*] Jupiter Ammon is call'd to witness, as the father of Alexander, to whom those Kings succeeded in the division of the Macedonian Empire, and whose *Horns* they wore on their Medals.

394. Douglas] A Physician of great Learning and no less Taste; above all curious in what related to *Horace*, of whom he collected every Edition, Translation, and Comment, to the number of several hundred volumes.

397.] The similitude of *Locusts* does not refer more to the numbers than to the qualities of the Virtuosi: who not only devour and lay waste every tree, shrub, and green leaf in their *Course*, i.e. of experiments; but suffer neither a moss nor fungus to escape untouched.

SCRIBL.

---

387 and n. Ammon: Originally an Egyptian god, represented with a ram's horns, later assimilated to the cult of Zeus/Jupiter (whose son Alexander the Great claimed to be). The insignia of horns was adopted by Alexander after his conquest of Egypt and continued by his successors. The note was initialled in 1751 as jointly by Pope and Warburton.

389. that thus I eat: As mentioned at line 350.

391. clear of all design: innocent of any plot.

393–4 and 394n. The lines hint at the involvement of the royal physician and obstetrician James Douglas (1675–1742) in the case of Mary Toft, who had in 1726 attracted the interest of 'the Learn'd' by her claim to have given birth to rabbits: Pope and Pulteney had ridiculed her dupes in 'The Discovery: or, The Squire turn'd Ferret' (*OAC*: I, 152; Nicolson & Rousseau 1968: 109–15). Douglas – despite the ridicule implicit in his being named in the present context – had in fact been quick to suspect fraud: he died only weeks after the appearance of *The New Dunciad* in 1742, in which these lines had first appeared (naming him as 'D—gl—s'), and there was a contemporary suspicion that seeing himself in the *Dunciad* had shortened his life (*TE*: V, 438; Nicolson & Rousseau 1968: 123–4). Although the note, initialled in 1751 as jointly by Pope and Warburton, cites Douglas's enthusiasm for Horace as if to deflect attention from the offensiveness of the verse, this is not (*pace* Nicolson & Rousseau) added in response to his death: the only change from 1742 is 'collected' instead of 'has collected', a change of tense in recognition of his death. Pope too read Horace with care and devotion, but the exhaustiveness of Douglas's collection and his pride in publishing its catalogue may have associated him in Pope's view with the lust for objects displayed by the collectors of antiquities (Douglas 1739).

397 and n. Introducing a well-established satirical topic, the study of natural history. According to *Tatler* 236 such studies 'do not so much tend to open and enlarge the Mind, as

A tribe, with weeds and shells fantastic crown'd,
Each with some wond'rous gift approach'd the Pow'r,
A Nest, a Toad, a Fungus, or a Flow'r.
But far the foremost, two, with earnest zeal,
And aspect ardent to the Throne appeal.
  The first thus open'd: Hear thy suppliant's call,
Great Queen, and common Mother of us all!
Fair from its humble bed I rear'd this Flow'r,
Suckled, and chear'd, with air, and sun, and show'r,
Soft on the paper ruff its leaves I spread,
Bright with the gilded button tipt its head,
Then thron'd in glass, and nam'd it CAROLINE:

405–9.] These Verses are translated from Catullus, Epith: 'Ut flos in septis secretus nascitur hortis, / Quam mulcent aurae, firmat Sol, educat imber, / Multi illum pueri, multae optavere puellae: / Idem quum tenui carptus defloruit ungui, / Nulli illum pueri, nullae optavere puellae', *etc.*

409. and nam'd it* Caroline:*] It is a compliment which the Florists usually pay to Princes and great persons, to give their names to the most curious Flowers of their raising: Some have been very jealous of vindicating this honour, but none more than that ambitious Gardiner at Hammersmith, who caused his Favourite to be painted on his Sign, with this inscription, *This is* My *Queen Caroline.*

---

to contract and fix it upon Trifles' (Bond 1987: III, 219). The note, initialled in 1751 as by Warburton, charges experimental science with destructiveness in its collection and dissection of living things. For Pope's involvement, despite his disapproval, with collecting and antiquarianism, and the suggestion that 'the entire *Dunciad* has become a sort of cabinet of curiosities', see Rogers 1993a: 253.

401–36. 'The Throne' strongly suggests an allusion to Queen Caroline, who had a keen interest in gardening. The destruction of the carnation 'Caroline' alludes to her death in 1737, and the image of the butterfly, which draws on a traditional figure for the favour briefly enjoyed by court favourites, might suggest her confidant Lord Hervey (Erskine-Hill 1972b: 56–9).

405–9n. The note cites a passage from a wedding poem by the Roman poet Gaius Valerius Catullus (*c.*84–*c.*54 BC) in which the bride is compared to a flower: 'As in a sheltered garden a hidden flower springs up, which the breezes caress, the sun strengthens, the showers help to grow ... many young men and many young women desire it; but when, nipped off by a sharp fingernail, it withers, no young men desire it, nor any young women' (LXII, 39, lines 41–4).

406. Suckled, and chear'd: The devotee talks about the flower as if it were a child.

407–9. A highly technical account of contemporary methods of producing and displaying perfect individual blooms on carnations (although Pope does not specify the type of flower until line 418). The 'leaves' (i.e. petals) were supported on a paper collar and protected by a glass with metal fittings (see the elaborate account given by Philip Miller in his *Gardeners Dictionary* (1733): entry under 'caryophyllus'). Although Pope was himself a keen gardener who ordered plants from Miller and alluded to his *Dictionary* as a standard work, as well as growing such labour-intensive specialities as hot-house pineapples, his recorded comments

Each Maid cry'd, charming! and each Youth, divine!
Did Nature's pencil ever blend such rays,
Such vary'd light in one promiscuous blaze?
Now prostrate! dead! behold that Caroline:
No Maid cries, charming! and no Youth, divine!
And lo the wretch! whose vile, whose insect lust
Lay'd this gay daughter of the Spring in dust.
Oh punish him, or to th' Elysian shades
Dismiss my soul, where no Carnation fades.

---

on gardening reveal an analogy with his humanistic interest in the classics, insofar as he professes less concern with the detail of individual plants than with larger effects of garden design (*Corr.*: III, 451; IV, 459; Martin 1984: 2–4).

409n. The note, initialled in 1751 as jointly by Pope and Warburton, satirises the practice of naming plant varieties after celebrities. The hybridising of ornamental varieties had gained pace from the seventeenth century, encouraging breeders to promote their products under distinct variety names; and naming plants after distinguished people both complimented the person and enhanced the status of the product. But such distinction was transient, as Miller noted in the article on carnations cited above: 'every County produces new Flowers almost every Year; so that those Flowers which at their first raising were greatly valu'd, are in two or three Years become so common, as to be of little worth'. He adds that it is therefore not worth recording the names of current favourites, 'which are generally borrow'd either from the Names and Titles of Noblemen, or from the Person's Name, or Place of Abode, who rais'd it' (Miller 1733: 'caryophyllus'). The story of the 'ambitious Gardiner' (Hammersmith was a village on the fashionable western side of London) mocks both his proprietorial aspirations and the reified status of the Queen herself.

410. 'Charming' and 'divine' are modish terms of facile approbation, overlaying Catullus's poignancy with elegant vacuity (see editor's note on lines 405–9).

411–12. The florist presents Nature as an inferior artist (the 'pencil' is a fine brush used for delicate work), who fails to equal the 'promiscuous blaze' that he has achieved artificially. For the epic connotations of the phrase, see Sherbo 1988: 223.

413–14. Queen Caroline's messy and excruciating death was, as her attendant Lord Hervey recorded in his private journal, preceded by agonising surgery and rupture of the intestine (Sedgwick 1931: II, 877–915). Epigrams by Pope suggest a complicated mixture of responses: 'HERE lies wrapt up in forty thousand towels / The only proof that C*** had bowels' combines a sneer at the indignity of her last hours with the old charge of her malice towards the Prince of Wales; but his compliment on Lady Burlington's picture of the Queen reserves its criticism for the 'blubbring Bishop' and 'flattring Dean', setting the tone of a soberer response in its first line: 'ALAS! what room for Flattry, or for Pride!' (*TE*: VI, 390, 392–3). Line 413 assimilates the dead flower to the dead queen, recalling the iconographic function of flowers as emblems of mortality.

415. insect lust: The rival, who speaks at lines 421–36, is characterised as low and disgusting like an insect; he destroys the flower as an insect might; and his lust is specifically to capture an insect, namely the butterfly. Carretta suggests this may be 'a particularly vicious hit at George II', implying that his 'lust' had caused Caroline's fatal illness, which may have arisen from complications of her last confinement (Carretta 1983: 269).

417–18. In the Elysian Fields of the classical underworld it was always spring, which this obsessive gardener visualises in terms of never-dying carnations.

He ceas'd, and wept. With innocence of mien,
Th' Accus'd stood forth, and thus address'd the Queen.
Of all th' enamel'd race, whose silv'ry wing
Waves to the tepid Zephyrs of the spring,
Or swims along the fluid atmosphere,
Once brightest shin'd this child of Heat and Air.
I saw, and started from its vernal bow'r
The rising game, and chac'd from flow'r to flow'r.
It fled, I follow'd; now in hope, now pain;
It stopt, I stopt; it mov'd, I mov'd again.
At last it fix'd, 'twas on what plant it pleas'd,
And where it fix'd, the beauteous bird I seiz'd:
Rose or Carnation was below my care;
I meddle, Goddess! only in my sphere.
I tell the naked fact without disguise,
And, to excuse it, need but shew the prize;
Whose spoils this paper offers to your eye,
Fair ev'n in death! this peerless *Butterfly*.
My sons! (she answer'd) both have done your parts:
Live happy both, and long promote our arts.
But hear a Mother, when she recommends
To your fraternal care, our sleeping friends.
The common Soul, of Heav'n's more frugal make,
Serves but to keep fools pert, and knaves awake:

421.] The poet seems to have an eye to Spenser, Muiopotmos: 'Of all the race of silver-winged Flies / Which do possess the Empire of the Air.'

427, 428.] 'I started back, / It started back; but pleas'd I soon return'd, / Pleas'd it return'd as soon'. Milton.

440. our sleeping friends.] Of whom see ver. 345 above.

---

420. Th' Accus'd: For the suggestion that the character is based on the entomologist Joseph Dandridge (1664–1755), see Means 1973.

421 and n. 'Enamel'd' evokes a glossy painted surface. The note cites Spenser's tale of a butterfly's entrapment by a spider (Oram 1989: 'Muiopotmos', lines 17–18).

422. Zephyrs: breezes.

425. vernal: pertaining to spring.

427–8 and n. The note cites Eve's account of first encountering her reflection in water, associating the collector's urge with narcissism and feminine self-absorption (Fowler 1998: *Paradise Lost* IV.462–4). Pope may also have taken a hint from the rhythm of the account of a child's chasing a butterfly in Shakespeare's *Coriolanus* (Alexander 1951: *Coriolanus* I.iii.57–65; Potts 1959).

430. bird: butterfly. For the unusual expression, see Loane 1944: 37.

435. The dead butterfly is mounted on paper.

440 and n. Dulness would like them to interest Paridell and his like in some such pointless but absorbing hobby.

A drowzy Watchman, that just gives a knock,
And breaks our rest, to tell us what's a clock.
Yet by some object ev'ry brain is stirr'd;
The dull may waken to a Humming-bird;
The most recluse, discreetly open'd, find
Congenial matter in the Cockle-kind;
The mind, in Metaphysics at a loss,
May wander in a wilderness of Moss;
The head that turns at super-lunar things,
Poiz'd with a tail, may steer on Wilkins' wings.
O! would the Sons of Men once think their Eyes

450. a wilderness of Moss;] Of which the Naturalists count I can't tell how many hundred species.

452.* Wilkins' *wings.] One of the first Projectors of the Royal Society, who, among many enlarged and useful notions, entertain'd the extravagant hope of a possibility to fly to the Moon; which has put some volatile Genius's upon making wings for that purpose.

453.] This is the third speech of the Goddess to her Supplicants, and completes the whole of what she had to give in instruction on this important occasion, concerning Learning, Civil

---

443–4. Watchmen patrolled the streets at night and called out the hours.

447–8. Developing an analogy between reclusive personalities and cockles (small shellfish which seal the serrated edges of their two shells tightly shut).

450 and n. Pope had compared the variety of human character with the variety between different kinds of moss in *Characters of Men*: he himself collected petrified mosses for his garden (line 18; *TE*: V, 384; Serle 1745; Nicolson & Rousseau 1968: 252–4). The note was initialled in 1751 as jointly by Pope and Warburton. Pope may have had in mind the magnificent *Historia Muscorum* published at Oxford in 1741 by Johann Jacob Dillenius (1684–1747), a German specialist in the classification and reproduction of moss who had been made Fellow of the Royal Society in 1724 and Sherardian Professor of Botany at Oxford in 1734 (Gillispie 1972: 'Dillenius, Johann Jacob'). About 600 species of moss are described, classified and illustrated.

451. super-lunar things: In ancient cosmology, things above the moon were immutable, things below subject to change and decay. The implication is that what is great and unchanging (like classics or theology as traditionally understood) is to be preferred to the empirical study of material objects basic to the then evolving conception of the natural sciences – a kind of study consistently ridiculed by traditional humanism as mere trifling.

452 and n. The note, initialled in 1751 as jointly by Pope and Warburton, refers to John Wilkins (1614–72), Bishop of Chester and a principal founder of the Royal Society, who is characterised as a 'projector', i.e. a deviser of schemes and inventions. Wilkins argued that the moon might be inhabited, and hoped that posterity would devise means to visit it (*The Discovery of a World in the Moone* 1638: 207–9). ***Poiz'd:*** weighted (to balance the flying machine). ***enlarged:*** liberated, enlightened.

453–6. For Dulness's preference for the trivial and minute in relation to notions of her sex's proper interests, and hence to a wider fear that culture was becoming feminised, see Ingrassia 1991: 46–8.

453 and n. For flies and other small creatures in Pope's thought, see particularly line 238 and editor's note and Nicolson & Rousseau 1968: 243–51. The note, initialled in 1751 as jointly by Pope and Warburton, charges 'the Investigators of Nature' with slighting the 'First'

And Reason giv'n them but to study *Flies*!
See Nature in some partial narrow shape,
And let the Author of the Whole escape:
Learn but to trifle; or, who most observe,
To wonder at their Maker, not to serve.
Be that my task (replies a gloomy Clerk,

Society, and Religion. In the first speech, ver. 119, to her Editors and conceited Critics, she directs how to deprave Wit and discredit fine Writers. In her second, ver. 175, to the Educators of Youth, she shews them how all Civil Duties may be extinguish'd, in that one doctrine of divine Hereditary Right. And in this third, she charges the Investigators of Nature to amuse themselves in Trifles, and rest in Second causes, with a total disregard of the First. This being all that Dulness can wish, is all she needs to say; and we may apply to her (as the Poet hath manag'd it) what hath been said of true Wit, that *She neither says too little, nor too much.*

459. a gloomy Clerk,] The Epithet gloomy in this line may seem the same with that of

---

cause (the divine creator) and contenting themselves instead with 'Second causes' (created things which, under divine authority, produce the effects with which the natural scientist is concerned). I have not been able to identify the closing quotation.

459–92. A satire on trends in religious thought that Pope and Warburton associate with deism and free-thinking. Like Dulness, the goddess Oblivion in Thomas Newcomb's anonymously published *Bibliotheca* (1712) had favoured such departures from orthodoxy (Lund 1991: 178). Warburton had initially won Pope's friendship by defending him from the accusation of having expressed such views in the *Essay on Man*; and this section, particularly in its commentary, works hard to set Pope's orthodoxy above reproach. Unlike Warburton, whose *Divine Legation* (1738–41) begins with a defiant challenge 'To the Free-Thinkers' and centres on a pugnacious reassertion of the orthodox case for the necessity of the belief in rewards and punishments after death, Pope was temperamentally ill at ease with systematic dogma and typically evasive on controversial points: it was characteristic that in his last days he still cherished the implausible hope that Bolingbroke, the extent of whose influence in slanting the *Essay on Man* towards deism has been much debated, could be drawn into friendship with the aggressively orthodox Warburton (Ruffhead 1769: 527–9). Though Warburton and Bolingbroke both argued from natural religion, i.e. using arguments derived from empirical experience, they argued in opposite directions, Warburton to bolster orthodoxy, Bolingbroke to undermine it – although it is unlikely that many realised during Bolingbroke's lifetime the full extent of his dissent from orthodoxy, which emerged most clearly from private papers published only after his death. Warburton, whose interest in maintaining Pope's orthodoxy makes him a partial witness, represented him after his death as duped by Bolingbroke (*OAC*: I, 127). Pope's friend the philosopher and defender of orthodoxy George Berkeley had in his anonymously published *Alciphron: or, The Minute Philosopher* (1732), which Pope read and admired, argued that natural religion was viable only in conjunction with the Christian doctrine of which he represented it as an intrinsic support (*Alciphron* 1732: I, 330–32, Dialogue V.xxix–xxx; Hollingshead 1982–3). Several of Pope's points in the present passage echo Berkeley's, whose adoption of the term 'minute philosopher' for 'free-thinker' anticipates Pope's repeated insistence that Dulness's votaries address themselves solely to small concerns so as to allow Dulness unchallenged control of larger issues. (For varying accounts of the religious issues raised in the passage, see Friedman in Clifford & Landa 1949: 89–95; Atkins in Mack & Winn 1980: 392–415; Hollingshead 1982–3; Sambrook 1993: 33–44; Young 1993; Rivers 1991, vol. 2.)

459. a gloomy Clerk: Punning on the name of the clergyman ('Clerk') Samuel Clarke

Sworn foe to Myst'ry, yet divinely dark;
Whose pious hope aspires to see the day
When Moral Evidence shall quite decay,
And damns implicit faith, and holy lies,
Prompt to impose, and fond to dogmatize:)

dark in the next. But *gloomy* relates to the uncomfortable and disastrous condition of an irreligious Sceptic, whereas *dark* alludes only to his puzzled and embroiled Systems.

462.] Alluding to a ridiculous and absurd way of some Mathematicians, in calculating the gradual decay of Moral Evidence by mathematical proportions: according to which calculation, in about fifty years it will be no longer probable that Julius Caesar was in Gaul, or died in the Senate House. See *Craig's Theologiae Christianae Principia Mathematica*. But as it seems evident, that facts of a thousand years old, for instance, are now as probable as they were five hundred years ago; it is plain that if in fifty more they quite disappear, it must be owing, not to their Arguments, but to the extraordinary Power of our Goddess; for whose help therefore they have reason to pray.

(1675–1729), author of *A Demonstration of the Being and Attributes of God* (1705) and *A Discourse Concerning the Unchangeable Obligations of Natural Religion, and the Truth and Certainty of the Christian Revelation* (1706), although it would be reductive to restrict the satire to a single individual. Clarke was one of the modernising theologians favoured by Queen Caroline (*TE*: V, 385–6; and see *To Burlington*, line 78, and Mack 1969: 47–8). Although he doubted the full divinity of Christ and hence the doctrine of the Trinity, and despite his use of 'a priori' reasoning (see line 471), he by no means went to the extremes here described (Sambrook 1993: 37, 40, 44). Bolingbroke apparently discussed his disagreements with Clarke's theology with Pope (St John 1844: Index, 'Clarke (Dr. Sam.)').

459n. Initialled in 1751 as jointly by Pope and Warburton.

460. Myst'ry: Religious propositions traditionally asserted as beyond the grasp of human reason. Freethinkers insisted on subjecting doctrine to rational enquiry in ways thought blasphemous by the orthodox. ***divinely dark:*** With a pun on 'divine' ('clergyman'). Prior describes in 'The Conversation' a theological argument which hinges on 'Points divinely dark', and rhymes 'Clarke' with 'dark' (Bawcutt 1958: 221; Wright & Spears 1971: I, 524, line 35).

462 and n. 'Moral' in this technical sense designates what is probable rather than demonstrable, a staple of orthodox apologetics. The note, initialled in 1751 as jointly by Pope and Warburton, focuses the notion of the decay of evidence through a particular example of a widespread seventeenth-century project for the resolution of moral, theological and philosophical problems by geometrical and mathematical methods (Bredvold 1951). John Craig (*d.* 1731), a distinguished mathematician and friend of Newton, proposed in his 'Mathematical Principles of Christian Theology' formulae for calculating the probability of past events according to distance in time and transmission of evidence. His dedication of the book to the Whig Bishop Gilbert Burnet would not have advanced his cause in Pope's eyes; and some of his calculations, notably 'In what space of time will the probability of the story of Christ disappear?', would have struck the orthodox as blasphemy of a peculiarly unhinged kind (Craig 1699: 23). Clarke also aspired to use quasi-mathematical proofs in metaphysics, and was criticised for the alleged inappropriateness of such a project (Young 1993: 441–8).

463–4. Freethinkers characteristically described established Christianity as a corrupt system under which the common people were required to place unquestioning trust ('implicit faith')

Let others creep by timid steps, and slow,
On plain Experience lay foundations low,
By common sense to common knowledge bred,
And last, to Nature's Cause thro' Nature led.
All-seeing in thy mists, we want no guide,
Mother of Arrogance, and Source of Pride!
We nobly take the high Priori Road,
And reason downward, till we doubt of God:

465–68.] In these lines are described the *Disposition* of the rational *Inquirer*, and the *means* and *end* of *Knowledge*. With regard to his *disposition*, the contemplation of the works of God with human faculties, must needs make a modest and sensible man timorous and fearful; and that will naturally direct him to the right *means* of acquiring the little knowledge his faculties are capable of, namely *plain and sure experience*; which tho' supporting only an humble *foundation*, and permitting only a very slow progress, yet leads, surely, to the *end*, the discovery of the *God of nature*.

471. the high Priori Road,] Those who, from the effects in this Visible world, deduce the Eternal Power and Godhead of the First Cause tho' they cannot attain to an adequate idea of the Deity, yet discover so much of him, as enables them to see the End of their Creation, and the Means of their Happiness: whereas they who take this high Priori Road (such as Hobbs, Spinoza, Des Cartes, and some better Reasoners) for one that goes right, ten lose themselves in Mists, or ramble after Visions which deprive them of all sight of their End, and mislead them in the choice of wrong means.

472.] This was in fact the case of those who, instead of reasoning from a *visible World* to an *invisible God*, took the other road; and from an *invisible God* (to whom they had given

---

in doctrines fabricated out of self-interest by their temporal and ecclesiastical superiors. The couplet suggests, however, that freethinkers really want to 'impose' and 'dogmatize' on their own account.

465–8 and n. The 'gloomy Clerk' despises the unpretentious reasoning from experience which the note, initialled in 1751 as by Warburton, characterises, in line with standard orthodox applications of natural religion, as the most devout and rational way of thinking about God.

468. Echoing Pope's application of natural religion in contrasting the narrow dogmatist with the truly enlightened man who 'looks thro' Nature, up to Nature's God' (*Essay on Man* IV.332).

471 and n. Punning on the technical expression *a priori*, denoting reasoning which proceeds from the assertion of causes to deduce their effects: the method is the reverse of *a posteriori*, in which effects are examined empirically and their causes induced from them. Pope, Warburton and Bolingbroke unite in condemning the former and approving the latter (cp. *Essay on Man* I.17–32; St John 1844: IV, 137–8, 144). Friedman cites Matthew Tindal's *Christianity as Old as the Creation* (1730) as prime example of *a priori* deism, and the method constituted one of Bolingbroke's objections to Clarke's *Demonstration* – although Clarke did also argue *a posteriori* (Clifford & Landa 1949: 91–5). The note, initialled in 1751 as jointly by Pope and Warburton, contrasts the humble *a posteriori* reasoner who learns the 'End' ('purpose') for which God created him with the ambitious philosophers whose *a priori* axioms lead them astray.

472n. The note, initialled in 1751 as by Warburton, explains that *a priori* reasoning from preconceived notions of God convinces the speculator that the world ought to be different

Make Nature still incroach upon his plan;
And shove him off as far as e'er we can:
Thrust some Mechanic Cause into his place;
Or bind in Matter, or diffuse in Space.

attributes agreeable to certain metaphysical principles formed out of their own imaginations) reasoned *downwards* to a *visible world* in theory, of Man's Creation; which not agreeing, as might be expected, to that of God's, they began, from their inability to account for *evil* which they saw in his world, to doubt of that God, whose being they had admitted, and whose attributes they had deduced *a priori*, on weak and mistaken principles.

473.] This relates to such as being ashamed to assert a mere Mechanic Cause, and yet unwilling to forsake it intirely, have had recourse to a certain *Plastic Nature, Elastic Fluid, Subtile Matter, etc.*

475–6.] The first of these Follies is that of Des Cartes, the second of Hobbs, the third of some succeeding Philosophers.

---

from what it actually is (notably as regards 'evil') and hence makes him doubt the existence of a God capable of creating the world that actually exists.

473–4 and n. The 'gloomy Clerk' seeks to 'incroach upon' the extent of God's activity in the world by attributing as much agency as possible to physical factors ('some Mechanic Cause': for contemporary controversies over materialist theories, as opposed to the traditional acceptance of immaterial as well as material substance, see Yolton 1983). The note, initialled in 1751 as jointly by Pope and Warburton, lumps together various attempts to define the dynamic potential of the universe, implying that they all represent an attempt to reassign God's creativity to created objects. **Plastic Nature:** The Cambridge Platonist Ralph Cudworth (1617–88), who was concerned to counter atheistic materialism, proposed the notion that 'plastic' ('formative') powers in nature were agents of God's activity (Passmore 1951: 19–25). The expression is used disapprovingly by the orthodox speaker in Berkeley's *Alciphron*, where belief in 'a plastic Nature, or Soul of the World' is presented as inadequate in comparison with belief in 'a Providence inspecting and taking care of Humane Affairs' (*Alciphron* 1732: I, 196, Dialogue III.xiv). **Elastic Fluid:** A contemporary term for the tendency of matter to expand when released from pressure, which might seem to the orthodox to attribute dynamic force to the substance rather than to God: see for example Bentley's statement that 'the Air is now certainly known to consist of elastick or springy Particles, that have a continual tendency and endeavour to expand and display themselves', made in the context of a work of Christian apologetics on Newtonian principles (Bentley 1693: 12). Newton himself had been accused by Berkeley of attributing to aspects of the physical universe what the orthodox regarded as unique to God; and he revised the *Principia* in order to distance himself explicitly from the suggestion that the universe could be understood without a conception of divine control (Cajori 1962: II, 544–6, 668–70, *Principia Mathematica* III, General Scholium). **Subtile Matter:** Descartes, who denied the possibility of a vacuum, posited 'some subtle and very fluid matter, which extends without interruption from the heavenly bodies to us' as a medium for the passage of light (Cottingham 1985–91: I, 154). The notion had been attacked by Bentley (Bentley 1693: 9–10).

475–6 and n. The note was initialled in 1751 as jointly by Pope and Warburton. ***The first of these Follies:*** The three expressions criticised in Pope and Warburton's note on line 473 could be cited as substituting a 'Mechanic Cause' for God. The reference to Descartes seems to allude to his theory of solar and planetary vortices ('the whole of the celestial

Or, at one bound o'er-leaping all his laws,
Make God Man's Image, Man the final Cause,

477.] These words are very significant: In their Physical and Metaphysical reasonings it was a *Chain* of pretended *Demonstrations* that drew them into all these absurd conclusions. But their errors in Morals rest only on bold and impudent *Assertions,* without the least shadow of proof, in which they *o'er-leap* all the laws of Argument as well as Truth.

478–80.] Here the Poet, from the errors relating to a Deity in Natural Philosophy, descends to those in Moral. Man was made according to *God's Image;* this false Theology, measuring his Attributes by ours, makes God after *Man's Image.* This proceeds from the imperfection of his *Reason.* The next, of imagining himself the Final Cause, is the effect of his *Pride:* as the making Virtue and Vice arbitrary, and Morality the imposition of the Magistrate, is of the *Corruption* of his *heart.* Hence he centers every thing in *himself.* The Progress of Dulness herein differing from that of Madness; one ends in *seeing all in God,* the other in *seeing all in Self.*

---

matter in which the planets are located turns continuously like a vortex with the sun at its centre'), by which he explained the movements of the heavens (Cottingham 1985–91: I, 253–4, 257). For Pope's interest in the theory of vortices, see Nicolson & Rousseau 1968: 199–206; for circular motion as expressive of Dulness's effects, see Sitter 1971: 37–9, 46–8. ***the second of Hobbs:*** Hobbes defines concepts of God and of spirit within a materialist framework, rather than accepting the traditional scheme in which spirit exists independently of matter (Oakeshott 1946: 255–60). ***the third of some succeeding Philosophers:*** Henry More (1614–87) asserted in his correspondence with Descartes that spirit was capable of extension in space, which Descartes denied (Cottingham 1985–91: III, 360–63). Sutherland suggests that Newton's conceptualising of divine activity, in which he was followed by Clarke, might also have been suspected as an attempt to 'diffuse' God 'in Space' (*TE*: V, 387).

477 and n. Echoing Satan's leap into Paradise: 'Due entrance he disdained, and in contempt, / At one slight bound high overleaped all bound' (Fowler 1998: *Paradise Lost* IV.180–81). The note, initialled in 1751 as by Warburton, expresses particular outrage at the freethinkers' sceptical approach to morality.

478. Reminiscent of Tindal's suggestion that living by right reason is to be like God (Tindal 1730: 20). ***Make God Man's Image:*** Reversing the biblical doctrine that man was made in God's image (Genesis 1:26). Anthropomorphic conceptions of God were criticised by Bolingbroke as flattering human vanity (St John 1844: III, 204, 532; IV, 134). Pope had stated in the *Essay on Man* that the idea of God was originally derived from the experience of paternal care, but had later been corrupted by the projection onto the divine of the worst human attributes, 'Such as the souls of cowards might conceive, / And, form'd like tyrants, tyrants would believe' (*Essay on Man* III.215–26, 241–68 (259–60)). Criticism of the *Essay* may have alerted Pope to the uncomfortable overlap between such theorising and the standard arguments of freethinkers, as rendered, for example, by Berkeley (*Alciphron* 1732: I, 23–4, Dialogue I.vii). Berkeley had also turned anthropomorphism against the freethinkers by making his orthodox speaker claim that freethinkers projected their own characteristics onto their idea of God, and then used the improbability of such a God as an argument for atheism (*Alciphron* 1732: I, 261–2, Dialogue IV.xxiv). ***the final Cause:*** The theological term for the divine purpose, conceived as the ultimate cause. The line seems to attribute to the freethinkers so exclusive a focus on man as to rule out the possibility of any purpose superior to human purposes.

478–80n. Initialled in 1751 as jointly by Pope and Warburton. ***Natural Philosophy:*** the physical sciences. ***making Virtue and Vice arbitrary:*** By arguing that since notions of

Find Virtue local, all Relation scorn,
See all in *Self,* and but for self be born:
Of nought so certain as our *Reason* still,
Of nought so doubtful as of *Soul* and *Will.*
Oh hide the God still more! and make us see
Such as Lucretius drew, a God like Thee:
Wrapt up in Self, a God without a Thought,
Regardless of our merit or default.

481.] Of which we have most cause to be diffident.

482.] Two things the most self-evident, the Existence of our Soul, and the Freedom of our Will.

484. Such as Lucretius drew,] Lib. I. ver. 57: 'Omnis enim per se Divom natura necesse'st / Immortali aevo *summa cum pace* fruatur, / *Semota* ab nostris rebus, *summotaque* longe ... / Nec bene pro *meritis* capitur, nec tangitur *ira.*' From whence the two verses following are translated, and wonderfully agree with the character of our Goddess. SCRIBL.

---

right and wrong vary, they are merely relative concepts, not divinely sanctioned absolutes. Hobbes had suggested that particular individuals and communities adopted particular definitions of good or evil appropriate to their own circumstances (Oakeshott 1946: 32–3). In his anonymously published *The Fable of the Bees* (1714), Mandeville had argued that appetites traditionally condemned as vices were vital to the nation's economy, and hence to the general good, a doctrine contested by Berkeley and by Warburton in the *Divine Legation* (*Alciphron* 1732: I, 66–152, Dialogue II; Warburton 1738–41: 78–86). ***Morality the imposition of the Magistrate:*** Freethinkers argued that the church served state power by using the threat of divine punishment to maintain social control, a suspicion which Pope could conceivably have been seen as supporting in the *Essay on Man* (see editor's note on line 478). ***that of Madness:*** The mystic's sense that all experience is centred in God is defined as a deviation from good sense as extreme as the self-centredness of Dulness's freethinkers.

479. local: dependent on place. ***all Relation scorn:*** scorn all sense of the responsibilities arising from relationship to God and to others.

480. Mandeville's *The Fable of the Bees,* with its subtitle of *Private Vices, Publick Benefits,* could be read as sanctifying self-indulgence by arguing that it was more conducive to the public good (conceived as economic prosperity) than traditional disciplines of altruism and self-restraint. Berkeley makes his freethinker maintain that 'every wise Man looks upon himself, or his own bodily Existence in this World, as the Center and ultimate End of all his Actions and Regards' (*Alciphron* 1732: I, 30, Dialogue I.ix).

481n and 482n. The notes, initialled in 1751 as jointly by Pope and Warburton, assert the orthodox view that while the soul and free will are self-evident facts, the claims of human reason are to be treated with caution.

484 and n. The note, initialled in 1751 as jointly by Pope and Warburton, quotes loosely from Lucretius's *De Rerum Natura* ('On the Nature of Things'): 'For the very nature of the gods is intrinsically such as must enjoy immortality in perfect peace, removed from our affairs, and quite separated .... Deity is not impressed by our deserving actions, nor is it touched by anger' (I.44–6, 49). The tendency of religious scepticism to undermine the teaching of rewards and punishments after death was widely viewed as subversive of morality.

Or that bright Image to our fancy draw,
Which Theocles in raptur'd vision saw,

***487. Or that* bright Image]** *Bright Image* was the Title given by the later Platonists to that Idea of *Nature,* which they had form'd in their fancy, so bright, that they call'd it *Αὔτοπτον Ἄγαλμα,* or the *Self-seen Image,* i.e. seen by its own light.

488.] Thus this Philosopher calls upon his Friend, to partake with him in these Visions:

'To-morrow, when the Eastern Sun
With his first Beams adorns the front
Of yonder Hill, if you're content
To wander with me in the Woods you see,
We will pursue those Loves of ours,
By favour of the Sylvan Nymphs:

and invoking first the *Genius* of the *Place,* we'll try to obtain at least some faint and distant view of the *Sovereign Genius* and *first Beauty.*' *Charact.* Vol. 2. pag. 245.

This *Genius* is thus apostrophized (pag. 345.) by the same Philosopher:

'—— O glorious *Nature!*
Supremely fair, and sovereignly good!
All-loving, and all-lovely! all divine!
Wise Substitute of Providence! *impower'd*
Creatress! or *impow'ring Deity,*
Supreme Creator!
Thee I invoke, and thee alone adore.'

Sir *Isaac Newton* distinguishes between these two in a very different manner. [Princ. Schol. gen. sub fin.] — *Hunc cognoscimus solummodo per proprietates suas et attributa, et per sapientissimas et optimas rerum structuras, et causas finales; veneramur autem et colimus ob dominium.* Deus *etenim sine dominio, providentia, et causis finalibus, nihil aliud est quam* Fatum *et* Natura.

487n. Initialled in 1751 as by Warburton.

488 and n. Theocles: The author's spokesman in 'The Moralists', anonymously published by Anthony Ashley Cooper (1671–1713), third Earl of Shaftesbury (included in *Characteristicks of Men, Manners, Opinions, Times* 1711). Shaftesbury was a major target of Warburton's 'To the Free-Thinkers', which attacks not only his doctrine, but also his use of rhetorical personae and his advocacy of a style less solemn than that conventionally deployed in theological discussion (Warburton 1738–41: I, i–xliv; but for a positive evaluation of his 'polite' style, see Klein 1994). Shaftesbury tended to assert a basic human impulse towards benevolence (rather than original sin requiring redemption through Christ), to rest morality on the love of virtue for its own sake (rather than on an afterlife of rewards and punishments), and to inculcate reverence for a somewhat remote deity conceived as a benign intelligence ordering the universe (rather than the Christian God, separate from but choosing to intervene in his creation, and capable of anger against his creatures) (Voitle 1984: Chs. IV and VII). ***Thus this Philosopher:*** The note, initialled in 1751 as jointly by Pope and Warburton, imitates Berkeley's joke of setting out Shaftesbury's prose (slightly adapted) as verse, implying a self-indulgent fluency of figurative language inappropriate for serious philosophical analysis (*Alciphron* 1732: I, 312–14, Dialogue V.xxii). To refer to Shaftesbury in this context as 'this Philosopher' thus implies a sneer. The choice of the first quotation seems humorously intended, inviting the

While thro' Poetic scenes the Genius roves,
Or wanders wild in Academic Groves;
That Nature our Society adores,
Where Tindal dictates, and Silenus snores.

489–90.] 'Above all things I lov'd *Ease*, and of all Philosophers those who reason'd most *at their Ease*, and were never angry or disturb'd, as those call'd *Sceptics* never were. I look'd upon this kind of Philosophy as the *prettiest, agreeablest, roving Exercise of the Mind*, possible to be imagined.' Vol. 2. p. 206.

492. Silenus] Silenus was an Epicurean Philosopher, as appears from Virgil, Eclog. 6. where he sings the Principles of that Philosophy in his drink.

---

reader to visualise Theocles pursuing 'Loves' rather less abstract than the divine image of Nature actually referred to. The second quotation is introduced to convict Shaftesbury of a heretical identification of God with nature; and Newton is cited to demonstrate by contrast that real intellectual distinction is not ashamed to submit to theological orthodoxy, in this case that the Creator is distinct from creation and rules over it within the context of a purposive design: 'We know him only through his properties and attributes, and through his most wise and excellent ordering of things, and his final causes; but we reverence and adore him on account of his dominion. For a God without dominion, providence, and final causes, is nothing else but Fate and Nature' (Cajori 1962: III, 'General Scholium').

489–90 and n. the Genius: the presiding spirit of Nature. ***'Above all things':*** The note, initialled in 1751 as jointly by Pope and Warburton, presents a quotation slightly adapted from *Characteristicks* to suggest that Shaftesbury's approach to philosophy is merely frivolous (cp. *Alciphron* 1732: I, 34–41, Dialogue I.xi). (Shaftesbury's stress on '*Ease*', contrasted with the state of those whose philosophy permits them to be 'angry or disturb'd', could be taken as a sign of his commitment to Stoic calm: see Voitle 1984: 135–63.)

491. Freethinkers are presented as a community or sect in *Alciphron* (*Alciphron* 1732: I, 8, Dialogue I.ii). Warburton suggested in 1751 a specific allusion to John Toland's pseudonymously published *Pantheisticon* (1720), a deist liturgy, in Latin, to be used by a so-called 'Socratic society'; but Warburton may simply have been reminded of Toland's work by the publication earlier in 1751 of an English translation.

492 and n. Virgil's Silenus is a drunken satyr who sings the story of creation in a style echoing the Epicurean atomism of Lucretius (*Eclogues* VI.31–40). The note, initialled in 1751 as jointly by Pope and Warburton, makes the commonplace but unjustified implication that the Epicurean system recommends unbridled hedonism as the highest good. Pope's Silenus alludes to Thomas Gordon (*d.* 1750), a strongly anti-clerical Whig, attacked by Warburton as a freethinker, who, despite writing against Walpole in the *London Journal* in the early 1720s, was later recruited by him, apparently as a literary (rather than financial) supervisor of government-subsidised journalism (Warburton 1738–41: I, i–xliv; Nichols 1812–15: I, 709–10; Harris 1987: 104; Gerrard 1994: 23–4, 28). An early manuscript draft had included him as one of the patron-ticklers in Book II, and Elwin and Courthope cite a couplet from a draft of *Epilogue to the Satires* which satirises his going over to Walpole (Mack 1984: 141; Elwin & Courthope 1871–86: III, 459). However, it appears from a letter from Pope to his and Walpole's friend William Fortescue, through whom Pope had sometimes met Walpole socially in earlier years, that in 1738 Pope had entertained Gordon at Twickenham, when they 'drank Sir Robert's health'; and Sherburn suggests that Pope's evocation of Silenus's relaxed self-revelation may reflect such an informal and unguarded encounter (*Corr.*: IV, 114). The

Rous'd at his name, up rose the bowzy Sire,
And shook from out his Pipe the seeds of fire;
Then snapt his box, and strok'd his belly down:
Rosy and rev'rend, tho' without a Gown.
Bland and familiar to the throne he came,
Led up the Youth, and call'd the Goddess *Dame*.
Then thus. From Priest-craft happily set free,
Lo! ev'ry finish'd Son returns to thee:

494. seeds of Fire;] The Epicurean language, *Semina rerum*, or Atoms. Virg. Eclog. 6. *Semina ignis — semina flammae.*

499, 500.] The learned Scriblerus is here very whimsical. It would seem, says he, by this, as if the *Priests* (who are always plotting and contriving mischief against the *Law of Nature*) had inveigled these harmless Youths from the bosom of their Mother, and kept them in open Rebellion to her, till Silenus broke the charm, and restored them to her indulgent arms. But

---

connection between Gordon and Silenus is initially through wine, as Walpole had made Gordon a Commissioner for Wine Licences; but a deeper parallel lies in their function as comically undercut unfolders of ultimate truths, since Pope uses his Silenus to reveal the key processes of political and moral corruption. For Gordon's possible resentment of his treatment at Pope's hands, see Tyers 1782: 109–10.

493. bowsy: intoxicated.

494 and n. Silenus prepares to speak by knocking the ash out of his pipe. The note, initialled in 1751 as jointly by Pope and Warburton, cites Virgilian parallels to Pope's 'Seeds of fire', which translates 'semina ignis' (*Eclogue* VI.32–3). To refer to atoms as 'semina' ('seeds') is characteristic of Epicurean atomism. 'Semina flammae' ('seeds of flame') also occurs in Virgil (*Aeneid* VI.6).

495. snapt his box: This would usually suggest a snuffbox, but in view of the previous line he may be refilling his pipe. ***his belly:*** Gordon was described as 'a very large man, and corpulent' (Nichols 1812–15: I, 709).

496. Drawing attention to Gordon's lack of academic or ecclesiastical status. The purchaser of his library after his death described it as 'not a learned one' (Nichols 1812–15: I, 709).

497. Bland and familiar: Silenus's over-familiarity has already been indicated by his knocking out his pipe in the Goddess's presence. There seems also to be an allusion to Gordon's translation of Tacitus (1728), which he dedicated to Walpole with the compliment that Tacitus was not an academic theorist but 'a man of Affairs, a great Minister', i.e. someone like Walpole. Pope alludes to Gordon's attempt at a style suited to this conception in *Peri Bathous*: 'Tacitus talks like a Coffee-House Politician' (*PW*: II, 220). Tacitus's contrast between the effete corruption of the Romans and the simple virtues of the Germans they oppressed made him a key author in debates on the political state of England, and Gordon's translation prompted *The Craftsman* to satirical applications of Tacitus to Walpole's regime (Erskine-Hill 1983: 324; Gerrard 1994: 113). Elwin & Courthope cite a couplet from a manuscript of *Epilogue to the Satires* which mocks Gordon as 'honest Tacitus' (Elwin & Courthope 1871–86: III, 459).

***498. call'd the Goddess* Dame:** 'Madam' was the form of address used by courtiers to the Queen.

499–500 and n. Priest-craft: A sceptical term, implying that the clergy inculcate superstition in order to serve their own interests. Gordon had concluded the first series of his

First slave to Words, then vassal to a Name,
Then dupe to Party; child and man the same;
Bounded by Nature, narrow'd still by Art,
A trifling head, and a contracted heart.
Thus bred, thus taught, how many have I seen,
Smiling on all, and smil'd on by a Queen.
Mark'd out for Honours, honour'd for their Birth,

this is so singular a fancy, and at the same time so unsupported by proof, that we must in justice acquit them of all suspicions of this kind.

501.] A Recapitulation of the whole Course of Modern Education describ'd in this book, which confines Youth to the study of *Words* only in Schools, subjects them to the authority of *Systems* in the Universities, and deludes them with the names of *Party-distinctions* in the World. All equally concurring to narrow the Understanding, and establish Slavery and Error in Literature, Philosophy, and Politics. The whole finished in modern Free-thinking; the completion of whatever is vain, wrong, and destructive to the happiness of mankind, as it establishes *Self-love* for the sole Principle of Action.

---

periodical *The Independent Whig* (1720–21) with the claim to have 'gone through most of the General Heads of Superstition and Priestcraft, by which the *Pagan* and *Popish* Clergy have, for so many Ages, deceived and afflicted Mankind; and ... unanswerably shown, that they are all inconsistent with the Establishment of our National Church, and in direct Opposition to Common Sense, as well as the Scriptures'. Thus he advocated a version of Anglicanism consistent with Whig constitutional thought, which he set in polemical contrast with the traditional high-church doctrines associated with Toryism. In the speech of Silenus Pope implies that Gordon's doctrine evacuates the notion of religion, so that it can be refilled by blind obedience to a political party. *The Independent Whig* had been singled out for attack in Warburton's preface 'To the Free-Thinkers'; and Berkeley had made his orthodox speaker ask satirically whether 'the overflowing Zeal of an Independent Whig' might not be more dangerous than 'the Fury and Folly of the ambitious Prelate', adding that 'the worst Tyranny this Nation ever felt was from the Hands of Patriots of that Stamp', i.e. under the Commonwealth (Warburton 1738–41: I, i–xliv; *Alciphron* 1732: I, 333, Dialogue V.xxx). ***The learned Scriblerus:*** The note is initialled in 1751 as by Warburton. ***their Mother:*** Dulness.

501. vassal to a Name: Satirising the medieval habit, still lingering in university study at this time, of citing an authority (notably Aristotle) rather than enquiring independently into the truth of a proposition – a habit that prepares the student to become a 'dupe to Party' in later life. Cp. Oldham's satire on the position of domestic chaplains: 'Slaves to an Hour, and Vassals to a Bell' (Brooks & Selden 1987: 'A Satyr Address'd to a Friend', line 91).

502. child and man the same: Dulness never allows her children to grow up into independent judgement.

504. Echoing a line applied to Lord Hervey in *To Arbuthnot*, 'The trifling Head, or the corrupted Heart!' (line 327).

506. smil'd on by a Queen: Following closely on the allusion to Hervey, this suggests a sneer at his close relationship with Caroline; but it also alludes to her much criticised patronage of the more sceptically inclined of the established clergy.

507–10. Gifted young aristocrats begin by being 'rebellious' towards Dulness; but in time they are rendered compliant by government pensions or loose women ('Punk' looks forward to the role of royal mistresses in the next couplet).

To thee the most rebellious things on earth:
Now to thy gentle shadow all are shrunk,
All melted down, in Pension, or in Punk!
So K* so B** sneak'd into the grave,
A Monarch's half, and half a Harlot's slave.
Poor W** nipt in Folly's broadest bloom,
Who praises now? his Chaplain on his Tomb.
Then take them all, oh take them to thy breast!
Thy *Magus*, Goddess! shall perform the rest.
  With that, a WIZARD OLD his *Cup* extends;

517.] Here beginneth the celebration of the *greater Mysteries* of the Goddess, which the Poet in his Invocation ver. 5. promised to sing. For when now each Aspirant, as was the custom, had proved his qualification and claim to a participation, the High-Priest of Dulness

---

511–12. The second line of the couplet points to men who made their way by servility to the King and currying favour with his mistresses. Plausible candidates are Henry de Grey (1671–1740), Duke of Kent, and James Berkeley (1680–1736), third Earl of Berkeley, both Knights of the Garter (*TE*: V, 392). Kent, notoriously malodorous but reputedly keen to impress women, was said to have gained office under Queen Anne by bribing her friend the Duchess of Marlborough, and he qualified himself for court favour under George I by deserting the Tories on his accession: Pope had contrasted him unfavourably with the Patriot MP Sir John Barnard, whose merit goes unrewarded because he comes from a merchant rather than an aristocratic background (Lord 1963–75: VII, 31–2; *Imitations of Horace, Epistles* I.i.85–90; *TE*: IV, 284–5, 364). Berkeley held many honorary appointments, and may have been the 'B**' associated with a royal 'Whore' in a draft of the *Essay on Man* (Mack 1984: 242). Dyce 7747 suggests Kent and Bolton: for the second Duke of Bolton, reputedly stupid, mean and immoral, see editor's note on III.330.

513–14. Although Horace Walpole thought the brilliant but volatile Philip Wharton (1698–1731), Duke of Wharton, was meant (in which case the reference would be to *Memoirs of the Life of ... Philip ... Duke of Wharton* (1731), attributed to 'an impartial hand', but conceivably by his chaplain, the poet Edward Young), Wharton lived into his thirties and was when he died a dissolute exile, distrusted even by the Jacobites to whose cause he claimed to have committed himself. (For Pope's estimate of Wharton, see 'To Richard Temple, Lord Cobham. Of the Knowledge and Characters of Men', lines 180–207.) A more convincing example of an aristocrat 'nipt in Folly's broadest Bloom' would have been the short-lived Earl of Warwick, whose dissipation had been unredeemed by any suspicion of brilliance (cp. Dyce 7747). Cibber, referring to him as 'a late young Nobleman ... who had a good deal of wicked Humour', blames him for organising the trip to the brothel with which Cibber embarrassed Pope in *A Letter from Mr. Cibber, To Mr. Pope* (Cibber 1742: 47; Fraser 1876: 104; *TE*: V, 392–3; Nokes 1995: 46). If Warwick is meant, the allusion to 'his Tomb' can be read literally of his epitaph in Kensington church.

516. **Magus**: magician (the 'WIZARD' of line 517).

517. The '*Cup*' represents such inducements as pensions and sinecures, used by Walpole to govern parliament, and alludes to the potion given by the witch Circe to Odysseus's companions, which turned them into pigs and was commonly read as an allegory of the

first initiateth the Assembly by the usual way of *Libation*. And then each of the Initiated, as was always required, putteth on a *new Nature*, described from ver. 518 to 528. When the High-Priest and Goddess have thus done their parts, each of them is delivered into the hands of his Conductor, an inferior Minister or *Hierophant*, whose names are *Impudence*, *Stupefaction*, *Self-conceit*, *Self-interest*, *Pleasure*, *Epicurism*, *etc.* to lead them thro' the several apartments of her Mystic Dome or Palace. When all this is over, the sovereign Goddess, from ver. 565 to 578 conferreth her *Titles* and *Degrees*; rewards inseparably attendant on the *participation* of the *Mysteries*; which made the ancient *Theon* say of them — *κάλλιστα μὲν οὖν, καὶ τῶν μεγίστων ἀγαθῶν, τὸ Μυστηρίων μετέχειν.* Hence being enriched with so many various Gifts and Graces, *Initiation* into the Mysteries was anciently, as well as in these our times, esteemed a necessary qualification for every high office and employment, whether in Church or State. Lastly the great Mother shutteth up the Solemnity with her gracious benediction, which concludeth in drawing the Curtain, and laying all her Children to rest. It is to be observed that Dulness, before this her Restoration, had her Pontiffs *in Partibus*; who from time to time held her Mysteries in secret, and with great privacy. But now, on her Re-establishment, she celebrateth them, like those of the *Cretans* (the most ancient of all Mysteries) in open day, and offereth them to the inspection of all men. SCRIBL.

517–19.] The *Cup* of *Self-love*, which causes a total oblivion of the obligations of Friendship, or Honour, and of the Service of God or our Country; all sacrificed to Vain-glory, Court-

---

degrading effect of sensual indulgence (*Odyssey* X.133–574). Relevant too is the Greek moral allegory known as 'The Table of Cebes', which personified Deceit as a woman who offered her cup to all as they entered into life (Fitzgerald & White 1983: V). The passage also participates in a tradition of identifying wicked ministers with the figure of a Merlin or Archimago (Spenser's evil enchanter in *The Faerie Queene*): cp. *Imitations of Horace*, *Epistles* II.i.131–3, and *To Bathurst*, line 136 (Gerrard 1994: 174–7).

517n. The note, initialled in 1751 as by Warburton, parallels the rites of Dulness with rites of initiation into sacred mysteries in the ancient world, which Warburton had treated in the *Divine Legation* as contrivances by rulers to maintain social order (Warburton 1738–41: I, 133–231; and see notes on line 4). He had also interpreted Aeneas's descent into the underworld in Virgil's *Aeneid* VI as an allegory of Augustus's initiation into the mysteries in preparation for the responsibilities of empire (cp. the characterisation of the prospective member of parliament as a 'young Aeneas' at line 290). Mack reads 'the portentous obliquity' of this note in the light of the opposition rhetoric of corrupt statecraft: 'this passage about Walpole is revealed as the goal to which the 1742 poem had been gravitating from the start' (Mack 1969: 155). **greater Mysteries:** Warburton argued that the greater mysteries were reserved for proven initiates, since they revealed that there were not many gods but one, and that the so-called gods had been no more than distinguished human beings (Warburton 1738–41: I, 148–59). Thus the chosen initiate ultimately shared the legislators' knowledge that conventional religion was merely a contrivance to control the masses. The enactment of Dulness's '*greater Mysteries*' similarly reveals her as the one source of power, and exposes social forms and authorities as self-interested imposture. **Libation:** A sacrificial offering of wine. **Hierophant:** A priest qualified to reveal sacred mysteries. ***the ancient* Theon:** The quotation, 'The finest of all and amongst the greatest goods is to share in the mysteries', is slightly adapted from a section on the use of commonplaces in the *Progymnasmata* (preliminary rhetorical exercises) of the rhetorician Libanius (AD 314–*c*.393) (VIII, 713). Warburton's confusion may have arisen from its being printed as an appendix to a work of the same title by the second-century AD rhetorician Aelius Theon of Alexandria (Camerarius 1541). ***her Pontiffs* in Partibus:** Roman Catholic bishops ('Pontiffs') in non-Catholic countries were

Which whoso tastes, forgets his former friends,
Sire, Ancestors, Himself. One casts his eyes
Up to a *Star*, and like Endymion dies:
A *Feather* shooting from another's head,
Extracts his brain, and Principle is fled,
Lost is his God, his Country, ev'ry thing;
And nothing left but Homage to a King!

worship, or yet meaner considerations of Lucre and brutal Pleasures. From ver. 520 to 528.

518–19.] Homer of the Nepenthe, Odyss. 4: *'Αὐτίκ' ἄρ' εἰς οἶνον βάλε φάρμακον, ἔνθεν ἔπινον / Νηπενθές τ' ἀχολόν τε, κακῶν ἐπίληθον ἁπάντων.'*

523, 524.] So strange as this must seem to a mere English reader, the famous Mons. de la Bruyere declares it to be the character of every good Subject in a Monarchy: 'Where (says he) *there is no such thing as Love of our Country*, the Interest, the Glory and Service of the *Prince* supply its place.' *De la Republique*, Chap. 10.

---

said to be 'in partibus infidelium' ('in regions of infidels'), as Dulness's disciples were before her triumph. ***those of the* Cretans:** Crete boasted the reputed birthplace and tomb of Zeus, which in Warburton's view (related to his belief that the mysteries culminated in a monotheistic refutation of faith in the gods of Olympus) would have made it ridiculous for the Cretans to have attempted to keep secret the fact that Zeus had been mortal, and would explain why the Cretans alone of all the Greeks are said to have imparted their mysteries freely to anyone who asked.

517–19n. Initialled in 1751 as jointly by Pope and Warburton. ***brutal Pleasures:*** Those befitting animals.

518–19 and n. Probably aimed at Pulteney, who had long been suspected of being willing to exchange opposition to Walpole for a peerage. He abandoned the Patriot programme on becoming Earl of Bath in 1742 (see editor's note on lines 167–70). The Homeric quotation refers to the drug ('nepenthe') which Helen puts into her guests' wine to dispel their sadness about friends lost in the Trojan war (*Odyssey* IV.220–26). It is so powerful that it would prevent someone from weeping even if they saw their whole family killed in front of them.

520–22. The star is worn by knights, the feather in the headdress of the Order of the Garter. Walpole was widely seen as abusing ancient orders of merit to reward himself and his clients (Gerrard 1994: 224). In 1725 George I had revived the Order of the Bath as a cheap way of recognising service for which a substantial place or pension might otherwise have been expected. When Walpole was admitted to the Order of the Garter by George I in 1726, he was the first commoner to be so honoured since 1660. Pope expressed contempt for such 'honours' in *Imitations of Horace*: *Satires* II.i.108 ('Bare the mean Heart that lurks beneath a Star'), setting up in contrast his conception of real worth in *Epilogue to the Satires* II.232–47.

520. Endymion: Endymion fell into an eternal sleep, sometimes said to be caused by the moon goddess, who was in love with him.

523–4n. A longer version of this note was initialled in 1751 as jointly by Pope and Warburton. Jean de la Bruyère (1645–96) entitles a section of his *Les Charactères ou les moeurs de ce siècle* 'Du souverain ou De la republique'. The original reads 'Il n'y a point de patrie dans le despotique; d'autres choses y suppléent: l'interêt, la gloire, le service du prince' (Garapon 1962: 276). In context, La Bruyère is concerned not with 'the character of every good Subject', but with the dynamics of particular forms of state organisation: to translate 'le despotique' ('despotism') as 'monarchy' is tendentious, suggesting the sycophantic passivity towards

The vulgar herd turn off to roll with Hogs,
To run with Horses, or to hunt with Dogs;
But, sad example! never to escape
Their Infamy, still keep the human shape.
  But she, good Goddess, sent to ev'ry child
Firm Impudence, or Stupefaction mild;
And strait succeeded, leaving shame no room,
Cibberian forehead, or Cimmerian gloom.
  Kind Self-conceit to some her glass applies,
Which no one looks in with another's eyes:
But as the Flatt'rer or Dependant paint,
Beholds himself a Patriot, Chief, or Saint.
  On others Int'rest her gay liv'ry flings,
Int'rest, that waves on Party-colour'd wings:

528. still keep the human shape.] The Effects of the Magus's Cup are just contrary to that of Circe. Hers took away the shape, and left the human mind: This takes away the mind, and leaves the human shape.

529.] The only comfort such people can receive, must be owing in some shape or other to Dulness; which makes some stupid, others impudent, gives Self-conceit to some, upon the Flatteries of their dependants, presents the false colours of Interest to others, and busies or amuses the rest with idle Pleasures or Sensuality, till they become easy under any infamy. Each of which species is here shadowed under Allegorical persons.

---

absolute monarchs typically attributed to the French by the English, and hence insinuating the standard Patriot claim that Walpole had brought in an equivalent tyranny.

525–6. Recalling the victims of Homer's Circe, who were turned into pigs if they failed to resist the refreshment she offered (*Odyssey* X.274–399). This was traditionally understood as a warning against animal appetite, and was reworked by Spenser as an allegory of enthralment by lust (Smith & De Selincourt 1912: *Faerie Queene* II.xii). Gluttony, horseracing and hunting are cited as distractions from moral and political responsibility.

528 and n. Their 'Infamy' consists in their falling short of the dignity implicit in the human image which they still retain. The note was initialled in 1751 as by Warburton.

529n. Initialled in 1751 as jointly by Pope and Warburton. ***Interest:*** In the sense of having something at stake; the hope of personal gain. ***easy:*** comfortable.

531–2. strait: immediately, but also implying 'narrow', in punning contrast with the 'room' that is not left for shame in a head like Cibber's (cp. the prefatory 'Ricardus Aristarchus of the Hero of the Poem'). The polarity of the line suggests that those who in line 530 receive the gift of 'Impudence' become actively dull like Cibber, while those who receive 'Stupefaction' become passively dull, like the Cimmerians, fabled to live where the sun never shone.

533. Self-conceit: Vanity, traditionally personified as a woman holding a looking-glass.

536. Patriot: Suggesting that the Patriot movement had praised some of its leaders beyond their real deserts.

537. 'Int'rest' (hope of gain, here identified with political venality) is personified as an employer whose servants wear her 'liv'ry'.

538. Party-colour'd: Punning on the favours worn by supporters of different parties and on the shifting multi-coloured effect of her wings in the changing light, an image suggesting

Turn'd to the Sun, she casts a thousand dyes,
And, as she turns, the colours fall or rise.
  Others the Syren Sisters warble round,
And empty heads console with empty sound.
No more, alas! the voice of Fame they hear,
The balm of Dulness trickling in their ear.
Great C**, H**, P**, R**, K*,
Why all your Toils? your Sons have learn'd to sing.
How quick Ambition hastes to ridicule!
The Sire is made a Peer, the Son a Fool.
  On some, a Priest succinct in amice white

544.] The true *Balm of Dulness*, called by the Greek Physicians *Κολακεία*, is a *Sovereign* remedy, and has its name from the Goddess herself. Its ancient Dispensators were *her Poets;* but it is now got into as many hands as Goddard's Drops or Daffy's Elixir. It is prepared by the *Clergy*, as appears from several places of this poem: And by ver. 535, 536, it seems as if the *Nobility* had it made up in their own houses. This, which *Opera* is here said to administer, is but a spurious sort. See my Dissertation on the *Silphium* of the *Antients*.

BENT.

---

the false allure of transient attractions (cp. Pope's imagery of unreliable historical tradition in *The Temple of Fame* (lines 129–36), but also the charm of the transparent sylphs in *The Rape of the Lock* (II.59–68): see Rosslyn 1985).

540. as she turns: The colours change depending on her alignment to the sun; but 'turns' may also suggest the traditional image of Fortune's wheel, representing the instability of such advantages as wealth and status.

541. the Syren Sisters: Personifying opera through an allusion to the mythical sirens, who lured sailors to their deaths by the beauty of their singing.

544n. Initialled in 1751 as by Warburton. ***called by the Greek Physicians:*** The Greek word means 'flattery'. **Sovereign:** The italicisation suggests an allusion to George II. ***Goddard's Drops or Daffy's Elixir:*** Patent medicines. ***my Dissertation:*** Bentley asserted that what the ancients called 'silphium' was modern assafoedita (Laurence 1726: 183–7).

545–8. Noting the irony by which titles earned in public service are handed down to dilettante heirs. Contemporary comment suggests that the five comprised four Lord Chancellors (William Cowper (*c.*1665–1723), first Earl Cowper; Simon Harcourt (1661–1727), first Viscount Harcourt; Thomas Parker (1667–1732), first Earl of Macclesfield; and Peter King (1669–1734), first Lord King, Baron of Ockham) and a Lord Chief Justice (Robert Raymond (1673–1733), first Baron Raymond). The elder Harcourt had been Pope's friend, as was Judith Cowper, a niece of the elder Cowper. For comparison between these peers and their heirs, including evidence that some of Pope's contrasts are exaggerated, see *TE*: V, 435, 442, 446, 451, 453. The placing of 'your Sons have learn'd to sing' in the passage is a striking instance of Pope's sense of opera as a touchstone of aristocratic degeneracy.

549–52. Although the description of the 'Priest' may initially suggest an ascetic detachment from the flesh, he turns out to be a chef devoted to indulging his clients with fantastic transformations of the flesh of their fellow-creatures; and his ability to reduce large animals to tiny quantities of jellied stock parodies Catholic and Anglican teaching (respectively the doctrines of transubstantiation and of the real presence) about the bread and wine received by the faithful at the Eucharist (and for possible allusions to miracles in the Bible, see Sherbo 1970: 512). ***succinct:*** wrapped round. ***amice:*** A white scarf worn with ecclesiastical

Attends; all flesh is nothing in his sight!
Beeves, at his touch, at once to jelly turn,
And the huge Boar is shrunk into an Urn:
The board with specious miracles he loads,
Turns Hares to Larks, and Pigeons into Toads.

553.] Scriblerus seems at a loss in this place. *Speciosa miracula* (says he) according to Horace, were the monstrous Fables of the Cyclops, Laestrygons, Scylla, *etc.* What relation have these to the transformation of Hares into Larks, or of Pigeons into Toads? I shall tell thee. The Laestrygons spitted Men upon Spears, as we do Larks upon Skewers; and the fair Pigeon turn'd to a Toad is similar to the fair Virgin Scylla ending in a filthy beast. But here is the difficulty, why Pigeons in so shocking a shape should be brought to a Table. Hares indeed might be cut into Larks at a second dressing, out of frugality: Yet that seems no probable motive, when we consider the extravagance before mention'd, of dissolving whole Oxen and Boars into a small vial of Jelly; nay it is expressly said, that *all Flesh is nothing in his sight.* I have searched in Apicius, Pliny, and the Feast of Trimalchio, in vain: I can only resolve it into some mysterious superstitious Rite, as it is said to be done by a *Priest,* and soon after called a *Sacrifice,* attended (as all ancient sacrifices were) with *Libation* and *Song.* SCRIBL.

This good Scholiast, not being acquainted with modern Luxury, was ignorant that these were only the miracles of *French Cookery,* and that particularly *Pigeons en crapeau* were a common dish.

---

vestments, originally arranged as a hood, and here perhaps used as an apron. ***all flesh is nothing:*** Cp. Isaiah 40:6, 8: 'All flesh *is* grass ... The grass withereth, the flower fadeth: but the word of our God shall stand for ever' (also echoed at 1 Peter 1:24; Sherbo 1970: 512). ***Beeves:*** beef carcasses.

553. specious: deceptively plausible.

553n. Initialled in 1751 as jointly by Pope and Warburton. **Speciosa miracula:** Quoting the Horatian original which Pope translates as 'specious miracles', but which in its original context could be read as 'impressive wonders' (*De arte poetica,* line 144). Horace is praising Homer's judicious use in the *Odyssey* of such fantastic creatures as the Cyclops, who had only one eye; the cannibal Laestrygonians; and Scylla, a sea-monster with twelve legs and six heads, each armed with three rows of teeth. Scriblerus's reference to Scylla as a 'fair Virgin ... ending in a filthy beast' recalls Virgil's depiction of her as a beautiful girl from the waist up, but a monster below, although it also recalls Horace's joke at the beginning of the same poem about the painter so lacking in judgement that he paints a woman with a fish's tail (*Aeneid* III.426–8). ***at a second dressing:*** when the leftovers reappear disguised as a fresh dish. ***Apicius, Pliny, and the Feast of Trimalchio:*** Marcus Gavius Apicius (AD 14–37) was a gourmet of reputation under the Emperor Tiberius, and was reputedly the author of a work on cookery – featuring much that is elaborately unpalatable to modern taste – which is now thought to be a later compilation. The dinner party given by the pretentious upstart Trimalchio forms a major episode in the *Satyricon* of Petronius Arbiter (*d.* AD 65), a favourite of the Emperor Nero famed for ingenious hedonism. ***the miracles of* French Cookery:** See editor's note on line 318; and cp. James Miller's *Of Politeness* (Miller 1738: 5). **en crapeau:** in the shape of a toad.

Another (for in all what one can shine?)
Explains the *Seve* and *Verdeur* of the Vine.
What cannot copious Sacrifice attone?
Thy Treufles, Perigord! thy Hams, Bayonne!
With French Libation, and Italian Strain,
Wash Bladen white, and expiate Hays's stain.

555. in all what one can shine?] Alludes to that of Virgil, Ecl. 8: 'non omnia possumus omnes.'

556. Seve *and* Verdeur*]* French Terms relating to Wines. St. Evremont has a very pathetic Letter to a *Nobleman in disgrace*, advising him to seek Comfort in a *good Table*, and particularly to be attentive to *these Qualities* in his Champaigne.

560. Bladen — Hays] Names of Gamesters. Bladen is a black man. Robert Knight Cashier of the South-sea Company, who fled from England in 1720, (afterwards pardoned in 1742.) — These lived with the utmost magnificence at Paris, and kept open Tables frequented by persons of the first Quality of England, and even by Princes of the Blood of France.

Ibid. Bladen, etc.] The former Note of *Bladen is a black man*, is very absurd. The Manuscript here is partly obliterated, and doubtless could only have been, *Wash Blackmoors white*, alluding to a known Proverb. SCRIBL.

---

555 and n. Virgil comments, with reference to a contest between two accomplished singers, that 'we cannot all do everything' (*Eclogues* VIII.63).

556 and n. Attacking two modish gallicisms and the obsessive gastronomy they are taken to imply. 'Sève', borrowed from French, denotes the strength and quality of flavour proper to a particular wine: *OED* cites this passage as the first use in English. 'Verdeur' is the French term for the tartness of new wine, cognate with but varying in application from the older-established English term 'verdure' or 'verdour', denoting a fresh or pleasant taste. Boileau's pretentious bore praises the wine he offers the poet by reference to 'sa sève et sa verdeur' (Vercruysse 1969: *Satire* III.24). ***St. Evremont:*** The note, initialled in 1751 as jointly by Pope and Warburton, cites the advice on the choice of champagne – which does not use the precise terms at issue here – given to a banished friend by Charles de Marguetel de Saint-Denys de Saint-Evremond (1613–1703), who had himself been exiled for satire against the King's minister (Saint-Evremond 1711: III, 98–9). A parallel is suggested between the distractions to which victims of French absolutism are reduced, and those that aid Walpole in setting up a similar tyranny.

558. Périgord is a district of France noted for truffles; the town of Bayonne is noted for its ham.

559. French wine and Italian opera.

560 and n. Identification of Bladen and Hays is problematic, although it seems clear that the line focuses on the analogy between the South Sea scheme and gambling. A Thomas Bladen was supposed to have lived by gambling and to have married a daughter of the disgraced South Sea director Theodore Janssen (Stephen & Lee 1885–1900: 'Theodore Janssen'; *TE*: V, 430, 473; editor's note on line 326; Stiker 1966). He may be deliberately blurred here with Martin Bladen (1680–1746), a playwright and translator who held office under Walpole and was in addition a Caribbean plantation owner and activist for the sugar interest. He was also presumably the 'Martin Bladin' included among the original investors in another joint-stock company of which Pope disapproved, the Royal Academy of Music set up to promote

Knight lifts the head, for what are crowds undone
To three essential Partriges in one?
Gone ev'ry blush, and silent all reproach,
Contending Princes mount them in their Coach.
  Next bidding all draw near on bended knees,
The Queen confers her *Titles* and *Degrees*.
Her children first of more distinguish'd sort,

562.] i.e. two dissolved into Quintessence to make sauce for the third. The honour of this invention belongs to France, yet has it been excell'd by our native luxury, an hundred squab Turkeys being not unfrequently deposited in one Pye in the Bishopric of Durham: to which our Author alludes in ver. 593 of this work.

Italian opera in 1719 (Milhous & Hume 1986: 51). His writing had been denigrated in an early manuscript draft of I.266 (Mack 1984: 103). The statement in the note, both paragraphs of which were initialled in 1751 as jointly by Pope and Warburton, that 'Bladen is a black man', may refer to his involvement with slavery, as well as giving occasion for the Bentleian argument for textual corruption which makes possible a satirical glance at the proverb 'wash blackamoors white'. Stiker proposes the connection that the Whig mathematician, theologian and placeman Charles Hayes (1678–1760) also profited from slavery (Stiker 1966). Hays, however, would seem in the context of the South Sea scheme more likely to have been the 'Lewis Hays, Esq; Factor to the S.S. Company at *Vera Cruz*' whose death was reported in the *Gentleman's Magazine* for 1737 (p. 767). To call him a 'gamester' would continue the insinuation that making a fortune by managing the South Sea scheme is no better than making it at cards (although before the collapse of the price of stock and the exposure of dishonest directors, Pope and other Scriblerians had themselves been keen investors: see Erskine-Hill 1972a; Nicholson 1994: 51–81).

The note then runs ahead to the career of Robert Knight (*d.* 1744: mentioned at line 561). Cashier to the South Sea Company, he had fled to France in 1722 on being found guilty of fraud, allegedly in order to protect the government from exposure (*TE*: IV, 210–11; V, 446). Pope heard that he subsequently attempted to bribe the Queen, and noted sardonically that it was a pity Hervey had left office just too soon to sign the pardon granted him in 1742 (*Corr.*: III, 80; IV, 414). The note stresses the corruption of aristocrats still prepared, despite Knight's exposure, to be entertained at his 'open Tables'.

561–2 and 562n. For Knight, see notes on line 560. He 'lifts the head' on realising that he is not, after all, condemned to ostracism on account of the 'crowds' he has 'undone' financially, since the sophistication of his cuisine ensures his continued popularity. The note may be by Pope, since Warburton omitted it in 1751, presumably to avoid the professional indecorum of satirising a bishop. As it stands, it avoids drawing attention to the blasphemous parody of the doctrine of the Trinity in line 562, but anticipates the criticism at lines 593–4 of William Talbot (1658?–1730), Bishop of Durham, who attracted criticism by his extravagance and by his dubious methods of augmenting his episcopal revenue. Pope echoes Chapman, who describes a clerical pluralist as 'Turning the rents of his superfluous Cures / Into your pheasants and your partridges; / Venting their Quintessence' (Maxwell & Stanley 1971; Brooke 1964: *Bussy D'Ambois* III.ii.44–6). 'Squab' denotes a young bird not fully fledged.

564. Princes argue over the honour of giving them a lift.

565. on bended knees: The traditional posture for receiving an academic degree.

Who study Shakespeare at the Inns of Court,
Impale a Glow-worm, or Vertù profess,
Shine in the dignity of F. R. S.
Some, deep Free-Masons, join the silent race
Worthy to fill Pythagoras's place:
Some Botanists, or Florists at the least,
Or issue Members of an Annual feast.
Nor past the meanest unregarded, one

571.] The Poet all along expresses a very particular concern for this silent Race: He has here provided, that in case they will not waken or open (as was before proposed) to a *Humming-Bird* or *Cockle*, yet at worst they may be made Free-Masons; where *Taciturnity* is the *only* essential Qualification, as it was the *chief* of the disciples of Pythagoras.

---

568. Students at the Inns of Court were ostensibly there to study law, but they were routinely satirised for preferring the pursuit of pleasure or a dilettante interest in the arts, and had been included in a list of targets in an early manuscript draft of Book II (Mack 1984: 127). Pope's Shakespearean antagonist Theobald was a lawyer by training. (For Warburton's later attempt to apply the reference to an attack on his Shakespeare edition, see *TE*: V, 398.)

569–70. The Royal Society was routinely satirised by writers of a traditional humanist outlook (for the conflict between the devaluation of language implicit in its stress on empirical investigation and the rhetorical ideal central to humanism, see Williams 1955: 111–15). Candidates for Royal Society fellowships are presented as qualifying by a range of interests which are not even clearly related to its scientific mission (i.e. as dilettantes of Shakespeare or the fine arts); but 'Impale a Glow-worm' implies that even when they pursue science, it is trivial and destructive. Pope retains the accent on the Italian *virtù* (i.e. connoisseurship in the fine arts), but spells it with an 'e' as if it were French, implying a dismissive gesture towards foreign refinements.

571–2 and n. The Grand Lodge of the Freemasons had been established in London in 1717, and the movement attracted a distinguished membership, since it offered, outside the constraints of established religious denominations, a quasi-religious ritual and a strong sense of shared idealism, framed within the belief in a harmonious and comprehensible universe (Jacobs 1981: 109–43). Membership was compatible with a variety of political affiliations, but it may be significant here that Walpole was a mason, along with various of his agents and correspondents. Although freemasonry was disapproved of and soon to be formally banned by the Roman Catholic Church, and despite the contemptuous tone of the present reference, there is documentary evidence to suggest that in 1730 Pope, along with Swift, had himself attended meetings (Mack 1985: 437–40, 889). The note, initialled in 1751 as jointly by Pope and Warburton, argues that whereas Pythagoras had some positive doctrines to counterbalance his implicitly negative insistence on silence (part of his ascetic programme for purifying the soul), freemasons insist *only* on silence (i.e. keeping their rituals secret). For humming-birds and cockles as hobbies for the more reserved of Dulness's disciples, see lines 445–8.

573. 'Botanists', who at least attempt to understand plants, are preferred to 'Florists', who are only interested in producing perfect blooms.

574. Sneering at the self-importance of those invited to the annual dinners of organisations such as the Royal Society and the masonic lodges.

Rose a Gregorian, one a Gormogon.
The last, not least in honour or applause,
Isis and Cam made Doctors of her Laws.
Then blessing all, Go Children of my care!
To Practice now from Theory repair.
All my commands are easy, short, and full:
My Sons! be proud, be selfish, and be dull.
Guard my Prerogative, assert my Throne:
This Nod confirms each Privilege your own.

576.] A sort of Lay-brothers, *Slips* from the Root of the Free-Masons.

581–2.] We should be unjust to the reign of *Dulness* not to confess that her's has one advantage in it rarely to be met with in Modern Governments, which is, that the public *Education* of her Youth fits and prepares them for the observance of her *Laws,* and the exertion of those Virtues she recommends. For what makes men *prouder* than the empty *knowledge of Words*; more *selfish* than the Free-thinker's *System of Morals*; or *duller* than the profession of true *Virtuosoship?* Nor are her *Institutions* less admirable in themselves than in the fitness of these their several relations, to promote the harmony of the whole. For she tells her Sons, and with great truth, that 'all her commands are *easy, short,* and *full.*' For is any thing in nature more *easy* than the exertion of *Pride,* more *short* and *simple* than the principle of *Selfishness,* or more full and ample than the sphere of *Dulness?* Thus Birth, Education, and wise Policy all concurring to support the throne of our Goddess, great must be the strength thereof.

584.] This speech of Dulness to her Sons at parting may possibly fall short of the Reader's expectation; who may imagine the Goddess might give them a Charge of more consequence, and, from such a Theory as is before delivered, incite them to the practice of something more extraordinary, than to personate Running-Footmen, Jockeys, Stage Coachmen, *etc.*

But if it be well consider'd, that whatever inclination they might have to do mischief, her sons are generally render'd harmless by their Inability; and that it is the common effect of Dulness (even in her greatest efforts) to defeat her own design; the Poet, I am persuaded,

576 and n. The Gregorians and the Gormogons were societies set up apparently in ridicule of freemasonry: the note, initialled in 1751 as jointly by Pope and Warburton, suggests that their function is to give spurious distinction to absolute nonentities who cannot gain admission to the societies previously mentioned. 'Lay-brothers', being disqualified by low rank and poor education from full participation in the spiritual and intellectual work of a religious order, serve it instead by manual labour. 'Slips' are cuttings taken from plants in order to propagate them.

578. A gesture of contempt for honorary degrees such as Warburton had been refused by Oxford (see editor's note on lines 115–18).

579. Dulness gives her disciples their final instructions.

581–2n. Initialled in 1751 as by Warburton.

582. Echoing Dryden's character of Og (a caricature of Shadwell): 'The Midwife laid her hand on his Thick Skull, / With this Prophetick blessing – *Be thou Dull*' (Kinsley 1958: *The Second Part of Absalom and Achitophel,* lines 476–7).

584 and n. The nod was the sign by which Zeus/Jupiter confirmed his decrees. The note was initialled in 1751 as jointly by Pope and Warburton.

The Cap and Switch be sacred to his Grace;
With Staff and Pumps the Marquis lead the Race;
From Stage to Stage the licens'd Earl may run,
Pair'd with his Fellow-Charioteer the Sun;
The learned Baron Butterflies design,
Or draw to silk Arachne's subtile line;

will be justified, and it will be allow'd that these worthy persons, in their several ranks, do as much as can be expected from them.

590.] This is one of the most ingenious employments assign'd, and therefore recommended only to Peers of Learning. Of weaving Stockings of the Webs of Spiders, see the Phil. Trans.

---

585. The 'Cap and Switch' (i.e. the short whip used in horseracing) are the insignia of the professional jockey. Hervey had described William Cavendish (*c.*1673–1729), second Duke of Devonshire, as 'more able as a virtuoso than a statesman, and a much better jockey than he was a politician', but this seems somewhat out of date for the present context (Sedgwick 1931: I, 24).

586. The Marquis seems to be engaged in an unseemly contest, having adopted the 'Pumps' (flat running shoes) and 'Staff' used by footmen, whose duty was to follow their master's coach on foot. William Cavendish (1720–64), son of the third Duke of Devonshire, styled Marquis of Hartington during his father's lifetime, has been suggested as a possible candidate (*TE*: V, 400). There may have been a contemporary fad for noblemen to dress as grooms and coachmen; organised races between the footmen of different nobles may also be alluded to.

587. James Cecil (1713–80), sixth Earl of Salisbury, apparently took his enthusiasm for driving to the extreme of driving a public stagecoach (Lewis 1937–83: X, 348). Stagecoaches, offering a public service along an advertised route, were so called from the 'stages' or advertised stops. 'Licens'd' refers literally to the licence required to run a coach for hire; but there is also a hint at the sense 'permitted to indulge in behaviour otherwise disapproved of'.

588. Helios, the sun, was imaged by the Greeks as driving a chariot from east to west during the day, and being carried back to the start during the night on the stream of Ocean. Like the stagecoach driver, he operates to a demanding timetable; and the comparison underlines the laboriousness of the obsessions by which the peers in lines 585–8 demean themselves.

589. An allusion to the Swedish entomologist Baron Charles de Geer (1720–78), celebrated for his observation of the process of insect metamorphosis, and for his ability to draw ('design') insects in such a way as to make clear their anatomy (Gillispie 1972: 'Geer, Charles de'). The seven lavish volumes of his *Mémoires pour servir à l'histoire des insectes* were to be published in 1752–78.

590 and n. Arachne was turned into a spider because she enraged the goddess Athena, patroness of weaving, by the skill and disrespect for the gods that she showed in a tapestry depicting their amorous adventures. *Philosophical Transactions*, the journal of the Royal Society, had published a paper read in 1710 by Monsieur Bon of Montpellier, advocating the spinning of silk from the egg cocoons (not the webs) of spiders (Bon 1710). Swift had included among the projectors of Lagado in *Gulliver's Travels* (1726) one who advocated the replacement of silk by spiders' webs (Davis 1939–68: XI, 164–5). The note was initialled in 1751 as jointly by Pope and Warburton. Cobwebs were an established image for pedantic learning, and for a man to interest himself in such traditionally feminine work as spinning, weaving and sewing carried damaging connotations of effeminacy. Young had argued derisively in the first satire

The Judge to dance his brother Sergeant call;
The Senator at Cricket urge the Ball;
The Bishop stow (Pontific Luxury!)
An hundred Souls of Turkeys in a pye;
The sturdy Squire to Gallic masters stoop,
And drown his Lands and Manors in a Soupe.
Others import yet nobler arts from France,
Teach Kings to fiddle, and make Senates dance.

591.] Alluding perhaps to that ancient and solemn *Dance* intitled *A Call of Sergeants.*

598. Teach Kings to fiddle] An ancient amusement of Sovereign Princes, (viz.) Achilles, Alexander, Nero; tho' despised by Themistocles, who was a Republican — *Make Senates dance,* either after their Prince, or to Pontoise, or Siberia.

---

of his *Love of Fame* that 'By *this* inspir'd (O! ne'er to be forgot) / Some Lords have learnt to *spell,* and some to *knot*' – where knotting is also a markedly feminine craft (Young 1728).

591 and n. Common-law judges were appointed from an order of barristers called serjeants, now abolished, whose members addressed each other as 'brother'. The note, initialled in 1751 as jointly by Pope and Warburton, suggests an allusion to the formal assemblies to which they were routinely summoned ('a call of serjeants'); but a near-contemporary witness states that the allusion is more specifically to the elaborate Revels of the Inns of Court, last held in 1733 (*Eunomus* 1768: IV, 58–89). This was attended by judges and sergeants, and included a ceremonial dance walked around the fireplace three times to the accompaniment of a traditional song. The 1768 account presents the ceremony as an absurd survival: it would have been hard by the mid-eighteenth century to see it as embodying any important aspect of the law.

592. 'Senator' stresses the parliamentary responsibility that goes with noble rank. Cricketing peers were not uncommon, but attracted disapproval since matches involved social contact with the lower orders on a footing of relative equality, and implied performance before a socially mixed audience, in marked contrast with the exclusive nature of traditional aristocratic diversions.

593–4. For the identification of Bishop Talbot of Durham, see Dyce 7747 and notes on lines 561–2. 'Pontific' ('relating to a bishop') is pointedly juxtaposed with 'Luxury'. 'Souls of Turkeys' (where something like 'carcasses' would have been expected) stresses by contrast the care of souls implicitly neglected by such a bishop: although Pope speculated that dogs might have souls, he was not a vegetarian (*OAC*: I, 118–19).

595–6. The expense of French cookery may bankrupt even a substantial landowner. 'Soupe', as distinguished from the English 'broth', is still a noticeable gallicism at this date. For the imagery, cp. *Sober Advice from Horace,* line 14: 'And Lands and Tenements go down her Throat', and James Miller's glutton in *Of Politeness,* who 'swallows down whole *Manors* at a Meal' (Miller 1738: 5). Pope may have in mind the glutton Oldfield twice mentioned in *Imitations of Horace* (*Satires* II.ii.25; *Epistles* II.ii.87; *TE*: IV, 375).

598 and n. Combining satire of the kind of tyrant who, in the proverbial allusion to Nero, fiddles while Rome burns (recalling royal participation in music and dancing at the French court, and possibly Prince Frederick's enthusiasm for playing the cello, or his father's for opera) with an attack on the absolutism that dictates policy to supposedly representative institutions (if Prince Frederick is a target, this would contrast with his depiction by more committed Patriot writers as ideal ruler in waiting). The note, initialled in 1751 as jointly by Pope and

Perhaps more high some daring son may soar,
Proud to my list to add one Monarch more;
And nobly conscious, Princes are but things
Born for First Ministers, as Slaves for Kings,
Tyrant supreme! shall three Estates command,
And MAKE ONE MIGHTY DUNCIAD OF THE LAND!
More she had spoke, but yawn'd — All Nature nods:
What Mortal can resist the Yawn of Gods?

606.] This verse is truly Homerical; as is the conclusion of the Action, where the great Mother composes all, in the same manner as Minerva at the period of the Odyssey. — It may

---

Warburton, refers to the Greek statesman Themistocles (*c.*524–*c.*459 BC), a major force in establishing the military security of the Athenian city state. As a figure of democratic independence he provides a contrast with the implicitly degenerate situation of later states ruled by the whim of 'Sovereign Princes'. The parliament of France had been exiled to Pontoise in 1720, and it was established practice in Russia for politicians out of favour to be exiled to Siberia (cp. *To Bathurst*, line 74, and Pope's explanatory note).

599–604. The 'daring son' is Walpole. Although he had left office early in 1742, shortly before the first publication of these lines in *The New Dunciad*, they were probably composed while he was still in power, when they could have been read as a warning about the pride that comes before a fall. Sutherland suggests that a note on the equivalent line in 1742 ('a wise advice to all first Ministers, but especially to any unable one') was probably aimed at Walpole's successor, Spencer Compton (*c.*1673?–1743), Lord Wilmington, who had in 1727–8 failed to prevail over Walpole in the contest for the favour of the new King, George II, but who replaced Walpole on his resignation in 1742 and died, a few months before the publication of *The Dunciad in Four Books*, in 1743 (*TE* V: 403; Sedgwick 1970: I, 568–9).

603. three Estates: Lords spiritual (i.e. bishops who sit in the House of Lords), lords temporal (the rest of the House of Lords), and commoners represented in the House of Commons. Traditional constitutional thinking rested the safety of the nation on the checks and balances between these representative bodies. (The three estates are sometimes taken to be the monarch, the Lords and the Commons, with similar stress on the need for a balance of power between them.)

604. Capitalisation underlines what Erskine-Hill calls the 'climactic moment, when land becomes poem' (Erskine-Hill 1996: 106).

605–6 and 606n. yawn'd: The Old Testament identifies creation with the word of God ('And God said, Let there be light: and there was light': Genesis 1:3), a theme taken up in the New Testament when Jesus is identified as the incarnation of the creative Word ('In the beginning was the Word, and the Word was with God, and the Word was God. ... All things were made by him; and without him was not any thing made that was made. ... And the Word was made flesh, and dwelt among us': John 1:1, 3, 14). Hence it would be inappropriate for Dulness to undo creation with effectively articulated words; she does it instead with a yawn, which, to the extent that it expresses anything, expresses her own boredom with herself and her unmaking of the world (for contextualisation of Pope's concern for the referentiality of words in his own practice, see Alderson 1996). Garth's God of Oblivion had comparable difficulties in staying awake: 'More he had spoke, but sudden Vapours rise, / And with their silken Cords tie down his eyes' (*The Dispensary* 1699: I.181–2, and cp. the falling asleep of Blackmore's leading suppliant to the God of Dulness in *The Kit-Cats* (1708) and of Newcomb's Oblivion

Churches and Chapels instantly it reach'd;

indeed seem a very singular Epitasis of a Poem, to end as this does, with a *Great Yawn*; but we must consider it as the *Yawn of a God*, and of powerful effects. It is not out of Nature, most long and grave counsels concluding in this very manner: Nor without Authority, the incomparable Spencer having ended one of the most considerable of his works with a *Roar*, but then it is the *Roar of a Lion*, the effects whereof are described as the Catastrophe of his Poem.

607.] The Progress of this Yawn is judicious, natural, and worthy to be noted. First it seizeth the Churches and Chapels; then catcheth the Schools, where, tho' the boys be unwilling to sleep, the Masters are not: Next Westminster-hall, much more hard indeed to subdue, and not totally put to silence even by the Goddess: Then the Convocation, which tho' extremely desirous to speak, yet cannot: Even the House of Commons, justly called the Sense of the Nation, is *lost* (that is to say *suspended*) during the Yawn (far be it from our Author to suggest it could be lost any longer!) but it spreadeth at large over all the rest of the Kingdom, to such a degree, that Palinurus himself (tho' as incapable of sleeping as Jupiter) yet nod-

---

(*Bibliotheca* 1712; Lund 1991: 176)). Dulness's interrupted speech, which draws on the convention of the monarch's speech from the throne (cp. 'the Queen's Speech' which sets the agenda for a new session of parliament), also parodies conservative celebrations of authority that assimilate royal decree to divine fiat: Dryden concludes his meditation on the challenge to Charles II by his illegitimate son with a coda to the royal speech beginning 'He said. Th' Almightly, nodding, gave consent' (*Absolom and Achitophel*, line 1026); and Pope looks forward to an age of peace under Queen Anne's ordering fiat in *Windsor Forest*: 'At length great ANNA said—Let Discord cease! / She said, the World obey'd, and all was *Peace*!' (lines 327–8). ***truly Homerical:*** The note, initialled in 1751 as jointly by Pope and Warburton, alludes to the conclusion of Homer's *Odyssey*, when the goddess Athene ('Minerva' in Pope's translation) intervenes to make peace in the battle between Odysseus and those who had worked against him in his absence. Pope's translation imports a resonant vision of political and moral order into Homer's ending (which simply says that Athene, in disguise, made peace between the two sides: *Odyssey* XXIV.545–8) by adopting as his last line the last line of Dryden's *Absolom and Achitophel*: 'And willing nations knew their lawful Lord'. The contrast with Dulness's undoing of order is especially ironic in this implied context of royal restoration. ***Epitasis:*** Properly, the central part of a plot, in which the action becomes more complicated; but here the term seems to be confused with 'catastrophe', i.e. denouement, as used later in the note. ***the incomparable Spencer:*** Spenser's *Mother Hubberds Tale*, an allegorical satire against the usurpation by commoners of royal authority (and therefore relevant to the *Dunciad*'s case against Walpole), tells how lower animals steal the lion's skin while he is asleep, but are exposed by the lion's roaring, which vindicates his royal identity. The roar, figuring the monarch's unique authority, stands in the tradition of assimilating royal to divine fiat parodied in line 605. ***Catastrophe:*** denouement of a plot.

607–18. Westminster, where George and Caroline had been crowned and where court and parliament were based, is the focus of Dulness's initial impact (Rogers 1985: 144).

607n. The church is the first institution to be affected: the anonymous *The State Dunces* (1733), dedicated to Pope by Paul Whitehead, had also stressed the role of the clergy in conniving at corruption. The note, initialled in 1751 as jointly by Pope and Warburton, glosses lines 607–18. ***far be it from our Author:*** The timid Scriblerus is anxious to protect his author from the consequences of the subversive implication that 'the Sense of the Nation' is permanently lost. ***Palinurus:*** Palinurus, mentioned at line 614, was Aeneas's helmsman, drowned when he fell asleep at the helm (*Aeneid* V.833–71). Young, however, had in his early

(St. James's first, for leaden Gilbert preach'd)
Then catch'd the Schools; the Hall scarce kept awake;
The Convocation gap'd, but could not speak:

deth for a moment: the effect of which, tho' ever so momentary, could not but cause some Relaxation, for the time, in all public affairs. SCRIBL.

608. leaden] An Epithet from the *Age* she had just then restored, according to that sublime custom of the Easterns, in calling new-born Princes after some great and recent Event. SCRIBL.

610.] Implying a great desire so to do, as the learned Scholiast on the place rightly observes. Therefore beware Reader lest thou take this *Gape* for a *Yawn*, which is attended with no desire but to go to rest: by no means the disposition of the Convocation; whose melancholy case in short is this: She was, it is *reported*, infected with the general influence of the Goddess, and while she was yawning at her ease, a wanton Courtier took her at this advantage, and in the very nick clap'd a *Gag* into her mouth. Well therefore may she be distinguished by her *gaping*; and this distressful posture it is our poet would describe, just as she stands at this day, a sad example of the effects of Dulness and Malice unchecked and despised. BENT.

---

satires *The Love of Fame* used the name to compliment Walpole's steadfastness in guiding the ship of state when the King was caught in a dangerous storm on his return voyage from one of his widely resented visits to Hanover: 'Our *Palinurus* slept not at the helm' (Young 1728: VII). Another figure of supposed vigilance was Zeus/Jupiter the all-seeing; but according to Homer he had been beguiled into sleep at a crucial moment in the Trojan War (*Iliad* XIV.352–60). Thus, as models for Walpole's vigilance, both figures are teasingly fallible; and the allusion to Young's compliment is a pointed reminder of the problem he faced in praising Walpole in satires posited on the folly and perversity of English society: 'How all mankind will be surpriz'd, to see / This flood of *British* folly charg'd on thee?', he exclaims, before diagnosing folly as the 'bad effect' of a 'pleasing cause' – namely the '*wealth*' and '*peace*' conferred by Walpole and his royal master.

608 and n. St. James's: The chapel royal. ***leaden Gilbert:*** John Gilbert (1693–1761), later to be Archbishop of York, had a reputation for arrogance unredeemed by spiritual or scholarly distinction, but was celebrated for the highly emotional delivery of his sermon on the death of Queen Caroline, during which he is said to have wept in the pulpit. Hence he seems not to be simply boring, but 'leaden' in the somewhat strained sense suggested in the note on line 608, i.e. insofar as his sycophancy is helping to bring about Dulness's age of lead (see I.28).

609. the Hall: Identified as Westminster Hall in the note on line 607 (and see editor's note on II.265), hence a metonymy for the judicial system.

610 and n. Convocation was the representative forum of the Anglican clergy, but, despite the government's progressive placing of Whig nominees in positions of power, it proved resistant to control, largely because the lower clergy persistently contested government indifference or even hostility to the church's traditional claims to authority. In 1717 the government had responded to the clerical outcry against the Whig Bishop Hoadly's sermon *The Nature of the Kingdom, or Church, of Christ* by dismissing Convocation (see editor's notes on II.370, 400). Thereafter it was routinely summoned only to be dismissed, angering not only Tory clergy, but also a wider constituency which combined Whig politics with a traditional sense of ecclesiastical authority. The silenced Convocation therefore had much in common with the Patriot opposition as a site of resistance to Walpole; and this was the more obvious in that in 1741,

Lost was the Nation's Sense, nor could be found,
While the long solemn Unison went round:
Wide, and more wide, it spread o'er all the realm;
Ev'n Palinurus nodded at the Helm:
The Vapour mild o'er each Committee crept;
Unfinish'd Treaties in each Office slept;
And Chiefless Armies doz'd out the Campaign;
And Navies yawn'd for Orders on the Main.
  O Muse! relate (for you can tell alone,
Wits have short Memories, and Dunces none)

616, 618.] These Verses were written many years ago, and may be found in the State Poems of that time. So that Scriblerus is mistaken, or whoever else have imagined this Poem of a fresher date.

620. Wits have short Memories,] This seems to be the reason why the Poets, whenever they give us a Catalogue, constantly call for help on the Muses, who, as the Daughters of

---

in the parliamentary session which led to Walpole's fall, it had briefly attempted to begin debate, only to be silenced again, as evoked in this line and in the note, which was initialled in 1751 as by Warburton (Langford 1988). The insult to Convocation would have been the more resonant for Pope insofar as his early friend Atterbury had first distinguished himself under William III by asserting the rights of the lower clergy in Convocation to transact business without royal licence (Bennett 1975: 48–62).

611. the Nation's Sense: parliament.

613. Echoing the simile of ripples at II.405–8.

614. Palinurus: See notes on line 607. Erskine-Hill suggests that this, 'the last of *The Dunciad*'s long series of allusions to the *Aeneid*, does a kind of honour to the great Prime Minister .... Palinurus did not desert the helm ... but was overwhelmed by the god of sleep and fell from the ship .... With Walpole gone ... the political world is left with neither direction nor life' (Erskine-Hill 1996: 108).

616–18 and n. The lines make the standard Patriot charge that Walpole had failed to respond adequately to Spanish depredations on English shipping: there are marked resemblances to passages in *Are These Things So?* (1740), an anonymously published diatribe supposed to be spoken by Pope, the work of his admirer James Miller (1706–44); and there are similarities also to *The State Dunces* (1733), published anonymously by the Patriot satirist Paul Whitehead (1710–74). The note, initialled in 1751 as jointly by Pope and Warburton, ostensibly disclaims contemporary reference by pointing out an allusion to a satire 'written many years ago' (parodying Bentley's arguments from anachronism; 'State Poems' denotes political verse, regularly published as collections (see Lord 1963–75)). The poem cited, 'Orpheus and Margarita' (sometimes attributed to Charles Montagu, Earl of Halifax (Montagu 1793: 770)), is a satire on the power of the singer Margherita de L'Epine (*c.*1683–1746) to seduce statesmen from duty: '*R—k* furls his Sails, and dozes on the Main; / Treaties unfinish'd in the Office sleep, / And *Sho—el* yawns for Orders on the Deep' (*A New Collection* 1705: 552–3; for Pope's ownership of this reprinted selection, see Mack 1982: 434–7). As well as permitting equivocation about the contemporaneity of the accusation, the allusion recalls the theme of operatic distraction from duty developed at lines 45–70, 314 and 322–4.

619–20 and 620n. Epic writers, rather than stressing their own agency as tellers, traditionally begin by calling upon the muse, envisaged as the divine power that knows what really

Relate, who first, who last resign'd to rest;
Whose Heads she partly, whose completely blest;
What Charms could Faction, what Ambition lull,
The Venal quiet, and intrance the Dull;
'Till drown'd was Sense, and Shame, and Right, and Wrong —
O sing, and hush the Nations with thy Song!
* * * * * * * * * *

Memory, are obliged not to forget any thing. So Homer, Iliad 2: '*Πληθὺν δ' οὐκ ἂν ἐγὼ μυθήσομαι, οὐδ' ὀνομήνω, / Εἰ μὴ Ὀλυμπιάδες Μοῦσαι, Διὸς αἰγιόχοιο / Θυγατέρες, μνησαίαθ*''. And Virgil, Aen. 7: 'Et meministis enim, Divae, et memorare potestis: / Ad nos vix tenuis famae perlabitur aura.' But our Poet had yet another reason for putting this Task upon the Muse, that all besides being *asleep*, she only could relate what passed. SCRIBL.

624.] It would be a Problem worthy the solution of *Aristarchus* himself, and (perhaps not of less importance than some of those weighty questions so long and warmly disputed amongst Homer's Scholiasts, as, *in which hand Venus was wounded*, and *what Jupiter whisper'd in the ear of Juno*) to inform us, which required the greatest effort of our Goddess's power, to *intrance the Dull*, or to *quiet the Venal*. For tho' the *Venal* may be more unruly than the *Dull*, yet, on the other hand, it demands a much greater expence of her Virtue to *intrance* than barely to *quiet*. SCRIBL.

---

happened. At the beginning of the *Dunciads*, however, Pope had called upon 'the Great', those who had brought about Dulness's triumph, to 'Say how' it happened; and the traditional invocation of the muse is displaced to this late and catastrophic stage (I.3; cp. *TE*: V, 61). The note, initialled in 1751 as jointly by Pope and Warburton, cites Homer's invocation of the muse at the beginning of the elaborate roll-call of the ships and men who went to Troy: 'I cannot tell the number nor name them unless the Olympian muses, daughters of aegis-bearing Zeus, relate them' (*Iliad* II.488, 491–2). As a prelude to the war between Aeneas and the natives of Italy from whom he must wrest possession of the land where Rome is to be founded, Virgil calls on the muses to detail the assembled hosts of Italy: 'Remember them, goddesses, for you can call them to mind; but hardly a vague breath of tradition comes down to us' (*Aeneid* VII.645–6).

621. The stress on 'first' and the general tenor of the request recall Milton's questions about the cause of the fall in his initial invocation of the muse (Fowler 1998: *Paradise Lost* I.27–33).

624 and n. The question posed in the note, initialled in 1751 as by Warburton, seems particularly pointless. Homer does not say which of Venus/Aphrodite's hands was wounded, but Virgil and Plutarch specify the right (*Iliad* V.334–7; *Aeneid* XI.277; *Moralia* IX.4). I have been unable to identify the incident between Jupiter/Zeus and Juno/Hera. 'Virtue' in this context denotes 'strength' or 'intrinsic quality'.

626. Of the asterisks that follow this line Erskine-Hill comments: 'The break in the poetry ... is entirely dramatic. It could easily have been smoothly linked with the preceding lines, as in 1729, but this would not have driven home to the reader its power over the poet himself' (Erskine-Hill 1972b: 62). In 1742 this line had been followed by a concluding couplet: 'While the Great Mother bids Britannia sleep, / And pours her Spirit o'er the Land and Deep', annotated to the effect that Britain was sleeping 'in company with all other Nations of Europe', with the possible exception of the proverbially lively French (*TE*: V, 406–7): 1743 presents the enormity uncompromised by comparisons. The 1742 note had also hinted that 'the rest of this Poem' would be forthcoming, citing Pope's declared intention to 'Publish the present

In vain, in vain, — the all-composing Hour
Resistless falls: The Muse obeys the Pow'r.
She comes! she comes! the sable Throne behold
Of *Night* Primaeval, and of *Chaos* old!
Before her, *Fancy*'s gilded clouds decay,
And all its varying Rain-bows die away.
Wit shoots in vain its momentary fires,
The meteor drops, and in a flash expires.
As one by one, at dread Medea's strain,
The sick'ning stars fade off th' ethereal plain;
As Argus' eyes by Hermes' wand opprest,
Clos'd one by one to everlasting rest;

629. the sable Throne behold] The sable Thrones of Night and Chaos, here represented as advancing to extinguish the light of the Sciences, in the first place blot out the Colours of *Fancy*, and damp the Fire of *Wit*, before they proceed to their greater work.

637–8.] 'Et quamvis sopor est oculorum parte receptus, / Parte tamen vigilat ... / ... Vidit Cyllenius omnes / Succubuisse oculos', *etc*. Ovid, Met. 2.

Age, but where my Text / Is Vice too high, reserve it for the next' (*Imitations of Horace*: *Satires* II.i.59–60). This note seems to have been written either in anticipation of or immediately after Walpole's resignation, and to suggest that in the changed context it would be safer for Pope to state explicitly his charges against Walpole's regime; but the revised ending of 1743 (lines 627–56) seems less concerned with party politics than with larger metaphysical issues. Goldgar suggests that 'Vice too high' may involve the royal family, and hence still be sensitive even after Walpole's fall (Goldgar 1976: 214).

627. Sitter points out that 'all-composing Sleep' is what Pope's grieving Achilles lacks at the end of the *Iliad*, but that 'in the inverted world of the *Dunciad* ... sleep always comes too easily' (*Iliad* XXIV.8; Sitter 1971: 114–15).

629–56. Reworking material which had in previous versions formed the conclusion of Book III. For its complex effects and an argument for its relation to the coming of the age of iron in Ovid's *Metamorphoses*, see Jones in Mack & Winn 1980: 645–50. For its relation to notions of 'ending' in the period, see Doody 1985: 190–92.

629–30 and n. For parallel epic acclamations, see Sherbo 1970: 512. 'The Sable [black] Throne' contrasts with Revelation 20:11: 'And I saw a great white throne, and him that sat on it, from whose face the earth and the heaven fled away; and there was found no place for them'. Chaos and Night were identified at I.12 as Dulness's parents: cp. Milton's 'behold the throne / Of Chaos, and his dark pavilion spread / Wide on the wasteful deep; with him enthroned / Sat sable-vested Night, eldest of things' (Fowler 1998: *Paradise Lost* II.959–62). The note was initialled in 1751 as by Warburton.

635–8 and 637–8n. Medea and Hermes are paralleled as agents of darkness and blindness. The sorceress Medea, in the Latin tragedy by Seneca (*c*.4 BC–AD 65), summons monsters outlined in the heavenly constellations as she prepares to murder her children in revenge for their father's infidelity (*Medea*, lines 694–700). She finally escapes into the heavens in a chariot drawn by dragons, leaving her husband to conclude that there are no gods (lines 1022–7). Argus, who had eyes all over his body which slept in rotation, was set by the jealous Hera to watch Io in order to prevent Zeus's adultery with her; but the god Hermes was able to put all Argus's eyes to sleep at once. The note quotes Ovid's account: 'And although

Thus at her felt approach, and secret might,
Art after *Art* goes out, and all is Night.
See skulking *Truth* to her old Cavern fled,
Mountains of Casuistry heap'd o'er her head!
Philosophy, that lean'd on Heav'n before,
Shrinks to her second cause, and is no more.

641.] Alluding to the saying of Democritus, That Truth lay at the bottom of a deep well, from whence he had drawn her: Though Butler says, *He first put her in, before he drew her out.*

643.] Philosophy has at length brought things to that pass, as to have it esteemed unphilosophical to rest in the *first cause*; as if its ends were an endless indagation of cause after cause, without ever coming to the first. So that to avoid this unlearned disgrace, some of the propagators of our best philosophy have had recourse to the contrivance here hinted at. For this Philosophy, which is founded in the principle of *Gravitation*, first considered that property in matter, as something extrinsical to it, and impressed immediately by God upon it. Which fairly and modestly coming up to the first Cause, was pushing natural enquiries as far as they should go. But this stopping, though at the extent of our ideas, was mistaken by foreign Philosophers as recurring to the *occult* qualities of the Peripatetics. To avoid which imaginary discredit to the new theory, it was thought proper to seek for the *cause* of *gravitation*

---

some of his eyes fall asleep, the others still keep watch .... Hermes sees that all the eyes have gone to sleep ...' (*Metamorphoses* I.686–7). Yet despite the obvious parallel between Medea/ Hermes and Dulness as enemies of light/perception, allegorists had used their conquests as emblems of reason/control making order from disorder, a tradition which underlays the passage with ironic contrast (Hauser 1961). A further analogue for line 636 suggests another contrast, as Prudentius describes the darkened sky during the harrowing of Hell, when, between the crucifixion and the resurrection, Christ went down into Hell to free souls condemned by the old law: 'tristia squalentis aethrae palluerunt sidera' ('the sky puts on mourning and the sad stars grow pale': *Liber Cathemerinon*, IX.76–8). The phraseology also recalls Pope's description of dawn: 'The Stars shine fainter on th' Aetherial Plains' (Pope's *Iliad* X.252). For the connotations of 'sick'ning', see Sherbo 1988: 223–4.

639. Recalling the Lady in Milton's *Comus*: as she approaches Comus says 'I feel the different pace, / Of some chaste footing'; and her brother declares that her chastity constitutes 'a hidden strength' (Carey 1968: lines 145–6, 414).

641 and n. Warburton initialled this note in 1751, although he had merely added the Butler reference, a paraphrase of *Hudibras* II.iii.665–6, to the existing note on the equivalent passage in 1729 (*TE*: V, 193). The Greek philosopher Democritus (460–*c*.357 BC) was pioneer of the atomic theory that underlay the later Epicurean system. Warburton's approval of Butler's gibe is in line with orthodox disapproval of such atomistic materialism (see notes on lines 15, 484 and 492).

643–4 and n. Returning to the accusations advanced at lines 473–6 that physicists were attempting to substitute mechanical necessity for divine action in their account of natural processes. The note was initialled in 1751 as by Warburton. ***indagation:*** investigation. **occult *qualities of the Peripatetics:*** The Peripatetics were the followers of Aristotle. In the pre-modern science derived from Aristotle, 'occult qualities' were posited as the unseen causes of perceived effects. In 1751 Warburton further explained what was at issue for him in these lines, quoting the version used in 1729: 'Philosophy, that touch'd the Heavens before, / Shrinks to her hidden cause, and is no more' (III.349–50 in 1729 version, but Warburton mistakenly

645 *Physic* of *Metaphysic* begs defence,
And *Metaphysic* calls for aid on *Sense!*

in a certain *elastic fluid,* which pervaded all body. By this means, instead of really advancing in natural enquiries, we were brought back again by this ingenious expedient to an unsatisfactory *second cause:* For it might still, by the same kind of objection, be asked, what was the *cause* of that *elasticity?* See this folly censured, ver. 475.

645, 646.] Certain writers, as Malbranch, Norris, and others, have thought it of importance, in order to secure the existence of the *soul,* to bring in question the reality of *body;* which they have attempted to do by a very refined *metaphysical* reasoning: While others of the same party, in order to persuade us of the necessity of a Revelation which promises immortality, have been as anxious to prove that those qualities which are commonly supposed to belong only to an immaterial Being, are but the result from the sensations of matter, and the soul naturally mortal. Thus between these different reasonings, they have left us neither Soul nor Body: nor the Sciences of Physics and Metaphysics the least support, by making them depend upon and go a begging to one another.

---

gives 'reach'd' for 'touch'd': Warburton 1751: V, 296–7). He claimed that when Pope wrote them he had been misled into criticising Newton by 'a man educated much abroad [presumably Bolingbroke], who had read every thing, but every thing superficially', who had suggested (what was in fact a commonplace criticism) that Newtonian gravitational theory implied a regression to the discredited notion of occult ('hidden') qualities (Yolton 1983: 193; *TE*: V, 193). Warburton claims to have 'hinted' to Pope that 'he had been imposed upon', prompting Pope to recast the lines as 'a compliment ... to that divine genius', a revision which Warburton took to constitute 'a satire on the folly by which he himself had been misled'. This would presumably imply that the first version had blamed Newton for substituting a 'hidden cause' (gravitation) for reliance on God, but that the second version had instead identified Newton as the one who relied properly on God, and had contrasted him with those who improperly looked only for a 'second cause' in the material world. This seems to represent a strained attempt to detach Pope posthumously from Bolingbroke's much-resented influence: it is highly unlikely that Pope intended a satire on Bolingbroke, since it was a basic strategy in his management of the two friends he most admired to refuse to admit the radical divisions between them – indeed in the last weeks of his life he was still hoping to cement a friendship between them (*Corr.*: IV, 488). **elastic fluid:** See notes on lines 473–4.

645–6 and n. Changed from the 1729 version 'See Physic beg the Stagyrite's defence! / See Metaphysic call for aid on Sence!' ('Physic' here denotes the natural sciences, assumed to rest on empirical knowledge of the material world: III.351–2 in 1729 version.) The couplet as revised seems to reflect Warburton's influence, since the earlier version is clearer and closer to Pope's characteristic concerns. Since Pope's disapproval of dependence on Aristotle (called 'the Stagyrite' in allusion to his birthplace) has already been made plain (see editor's notes on line 192), the two lines of 1729 can be read as parallel structures in which a discipline looks for inappropriate support (and the following line, substantially the same as line 647 in 1743, follows easily with a third parallel). In 1743, however, the substitution of '*Metaphysic*' for 'the Stagyrite' shifts the couplet into a vicious circle of mutual and implicitly inappropriate appeal which the note, initialled in 1751 as by Warburton, elaborates. The note rests on Warburton's orthodox acceptance of the separate existence of matter and spirit, and elaborates the irony by which, in his view, some defenders of the reality of spirit go to the perverse extreme of denying the reality of matter. Nicolas de Malebranche (1638–1715), priest and philosopher, developed from Descartes a system characterised by two leading principles:

See *Mystery* to *Mathematics* fly!
In vain! they gaze, turn giddy, rave, and die.
Religion blushing veils her sacred fires,
And unawares *Morality* expires.

647.] A sort of men (who make human Reason the adequate measure of all Truth) having pretended that whatsoever is not fully comprehended by it, is contrary to it; certain defenders of Religion, who would not be outdone in a paradox, have gone as far in the opposite folly, and attempted to shew that the mysteries of Religion may be mathematically demonstrated; as the authors of Philosophic, or Astronomic Principles, natural and reveal'd.

649.] *Blushing*, not only at the view of these her false supports in the *present* overflow of dulness, but at the memory of the *past*; when the barbarous learning of so many ages was solely employed in corrupting the simplicity, and defiling the purity of Religion. Amidst the extinction of all other Lights, she is said only to withdraw hers; as hers alone in its own nature is unextinguishable and eternal.

650.] It appears from hence that our Poet was of very different sentiments from the Author of the Characteristics, who has written a formal treatise on Virtue, to prove it not only real but durable, without the support of Religion. The word *unawares* alludes to the confidence

---

perception is not directly of objects but of the divine ideas of objects (called 'vision in God'); and events are caused not by any intrinsic power in objects or people, but by the particular will of God that such events should occur (called 'occasionalism'). John Norris (1657–1711), clergyman and philosopher, was a disciple of Malebranche. Warburton goes on to claim that others, equally intent on countering deist arguments for the superfluity of the Christian 'Revelation which promises immortality', insist that attributes conventionally seen as specific to spirit (and hence vulnerable to materialist analysis) are actually no more than attributes of matter: hence the soul, being an effect of the body, would naturally die with it, were it not for the revealed promise of eternal life.

647 and n. For satire on mathematical divinity, see editor's note on line 462. The note, initialled in 1751 as by Warburton, could also imply a sneer at William Derham's *Astro-Theology: or, A Demonstration of the Being and Attributes of God, from a Survey of the Heavens* (1715), or at George Cheyne's *Philosophical Principles of Natural Religion: Containing the Elements of Natural Philosophy, and the Proofs for Natural Religion, arising from them* (1705). Pope, however, said of Cheyne that 'There lives not an Honester Man, nor a Truer Philosopher' (*Corr.*: IV, 242).

648. they: The personifications whose desperate shifts for survival have been described in lines 641–7.

649 and n. Sutherland is surely correct to play down the shame for the past (i.e. the Middle Ages) attributed to Religion in the note, which was initialled in 1751 as by Warburton; although there is much in Book IV to suggest that Dulness's final triumph recapitulates the earlier, and milder, process of Gothic corruption (*TE*: V, 409; Rumbold 1983: 36–43). Warburton's insistence that Religion's light 'is unextinguishable and eternal' sits uneasily with the closing paragraph of the verse.

650 and n. Morality is made to die as an unintended consequence of the suppression of religion. The note, initialled in 1751 as by Warburton, attacks Shaftesbury, the author of *Characteristicks* (1711), for his argument, in his *Inquiry concerning Virtue*, that belief in God was not absolutely necessary in order to attain virtue (*Inquiry* 1699: 81; Voitle 1984: 119–33). Deists, with their belief in the oppressive corruption of established religion, tended to argue that morality would actually benefit by separation from religion: Warburton implies that such claims are too preposterous to be sincere, and are more likely a cover for libertinism.

Nor *public* Flame, nor *private*, dares to shine;
Nor *human* Spark is left, nor Glimpse *divine!*
Lo! thy dread Empire, CHAOS! is restor'd;
Light dies before thy uncreating word:
Thy hand, great Anarch! lets the curtain fall;
And Universal Darkness buries All.

of those men who suppose that Morality would flourish best without it, and consequently to the surprize such would be in (if any such there are) who indeed love Virtue, and yet do all they can to root out the Religion of their Country.

FINIS.

---

653. Restoring the condition that existed before creation.

654. Cp. 'And God said, Let there be light: and there was light' (Genesis 1:3; and see editor's note on line 605).

655–6. For contextualisation of the 'fall'/'all' rhyme and the sentiments to which it lends itself, see Jones in Mack & Winn 1980: 650–51. Dryden, translating *Iliad* VI, makes Hector describe the coming fall of Troy: 'The fatal Day draws on, when I must fall; / And Universal Ruine cover all' (Kinsley 1958: 'The Last Parting of Hector and Andromache', lines 116–17; Smith 1965; Erskine-Hill 1972b: 60). The closing lines of his tragedy *Amboyna*, whose hero also invokes the idea of theatrical representation in terms that may anticipate Pope's reference to the fall of the curtain, prophesy an apocalyptic flood in markedly similar terms: 'Till at the last, your sapped foundation fall, / And universal ruin swallows all' (Corman & Stone 1988). Other late seventeenth-century couplets use the rhyme for comparable forebodings (Maxwell & Stanley 1967). Pope used such couplets three times in his *Iliad* (IV.198–9; VI.73–4; XII.79–80).

655. Anarch: Milton calls Chaos 'anarch' (Fowler 1998: *Paradise Lost* II.988). His 'faltering speech and visage incomposed' mark his kinship with his portentously yawning daughter. ***the curtain:*** Most obviously, a stage curtain, assimilating the end of the world to the triteness of theatrical apocalypse (cp. III.231–72); but also, in view of Dulness's characterisation as a nursing mother (I.311–18; IV.20; Warburton's note on IV.517), perhaps a bed-curtain, as she tucks up her children for the last time.

656. Cp. Shakespeare's *2 Henry IV*, where the end of the world is also described in terms of stage effects: 'Let order die! / And let this world no longer be a stage / To feed contention in a ling'ring act; / But let one spirit of the first-born Cain / Reign in all bosoms, that, each heart being set / On bloody courses, the rude scene may end / And darkness be the burier of the dead!' (Alexander 1951: *2 Henry IV*, I.i.154–60). This speech was admired by Pope as a 'curse ... where that admirable Master of Nature makes *Northumberland*, in the Rage of his Passion, wish for an universal Destruction' (Pope's note to his *Iliad*, XVI.122). The allusion could imply that Pope recognises that, like Northumberland, the speaker, he has set his face against the course of history with a passion that others find excessive: Northumberland's outburst is received with the words, 'This strained passion doth you wrong'; and it may also be relevant to the *Dunciads*' concern with the inadequacies of Hanoverian rule that Northumberland's rage stems from his son's death in an attempt to redivert the succession from a usurper. There may also be an ironic allusion to Cibber's incorporation of these lines into his adaptation of *Richard III*, where they serve as the murderous usurper's dying words (Potter 1983).

APPENDIX

APPENDIX.

I.

PREFACE

Prefixed to the five first imperfect Editions of the DUNCIAD, in three books, printed at DUBLIN and LONDON, in octavo and duodecimo, 1727.

The PUBLISHER [a] to the READER.

IT will be found a true observation, tho' somewhat surprizing, that when any scandal is vented against a man of the highest distinction and character, either in the state or in literature, the public in general afford it a most quiet reception; and the larger part accept it as favourably as if it were some kindness done

[a] *The Publisher*] Who he was is uncertain; but Edward Ward tells us, in his preface to Durgen, 'that most judges are of opinion this preface is not of English extraction, but Hibernian,' *etc.* He means it was written by Dr. Swift, who, whether publisher or not, may be said in a sort to be author of the poem: For when he, together with Mr. Pope (for reasons specified in the preface to their Miscellanies) determined to own the most trifling pieces in which they had any hand, and to destroy all that remained in their power; the first sketch of this poem was

PREFACE: Reprinted as Appendix I from 1729.

five first imperfect Editions: Of the three-book version without commentary, in which many victims were indicated only by initials (Griffith 1922–7: I, 147, 152–61).

1727: Actually 1728 (compare original note on title at the beginning of Book I).

Note a. Pope himself arranged for the anonymous publication of the *Dunciad*. Ward's attribution was more offensively expressed than the paraphrase suggests (Guerinot 1969: 158). In a letter of 1728 Pope gave a sadder turn to the compliment to Swift: 'It had never been writ but at his Request, and for his Deafness: For had he been able to converse with me, do you think I had amus'd my Time so ill?' (Mack 1985: 441–2, 890; *Corr.*: II, 523). For the early stages of composition, see Vander Meulen 1991: 3–28.

The preface to Swift and Pope's *Miscellanies* (1727) stated that they would publish all the 'loose Papers in Prose and Verse, we have formerly written' so that publishers such as Curll could no longer attribute to them 'whole Volumes of mean Productions ... which we never saw or heard of till they appeared in Print'.

The final paragraph of the note is adapted from the Dedication to Richard Savage's *A Collection of Pieces* (1732), signed by Savage, but said by Johnson to be by Pope (Hill 1905: III, 147). The 'Treatise of the Bathos', or *Peri Bathous*, published early in 1728 in the so-called 'Last Volume' of the *Miscellanies*, is closely related to the genesis of the *Dunciads* (*PW*: II, 171–276). Chapter VI gives initials as examples of various kinds of bad poets: far from being

to themselves: whereas if a known scoundrel or blockhead but chance to be touch'd upon, a whole legion is up in arms, and it becomes the common cause of all scriblers, booksellers, and printers whatsoever.

Not to search too deeply into the reason hereof, I will only observe as a fact, that every week for these two months past, the town has been persecuted with [b] pamphlets, advertisements, letters, and weekly essays, not only against the wit and writings, but against the character and person of Mr. Pope. And that of all those men who have received pleasure from his works, which by modest computation may be about a [c] hundred thousand in these kingdoms of England and Ireland;

snatched from the fire by Dr. Swift, who persuaded his friend to proceed in it, and to him it was therefore inscribed. But the occasion of printing it was as follows.

There was published in those Miscellanies, a Treatise of the Bathos, or Art of Sinking in Poetry, in which was a chapter, where the species of bad writers were ranged in classes, and initial letters of names prefixed, for the most part at random. But such was the Number of Poets eminent in that art, that some one or other took every letter to himself. All fell into so violent a fury, that for half a year, or more, the common Newspapers (in most of which they had some property, as being hired writers) were filled with the most abusive falshoods and scurrilities they could possibly devise: A liberty no ways to be wondered at in those people, and in those papers, that, for many years, during the uncontrolled Licence of the press, had aspersed almost all the great characters of the age; and this with impunity, their own persons and names being utterly secret and obscure. This gave Mr. Pope the thought, that he had now some opportunity of doing good, by detecting and dragging into light these common Enemies of mankind; since to invalidate this universal slander, it sufficed to shew what contemptible men were the authors of it. He was not without hopes, that by manifesting the dulness of those who had only malice to recommend them, either the booksellers would not find their account in employing them; or the men themselves, when discovered, want courage to proceed in so unlawful an occupation. This it was that gave birth to the Dunciad; and he thought it an happiness, that by the late flood of slander on himself, he had acquired such a peculiar right over their Names as was necessary to his design.

[b] *Pamphlets, advertisements, etc.*] See the List of those anonymous papers, with their dates and authors annexed, inserted before the Poem.

[c] *About a hundred thousand*] It is surprizing with what stupidity this preface, which is almost a continued irony, was taken by those authors. All such passages as these were understood by Curl, Cook, Cibber, and others, to be serious. Hear the Laureate (Letter to Mr. Pope, p. 9.) 'Though I grant the Dunciad a better poem of its kind than ever was writ; yet, when I read

allocated 'for the most part at random', they deliberately provoked a new round of attacks in advance of the appearance of the *Dunciad*. The victims are said to have had 'some property' in the newspapers in which they published their responses since as 'hired writers' they had ready access to the press for their own ends. These writers are also said to have 'aspersed' ('slandered') their betters.

Note b. See Appendix II.

Note c. Cibber implies that Pope resembles the Duke of Wharton, in Pope's estimate 'the scorn and wonder of our days, / Whose ruling Passion was the Lust of Praise' (*Characters of Men*, 180–81). Except for the use of 'Virgilius Restauratus' (probably by Arbuthnot), some early assistance from Gay while Pope had been unable to write owing to an injury to his hand,

(not to mention Jersey, Guernsey, the Orcades, those in the new world, and foreigners who have translated him into their languages) of all this number not a man hath stood up to say one word in his defence.

The only exception is the [d] author of the following poem, who doubtless had either a better insight into the grounds of this clamour, or a better opinion of Mr. Pope's integrity, join'd with a greater personal love for him, than any other of his numerous friends and admirers.

Farther, that he was in his particular intimacy, appears from the knowledge he manifests of the most private authors of all the anonymous pieces against him, and from his having in this poem attacked [e] no man living, who had not before printed, or published, some scandal against this gentleman.

How I came possest of it, is no concern to the reader; but it would have been a wrong to him had I detain'd the publication; since those names which are its chief ornaments die off daily so fast, as must render it too soon unintelligible. If it provoke the author to give us a more perfect edition, I have my end.

Who he is I cannot say, and (which is great pity) there is certainly [f] nothing in his style and manner of writing which can distinguish or discover him: For if it

it with those *vain-glorious* encumbrances of Notes and Remarks upon it, *etc.* — it is amazing, that you, who have writ with such masterly spirit upon the ruling Passion, should be so blind a slave to your own, as not to see how far a *low avarice of Praise,' etc.* (taking it for granted that the notes of Scriblerus and others, were the author's own.)

[d] *The author of the following poem, etc.*] A very plain irony, speaking of Mr. Pope himself.

[e] The publisher in these words went a little too far: But it is certain whatever names the reader finds that are unknown to him, are of such; and the exception is only of two or three, whose dulness, impudent scurrility, or self-conceit, all mankind agreed to have justly entitled them to a place in the Dunciad.

[f] *There is certainly nothing in his style, etc.*] This irony had small effect in concealing the author. The Dunciad, imperfect as it was, had not been published two days, but the whole Town gave it to Mr. Pope.

---

one note initialled 'C' which may denote Cleland's authorship, and Warburton's initialling of some of his own and Pope's contributions to the commentary in 1751, specific contributions are unclear, although Pope certainly invited Swift to contribute, probably used information derived from Savage's contacts with the lower end of the book trade, and probably used epigrams sent in by readers (editor's note on I.1n.; Nokes 1995: 373; III.179n.; *Corr.*: II, 503, 523). At the very least, Pope closely supervised the commentary of the three-book versions, and probably wrote most of it himself, although he was to give a freer hand to Warburton in the preparation of 1743 (*TE*: V, xxiv–xxvii).

the Orcades: the Orkney Islands.

Note d. Pope did not put his name on the title-pages of the *Dunciads*, although authorship was very soon an open secret, and he owned it implicitly by including it in his collected works.

the most private authors: Those whose anonymity was hardest to penetrate, i.e. the most obscure and insignificant.

I have my end: I shall have achieved my purpose. Readers are encouraged to look out for further expansions.

bears any resemblance to that of Mr. Pope, 'tis not improbable but it might be done on purpose, with a view to have it pass for his. But by the frequency of his allusions to Virgil, and a labour'd (not to say affected) *shortness* in imitation of him, I should think him more an admirer of the Roman poet than of the Grecian, and in that not of the same taste with his friend.

I have been well inform'd, that this work was the labour of full [g] six years of his life, and that he wholly retired himself from all the avocations and pleasures of the world, to attend diligently to its correction and perfection; and six years more he intended to bestow upon it, as it should seem by this verse of Statius which was cited at the head of his manuscript: 'Oh mihi bissenos multum vigilata per annos, / Duncia[h]!'

Hence also we learn the true title of the poem; which with the same certainty as we call that of Homer the Iliad, of Virgil the Aeneid, of Camoens the Lusiad, we may pronounce could have been, and can be no other than

The DUNCIAD.

It is styled *Heroic*, as being *doubly* so; not only with respect to its nature, which according to the best rules of the ancients, and strictest ideas of the moderns, is critically such; but also with regard to the heroical disposition and high courage

[g] *The labour of full six years, etc.*] This also was honestly and seriously believed by divers gentlemen of the Dunciad. J. Ralph, pref. to Sawney. 'We are told it was the labour of six years, with the utmost assiduity and application: It is no great compliment to the author's sense, to have employed so large a part of his life,' *etc.* So also Ward, pref. to Durgen, 'The Dunciad, as the publisher very wisely confesses, cost the author six years retirement from all the pleasures of life; though it is somewhat difficult to conceive, from either its bulk or beauty, that it could be so long in hatching, *etc.* But the length of time and closeness of application were mentioned to prepossess the reader with a good opinion of it.'

They just as well understood what Scriblerus said of the Poem.

[h] The prefacer to Curl's Key, p. 3. took this word to be really in Statius: 'By a quibble on the word *Duncia*, the *Dunciad* is formed.' Mr. Ward also follows him in the same opinion.

***a labour'd (not to say affected)* shortness:** The writer attributes to Pope a careful and deliberate imitation of Virgil's succinctness, and goes so far as to imply it may be assumed for effect, in order to imply that the writer cannot be Pope, whose devotion to Homer ('the Grecian') as in some respects Virgil's superior was well known from his Preface to his translation. ('Labour'd' and 'affected' need not carry the pejorative charge of modern usage.)

Note g. Pope tones down the offensiveness of the quotations.

avocations: distractions.

Statius: Pope has substituted 'Duncia' for the original 'Thebai' ('I have sat up at night for twelve years to work on you, my *Thebaid*': *Thebaid* XII.811–12).

Note h. The *Compleat Key* (1728) really does fail to recognise Pope's alteration of the quotation from Statius: 'By a dull Pun, from the word *Duncia* in *Statius*, the *Dunciad* is formed' (p. iv); but the parallel charge against Ward's Preface to *Durgen* (1728) is exaggerated.

Camoens: Luís de Camòes (*c.*1525–80), author of *Os Lusíadas*, (from 'Lusitania', the classical name for Portugal), the Portuguese national epic.

of the writer, who dar'd to stir up such a formidable, irritable, and implacable race of mortals.

There may arise some obscurity in chronology from the *Names* in the poem, by the inevitable removal of some authors, and insertion of others, in their niches. For whoever will consider the unity of the whole design, will be sensible, that the *poem was not made for these authors, but these authors for the poem.* I should judge that they were clapp'd in as they rose, fresh and fresh, and chang'd from day to day; in like manner as when the old boughs wither, we thrust new ones into a chimney.

I would not have the reader too much troubled or anxious, if he cannot decypher them; since when he shall have found them out, he will probably know no more of the persons than before.

Yet we judg'd it better to preserve them as they are, than to change them for fictitious names; by which the satire would only be multiplied, and applied to many instead of one. Had the hero, for instance, been called Codrus, how many would have affirm'd him to have been Mr. T. Mr. E. Sir R.B. *etc.* but now all that unjust scandal is saved by calling him by a name, which by good luck happens to be that of a real person.

II.

A LIST of

BOOKS, PAPERS, and VERSES,

In which our Author was abused, before the Publication of the DUNCIAD; with the true Names of the Authors.

REFLECTIONS critical and satyrical on a late Rhapsody, called An Essay on Criticism. By Mr. Dennis, printed by B. Lintot, price *6d.*

***the* poem was not made for these authors:** In accordance with Le Bossu's dictum that the characters of epics were contingent on the poet's predetermined moral and fable (Keener 1991: 43–4).

when the old boughs wither: Foliage was used to decorate unused fireplaces.

he will probably know no more: Because he will never have heard of them.

Mr. T. Mr. E. Sir R.B.: Tibbald actually was the hero in 1728; and Eusden and Blackmore were attacked in all versions.

A LIST of BOOKS, PAPERS, and VERSES: An incomplete list, only slightly updated from its first appearance as Appendix II in 1729, but sufficient to be presented as justification for Pope's claim to be retaliating against continuous persecution. For individual items, including Pope's attributions of anonymous pieces, see Bibliography and Guerinot 1969.

REFLECTIONS critical and satyrical: Dennis 1711.

A New Rehearsal, or Bays the younger; containing an Examen of Mr. Row's plays, and a word or two on Mr. Pope's Rape of the Lock. Anon. [by Charles Gildon] printed for J. Roberts, 1714. price 1*s*.

Homerides, or a Letter to Mr. Pope, occasioned by his intended translation of Homer. By Sir Iliad Dogrel. [Tho. Burnet and G. Ducket esquires] printed for W. Wilkins, 1715. price 9*d*.

Aesop at the Bear-garden; a vision, in imitation of the Temple of Fame. By Mr. Preston. Sold by John Morphew, 1715. price 6*d*.

The Catholic Poet, or Protestant Barnaby's Sorrowful Lamentation; a Ballad about Homer's Iliad. By Mrs. Centlivre, and others, 1715. price 1*d*.

An Epilogue to a Puppet-shew at Bath, concerning the said Iliad. By George Ducket esq. printed by E. Curl.

A complete Key to the What d'ye call it. Anon. [by Griffin a player, supervised by Mr. Th——] printed by J. Roberts, 1715.

A true Character of Mr. P. and his writings, in a letter to a friend. Anon. [Dennis] printed for S. Popping, 1716, price 3*d*.

The Confederates, a Farce. By Joseph Gay [J.D. Breval] printed for R. Burleigh, 1717, price 1*s*.

Remarks upon Mr. Pope's translation of Homer; with two letters concerning the Windsor Forest, and the Temple of Fame. By Mr. Dennis, printed for E. Curl, 1717, price 1*s*. 6*d*.

Satyrs on the translators of Homer, Mr. P. and Mr. T. Anon. [Bez. Morris] 1717, price 6*d*.

The Triumvirate; or, a Letter from Palaemon to Celia at Bath. Anon. [Leonard Welsted] 1711, Folio, price 1*s*.

The Battle of Poets, an heroic poem. By Tho. Cooke, printed for J. Roberts, Folio, 1725.

Memoirs of Lilliput. Anon. [Eliza Haywood] octavo, printed in 1727.

A New Rehearsal: *A New Rehearsal* 1714.

Homerides: *Homerides* 1715.

Aesop: Preston 1715.

The Catholic Poet: *The Catholick Poet* 1716.

An Epilogue: Included in *Homerides* 1715.

A complete Key: *A Complete Key to ... The What D'Ye Call It* 1715. Attacking Gay and his presumed collaborator Pope for disrespectful parody of the English tragic repertory, the *Key* is identified by Pope as the work of theatrical professionals, and may have provided an early motive for his dislike of Theobald.

A true Character: *A True Character* 1716.

The Confederates: *The Confederates* 1717.

Remarks: Dennis 1717.

Satyrs: Pope misdates publication (*Three Satires* 1719). 'Mr. T.' was Tickell.

The Triumvirate: *Palaemon to Caelia*, actually published in 1717.

The Battle: *The Battle of the Poets* 1725.

Memoirs: *Memoirs of the Court of Lilliput* 1727.

An Essay on Criticism, in prose. By the Author of the Critical History of England [J. Oldmixon] octavo, printed 1728.

Gulliveriana and Alexandriana; with an ample preface and critique on Swift and Pope's Miscellanies. By Jonathan Smedley, printed by J. Roberts, octavo, 1728.

Characters of the Times; or, an account of the writings, characters, *etc.* of several gentlemen libelled by S—— and P——, in a late Miscellany. Octavo, 1728.

Remarks on Mr. Pope's Rape of the Lock, in letters to a friend. By Mr. Dennis; written in 1714, though not printed till 1728, octavo.

Verses, Letters, Essays, or Advertisements, in the public Prints.

British Journal, Nov. 25, 1727. A Letter on Swift and Pope's Miscellanies. [Writ by M. Concanen.]

Daily Journal, March 18, 1728. A Letter by Philo-mauri. James-Moore Smith.

Id. March 29. A Letter about Thersites; accusing the author of disaffection to the Government. By James-Moore Smith.

Mist's Weekly Journal, March 30. An Essay on the Arts of a Poet's sinking in reputation; or, a Supplement to the Art of Sinking in Poetry. [Supposed by Mr. Theobald.]

Daily Journal, April 3. A Letter under the name of Philoditto. By James-Moore Smith.

Flying Post, April 4. A Letter against Gulliver and Mr. P. [By Mr. Oldmixon.]

Daily Journal, April 5. An Auction of Goods at Twickenham. By James-Moore Smith.

The Flying Post, April 6. A Fragment of a Treatise upon Swift and Pope. By Mr. Oldmixon.

The Senator, April 9. On the same. By Edward Roome.

Daily Journal, April 8. Advertisement by James-Moore Smith.

Flying Post, April 13. Verses against Dr. Swift, and against Mr. P—'s Homer. By J. Oldmixon.

Daily Journal, April 23. Letter about the translation of the character of Thersites in Homer. By Thomas Cooke, *etc.*

An Essay on Criticism: Oldmixon 1728a. His *Critical History of England* (1724–6) had been published anonymously.

Gulliveriana: *Gulliveriana* 1728.

Characters: *Characters of the Times* 1728.

Remarks: Dennis 1728. Dennis's Preface states that he had written it by 1714 and used it as a threat to ensure Pope's good behaviour, publishing it only when his behaviour became intolerable.

Verses, Letters, Essays: Only those reprinted in *A Compleat Collection* 1728.

Daily Journal, March 18: Pope had been accused of writing this letter himself, but see Guerinot 1969: 105.

Thersites: An ugly and obstreperous member of the lower ranks in Homer's *Iliad*, whose insubordination is punished, to universal acclaim, by a beating from Odysseus (*Iliad* II.211–77).

Mist's Weekly Journal, April 27. A Letter of Lewis Theobald.

Daily Journal, May 11. A Letter against Mr. P. at large. Anon. [John Dennis.]

All these were afterwards reprinted in a pamphlet, entituled A Collection of all the Verses, Essays, Letters, and Advertisements occasioned by Mr. Pope and Swift's Miscellanies, prefaced by Concanen, Anonymous, octavo, and printed for A. Moore, 1728, price 1*s*. Others of an elder date, having lain as waste Paper many years, were, upon the publication of the Dunciad, brought out, and their Authors betrayed by the mercenary Booksellers (in hope of some possibility of vending a few) by advertising them in this manner — 'The Confederates, a farce. By Capt. Breval (for which he was put into the Dunciad.) An Epilogue to Powel's Puppet-show. By Col. Ducket (for which he is put into the Dunciad.) Essays, *etc*. By Sir Richard Blackmore. (N. B. It was for a passage of this book that Sir Richard was put into the Dunciad.)' And so of others.

After the Dunciad, 1728.

An Essay on the Dunciad. Octavo, printed for J. Roberts. [In this book, p. 9. it was formally declared, 'That the complaint of the aforesaid Libels and Advertisements was forged and untrue; that all mouths had been silent, except in Mr. Pope's praise; and nothing against him published, but by Mr. Theobald.']

Sawney, in blank verse, occasioned by the Dunciad; with a Critique on that Poem. By J. Ralph [a person never mentioned in it at first, but inserted after] printed for J. Roberts, octavo.

A complete Key to the Dunciad. By E. Curl, 12mo. price 6*d*.

A second and third edition of the same, with additions, 12mo.

The Popiad. By E. Curl, extracted from J. Dennis, Sir Richard Blackmore, *etc*. 12mo. price 6*d*.

The Curliad. By the same E. Curl.

The Female Dunciad. Collected by the same Mr. Curl, 12mo. price 6*d*. With the Metamorphosis of P. into a stinging Nettle. By Mr. Foxton, 12mo.

It was for a passage of this book: For the offence given by Blackmore's condemnation in his *Essays* of the poem Curll printed in 1716 as 'A Roman Catholick Version of the First Psalm', see notes on II.268.

An Essay on the Dunciad: *An Essay on the Dunciad* 1728. The loose quotation is from a passage denying Pope's claim that he had been persecuted by a flood of attacks in the press.

Sawney: *Sawney* 1728. Pope notes that it was entirely owing to this attack that he later included Ralph among the dunces.

A complete Key: *A Compleat Key to the Dunciad* 1728, which appeared in three editions in that year.

The Popiad: *The Popiad* 1728.

The Curliad: Curll 1729.

The Female Dunciad: *The Female Dunciad* 1728. This includes 'The New Metamorphosis', attributed by Pope to the poet and translator Thomas Foxton (1697–1769), who had worked for Curll, but was dropped from the *Dunciad* in 1743 (*TE*: V, 164, 440).

The Metamorphosis of Scriblerus into Snarlerus. By J. Smedley, printed for A. Moore, folio, price *6d.*

The Dunciad dissected. By Curl and Mrs Thomas, 12mo.

An Essay on the Taste and Writings of the present times. Said to be writ by a gentleman of C.C.C. Oxon, printed for J. Roberts, octavo.

The Arts of Logic and Rhetoric, partly taken from Bouhours, with new Reflections, *etc.* By John Oldmixon, octavo.

Remarks on the Dunciad. By Mr. Dennis, dedicated to Theobald, octavo.

A Supplement to the Profund. Anon. by Matthew Concanen, octavo.

Mist's Weekly Journal, June 8. A long Letter, signed W. A. Writ by some or other of the Club of Theobald, Dennis, Moore, Concanen, Cooke, who for some time held constant weekly meetings for these kind of performances.

Daily Journal, June 11. A Letter, signed Philoscriblerus, on the name of Pope — Letter to Mr. Theobald, in verse, signed B. M. [Bezaleel Morris] against Mr. P. — Many other little epigrams about this time in the same papers, by James Moore, and others.

Mist's Journal, June 22. A Letter by Lewis Theobald.

Flying Post, August 8. Letter on Pope and Swift.

Daily Journal, August 8. Letter charging the Author of the Dunciad with Treason.

Durgen; a plain satyr on a pompous satyrist. By Edward Ward, with a little of James Moore.

Apollo's Maggot in his Cups. By E. Ward.

Gulliveriana secunda. Being a Collection of many of the Libels in the News-papers, like the former Volume, under the same title, by Smedley. Advertised in the Craftsman, Nov. 9, 1728, with this remarkable promise, that '*any thing* which

---

The Metamorphosis: *The Metamorphosis* 1728.

The Dunciad dissected: *Codrus* 1728.

An Essay on the Taste and Writings: Published in 1728 as by a member of Christ Church, its anonymity teased Pope, who was usually able to identify authors with some plausibility. It was dedicated to Walpole; but Pope seems to have been unsuccessful in finding out the author's identity via their mutual friend Fortescue (Guerinot 1969: 130).

The Arts of Logic and Rhetoric: Oldmixon 1728b.

Remarks on the Dunciad: Dennis 1729.

A Supplement: *A Supplement* 1728.

Mist's Weekly Journal, June 8: 8 June 1728. Pope's circumstantial account of the letter's authorship may be derived in part from a 1729 letter from William Arnall, an attempt to clear himself with Pope which proved only temporarily successful (see editor's note on II.315).

Daily Journal, June 11: 11 June 1728.

Mist's Journal, June 22: 22 June 1728.

Flying Post, August 8: I have been unable to inspect a copy.

Durgen: *Durgen* 1728.

Apollo's Maggot: Ward 1729. 'In his Cups' means 'drunk'.

Gulliveriana secunda: Apparently planned but never published (Guerinot 1969: 145). As paraphrased, the promise was 'remarkable' in suggesting that no degree of implausibility

any body should send as Mr. Pope's or Dr. Swift's, should be inserted and published as theirs.'

Pope Alexander's supremacy and infallibity examined, *etc*. By George Ducket and John Dennis, quarto.

Dean Jonathan's Paraphrase on the 4th chapter of Genesis. Writ by E. Roome, folio, 1729.

Labeo. A paper of verses by Leonard Welsted, which after came into *One Epistle*, and was published by James Moore, quarto, 1730. Another part of it came out in Welsted's own name, under the just title of Dulness and Scandal, folio, 1731.

There have been since published

Verses on the Imitator of Horace. By a Lady [or between a Lady, a Lord, and a Court-'squire.] Printed for J. Roberts, folio.

An Epistle from a Nobleman to a Doctor of Divinity, from Hampton-court [Lord H——y.] Printed for J. Roberts also, folio.

A Letter from Mr. Cibber to Mr. Pope. Printed for W. Lewis in Covent-garden, octavo.

III.

ADVERTISEMENT

To the First Edition with Notes, in Quarto, 1729.

It will be sufficient to say of this edition, that the reader has here a much more correct and complete copy of the Dunciad, than has hitherto appear'd.

---

whatsoever would deter the publisher from ascribing contributions to Pope or to Swift. As originally printed it was slightly less shameless: 'Persons, possessed of any Thing written by Pope and Swift, not publish'd in the Four Volumes [i.e. the *Miscellanies* in which they said they had printed everything they had not destroyed], or who can furnish any Thing fit for this Miscellany, may have it inserted' (*The Craftsman*, 9 November 1728).

Pope Alexander's supremacy: *Pope Alexander's Supremacy* 1729.

Dean Jonathan's Paraphrase: *Dean Jonathan's Parody* 1729.

Labeo: A verse attack supposedly projected by Welsted, who is here assumed to have incorporated it into the anonymous *One Epistle* 1730 (Guerinot 1969: 189).

Verses on the Imitator of Horace: *Verses Address'd to the Imitator of Horace* 1733 was written by Lady Mary Wortley Montagu and Lord Hervey. Which other courtier ('Court-'squire') may have been thought to be involved is unclear.

An Epistle from a Nobleman: *An Epistle from a Nobleman* 1733.

A Letter from Mr. Cibber: Cibber 1742.

ADVERTISEMENT: Written, presumably by Pope, as if by the publisher.

I cannot answer but some mistakes may have slipt into it, but a vast number of others will be prevented by the names being now not only set at length, but justified by the authorities and reasons given. I make no doubt, the author's own motive to use real rather than feign'd names, was his care to preserve the innocent from any false application; whereas in the former editions, which had no more than the initial letters, he was made, by keys printed here, to hurt the inoffensive; and (what was worse) to abuse his friends, by an impression at Dublin.

The commentary which attends this poem was sent me from several hands, and consequently must be unequally written; yet will have one advantage over most commentaries, that it is not made upon conjectures, or at a remote distance of time: And the reader cannot but derive one pleasure from the very *Obscurity* of the persons it treats of, that it partakes of the nature of a *Secret*, which most people love to be let into, tho' the men or the things be ever so inconsiderable or trivial.

Of the *Persons* it was judg'd proper to give some account; For since it is only in this monument that they must expect to survive (and here survive they will, as long as the English tongue shall remain such as it was in the reigns of queen ANNE and king GEORGE,) it seem'd but humanity to bestow a word or two upon each, just to tell what he was, what he writ, when he liv'd, and when he died.

If a word or two more are added upon the chief offenders, 'tis only as a paper pinn'd upon the breast, to mark the enormities for which they suffer'd; lest the correction only should be remember'd, and the crime forgotten.

In some articles it was thought sufficient, barely to transcribe from Jacob, Curl, and other writers of their own rank, who were much better acquainted with them than any of the authors of this comment can pretend to be. Most of them had

---

the names being ... set at length: Many names were given in full for the first time in 1729.

by keys printed here: Notably Curll 1728.

an impression at Dublin: See Griffith 1922–7: no. 206; *TE*: V, 8.

sent me from several hands: See editor's note on note c to Appendix I.

as long as the English tongue: Pope had lamented that 'Short is the Date, alas, of *Modern Rhymes*' in *An Essay on Criticism* (line 476); and Swift had proposed an academy to reform the language and fix it for perpetuity (Davis 1939–68: IV, 5–21). Rapid language change had made Chaucer almost unintelligible within 300 years (the more so since scholars had not yet reconstructed the grammar of earlier states of the language), and Pope's generation feared, unnecessarily as it turned out, that this rate of change would continue.

just to tell what he was: After seeing the mistaken identifications in the Dublin edition mentioned above, Swift had suggested that readers outside London, or in the future even in London, would need help with the personal allusions (*Corr.*: II, 504–5).

a paper: Criminals put into the pillory wore a placard to inform passers-by of their crime.

other writers of their own rank: Implying that no gentleman could possibly associate on familiar terms with the dunces – although Pope apparently profited from Savage's anomalous position in this respect.

comment: commentary.

drawn each other's characters on certain occasions; but the few here inserted are all that could be saved from the general destruction of such works.

Of the part of Scriblerus I need say nothing; his manner is well enough known, and approv'd by all but those who are too much concern'd to be judges.

The Imitations of the Ancients are added, to gratify those who either never read, or may have forgotten them; together with some of the parodies and allusions to the most excellent of the Moderns. If, from the frequency of the former, any man think the poem too much a Cento, our poet will but appear to have done the same thing in jest which Boileau did in earnest; and upon which Vida, Fracastorius, and many of the most eminent Latin poets, professedly valued themselves.

IV.

ADVERTISEMENT

To the First Edition, separate, of

The Fourth Book of the DUNCIAD.

WE apprehend it can be deemed no injury to the author of the three first books of the Dunciad, that we publish this Fourth. It was found merely by

---

the general destruction of such works: Implying that the dunces' publications will be thrown away as soon as read.

his manner is well enough known: *Peri Bathous*, which was ascribed to Martinus Scriblerus, had appeared early in 1728 in Pope and Swift's *Miscellanies* (*PW*: II, 171–276).

The Imitations of the Ancients: Not the imitations themselves, but the footnotes which set out the passages imitated, another idea that Pope and Swift had discussed by letter (*Corr.*: II, 503, 523).

who either never read: People who have not had the classical training assumed to be the basis of a gentleman's education.

a Cento: A literary patchwork, made of phrases from other writers.

which Boileau did in earnest: In a Latin poem Boileau describes himself as having learned from childhood how to take apart and re-use elements of Latin verse (Vercruysse 1969: II, 168).

Vida, Fracastorius: Marco Girolamo Vida (1485–1566), bishop and poet, and Girolamo Fracastoro (1478–1553), physician and poet, both composed Latin hexameter verse in the style of Virgil. Vida is best known for his life of Christ in verse, and Fracastoro for his account of syphilis. Neo-Latin verse was one of Pope's particular enthusiasms, and both poets are represented at length in his 1740 anthology, *Selecta Poemata Italorum qui Latine scripserunt* ('Select poems by Italians who have written in Latin') (*OAC*: I, 233).

the First Edition, separate: *The New Dunciad* 1742.

no injury to the author: Playing with the notion that the addition may be by another hand.

accident, in taking a survey of the *Library* of a late eminent nobleman; but in so blotted a condition, and in so many detach'd pieces, as plainly shewed it to be not only *incorrect*, but *unfinished*. That the author of the three first books had a design to extend and complete his poem in this manner, appears from the dissertation prefixt to it, where it is said, that *the design is more extensive, and that we may expect other episodes to complete it:* And from the declaration in the argument to the third book, that *the accomplishment of the prophecies therein, would be the theme hereafter of a greater Dunciad*. But whether or no he be the author of this, we declare ourselves ignorant. If he be, we are no more to be blamed for the publication of it, than Tucca and Varius for that of the last six books of the Aeneid, tho' perhaps inferior to the former.

If any person be possessed of a more perfect copy of this work, or of any other fragments of it, and will communicate them to the publisher, we shall make the next edition more complete: In which, we also promise to insert any *Criticisms* that shall be published (if at all to the purpose) with the *Names* of the *Authors*; or any letters sent us (tho' not to the purpose) shall yet be printed under the title of *Epistolae Obscurorum Virorum*; which, together with some others of the same kind formerly laid by for that end, may make no unpleasant addition to the future impressions of this poem.

---

a late eminent nobleman: Readers might think of the recently deceased Edward Harley (1689–1741), second Earl of Oxford, proprietor of the famous Harleian Library, where Pope had deposited letters, and whence, in order to avert any charge of immodesty in seeking to publish his own correspondence, he had suggested they had been published without his consent (*TE*: V, 410; *Corr.*: I, xii–xiii).

unfinished: Preparing readers for the version of 1743.

the dissertation prefixt to it: See Appendix I, which speaks of six years' work, and a further six to come.

Tucca and Varius: Varius Rufus and Plotius Tucca, friends of Virgil who published the *Aeneid* after his death, despite its evidently incomplete and unrevised state.

tho' not to the purpose: Like Curll, this bookseller will print anything that serves his purpose, however irrelevant.

Epistolae Obscurorum Virorum: Pope gave Swift a copy of the 'Letters from obscure men', an early sixteenth-century satire on the self-satisfaction and pointlessness of monastic culture (Mack 1982: 411; for analogies with the *Dunciad*s, see Williams 1955: 61–2, and Jones in Mack & Winn 1980: 617–18). Pope would presumably have been amused that when Steele had received the dedication of an edition in 1710 neither editor nor dedicatee had seemed to realise that the letters were fictitious (Bond 1987: III, 57–61).

V.

THE

GUARDIAN.

Being a continuation of some former Papers on the Subject of PASTORALS.

Monday, April 27, 1713.

Compulerantque greges Corydon et Thyrsis in unum. —
Ex illo Corydon, Corydon est tempore nobis.

I Designed to have troubled the reader with no farther discourse of Pastoral; but being informed that I am taxed of partiality, in not mentioning an author whose Eclogues are published in the same volume with Mr. Philips's; I shall employ this paper in observations upon him, written in the free spirit of criticism, and without any apprehension of offending that gentleman, whose character it is, that he

THE GUARDIAN: A periodical edited and principally written by Steele (Stephens 1982). In 1709 Pope and Ambrose Philips had both had pastorals published in the same collection (*Poetical Miscellanies* 1709); and in 1713 *Guardian* articles (probably written by Addison's confidant Tickell) had repeatedly praised Philips's while neglecting Pope's (Stephens 1982: 29). Philips's work, in contrast to the sophisticated distillation of classical and later tradition that characterised Pope's, imitated from Spenser's *The Shepheardes Calender* characters conceived as specifically English and specifically rustic, using a language marked by supposedly rustic deviations from refined usage: Pope was to summarise his own contrasting view of the aims of pastoral in the 'Discourse on Pastoral Poetry' in his *Works* of 1717 (*PW*: I, 297–302). He managed to slip his ironic praise of Philips past Steele, providing a paper that at first sight seemed simply to pick up where Tickell had left off, but which on a closer reading argued plainly – and offensively – for the superiority of Pope's conception of the genre. (An early draft of the *Dunciad* had cited Steele as one of those who 'Sleep and Wake by fits', which Mack connects with his failure to see through Pope's ploy (Mack 1984: 98–9, 116, 146).) The controversy also reflected political agendas: Pope had hoped to be accepted in Addison's circle without abandoning his Tory connections, but the favour shown to the Whig Philips helped to convince him of the covert party-political programme which underlay Addison's ostensible friendship. Gay joined the controversy on Pope's behalf with his *The Shepherd's Week*; it has been suggested that he may have collaborated with Pope in writing the present essay (Stephens 1982: 640).

Compulerantque: Pope quotes the beginning and end of Virgil's account of Corydon's triumph in his singing contest with Thyrsis: 'Corydon and Thyrsis had driven their flocks together ... From now on, it's Corydon, Corydon for us' (*Eclogues* VIII.2, 70).

I Designed: Adopting the persona of the regular *Guardian* writer.

that gentleman: Pope need not fear readers' criticism, since he publishes only when he is confident that the work needs no further revision.

takes the greatest care of his works before they are published, and has the least concern for them afterwards.

I have laid it down as the first rule of Pastoral, that its idea should be taken from the manners of the *Golden Age*, and the moral form'd upon the representation of innocence; 'tis therefore plain that any deviations from that design degrade a poem from being truly pastoral. In this view it will appear that Virgil can only have two of his Eclogues allowed to be such: his first and ninth must be rejected, because they describe the ravages of armies, and oppressions of the innocent; Corydon's criminal passion for Alexis throws out the second; the calumny and railing in the third are not proper to that state of concord; the eighth represents unlawful ways of procuring love by inchantments, and introduces a shepherd whom an inviting precipice tempts to self-murder: As to the fourth, sixth, and tenth, they are given up by Heinsius, Salmasius, Rapin[a], and the critics in general. They likewise observe that but eleven of all the Idyllia of Theocritus are to be admitted as Pastorals; and even out of that number the greater part will be excluded for one or other of the reasons above mentioned. So that when I remark'd in a former paper, that Virgil's Eclogues taken altogether are rather select poems than Pastorals; I might have said

[a] See Rapin de Carm. Par. 2.

***the* Golden Age:** In classical thought, the age before corruption set in.

Virgil can have only two: The set consists of ten, and the argument is developed that by the rules declared, hardly any of these foundation texts in the pastoral tradition are really pastorals. The tradition is in effect reduced to its most vacuous and unsophisticated elements in order to make possible the triumphant turn of the essay's final sentence.

ravages of armies: Virgil's first and ninth eclogues allude to the sufferings of farmers evicted from their land as part of Augustus's policy of confiscating land to reward military veterans.

Corydon's criminal passion: *Eclogue* II is a monologue of frustrated homosexual desire.

calumny and railing: In *Eclogue* III two shepherds exchange insults as a prelude to a singing contest.

unlawful ways: *Eclogue* VIII recounts the suicide for love of a disappointed shepherd and the spells used by a deserted woman to reclaim her faithless lover.

the fourth, sixth, and tenth: *Eclogue* IV, traditionally read as a prophecy of the coming of Christ, looks forward to the birth of a child under whom the world would be reborn; VI contains an account of the origins of the universe; X depicts the despair in love of Virgil's friend Gallus. It could be argued that these subjects are too serious for pure pastoral.

Heinsius, Salmasius, Rapin: Daniel Heins (1580–1655), Dutch poet and classicist; Claude Saumaise (1588–1653), French classicist, and René Rapin (1621–87), French Jesuit poet and classicist, were all authorities on pastoral verse. Pope owned a translation of Theocritus which also included a translation of Rapin's 'De Carmine Pastorali' ('On Pastoral Verse') (Creech 1684; Mack 1982: 443). Pope gives a negative turn to Rapin's consideration of precisely what may and what may not be considered to belong to the pastoral genre, a discussion in which the views of Heins and Saumaise are cited (Creech 1684: 26–7; Congleton 1952: 56).

but eleven: The *Idylls* of Theocritus, Virgil's principal model, are usually numbered at thirty.

I remark'd in a former paper: *Guardian* 28.

select poems: A collection of various poems, rather than a set of pastorals as such. *Guardian* 28 had pointed out that 'eclogue', though commonly used as a synonym for 'pastoral', had originally meant 'selection' (Stephens 1982: 160).

the same thing with no less truth of Theocritus. The reason of this I take to be yet unobserved by the critics, viz. They never meant them all for pastorals.

Now it is plain Philips hath done this, and in that particular excelled both Theocritus and Virgil.

As Simplicity is the distinguishing characteristic of Pastoral, Virgil hath been thought guilty of too courtly a style; his language is perfectly pure, and he often forgets he is among peasants. I have frequently wondered that since he was so conversant in the writings of Ennius, he had not imitated the rusticity of the Doric, as well by the help of the old obsolete Roman language, as Philips hath by the antiquated English: For example, might not he have said *quoi* instead of *cui, quoijum* for *cujum, volt* for *vult, etc.* as well as our modern hath *welladay* for *alas, whilome* for *of old, make mock* for *deride,* and *witless younglings* for *simple lambs, etc.* by which means he had attained as much of the air of Theocritus, as Philips hath of Spencer.

Mr. Pope hath fallen into the same error with Virgil. His clowns do not converse in all the simplicity proper to the country; his names are borrowed from Theocritus

---

Ennius: The language of the early Latin poet Quintus Ennius (239–169 BC) seemed clumsy and primitive by the standards of the Augustan age.

the rusticity of the Doric: Later writers of Greek pastoral imitated the Doric-based dialect used by Theocritus in his *Idylls.* Hence, Doric came to be seen as rustic and uncultivated.

by the antiquated English: Philips had pointedly included Spenser with Theocritus and Virgil as 'the only Writers, that seem to have hit upon the true Nature of *Pastoral* Poems', and had imitated him in incorporating archaism and dialect into his style (*Poetical Miscellanies* 1709: Preface). Modern Spenser scholarship would see Spenser not so much as impersonating peasants as blending archaism and dialect into a sophisticated and flexible medium; and his topics range far beyond the rustic trivia which Pope's mock argument defines as proper to pastoral (Hamilton 1990: 52–3, 215). In fact, Pope had considerable respect for Spenser, despite disapproving of the non-standard elements in his language: he suffers in this essay by association with Philips. Pope had alluded conspicuously to Spenser's pastorals in his own, and had once intended to use a stanza from the *Faerie Queene* (in which the shepherd swats gnats which annoy him, a simile for Redcross Knight's battle with the offspring of Error) as epigraph to the *Dunciad* (*TE*: I, 13–20; *OAC*: I, 182–3; Rumbold 1983: 86–93, 118–22; Hamilton 1990: 555–6; cp. *Tatler* 229). His decision to cancel a paragraph in a draft of the 'Discourse on Pastoral Poetry' expressing his aspiration to be recognised as Spenser's heir appears to be a disgusted response to Philips's effective devaluation of that role.

might not he have said: Virgil could perfectly easily have put archaic forms of common words into the mouths of his characters to mark their rustic and uncultivated status; but by implication he showed his judgement in not doing so.

he had attained: he would have attained.

as Philips hath of Spencer: Since readers of Virgil are hardly likely to wish he had changed a vocabulary and grammar proverbial for its elegance and refinement for one distorted by archaism, the implication is that Philips has attained not the essence, but only the oddities of Spenser.

clowns: rustics.

his names: While Pope retained the classical names long associated with pastoral, Philips used names of the kind found in Spenser, which sounded clumsy and awkward to a neoclassical ear.

and Virgil, which are improper to the scene of his Pastorals: He introduces Daphnis, Alexis, and Thyrsis on British plains, as Virgil hath done before him on the Mantuan. Whereas Philips, who hath the strictest regard to propriety, makes choice of names peculiar to the country, and more agreeable to a reader of delicacy, such as Hobbinol, Lobbin, Cuddy, and Colin-Clout.

So easy as pastoral writing may seem (in the simplicity we have described it) yet it requires great reading, both of the ancients and moderns, to be a master of it. Philips hath given us manifest proofs of his knowledge of books. It must be confessed his competitor hath imitated *some single thoughts* of the ancients well enough (if we consider he had not the happiness of an University education) but he hath dispersed them, here and there, without that order and method which Mr. Philips observes, whose *whole* third Pastoral is an instance how well he hath studied the fifth of Virgil, and how judiciously reduced Virgil's thoughts to the standard of Pastoral; as his contention of Colin-Clout and the Nightingale shows with what exactness he hath imitated every line in Strada.

When I remarked it as a principal fault to introduce fruits and flowers of a foreign growth, in the descriptions where the scene lies in our own country, I did not design that observation should extend also to animals, or the sensitive life; for Mr. Philips hath with great judgment described Wolves in England in his first Pastoral. Nor would I have a poet slavishly confine himself (as Mr. Pope hath done) to one particular season of the year, one certain time of the day, and one unbroken scene in each Eclogue. 'Tis plain Spencer neglected this pedantry, who in his Pastoral of November mentions the mournful song of the Nightingale: 'Sad Philomel her song in tears doth steep.' And Mr. Philips, by a poetical creation, hath raised up finer beds of flowers than the most industrious gardiner; his roses, endives, lillies, king-cups, and daffidils blow all in the same season.

But the better to discover the merits of our two contemporary Pastoral writers, I shall endeavour to draw a parallel of them, by setting several of their particular

---

Mantuan: Virgil came from Mantua.

some single thoughts: Preparing the ground for the accusation that Philips's use of his models is so extensive and mechanical as to amount to plagiarism.

the happiness of an University education: Reminding readers of Philips's superior opportunities.

whose* whole *third Pastoral: Philips's third pastoral mourns the death of Queen Anne's only surviving son, and is a close imitation of Virgil's fifth, traditionally taken as an allegory of the apotheosis of the assassinated Julius Caesar. The Whig Philips excites Pope's contempt by his attempt to represent his role in relation to Queen Anne as analogous to Virgil's in relation to Augustus, and Spenser's in relation to Elizabeth I.

Colin-Clout and the Nightingale: The subject of Philips's fifth pastoral, based on a poem from Strada's *Prolusiones academicae* (Strada 1631: 240–41).

Wolves in England: Wolves had long been extinct in England.

slavishly confine himself: An ironically negative way of specifying standards of focus and consistency crucial to neo-classical taste.

in his Pastoral of November: *The Shepheardes Calender*, 'November', line 141.

blow: blossom.

thoughts in the same light, whereby it will be obvious how much Philips hath the advantage. With what simplicity he introduces two shepherds singing alternately!

Hobb. *Come, Rosalind, O come, for without thee*
What pleasure can the country have for me!
Come, Rosalind, O come; my brinded kine,
My snowy sheep, my farm, and all are thine.

Lanq. *Come, Rosalind, O come; here shady bow'rs,*
Here are cool fountains, and here springing flow'rs,
Come, Rosalind; here ever let us stay,
And sweetly waste our live-long time away.

Our other Pastoral writer, in expressing the same thought, deviates into downright Poetry:

Streph. *In spring, the fields, in autumn, hills I love;*
At morn the plains, at noon the shady grove;
But Delia always; forc'd from Delia's sight,
Nor plains at morn, nor groves at noon delight.

Daph. *Sylvia's like autumn ripe, yet mild as May,*
More bright than noon, yet fresh as early day;
Ev'n spring displeases when she shines not here,
But blest with her 'tis spring throughout the year.

In the first of these authors, two shepherds thus innocently describe the behaviour of their mistresses:

Hobb. *As Marian bath'd, by chance I passed by,*
She blush'd, and at me cast a side-long eye;
Then swift beneath the crystal wave she try'd
Her beauteous form, but all in vain to hide.

Lanq. *As I to cool me bath'd one sultry day,*
Fond Lydia lurking in the sedges lay;
The wanton laugh'd, and seem'd in haste to fly;
Yet often stopp'd, and often turn'd her eye.

The other modern (who, it must be confessed, hath a knack of versifying) hath it as follows:

Come, Rosalind ...: From Philips's sixth pastoral. In common with the quotations that follow, Pope's transcription is accurate except for accidentals and a few minor variants.

deviates into downright Poetry: One of the points in the essay where the irony becomes most transparent.

In spring ...: Pope, *Pastorals*, 'Spring', lines 77–80 in the version of 1709.

innocently: Perhaps at first likely to be taken in the sense of 'without sophistication'; but in the light of what follows, the word asks to be taken ironically of Hobbinol's lewdness.

As Marian bath'd ...: From Philips's sixth pastoral.

Streph. *Me gentle Delia beckons from the plain,*
Then, hid in shades, eludes her eager swain;
But feigns a laugh, to see me search around,
And by that laugh the willing fair is found.

Daph. *The sprightly Sylvia trips along the green,*
She runs, but hopes she does not run unseen,
While a kind glance at her pursuer flies,
How much at variance are her feet and eyes!

There is nothing the writers of this kind of poetry are fonder of, than descriptions of pastoral presents. Philips says thus of a sheep-hook:

Of season'd elm, where studs of brass appear,
To speak the giver's name, the month and year;
The hook of polish'd steel, the handle turn'd,
And richly by the graver's skill adorn'd.

The other of a bowl embossed with figures:

—— *where wanton ivy twines,*
And swelling clusters bend the curling vines;
Four figures rising from the work appear,
The various seasons of the rolling year;
And what is that which binds the radiant sky,
Where twelve bright signs in beauteous order lie?

The simplicity of the swain in this place, who forgets the name of the zodiac, is no ill imitation of Virgil: but how much more plainly and unaffectedly would Philips have dressed this thought in his Doric?

And what that hight which girds the welkin sheen,
Where twelve gay signs in meet array are seen?

If the reader would indulge his curiosity any farther in the comparison of particulars, he may read the first Pastoral of Philips with the second of his contemporary; and the fourth and sixth of the former with the fourth and first of the latter; where several parallel places will occur to every one.

Having now shown some parts in which these two writers may be compared, it is a justice I owe to Mr. Philips, to discover those in which no man can compare with him. First, that beautiful rusticity, of which I shall only produce two instances of an hundred not yet quoted:

Me gentle Delia ...: Pope's *Pastorals*, 'Spring', lines 53–6.
Of season'd elm ...: From Philips's fourth pastoral.
where wanton ivy twines ...: Pope's *Pastorals*, 'Spring', lines 35–40.
no ill imitation of Virgil: In the singing contest of *Eclogue* III one of the characters forgets the name of a famous astronomer (lines 40–42). Pope goes on to ridicule the way Philips might have paid homage to the passage.

O woeful day! O day of woe! quoth he;
And woeful I, who live the day to see!

The simplicity of the diction, the melancholy flowing of the numbers, the solemnity of the sound, and the easy turn of the words in this dirge (to make use of our author's expression) are extremely elegant.

In another of his Pastorals, a shepherd utters a dirge not much inferior to the former, in the following lines:

Ah me, the while! ah me! the luckless day!
Ah luckless lad! the rather might I say!
Ah silly I! more silly than my sheep,
Which on the flow'ry plain I once did keep.

How he still charms the ear with these artful repetitions of the epithets; and how significant is the last verse! I defy the most common reader to repeat them without feeling some motions of compassion.

In the next place I shall rank his Proverbs, in which I formerly observed he excels. For example:

A rolling stone is ever bare of moss;
And, to their cost, green years old proverbs cross.

— *He that late lies down, as late will rise,*
And, sluggard-like, 'till noon-day snoring lies.

— *Against ill luck all cunning foresight fails;*
Whether we sleep or wake, it nought avails.

— *Nor fear, from upright sentence, wrong.*

Lastly, his elegant dialect, which alone might prove him the eldest born of Spencer, and our only true Arcadian. I should think it proper for the several

---

O woeful day! ...: From Philips's fourth pastoral.

dirge: The speaker in Philips's fourth pastoral, lamenting the death of his love, says he will hang his pipe 'upon this blasted Oak, / Whence Owls their Dirges sing, and Ravens croak'. The funereal connotations of 'Dirges' are fitting in this context of pathetic fallacy; but Pope contrives to suggest that Philips equates his own verse with such a proverbially dreary performance.

Ah me, the while! ...: From Philips's second pastoral. Pope omits a couplet which comes between the two quoted.

compassion: Presumably for the writer.

his Proverbs: Neo-classical taste disdained popular proverbs as vulgar and banal.

A rolling stone ...: From Philips's second pastoral.

He that late lies down ...: From Philips's fourth pastoral, omitting the initial 'For' which completes the metre.

Against ill luck ...: From Philips's second pastoral.

Nor fear ...: From Philips's sixth pastoral. Pope omits the name of the judge in the singing contest, which makes the line appear metrically deficient. 'Sentence' is used in the sense of 'judgment'.

Arcadian: The dialect of Arcadia, a district of Greece remote from outside influences,

writers of Pastoral to confine themselves to their several counties. Spencer seems to have been of this opinion; for he hath laid the scene of one of his Pastorals in Wales; where with all the simplicity natural to that part of our island, one shepherd bids the other good-morrow, in an unusual and elegant manner:

Diggon Davy, I bid hur God-day;
Or Diggon hur is, or I mis-say.

Diggon answers,

Hur was hur while it was day-light;
But now hur is a most wretched wight, etc.

But the most beautiful example of this kind that I ever met with, is in a very valuable piece which I chanced to find among some old manuscripts, entituled a Pastoral Ballad; which I think, for its nature and simplicity, may (notwithstanding the modesty of the title) be allowed a perfect Pastoral. It is composed in the Somersetshire dialect, and the names such as are proper to the country people. It may be observed, as a farther beauty of this Pastoral, the words Nymph, Dryad, Naiad, Fawn, Cupid, or Satyr, are not once mentioned throughout the whole. I shall make no apology for inserting some few lines of this excellent piece. Cicily breaks thus into the subject as she is going a milking:

Cicily. *Rager, go vetch tha kee*[b]*, or else tha zun*
Will quite be go, bevore c'have half a don.

Roger. *Thou shouldst not ax ma tweece, but I've a bee*
To dreave our bull to bull tha parson's kee.

It is to be observed, that this whole dialogue is formed upon the passion of *jealousy*; and his mentioning the parson's kine naturally revives the jealousy of the shepherdess Cicily, which she expresses as follows:

[b] That is, the *kine*, or *cows*.

---

preserves primitive features and is not used in surviving literature. Shepherds in pastoral are traditionally represented as Arcadians, although pastoral uses the Doric dialect. The implication is that Philips, in keeping with his subject, has regressed in the cause of authenticity to something even more uncouth than Doric.

he hath laid the scene of one of his Pastorals in Wales: 'September', in *The Shepheardes Calender*, begins, as quoted below, by evoking English as spoken by a Welshman, an allusion to its concern with the difficulties encountered by a Welsh reforming bishop (Oram 1989: 149).

a very valuable piece: Apparently Pope's fabrication.

as a farther beauty: Drawing ironic attention to the importance of such links between modern pastoral and its classical origins.

Fawn: faun.

his mentioning the parson's kine: The paralleling of the human lovers to the bull and cow, implying a coarseness which has no part in traditional literary pastoral, recalls the resolution of 'Tuesday' in Gay's *The Shepherd's Week*.

Cicily. *Ah Rager, Rager! ches was zore avraid*
When in yon vield you kiss'd the parson's maid;
Is this the love that once to me you zed,
When from the wake thou brought'st me ginger-bread!

Roger. *Cicily, thou charg'st me valse, — I'll zwear to thee*
The parson's maid is still a maid for me.

In which answer of his are expressed at once that spirit of Religion, and that Innocence of the Golden age, so necessary to be observed by all writers of Pastoral.

At the conclusion of this piece, the author reconciles the lovers, and ends the eclogue the most simply in the world:

So Rager parted, vor to vetch tha kee;
And vor her bucket in went Cicily.

I am loth to shew my fondness for antiquity so far as to prefer this ancient British author to our present English writers of Pastoral; but I cannot avoid making this obvious remark, that Philips hath hit into the same road with this old West-country bard of ours.

After all that hath been said, I hope none can think it any injustice to Mr. Pope, that I forbore to mention him as a Pastoral writer; since upon the whole, he is of the same class with Moschus and Bion, whom we have excluded that rank; and of whose eclogues, as well as some of Virgil's, it may be said, that (according to the description we have given of this sort of poetry) they are by no means Pastorals, but something better.

VI.

OF THE
POET LAUREATE.

November 19, 1729.

THE time of the election of a Poet Laureate being now at hand, it may be proper to give some account of the *rites* and *ceremonies* anciently used at that

---

for me: 'As far as I've got anything to do with it'.

Moschus and Bion: Greek poets of the later second century BC. Their work displays pastoral features, but is not confined to pastoral.

OF THE POET LAUREATE: Adapted from an article first printed in *The Grub-Street Journal*, 19 November 1730 (not 1729 as given in the heading), when it was rumoured that the next Laureate was to be Stephen Duck, a farm labourer whose poetry had attracted the Queen's patronage (Williams 1965: III, 415). The post in fact went to Cibber. The essay uses the same material on Camillo Querno as in the original note on II.15: see editor's notes for commentary.

Solemnity, and only discontinued through the neglect and degeneracy of later times. These we have extracted from an historian of undoubted credit, a reverend bishop, the learned Paulus Jovius; and are the same that were practised under the pontificate of Leo X, the great restorer of learning.

As we now see an *age* and a *court*, that for the encouragement of poetry rivals, if not exceeds, that of this famous Pope, we cannot but wish a restoration of all its *honours* to *poesy*; the rather, since there are so many parallel circumstances in the *person* who was then honoured with the laurel, and in *him*, who (in all probability) is now to wear it.

I shall translate my author exactly as I find it in the 82d chapter of his Elogia Vir. Doct. He begins with the character of the poet himself, who was the original and father of all Laureates, and called Camillo. He was a plain country-man of Apulia, whether a *shepherd* or *thresher*, is not material. 'This man (says Jovius) excited by the fame of the great encouragement given to poets at court, and the high honour in which they were held, came to the city, bringing with him a strange kind of lyre in his hand, and at least some *twenty thousand of verses*. All the wits and critics of the court flock'd about him, delighted to see a *clown*, with a ruddy, hale complexion, and in his own long hair, so top full of poetry; and at the first sight of him all agreed he was born to be *Poet Laureate*[a]. He had a most hearty welcome in an *island* of the river Tiber (an agreeable place, not unlike our Richmond) where he was first made to *eat* and *drink plentifully*, and *to repeat his verses to every body*. Then they adorn'd him with a new and elegant garland, composed of *vine-leaves, laurel*, and *brassica* (a sort of cabbage) so composed, says my author, emblematically, *ut tam sales, quam lepide ejus temulentia, Brassicae remedio cohibenda, notaretur*. He was then saluted by common consent with the title of *archi-poeta*, or *arch-poet*, in the style of those days, in ours, *Poet Laureate*. This honour the poor man received with the most sensible demonstrations of joy, his eyes drunk with tears and gladness[b]. Next the public acclamation was expressed in a *canticle*, which is transmitted to us, as follows:

[a] Apulus praepingui vultu alacer, & prolixe comatus, omnino dignus festa laurea videretur.
[b] Manantibus prae gaudio oculis.

Leo X: Giovanni de'Medici (1475–1521), lavish supporter of humanistic literary study and of the arts in general, became pope in 1513.

***whether a* shepherd *or* thresher:** Duck had been a thresher, and had written about his experiences in *The Thresher's Labour* (Lonsdale 1989: 224–5).

Note a. 'A man from Apuleia, with an enthusiastic expression on his pudgy face and luxuriant long hair, he seemed thoroughly worthy of the solemn laurel'.

Richmond: The Queen gave Duck a home at Richmond, and put him in charge of the Hermitage and Merlin's Cave, emblematic buildings in which during the 1730s she attempted to assimilate the Hanoverian line to a vision of Britain's past and future destiny (Gerrard 1994: 169–74).

ut tam sales ...: 'So that the cabbage cure was observed to keep his wit under control as elegantly as it did his drunkenness'. Cabbage was reputedly a hangover cure.

sensible: acutely felt.

Note b. 'With eyes streaming for joy'.

Salve, brassicea virens corona,
Et lauro, archipoeta, pampinoque!
Dignus principis auribus Leonis.

All hail, arch-poet without peer!
Vine, bay, or cabbage fit to wear,
And worthy of the prince's ear.

From hence he was conducted in pomp to the *Capitol* of Rome, mounted on an *elephant,* thro' the shouts of the populace, where the ceremony ended.

The historian tells us farther, 'That at his introduction to Leo, he not only poured forth verses innumerable, like a torrent, but also *sung* them with *open mouth.* Nor was he only *once* introduced, or on *stated* days (like our Laureates) but made a *companion* to his *master,* and entertained as one of the instruments of his *most elegant pleasures.* When the prince was at table, the poet had his place at the window. When the prince had[c] half eaten his meat, he gave with his own hands the rest to the poet. When the poet drank, it was out of the prince's own flaggon, insomuch (says the historian) that thro' so great good eating and drinking he contracted a most terrible gout.' Sorry I am to relate what follows, but that I cannot leave my reader's curiosity unsatisfied in the catastrophe of this extraordinary man. To use my author's words, which are remarkable, *mortuo Leone, profligatisque poetis, etc.* 'When Leo died, and poets were no more' (for I would not understand *profligatis* literally, as if poets then were *profligate*) this unhappy Laureate was forthwith reduced to return to his country, where, oppress'd with *old age* and *want,* he miserably perish'd in a *common hospital.*

We see from this sad conclusion (which may be of example to the poets of our time) that it were happier to meet with no encouragement at all, to remain at the plough, or other lawful occupation, than to be elevated above their condition, and taken out of the common means of life, without a surer support than the *temporary,* or, at best, *mortal* favours of the great. It was doubtless for this consideration, that when the Royal Bounty was lately extended to a *rural genius,* care was taken to *settle it upon him for life.* And it hath been the practice of our Princes, never to remove from the station of Poet Laureate any man who hath once been chosen, tho' never so much greater Genius's might arise in his time. A noble instance, how much the *charity* of our monarchs hath exceeded their *love of fame.*

[c] Semesis opsoniis.

Note c. 'When the food was half eaten'.

mortuo Leone, profligatisque poetis: In modern usage, 'profligate' implies blame, but the Latin word can simply mean 'defeated' or 'ruined' (in the sense that after Leo's death, poets were ruined in having lost a patron of unprecedented generosity).

hospital: a poor-house.

the Royal Bounty: Duck was granted a royal salary.

never so much greater Genius's: The reader is obviously expected to think of Pope, although as a Roman Catholic he was ineligible for the post. The catholic Laureate Dryden had, moreover, been removed on the accession of the protestant William and Mary.

To come now to the intent of this paper. We have here the whole ancient *ceremonial* of the Laureate. In the first place the crown is to be mix'd with *vine-leaves*, as the vine is the plant of Bacchus, and full as essential to the honour, as the *butt of sack* to the salary.

Secondly, the *brassica* must be made use of as a qualifier of the former. It seems the *cabbage* was anciently accounted a remedy for *drunkenness*; a power the French now ascribe to the onion, and style a soupe made of it, *soupe d'Yvronge*. I would recommend a large mixture of the *brassica* if Mr. Dennis be chosen; but if Mr. Tibbald, it is not so necessary, unless the cabbage be supposed to signify the same thing with respect to *poets* as to *taylors*, viz. *stealing*. I should judge it not amiss to add another plant to this garland, to wit, *ivy*: Not only as it anciently belonged to poets in general; but as it is emblematical of the three virtues of a court poet in particular; it is *creeping*, *dirty*, and *dangling*.

In the next place, a *canticle* must be composed and sung in laud and praise of the new poet. If Mr. CIBBER be laureated, it is my opinion no man can *write* this but himself: And no man, I am sure, can *sing* it so affectingly. But what this canticle should be, either in his or the other candidates case, I shall not pretend to determine.

Thirdly, there ought to be a *public show*, or entry of the poet: To settle the order or procession of which, Mr. Anstis and Mr. DENNIS ought to have a conference. I apprehend here two difficulties: One, of procuring an *elephant*; the other of teaching the poet to ride him: Therefore I should imagine the next animal in size or dignity would do best; either a *mule* or a large *ass*; particularly if that noble one could be had, whose portraiture makes so great an ornament of the *Dunciad*, and which (unless I am misinform'd) is yet in the park of a nobleman near this city: —— Unless Mr. CIBBER be the man; who may, with great propriety and beauty, ride on a *dragon*, if he goes by land; or if he chuse the water, upon one of his own *swans* from *Caesar in Egypt*.

We have spoken sufficiently of the *ceremony*; let us now speak of the *qualifications* and *privileges* of the Laureate. First, we see he must be able to make verses

---

***the* butt of sack:** A traditional emolument of the laureate.

soupe d'Yvronge: drunkards' soup.

Mr. Dennis: Not literally a drunkard, but habitually intemperate in tone and judgement.

taylors: 'Cabbage' was a term for the bundle of offcuts from cutting out a garment, which the tailor would keep for his own use, although it could be argued that the customer had paid for the whole piece of cloth. Hence 'to cabbage' was a term for stealing, here implying that Theobald is a plagiarist.

ivy: Cp. I.303–4.

Mr. Anstis: As Garter King of Arms, John Anstis (1669–1744) was the official expert on heraldry and other matters of precedence and played a key role in the organisation of official ceremonies.

***so great an ornament of the* Dunciad:** The frontispiece introduced in 1729.

a nobleman near this city: Hervey had resorted to an invalid diet featuring asses' milk.

with great propriety: Mocking stage effects associated with Cibber's career as actor and dramatist. For Cibber's denial of the charge that he 'was Dunce enough to mount a Machine', see editor's note on III.268. A member of the audience at the first night of *Caesar in Egypt*

extempore, and to pour forth innumerable, if requir'd. In this I doubt Mr. TIBBALD. Secondly, he ought to *sing*, and intrepidly, *patulo ore:* Here, I confess the excellency of Mr. CIBBER. Thirdly, he ought to carry a *lyre* about with him: If a large one be thought too cumbersome, a small one may be contrived to hang about the neck, like an order, and be very much a grace to the person. Fourthly, he ought to have a good *stomach*, to eat and drink whatever his betters think fit; and therefore it is in this high office as in many others, no puny constitution can discharge it. I do not think CIBBER or TIBBALD here so happy: but rather a stanch, vigorous, season'd, and dry *old gentleman*, whom I have in my eye.

I could also wish at this juncture, such a person as is truly jealous of the *honour* and *dignity* of *poetry*; no joker, or trifler; but a bard in *good earnest*; nay, not amiss if a critic, and the better if a little *obstinate*. For when we consider what great privileges have been lost from this office (as we see from the forecited authentic record of Jovius) namely those of *feeding* from the *prince's table*, *drinking* out of his *own flaggon*, becoming even his *domestic* and *companion*; it requires a man warm and resolute, to be able to claim and obtain the restoring of these high honours. I have cause to fear the most of the candidates would be liable, either through the influence of ministers, or for rewards or favours, to give up the glorious rights of the Laureate: Yet I am not without hopes, there is *one*, from whom a *serious* and *steddy* assertion of these privileges may be expected; and, if there be such a one, I must do him the justice to say, it is Mr. DENNIS the worthy president of our society.

VII.

ADVERTISEMENT

Printed in the JOURNALS, 1730.

WHEREAS, upon occasion of certain Pieces relating to the Gentlemen of the Dunciad, some have been willing to suggest, as if they looked upon them

remembered laughing 'at his Pasteboard Swans which the Carpenters pulled along the *Nile*', although Horace Walpole claimed that they were real geese in disguise (Victor 1761: II, 164; *The World*: No. 6, 8 February 1753).

patulo ore: with his mouth wide open.

an order: Such as the Order of the Garter.

stanch: staunch, i.e. firm, determined.

old gentleman: Presumably Dennis.

assertion: One of Dennis's most characteristic modes of expression.

our society: The society of authors from which the *Grub Street Journal* is supposed to emanate.

Printed in the JOURNALS: The original is untraced, but a longer version was printed as the final item in Savage 1732.

as an *abuse*: we can do no less than own, it is our opinion, that to call these Gentlemen *bad authors* is no sort of *abuse*, but a great *truth*. We cannot alter this opinion without some reason; but we promise to do it in respect to every person who thinks it an injury to be represented as no *Wit*, or *Poet*, provided he procures a Certificate of his being really such, from any *three of his companions* in the Dunciad, or from Mr. *Dennis singly*, who is esteemed equal to any three of the number.

VIII.

A PARALLEL OF THE CHARACTERS OF Mr. DRYDEN and Mr. POPE.

As drawn by certain of their Contemporaries.

Mr. DRYDEN.

His POLITICS, RELIGION, MORALS.

MR. Dryden is a mere renegado from monarchy, poetry, and good sense[a]. A true republican son of monarchical Church[b]. A republican Atheist[c]. Dryden was from the beginning an ἀλλοπρόσαλλος, and I doubt not will continue so to the last[d].

In the poem call'd *Absalom* and *Achitophel* are notoriously traduced, The KING, the QUEEN, the LORDS and GENTLEMEN, not only their honourable persons exposed, but the whole NATION and its REPRESENTATIVES notoriously libell'd. It is *scandalum magnatum*, yea of MAJESTY itself[e].

He looks upon God's gospel as a foolish fable, like the Pope, to whom he is a pitiful purveyor[f]. His very christianity may be questioned[g]. He ought to expect more severity than other men, as he is most unmerciful in his own reflections on others[h]. With as good a right as his Holiness, he sets up for poetical infallibility[i].

[a] Milbourn on Dryden's Virgil, 8vo. 1698. p. 6. [b] pag. 38. [c] pag. 192. [d] pag. 8.
[e] Whip and Key, 4to. printed for R. Janeway, 1682. Preface. [f] Ibid. [g] Milbourn, p. 9.
[h] Ibid. p. 175. [i] pag. 39.

A PARALLEL OF THE CHARACTERS OF Mr. DRYDEN and Mr. POPE: First used in 1729, it helps to suggest that the obloquy Pope shared with Dryden has more to do with belonging to the church and party excluded from power than with individual merit.

Note a. Milbourn 1698.

Note d. A turncoat, 'all things to all men'.

Note e. *A Key (With the Whip)* 1682.

scandalum magnatum: Scandalous utterance or writing against a person in a position of authority.

VIII.

A PARALLEL OF THE CHARACTERS OF Mr. POPE and Mr. DRYDEN.

As drawn by certain of their Contemporaries.

Mr. POPE.

His POLITICS, RELIGION, MORALS.

MR. Pope is an open and mortal enemy to his country, and the commonwealth of learning[a]. Some call him a popish whig, which is directly inconsistent[b]. Pope, as a papist, must be a tory and high flyer[c]. He is both a whig and tory[d].

He hath made it his custom to cackle to more than one party in their own sentiments[e].

In his Miscellanies, the Persons abused are, The KING, the QUEEN, His late MAJESTY, both Houses of PARLIAMENT, the Privy-Council, the Bench of BISHOPS, the Establish'd CHURCH, the present MINISTRY, *etc.* To make Sense of some passages, they must be construed into ROYAL SCANDAL[f].

He is a Popish Rhymester, bred up with a contempt of the Sacred Writings[g]. His Religion allows him to destroy Hereticks, not only with his pen, but with fire and sword; and such were all those unhappy Wits whom he sacrificed to his accursed Popish Principles[h]. It deserved Vengeance to suggest, that Mr. Pope had less Infallibility than his Namesake at Rome[i].

[a] Dennis's Rem. on the Rape of the Lock, Pref. p. xii. [b] Dunciad dissected.
[c] Pref. to Gulliveriana. [d] Dennis, Character of Mr. Pope.
[e] Theobald, Letter in Mist's Journal, June 22, 1728.
[f] List, at the end of a Collection of Verses, Letters, Advertisements, 8vo. Printed for A. Moore, 1728, and the Preface to it, p. 6. [g] Dennis's Remarks on Homer, p. 27.
[h] Preface to Gulliveriana, p. 11. [i] Dedication to the Collection of Verses, Letters, *etc.* p. 9.

A PARALLEL OF THE CHARACTERS OF Mr. POPE AND Mr. DRYDEN: The number of different published attacks on Pope here cited is striking in comparison to the very few (but admittedly intemperate) works repeatedly cited in the account of Dryden: although both lists are highly selective, the impression is correctly given that Pope was more frequently attacked in print than previous writers.

Note b. Dunciad dissected: *Codrus* 1728. ***Note d.*** The reference is to *A True Character* 1716. ***Note f.*** The reference is to *A Compleat Collection* 1728. ***Note i.*** *A Compleat Collection* 1728.

Mr. DRYDEN only a Versifier.

His whole Libel is all bad matter, beautify'd (which is all that can be said of it) with good metre[k]. Mr. Dryden's genius did not appear in any thing more than his Versification, and whether he is to be ennobled for that only, is a question[l].

Mr. DRYDEN's VIRGIL.

Tonson calls it *Dryden's Virgil*, to shew that this is not that Virgil so admir'd in the Augustaean age; but a Virgil of another stamp, a silly, impertinent, nonsensical writer[m]. None but a Bavius, a Maevius, or a Bathyllus carp'd at Virgil; and none but such unthinking Vermin admire his Translator[n]. It is true, soft and easy lines might become Ovid's Epistles or Art of Love — But Virgil, who is all great and majestic, *etc.* requires strength of lines, weight of words, and closeness of expressions; not an ambling Muse running on Carpet-ground, and shod as lightly as a Newmarket-racer. — He has numberless faults in his Author's meaning, and in propriety of expression[o].

Mr. DRYDEN understood no Greek nor Latin.

Mr Dryden was once, I have heard, at Westminster School: Dr. Busby would have whipt him for so childish a Paraphrase[p]. The meanest Pedant in England would whip a Lubber of twelve for construing so absurdly[q]. The Translator is mad, every line betrays his Stupidity[r]. The faults are innumerable, and convince me that Mr. Dryden did not, or would not understand his Author[s]. This shews how fit Mr. D. may be to translate *Homer!* A mistake in a single letter might fall on the Printer well enough, but εἴχωρ for ἰχὼρ must be the error of the Author: Nor had he art enough to correct it at the Press[t]. Mr. Dryden writes for the Court Ladies. — He writes for the Ladies, and not for use[v].

The Translator puts in a little Burlesque now and then into Virgil, for a Ragout to his cheated Subscribers[w].

[k] Whip and Key, Pref.
[l] Oldmixon, Essay on Criticism, p. 84. [m] Milbourn, pag. 2.
[n] Pag. 35. [o] Pag. 22 and 192. [p] Milbourn, p. 72. [q] Pag. 203. [r] Pag. 78.
[s] Pag. 206. [t] Pag. 19. [v] Pag. 144, 190. [w] Pag. 67.

Tonson: Jacob Tonson, the publisher.
Note m. Actually p. 4.
Note p. For Busby, see Book IV.141–74 and notes.
Note q. Lubber: 'lout', 'idler'.
Note t. Drawing attention to the flagrant misspelling of the Greek word for the divine equivalent of blood (*ichor*) in the first edition of Dryden's Dedication to his *Aeneid* (Hooker 1956–89: 315).
Note v. These allegations are not on the pages cited.

Mr. POPE only a Versifier.

The smooth numbers of the Dunciad are all that recommend it, nor has it any other merit[k]. It must be own'd that he hath got a notable knack of rhyming and writing smooth verse[l].

Mr. POPE's HOMER.

The Homer which Lintot prints, does not talk like Homer, but like Pope; and he who translated him one would swear had a Hill in Tipperary for his Parnassus, and a puddle in some Bog for his Hippocrene[m]. He has no Admirers among those that can distinguish, discern, and judge[n].

He hath a knack at smooth verse, but without either Genius or good sense or any tolerable knowledge of English. The qualities which distinguish Homer are the beauties of his Diction and the Harmony of his Versification. — But this little Author, who is so much in vogue, has neither sense in his Thoughts, nor English in his Expressions[o].

Mr. POPE understood no Greek.

He hath undertaken to translate Homer from the Greek, of which he knows not one word, into English, of which he understands as little[p]. I wonder how this Gentleman would look, should it be discover'd, that he has not translated ten verses together in any book of Homer with justice to the Poet, and yet he dares reproach his fellow-writers with not understanding Greek[q]. He has stuck so little to his Original as to have his knowledge in Greek call'd in question[r]. I should be glad to know which it is of all Homer's Excellencies which has so delighted the Ladies, and the Gentlemen who judge like Ladies[s].

But he has a notable talent at Burlesque; his genius slides so naturally into it, that he hath burlesqu'd Homer without designing it[t].

[k] Mist's Journal of June 8, 1728. [l] Character of Mr. P. and Dennis on Hom.
[m] Dennis's Remarks on Pope's Homer, p. 12.
[n] Dennis's Remarks on the Rape of the Lock, p. vi.
[o] Character of Mr. P. p. 17. and Remarks on Homer, p. 91.
[p] Dennis's Remarks on Homer, p. 12. [q] Daily Journal of April 23, 1728.
[r] Supplement to the Profund, Pref. [s] Oldmixon, Essay on Criticism, p. 66.
[t] Dennis's Remarks, p. 28.

Note m. Dennis insults Pope ('he who translated him') by calling his style more Irish than Greek.

Note n. Dennis 1728.

Note q. Reprinted in *A Compleat Collection* 1728: 36.

Note s. The quotation from Oldmixon 1728a is slightly edited.

Note t. The reference is to *Remarks upon ... Homer* (Dennis 1717).

Mr. DRYDEN trick'd his Subscribers.

I wonder that any man, who could not but be conscious of his own unfitness for it, should go to amuse the learned world with such an undertaking! A man ought to value his Reputation more than Money; and not to hope that those who can read for themselves, will be imposed upon, merely by a partially and unseasonably celebrated Name[x]. *Poetis quidlibet audendi* shall be Mr. Dryden's Motto, tho' it should extend to Picking of Pockets[y].

Names bestow'd on Mr. DRYDEN.

An APE] A crafty Ape drest up in a gaudy gown — Whips put into an Ape's paw, to play pranks with — None but Apish and Papish brats will heed him[z].

An ASS.] A Camel will take upon him no more burden than is sufficient for his strength, but there is another beast that crouches under all[a].

A FROG.] Poet Squab endued with Poet Maro's Spirit! an ugly, croaking kind of Vermin, which would swell to the bulk of an Ox[b].

A COWARD.] A Clinias or a Damaetas, or a man of Mr. Dryden's own Courage[c].

A KNAVE.] Mr. Dryden has heard of Paul, the Knave of Jesus Christ: And if I mistake not, I've read somewhere of John Dryden, Servant to his Majesty[d].

A FOOL.] Had he not been such a self-conceited Fool[e]. — Some great Poets are positive Blockheads[f].

A THING.] So little a Thing as Mr. Dryden[g].

[x] Pag. 192. [y] Pag. 125. [z] Whip and Key, Pref. [a] Milb. p. 105. [b] Pag. 11.
[c] Pag. 176. [d] Pag. 57. [e] Whip and Key, Pref. [f] Milbourn, p. 34. [g] Ibid. p. 35.

***Note y.* Poetis quidlibet audendi:** Milbourn cites a tag from Horace, where the poet's friend argues that '[painters and] poets [have always had the power] of taking whatever liberties they like' (*De arte poetica*, line 7).

A Clinias or a Damaetas: Disreputable cowards in Sir Philip Sidney's *The Countess of Pembroke's Arcadia* (Evans 1977: particularly III.13).

Note c. Actually p. 178.

Note d. Milbourn objects to the use of 'knave' (originally 'boy', but later with connotations of 'rascal', 'criminal'), and makes his point by rephrasing the familiar biblical language of St Paul, who describes himself as 'servant' of Jesus Christ: if in that context 'knave' is to mean 'servant', the reader is left to infer what 'servant' must mean when applied to Dryden.

Mr. POPE trick'd his Subscribers.

'Tis indeed somewhat bold, and almost prodigious, for a single man to undertake such a work: But 'tis too late to dissuade by demonstrating the madness of the Project. The Subscribers expectations have been rais'd in proportion to what their Pockets have been drain'd of[v]. Pope has been concerned in Jobs, and hired out his Name to Booksellers[w].

Names bestow'd on Mr. POPE.

An APE.] Let us take the initial letter of his Christian name, and the initial and final letters of his surname, *viz.* APE and they give you the same Idea of an Ape as his Face[x], *etc.*

An ASS.] It is my duty to pull off the Lion's skin from this little Ass[y].

A FROG.] A squab short Gentleman — a little creature that, like the Frog in the Fable, swells and is angry that it is not allow'd to be as big as an Ox[z].

A COWARD.] A lurking way-laying coward[a].

A KNAVE.] He is one whom God and nature have mark'd for want of common honesty[b].

A FOOL.] Great Fools will be christen'd by the names of great Poets, and Pope will be call'd Homer[c].

A THING.] A little abject Thing[d].

[v] Homerides, p. 1, *etc.* [w] British Journal, Nov. 25, 1727.
[x] Dennis, Daily Journal, May 11, 1728. [y] Dennis, Rem. on Homer, Pref.
[z] Dennis's Remarks on the Rape of the Lock, Pref. p. 9. [a] Char. of Mr. P. pag. 3.
[b] Ibid. [c] Dennis Rem. on Homer, p. 37. [d] Ibid. p. 8.

---

note w. Reprinted in *A Compleat Collection* 1728: 2. 'Jobs' ('transactions for profit') has a prejorative sense in this context.

Note x. Reprinted in *A Compleat Collection* 1728: 49.

Note a. *A True Character* 1716: 4.

By the AUTHOR
A DECLARATION.

WHEREAS certain Haberdashers of Points and Particles, **being instigated by the spirit of** Pride, **and assuming to themselves the name of** Critics **and** Restorers, **have taken upon them to adulterate the common and current sense of our** Glorious Ancestors, Poets of this Realm, **by clipping, coining, defacing the images, mixing their own base allay, or otherwise falsifying the same; which they publish, utter, and vend as genuine: The said haberdashers having no right thereto, as neither heirs, executors, administrators, assigns, or** in any sort related **to such Poets, to all or any of them:** Now We, **having carefully revised this our** Dunciad, [a]**beginning with the words** The Mighty Mother, **and ending with the words** buries all, **containing**

[a] Read thus confidently, instead of 'beginning with the word *Books*, and ending with the word *flies*,' as formerly it stood; Read also 'containing the entire sum of *one thousand, seven hundred, and fifty four* verses,' instead of '*one thousand and twelve* lines;' such being the initial and final words, and such the true and entire contents, of this Poem.

Thou art to know, reader! that the first Edition thereof, like that of Milton, was never

---

By the AUTHOR A DECLARATION: First used in 1735. The pomp and authority of the mock-legal language is supported by the use of blackletter type and the spoof royal arms.

Haberdashers of Points and Particles: Editors like Theobald, who emphasise such details as punctuation, are contemptuously compared with tradesmen who live by selling such implicitly trivial items as thread, tape and buttons (see Jarvis 1995: 25–6, 79).

utter: publish.

Note a. 'Bentley' declares that he has amended the specifications originally given in the Declaration to match the facts of 1743. ***Thou art to know:*** 'Bentley' alludes to his argu-

the entire sum of one thousand seven hundred and fifty four verses, **declare every word, figure, point, and comma of this impression to be authentic: And do therefore strictly enjoin and forbid any person or persons whatsoever, to erase, reverse, put between** hooks, **or by any other means directly or indirectly change or mangle any of them.** And **we do hereby earnestly exhort all our brethren to follow** this our example, **which we heartily wish our Great Predecessors had heretofore set, as a remedy and prevention of all such abuses.** Provided always, **that nothing in this Declaration shall be construed to limit the lawful and undoubted right of every subject of this Realm, to judge, censure, or condemn, in the whole or in part, any Poem or Poet whatsoever.**

Given under our hand at London, this third day of January, in the year of our Lord One thousand, seven hundred, thirty and two.

Declarat' cor' me,
JOHN BARBER, Mayor.

seen by the Author, (though living and not blind;) The Editor himself confest as much in his Preface: And no two poems were ever published in so arbitrary a manner. The Editor of this, had as boldly suppressed whole Passages, yea the entire last book; as the Editor of Paradise lost, added and augmented. Milton himself gave but *ten* books, his editor *twelve*; this Author gave *four* books, his Editor only *three*. But we have happily done justice to both; and presume we shall live, in this our last labour, as long as in any of our others.

BENTLEY.

---

ment about the alleged corruption of the text of *Paradise Lost* on account of the blind Milton's inability to supervise publication. ***The Editor himself confest as much:*** In the Preface, printed as Appendix I, the publisher suggests that he does not even know who the author is, and that he publishes entirely on his own initiative. ***had as boldly suppressed:*** Asserting that the 1743 text was cut for earlier editions, rather than expanded from them. ***gave but* ten *books:*** Whereas the first edition of *Paradise Lost* is divided into ten books, the second is divided into the now-familiar twelve. ***both:*** Milton and Pope.

hooks: The angle brackets used by Bentley to distinguish what he considered to be spurious.

the year of our Lord: Actually early 1733 (Barber uses the archaic legal dating system). Arbuthnot described the Declaration in a letter to Swift on 13 January 1733 (Williams 1965: IV, 102).

Declarat' cor' me: Imitating the formal subscription of an official witnessing that a declaration has been made in his presence.

INDEX

OF

PERSONS celebrated in this POEM.

The first number shews the Book, the second the Verse.

INDEX OF PERSONS. Alphabetical indexing was a considerable selling point in early eighteenth-century books (see Lund 1998). Current conventions allowed items to be grouped by initial without regard to the alphabetical order of second and subsequent letters. Some individuals appear under both christian name and surname; the christian names of others who are named by surname only in the main text are not given. These features, taken in conjunction with the relatively factual approach of this Index (cp. Index of Matters following), could suggest that it was compiled by an assistant.

Log, King: *lin. ult.*, 'The last line'.

Walpole [late Sir Robert]: Formerly Sir Robert Walpole, but now ennobled as Earl of Orford.

INDEX

OF

MATTERS

Contained in this

POEM and NOTES.

[The first Number denotes the BOOK, the second the VERSE and NOTE on it. *Test.* Testimonies. *Ap.* Appendix.

NOTE ON TITLE. Pope uses this index as an opportunity for a sardonic review of his various targets. Again, the entries under each initial letter are not in alphabetical order, and many references are somewhat approximate. The rubric makes it clear that the original notes and accompanying documents are to be taken as an integral part of *The Dunciad in Four Books.*

ADDISON: False Facts: Referring to the controversy as to whether Addison had encouraged Tickell to make a rival translation of the *Iliad.* See editor's notes to 'Testimonies of Authors'.

Alehouse, The Birth-place of Mr. Cook: An offensive way of stating that his father was an innkeeper.

CIBBER: ***yet not without Furniture:*** not empty.
—— ***His Entry:*** usque ad fin., 'up to the end'.

Critics: Postulata: propositions which must be granted.

DULLNESS, Her Critics: Referring to the lines on Hanmer's Shakespeare which had been cancelled in ordinary copies of 1743 (IV.115–18). This entry appeared even in such cancelled copies.

Log (King): ver. ult., 'the last line'.

MOORE (James): What he was real author of: Vide, 'see'.
Pope (Mr.) his Life] Educated: Test. init., 'at the beginning of "Testimonies of Authors"'.
Poverty: When, and how far Poverty may be satirized: i.e. the prefatory 'Letter to the Publisher'. The page number refers to the original edition.

Personal abuses on our Author, by ... Edw. Ward: The subject of the passage is actually John Ward, although the note prevaricates as to the possibility that Edward Ward may be meant.

Personal abuses of others. D. Smedley: i.e. Jonathan Smedley (the 'D.' stands for 'Dr').

Resemblance of the* Hero: *To Querno: *ut supra*, 'as above'.

Round-house: *prope fin.*, 'near the end'.

FINIS.

Sawney, a Poem: The Author's great Ignorance —— In Languages: The index refers by mistake to a part of the 1729 note (on III.159) omitted from the equivalent note in 1743.

BIBLIOGRAPHY

Most works referred to in the editorial matter are cited by author and date. In this bibliography they are arranged alphabetically by author (except that edited works are arranged by editor and cross-referenced under author; and anonymously published works are arranged by title and cross-referenced under author where known). The original texts of classical works quoted in the commentary – but not the translations, which are editorially supplied – are from the Loeb Classical Library (hereafter LCL): the relevant Loeb volumes are arranged by editor/translator and cross-referenced under author. Unless otherwise specified, a reference to book and line (e.g. 'IV.230') refers to a book of *The Dunciad in Four Books* other than the current one, and a reference to line only (e.g. 'line 230') refers to the current book. A few frequently cited editions are referred to by short titles (for full details, see main entries in bibliography):

Corr.	George Sherburn, ed., *The Correspondence of Alexander Pope* (1956)
OAC	Joseph Spence, *Observations, Anecdotes, and Characters of Books and Men*, ed. James M. Osborn (1966)
PW	Norman Ault and Rosemary Cowler, eds, *The Prose Works of Alexander Pope* (1936–86)
TE	John Butt *et al.*, eds, *The Twickenham Edition of the Poems of Alexander Pope* (1939–69)

Manuscript annotations in a copy of the *New Dunciad* (1742) in the National Art Library at the Victoria and Albert Museum (Dyce 7747) are cited as Dyce 7747.

A few frequently cited texts by Pope, some with a confusing history of title variants, are also referred to in the commentary by short titles:

To Arbuthnot	*An Epistle from Mr. Pope, to Dr. Arbuthnot*
To Bathurst	*Epistles to Several Persons* [sometimes called *Moral Essays*], *Epistle III. To Allen Lord Bathurst* [sometimes subtitled *Of the Use of Riches*]
To Burlington	*Epistles to Several Persons* [sometimes called *Moral Essays*], *Epistle IV. To Richard Boyle, Earl of Burlington* [sometimes subtitled *Of the Use of Riches*]
Characters of Men	*Epistles to Several Persons* [sometimes called *Moral Essays*], *Epistle I. To Sir Richard Temple, Lord Viscount Cobham* [sometimes subtitled *Of the Knowledge and Characters of Men*]

Characters of Women	*Epistles to Several Persons* [sometimes called *Moral Essays*], *Epistle II. To a Lady. Of the Characters of Women*
Peri Bathous	*Peri Bathous: or, Martinus Scriblerus, His Treatise of the Art of Sinking in Poetry*

Periodicals are cited in the bibliography by the following abbreviations:

ELH	*English Literary History*
ELN	*English Language Notes*
HLQ	*Huntington Library Quarterly*
JEGP	*Journal of English and Germanic Philology*
MLN	*Modern Language Notes*
MLR	*Modern Language Review*
MP	*Modern Philology*
NQ	*Notes & Queries*
PBA	*Proceedings of the British Academy*
PMLA	*Publications of the Modern Language Association of America*
PQ	*Philological Quarterly*
RES	*Review of English Studies*
SEL	*Studies in English Literature*
SP	*Studies in Philology*

A selection of critical books and articles that are particularly helpful for newcomers to the *Dunciads* are marked with an asterisk. (These include not only recent work but also some classic older accounts which need to be read with careful attention to changing critical contexts.) Essential sources for exploring books mentioned in the *Dunciads* are *The Eighteenth-Century Short-Title Catalogue on CD-rom* (The British Library, 1992) and its associated microfilm series. For details of contemporary newspapers, see listings in Watson 1969–77 and the microfilm collection *Early English Newspapers*, with accompanying handbook, compiled by Susan M. Cox and Janice L. Budeit, 1207 reels, Research Publications, Woodbridge, 1983.

All works are published in London unless otherwise indicated.

Absolom Senior: or, Achitophel Transpros'd. A Poem (1682), by Elkanah Settle.

Addison, Joseph (1719), *Poems on Several Occasions. With a Dissertation upon the Roman Poets.*

——: for *Miscellaneous Works*, see Guthkelch 1914.

——: for *The Freeholder*, see Leheny 1979.

——: for *The Spectator*, see Bond 1965.

Aesop: see Ogilby 1651.

——: see Perry 1965.

Alciphron: or, The Minute Philosopher. In Seven Dialogues (1732), by George Berkeley, 2 vols.

Alderson, Simon (1996), 'Alexander Pope and the nature of language', *RES* 47, 23–34.

Alexander, Peter, ed. (1951), *William Shakespeare: The Complete Works.*

Allen, Thomas W. (1946), *Homeri Opera*, corrected edn, 5 vols, Oxford.

Alston, R.C., and M.J. Janetta (1978), *Bibliography, Machine-Readable Cataloguing and the ESTC* (includes catalogue of British Library holdings of Pope's works published 1711–1800).

Amherst, Nicholas: see *The Craftsman*.

Amores Britannici, Epistles Historical and Gallant (1703), by John Oldmixon, 2 parts.

Amory, Thomas: see *The Life of John Buncle* 1770.

Are These Things So? The Previous Question, from an Englishman in his Grotto, to a Great Man at Court (1740), by James Miller.

Aristarchus ampullans in curis horationis (1712), by Joshua Barnes.

Aristotle: for *The Poetics*, see Fyfe & Roberts 1932.

——: for *Nicomachean Ethics*, see Rackham 1943.

——: for *Generation of Animals*, see Peck 1943.

Arnall, William: see *The Daily Gazetteer*.

The Art of Politicks (1729), by James Bramston. Reprinted in Augustan Reprint Society 177.

Aston, T.H., ed. (1984–94), *The History of the University of Oxford*, 8 vols, Oxford.

Atkins, G. Douglas (1972), 'Pope and deism: a new analysis', *HLQ* 35, 257–78, reprinted in Mack & Winn 1980: 392–415.

Atterbury, Francis (1731), *I have lately seen ... Mr. Oldmixon's History*, Paris. (Title from opening of text, later reprints entitled *The Late Bishop of Rochester's Vindication*.)

Attridge, Derek (1974), *Well-Weighed Syllables: Elizabethan Verse in Classical Metres*, Cambridge.

Audra, Emile (1931), *Les traductions françaises de Pope (1717–1825), étude de bibliographie*, Paris.

Ault, Norman (1949), *New Light on Pope with Some Additions to his Poetry hitherto Unknown*.

Ault, Norman, and Rosemary Cowler, eds (1936–86), *The Prose Works of Alexander Pope*, 2 vols, Oxford (hereafter *PW*).

Austin, R.G., ed. (1977), *P. Vergili Maronis Aeneidos Liber Sextus*, Oxford.

An Author to be Lett (1729), attributed on title-page to Iscariot Hackney, actually Richard Savage. (Facsimile in Augustan Reprint Society 84 (1960), ed. James Sutherland.)

Avery, Emmet L., ed. (1960), *The London Stage 1600–1800. Part 2: 1700–1729*, 2 vols, Carbondale, Ill.

B., E. (i.e. Edward Benlowes) (1652), *Theophila, or Loves Sacrifice. A Divine Poem*.

B., J. (i.e. John Breval) (1729), *Henry and Minerva. A Poem*.

Babrius: see Perry 1965.

Backscheider, Paula R. (1989), *Daniel Defoe: His Life*.

Baker's News: or, The Whitehall Journal, ed. Jonathan Smedley. Issued 1722; continued as *Whitehall Journal*, 1722–3.

Ballaster, Ros (1992), *Seductive Forms: Women's Amatory Fiction from 1684 to 1740*, Oxford.

Banier, Antoine (1738–40), *La mythologie et les fables expliquées par l'histoire*, Paris.

—— (1739–40), *The Mythology and Fables of the Ancients, Explain'd from History. By the Abbé Banier .... Translated from the original French*, 4 vols.

Banks, Theodore Howard, ed. (1969), *The Poetical Works of Sir John Denham*, Archon Books.

Barnes, Joshua, ed. (1711), *Homeri Ilias & Odyssea*, 2 vols, Cambridge.

——: see *Aristarchus ampullans* 1712.

*Battestin, Martin (1974), *The Providence of Wit: Aspects of Form in Augustan Literature and the Arts*, Oxford.

The Battle of the Poets. An Heroick Poem (1725), by Thomas Cooke. (See Guerinot 1969: 91–3. A revised and expanded version is included in Cooke's anonymous *Tales, Epistles, Odes, Fables, &c.* 1729: facsimile in *Popeiana* 9.)

Bawcutt, N.W. (1958), 'More echoes in Pope's poetry', *NQ* 203, 220–21.

—— (1961), 'Pope's "Duchesses and Lady Mary's": more evidence', *NQ* 206, 253–4.

Bayle, Pierre (1710), *An Historical and Critical Dictionary. ... Translated into English*, 4 vols.
Beaumont, Joseph (1648), *Psyche: or, Loves Mysterie.*
Bedford, Arthur (1719), *A Serious Remonstrance in Behalf of the Christian Religion against the Horrid Blasphemies and Impieties which are still Used in the English Playhouse.*
Bedford, Hilkiah: see *The Hereditary Right* 1713.
Benlowes, Edward: for *Theophila*, see B., E. 1652.
Bennett, C.E., ed. and trans. (1968), *Horace: Odes, Epodes*, revised edition, LCL 33.
Bennett, G.V. (1957), *White Kennett, 1660–1728: Bishop of Peterborough.*
—— (1975), *The Tory Crisis in Church and State, 1688–1730: The Career of Francis Atterbury, Bishop of Rochester*, Oxford.
Benson, Larry, ed. (1987), *The Riverside Chaucer*, 3rd edn, Oxford.
Benson, William: see Johnston 1741.
——: see *A Prefatory Discourse* 1741.
Bentley, Richard (1693), *A Confutation of Atheism ... Part II. A Sermon ... Being the Seventh of the Lecture Founded by the Honourable Robert Boyle.*
—— (1699), *A Dissertation upon the Epistles of Phalaris: with an Answer to the Objections of the Hon. Charles Boyle.*
——, ed. (1711), *Q. Horatius Flaccus*, Cambridge.
—— (1713), *Emendationes in Menandri et Philemonis reliquias ... Accedit epistola critica Richardi Bentleii*, Cambridge. (For first edition, see *Emendationes in Menandri et Philemonis reliquias* 1710.)
——, ed. (1726), *Publii Terentii Afri comoediae*, Cambridge.
——, ed. (1732), *Milton's Paradise Lost. A New Edition.*
——, ed. (1739), *M. Manilii astronomicon.*
Bentley, Thomas, ed. (1713), *Q. Horatius Flaccus ad nuperam Richardi Bentleii editionem ... Notas addidit Thomas Bentleius*, Cambridge.
——: see *A Letter to Mr. Pope, Occasioned by Sober Advice from Horace* 1735.
Berkeley, George: see *Alciphron* 1732.
Berry, Reginald (1988), *A Pope Chronology.*
Bibliotheca: A Poem. Occasion'd by the Sight of a Modern Library (1712), by Thomas Newcomb.
Black, Jeremy (1987a), *The English Press in the Eighteenth Century.*
—— (1987b), 'An underrated journalist: Nathaniel Mist and the opposition press', *British Journal for Eighteenth Century Studies* 10, 27–41.
—— (1992), *The British Abroad: The Grand Tour in the Eighteenth Century*, Stroud.
Blackmore, Sir Richard (1695), *Prince Arthur. An Heroick Poem. In Ten Books.*
—— (1697), *King Arthur. An Heroic Poem. In Twelve Books.*
—— (1700), *A Paraphrase on the Book of Job.*
—— (1705), *Eliza: An Epick Poem. In Ten Books.*
—— (1708), *The Kit-Cats. A Poem.*
—— (1711), *The Nature of Man. A Poem. In Three Books.*
—— (1716–17), *Essays upon Several Subjects*, 2 vols.
—— (1721), *A New Version of the Psalms of David, Fitted to the Tunes Used in Churches.*
—— (1722), *Redemption: A Divine Poem, in Six Books.*
—— (1723), *Alfred. An Epick Poem. In Twelve Books.*
—— (1727), *Creation. A Philosophical Poem. In Seven Books.*
Blain, Virginia, Patricia Clements and Isobel Grundy (1990), *The Feminist Companion to Literature in English: Women Writers from the Middle Ages to the Present.*
Blanchard, Rae, ed. (1941), *The Correspondence of Richard Steele*, Oxford.
——, ed. (1959), *Richard Steele's Periodical Journalism, 1714–16*, Oxford.

Bloom, Lillian (1948), 'Pope as textual critic: a bibliographical study of his Horatian text', *JEGP* 47, 150–55. Reprinted in Mack 1964: 495–506.

Blouch, Christine (1991), 'Eliza Haywood and the romance of obscurity', *SEL* 31, 535–51.

Blount, Charles, and Charles Gildon (1693), *The Oracles of Reason ... by Char. Blount ... Mr. Gildon, and Others.*

——: for *The Miscellaneous Works*, see 'Lindamour' 1695.

*Bogel, Fredric V. (1982), 'Dulness unbound: rhetoric and Pope's *Dunciad*', *PMLA* 97, 844–55.

Boileau, Nicolas (1701), *Oeuvres diverses*, 2 vols, Paris.

——: see Ozell 1708.

——: see Vercruysse 1969.

Bolingbroke, Henry, Viscount: see St John, Henry.

Bon, Monsieur (1710), 'A Discourse upon the Usefulness of the Silk of Spiders', *Philosophical Transactions* 27, no. 325, 2–16.

Bond, Donald F., ed. (1965), *The Spectator*, 5 vols, Oxford.

——, ed. (1987), *The Tatler*, 3 vols, Oxford.

Bond, William: see *The Progress of Dulness* 1728.

Borgman, Albert S. (1928), *Thomas Shadwell: His Life and Comedies*, New York.

Bossu: for René Le Bossu, see Le Bossu, René 1695.

Boswell, James: for *Boswell's Life of Johnson*, see Hill 1934–5.

Bowles, William Lisle, ed. (1806), *The Works of Alexander Pope*, 10 vols.

Boyer, Abel (1702), *Dictionnaire royal, françois et anglois*, The Hague.

——: see *The History of the Reign of Queen Anne* 1711–13.

——: see *The Political State of Great Britain* 1711–29.

Boyle, Charles, ed. (1695), *Phalaridis Agrigentinorum tyranni epistolae*, Oxford.

Boyle, Richard, Earl of Burlington, ed. (1730), *Fabbriche antiche designate da A. Palladio.*

Bramston, James: see *The Art of Politicks* 1729.

——: see *The Man of Taste* 1733.

Bredvold, Louis I. (1951), 'The invention of the ethical calculus', in *The Seventeenth Century: Studies in the History of English Thought and Literature from Bacon to Pope*, by Richard Foster Jones *et al.*, 165–80, Stanford.

Breval, John Durant (1726), *Remarks on Several Parts of Europe: Relating chiefly to the History, Antiquities and Geography, Of those Countries through which the Author has travel'd.*

——: see B., J. 1729.

——: see *A Complete Key to the Non-Juror* 1718.

——: see *The Confederates* 1717.

Brice's Weekly Journal, printed by Andrew Brice. Issued 1727–8.

A Brief Examination of the Rev. Mr. Warburton's Divine Legation of Moses ... By a Society of Gentlemen (1742), by Thomas Morgan.

Brink, C.O. (1986), *English Classical Scholarship: Historical Reflections on Bentley, Porson, and Housman*, Cambridge.

The British Enchanters: or, No Magick like Love. A Tragedy (1706), by George Granville, Lord Lansdowne.

The British Journal, ed. J. Trenchard *et al.* Issued 1722–8; continued as *The British Journal: or, The Censor*, 1728–30; continued as *The British Journal: or, The Traveller*, 1730–31.

The British Muse: or, Tyranny Expos'd. A Satyr, occasion'd by all the Fulsome and Lying Poems and Elegies, that have been written on the Death of the Late King James (1701), by John Tutchin.

The British Stage: or, The Exploits of Harlequin: A Farce (1724).

Brockbank, J. Philip (1979), 'The Book of Genesis and the genesis of books: the creation of Pope's *Dunciad*', in *The Art of Alexander Pope*, ed. Howard Erskine-Hill and Anne Smith, 192–211.

Brooke, Nicholas, ed. (1964), *George Chapman: Bussy D'Ambois*, The Revels Plays.

Brooks, Harold F., and Raman Selden, eds (1987), *The Poems of John Oldham*, Oxford.

Brooks-Davies, Douglas (1985), *Pope's 'Dunciad' and the Queen of Night: A Study in Emotional Jacobitism*, Manchester.

Broome, William (1727), *Poems on Several Occasions*.

Brower, Reuben A. (1959), *Alexander Pope: The Poetry of Allusion*, Oxford.

Brown, F.C. (1910), *Elkanah Settle: His Life & Works*, Chicago.

Brown, Laura (1985), *Alexander Pope*, Rereading Literature, Oxford.

Brownell, Morris R. (1976), 'Ears of an untoward make: Pope and Handel', *Musical Quarterly* 62, 554–70.

—— (1978), *Alexander Pope and the Arts of Georgian England*, Oxford.

Buckingham, George Villiers, Duke of: for *The Rehearsal*, see Stone 1969.

Buckingham, John Sheffield, Duke of: for *Works*, see Pope 1723.

Buckley, Samuel: see *The Daily Courant*.

Budgell, Eustace, trans. (1714), *The Moral Characters of Theophrastus*.

—— (1720a), *The Case of the Annuitants and Proprietors of the Redeemable Debts*.

—— (1720b), *The Speech made by Eustace Budgell, Esq; at a General Court of the South-Sea Company*.

—— (1720c), *The Second Speech made by Eustace Budgell Esq; at the General Court of the South-Sea Company*.

—— (1721), *A Letter to a Friend in the Country, occasioned by ... the Late Directors of the South-Sea Company*.

—— (1730a), *A Poem upon His Majesty's Late Journey to Cambridge and New-Market ... To this New Edition is added, Some Observations on the said Poem by Caleb D'Anvers*.

—— (1730b), *On Tuesday being April the 21st, Eustace Budgell ... deliver'd into His Majesty's Own Hand ... an Humble Memorial or Petition*.

—— (1730c), *A Letter to the Craftsman from Eustace Budgell; Occasion'd by his Late Presenting an Humble Complaint to His Majesty against the Rt. Honble Sir Robert Walpole*.

Bukofzer, Manfred (1939), 'Allegory in Baroque music', *Journal of the Warburg and Courtauld Institute* 3, 1–21.

Bull, George, and Peter Porter, eds and trans (1987), *Michelangelo: Life, Letters, and Poetry*, Oxford.

Buonarotti, Michelangelo: see Bull & Porter 1987.

Burgess, C.F., ed. (1966), *The Letters of John Gay*, Oxford.

Burke, Peter (1978), *Popular Culture in Early Modern Europe*.

—— (1992), *The Fabrication of Louis XIV*.

Burlington, Richard, Earl of: see Boyle 1730.

Burnet, Thomas: see *The Grumbler*.

——: see *Homerides: or, A Letter to Mr. Pope* 1715.

Burney, Charles: see Mercer 1935.

Burrows, Donald (1994), *Handel*, The Master Musicians, Oxford.

Butler, H.E., ed. and trans. (1921–2), *The Institutio Oratoria of Quintilian*, 4 vols, LCL 124–7.

Butler, Samuel: see Wilders 1967.

Butt, John (1954), 'Pope's poetical manuscripts', *PBA* 40, 23–39. Reprinted in Mack 1964: 507–27.

Butt, John *et al.*, eds (1939–69), *The Twickenham Edition of the Poems of Alexander Pope*, 11 vols. All references are to the most recent revision of each volume, i.e.: I, *Pastoral Poetry and an Essay on Criticism*, ed. E. Audra and Aubrey Williams (1961); II, *The Rape of the Lock and Other Poems*, ed. Geoffrey Tillotson (1962); III.i, *An Essay on Man*, ed. Maynard Mack (1950); III.ii, *Epistles to Several Persons*, ed. F.W. Bateson (1961); IV, *Imitations of Horace with An Epistle to Dr Arbuthnot and The Epilogue to the Satires*, ed. John Butt (1961); V, *The Dunciad*, ed. James Sutherland (1963); VI, *Minor Poems*, ed. Norman Ault and John Butt (1964); VII–X, *Homer's Iliad and Odyssey*, ed. Maynard Mack *et al.* (1967); XI, *Index*, ed. Maynard Mack (1969). (Hereafter *TE.*)

Byrd, Max (1975), *Visits to Bedlam: Madness and Literature in the Eighteenth Century*, Columbia.

—— (1978), *London Transformed: Images of the City in the Eighteenth Century*.

Cajori, Florian, ed. and rev. (1962), *Sir Isaac Newton's Mathematical Principles*, trans. Andrew Motte (originally published in London in 1729), 2 vols, Berkeley.

Camerarius, J., ed. (1541), *Theonis sophistae ... exercitationes*, Basle.

A Canto of the Fairy Queen. Written by Spenser. Never before Published (1739), by Gilbert West.

Capp, Bernard (1994), *The World of John Taylor the Water-Poet, 1578–1653*, Oxford.

Carew, Thomas: see Dunlap 1949.

Carey, John, ed. (1968), *John Milton: Complete Shorter Poems*.

Carretta, Vincent (1983), *The Snarling Muse: Verbal and Visual Political Satire from Pope to Churchill*, Philadelphia.

Caryll, John: see *The Duumvirate c.*1704.

Castle, Terry (1986), *Masquerade and Civilization: The Carnivalesque in Eighteenth-Century English Culture and Fiction*.

The Catholick Poet: or, Protestant Barnaby's Sorrowful Lamentation: An Excellent New Ballad (1716), by John Oldmixon, but attributed by Pope to Susannah Centlivre.

Catullus: see Cornish 1912.

Caxton, William, trans. (1473–4), *The Recuyell of the Historyes of Troye*, Bruges.

——, trans. (1490), *Eneydos*. (See also Culley & Furnivall 1890.)

Cebes, tabula of: see Fitzgerald & White 1983.

The Censor (1717), 3 vols, by Lewis Theobald.

Centlivre, Susannah: see *The Catholick Poet* 1716.

Cervantes, Miguel de: see Riley 1992.

Chambers, E.K., and F. Sidgwick, eds (1907), *Early English Lyrics*.

Chambers, Jessie Rhodes (1964), 'The episode of Annius and Mummius: "Dunciad" IV, 347–96', *PQ* 43, 185–92.

The Champion: or, British Mercury, by 'Captain Hercules Vinegar, of Pall-Mall', i.e. Henry Fielding and others. Issued 1739–40; continued as *The Champion: or, Evening Advertiser* 1740–42; continued as *The British Champion: or, The Impartial Advertiser* 1743.

Chapman, George, trans. ([1611]), *The Iliad of Homer Prince of Poets*.

——, trans. ([1615]), *Homer's Odysses*.

——: for *Bussy D'Ambois*, see Brooke 1964.

Character of Mr. P. and his Writings: see *A True Character of Mr. Pope* 1716.

The Character of a Popish Successour, and what England may Expect from Such a One (1681), by Elkanah Settle.

Characteristicks of Men, Manners, Opinions, Times (1711), by Anthony Ashley Cooper, third Earl of Shaftesbury, 3 vols, n.p. A revised edition of 1714 is the basis for subsequent texts.

Characters of the Times: or, An Impartial Account of the Writings, Characters, Education, &c. of Several Noblemen and Gentlemen, Libell'd in a Preface to a late Miscellany Publish'd by P—pe and S—ft (1728). (Facsimile in *Popeiana* (1974–5), vol. 7. After 1735 Pope dropped his attribution to Edmund Curll and Leonard Welsted: see Guerinot 1969: 151–3.)

Charke, Charlotte (1755), *A Narrative of the Life of Mrs. Charlotte Charke*. (Facsimile of 2nd edn 1755, ed. Leonard R.N. Ashley, in *Scholars' Facsimiles and Reprints*, Gainesville, Fla., 1969.)

Chaucer, Geoffrey: see Benson 1987.

Cheyne, George (1705), *Philosophical Principles of Natural Religion: Containing the Elements of Natural Philosophy, and the Proofs for Natural Religion, arising from them.*

Cibber, Colley (1705), *The Careless Husband. A Comedy.*

—— (1706), *Perolla and Izadora. A Tragedy.*

—— (1718), *The Non-juror. A Comedy.*

—— (1719), *Ximena: or, The Heroick Daughter. A Tragedy.*

—— (1725), *Caesar in Aegypt. A Tragedy.*

—— (1740), *An Apology for the Life of Mr. Colley Cibber ... Written by Himself. The Second Edition.* (The octavo cited by Pope. For a reprint from the first edition, quarto, also 1740, see B.R.S. Fone 1968.)

—— (1742), *A Letter from Mr. Cibber, To Mr. Pope.* There were three editions in this year. (Facsimile of first edition in *Popeiana* (1974–5), vol. 15. See Guerinot 1969: 288–94.)

—— (1743), *A Second letter from Mr. Cibber to Mr. Pope.* (See Guerinot 1969: 310–11.)

—— (1744), *Another Occasional Letter from Mr. Cibber to Mr. Pope.* (Facsimile in *Popeiana* (1974–5), vol. 15. See Guerinot 1969: 316–19.)

—— (1745), *Papal Tyranny in the Reign of King John. A Tragedy.*

Claremont (1715), by Samuel Garth.

Clarendon, Earl of: see Hyde, Edward.

Clarke, Samuel (1705), *A Demonstration of the Being and Attributes of God.*

—— (1706), *A Discourse Concerning the Unchangeable Obligations of Natural Religion, and the Truth and Certainty of the Christian Revelation.*

Claudian: see Platnauer 1922.

Clifford, James L., and Louis A. Landa, eds (1949), *Pope and his Contemporaries: Essays Presented to George Sherburn*, Oxford.

Codrus: or, The Dunciad Dissected. ... To which is added, Farmer Pope and his Son. A Tale. By Mr. Philips. (1728). (Facsimile in *Popeiana* (1974–5), vol. 7. Attributed by Pope to Edmund Curll and Elizabeth Thomas: see Guerinot 1969: 153–6.)

A Collection of Several Curious Pieces Lately Inserted in the Daily Journal (1728). (No. 7 by Aaron Hill, the rest attributed by Pope to James Moore Smythe: see Guerinot 1969: 104–7.)

Collier, Jeremy (1698), *A Short View of the Immorality and Profaneness of the English Stage.*

—— (1703), *Mr. Collier's Dissuasive from the Play-House ... Occasion'd by the Late Calamity of the Tempest.*

*Colomb, Gregory G. (1992), *Designs on Truth: The Poetics of the Augustan Mock-Epic*, Pennsylvania.

A Compleat Collection of all the Verses, Essays, Letters and Advertisements ... occasioned by ... Miscellanies, by Pope and Company (1728). (Preface attributed by Pope to Matthew Concanen. Facsimile in *Popeiana* (1974–5), vol. 6. See Guerinot 1969: 116–22.)

A Compleat Key to the Dunciad (1728), by Edmund Curll. (There were three editions in this year, of which Pope cites the third. Facsimile of first edition in *Popeiana* (1974–5), vol. 6. See Guerinot 1969: 110–14.)

A Complete History of England (1706), 3 vols. (Vols I–II ed. John Hughes; Vol. III written by White Kennett; overall editing ascribed to John Oldmixon.)

A Complete Key to the Last New Farce, The What D'Ye Call It (1715), attributed by Pope to Benjamin Griffin and Lewis Theobald. (Facsimile in *Popeiana* (1974–5), vol. 4; see Guerinot 1969: 28–32.)

A Complete Key to the Non-Juror (1718), attributed on title-page to 'Joseph Gay', actually by John Durant Breval. (Facsimile in *Popeiana* (1974–5), vol. 4.)

Concanen, Matthew, ed. and contributor (1724), *Miscellaneous Poems ... by Several Hands.*

——: see *A Compleat Collection* 1728.

——: see Theobald 1732.

——: see *The Speculatist* 1730.

——: see *A Supplement to the Profund* 1728.

The Confederates (1717), attributed on title-page to 'Mr. Gay', dedication signed 'Joseph Gay', actually by John Durant Breval. (Facsimile in *Popeiana* (1974–5), vol. 4; see Guerinot 1969: 64–7.)

Congleton, J.E. (1952), *Theories of Pastoral Poetry in England, 1684–1798*, Gainesville, Fla.

Congreve, William: see Summers 1923.

Cooke, Thomas (1728), *The Works of Hesiod Translated from the Greek*, 2 vols.

——: see *The Battle of the Poets* 1725.

——: see *Penelope* 1728.

Cooper, Anthony Ashley: see *Characteristicks* 1711.

——: see *An Inquiry concerning Virtue* 1699.

A Copy of the Will of Dr. Matthew Tindall, with an Account of what Pass'd Concerning the Same, between Mrs. Lucy Price, Eustace Budgell Esq; and Mr. Nicolas Tindal (1733).

Corman, Brian, and Paul R. Stone (1988), 'A possible source for the *Dunciad* (B. IV.655–656)', *Scriblerian* 20, 194–6.

The Corn-Cutter's Journal. Issued 1733–5.

Cornish, F.W., *et al.*, eds and trans (1912), *Catullus, Tibullus and Pervigilium Veneris*, LCL 6.

Corse, Taylor (1991), '"Another yet the Same": Joseph Hall and *The Dunciad*', *NQ* 236, 183–4.

Cosgrove, Peter (1991), 'Undermining the text: Edward Gibbon, Alexander Pope, and the anti-authenticating footnote', in *Annotation and its Texts*, ed. Stephen A. Barney, 130–51, Oxford.

Cottingham, John, *et al.*, trans (1985–91), *The Philosophical Writings of Descartes*, 3 vols, Cambridge.

The Country Journal: see *The Craftsman*.

Courthope, William John: for *The Works of Alexander Pope*, see Elwin & Courthope 1871–86.

Cowler, Rosemary: for *The Prose Works of Alexander Pope*, see Ault & Cowler 1936–86.

Cowley, Abraham (1689), *The Works of Mr. Abraham Cowley. In Three Volumes.*

——: for *The English Writings*, see Waller 1905.

——: for *Essays*, see Gough 1915.

The Craftsman, ed. Nicholas Amherst *et al.* Issued 1726–7; continued as *The Country Journal: or, The Craftsman*, 1727–47.

Craig, John (1699), *Theologiae Christianae principia mathematica.*

Creech, Thomas, trans. (1684), *The Idylliums of Theocritus with Rapin's Discourse of Pastorals. Done into English*, Oxford.

The Critical History of England (1724–6), by John Oldmixon, 2 vols.

A Critical History of the Administration of Sir Robert Walpole ... By a Gentleman of the Middle Temple (1743), by James Ralph.

Cruickshanks, Eveline (1986), *Lord Cornbury, Bolingbroke and a Plan to Restore the Stuarts, 1731–35*, Royal Stuart Papers 27, Huntingdon.

Culley, W.T., and Furnivall, F.J., eds (1890), *Eneydos*, trans. William Caxton, Early English Text Society, extra series 57.

Curll, Edmund (1729), *The Curliad. A Hypercritic upon the Dunciad Variorum. With a farther key to the New Characters*. (Facsimile in *Popeiana* (1974–5), vol. 8; see Guerinot 1969: 164–6.)

——: see *Characters of the Times* 1728.

——: see *Codrus: or, The Dunciad Dissected* 1728.

——: see *A Compleat Key* 1728.

——: see *The Female Dunciad* 1728.

——: see *The Popiad* 1728.

D., S. (i.e. Samuel Daniel) (1618), *The Collection of the History of England*.

Dacier, Anne Lefebvre (1724), *Remarks upon Mr. Pope's Account of Homer*, translation from the French attributed on title-page to one T. Parnell (not Pope's friend Thomas, but probably an invention by Curll).

The Daily Courant, ed. Samuel Buckley. Issued 1702–35.

The Daily Gazetteer, ed. William Arnall *et al*. Issued 1735–46; continued as *The Daily Gazetteer: or Advertiser*, 1746–8, and thereafter under varying titles until absorbed by *The Morning Post* in 1797.

The Daily Journal. Issued 1720–42.

——: for reprinted articles, see *A Collection of Several Curious Pieces* 1728.

*Damrosch, Leopold (1990), 'Pope's *Dunciad*', in *Teaching Eighteenth-Century Poetry*, ed. Christopher Fox, 263–72, New York.

Daniel, Samuel: for *The Complete Works*, see Grosart 1885–96.

——: for *The Collection of the History of England*, see D., S. 1618.

Davies, Thomas (1780), *Memoirs of the Life of David Garrick*, 2 vols.

Davis, Herbert, *et al.*, eds (1939–68), *The Prose Works of Jonathan Swift*, 14 vols, Oxford.

Dean Jonathan's Parody on the 4th Chap. of Genesis (1729). (Attributed by Pope to Edward Roome: see Guerinot 1969: 182–3.)

Dean, Winton, and John Merrill Knapp (1987), *Handel's Operas, 1704–1726*, Oxford.

Dearing, Vinton A., ed. (1974), *John Gay: Poetry and Prose*, 2 vols, Oxford.

De Beer, E.S., ed. (1976–89), *The Correspondence of John Locke*, 8 vols, Oxford.

A Defence of our Present Happy Establishment; and the Administration Vindicated (1722), by Matthew Tindal.

Defoe, Daniel (1706), *Jure Divino: A Satyr. In Twelve Books.*

—— (1855), *The Novels and Miscellaneous Works*, Bohn's British Classics.

——: see *The Shortest Way with the Dissenters* 1702.

Denham, Sir John: for *Poetical Works*, see Banks 1969.

Dennis, John (1696a), *Letters upon Several Occasions: Written by and between Mr. Dryden, Mr. Wycherly, Mr. Congreve, and Mr. Dennis.*

—— (1696b), *Remarks on a Book Entituled, Prince Arthur*. (Repr. in Hooker 1939–43.)

—— (1711), *Reflections Critical and Satyrical, upon a Late Rhapsody, Call'd, An Essay Upon Criticism*. (Facsimile in *Popeiana* (1974–5), vol. 1; repr. in Hooker 1939–43. See Guerinot 1969: 1–11.)

—— (1717), *Remarks upon Mr. Pope's Translation of Homer. With Two Letters concerning Windsor Forest, and the Temple of Fame*. (Facsimile in *Popeiana* (1974–5), vol. 2; repr. in Hooker 1939–43. See Guerinot 1969: 51–8.)

—— (1726), *The Stage Defended ... Occasion'd by Mr. Law's Late Pamphlet against Stage-entertainments*. (Repr. in Hooker 1939–43.)
—— (1728), *Remarks on Mr. Pope's Rape of the Lock ... With a Preface, Occasion'd by the Late Treatise on the Profund, and the Dunciad*. (Facsimile in *Popeiana* (1974–5), vol. 7, omitting dedication to George Duckett; repr. in Hooker 1939–43. See Guerinot 1969: 135–40.)
—— (1729), *Remarks upon ... the Dunciad*. (Facsimile in *Popeiana* (1974–5), vol. 8; repr. in Hooker 1939–43. See Guerinot 1969: 173–7.)
——: for *Critical Works*, see Hooker 1939–43.
——: see *A True Character of Mr. Pope* 1716.
Derham, William (1715), *Astro-Theology: or, A Demonstration of the Being and Attributes of God, from a Survey of the Heavens*.
Descartes: see Cottingham 1985–91.
Deutsch, Otto Erich (1955), *Handel: A Documentary Biography*.
Dickinson, H.T. (1970), *Bolingbroke*.
Dillenius, Johann Jacob (1741), *Historia muscorum, in qua circiter sexcentae species veteres et novae ad sua genera relatae describuntur et iconibus genuinis illustrantur*, Oxford.
Dillon, Wentworth, Earl of Roscommon (1749), *The Poetical Works*, Glasgow.
Diodorus Siculus: see Oldfather 1933–67.
The Discovery of a World in the Moone: or, A Discourse Tending to Prove, that 'tis Probable there may be another Habitable World in that Planet (1638), by John Wilkins.
The Dispensary; A Poem (1699), by Sir Samuel Garth. Text cited from Lord 1963–75: VI, 58–128.
A Dissertation upon Parties (1735), by Henry St John, Viscount Bolingbroke, repr. from *The Craftsman*.
Dobson, Michael (1992), *The Making of the National Poet: Shakespeare, Adaptation and Authorship, 1660–1769*, Oxford.
Donne, John: for *Satires, Epigrams and Verse Letters*, see Milgate 1967.
Doody, Margaret Anne (1985), *The Daring Muse: Augustan Poetry Reconsidered*, Cambridge.
Dorris, George E. (1967), *Paolo Rolli and the Italian Circle in London, 1715–1744*, Studies in Italian Literature II, The Hague and Paris.
Douglas, David C. (1939), *English Scholars*.
Douglas, James (1739), *Catalogus editionum Quinti Horatii Flacci ... quae in bibliotheca Jacobi Douglas ... adservantur*.
Downie, J.A., and Thomas N. Corns, eds (1993), *Telling People what to Think: Early Eighteenth-Century Periodicals from 'The Review' to 'The Rambler'*. (First published as *Prose Studies* 16, no. 1.)
A Dramatic Entertainment, Call'd Harlequin a Sorcerer: With the Loves of Pluto and Proserpine (1725), by Lewis Theobald. (For revised issue under the author's name, see Theobald 1727.)
Drury, G. Thorn, ed. (1893), *The Poems of Edmund Waller*, 2 vols, The Muses' Library.
Dryden, John: for *Letters*, see Ward 1942.
——: for *Poems*, see Kinsley 1958.
——: for *Works*, see Hooker 1956–89.
Drydeniana (1974–5), 12 vols, The Life and Times of Seven Major British Writers, Garland Publishing. (Facsimiles of original publications relating to Dryden.)
Duckett, George: see Dennis 1728.
——: see *Homerides: or, A Letter to Mr. Pope* 1715.
——: see *Pasquin*.
Duff, J.D., ed. and trans. (1928), *Lucan, The Civil War*, LCL 220.
The Dunciad Dissected: see *Codrus: or, The Dunciad Dissected* 1728.

The Dunciad. An Heroic Poem. In Three Books (1728), by Alexander Pope. (Three books of verse, Tibbald as hero, no commentary. Griffith (*Bibliography*) 198 etc.; Foxon (*English Verse*) P764 etc. For discussion and facsimile, see Vander Meulen 1991.)

The Dunciad, Variorum (1729), by Alexander Pope. (Three books of verse, Tibbald as hero, commentary added. Griffith (*Bibliography*) 211 etc.; Foxon P771 etc. For discussion and facsimile, see Root 1929; a further facsimile was published by the Scolar Press in 1966.)

The Dunciad, in Four Books (1743), by Alexander Pope. (Four books, Cibber as hero, commentary. Griffith (*Bibliography*) 578 etc.; Foxon (*English Verse*) P796 etc. The present edition is based on the fine-paper copy in the British Library, 641.l.17. For the 1742 publication of what would become Book IV, see *The New Dunciad* 1742. For a preliminary octavo of the four-book version, see Pope 1743, 1742 (*The Works ... Vol. III. Part I*).

Dunlap, Rhodes, ed. (1949), *The Poems of Thomas Carew*, Oxford.

Dunton, John: see *The Hazard of a Death-Bed-Repentance* 1708.

——: see *Neck or Nothing* 1713.

D'Urfey, Thomas (1691), *Love for Money: or, The Boarding School*, London.

—— (1692), *The Marriage Hater Match'd.*

Durgen: or, A Plain Satyr upon a Pompous Satyrist (1728), by Edward Ward. Issued in December 1728, bearing date of 1729 on title. (Facsimile in *Popeiana* (1974–5), vol. 8; see Guerinot 1969: 157–9.)

The Duumvirate (*c.*1704), by John Caryll, n.p. (For attribution, see Erskine-Hill 1996: 102.)

Dyce: for Dyce 7747 see list of short titles.

E.B.: see B., E.

Edmonds, J.M., ed. and trans. (1912), *The Greek Bucolic Poets*, LCL 28.

Ehrenpreis, Irvin (1960–83), *Swift: The Man, his Works, and the Age*, 3 vols.

Elwin, Whitwell, and William John Courthope, eds (1871–86), *The Works of Alexander Pope*, 10 vols (*The Dunciad* is in Vol. IV).

Emendationes in Menandri et Philemonis reliquias . . . auctore Phileleuthero Lipsiensi (1710) by Richard Bentley, Amsterdam.

English, Sarah (1979), 'John Rich and the pease: a footnote to "The Dunciad" ', *NQ* 224, 533–4.

Eoganesius, Janus Junius (1720), *Pantheisticon. Sive formula celebrandae sodalitatis Socraticae*, by John Toland, 'Cosmopoli'.

An Epistle from a Nobleman to a Doctor of Divinity (1733), by John, Lord Hervey. (See Guerinot 1969: 239–41.)

An Epistle to Eustace Budgell Esq; Occasioned by the Death of the Late Dr. Tindall (1734).

An Epistle to Mr. Pope, On Reading his Translations of the Iliad and Odyssy (1731). (Facsimile in *Popeiana* (1974–5), vol. 3, sometimes attributed to Walter Harte. For doubts of the attribution, see Guerinot 1969: 199–201.)

An Epistle to Mr. Welsted; And a Satyre on the English Translations of Homer (1721), by Bezaleel Morrice.

An Epistle to the ... Earl of Dorset (1690), by Charles Montagu, Earl of Halifax.

Erasmus: see Levi 1971.

Erskine-Hill, Howard, (1962), 'The "new world" of Pope's *Dunciad*', *Renaissance and Modern Studies* 6, 47–67. Repr. in Mack 1964: 739–60.

—— (1972a), 'Pope and the financial revolution', in *Writers and their Background: Alexander Pope*, ed. Peter Dixon, 200–29, Athens, Ohio.

*—— (1972b), *Pope: 'The Dunciad'.*

—— (1975), *The Social Milieu of Alexander Pope: Lives, Example, and the Poetic Response.*

—— (1983), *The Augustan Idea in English Literature.*
—— (1988), 'Life into letters, death into art: Pope's epitaph on Francis Atterbury', *Yearbook of English Studies* 18, 200–20.
*—— (1996), *Poetry of Opposition and Revolution, Dryden to Wordsworth*, Oxford.
An Essay on the Dunciad. An Heroick Poem (1728). (Facsimile in *Popeiana* (1974–5), vol. 7. See Guerinot 1969: 127–9.)
An Essay on the Universe: A Poem (1733). (By Bezaleel Morrice, who had signed the dedication when the poem was first printed in 1725.)
An Essay towards the Character of her Late Majesty Caroline (1738), by Alured Clarke.
An Essay upon the Taste and Writings of the Present Times (1728), 'by a Gentleman of C.C., [Christ Church] Oxon.'. (See Guerinot 1969: 130–31.)
Eunomus: or, Dialogues Concerning the Law and Constitution of England (1768), by Edward Wynne, 4 vols.
Evans, A.W. (1932), *Warburton and the Warburtonians: A Study in some Eighteenth-Century Controversies*, Oxford.
Evans, Maurice, ed. (1977), *Sir Philip Sidney: The Countess of Pembroke's Arcadia*, Harmondsworth.
Evelyn-White, Hugh G., ed. and trans. (1936), *Hesiod*, rev. D.L. Page, LCL 57.

The Fable of the Bees: or, Private Vices, Publick Benefits (1714), by Bernard Mandeville.
Faction Display'd (1704), by William Shippen.
Fairclough, H.R., ed. and trans. (1926), *Horace: Satires, Epistles, Ars Poetica*, LCL 194.
——, ed. and trans. (1935, 1934), *Virgil*, rev. edn, 2 vols, LCL 63–4.
Farmer Pope and his Son (1728): see *Codrus* 1728.
Faulkner, Thomas C., and Rhonda L. Blair (1980), 'The classical and mythographic sources of Pope's Dulness', *HLQ* 43, 213–46.
The Female Dunciad ... being a Continuation of the Twickenham Hotch-Potch (1728). (Facsimile in *Popeiana* (1974–5), vol. 7. Attributed by Pope to Edmund Curll: see Guerinot 1969: 142–4.)
Fielding, Henry (1730), *The Author's Farce ... Written by Scriblerus Secundus* (i.e. Henry Fielding).
—— (1736), *Pasquin.*
—— ([1737]), *The Historical Register, for the year 1736 ... by the Author of Pasquin* (i.e. Henry Fielding).
——: see *The Champion.*
Firmager, Gabrielle M., ed. (1993), *The Female Spectator: Being selections from Mrs Eliza Haywood's periodical, first published in monthly parts (1744–6).*
Fitzgerald, C.P. (1986), *China: A Short Cultural History.*
Fitzgerald, John T., and L. Michael White, eds and trans (1983), *The Tabula of Cebes*, Society of Biblical Literature: Texts and Translations, Chico, Calif.
The Flying-Post from Paris and Amsterdam, ed. George Ridpath *et al.* Issued 1695; continued as *The Flying-Post*, 1695–6, then as *The Flying-Post: or, The Post-Master*, 1696–1733.
The Flying-Post: or, Weekly Medley, French and English, ed. J.M. Smith, James Ralph. Issued 1728–9; continued as *The Weekly Medley*, 1729, then as *Weekly Medley and Literary Journal*, 1729–30.
Foerster, Richard, ed. (1903–23), *Libanii opera*, 12 vols, Bibliotheca Scriptorum Graecorum et Romanorum Teubneriana, Leipzig.
Fog's Weekly Journal: see *The Weekly Journal: or, Saturday's Post.*
Fone, B.R.S., ed. (1968), *An Apology for the Life of Colley Cibber ... Written by Himself*, Ann Arbor, Mich. (From the first edition, in quarto, 1740.)

Fowler, Alastair (1959), 'Six knights at Castle Joyous', *SP* 56, 583–99.
—— ed. (1998), *John Milton: Paradise Lost*, 2nd edn, Harlow.
Foxon, David (1964), *Libertine Literature in England, 1660–1745*.
—— (1975), *English Verse, 1701–1750*, 2 vols, Cambridge.
*—— (1991), *Pope and the Early Eighteenth-Century Book Trade*, rev. James McLaverty, Oxford.
*Francus, Marilyn (1994), 'The monstrous mother: reproductive anxiety in Swift and Pope', *ELH* 61, 829–51.
Fraser, Sir William Augustus, ed. (1876), *Notes on the Poems of Alexander Pope, by Horatio Earl of Orford* (i.e. Horace Walpole).
The Freeholder: see Leheny 1979.
The Free-thinker (1722–3), by Ambrose Philips *et al.*, 3 vols.
Friedman, Arthur (1949), 'Pope and deism', in Clifford & Landa 1949: 89–95.
Fuller, John, ed. (1983), *John Gay: Dramatic Works*, 2 vols, Oxford.
A Further Report from the Committee of Secresy, Appointed to Enquire into the Conduct of Robert Earl of Orford (1742). (Many of the frequent impressions printed in this year lack Appendix 13, which details government subsidies to newspapers.)
Fyfe, W. Hamilton, and W. Rhys Roberts, eds and trans (1932), *Aristotle: The Poetics; Longinus on the Sublime; Demetrius on Style*, rev. edn, LCL 199.

Garapon, Robert, ed. (1962), *La Bruyère: Les Charactères de Théophraste traduits du grec, avec Les Charactères ou les moeurs de ce siècle*, Paris.
Garth, Sir Samuel: see *Claremont* 1715.
——: see *The Dispensary* 1699.
Gay, John: for *Dramatic Works*, see Fuller 1983.
——: for *Letters*, see Burgess 1966.
——: for *Poetry and Prose*, see Dearing 1974.
Gay, 'Joseph': see *The Confederates* 1717.
GEC: for *The Complete Peerage*, see Gibbs 1910–40.
Geer, Charles de (1752–78), *Mémoires pour servir à l'histoire des insectes*, 7 vols, Stockholm.
The Gentleman's Magazine: or, Monthly Intelligencer, ed. Edward Cave. Issued monthly from 1731, each year's issues being continuously paginated.
Geoffrey of Monmouth: for *The British History*, see Thompson 1718.
*Gerrard, Christine (1994), *The Patriot Opposition to Walpole: Politics, Poetry, and National Myth, 1725–1742*, Oxford.
Gibbs, Vicary, *et al.*, eds (1910–40), *The Complete Peerage*, by G[eorge] E[dward] C[okayne], 13 vols.
Gibson, Elizabeth (1989), *The Royal Academy of Music, 1719–1728: The Institution and its Directors*, Outstanding Dissertations in Music from British Universities.
Gildon, Charles (1718), *The Complete Art of Poetry*, 2 vols.
—— (1721), *The Laws of Poetry, as Laid Down by the Duke of Buckinghamshire ..., the Earl of Roscommon ... and by the Lord Lansdowne.*
——: see *Memoirs of the Life of William Wycherley* 1718.
——: for *The Miscellaneous Works of Charles Blount*, see 'Lindamour' 1695.
——: see *A New Rehearsal* 1714.
——: see Blount & Gildon 1693.
——: see *A True Character of Mr. Pope* 1716.
Gillispie, Charles Coulston, ed. (1972), *Dictionary of Scientific Biography*, 16 vols, New York.
Gneiting, Teona Tone (1975), 'Pictorial imagery and satiric inversion in Pope's *Dunciad*', *Eighteenth-Century Studies* 8, 420–30.

Godley, A.D., ed. and trans. (1920–24), *Herodotus*, 4 vols, LCL 117–20.
*Goldgar, Bertrand A. (1976), *Walpole and the Wits: The Relation of Politics to Literature, 1722–1742.*
Goold, G.P., ed. and trans. (1990), *Propertius: Elegies*, LCL 18.
Gordon, Thomas: see *The Independent Whig* 1720–21.
Gough, Alfred B., ed. (1915), *Abraham Cowley: The Essays and Other Prose Writings*, Oxford.
Granville, George, Lord Lansdowne: see *The British Enchanters* 1706.
Grassineau, James (1740), *A Musical Dictionary* (from the French of Sébastien Brossard).
Graves, Richard: for *The Spiritual Quixote*, see Tracy 1967.
Griffin, Dustin (1986), *Regaining Paradise: Milton and the Eighteenth Century*, Cambridge.
Griffith, Reginald H. (1922–7), *Alexander Pope: A Bibliography*, 2 vols, Austin, Texas.
Grosart, Alexander B., ed. (1885–96), *The Complete Works in Verse and Prose of Samuel Daniel*, 5 vols, printed for private circulation.
The Grub Street Journal. Issued 1730–37.
The Grumbler, by Thomas Burnet. Issued 1715.
Grundy, Isobel: see Halsband & Grundy 1977.
The Guardian: see Stephens 1982.
Gubar, Susan (1977), 'The female monster in Augustan satire', *Signs* 3, 380–94.
Guerinot, J.V. (1969), *Pamphlet Attacks on Alexander Pope, 1711–1744: A Descriptive Bibliography*, New York.
Gulliveriana: or, A Fourth Volume of Miscellanies ... To which is added, Alexanderiana (1728). (Facsimile in *Swiftiana* (1974–5), vol. 8. Attributed by Pope to Jonathan Smedley: see Guerinot 1969: 144–8.)
Guthkelch, A.C., ed. (1914), *The Miscellaneous Works of Joseph Addison*, 3 vols.

Hackney, Iscariot: see *An Author to be Lett* 1729.
Haig, Robert L. (1960), *The Gazetteer, 1735–1797: A Study in the Eighteenth-Century English Newspaper*, Carbondale, Ill.
Halifax, Charles Montagu, Earl of (1690): see *An Epistle to the ... Earl of Dorset* 1690.
Halsband, Robert (1960), *The Life of Lady Mary Wortley Montagu*, Oxford.
—— (1973), *Lord Hervey: Eighteenth-Century Courtier*, Oxford.
Halsband, Robert, and Isobel Grundy (1977), *Essays and Poems; and, Simplicity, a Comedy*, Oxford.
Hamilton, A.C., ed. (1990), *The Spenser Encyclopaedia.*
Hammond, Brean (1984), *Pope and Bolingbroke: A Study of Friendship and Influence*, Columbia.
*—— (1986), *Pope*, Harvester New Readings, Brighton.
—— (1990), '"Guard the sure barrier": Pope and the partitioning of culture', in *Pope: New Contexts*, ed. David Fairer, 225–40.
*—— (1997), *Professional Imaginative Writing in England, 1670–1740: 'Hackney for Bread'*, Oxford.
Hammond, James: see *Love Elegies* 1743.
Handasyde, Elizabeth (1933), *Granville the Polite: The Life of George Granville, Lord Lansdowne, 1666–1735*, Oxford.
Hanmer, Sir Thomas, ed. (1743–4), *The Works of Shakespear*, 6 vols, Oxford.
Hanson, Laurence (1936), *Government and the Press, 1695–1763.*
Harbin, George: see *The Hereditary Right* 1713.
Harlequin a Sorcerer: see *A Dramatic Entertainment* 1725.
Harmon, A.M., K. Kilburn and M.D. Macleod, eds and trans (1913–67), *Lucian*, 8 vols, LCL 14, 54, 130, 162, 302, 430–32.

Harris, Michael (1987), *London Newspapers in the Age of Walpole: A Study of the Origins of the Modern English Press.*
Harte, Walter (1727), *Poems on Several Occasions.*
—— (1730), *An Essay on Satire, particularly on the Dunciad.* (Facsimile in *Popeiana* (1974–5), vol. 10.)
——: see *An Epistle to Mr. Pope, On Reading his Translations of the Iliad and Odyssy* 1731.
Hauser, David R. (1961), 'Medea's strain and Hermes' wand: Pope's use of mythology', *MLN* 76, 224–9.
Haywood, Eliza (1724), *Secret Histories, Novels and Poems,* 4 vols.
—— (1725), *Memoirs of a Certain Island adjacent to the Kingdom of Utopia.*
—— (1727), *The Secret History of the Present Intrigues of the Court of Carimania.*
——: see *Memoirs of the Court of Lilliput* 1727.
——: see Firmager 1993.
The Hazard of a Death-Bed-Repentance (1708), by John Dunton.
Hearne, Thomas, ed. (1724), *Robert of Gloucester's Chronicle,* 2 vols, Oxford.
Henley, John (1728), *Oratory Transactions N° 1. to be occasionally publish'd, by J. Henley, M.A.*
——: see *The Hyp-Doctor.*
The Hereditary Right of the Crown of England Asserted (1713), by George Harbin. (Hilkiah Bedford, the probable editor, was convicted as its author when the work was condemned as seditious.)
Herford, C.H., and Percy Simpson, eds (1925–52), *Ben Jonson,* 11 vols, Oxford.
Herodotus: see Godley 1920–24.
Hervey, John Lord: see *Some Remarks on the Minute Philosopher* 1732.
——: see *An Epistle from a Nobleman to a Doctor of Divinity* 1733.
——: see *Verses Address'd to the Imitator of ... Horace* 1733.
——: see *A Letter to Mr. C—b—r, on his Letter to Mr. P—* 1742.
——: for *Memoirs,* see Sedgwick 1931.
Hesiod: see Cooke 1728, Evelyn-White 1936.
The High German Doctor, ed. Philip Horneck. Issued 1714–15.
Hill, Aaron: see *A Collection of Several Curious Pieces* 1728.
Hill, George Birkbeck, ed. (1905), *Lives of the English Poets by Samuel Johnson,* 3 vols, Oxford.
——, ed. (1934–5), *Boswell's Life of Johnson,* rev. L.F. Powell, 6 vols, Oxford.
An Historical Rhapsody on Mr. Pope (1782), by Thomas Tyers, 2nd edn.
The History of England, during the Reigns of the Royal House of Stuart. Wherein the Errors of Late Histories are Discover'd ... With some Account of the Liberties Taken with Clarendon's History before it Came to the Press (1730), by John Oldmixon.
The History of the Reign of Queen Anne, Digested into Annals (1711–13), by Abel Boyer, 11 vols.
Hoadly, Benjamin (1717), *The Nature of the Kingdom, or Church, of Christ: A Sermon Preach'd before the King.*
Hobbes, Thomas, trans. (1676), *Homer's Iliads in English.*
——: for *Leviathan,* see Oakeshott 1946.
Hodges, John C. (1936), 'Pope's debt to one of his dunces', *MLN* 51, 154–8.
Hollingshead, Greg (1982–3), 'Bishop Berkeley and the Gloomy Clerk: Pope's final satire on deism', *Durham University Journal* 75, 19–27.
Homer: for *Homeri Ilias & Odyssea,* see Barnes 1711.
——: for *The Iliad,* see Murray 1924–5.

——: for *The Iliad of Homer Prince of Poets*, see Chapman 1611.
——: for *The Odyssey*, see Murray 1919.
Homerides: or, A Letter to Mr. Pope, Occasion'd by his Intended Translation of Homer (1715). (Facsimile in *Popeiana* (1974–5), vol. 2, which also gives the version of 1716. By Thomas Burnet and George Duckett: see Guerinot 1969: 20–23.)
Homer's Battle of the Frogs and Mice. With the Remarks of Zoilus (1717), by Thomas Parnell.
Hooker, Edward Niles, ed. (1939–43), *The Critical Works of John Dennis*, 2 vols, Baltimore.
Hooker, Edward Niles, *et al.*, eds (1956–89), *The Works of John Dryden*, 20 vols, Berkeley and Los Angeles.
Hopkins, Robert H. (1966), '"The Good Old Cause" in Pope, Addison, and Steele', *RES* 17, 62–8.
Horace: for *Satires, Epistles, Ars Poetica*, see Fairclough 1926.
——: for *Odes, Epodes*, see Bennett 1968.
Horneck, Philip: see *The High German Doctor*.
Howard, William J. (1968), 'The mystery of the Cibberian *Dunciad*', *SEL* 8, 463–74.
Howatson, M.C. (1993), *The Oxford Companion to Classical Literature*, 2nd edn, Oxford.
Hughes, John: see *A Complete History of England* 1706.
Hume, Robert D. (1988), *Henry Fielding and the London Theatre, 1728–1737*, Oxford.
Hunter, J. Paul (1990), *Before Novels: The Cultural Contexts of Eighteenth-Century English Fiction*.
Hyde, Edward, Earl of Clarendon (1702–4), *The History of the Rebellion and Civil Wars in England*, 3 vols, Oxford.
——: for *The History of the Rebellion*, see also Macray 1888.
*Hyde, Ralph, ed. (1981), *The A–Z of Georgian London*, Lympne Castle, Kent. (Derived from John Rocque's *Plan of the Cities of London and Westminster and Borough of Southwark* (1746 on title, actually 1747).)
Hyland, Paul, ed. (1993), *Ned Ward: The London Spy*, East Lansing.
A Hymn to the Creator. Written by a Gentleman, on the Occasion of the Death of his Only Daughter (1727), by Leonard Welsted.
The Hyp-Doctor, by 'Sir Isaac Ratcliffe of Elbow Lane' (John Henley). Issued 1730–41; subtitles vary.

The Independent Whig, issued 1720–21 by Thomas Gordon, possibly with John Trenchard.
*Ingrassia, Catherine (1991), 'Women writing/writing women: Pope, Dulness, and "feminization" in the *Dunciad*', *Eighteenth-Century Life* 14, 40–58.
An Inquiry concerning Virtue (1699), by Anthony Ashley Cooper, third Earl of Shaftesbury.

J., W., trans. (1695), *Monsieur Bossu's Treatise of the Epick Poem ... Done into English from the French ... by W.J. ... to which are Added, An Essay upon Satyr, by Monsieur D'Acier; and A Treatise upon Pastorals, by Monsieur Fontanelle.*
Jack, Ian (1942), *Augustan Satire: Intention and Idiom in English Poetry, 1660–1750*, Oxford.
Jacob, Giles (1719–20), *The Poetical Register: or, The Lives and Characters of the English Dramatic Poets*. (Vol. II is entitled *An Historical Account of the Lives and Writings of our most Considerable English Poets*. See Guerinot 1969: 72–3.)
—— (1744), *A Law Grammar: or, Rudiments of the Law*.
——: for *Lives*, see Jacob 1719–20, Vol. II.
——: see *The Mirrour* 1733.
Jacobs, Margaret (1981), *The Radical Enlightenment: Pantheists, Freemasons and Republicans*.
Jarvis, Charles: see Riley 1992.

*Jarvis, Simon (1995), *Scholars and Gentlemen: Shakespearian Textual Criticism and Representations of Scholarly Labour, 1725–1765*, Oxford.

J.B.: see B., J.

Jebb, R.C. (1902), *Bentley*, English Men of Letters.

Jenkins, Harold (1952), *Edward Benlowes (1602–1676): Biography of a Minor Poet.*

Jervas, Charles: see Riley 1992.

Johnson, Richard (1717), *Aristarchus anti-Bentleianus quadriginta sex Bentleii errores super Q. Horatii Flacci odarum libro primo ... ostendens*, 2 vols, Nottingham.

Johnson, Samuel: for *Lives of the English Poets*, see Hill 1905.

Johnston, Arthur, trans. (1741), *Psalmorum Davidis paraphrasis poetica*, ed. William Benson.

*Jones, Emrys (1968), 'Pope and Dulness', *PBA* 54, 231–63, repr. in Mack & Winn 1980: 612–51.

Jones, George Hilton (1954), *The Main Stream of Jacobitism*, Cambridge, Mass.

Jones, Inigo: see Kent 1727.

Jones, R.F. (1919), *Lewis Theobald: His Contribution to English Scholarship, with some Unpublished Letters*, Columbia, Ohio.

Jonson, Ben: see Herford & Simpson 1925–52.

Jovius, Paulus (1557), *Elogia doctorum virorum ab avorum memoria publicatis ingenii monumentis illustrium*, Antwerp.

Juvenal: see Ramsay 1969.

Keener, Frederick M. (1991), 'Pope, *The Dunciad*, Virgil, and the new historicism of Le Bossu', *Eighteenth-Century Life* 15, 37–57.

Kennett, White: see *A Complete History of England* 1706.

Kent, William, ed. (1727), *The Designs of Inigo Jones*, 2 vols.

Ker, Walter C.A., ed. and trans. (1925), *Martial: Epigrams*, 2 vols, LCL 94–5.

Kerby-Miller, Charles, ed. (1950), *Memoirs of the Extraordinary Life, Works, and Discoveries of Martinus Scriblerus*, New York.

A Key (With the Whip) to Open the Mystery and Iniquity of the Poem called Absolom and Achitophel (1682). (Facsimile in *Drydeniana* (1974–5), vol. 6.)

King, William: see *Rufinus* 1712.

Kingsford, Charles Lethbridge, ed. (1971), *A Survey of London*, by John Stow, 2 vols, repr. from the text of 1603, Oxford.

Kinsley, James, ed. (1958), *The Poems of John Dryden*, 4 vols, Oxford.

*Kinsley, William (1971), 'The *Dunciad* as mock-book', *HLQ* 35, 29–47; repr. in Mack & Winn 1980: 707–30.

—— (1975), 'Physico-demonology in Pope's "Dunciad"', *MLR* 70, 20–31.

Kippis, Andrew, and Joseph Towers, eds (1778–95), *Biographia Britannica: or, The Lives of the Most Eminent Persons who have Flourished in Great Britain and Ireland*, 2nd edn, only 6 vols published.

Klein, Lawrence E. (1994), *Shaftesbury and the Culture of Politeness*, Cambridge.

Knecht, Robert (1991), *Richelieu.*

Knight, Charles (1842), *London.*

*Koon, Helene (1986), *Colley Cibber: A Biography*, Lexington, Ky.

Kowalk, Wolfgang (1981), *Alexander Pope: An Annotated Bibliography of Twentieth-Century Criticism, 1900–1979*, Frankfurt.

Kropf, C.R. (1973), 'Education and the Neoplatonic idea of Wisdom in Pope's *Dunciad*', *Texas Studies in Literature and Language* 14, 593–604.

Küster, Ludolph, ed. (1705), *Suidae lexicon*, 3 vols, Cambridge.

La Bruyère: for *Les Charactères*, see Garapon 1962.
Lactantius: see Migne 1844.
Langbaine, Gerard (1691), *An Account of the English Dramatic Poets*, Oxford.
Langford, Paul (1988), 'Convocation and the Tory clergy, 1717–61', in *The Jacobite Challenge*, ed. Eveline Cruickshanks and Jeremy Black, Edinburgh, 107–22.
LaRue, C. Steven (1995), *Handel and his Singers: The Creation of the Royal Academy Operas, 1720–1728*, Cambridge.
Laurence, John (1726), *A New System of Agriculture. Being a Complete Body of Husbandry and Gardening*.
Law, William (1726), *The Absolute Unlawfulness of the Stage-entertainment Fully Demonstrated*.
Lawler, Traugott (1974), '"Wafting Vapours from the Land of Dreams": Virgil's fourth and sixth eclogues and the *Dunciad*', *SEL* 14, 373–86, repr. in Mack & Winn 1980: 731–48.
Le Bossu, René (1695), *Traité du poème épique*, 2 vols, Paris.
——: for a translation of the above work, see J. 1695.
Leheny, James, ed. (1979), *The Freeholder*, by Joseph Addison (originally published 1715–16), Oxford.
Lepre, J.P. (1990), *The Egyptian Pyramids: A Comprehensive, Illustrated Reference*.
Leranbaum, Miriam (1977), *Alexander Pope's 'Opus Magnum', 1729–1744*, Oxford.
A Letter from the Facetious Doctor Andrew Tripe (1714). (Attributed to Pope in *A True Character of Mr. Pope*, and by Pope to William Wagstaffe.)
A Letter to Mr. C–b–r, on his Letter to Mr. P— (1742), by John Lord Hervey. (Facsimile in *Popeiana* (1974–5), vol. 15. See Guerinot 1969: 295–8.)
A Letter to Mr. Pope, Occasioned by Sober Advice from Horace (1735), by Thomas Bentley. (See Guerinot 1969: 251–4.)
A Letter to Polly. To One of her Own tunes (1728).
Letters in Prose and Verse, to the Celebrated Polly Peachum (1728).
Levi, A.H.T., trans. (1971), *Erasmus: The Praise of Folly*, Harmondsworth.
Levine, Joseph (1977), *Dr. Woodward's Shield: History, Science, and Satire in Augustan England*.
*—— (1991), *The Battle of the Books: History and Literature in the Augustan Age*.
Lewis, David, ed. and contributor (1730), *Miscellaneous Poems*.
Lewis, Peter, and Nigel Wood (1989), *John Gay and the Scriblerians*.
Lewis, W.S., ed. (1937–83), *The Yale Edition of Horace Walpole's 'Correspondence'*, 48 vols, Oxford.
Libanius: see Foerster 1903–23.
The Life of John Buncle (1770), by Thomas Amory, 4 vols.
The Life of Lavinia Beswick, alias Fenton, alias Polly Peachum (1728).
'Lindamour', pseud., ed. (1695), *The Miscellaneous Works of Charles Blount*. ('Lindamour' was Charles Gildon.)
Lindsay, Wallace M., ed. (1913), *Sexti Pompei Festi de verborum significatu quae supersunt*, Leipzig.
Loane, G.G. (1944), 'Remarks on the new Pope', *NQ* 186, 36–7.
**London and its Environs Described* (1761), published by R. and J. Dodsley, 6 vols. (Fold-out map in Vol. IV.)
The London Journal: see *The Thursday's Journal*.
The London Spy: see Hyland 1993.
Longinus: see Welsted 1712.
——: see Fyfe & Roberts 1932.

Lonsdale, Roger (1965), *Dr. Charles Burney: A Literary Biography*, Oxford.
——, ed. (1989), *Eighteenth-Century Women Poets: An Anthology*, Oxford.
Lord, George deF., *et al.*, eds (1963–75), *Poems on Affairs of State: Augustan Satirical Verse, 1660–1714*, 7 vols.
Lounsbury, T.R. (1906), *The Text of Shakespeare*, New York.
Love Elegies. Written in the Year 1732 (1743 [1742]), by James Hammond.
Lovelace, Richard: see Wilkinson 1930.
Lucan: see Duff 1928.
Lucian: see Harmon, Kilburn & Macleod 1913–67.
Lucretius: see Smith 1975.
Lund, Roger D. (1984), '*Rufinus* and the *Dunciad*: Pope's debt to William King', *Papers on Language and Literature* 20, 293–300.
—— (1991), 'From oblivion to Dulness: Pope and the poetics of appropriation', *British Journal for Eighteenth-Century Studies* 14, 171–89.
—— (1998), 'The eel of science: index learning, Scriblerian satire, and the rise of information culture', *Eighteenth Century Life* 22, 18–42.

McAdam, E.L., ed. (1958), *Samuel Johnson: Diaries, Prayers, and Annuals*, The Yale Edition of the Works of Samuel Johnson I, Oxford.
*Mack, Maynard, ed. (1964), *Essential Articles for the Study of Alexander Pope*.
*—— (1969), *The Garden and the City: Retirement and Politics in the Later Poetry of Pope*.
—— (1979), 'Pope's copy of Chaucer', in *Evidence in Literary Scholarship: Essays in Memory of James Marshall Osborn*, ed. René Wellek and Alvaro Ribeiro, Oxford, 105–21.
—— (1982), *Collected in Himself: Essays Critical, Biographical, and Bibliographical on Pope and Some of his Contemporaries*.
—— (1984), *The Last and Greatest Art: Some Unpublished Poetical Manuscripts of Alexander Pope*.
*—— (1985), *Alexander Pope: A Life*.
*Mack, Maynard, and James A. Winn, eds (1980), *Pope: Recent Essays by Several Hands*, Brighton.
Mackail, J.W. (1924–5), 'Bentley's Milton', Warton Lecture on English Poetry XV, *PBA* XI, 55–73.
Mackenzie, Alan T. (1976), 'The solemn owl and the laden ass: the iconography of the frontispieces to *The Dunciad*', *Harvard Library Bulletin* 29, 25–39.
McKenzie, D.F. (1966), *The Cambridge University Press, 1696–1712*, 2 vols, Cambridge.
*McLaverty, James (1984), 'The mode of existence of literary works of art: the case of the *Dunciad Variorum*', *Studies in Bibliography* 37, 82–105, Charlottesville, Virginia.
—— (1985), 'Pope and Giles Jacob's *Lives of the Poets*: the *Dunciad* as alternative literary history', *MP* 83, 22–32.
—— (1993), 'Facsimiles and the bibliographer: Pope's *Dunciad*', *Review* 15, 1–15.
——: for *Pope and the Early Eighteenth-Century Book Trade*, see Foxon 1991.
Macray, W. Dunn, ed. (1888), *The History of the Rebellion and Civil Wars in England ... by Edward, Earl of Clarendon*, 6 vols, Oxford.
Maitland, William (1739), *The History of London, from its Foundation by the Romans, to the Present Time*.
Mallet, David: see *Of Verbal Criticism* 1733.
The Man of Taste. Occasion'd by an Epistle of Mr. Pope's on that Subject. By the Author of the Art of Politicks (1733), by James Bramston.
Mandeville, Bernard: see *The Fable of the Bees* 1714.
Marshall, W.H. (1961), 'Medea's strain and Hermes' wand: Pope's use of mythology', *MLN* 76, 224–32.

Martin, Peter (1984), *Pursuing Innocent Pleasures: The Gardening World of Alexander Pope*, Hamden, Conn.

Maslen, Keith (1993), *An Early London Printing House at Work: Studies in the Bowyer Ledgers*, New York.

——: see Wise 1973.

Maslen, Keith, and John Lancaster, eds (1991), *The Bowyer Ledgers ... reproduced on Microfiche with a Checklist of Bowyer Printing, 1699–1777.*

Mather, Cotton (1726), *Manuductio ad ministerium. Directions for a Candidate of the Ministry*, Boston, Mass.

Maxwell, J.C. (1962), '"Look ... what": a late instance', *NQ* 207, 19.

Maxwell, J.C., and E.G. Stanley (1967), 'An echo of Dryden in Pope', *NQ* 212, 146.

—— (1971), 'Partridges in Pope and Chapman', *NQ* 216, 156.

Means, J.A. (1973), 'Pope's butterfly-collector: "Dandridge the Aurelian"', *NQ* 218, 209–11.

Means, James (1983), 'Pope's silkworm and Dryden', *NQ* 228, 509.

Memoirs of the Court of Lilliput (1727), attributed by Pope to Eliza Haywood. (See Guerinot 1969: 99.)

Memoirs of the Life of ... Philip ... Duke of Wharton. By an impartial hand. (1731).

Memoirs of the Life of William Wycherley (1718), by Charles Gildon. (See Guerinot 1969: 71–2.)

Mengel, Elias F. (1973), 'The Dunciad illustrations', *Eighteenth-Century Studies* 7, 161–78, repr. in Mack & Winn 1980: 749–73.

Mercer, Frank, ed. (1935), *A General History of Music ... by Charles Burney*, 2 vols.

The Metamorphosis: A Poem (1728). (Attributed by Pope to Jonathan Smedley; see Guerinot 1969: 133–4.)

Michelangelo: see Bull & Porter 1987.

Middleton, Conyers (1741), *The History of the Life of Marcus Tullius Cicero*, 2 vols.

Midgley, Graham (1973), *The Life of Orator Henley*, Oxford.

Migne, J.-P., *et al.*, eds (1844), *Lucii Caecilii Firmiani Lactantii opera omnia*, 2 vols, Patrologiae cursus completus 6–7, Paris.

Milbourn (1698), *Notes on Dryden's Virgil*. (Facsimile in *Drydeniana* (1974–5), vol. 12.)

Milgate, W., ed. (1967), *John Donne: The Satires, Epigrams and Verse Letters*, Oxford.

Milhous, Judith, and Robert D. Hume (1986), 'The charter for the Royal Academy of Music', *Music and Letters* 67, 50–58.

Miller, Frank Justus, ed. and trans. (1953), *Seneca's Tragedies*, 2 vols, LCL 62, 78.

——, ed. and trans. (1977–84), *Ovid: Metamorphoses*, edn rev. G.P. Goold, 2 vols, LCL 42–3.

Miller, James (1738), *Of Politeness. An Epistle ... By the Author of Harlequin Horace* (i.e. James Miller).

——: see *Are These Things So?* 1740.

Miller, Philip (1733), *The Gardeners Dictionary: Containing the Methods of Cultivating and Improving the Kitchen, Fruit and Flower Garden.*

Milton, John: for *Complete Shorter Poems*, see Carey 1968.

——: for *Paradise Lost*, see Bentley 1732; Fowler 1998.

The Mirrour ... To which is added A Legal Conviction of Mr. Alexander Pope of Dulness and Scandal (1733), by Giles Jacob. (See Guerinot 1969: 229–33.)

Miscellanea. In Two Volumes. Never before Published. Viz. I. Familiar Letters written to Henry Cromwell Esq; by Mr. Pope ... Vol. I (1727: actually 1726), published by Edmund Curll without Pope's consent and with the connivance of Elizabeth Thomas.

The Miscellany, by 'Richard Hooker, of the Temple Esq.' (William Webster). Issued 1732; continued as *The Weekly Miscellany*, 1732–41.

A Miscellany on Taste: see Theobald 1732.

Mr. Oldmixon's Reply to the Late Bishop of Rochester's Vindication ... Examin'd (1732).

Mist's Weekly Journal: see *The Weekly Journal: or, Saturday's Post.*

Moderation Display'd (1704), by William Shippen.

Monk, James Henry (1833), *The Life of Richard Bentley*, 2nd edn, 2 vols.

Monk, Samuel Holt, ed. (1963), *Five Miscellaneous Essays by Sir William Temple*, Ann Arbor, Mich.

Monmouth, Geoffrey of: for *The British History*, see Thompson 1718.

Montagu, Charles, Earl of Halifax (1690): see *An Epistle to the ... Earl of Dorset* 1690.

—— (1793), *The Poetical Works*, Edinburgh.

Montagu, Lady Mary Wortley: see *Verses Address'd to the Imitator of ... Horace* 1733.

The Moral Philosopher. In a Dialogue between Philalethes a Christian Deist, and Theophanes a Christian Jew (1737), by Thomas Morgan.

Morgan, Thomas: see *The Moral Philosopher* 1737.

——: see *A Brief Examination* 1742.

Morley, Henry (1869), *Memoirs of Bartholomew Fair.*

Morrice, Bezaleel (1721), *An Epistle to Mr. Welsted; and a Satyre on the English Translators of Homer.*

——: see *An Essay on the Universe* 1733.

——: see *On the English Translators of Homer* 1733.

Morris, David (1984), *Alexander Pope: The Genius of Sense.*

Morrison, Lois G. (1971), 'Lewis Theobald's early step to the throne of *The Dunciad*', *Scriblerian* 4, 31–3.

Moschus: see Edmonds 1912.

Motte, Andrew: see Cajori 1962.

Mottley, John: see *Penelope* 1728.

Mozley, J.H., ed. and trans. (1928), *Statius*, 2 vols, LCL 206–7.

——, ed. and trans. (1934), *Valerius Flaccus*, LCL 286.

Murray, A.T., ed. and trans. (1919), *Homer: The Odyssey*, 2 vols, LCL 104–5.

——, ed. and trans. (1924–5), *Homer: The Iliad*, 2 vols, LCL 170–71.

Murray, Oswyn (1968), 'Divine right in the *Dunciad* (IV, 175–88)', *NQ* 213, 208–11.

Nash, Mary (1977), *The Provoked Wife: The Life and Times of Susannah Cibber.*

Nash, Richard (1992), 'Translation, editing, and poetic invention in Pope's *Dunciad*', *SP* 89, 470–84.

Neck or Nothing (1713), by John Dunton.

Ness, Robert (1986), '*The Dunciad* and Italian opera in England', *Eighteenth Century Studies* 20, 173–94.

A New Ballad Inscrib'd to Polly Peachum (1728).

A New Collection of Poems Relating to State Affairs (1705).

The New Dunciad: As it was Found in the Year 1741 (1742), by Alexander Pope. (Griffith (*Bibliography*) 546 etc.; Foxon (*English Verse*) P787 etc. A single book of verse, with commentary. It forms a sequel to previous *Dunciads* and was in 1743 adapted as the fourth book of *The Dunciad in Four Books*.)

A New Rehearsal: or, Bays the Younger (1714), by Charles Gildon. (Facsimile in *Popeiana* (1974–5), vol. 2. See Guerinot 1969: 11–14.)

Newcomb, Thomas: see *Bibliotheca* 1712.

Newton, Sir Isaac: see Cajori 1962.

Nichol, Donald W. (1992), *Pope's Literary Legacy: The Book-Trade Correspondence of William Warburton and John Knapton, 1744–1780*, Oxford Bibliographical Society, Oxford.

Nichols, James, ed. (1854), *The Complete Works, Poetry and Prose, of the Rev. Edward Young*, 2 vols.
Nichols, John, ed. (1787), *The Works in Verse and Prose of Leonard Welsted.*
—— (1812–15), *Literary Anecdotes of the Eighteenth Century*, 9 vols.
—— (1817–58), *Illustrations of the Literary History of the Eighteenth Century*, 8 vols.
Nicholson, Colin (1994), *Writing and the Rise of Finance: Capital Satires of the Early Eighteenth Century*, Cambridge.
Nicolson, Marjorie, and G.S. Rousseau (1968), *'This Long Disease, My Life': Alexander Pope and the Sciences*, Princeton.
Nidditch, Peter H., ed. (1975), *John Locke: An Essay Concerning Human Understanding*, Oxford.
Nokes, David (1995), *John Gay: A Profession of Friendship*, Oxford.
Notzon, Mark (1979), 'A new source for Pope's "Dunciad", Book IV, 21–24', *NQ* 224, 543.

Oakeshott, Michael (1946), *Thomas Hobbes: Leviathan: or, The Matter, Forme and Power of a Commonwealth, Ecclesiasticall and Civil*, Oxford.
Of Verbal Criticism: An Epistle to Mr Pope, Occasioned by Theobald's Shakespear and Bentley's Milton (1733), by David Mallet.
Ogilby, John, trans. (1651), *The Fables of Aesop Paraphrasd in Vers, and Adorn'd with Sculpture.*
O'Grady, Deirdre (1986), *Alexander Pope and Eighteenth-Century Italian Poetry*, Berne, Frankfurt am Main, New York.
Oldfather, C.H., *et al.*, eds and trans (1933–67), *Diodorus of Sicily*, 12 vols, LCL 279, 303, 340, 375, 384, 399, 389, 422, 377, 390, 409, 423.
Oldham, John: see Brooks & Selden 1987.
Oldmixon, John (1700), *The Grove: or, Love's Paradice, an Opera.*
—— (1703), *The Governour of Cyprus: A Tragedy.*
—— (1728a), *An Essay on Criticism; As it regards Design, Thought, and Expression, in Prose and Verse.* (Facsimile published by Augustan Reprint Society (nos. 107–8); see Guerinot 1969: 102–4.)
—— (1728b), *The Arts of Logick and Rhetorick ... Interpreted ... By ... Father Bouhours.* (See Guerinot 1969: 140–42.)
—— (1732), *Mr. Oldmixon's Reply to the Late Bishop Atterbury's Vindication.*
——: see *Amores Britannici* 1703.
——: see *The Catholick Poet* 1716.
——: see *A Complete History of England* 1706.
——: see *The Critical History of England* 1724–6.
——: see *The History of England, during the Reigns of the Royal House of Stuart* 1730.
On the English Translators of Homer (1733), by Bezaleel Morrice.
One Epistle to Mr. A. Pope (1730), by Leonard Welsted and James Moore Smythe. (Facsimile in *Popeiana* (1974–5), vol. 10; see Guerinot 1969: 188–93.)
O'Neill, Hugh B. (1987), *Companion to Chinese History*, Oxford.
Oram, William A., *et al.*, eds (1989), *The Yale Edition of the Shorter Poems of Edmund Spenser.*
Osborn, James M., ed. (1966), *Joseph Spence: Observations, Anecdotes, and Characters of Books and Men*, 2 vols, Oxford. (Hereafter *OAC*.)
Ovid: for *Heroides and Amores*, see Showerman 1977.
——: for *Metamorphoses*, see Miller 1977–84; Sewell 1717.
Ozell, John, trans. (1708), *Boileau's Lutrin: A Mock-Heroic Poem ... render'd into English Verse.* (Dedication signed by translator.)

Ozell, John, trans. (1710), *La secchia rapita: The Trophy-bucket, A Mock-Heroic Poem.*
—— (1722), *Common-Prayer not Common Sense, in Several Places of the Portuguese, Spanish, Italian, French, Latin, and Greek Translations of the English Liturgy.*

Painter, George (1976), *William Caxton.*
Palaemon to Caelia, at Bath: or, The Triumvirate (1717), by Leonard Welsted. (See Guerinot 1969: 60–62.)
Palladio, Andrea: see Boyle 1730.
Parnell, Thomas: see *Homer's Battle of the Frogs and Mice* 1717.
——: for *Poems*, see Pope 1721.
——: for *Collected Poems*, see Rawson & Lock 1989.
——: for the misleading attribution of a translation from Anne Dacier, see Dacier 1724.
Pasquin, by George Duckett *et al*. Issued 1722–4.
Passmore, J.A. (1951), *Ralph Cudworth: An Interpretation*, Cambridge.
Paul, H.G. (1911), *John Dennis: His Life and Criticism*, New York.
Peck, A.L., ed. and trans. (1943), *Aristotle: Generation of Animals*, LCL 366.
Penelope, a Dramatic Opera (1728), by John Mottley and Thomas Cooke.
Perry, Ben Edwin, ed. and trans. (1965), *Babrius and Phaedrus*, LCL 436.
Persius: see Ramsay 1969.
Peterson, R.G. (1975), 'Renaissance classicism in Pope's *Dunciad*', *SEL* 15, 431–45.
Phaedrus: see Perry 1965.
'Philalethes' (1723), *Memoirs of the Life, and Conduct, of Dr. Francis Atterbury*, by Thomas Stackhouse.
Philips, Mr.: for *Farmer Pope and his Son*, see *Codrus* 1728.
Philips, Ambrose (1712), *The Distrest Mother. A Tragedy.*
—— (1748), *Pastorals, Epistles, Odes, and other original poems, with translations from Pindar, Anacreon, and Sappho.*
——: see *Poetical Miscellanies* 1709.
——: see *The Free-thinker* 1722–3.
Pilkington, Laetitia (1748–54), *Memoirs*, 3 vols, Dublin. (Facsimile in *Swiftiana* (1974–5), vols 17–19.)
Platnauer, Maurice, ed. and trans. (1922), *Claudian*, 2 vols, LCL 135–6.
Pliny the Elder: for *Natural History*, see Rackham 1938.
Plomer, Henry R. (1922), *A Dictionary of the Printers and Booksellers who were at Work in England, Scotland and Ireland from 1668 to 1725*, Oxford.
Plomer, H.R., G.H. Bushnell and E.R.McC. Dix (1932), *A Dictionary of the Printers and Booksellers who were at Work in England, Scotland and Ireland from 1726 to 1775*, Oxford.
Pocock, J.G.A. (1985), *Virtue, Commerce, and History: Essays on Political Thought and History, Chiefly in the Eighteenth Century*, Cambridge.
Poems on Affairs of State: see *A New Collection* 1705; Lord 1963–75.
Poetical Miscellanies: The Sixth Part (1709). (Griffith (*Bibliography*) no. 1; contains pastorals by Pope and by Ambrose Philips.)
The Political State of Great Britain ... To be continu'd monthly (1711–29), by Abel Boyer.
Polly Peachum's Jests (1728).
Pope, Alexander (1713), *Guardian* no. 40. (Repr. as Appendix V to *The Dunciad in Four Books* and in Stephens 1982.)
——, trans. (1715–20), *The Iliad of Homer*, 6 vols. William Broome contributed to the annotation.
—— (1717), *The Works of Mr. Alexander Pope.*

——, ed. (1721), *Poems on Several Occasions*, by Thomas Parnell.
——, ed. (1723), *The Works of John Sheffield ... Duke of Buckingham*, 2 vols.
——, ed. (1725; vols II–VI misdated 1723), *The Works of Shakespear in Six Volumes, Collated and Corrected by the Former Editions by Mr. Pope*, 6 vols.
——, trans. (1725–6), *The Odyssey of Homer*, 5 vols. (Elijah Fenton and William Broome did part of the translation.)
—— (1727 [1726]), *Miscellanea ... Viz. I. Familiar Letters written to Henry Cromwell Esq. ... Vol. I.*
—— (1735), *The Works of Mr. Alexander Pope. Volume II.* (Griffith 370. Contains a revised version of *The Dunciad Variorum.*)
——, ed. (1740), *Selecta Poemata Italorum qui Latine scripserunt*, 2 vols.
—— (1743, 1742), *The Works ... Vol. III. Part I. Containing the Dunciad. Now first published according to the complete copy found in the year MDCCXLI. [Part II. Containing the Dunciad, Book IV. And the memoirs of Scriblerus]* (A preliminary *Dunciad in Four Books* in octavo: for its relation to the 1743 quarto, see Vander Meulen 1989; Maslen & Lancaster 1991: Checklist nos 3080–81.)
——: for *Correspondence*, see Sherburn 1956.
——: for the *Dunciads*, regularly published without Pope's name on the title, see *The Dunciad. An Heroic Poem* 1728; *The Dunciad Variorum* 1729 and Pope 1735; *The New Dunciad* 1742; Pope 1743, 1742 (*The Works ... Vol. III*); *The Dunciad, in Four Books* 1743.
——: for *Miscellanies*, see Swift & Pope 1727.
——: for *Pastorals*, see *Poetical Miscellanies* 1709.
——: for *Poems*, see Butt 1939–69.
——: for *Prose Works*, see Ault & Cowler 1936–86.
——: for *Works*, see Bowles 1806; Elwin & Courthope 1871–86.
Pope Alexander's Supremacy and Infallibility Examin'd (1729), variously ascribed by Pope to George Duckett, Thomas Burnet and John Dennis. (Facsimile in *Popeiana* (1974–5), vol. 8; see Guerinot 1969: 166–70.)
Popeiana (1974–5), 24 vols, The Life and Times of Seven Major British Writers, Garland Publishing. (Facsimiles of original publications relating to Pope.)
The Popiad (1728), attributed by Pope to Edmund Curll. (See Guerinot 1969: 132–3.)
Popple, William (1734), *The Lady's Revenge: or, The Rover Reclaim'd. A Comedy.*
Porpora, Nicolò (1735), *The Favourite Songs in the Opera call'd Polypheme.*
The Post Boy, printed by Abel Roper. Issued, spasmodically and with title variations, 1695–1728.
Potter, John, ed. (1697), *Lycophronis ... Alexandra, cum Graecis J. Tzetzis commentariis*, Oxford.
Potter, Lois (1983), 'Cibber's *Richard III* and the end of *The Dunciad*', *NQ* 228, 509–10.
Potts, Abbie Findlay (1959), 'The case for internal evidence (7): butterflies and butterfly-hunters', *Bulletin of the New York Public Library* 63, 148–52.
A Prefatory Discourse to a New Edition of the Psalms. Translated into Latin Verse. By Dr. Arthur Johnston (1741), by William Benson.
Preston, Mr. (1715), *Aesop at the Bear-Garden: A Vision.* (Facsimile in *Popeiana* (1974–5), vol. 1. 'Mr. Preston' is apparently a pseudonym: see Guerinot 1969: 24–6.)
Prior, Sir James (1860), *Life of Edmond Malone ... with selections from his manuscript anecdotes.*
Prior, Matthew: for *Literary Works*, see Wright & Spears 1971.
Probyn, Clive T. (1979), 'Pope's bestiary', in *The Art of Alexander Pope*, ed. Howard Erskine-Hill and Anne Smith, 212–30.

The Progress of Dulness. By an Eminent Hand. Which will Serve for an Explanation of the Dunciad (1728). (Facsimile in *Popeiana* (1974–5), vol. 6. The first item is signed 'H. Stanhope', identified by Edmund Curll as William Bond; see Guerinot 1969: 122–4.)
The Prompter, ed. Aaron Hill *et al.* Issued 1734–6.
Propertius: see Goold 1990.
Prudentius: see Thomson 1949–53.
Prynne, William (1641), *Mount-Orgueil: or, Divine and Profitable Mediations.*

Quintilian: see Butler 1921–2.

Rackham, H., ed. and trans. (1938), *Pliny: Natural History*, Vol. I, LCL 330.
——, ed. and trans. (1943), *Aristotle: Nicomachean Ethics*, rev. edn, LCL 73.
Ralph, James (1728), *Night: A Poem. In four Books.*
——: see *A Critical History of the Administration* 1743.
——: see *The Flying-Post: or, Weekly Medley.*
——: see *Sawney. An Heroic Poem* 1728.
Ramsay, G.G., ed. and trans. (1969), *Juvenal and Persius*, LCL 91.
Rapin, René: see Creech 1684.
Rawson, Claude, and F.P. Lock, eds (1989), *Collected Poems of Thomas Parnell.*
Read's Weekly Journal: see *The Weekly Journal: or, British Gazetteer.*
Redford, Bruce (1996), *Venice and the Grand Tour.*
Regan, John V. (1975), 'Orpheus and the *Dunciad*'s narrator', *Eighteenth-Century Studies* 9, 87–101.
Remarks on the Divine Legation of Moses, &c. in Several Letters. By the Author of the Miscellany (i.e. William Webster) (1739).
Ricks, Christopher (1963), *Milton's Grand Style*, Oxford.
Ridpath, George: see *The Flying-Post from Paris and Amsterdam.*
Riley, E.C., ed. (1992), *Miguel de Cervantes Saavedra: Don Quixote de la Mancha*, trans. Charles Jarvis [i.e. Jervas], The World's Classics, Oxford.
Rivero, Albert J. (1989), *The Plays of Henry Fielding: A Critical Study of his Dramatic Career*, Charlottesville, Va.
Rivers, Isabel (1991), *Reason, Grace and Sentiment: A Study of the Language of Religion and Ethics in England, 1660–1880*, 2 vols (second volume forthcoming), Cambridge.
Rivers, William E. (1979), 'Pope, the spectre, and Mr. Busby', *Eighteenth-Century Life* 5, 43–53.
Rochester, John Wilmot, Earl of: see Vieth 1968.
Rocque, John: see Hyde 1981.
*Rogers, Pat (1972), *Grub Street: Studies in a Subculture.* (An abridged version appeared in 1980 as *Hacks and Dunces.*)
*—— (1975), *An Introduction to Pope.*
*—— (1985), *Literature and Popular Culture in Eighteenth Century England*, Brighton.
—— (1988), 'Gay and the world of opera', in *John Gay and the Scriblerians*, ed. Peter Lewis and Nigel Wood, 147–62.
*—— (1993a), *Essays on Pope*, Cambridge.
—— (1993b), *Alexander Pope: A Critical Edition of the Major Works*, The Oxford Authors, Oxford.
——: see Rousseau & Rogers 1988.
Rolfe, J.C., ed. and trans. (1920), *Sallust*, LCL 116.
Rolli, Paolo (1734 [1735]), *Polifemo.*
Roome, Edward: see *Dean Jonathan's Parody* 1729.

Root, Robert Kilburn, ed. (1929), *The Dunciad Variorum ... reproduced in facsimile*, Princeton, NJ.
Roscommon, Earl of: see Dillon, Wentworth.
Rosenblum, Michael (1972), 'Pope's illusive temple of infamy', in *The Satirist's Art*, ed. H. James Jensen and Malvin R. Zirker, Bloomington; repr. in Mack & Winn 1980: 652–77.
Rosselli, John (1992), *Singers of Italian Opera: The History of a Profession*, Cambridge.
Rosslyn, Felicity (1985), '"Dipt in the Rainbow": Pope on women', *Parnassus* 12–13, 179–93.
Rousseau, G.S., and Pat Rogers, eds (1988), *The Enduring Legacy: Alexander Pope Tercentenary Essays*, Cambridge.
Rowe, Nicholas, ed. (1709), *The Works of Mr. William Shakespear*.
Ruffhead, Owen (1769), *The Life of Alexander Pope, Esq., Compiled from Original Manuscripts, with a Critical Essay on his Writings and Genius*.
Rufinus: or, An Historical Essay on the Favourite-Ministry under Theodosius the Great and his Son Arcadius (1712). (Attributed to William King.)
Rumbold, Valerie (1983), 'Pope and the Gothic past', PhD dissertation, University of Cambridge.
—— (1989), *Women's Place in Pope's World*, Cambridge.

Sadie, Stanley, ed. (1980), *The New Grove Dictionary of Music and Musicans*, 20 vols.
Sadie, Stanley, and Anthony Hicks, eds (1987), *Handel Tercentenary Collection*.
Saint-Evremond, Charles de (1711), *Oeuvres de Monsieur de Saint-Evremond*, 7 vols.
St John, Henry, Viscount Bolingbroke (1844), *The Works of Lord Bolingbroke*, 4 vols.
——: see *The Craftsman*.
——: see *A Dissertation upon Parties* 1735.
Sallust: see Rolfe 1920.
Sambrook, James (1967), 'A possible source for "Master of the sev'nfold face" in "The Dunciad (B)"', *NQ* 212, 409–10.
——, ed. (1986), *James Thomson: Liberty, The Castle of Indolence and Other Poems*, Oxford.
—— (1991), *James Thomson, 1700–1748: A Life*, Oxford.
—— (1993), *The Eighteenth Century: The Intellectual and Cultural Context of English Literature, 1700–1789*, 2nd edn.
Sandys, George (1615), *A Relation of a Journey begun An: Dom: 1610. Foure Bookes. Containing a description of the Turkish Empire, of Aegypt, of the Holy Land, of the Remote parts of Italy, and Ilands adioyning*.
Sarasin, Jean-François (1649), *Dulot vaincu ou la défaite des bouts-rimés*, Paris.
Saunders, J.J. (1965), *A History of Medieval Islam*.
Savage, Richard, ed. (1732), *A Collection of Pieces in Verse and Prose which have been published on Occasion of the Dunciad*. (Facsimile in *Popeiana* (1974–5), vol. 11.)
——: see *An Author to be Lett* 1729.
Sawney. An Heroic Poem. Occasion'd by the Dunciad (1728), by James Ralph. (Facsimile in *Popeiana* (1974–5), vol. 6. See Guerinot 1969: 124–7.)
Sawyer, Paul (1972), 'John Rich's contribution to the eighteenth-century London stage', in *Essays on the Eighteenth-Century English Stage*, ed. Kenneth Richards and Peter Thomson, 85–104.
Schenkl, H., *et al.*, eds (1965–74), *Themistii orationes quae supersunt*, 3 vols, Bibliotheca Scriptorum Graecorum et Romanorum Teubneriana, Leipzig.
Schnapper, Edith B., ed. (1957), *The British Union-Catalogue of Early Music printed before the year 1801*, 2 vols.
Schoenbaum, S. (1975), *William Shakespeare: A Documentary Life*, Oxford.

Schwartz, Richard B. (1979), 'Berkeley, Newtonian space, and the question of evidence', in *Probability, Time and Space in Eighteenth-Century Literature*, ed. Paula R. Backscheider, 295–73, New York.

Scouten, Arthur H., ed. (1961), *The London Stage, 1660–1800. Part 3: 1729–1747*, 2 vols, Carbondale, Ill.

*Seary, Peter (1990), *Lewis Theobald and the Editing of Shakespeare*, Oxford.

Sedgwick, Romney, ed. (1931), *Some Materials towards Memoirs of the Reign of King George II*, by John Lord Hervey, 3 vols.

——, ed. (1970), *The House of Commmons, 1715–1754*, 2 vols, The History of Parliament.

Seidel, Michael (1979), *Satiric Inheritance: Rabelais to Sterne*, Princeton, NJ.

Selden, Raman (1984), 'Oldham, Pope, and Restoration satire', in *English Satire and the Satiric Tradition*, ed. Claude Rawson and Jenny Mezciems, 109–26, Oxford.

Seneca: see Miller 1953.

Serle, John (1745), *A Plan of Mr. Pope's Garden, As it was left at his Death.*

The Session of Musicians. In Imitation of the Session of Poets (1724).

Settle, Elkanah (1673), *The Empress of Morocco. A Tragedy. With Sculptures.*

—— (1683), *A Narrative.*

—— (1685), *An Heroick Poem on the Coronation of the High and Mighty Monarch James II.*

—— (1701), *The Virgin Prophetess: or, The Fate of Troy. An Opera.*

——: see *Absolom Senior* 1682.

——: see *The Character of a Popish Successour* 1681.

——: see *The Siege of Troy* 1707.

Sewell, George, ed. (1717), *Ovid's Metamorphoses ... By Several Hands*, 2 vols. (Contains versions by Lewis Theobald, with Pope's 'Vertumnus and Pomona'.)

Shaftesbury, Anthony Ashley Cooper, third Earl of: see *An Inquiry concerning Virtue* 1699.

——: see *Characteristicks* 1711.

Shakespeare, William: for editions see Rowe 1709; Pope 1725; Theobald 1733, 1740; Hanmer 1743–4; Warburton 1747; Alexander 1951.

Sheffield, John, Duke of Buckingham: see Pope 1723.

Sherbo, Arthur (1951), 'Pope and Boileau', *NQ* 196, 495.

—— (1970), 'No single scholiast: Pope's "The Dunciad"', *MLR* 65, 503–16.

—— (1988), 'More Pope scholia', *Yearbook of English Studies* 18, 221–30.

Sherburn, George (1934), *The Early Career of Alexander Pope*, Oxford.

*—— (1944), 'The *Dunciad*, Book IV', *Texas Studies in Literature and Language*, 24, 174–90. Repr. in Mack 1964: 666–82.

——, ed. (1956), *The Correspondence of Alexander Pope*, 5 vols, Oxford. (Hereafter *Corr.*)

—— (1958), 'New anecdotes about Alexander Pope', *NQ* 203, 343–9.

Shipley, John Burke (1963), 'James Ralph: pretender to genius', unpublished PhD dissertation, Columbia University, Ohio.

Shippen, William: see *Faction Display'd* 1704; *Moderation Display'd* 1704.

The Shortest Way with the Dissenters: or, Proposals for the Establishment of the Church (1702), by Daniel Defoe.

Showerman, Grant, ed. and trans. (1977), *Ovid: Heroides and Amores*, edn rev. G.P. Goold, LCL 41.

Sidney, Sir Philip: see Evans 1977.

The Siege of Troy, a Dramatic Performance. Presented in Mrs. Mynn's Booth ... during the Bartholomew Fair (1707), by Elkanah Settle, adapted from his opera *the Virgin Prophetess.*

*Sitter, John E. (1971), *The Poetry of Pope's 'Dunciad'*, Minneapolis.

Smedley, Jonathan: see *Baker's News*.
——: see *Gulliveriana* 1728.
Smith, Constance (1965), 'An echo of Dryden in Pope', *NQ* 210, 451.
Smith, D. Nichol, ed. (1963), *Eighteenth Century Essays on Shakespeare*, 2nd edn, Oxford.
Smith, J.C., and E. De Selincourt, eds (1912), *The Poetical Works of Edmund Spenser*, Oxford.
Smith, J.M.: see *The Flying-Post: or, Weekly Medley*.
Smith, Martin Ferguson, *et al.*, eds and trans (1975), *Lucretius: De Rerum Natura*, LCL 181.
Smith, Ruth (1995), *Handel's Oratorios and Eighteenth-Century Thought*, Cambridge.
Smythe, James Moore (1727), *The Rival Modes. A Comedy*.
——: see *A Collection of Several Curious Pieces* 1728.
Some Remarks on the Minute Philosopher (1732), by John, Lord Hervey.
South, Robert (1842), *Sermons Preached upon Several Occasions*, 5 vols, Oxford.
The Spectator: see Bond 1965.
The Speculatist. A Collection of Letters and Essays (1730), by Matthew Concanen. (Articles reprinted from the *London Journal* and *British Journal*.)
Spence, Joseph: for *Anecdotes*, see Osborn 1966.
Spenser, Edmund: for *The Faerie Queene*, see Smith & De Selincourt 1912.
——: for *Shorter Poems*, see Oram 1989.
Spon, Jacob (1678), *Voyage d'Italie, de Dalmatie, de Grece, et du Levant*, 3 vols, Lyons.
Stackhouse, Thomas (1729), *A Complete Body of Divinity ... extracted from the best ancient and modern writers*.
——: for *Memoirs ... of Atterbury*, see 'Philalethes' 1723.
*Stallybrass, Peter, and Allon White (1986), *The Politics and Poetics of Transgression*, Ithaca, NY.
Stanhope, H.: see *The Progress of Dulness* 1728.
The State Dunces: Inscrib'd to Mr. Pope (1733), by Paul Whitehead.
Statius: see Mozley 1928.
Steele, Richard: for *Correspondence*, see Blanchard 1941.
——: for *The Spectator*, see Bond 1965.
Stephen, Leslie, and Sidney Lee, eds (1885–1900), *Dictionary of National Biography*, 63 vols.
Stephens, John Calhoun, ed. (1982), *The Guardian*, Lexington, Ky.
Stiker, J.M. (1966), '"Bladen" and "Hays": Pope's "Dunciad", IV, 560', *NQ* 211, 458–9.
Stone, George Winchester, *et al.*, eds (1969), *British Dramatists from Dryden to Sheridan*, Carbondale, Ill.
Stow, John: for *A Survey of London*, see Kingsford 1971.
Strada, R.P. Faminius (1631), *Prolusiones academicae*, Oxford.
Strahle, Graham (1995), *An Early Music Dictionary: Musical Terms from British Sources, 1500–1740*, Cambridge.
Straub, Kristina (1992), *Sexual Suspects: Eighteenth-Century Players and Sexual Ideology*, Princeton, NJ.
Straus, Ralph (1927), *The Unspeakable Curll*.
Strohm, Reinhard (1985), *Essays on Handel and Italian Opera*, Cambridge.
Summers, Montagu, ed. (1923), *The Complete Works of William Congreve*, 4 vols.
A Supplement to the Profund (1728), attributed by Pope to Matthew Concanen. (Facsimile in *Popeiana* (1974–5), vol. 7; see Guerinot 1969: 148–50.)
Sutherland, James (1945), '"The dull duty of an editor"', *RES* 21, 202–15. (Repr. in Mack 1964: 630–49.)
—— (1986), *The Restoration Newspaper and its Development*, Cambridge.
——: for *The Dunciad*, see Butt 1939–69 (hereafter *TE*): V.
Swift, Jonathan: for *Prose Works*, see Davis 1939–68.

Swift, Jonathan, and Alexander Pope (1727), *Miscellanies in Prose and Verse*, 2 vols.
Swiftiana (1974–5), 11 vols, The Life and Times of Seven Major British Writers, Garland Publishing. (Facsimiles of original publications relating to Swift.)

Tales, Epistles, Odes, Fables, &c. (1729), by Thomas Cooke. (See Guerinot 1969: 160–64.)
Taylor, John (1630), *All the Workes of John Taylor the Water-Poet. Beeing Sixty and three in Number. Collected into one Volume by the Author.* (Facsimile by Scolar Press 1973.)
Temple, Sir William: see Monk 1963.
Terence: see Bentley 1726.
Themistius: see Schenkl 1965–74.
Theobald, Lewis (1714), *The Cave of Poverty, a Poem. Written in Imitation of Shakespeare.*
—— (1726), *Shakespeare Restored: or, A Specimen of the Many Errors, as well Committed, as Unamended, by Mr. Pope in his late Edition of this Poet.* (Facsimile in *Popeiana* (1974–5), vol. 5. See Guerinot 1969: 96–8.)
—— (1727), *The Rape of Proserpine.* (Rev. of *A Dramatic Entertainment* 1725.)
——, ed. (1728), *The Posthumous Works of William Wycherley Esq., in Prose and Verse.*
—— (1732), 'Of Mr. Pope's taste of Shakespeare', No. III in *A Miscellany on Taste. By Mr. Pope, &c.*, ed. Matthew Concanen. (Facsimile in *Popeiana* (1974–5), vol. 11; see Guerinot 1969: 207–10.)
——, ed. (1733), *The Works of Shakespeare*, 7 vols.
——, ed. (1740), *The Works of Shakespeare*, 8 vols.
——: see *The Censor* 1717.
——: see *A Compleat Collection* 1728.
——: see *A Complete Key to the Last New Farce* 1715.
——: for *Harlequin ... With the Loves of Pluto and Proserpine*, see *A Dramatic Entertainment* 1725.
——: see *Mist's Weekly Journal* for 1728.
——: for *Ovid's Metamorphoses*, see Sewell 1717.
Theocritus: see Edmonds 1912.
Theon: see Camerarius 1541.
Thomas, Elizabeth (1731–2), *Pylades and Corinna; or, Memoirs of the Lives, Amours, and Writings of Richard Gwinnett ... and Mrs Elizabeth Thomas*, 2 vols.
——: see *Codrus: or, The Dunciad Dissected* 1728.
Thompson, Aaron, trans. (1718), *The British History, Translated into English from the Latin of Jeffrey of Monmouth.*
Thomson, H.J., ed. and trans. (1949–53), *Prudentius*, 2 vols, LCL.
Three Satires. Most Humbly Inscribed ... to that Little Gentleman ... who has just Published, A Fourth Volume of Homer (1719), by Bezaleel Morrice. (Facsimile in *Popeiana* (1974–5), vol. 2; see Guerinot 1969: 77–8; and for later expansions, 82–3, 228–9.)
Thurmond, John (1724), *Harlequin Doctor Faustus. With the Masque of the Deities.*
The Thursday's Journal, ed. J. Pitt. Issued 1719; continued as *The London Journal: or, The Thursday's Journal*, 1719–20; then continued as *The London Journal*, 1720–44.
Tickell, Thomas (1713 [1712]), *A Poem, to His Excellency the Lord Privy-Seal, on the Prospect of Peace.*
—— (1715), *The First Book of Homer's Iliad.*
*Tillotson, Geoffrey (1950), *On the Poetry of Pope*, 2nd edn, Oxford.
Tindal, Matthew (1730), *Christianity as Old as the Creation: or, The Gospel, a Republication of the Religion of Nature.*
——: see *A Copy of the Will* 1733.
——: see *A Defence of our Present Happy Establishment* 1722.

Tinniswood, Adrian (1989), *A History of Country House Visiting: Five Centuries of Tourism and Taste*, Oxford.

Todd, Dennis (1982), 'The "blunted arms" of Dulness: the problem of power in the *Dunciad*', *SP* 79, 177–204.

—— (1986), 'An echo of Granville in Pope's *Dunciad* I, 202', *NQ* 231, 512–13.

—— (1989), '"One vast egg": Leibniz, the new embryology, and Pope's *Dunciad*', *ELN* 26, no. 4, 24–49.

Toland, John (1702), *Christianity not Mysterious ... Shewing, that there is Nothing in the Gospel Contrary to Reason.*

—— (1710), *The Jacobitism, Perjury and Popery of High-Church-Priests*, Edinburgh.

—— (1711), *High-Church Display'd: Being a Complete History of the Affair of Dr. Sacheverel.*

——: see Eoganesius 1720.

Tracy, Clarence, ed. (1967), *Richard Graves: The Spiritual Quixote.*

——, ed. (1971), *Samuel Johnson: Life of Savage*, Oxford.

Trenchard, J.: see *The British Journal.*

——: see *The Independent Whig* 1720–21.

A True Character of Mr. Pope, and his Writings (1716). (Facsimile in *Popeiana* (1974–5), vol. 1; repr. in Hooker 1939–43. By John Dennis, apparently incorporating material by Charles Gildon: see Guerinot 1969: 40–47.)

Tucker, Susie I. (1959), 'A note on Colley Cibber's name', *NQ* 204, 400.

Tutchin, John: see *The British Muse* 1701.

The Twickenham Edition of the Poems of Alexander Pope: see Butt 1939–69.

Tyers, Thomas: see *An Historical Rhapsody* 1782.

Valerius Flaccus: see Mozley 1934.

Vander Meulen, David L. (1981), 'A descriptive bibliography of Alexander Pope's Dunciad, 1728–1751', PhD thesis, University of Wisconsin.

—— (1989), '*The Dunciad in Four Books* and the bibliography of Pope', in *The Papers of the Bibliographical Society of America*, 83, 293–310.

—— (1991), *Pope's Dunciad of 1728: A History and Facsimile.*

Vanini, Lucilio (called Julius Caesar) (1616), *De admirandis naturae reginae deaque mortalium arcanis libri quatuor*, Paris.

Varey, Simon, ed. (1982), *Lord Bolingbroke: Contributions to the Craftsman*, Oxford.

Vercruysse, Jérôme, ed. (1969), *Boileau: Oeuvres*, 2 vols, Paris.

Verses Address'd to the Imitator of the First Satire of the Second Book of Horace ... by a Lady (1733), by Lady Mary Wortley Montagu and John, Lord Hervey. (See Guerinot 1969: 224–6.)

Victor, Benjamin (1722), *An Epistle to Sir Richard Steele, on his Play, call'd, The Conscious Lovers.*

—— (1761), *The History of the Theatres of London and Dublin, from the Year 1730 to the present Time*, 2 vols.

Vieth, David M., ed. (1968), *The Complete Poems of John Wilmot, Earl of Rochester.*

Villiers, George, Duke of Buckingham: for *The Rehearsal*, see Stone 1969.

A Vindication of Eustace Budgell (1733), by William Webster.

Virgil: for *Eneydos*, see Caxton 1490.

——: see Fairclough 1935, 1934.

Voitle, Robert (1984), *The Third Earl of Shaftesbury, 1671–1713.*

Voltaire (pseudonymn of François-Marie Arouet) (1732), *The History of Charles XII. King of Sweden. ... Translated from the French.*

Voss, Gerhard Johann (1627), *De historicis latinis libri tres*, Leiden.

Waller, A.R., ed. (1905), *The English Writings of Abraham Cowley*, Cambridge.
Waller, Edmund: for *Poems*, see Drury 1893.
Walpole, Horace: for *Correspondence*, see Lewis 1937–83.
——: for *Notes on the Poems of Alexander Pope*, see Fraser 1876.
——: see *The World* 1787–94.
Warburton, William (1738–41), *The Divine Legation of Moses Demonstrated*, 2 vols.
—— (1738), *A Vindication of the Author of the Divine Legation of Moses from the Aspersions ... in the Weekly Miscellany of February 24, 1737.*
—— (1742), *A Critical and Philosophical Commentary on Mr. Pope's Essay on Man.* (An enlarged edition of a series of articles begun in 1738: see Sherburn 1956: IV, 163, n.)
——, ed. (1747), *The Works of Shakespear*, 8 vols.
——, ed. (1751), *The Works of Alexander Pope ... with the Commentaries and Notes of Mr. Warburton*, 9 vols. (*The Dunciad* occupies Vol V.)
—— (1763), *The Doctrine of Grace ... Vindicated from the Insults of Infidelity, and the Abuses of Fanaticism.*
Ward, Charles E., ed. (1942), *The Letters of John Dryden*, Durham, NC.
Ward, Edward (1729), *Apollo's Maggot in his Cups: or, The Whimsical Creation of a Little Satyrical Poet.* (Author named in Postscript. Facsimile in *Popeiana* (1974–5), vol. 8. See Guerinot 1969: 177–9.)
——: see *Durgen* 1728.
——: for *The London Spy*, see Hyland 1993.
Warton, Joseph, ed. (1797), *The Works of Alexander Pope*, 9 vols. (*The Dunciad* occupies Vol V.)
Wasse, Joseph, ed. (1710), *C. Crispi Sallusti quae extant*, Cambridge.
——, ed. (1731), *Thucydidis de bello peloponnesiaco libri octo*, 2 parts, Amsterdam.
Watson, George, ed. (1969–77), *The New Cambridge Bibliography of English Literature*, 5 vols, Cambridge.
Webster, William: see *Remarks on The Divine Legation of Moses* 1739.
——: see *A Vindication of Eustace Budgell* 1733.
——: see *The Miscellany.*
The Weekly Journal: or, British Gazeteer, published by James Read. Issued 1715–25; continued as *Read's Weekly Journal: or, British Gazetteer*, 1730–61.
The Weekly Journal: or, Saturday's Post, ed. Nathaniel Mist *et al.* Issued 1716–25; continued as *Mist's Weekly Journal*, 1725–8, then as *Fog's Weekly Journal*, 1728–37.
The Weekly Medley: see *The Flying-Post.*
The Weekly Miscellany: see *The Miscellany.*
Weinbrot, Howard D. (1978), *Augustus Caesar in 'Augustan' England: The Decline of a Classical Norm*, Princeton, NJ.
Welsted, Leonard, trans. (1712), *The Works of Dionysius Longinus, On the Sublime ... with some Remarks on the English Poets.*
—— (1724), *Epistles, Odes, &c. ... To which is prefix'd, A Dissertation concerning the Perfection of the English Language, the State of Poetry, &c.* (There were two editions in this year: see Guerinot 1969: 88–90.)
——: see *Palaemon to Caelia* 1717.
——: see *Characters of the Times* 1728.
——: see Nichols 1787.
West, Gilbert: see *A Canto of the Fairy Queen* 1739.
West, M.L. (1992), *Ancient Greek Music*, Oxford.
Wheeler, David (1983), 'Hoadly, Henley, and *The Dunciad*', *Scriblerian* 16, 59–61.

Whip and Key: see *A Key (With the Whip)* 1682.

Whitefield, George (1763), *Observations on Some Fatal Mistakes in ... The Doctrine of Grace ... By William Lord Bishop of Gloucester* (William Warburton).

The Whitehall Journal: see *Baker's News*.

Whitehead, Paul: see *The State Dunces* 1733.

The Whole Life of Polly Peachum (1730?).

Wilders, John, ed. (1967), *Samuel Butler: Hudibras*, Oxford.

Wilkins, John: see *The Discovery of a World in the Moone* 1638.

Wilkinson, C.H. (1930), *The Poems of Richard Lovelace*, Oxford.

Williams, Aubrey L. (1953a), 'Literary backgrounds to Book IV of the *Dunciad*', *PMLA* 68, 806–13.

—— (1953b), 'Pope's "duchesses and Lady Mary's"', *RES* 4, 359–61.

*—— (1955), *Pope's 'Dunciad': A Study of its Meaning*.

Williams, Carolyn D. (1993), *Pope, Homer, and Manliness: Some Aspects of Eighteenth-Century Classical Learning*.

Williams, Harold, ed. (1958), *The Poems of Jonathan Swift*, 2nd edn, 3 vols, Oxford.

——, ed. (1965), *The Correspondence of Jonathan Swift*, 5 vols, rev. edn, Oxford.

Wilmot, John, Earl of Rochester: see Vieth 1968.

Wilson, Arthur (1653), *The History of Great Britain, being the Life and Reign of King James the First*.

Winn, James Anderson (1981), *Unsuspected Eloquence: A History of the Relations between Poetry and Music*.

—— (1987), *John Dryden and his World*.

Winstanley, William (1687), *The Lives of the Most Famous English Poets*. (Facsimile, with introduction by William Riley Parker, in Scholars' Facsimiles and Reprints (1963), Gainesville, Fla.)

Winton, Calhoun (1993), *John Gay and the London Theatre*, Lexington, Ky.

Wise, Thomas James (1973), *A Pope Library: A Catalogue of Plays, Poems, and Prose Writings by Alexander Pope*, repr. with a new introduction by K.I.D. Maslen, Folkestone.

Wood, Nigel: see Lewis & Wood 1989.

*Woodman, Thomas (1990), '"Wanting nothing but the Laurel": Pope and the idea of the Laureate Poet', in *Pope: New Contexts*, ed. David Fairer, 45–58.

Wooton, William (1697), *Reflections upon Ancient and Modern Learning ... the Second Edition ... with a Dissertation upon the Epistles of Phalaris, Themistocles, Socrates, Euripides; &c. and Aesop's Fables, by Dr. Bentley*.

The World, written by Edward Moore, Lord Chesterfield, Horace Walpole *et al*. Issued 1753–6.

Wright, H. Bunker, and K. Monroe Spears, eds (1971), *The Literary Works of Matthew Prior*, 2 vols, Oxford.

Wynne, Edward: see *Eunomus* 1768.

Yolton, John W. (1983), *Thinking Matter: Materialism in Eighteenth-Century Britain*, Minneapolis.

Young, Edward (1728), *Love of Fame, the Universal Passion. In Seven Characteristical Satires ... The Second Edition*.

——: for *Memoirs of ... Wharton*, see *Memoirs* 1731.

——: for *Complete Works*, see Nichols 1854.

Young, W.B. (1993), '"See mystery to mathematics fly!": Pope's *Dunciad* and the critique of religious rationalism', *Eighteenth-Century Studies* 26, 435–48.

SELECTIVE INDEX TO EDITORIAL MATTER

This index supplements the two indexes which Pope provided for his text by listing the most important references to persons and topics in the editor's Introduction and commentary: page numbers in **bold** type locate basic biographical information, and analytical entries are provided for the most frequently recurring topics. Members of the nobility are indexed by family name, cross-referenced to title.